Korea

Martin Robinson, Andrew Bender,
Rob Whyte

Contents

NORTH KOREA
p323

GANGWON-DO
p140

SEOUL p65
GYEONGGI-DO
p117

CHUNGCHEONGBUK-DO
p309

CHUNGCHEONGNAM-DO
p291

GYEONGSANGBUK-DO
p165

JEOLLABUK-DO
p277

GYEONGSANGNAM-DO
p206

JEOLLANAM-DO
p232

JEJU-DO p254

Destination Korea

Sandwiched between China and Japan, lesser-known Korea is a country with its own unique and distinctive language, culture and food. An Asian economic tiger which exports container ships, cars, cameras and computers around the globe, South Korea's safe and buzzing modern cities are crowded with Internet cafés, restaurants and all-night entertainment dens. Yet palaces, fortresses and wooden, tiled *yangban* (aristocrat) houses are reminders of the country's feudal past.

The countryside is another world, where well-maintained hiking trails take visitors up densely forested mountains and along river valleys that are graced by some of Asia's finest Buddhist temples and reveal the Koreans' spiritual side. An excellent and cheap public transportation system whisks visitors to every village, national park and beach-encrusted island.

Take the time to discover this compact and little-explored country and be surprised by dramatic national and provincial parks, World Heritage monuments, traditional music and dance, a diverse cuisine and helpful, lively people. Many good buys await in traditional open-air markets, underground arcades and brand-new shopping malls.

The peninsula is a mosaic of old and new – rural folk villages and DVD mini-cinemas, ancient stone pagodas and rock music bars, Buddhas and bowling alleys. Asian traditions and Western fashions, Confucian ideals and democratic ideas, yin and yang, East and West mix and mingle together.

A visit to the Demilitarized Zone (DMZ) reveals the country's dangerous division. The North is still trapped in the totalitarian straight-jacket that was imposed after Japanese colonial rule collapsed in 1945. Relations between the two Koreas are another complex but fascinating topic.

JULIET COOMBE

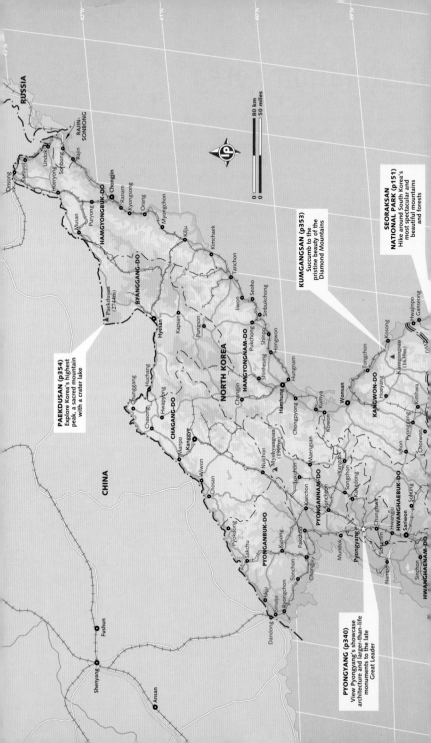

PYONGYANG (p340)
View Pyongyang's showcase architecture and larger-than-life monuments to the late Great Leader

PAEKDUSAN (p354)
Explore Korea's highest peak, a sacred mountain with a crater lake

KUMGANGSAN (p353)
Succumb to the pristine beauty of the Diamond Mountains

SEORAKSAN NATIONAL PARK (p151)
Hike around South Korea's most spectacular and beautiful mountains and forests

80 km
50 miles

RUSSIA

CHINA

NORTH KOREA

Shenyang

Fushun

Ansan

Dandong

Sinuiju

Ryongchon

Sonchon

Sakchu

Pyoktong

Chongju

Kusong

Pakchon

PYONGANBUK-DO

Chongju

Huchang

Chunggang

Chasong

Manpo

Wiwon

Chosan

Kanggye

CHAGANG-DO

Hwapyong

Nujchon

Myohyangsan
(1909m)

RYANGGANG-DO

Paektusan
(2744m)

Hyesan

Kapsan

Pungdong

Chunggang

Sinpho

HAMGYONGNAM-DO

Pukchong

Iwon

Seoho

Sinbukchong

Hongwon

Hamhung

Hungnam

Sumya

Kowon

HAMGYONGBUK-DO

Onsong

Saebyol

Undok

Hoeryong

Sonbong

Rajin

RAJIN-SONBONG

Puryong

Ranam

Kyongsong

Orang

Myongchon

Musan

Kilju

Kimchaek

Tanchon

Changjin

Maengsan

Kakhtron

Songchon

Kujang

Kaechon

Sunchon

Songchon

Muldok

Murdok

Nampo

Pyongyang

PYONGANNAM-DO

Kangdong

Yangdok

Hwangju

Sohung

Chunghwa

Sinchon

Sinmi

HWANGHAEBUK-DO

Sariwon

Hwangju

HWANGHAENAM-DO

KANGWON-DO

Wonsan

Hoeyang

Pyonggang

Ichon

Chorwon

Kimhwa

Tongchon

Kosong

Kumgangsan
(1638m)

Hwaljinpo

Ganseong

Seoho

Kowon

Hamhung

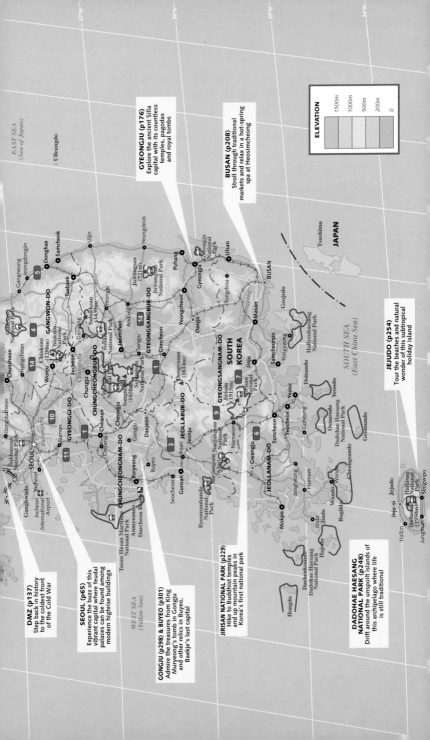

EAST SEA
(Sea of Japan)

Ulleungdo

GYEONGJU (p176)
Explore the ancient Silla capital with its countless temples, pagodas and royal tombs

BUSAN (p208)
Stroll through traditional markets and relax in a hot-spring spa at Heosimcheong

ELEVATION

1500m
1000m
500m
200m
0

Uljin
Yeongdeok

Gangneung
Jeongdongjin
Donghae
Samcheok

5

GANGWON-DO

Taebaek

Juwangsan (721m)
Juwangsan National Park

Pohang

Gyeongju National Park

14

Chiaksan (1288m)
Chiaksan National Park

Wonju

Jecheon
Danyang

Sobaeksan (1439m)
Sobaeksan National Park

Gimcheon
Sangju

GYEONGSANGBUK-DO

Yeongju
Andong
Yeongcheon

Gyeongju
Dongdaesan

Ulsan

BUSAN

JAPAN

Tsushima

10

Suwon

GYEONGGI-DO

Cheonan
Onyang

CHUNGCHEONGNAM-DO

Cheongju

Songnisan (1058m)
Songnisan National Park

Chungju

Dongducheon

Chuncheon
Hongcheon

14

Bukhansan National Park

SEOUL

11

Daejeon

Gongju
Boryeong

Buyeo

CHUNGCHEONGBUK-DO

Seocheon
Gunsan

Taean Haean Maritime National Park
Anmyeondo
Daecheon Beach

1

Deogyusan (1614m)

Daegu

Masan
Jinju

Jinhae

SOUTH KOREA

Yeongnam

GYEONGSANGNAM-DO

7

Jirisan (1915m)
Jirisan National Park

Geochang

Masan

Samcheonpo

Tongyeong

Geojedo

Hallyeohaesang National Park

9

JEOLLABUK-DO

Jeonju

Iksan

Naejangsan National Park

Namwon

Byeonsanbando National Park

3

Gwangju

Suncheon

Yeocheon
Yeosu

Goheung

JEOLLANAM-DO

6

Mokpo

Jangheung

Haenam

Wando

Dadohae Haesang National Park

Bogildo

Cheongsando

Oenarodo
Yeondo

Geomundo

Jindo
Jindo

Hongdo

Daeheuksando
Dadohae Haesang National Park

Hajodo

DADOHAE HAESANG NATIONAL PARK (p248)
Drift around the unspoilt islands of this archipelago where life is still traditional

SOUTH SEA
(East China Sea)

JEJUDO (p254)
Tour the beaches and natural wonder of this subtropical holiday island

Jeju-si
Jejudo

Hallim

Hallasan (1950m)
Hallasan National Park

Seogwipo
Jungmun

WEST SEA
(Yellow Sea)

SEOUL (p65)
Experience the buzz of this vibrant capital where feudal palaces can be found among modern highrise buildings

Incheon International Airport

Gamhwado
Incheon

Pyeongtaek

Imjingang

DMZ (p137)
Step back in history to the coldest front of the Cold War

GONGJU (p298) & BUYEO (p301)
Admire the treasures from King Muryeong's tomb in Gongju and other relics in Buyeo, Baekje's last capital

JIRISAN NATIONAL PARK (p229)
Hike to Buddhist temples and up mountain peaks in Korea's first national park

Twenty scenic national parks are packed with hiking trails, densely forested mountains, rivers, waterfalls, ancient fortresses and colourful Buddhist temples. Sandy beaches, water sports and seafood restaurants lure visitors to the beaches and relaxing islands that dot Korea's coastline. A youthful buzz pervades the market, entertainment and shopping districts in modern, almost crime-free cities.

JEFF YATES

Soak up the atmosphere of the feudal court at Changdeokgung (p87)

JOHN BORTHWICK

Enjoy traditional royal court food while watching folk music and dance shows at Korea House (p105)

Strap on skis or a snowboard, or jump on a sled at Muju Ski Resort (p284)

MARTIN VINCENT

BILL WASSMAN

View the imposing Genjeongjeon (p85) at Gyeongbokgung and immerse yourself in the splendour of the Joseon dynasty

JEFF YATES

Be dazzled by the bright lights of Seoul (p65) after dark

Hike the rugged Wolchulsan National Park (p249)

MARTIN MOOS

MICHAEL S. YAMASHITA/

Join the honeymooners on the semitropical island of Jeju-do (p254)

Marvel at the skill of the artisans who created
Bulguksa (p182)

JOHN BORTHWICK

BIL

Explore the rich culinary traditions of one of Asia's most distinctive cuisines (p50)

Getting Started

South Korea is a small and generally safe country, easy and relatively cheap to travel around, with plenty of national parks, temples, mountains and unspoilt islands to explore, good buys (especially clothing, accessories and electronic items) in the busy city shopping areas, and lots to see, do and eat. The country has one of the world's most dynamic economies, so be prepared for changes – restaurants and motels are demolished or change owners, and even museums disappear.

The government introduced a new romanisation system in 2000, but the changeover is taking time. You will see lots of different spellings – Pusan for Busan, Chongju for Jeonju and *kimbap* for *gimbap*. This guidebook uses the new system, so what you see on a sign may not be exactly what is written in the guidebook. Keep this in mind and you shouldn't have any problems – you'll soon realise that *vivimbop* is *bibimbap* in disguise!

Few Koreans can communicate well in English, especially in more remote areas, so learn a few Korean phrases, and spend a couple of hours learning the *hangeul* letters – it's not difficult. See p394 for the language chapter. Lonely Planet's *Korean Phrasebook* is a good investment.

WHEN TO GO

Korea has four very distinct seasons. The best time of year to visit is probably autumn, from September to November, when the weather is usually sunny and warm and the mountainsides are ablaze with bright colours.

Spring, from April to May, is another beautiful season, with mild temperatures and cherry blossoms spreading north across the country in April. Camellias, azaleas and other plants and trees flower and blossom as well.

See p368 for climate charts

Winter, from December to March, is dry but can be bitterly cold, with Siberian winds dragging January temperatures in most of the country to below zero. It can be dangerous in the mountains, so pack crampons and the proper clothing. This is the time when you really appreciate *ondol*

DON'T LEAVE HOME WITHOUT...

- Checking the tourist visa situation (see p374). Many nationalities can stay 90 days without a visa but Americans can only stay for 30 days.

- Taking out travel insurance (p371). Korea is generally a safe country but accidents do happen and they can be expensive.

- Packing your hiking boots, as Korea is full of national parks, scenic mountains and well-marked trails (p48).

- Learning a bit of the local language (see p394) as English isn't widely spoken.

- Studying the food chapter (p50) so you can sample the unique and varied local cuisine such as *bibimbap*, *samgyetang* and *samgyeopsal*.

- Packing your swimming costume, especially if you are visiting in July and August.

- Buying a diary to record all your Korean experiences and adventures.

- Packing a pair of sheets if you're planning to stay in budget accommodation, which often have just a sheet and a quilt.

- Packing personal hygiene and brand-name medical items that may be difficult to obtain.

(underfloor heating), hot spring baths and the ubiquitous saunas. White snow on temple roofs is very picturesque and winter is a good time to visit if you enjoy skiing, snowboarding or ice-skating. All sorts of snowy fun and games take place during festivals in January.

Try to avoid peak summer – late June to late August – which is the monsoon season, when the country receives some 60% of its annual rainfall, and the weather is often unpleasantly hot and humid. Visit in August and you will find out why everyone is keen to install air-conditioning. The locals flee the muggy cities for the national parks and beaches, which become overcrowded, and the hotels in these areas double their prices. As if that wasn't enough, typhoons can also occur in this season.

Jejudo, off the south coast, is the warmest place in Korea, with an almost sub-tropical climate along its south coast. Here the rain is more spread out through the year but autumn and winter are still the driest months, as they are throughout the country.

Visit www.kma.go.kr for daily weather forecasts in English.

COSTS & MONEY

Korea is a developed country but prices are reasonable and you can get by on a low budget. Public transport, basic meals, admission prices and accommodation are all relatively cheap, although luxury hotels and duty-free shops can be expensive. The exchange rate is a key factor and the stronger the won is, the more expensive Korea is for foreign visitors.

TRAVEL LITERATURE

A Walk Through the Land of Miracles by Simon Winchester describes a classic walk from Jejudo to Seoul. This well-known English journalist vividly describes his encounters with the locals – monks, nuns, artists, marriage arrangers – and US generals, but the highlight of his trip is a visit to a barber shop.

To Dream of Pigs by Clive Leatherdale is a journalist's account of his jaunt around North and South Korea and the oddball characters he meets on his travels.

Korea and Her Neighbours by Isabella Bird (originally published in 1898) is a detailed and readable account of the author's intrepid travels around Korea and her insightful comments on life in the country over a century ago.

Korea Unmasked by Rhe Won-bok (Gimm Young Int, 2002) provides an illuminating look at contemporary Korean attitudes in a cartoon format that compares Korea to neighbours China and Japan to highlight differences between these three Asian cultures.

Unforgettable Things by So Chong-ju (translated by D McCann) is a wonderful collection of highly original poems that reflects the author's varied life and unusual philosophy.

Seoul Food Finder by A and J Salmon includes reviews of over 100 of Seoul's best restaurants.

INTERNET RESOURCES

KNTO (www.knto.or.kr) Tons of useful tourist info and links to other sites.
Korean Films (www.koreanfilm.org) All about the Korean film industry plus hundreds of film reviews.
Korean News (www.koreaherald.co.kr) Daily updated news, a weekender section and links to magazines.
Korean Society and Culture (www.korea.net) A treasure trove of all things Korean.
Korean Traditional Music (www.gugakfm.co.kr) Listen to traditional Korean music.
Lonely Planet (www.lonelyplanet.com) Read the latest traveller's tips on Korea.

LONELY PLANET INDEX

Litre of petrol
W1250

Litre of bottled water
W800

Bottle of beer (500mL)
W1500

Souvenir T-shirt
W5000

Tteokbokki snack
W2000

HOW MUCH?

Local newspaper
W600

Food-court lunch
W6000

Cinema ticket
W7000

Steak dinner
W25,000

Tailor-made suit
W200,000

Itineraries

In general, buses are the most convenient way to tour the country, but go by train if you need to take a long journey.

CLASSIC ROUTES

EAST COAST RUN   1 week / 750km

From Seoul this favourite route traverses mountains, rice fields and lakes to the sandy beaches, seafood restaurants and romantic sunrises of the rocky east coast. Ancient caves, temples and tombs, traditional villages and a remote island of squid fishermen are highlights on the way to cosmopolitan Busan city.

Catch a train from Seoul to **Gangchon** (p145) and cycle to the waterfall and bungee jump spot. Hop on a bus to the lakeside city of **Chuncheon** (p142), eat *dakgalbi* (diced, grilled chicken) and cycle along the lake shore. Head to Soyang Dam, take a boat trip to Yanggu and sample some adventure sports in **Inje** (p146).

Dine in a seafood restaurant in the east-coast port of **Sokcho** (p146) before journeying up the coast to the sandy beach at **Hwajinpo** (p150). Then hike around **Seoraksan National Park** (p151) and stay in Seorak-dong. Visit Naksan temple and beach (p150) and continue south along the coast to **Jeongdongjin** (p157) and view a North Korean spy submarine. At **Samcheok** (p160) see

The East Coast Run is 750km of shifting countryside, historical sights and seafood, with a relaxing hot spring spa waiting at the end of the road.

the caves exhibition and nearby **Hwanseondonggul** (p161) before checking out some **beach coves** (p161) and the unusual **penis park**.

Travel back in time at **Hahoe folk village** (p194) and don't miss the nearby **mask museum** or the cultural museums of **Andong** (p191). Then on to the highlight – **Gyeongju** (p176), the ancient capital of the Silla kingdom, for two or more days of hiking or cycling among the tombs and Buddhist treasures. Board a ferry to rugged **Ulleungdo** (p200) for a complete change of scene. Finally arrive in **Busan** (p208), a port city with markets, beaches, a hot spring spa and fast ferry connections to Japan.

HONEYMOON ISLAND

1 week / 300km

Plenty of flights and ferries provide fast and easy transport to Jeju-do, Korea's holiday island where honeymooners stay in resort hotels among the palm trees, bask on the south coast's sandy subtropical beaches, and enjoy water sports and fresh seafood meals. Volcanic craters, waterfalls and unusual rock formations add to the island's scenic attractions.

Hallasan (p275), an extinct volcano, is Korea's highest peak and domi-nates the island. You can climb it or admire it from a distance. Closer to sea level, walk along the rim of **Sangumburi Crater** (p265) and through part of **Manjanggul** (p265), one of the world's longest lava tubes. Don't miss the spectacular 'sunrise peak' **Seongsan Ilchulbong** (p266). Cycle around **Udo** (p267), a small offshore island where wet-suited *haenyeo* (female divers) still gather seafood from the ocean floor. **Seong-eup** (p268) and **Jeju Folk Village** (p268) give you a glimpse of the island's past.

Traditional *harubang* ('grandfather' statues) hewn out of volcanic rock can be seen everywhere including the outdoor **sculpture parks**, Jeju Art Park (p273) and Shincheonji Art Museum (p275).

To the south, near Seogwipo, are famous **waterfalls** including Jeong-bangpokpo (p269), which enters the sea, as well as **boat and submarine tours** (p270). Tiny offshore islands are best for **scuba diving** (p270). **Yakcheonsa** (p271) has a striking hall and beautiful murals. Two giant glasshouses are near Jungmun – a new conference centre and **Yeomiji botanical garden** (p272). **Dolphin shows** (p272), a **tea plantation** (p274) with a teacup-shaped museum, and a **bonsai tree park** (p274) will occupy you. But the highlight is the **Chinese circus** (p274), with wonderful acrobatics on horseback.

Lurk in lava tube caves, venture up an extinct volcano, wander past waterfalls, sup on seafood, and bask on subtropical beaches – you'll soon discover why Jeju-do is Korea's holiday island.

ROADS LESS TRAVELLED

COAST TO COAST
2 weeks / 800km

Journey through glorious mountain scenery, hike along river valleys, feast on pheasant and duck in small resort towns, and unwind on sandy beaches, and in hot spring baths. Along the way visit the presidential summer villa and admire 1300-year-old treasures from the Baekje dynasty.

From Seoul take the subway to **Suwon** (p124), hike around the World Heritage fortress, eat *galbi* (beef ribs) and spend some hours in the **Korean Folk Village** (p126). Next stop is the **Independence Hall of Korea** (p308) near Cheonan, followed by two more days of history in the Baekje kingdom's capitals of **Gongju** (p298) and **Buyeo** (p301).

Then head to **Daecheon** (p305) for the best beach and seafood on the west coast. Cruise around small islands and stay with a fisherman's family on **Sapsido** (p306) before touring **Anmyeondo** (p307) and watching the sunset from **Mallipo beach** (p307). Travel inland via **Haemi fortress** (p308) to Daejeon and **Yuseong Hot Springs** (p295). Buy ginseng in **Geumsan** (p297), then stay in a motel castle in **Cheongju** (p311), eating in a **mountain fortress** (p312) and touring the **presidential villa** (p314), if it's unoccupied.

Spot a goral antelope in **Woraksan National Park** (p318), rejuvenate tired limbs in **Suanbo Hot Springs** (p317), and dine on pheasant. Take a scenic ferry trip across Chungju Lake to **Danyang** (p319). From there explore nearby **limestone caves** (p321) and **Guinsa** (p322), an amazing temple complex. Go bush in remote **Jeongseon** (p163) where you might see an ox-drawn plough. In Taebaeksan Provincial Park visit the mountain-top **Dangun altar** (p162). Finally dip your toe into the East Sea at a beach near **Samcheok** (p160). See p11 for Samcheok and beyond.

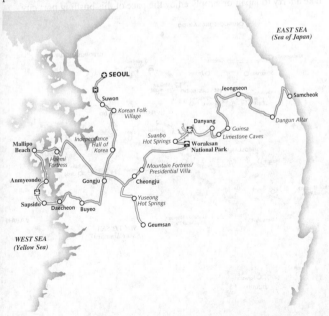

From busy to Seoul to remote fishing villages, a motel castle to a mountain fortress, and a presidential villa to limestone caves: travelling coast to coast is a great way to experience the variety on offer in Korea.

JEOLLA PROVINCES & THE SOUTH COAST ISLANDS

2 weeks / 1200km

The Jeolla provinces make up the rice bowl of Korea and are the main-stays of tradition. Besides *bibimbap* (rice, egg, meat and vegetables in hot sauce) the area is famous for *pansori* opera, poets, pottery and political protests. The south coast is Korea's most captivating coastline where re-laxing islands and their pristine beaches invite island-hopping jaunts.

Jeonju city's fascinating **hanok village** (p279) is crammed with traditional houses and buildings. Try local specialities like *bibimbap* and *kongnam-ulgukbap* (spicy red bean sprout porridge) and drink *moju* (a sweet, gingery drink that is served warm). See the rock pinnacle garden and climb a horse's ear at **Maisan Provincial Park** (p284), then go skiing or hiking in **Deogyusan National Park** (p284). Scenic splendours also await at **Naejangsan National Park** (p286) or **Seonunsan Provincial Park** (p287). Take a ferry from Gunsan to relax-ing **Seonyudo** (p290). **Eocheongdo** (p290) has Korea's best bird-watching.

In Gwangju visit the **May 18th Memorial Park** (p235), a sombre reminder of the 1980 student uprising; admire the ceramics in **Gwangju National Museum** (p234), explore **Art Street** (p238) and eat in **Duck Street** (p237).

At Mokpo visit the **Maritime Museum** (p245) before exploring the 'red island' **Hongdo** (p248), the 'fisherfolk island' **Heuksando** (p248), the 'dog island' **Jindo** (p252) or the 'poet island' **Bogildo** (p252). In Yeosu, taste *gakkimchi* (leafy *kimchi*) and board a replica of **Admiral Yi's turtle ship** (p242) on Namhae Island before visiting handsome **Hwa-eomsa** (p239) in Jirisan National Park. Sip freshly picked green tea at the **Boseong tea plantation** (p244) and mould your own pot in **Gangjin** (p244) or **Yeong-am** (p249).

Jinju fortress (p224) has a terrible story to tell, and don't miss the Korean War POW camp and museum on **Geoje Island** (p226) or the botanical garden on tiny **Oe Island** (p227). Finally you reach **Busan** (p208), from where you can take a ferry to Japan or simply enjoy the pace of this bustling port city.

Eat your way across the Jeolla prov-inces, admire the vista of Jeollabuk-do's national and provincial parks, and soak up the history of the south coast islands.

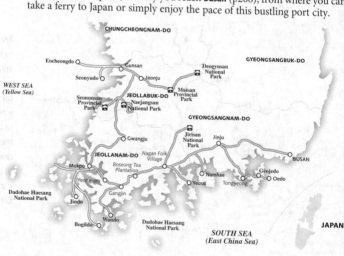

TAILORED TRIPS

TEMPLE PILGRIMAGE

10 days / 1500km

Located in beautiful forest-covered mountain areas are some of Asia's most outstanding Buddhist temples. Their remoteness makes the pilgrimage by bus difficult and the journey covers around 1500km but it begins with a single step. Nearly all the temples date back many centuries, and although the buildings are often relatively new, they follow the traditional style with colourful decoration around the eaves, murals, striking roof lines, latticework doors, and superbly carved and painted ceilings.

Buses from Seoul run to **Guinsa** (p322), which is the impressive headquarters of the Cheontae sect and quite different from any other Korean temple, with multistorey modern buildings lining both sides of a steep valley. It has a Utopian atmosphere and free vegetarian meals are available. From here take a bus to Danyang and on to Gongju and **Magoksa** (p301), which is an ancient and traditional temple with a hall of 1000 pint-sized disciples that are all slightly different. Then head southeast to Daegu and on to stunning **Haeinsa** (p174), which houses an amazing library of 80,000 World Heritage 14th-century woodblocks that were carved in an effort to ward off Mongolian invaders. Back in Daegu, an hour on the bus takes you to Gimcheon, the gateway to **Jikjisa** (p190), an impressive temple dating back to the 5th century. A soldier monk from here, Sa-myeong, led the fight against Japanese invaders in 1592. Monks were not pacifists in those days when the nation was under threat. Return to Daegu and take a bus to Jeonju and another bus to Jinan the access town for **Tapsa** (p284), a tiny temple surrounded by two 'horse ear' mountains and an extraordinary garden of stone pinnacles that were built by a Buddhist mystic. Return to Jeonju via Jinan and go south to Gwangju and on to **Unjusa** (p239). This temple is unique with pagodas and Buddhas, including unusual twin and reclining Buddhas. Returning to Gwangju, catch a bus to Busan and on to **Tongdosa** (p223), Korea's largest temple, which houses an excellent Buddhist art museum. Catch a bus to Ulsan and from there to **Seongnamsa** (p222), a visual masterpiece set in a provincial park. Finally return to Ulsan and on to Gyeongju and **Bulguksa** (p182), a temple replica that represents the crowning glory of Silla architecture and is constructed on a stone terrace. Nearby is a superb mid-8th-century stone Buddha in the Seokguram Grotto.

Journey along the path to spiritual enlightenment by visiting some of Asia's most beautiful Buddhist temples.

NORTH KOREA

THREE-DAY TOUR

Three days in North Korea will be enough to give you a generous taste of the surreal. For those unsure of how much they will enjoy an ideologically charged guided tour through a Stalinist country, this is perhaps the safe option.

That said, three days gives very little choice – the authorities will expect you to visit a long-trodden route of cities deemed desirable for tourists, beginning with the remarkable revolutionary showcase of **Pyongyang** (p340). The incredible North Korean capital has both the look and feel of a vast urban museum, with its timid population scuttling between monolithic architecture and its roads spookily empty of traffic. It is a fascinating place, built to impress – absolute power expressed in concrete.

The second day will include a trip south through the ancient Korean capital of **Kaesong** (p350) and then on to nearby **Panmunjeom** (p351), where you'll get your last chance to see the Cold War at its frosty height. Watching South Korean soldiers eyeballing the Northern troops is a bizarre experience, especially when witnessing it on the north of the Demilitarized Zone. The final day is likely to be a day trip into the mountains – beautiful **Myohyangsan** (p352), is deservedly famous for its stunning mountain walks, and also offers proximity to the **International Friendship Exhibition** – a frankly vulgar collection of staggeringly useless gifts from foreign dictators sent to the leaders Great and Dear.

North Korea has to be seen to be believed. You can do it in three days, but a week will give you a chance to really experience this fascinating country.

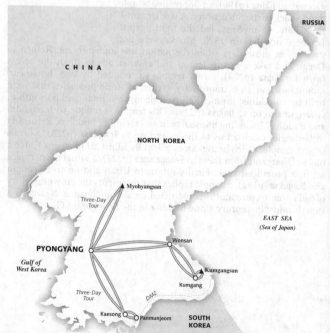

EVEN-DAY TOUR

To really get to grips with Democratic People's Republic of Korea, a week in the country is ideal – this gives you time to see much of what is open in the country without being too overwhelmed by the relentless propaganda. Even during a slower paced tour, however, visitors still frequently complain that they have no chance simply to absorb the local atmosphere or relax in any way other than karaoke.

As well as **Pyongyang**, **Kaesong**, **Panmunjeom**, and **Myohyangsan** you will be able to see some of the more remote parts of the country including more of North Korea's idyllic and dramatic mountain scenery. The resort of **Kumgangsan** (p353), with its unspoilt alpine environment is a truly different world from the frenetic propaganda of Pyongyang. The journey there also gives you the opportunity to stop in the port city of **Wonsan** (p355) and, in the summer, a stop off for swimming at one of the pristine sandy beaches. How many people can claim to have swum at a North Korean beach?

The Authors

MARTIN ROBINSON
Seoul, Gyeonggi-do, Gangwon-do, Jeollabuk-do, Chungcheongnam-do, Chungcheongbuk-do

Martin, the coordinating author of this guide, researched and wrote the non-regional chapters (except Food & Drink) plus Seoul and the five northern-most provinces of South Korea. He is also the author of Lonely Planet's *Seoul* guide. Martin lived in South Korea for two years teaching English, working in a provincial governor's office and writing a hiking guide to Jeollabuk-do. Before that he worked for the British Council in Tokyo, explored Asia and contributed travel articles and photographs to newspapers and magazines. Born in London and educated at Oxford University, he is married and lives in New Zealand when not roaming around our small but complicated planet.

The Coordinating Author's Favourite Trip

Scenic lakes, impressive forest-covered mountains and a serene sunrise over the East Sea made my trip from Seoul to the east coast memorable. In Chuncheon (p142), cycling along the lake (p144) as the sun set behind misty mountains and eating delicious *dakgalbi* (spicy chicken). After speeding across pristine Soyang lake (p146) on a ferry, staying in a castle-shaped motel and feasting on fresh seafood in Sokcho (p146). In Seoraksan National Park, climbing up granite cliffs to Ulsanbawi (p151) where a glass of *soju* (Korean vodka) added to my 'top-of-the-world' feeling. Then down to Naksan Beach (p151) for the night, and getting up early to walk up to Naksan Temple (p150), where the monks were already greeting the magical sunrise with rhythmic chants.

ANDREW BENDER
Food & Drink, Gyeongsangbuk-do, Jeollanam-do, Jeju-do

Andy began learning about Korea without intending to, practising the *hangeul* of designer names in the Korean Air in-flight catalogue. This New England native has got an MBA, lived in Japan and travelled all over Asia before settling in Los Angeles, home of the world's largest overseas Korean community (to satisfy those *bibimbap* cravings). His work has appeared in *Travel & Leisure*, *Fortune* and in-flight magazines and he has written four other LP titles. When not on the road, he consults on cross-cultural communication, sees friends and family as much as he can, bikes at the beach, and schemes ways to spoil his nieces and nephews, especially Dayna, who was born while he was working on this book.

ROB WHYTE
Gyeongsangnam-do

Rob has lived in Busan, South Korea, for seven years. A battle-hardened veteran of Korea's English education industry, he earned his scars and stripes in private language academies, jaebol (family-owned conglomerates) and numerous post-secondary institutions. In between travels across Gyeongsangnam province, he worked as a lowly bureaucrat for the Busan Metropolitan City government where he immersed himself in the heady issues of local government finance and municipal governance. Rob, along with four other foreign nationals, was the first expatriate hired by a local government in Korea. Originally from Canada, Rob lives with his family in Busan where he continues to work, write and dream of lands where a round of golf doesn't cost US$200.

CONTRIBUTING AUTHORS

North Korea was newly researched for this edition, but we have chosen not to identify our author so as to protect his identity and that of those North Koreans who assisted him on his travels.

Dr Trish Batchelor wrote the Health chapter. She is a general practitioner and travel medicine specialist who works at the CIWEC Clinic in Kathmandu, Nepal, as well as being a Medical Advisor to the Travel Doctor New Zealand clinics. Trish teaches travel medicine through the University of Otago, and is interested in underwater and high-altitude medicine, and in the impact of tourism on host countries. She has travelled extensively through Southeast and East Asia and particularly loves high-altitude trekking in the Himalayas.

Snapshot

South Korea's president Roh Moo-hyun won an unexpected victory in 2002 riding a wave of support from young voters. However the 56-year-old human rights lawyer from a humble background had a very tough start to his five-year term (presidents are limited to one term). Revelations about North Korea's nuclear weapon ambitions, widespread labour unrest and aggressive environmental protests gave him a baptism of fire. The euphoria of Korea's epic World Cup soccer victories soon wore off as the SARS epidemic reduced economic growth to 3%, and a fatal traffic accident involving an American army driver sparked off large anti-American demonstrations.

As the democratic process broadens and new freedoms emerge, the road ahead will be rocky. Traditional authority figures (fathers, husbands, teachers, company bosses, mayors and presidents) are losing their grip on society, and nobody is sure how the next generation will behave. The ruling elite has had amazing success at building up export industries and improving living standards, but it is widely viewed as greedy and corrupt, so lacks the moral authority of leaders who are respected and loved. A new balance of power between the regions, between central and local government, between young and old, between unions and management must be forged. An updated national consensus needs to replace the old dogmas of centralisation and industrialisation.

Despite all this the future is bright. South Korea is a wired society of hardworking, highly educated and motivated people. Crime rates are low except in top political and business circles. Many local industries are world class or becoming so, and the local film industry is now successfully taking on Hollywood in terms of box-office sales within Korea – see p42. With the right leadership miracles can be achieved – and not just on the soccer field. The public's high hopes for their unconventional and youthful leader may yet be fulfilled despite his stormy start.

The South's lenient 'Sunshine Policy' towards the North since 1997 has hardly improved relations, although mines in the DMZ have been cleared to allow road and train routes to again link the two countries sometime in the future. But the slow progress of years is often undone in one day by some extraordinary admission by the North about nuclear weapons or kidnapped Japanese nationals. Kim Jong-il has proved to be no improvement on his father, so the sufferings of the North Koreans continue, and the future is unpredictable and therefore dangerous.

One day the DMZ (Demilitarized Zone) will disappear but as South Korea prospers and North Korea continues to suffer almost famine conditions, the cost of any future unification grows year by year. To raise the standard of living in the North to equal that of the South would be a far greater challenge than that faced by West Germany when it reunited with East Germany. Also, after living for so long under two completely different economic and political systems, the mind-set in the two halves of Korea is very different. Defectors from the North can have considerable difficulty adapting to southern ways.

FAST FACTS:

Growth, inflation & unemployment: all 3-4% in 2003

Leading exports in 2003: semiconductors, computers, mobile phones, cars, ships

Leading exports in 1903: gold, rice, beans, timber, hides

Korea produces 3 million cars each year and exports 50% of them

Thirteen percent of households have a high-speed Internet connection

Koreans chomp through over 10 million packets of instant noodles every day

Korea exported US$80 million of *kimchi* in 2002

Foreigners own one-third of the shares quoted on the stock exchange

History

BUDDHISM IN KOREA

Buddhism was introduced to Korea from China during the Three Kingdoms era, establishing itself in Goguryeo and Baekje in the late 4th century and in Silla in the early 6th century. With royal support, the faith spread throughout the peninsula and incorporated indigenous shamanist beliefs. Many temples still have a small hall dedicated to shamanist deities such as the mountain god.

Many of the colourful wooden temples you can see in the mountains today have a history that stretches back over a thousand years. Although the existing buildings are usually modern, they follow the traditional style.

Buddhism became the official religion in all three states, and some monasteries became wealthy and owned large estates and thousands of slaves. Some monks dressed in silk robes, rode fine horses, and indulged in wine, women and song.

After General Yi Song-gye proclaimed himself King Taejo and founded the Joseon dynasty in 1392, Buddhism was gradually replaced as the state religion by Neo-Confucianism. King Taejo's son, Taejong, took over the monasteries' estates and their 80,000 slaves, and many temples were closed. Buddhists suffered severe discrimination throughout the Joseon era, although occasionally a sympathetic queen offered patronage and encouragement.

Koreans have adapted various foreign religions to their own patterns of thinking and behaviour. So Korean monks, especially in the past, made up their own rules rather than following those laid down by Buddha in his teachings. Far from being pacifists who didn't even kill flies, Korean monks were often called upon to defend their country in times of crisis. The mountain fortresses found throughout the Korean peninsula often contained temples and were garrisoned by warrior monks. Toughened by their spartan lifestyle and trained in martial arts, monk warriors played a major part in resisting the Japanese invasions in the 1590s.

The monks put saving their country before their Buddhist vows, even though their Neo-Confucian rulers treated them as low-born and no better than beggars. Monks were not allowed to enter the gates of Seoul, and even today just about all the famous temples are hidden away on remote mountainsides.

Nowadays monks and nuns are vegetarian and very disciplined, getting up at 4am and spending their time praying, meditating or working. The Seon (Zen) style of Buddhism is the most common.

Buddhism in South Korea is still a powerful force, and Buddhists, both lay and monastic, have figured prominently in recent environmental campaigns. Unfortunately in the North the two Kims have treated the Buddhists even worse than the Joseon kings did. Religious practice is forbidden and persistent offenders are sent to forced labour camps. Few temples were maintained or rebuilt after the Korean War and the only worship allowed is at the numerous shrines and monuments to Kim Il-sung.

Sourcebook of Korean Civilisation, edited by Peter Lee (Columbia University Press, 1993), has a wide selection of themed original historical documents with a commentary.

A New History of Korea by Lee Ki-baik (Kchokak, 1984) takes a cultural and sociological perspective on the country's tortured history.

Korea by Angus Hamilton (Heinemann, 1904) is a journalist's lively description of life in Korea under the Joseon dynasty.

CHINA'S LITTLE BROTHER

The Joseon dynasty was founded in 1392 when General Yi Song-gye refused to send his troops into battle against a Chinese army, and used them to overthrow his own government and make himself king. Not surprisingly, he received the blessing and support of the Chinese emperor, and Korea became the most loyal of the many 'tribute' countries that bordered China. In return for Chinese protection, the Joseon kings accepted the Chinese emperor's suzerainty and delivered tribute to him up to four times a year. This policy was known as *sadae* or serving the great. Except for the onerous tribute, the Korean kings retained their independence.

Because of this special relationship, when Japan attacked Korea in the 1590s, Chinese troops were sent to help Korea repel them. In just one battle at Sanchon 30,000 Chinese soldiers died. The problem was that the Japanese samurai had already laid waste to most of the country before the Chinese arrived.

Sadae was revived as foreign policy in 1950 during the Korean War, when a huge Chinese army suddenly attacked the UN forces (primarily American and South Korean troops), and rescued the North from certain defeat. Mao Zedong, the Communist Chinese emperor, was protecting his Communist

TRIBUTE TO CHINA

The tribute taken to Beijing three or four times a year during most of the Joseon period provides an interesting insight into Korean products at this time. The tribute was a symbol of Korea's vassal status, which began during the Three Kingdoms period, and the Koreans delivering it had to prostrate themselves in front of the Chinese emperor. Although the emperor sent gifts in return, they did not match what he received, and the lavish hospitality that had to be provided to the Chinese emissaries in Seoul was very expensive and could take up 15% of the government's revenue.

The Chinese would arrive at Seodaemun, the West Gate of Seoul (demolished by the Japanese in 1915) and be greeted by the king. In 1898 the Independence Gate was built nearby after Korea threw off Chinese suzerainty in 1897 when King Gojong declared himself as Emperor Kwangmu. But Korean independence did not last long and was soon followed by Japanese colonial rule which exacted far more tribute than China ever did.

The goods carried to the Forbidden Palace in Beijing varied, but one agreement stipulated a wide range of goods to be delivered. Top of the list was 100 *tael* of gold and 1000 *tael* of silver. A *tael* weighed about 40g, so that meant 4kg of gold and 40kg of silver. The emperor was also to receive 100 tiger skins, 100 deer skins and 400 other skins. A thousand packs of green tea was also on the gift list as well as rice, ginseng and pine seeds. Horses, swords and buffalo horn bows were sent as well as large quantities of paper, cotton, *ramie* cloth (an almost transparent textile made from bark) and floral-patterned straw mats from Ganghwado. Less publicised were the eunuchs and virgins that were destined for the emperor's vast harem.

In return the Chinese emperor would send the best quality silk, herbal medicines, exquisite porcelain and a library of books, amounting to hundreds of volumes. Tribute trade was a cultural and economic exchange between the two countries.

The 300-strong tribute party took one to two months to cover the 1200km route to Beijing, and spent the same amount of time there before beginning the arduous journey home. The embassy included generals, scholars, painters, doctors, interpreters, heralds, secretaries, grooms, umbrella holders and sedan chair carriers.

Buddhism and Confucianism introduced from China.	Silla kingdom rules a unified Korea from its capital Gyeongju.

Little Brother Kim Il-sung from foreign conquest. The Chinese military assistance was not so surprising in the light of the two countries' history.

For the Joseon kings and officials, *sadae* seemed a sensible policy, but the drawback was that Korea depended on China for defence and did not train or equip strong armed forces of their own. The *yangban* (elite or aristocratic class) was divided into civil and military sections, but the civil section had a much higher status. In 1894 China was defeated by Japan, and defenceless Korea was taken over almost without the Japanese firing a shot. It wasn't just technological backwardness and lack of money, but the traditional reliance on China that left King Gojong and his country weak and vulnerable.

Not only was China the protective big brother, it was the sun around which *yangban* culture circled. The Korean ruling elite looked up to China as the source of all philosophical, political, economic, literary and cultural knowledge. This led them to despise Japan and the West, and explains why modernisation and reform movements always failed.

The *yangban* were enthusiastic Confucianists – China and everything Chinese was their god. The heaven-appointed Chinese emperor was ordained to rule the world and he was their emperor too. Whether it was weapons or theories of warfare, painting or poetry, music, politics, philosophy or the concubine and eunuch system, they copied and admired China, the ultimate in civilisation, fashion and style.

The complicated Chinese script was used for virtually all government and cultural activities throughout the Joseon period. The *hangeul* script, invented during the reign of Sejong the Great in 1443, didn't come into general use until after 1945. The *yangban* opposed the use of *hangeul* because they wanted to keep the government exam as difficult as possible so that only their children had the time and money to pass. Although universally revered in Korea nowadays, the *yangban* in those days regarded *hangeul* as 'mean, vulgar and profitless', and only fit for women and children. Even in the 1960s South Korean newspapers still used many Chinese characters.

Since 1945, South Korea has admired and copied the West rather than China. South Korea still has a protective big brother in America, which plays a similar role to that played by China in the Joseon era, except that US armed forces are permanently stationed in the country. Korea is a small country with powerful neighbours and is used to swallowing its national pride when necessary.

North Korea had two big brothers (China and Russia) who provided large amounts of military and economic aid. But in the early 1990s the tap was turned off with disastrous consequences. Living with a big brother or two has its drawbacks, but North Korea is finding out the hard way that Juche – self-reliance or living on your own – can be a nightmare.

ROYAL POMP & CEREMONY

The apex of the Confucian Joseon system was the king who was heaven-sent and had absolute power, although he was expected to be benevolent towards his people. It is difficult to imagine the wealth, power and status of Joseon kings in these more democratic times. The main palace, Gyeongbokgung, contained 800 buildings and over 200 gates, and in 1900, palace costs accounted for 10% of government expenditure. Four hundred eunuchs, 500 ladies-in-waiting, 800 other court ladies and 70 *kisaeng*

DID YOU KNOW?

Wearing a topknot was a traditional male custom that had prevailed for centuries. In 1895 King Gojong had his topknot of hair cut off, but few followed his example or shared his enthusiasm for reforms.

Goryeo dynasty rules Korea – slaves produced exquisite celadon pottery.	Mongols conquer Korea and dominate the country for over a century.

(female entertainers who were expert singers and dancers) made up the royal household. Only women and eunuchs were allowed to live inside the palace – male servants, guards, officials and visitors had to leave at sunset. Most of the women lived like nuns and never left the palace.

> The court ladies were locked up behind the nine gates of the palace where they waited upon the king and queen, princes and princesses. Only the lucky ones became favourites of the royal lovers but the rest wasted their sweetness in drudgery.
>
> Ha Tae-hung, *Guide to Korean Culture*

Angus Hamilton watched 18 *kisaeng* perform an outdoor dance for King Gojong. Wearing long silk gowns and huge wigs, they were 'lithe and graceful' as they danced and sang to the 'strange eerie notes' of the music. 'The dance epitomised the poetry and grace of human motion. The dainty attitude of the performers had a gentle delicacy which was delightful.'

At the Court of Korea by William Franklin Sands gives a first-hand account of King Gojong and his government at the turn of the century.

First-hand accounts of King Gojong's court reveal the grandeur of a vanished age. In 1895 Isabella Bird visited King Gojong and Queen Min in the newly restored Gyeongbokgung:

> What with 800 troops, 1500 attendants and officials of all descriptions, courtiers and ministers and their attendants, secretaries, messengers and hangers-on, the vast enclosure of the palace seemed as crowded and populated as the city itself.
>
> Isabella Bird, *Korea and Her Neighbours*

A missionary's wife, Harriet Heron Gale, observed the pampered life of the crown prince, who later became Emperor Sunjong:

DID YOU KNOW?

Soup, fish, quail, wild duck, pheasant, stuffed and rolled beef, vegetables, creams, glacé walnuts, fruits, claret and coffee were on the menu when Isabella Bird had dinner with King Gojong and Queen Min.

> An army of attendants and maids in long blue silk shirts and yellow jackets hover about his little kingship all day long, powdering his face, painting his lips and finger tips, shaving the top of his head, pulling out his eyebrows, cutting his food into the daintiest of morsels, fanning him with monstrous long-handled fans, never leaving him alone for a moment..., even at night guarding and watching by his bedside, singing him to sleep with a queer little lullaby.
>
> James Scarth Gale, *History of the Korean People*

Families provided the royal family with young eunuchs, the only 'male' staff allowed to live inside the palaces. The eunuchs were privy to all the secrets of the state, and their influence stemmed from the fact that they were the only people who could wait upon the king:

> They sweep his room, make his bed, draw the blinds, spread the quilt, put on his clothes, tie his topknot, fix his head-band and hat, bring in his table, light his pipe. They are all around and about him with their sallow, clammy existences. They move in and out of the kitchen and among the serving maids. There is not a corner of the palace, be it the emperor's or queen's apartments, that is not free to them.
>
> James Scarth Gale, *History of the Korean People*

1392	1443
Establishment of Joseon dynasty by General Yi Seong-gye, who makes Seoul the capital.	Invention of *hangeul*, Korea's unique script, by scholars working for King Sejong the Great.

LIVES OF THE EUNUCHS

The eunuchs were the most extraordinary people. They could become as powerful as leading government officials because they were around the king and the royal family for 24 hours a day. All access to the king was through them, as they were the royal bodyguards and responsible for the safety of their master. This was an easy way to earn money and they usually exploited it to the full.

These bodyguard eunuchs, toughened by a harsh training regime of martial arts, were also personal servants to the king and even nursemaids to the royal children. They played so many roles that life must have been very stressful for them, particularly as any mistake could lead to horrific physical punishments.

Although often illiterate and uneducated, a few became important advisors to the king, attaining high government positions and amassing great wealth. Most were from poor families and their greed for money was a national scandal, although some *yangban* aristocrats were no better. Eunuchs were supposed to serve their sacred master the king with total devotion, like monks serving Buddha, never thinking about mundane matters like money or status – but of course few were that high-minded.

A surprising aspect is that the eunuchs were usually married and adopted young eunuch boys who they brought up as their sons to follow in their footsteps. The eunuch in charge of the king's health would pass on his medical knowledge to his 'son'. Under the Confucian system not only gays but also eunuchs had to get married.

The system continued until 1910 when the country's new Japanese rulers summoned all the eunuchs to Deoksu palace and dismissed them from government service. In Japan, unlike in China, Vietnam and Korea, the ruler had no large harem guarded by eunuchs.

Diplomat William Franklin Sands found he could not escape from them:

> These curious eunuch people wandered in and out of my quarters at all times, questioning about everything, restless, eternally dissatisfied and greedy. Under no other conditions could one possibly gain so complete an insight into the secret workings of palace diplomacy in the East as by living among them.
> William Franklin Sands, *At the Court of Korea*

Eunuch (1968), an artistic film directed by Shin Sang-ok, is based on true events. The story concerns a lady who is forced by her father to become the king's concubine although she loves someone else. The film reveals what went on in those now-empty and dusty palaces.

THE JOSEON CLASS & CASTE SYSTEM

Neo-Confucianism was the ruling ideology of the entire Joseon era, which lasted over 500 years, from 1392 to 1910, and it strengthened the class and caste system that was inherited from the previous dynasties. Rule by Confucian scholars was not much fun for most of the population.

Traditional Korean society was divided into four hereditary groups. At the top were the bilingual *yangban* who used Chinese characters when they wrote. Most of them were landowners who collected rent for themselves and taxes for the government, both of which the peasant farmers usually paid with crops or textiles, which were the currency of those times. The *yangban* frequently imposed additional unauthorised taxes, which they kept for themselves.

Local magistrates supported the *yangban* and enforced the laws vigorously. Torture-induced confessions were routine and dreadful floggings were the usual punishment. When some Dutch shipwrecked sailors were beaten for trying to escape, one of their companions Hendrik Hamel wrote that 'as a result they had to stay in bed for about a month'. They had only received 25 blows, but locals often received 50 to 90 blows, even for minor offences. In very serious cases an entire family would be punished – a practice still prevalent in the North.

The top *yangban* lived in Seoul and aspired to be Confucian scholars and gentlemen who entertained their male friends lavishly while discussing art, music and philosophy. Their lifestyle is portrayed in the award-winning film *Chihwaseon*.

The *yangban* disdained military and business occupations but admired teachers, scholars, poets and artists. These attitudes are still around. A picnic party in the mountains with *kisaeng* dancing girls, *sijo* (three-line poems usually about nature), songs, green tea and rice wine was what life was all about.

They rarely paid taxes or did military service, and the symbols of their high rank included a tiled house, silk robes, black hats of woven horsehair, long pipes, ink stones and calligraphy brushes. In the 19th century many *yangban* sold places in their family registers to non-*yangban* who wanted the status and military service and tax exemptions of the hereditary aristocrats. Not all *yangban* were wealthy – extravagant spending, bad luck, failing the government exam, political exile, runaway slaves, and not obtaining a government job could all result in impoverishment.

Their position within their class depended on the size of their estate, the number of slaves and concubines (secondary wives) they possessed, and their government job. To become an important government official they had to learn to read and write the Chinese language and memorise key Confucian texts. Then they could pass the all-important government exams, the narrow and only gateway to a good job, wealth and high status.

Scholars and teachers are still highly respected and in both North and South Korea the university entrance exams dominate the lives of most children and their mothers, whose primary duty is to make sure their children pass the university entrance exam and go to a good university. A mania for education unites Koreans of all ages and eras, wherever they live.

Unfortunately the top-level *yangban* often joined factions based on powerful family and regional groups. For long periods of Joseon history, weak kings were dominated by feuding *yangban* factions who threw off Confucian restraints and indulged in assassinations and massacres. Factions grouped around powerful individuals still dominate politics on both sides of the DMZ.

Often the *yangban* factions were divided into westerners and northerners, following the pattern of the Baekje, Silla and Goguryeo kingdoms. This regional division still bedevils the peninsula today. The North is a separate and hostile country, while in the 2002 presidential election in South Korea, 90% of westerners in Jeolla province voted for 'their man' Roh Moo-hyun.

Below the *yangban* were the *chungin*, the middle people, who were accountants, high-ranking soldiers, successful merchants or local magistrates.

1866	1876
Thousands of Korean Catholics executed.	Korea opens its ports to foreign trade.

Most of this small class had specialist government jobs in Seoul which they passed on to their children. The merchants were few because the government taxed everything that moved, and generally controlled and restricted the economy. Market sellers and travelling peddlers became common in the later stages of the dynasty, but they never achieved *chungin* status.

One troublesome group in this middle class were the numerous offspring of the *yangban* and their concubines. 'We marry our wives but we love our concubines', a *yangban* explained to Isabella Bird. The children of concubines were not allowed to take the government exams and were not usually accepted as *yangban* and so fell into the *chungin* group or even lower.

The *sangmin* or common people were the largest group, consisting of peasant farmers, free labourers and fishermen. They spent their lives working hard for little or no reward. Forced to pay high levels of rent and tax (perhaps 50% of what they produced), they were also subject to regular military conscription and forced labour on government projects such as building roads, irrigation dams, fortresses and palaces.

At the mercy of freezing winters, fickle nature and remorseless moneylenders, the peasants generally led a miserable, downtrodden life enlivened by the occasional shamanist festival or bout of *makgeolli* (fermented rice wine) drinking.

South Korean folk museums present an image of happy peasants who spent their time singing and dancing, but museums in the North go to the opposite extreme and portray the peasants leading a hellish life due to the evil money-and-daughter-grabbing landowning class.

The peasants were hardly better off than the *chonmin* or low-born who were at the bottom level of society. The largest element of this level was the 30% of the population who were slaves. The slave system went back to the Three Kingdoms period and could have started with prisoners of war being made slaves; slavery being a punishment for criminal behaviour; or parents being forced to sell their children into slavery. The government owned many slaves (450,000 in 1467), and the rest were privately owned and worked on farms or in households.

A wealthy family might have 50 slaves on their household register, but just a handful was more common. One Confucian academy had 757 slaves on its register. Slaves had no family name (only a degrading personal name), cost less than a cow or a horse, and their children could be taken away or sold when they reached working age. Adult and child slaves, male and female, were bought and sold at prices fixed by the government. Slaves were a popular wedding present.

Slavery was hereditary so they were trapped forever. Even if a slave married a non-slave their children were still slaves. About the only way of escaping was by joining the military, since slaves were sometimes given their freedom as a reward for some brave action. Many were ill-treated, but escaped and led a wandering life. Runaway slaves (around 100,000 in 1467) were a major social problem, which suggests they were often harshly treated by their masters, who were never punished for abusing or even murdering their slaves. A 1692 report

'Slavery was hereditary... Even if a slave married a non-slave their children were still slaves'

1894	1894–95
Donghak peasant uprising defeated.	Japan defeats China.

DONGHAK DEMANDS

The Donghak rebellion, which began in 1893 in Jeolla province, attracted huge numbers of peasants and low-born groups. The rebels were only armed with primitive, homemade weapons but they defeated the government army sent against them. The rebellion spread to neighbouring provinces and when King Gojong called in Chinese troops, Japanese troops also arrived. The rebels were defeated and their leaders, including Chon Pong-jun who was known as the 'Green Pea General' because of his small size, were executed by Japanese firing squads.

The demands of the rebels reveal their many grievances against the Joseon social system:

- Slaves should be freed.
- The low-born should be better treated.
- Land should be redistributed.
- Taxes on fish and salt should be scrapped.
- No unauthorized taxes should be levied and any corrupt *yangban* should be severely punished.
- All debts should be cancelled.
- Regional favouritism and factions should be abolished.
- Widows should be allowed to remarry.
- Traitors who support foreign interference should be punished.

complained that 'local governors are raping state-owned female slaves on their whim'.

The slavery system was a cause of the country's weakness – slaves didn't pay taxes, nor did they serve in the army, and their productivity was low since they received no wages and had no reason to work hard. A peasant and slave rebellion (see the Donghak Demands boxed text, above) played a major role in the dynasty's downfall and the Japanese takeover.

Most male government slaves were freed in 1801, but slavery was not finally abolished until 1897. Some slaves were slave owners, and those with special talents could improve their position – for instance one slave became a famous painter Many artisans were slaves, so these occupations had a low status. Most of the magnificent Goryeo and Joseon celadon pottery was made by slaves.

Workers in certain occupations called *paekchong* were particularly despised, like *burakumin* in Japan. Gravediggers, prison wardens, wicker workers, *kisaeng* hostesses, travelling entertainers, shamanist healers, monks and nuns were all in this unfortunate group. The lowest of the low were butchers and tanners, who had to wear a special hat and clothes and walk in a funny way. They were outcasts who were forced to live in segregated hamlets outside ordinary towns and villages. In 1923 *paekchong* formed Hyongpyongsa (Equity Society), an organisation that campaigned against discrimination, and for the right of their children to attend schools. Social apartheid took a long time to die.

The strict, hereditary hierarchy helps to explain why Korea is one of the few Asian countries where large numbers adopted Christianity. The Christian concept of the equality of man (and woman) outraged the

www.kf.or.kr has video lectures on history (though the sound is not very good) and a link to *Koreana*, a magazine with some history articles.

Confucian *yangban*, but represented a hope for a better life and future to women and to the despised and oppressed masses. Protestant missionaries arrived in 1884 and founded many schools and hospitals which are still running today. Religions that promise a good education for their children appeal to Koreans.

Today the legacy of the traditional social system is still strong – everyone wants a white-collar job and manual labour is looked down on. There is a strong feeling that authority – whether that of parents, teachers, older people, or the government and police – should be respected and obeyed. Men are perceived as more important than women.

This acceptance of hierarchy and hardship helps to explain public passivity in North Korea, which went from the Joseon slave system to the Japanese colonial system to the totalitarian communist rule of the two Kims. The people there have never experienced a day of democracy and civil rights.

The Kims have divided North Korean society into three hereditary groups – the 'reliables' include Communist Party members, armed forces personnel and those with peasant ancestors; the 'unreliables' are those with family members who were *yangban*, worked for the Japanese during colonisation, were religious leaders or have defected abroad; the 'neutrals' include everyone not in the first two categories. As with the Joseon system, your life (and the lives of your children and your children's children and so on) depends on your family classification. Only 'reliables' are allowed to live in Pyongyang, study at a good university or marry a 'reliable'.

Isolated from the outside world, inundated with relentless propaganda, and threatened by police torture chambers, forced labour in prison camps and the punishment of their entire family for generations in the event of any sign of rebellion, the North Koreans, unable to move or think freely, are completely at the mercy of their government. The most desperate flee to China while the rest helplessly await their fate.

KOREA & JAPAN

Relations between these two countries have always been difficult and controversial. Koreans claim that their early dynasties, especially Baekje, were a major influence on Japanese culture, and that Chinese civilization was filtered to Japan through Korea. But Japanese historians usually see it differently. There isn't much about their historical relationship that the two rivals agree on.

During the Joseon era, Japanese pirates caused endless trouble, but the real disaster occurred when the warlord, Toyotomi Hideyoshi, united Japan and decided to attack Korea and then China. In 1592, 150,000 well-armed Japanese troops, divided into nine armies, rampaged throughout Korea looting, raping and killing. Palaces and temples were burnt to the ground and priceless cultural treasures were destroyed or stolen. Entire villages of ceramic potters were shipped back to Japan.

Fortunately a series of brilliant naval victories by Admiral Yi Sun-sin helped to turn the tide against the Japanese. His iron-clad warships, called *geobukseon* (turtle ships), played their part although only five

Korea's Place in the Sun by Bruce Cumings (WW Norton, 1997) is a well-written history of Korea from 1860.

Samurai Invasion by Stephen Turnbull (Cassell & Co, 2002) is a detailed account of the Japanese invasions of Korea in the 1590s.

1910	1919
Japan annexes Korea and abolishes the monarchy.	Nationwide protests against Japanese rule crushed.

War Diary of Admiral Yi Sun-sin, edited by Sohn Pow-key (Yonsei University Press, 1977), is a straightforward and fascinating account by Korea's greatest admiral of the battles, floggings and court intrigues that were his daily preoccupations.

were deployed. With the arrival of Chinese troops and counter attacks by guerrilla bands and monk warriors, the Japanese were forced to withdraw in 1593.

However, the Japanese retained a handful of forts in the south of Korea and in 1597 they returned. They massacred everything that moved in Namwon and killed 30,000 Chinese soldiers at Sanchon, but Admiral Yi again destroyed their navy. Stout resistance on land and Hideyoshi's death in 1598 again thwarted Japanese ambitions of Asian domination, but only at the cost of massive destruction and economic dislocation in Korea.

Grand plans of conquering Korea and China resurfaced in Japan three hundred years later, at the end of the 19th century. After defeating China and Russia in quick succession, defenceless Korea became a Japanese protectorate in 1905 and a colony in 1910.

Heroes & Collaborators

The Japanese occupation of Korea was not particularly long – annexation lasted for 35 years, from 1910 until 1945 – but it was a traumatic experience that has not been forgotten or forgiven. The occupation ended more than 50 years ago but the scars remain.

In the North, countless films and TV programmes still focus on atrocities committed by the Japanese during their rule. This is designed to make the public feel grateful to Kim Il-sung who claims (falsely) to have kicked the Japanese out of Korea. The descendants of Koreans deemed by the government to have worked for the Japanese occupation authorities are still subject to severe discrimination.

South Korea, however, punished very few collaborators, partly because they were needed in the fight against communism. If you visit Independence Hall, near Cheonan in Chungcheongnam-do, the South Korean shrine to the heroes of the anti-Japanese resistance, keep in mind that for every independence fighter there were a hundred who collaborated in one way or another.

My Innocent Uncle by Chae Man-shik (Jimoondang) is a shocking short story, written in a direct, colloquial style, that portrays a pro-Japanese Korean opportunist who refers to Japan as his home country and wants to marry a Japanese girl. His uncle is innocent of such treacherous views but his opposition to Japanese rule is ineffective.

On 1 March 1919 the death of ex-king Gojong sparked off massive pro-independence demonstrations throughout the country. The protests were ruthlessly suppressed, however. The Japanese at the time claimed that 500 were killed, 1400 injured and 12,000 arrested, but Korean estimates put the casualties at ten times these figures.

A certain amount of collaboration was unavoidable, especially in the later war years. But Koreans made up half the police force who hunted down and tortured thousands of Korean independence fighters; Koreans went around the country urging students to join the Japanese army and 800,000 volunteered; Koreans also made money forcing young Korean girls to have sex with Japanese soldiers; and pro-Japanese *yangban* were rewarded with special titles. Collaboration was widespread but has never been fully and frankly debated in South Korea. The most painful memories of Japanese rule concern not what the Japanese did but what some Koreans did.

Westernised Japanese bureaucrats ran the colonial government and they implemented policies that developed industries and modernised the government. Thus the main trauma of the occupation was psychological

1945	1948
Korea liberated following the surrender of Japanese forces to the Allies.	Republic of Korea established.

rather than economic or political, and during the 1930s Japan adopted the policy of trying to destroy the Korean sense of national identity. Koreans were forced to use Japanese names, to speak and write Japanese, to bow to the Japanese emperor's picture, and to pray at Shinto shrines; they read and saw Japanese propaganda every day; they shopped in Japanese department stores, banked at Japanese banks, drank Japanese beer, travelled on the Japanese-run railway, and dreamed of attending a university in Tokyo. Cities were renamed, *hangeul* was banned in schools and Korean history books were burnt. It was no wonder that some Koreans began to think of themselves as Japanese. Korea had officially ceased to exist; it was a province of mighty Japan.

By 1940, the Japanese owned 40% of the land and 700,000 of them were living and working in Korea. Around 3 million Korean men and women were uprooted and sent to work as miners, farm labourers, factory workers and soldiers abroad, mainly in Japan and China. Over 130,000 Korean miners in Japan worked 12 hours a day, were paid meagre (if any) wages, poorly fed and subjected to brutal, club-wielding overseers. More than 100,000 young Korean girls were forced to work as 'comfort women' (see A Long Protest, on this page).

It was Korea's darkest hour but resistance was continued by guerrilla groups in China and the Soviet Union, and campaigns to 'Buy Korean' and preserve *hangeul* inside Korea.

Japan's surrender to the Allies in 1945 opened a new chapter in the stormy relationship between the two countries. Companies and workers in both countries now battle each other to produce the best ships, cars, steel products, computer chips, mobile phones and other electronic equipment. The new rivalry is a never-ending competition for world markets. Sports are another modern-day battleground to decide who is top dog.

POST-WAR PERIOD

The 40-year period from 1953 until 1992 was a time of rapid economic development (especially after 1960) but was a dark era in South Korea's political history. Corrupt, autocratic and military rulers censored the media, imprisoned and tortured political opponents, manipulated elections, and continually changed the country's constitution to suit themselves. Student protests and less frequent trade union street protests were often violent, as were the police or military forces sent to suppress them.

DID YOU KNOW?

The marathon at the 1936 Berlin Olympics was won by Kitei Son of Japan, but his real name was Sohn Kee-chung and he was from Korea.

www.twotigers.org has a dozen personal testimonies by Korean 'comfort women' that give a unique insight into their horrifying ordeals.

A LONG PROTEST

Hwang Geum-joo and a handful of other Korean comfort women, survivors of the WWII camps where they were forced to have sex with Japanese soldiers, have been protesting outside the Japanese embassy in Seoul every Wednesday at noon since 1992. 'Our numbers are dwindling every year' she says, 'and nothing has changed'. With their young supporters, the old ladies hold up placards demanding an apology and financial compensation. Hwang Geum-joo has taken part in over 554 protests outside the embassy but she refuses to give up. 'We are still full of anger and they should apologise for what they did to us!'

1950–53	1988
Korean War.	Olympic Games held in Seoul; publication of Lonely Planet's first guide to Korea.

When the Korean War ended in 1953, Syngman Rhee continued his dictatorial rule until 1961, when he and his wife fled to Hawaii following a widespread campaign against him that included university professors demonstrating in the streets of Seoul. Following a military coup later in 1961, three generals ruled in turn and often won elections despite almost continuous student protests. Finally, in 1992, a civilian, Kim Young-sam, took over and ushered in a period of more genuine democracy – although he failed to eradicate widespread corruption inherited from the era of military rule. His successors, Kim Dae-jung and Roh Moo-hyun, have introduced more democratic reforms, but the country's economic system continues to be far more developed and sophisticated than its political system.

1992	1996
Kim Young-sam elected president and ushers in a more democratic political era.	Korea achieves US$10,000 per capita income.

The Culture

THE NATIONAL PSYCHE

Korea is probably the most Confucian nation in Asia. At the heart of the Confucian doctrine are the Five Relationships, which prescribe behaviour between ruler and subject, father and son, husband and wife, old and young and between friends. Understanding this structuring of relationships is very important in making sense of Korean society.

All relationships require a placement in some sort of hierarchy so that everybody knows how to behave and speak with respect towards each other. The middle-aged male office worker who jumps the queue to pay for a Coke at a 7-Eleven store does not even register your presence because you have not been introduced and he has nowhere to place you on the scale of relationships. An introduction and an exchange of business cards would immediately place you into a category that would demand certain behaviour from him.

Once contact has been established, everything changes. Courtesy is highly valued and most Koreans will go out of their way to be pleasant and helpful. And you should return the favour – be polite and smile even when bargaining over prices in the market.

KOREA AND YOU

Although shyness and poor English skills are obstacles that have to be overcome, Koreans are often kinder to foreigners than to their own people. This is partly because they want visitors to have a good impression of their nation. Like citizens of other small countries, Koreans worry about their national identity and image.

Not everything is perfect and there are annoyances – people block your way and push in front of you, drivers go too fast and ignore red lights, and all the 'hurry, hurry' can be tiresome. Walking around with a stern unsmiling face and ignoring strangers are also part of Korean custom. Koreans are often reserved initially but if you are friendly and outgoing they respond in like manner. The key to an enjoyable and enlightening trip is to be open-minded and positive rather than critical and judgemental. Korea is different from what you've been used to, but that's the reason for going there.

The main problem you are likely to encounter is a scarcity of English speakers, so the best preparation is to spend time learning the *hangeul* script, the numbers and some simple phrases. It doesn't take long – see p394 for the Language chapter. Most restaurants lack English menus so study the Food & Drink chapter (p50). Korea is a relatively crime-free country, but the usual precautions should be taken. You will see women walking around alone very late at night but there is always an element of risk.

Respect for seniors is one of the more admirable legacies of Confucianism, and elderly visitors will find that some young people will offer them seats on buses and subway trains. Youthful visitors can follow the local custom and get into a Confucian state of mind.

When visiting temples, private homes, Korean-style restaurants and guesthouses, take off your shoes and leave them by the front door. Wearing socks is more polite than bare feet. In Korea you are judged by your appearance so dress casually but neatly.

It's customary to bring along a small gift when visiting somebody at their home. When presented with a gift, your host may at first refuse it. This doesn't mean that he or she doesn't want it – the idea is not to look greedy. You should insist that they take it, and they will accept it 'reluctantly'. For the same reason, the recipient of a gift is not supposed to open the package immediately, but rather put it aside and open it later. If you want to follow polite Korean custom, receive gifts using both hands.

Korean relationships are complicated by the social hierarchy. Neo-Confucian ideals dictated that fathers, husbands, teachers, bosses and governments should be authoritarian rather than democratic and this is changing only slowly. People with a high status may still act arrogantly towards those with lower status. Status is governed by a few key factors: who is older? who has the more prestigious job? who attended the better university? who comes from the most respectable family?

This notion of social status is one aspect of Korean culture that many foreigners (or those who prefer equality) find difficult to accept. If you are working in Korea, your employer might make it all too clear that he or she is on the top of the social totem pole and you are lower. But for short-term tourists, this is seldom a problem and since most Koreans are anxious to make a good impression, visitors are accorded considerable kindness and respect. Although even this depends on which country you are from – people from rich countries have a higher position in the social hierarchy than those from poorer countries.

The Korean character has a fanatical streak – computer game addicts fill the Internet rooms, obsessive students study all night, sports training programmes are relentless, and working hours are frequently excessive. Everything is taken seriously, including what are relaxing leisure pursuits in other countries like ten-pin bowling, hiking and golf. Drivers are aggressive, and protests by students, trade unionists and environmentalists can turn threatening and violent.

Life is competitive and stressful with no safety net provided by a welfare state. Health insurance and pensions are only there if you work. The lack of welfare benefits means that taxes are low but on the flipside, everyone has to depend on their own efforts. The lazy and the unlucky have a hard time unless they have support from their family and friends. Working hours are agonisingly long although a five-day week is gradually being introduced.

Computer gamers may spend all their spare time sitting in front of a screen and live on instant noodles, but many Koreans are very health-conscious. The millions of hikers who stream into the mountains at weekends are not only enjoying nature but are also keeping fit. Saunas and hot spring baths are big attractions. Thousands of health foods and drinks are sold in markets and pharmacies, which stock traditional as well as Western medicines. Health drinks include fruit teas, vitamin-packed canned drinks and traditional alcoholic drinks that are flavoured with medicinal herbs and roots such as the elixir ginseng. Nearly every food claims to be an aphrodisiac – 'good for stamina' is the local phrase.

Family life is rapidly becoming Westernised with small nuclear families the norm and a high percentage of divorces and abortions. Education and other costs deter families from having more than two children. Many marriages are still arranged by parents or matchmakers, although dating and love marriages are on the increase. The position of women is improving but equality of the sexes is a long way off.

Another aspect of the Korean character you will come across is their generosity. Fighting to pay the bill is a common phenomenon and if a Korean takes you under his or her wing it is difficult to pay for anything. If you work in Korea, fellow workers may ply you with small gifts of drinks or snacks. When someone comes back from a holiday they often hand out a small souvenir to everyone. Cash collections are always being made for meals, trips or a colleague who has fallen ill. At New Year and Chuseok (Thanksgiving Day) gift-giving reaches fever pitch and general stores are so filled with mountains of gift packages – 10kg cartons of grapes, 10kg packs of pears and 5kg jars of *kimchi* – that you can hardly squeeze inside.

'Nearly every food claims to be an aphrodisiac – "good for stamina" is the local phrase.'

The Confucian Mindset

Despite rapid economic development and modernisation in recent years, Korea is still Confucian. A Western woman who dates a Korean man soon finds this out as does a Westerner who teaches English in a Korean high school. Of course not everyone follows all the Confucian rules but they are still around inside people's heads to a greater or lesser extent. It's what makes Koreans different from Westerners.

The Confucian legacy of the 500-year Joseon dynasty that ended less than a century ago still lingers. But what exactly is Confucianism? It is not a religion, although in the past it did involve ancestral rites, shrines dedicated to important Chinese and Korean Confucian scholars, and offerings to the Sky by the king. It is more a philosophy, an ideology and a mindset:

- Respect and obedience towards authority and seniors at all times is crucial. Never argue back to your parents, teachers or your boss. Be polite to older brothers and sisters. Give up your seat on the bus or train to an older person. Don't start eating before your seniors. Use polite terms when speaking to or about someone older than you. Expect a heavy penalty (including physical punishment) if you step out of line.
- Education is very, very important and only educated people are civilised and respected. Passing the university entrance exam and going to a good university is the key ambition in life.
- Men and women have separate roles and should live separate lives. In *yangban* (aristocratic) houses men and women lived in different quarters. A woman's role is life-long service and obedience, although inside the home mothers may rule the roost. Men shouldn't have to do housework, cook or look after children. In the past women rarely inherited anything and widows couldn't remarry. Even now women cannot be head of a household, although this may change.
- Status and dignity are very important. Every action you take reflects on your family, your school, your company, and your country. Criminals hide their faces and feel shame. Don't do anything that would make your boss lose face, even in a very minor way, and he will always pay the bill when you go out eating and drinking.
- There is always a pecking order rather than equality. Never forget who is senior and who is junior to you. Even different types of rice and fruit are in a hierarchy, as are mountains, rivers, hats and brand names. Everything on and beyond the earth is in a hierarchy. Schools and universities are not equal, people are not equal and manual workers are looked down on.
- Families are more important than individuals. Individuals are just an insignificant part of a family that stretches backwards and forwards in time. Everyone's purpose in life is to raise up their family's reputation and wealth, and so they must study and work hard. No one should choose a career or marry someone against their parents' wishes – a bad choice could bring ruin to a family that has been built up over generations. Everyone must marry and have a son to continue the family line. Homosexuals are therefore perverts.
- Loyalty is important. In the Joseon period thousands of Catholic converts suffered appalling tortures and death rather than renounce their faith, and a wife who committed suicide when her husband died was praised by Neo-Confucian scholars as a loyal woman. A loyal liar is a virtuous person, and you are obliged to help relatives or friends in trouble.
- Save money and don't be extravagant. Wear pastel shades rather than bright colours. Revealing clothes are only worn by immoral women. Don't show off. Be frugal with praise. Life is serious rather than fun.

The Koreans by Michael Breen (St Martin's Press, 1999) is an expat view of the Korean psyche but is more accurate than what you usually hear in Itaewon bars.

LIFESTYLE

The traditional Korean style is to sleep on a *yo* mattress (similar to a futon) on the floor, and to sit on floor cushions at low tables for meals. Floors are heated from underneath by the *ondol* system. Hotels often offer a choice between a *yo* or a bed. Although tables and chairs are increasingly common, customers at traditional restaurants have to sit on the floor.

The Way Home (2002), written and directed by Lee Jeong-hyang, is an unsentimental but poetic study of an ancient rural grandma and her selfish, rude young grandson from Seoul who comes to stay with her. This unusual and engaging low-budget film about rural and city contrasts was a huge hit with local audiences.

Koreans rarely entertain at home, as 'inside' female-dominated family life is traditionally kept separate from 'outside' male-dominated working life. Therefore restaurants, cafés and bars are popular places to meet and entertain friends and work colleagues. Few people like to eat alone – they prefer being part of a group.

In one generation the country has been transformed from a rural to an urban society and although nearly everyone prefers the urban lifestyle there is widespread nostalgia for rural hometowns.

Work and study hours are long and tedious, although a five-day week is being introduced for some workers. Car mechanics are still banging away at 9pm on a Saturday evening and junior high school children may be studying until 2am. Everyone rushes around – and this trend is particularly evident when it comes to driving behaviour on the roads. Most people live in city apartment blocks surrounded by the latest gadgets and wear brand-name clothes.

An outstanding characteristic of Korean society is an obsession with education. An old saying is that 'a person without education is like a beast wearing clothes'. These days one university degree is not enough and two or three is becoming the norm, preferably including one from overseas. To get into one of the top universities, high-school students go through 'examination hell', studying 14 hours a day and torturing their brains with multiple-choice questions on calculus, the bizarre intricacies of English grammar and many other topics. From the moment of birth, 'education mamas' prepare their offspring for the all-important exams that will determine their child's fate and status in life. There is an inexhaustible desire for studying English in *hagwon* (private language schools) by people of all ages – see p375 for information on teaching English in Korea.

The minimum wage in Korea is W567,000 a month but the average worker receives W1.6 million a month. An expat English teacher could

---

PROVERBS

Traditional sayings provide an uncensored insight into a nation's psyche.

- Koreans' strong belief in the importance of education is reflected in this proverb: 'Teaching your child one book is better than leaving him a fortune.'

- The hope of all Koreans of humble origins is to improve their lifestyle and be 'a dragon that rises from a ditch'.

- The blunt, peasant humour of the Korean character is expressed by this poor man's lament: 'I have nothing but my testicles'.

- Koreans distrust lawyers and governments and prefer to settle disputes in their own way: 'The law is far but the fist is near.'

- An unblemished character is a Korean's most treasured possession. To avoid any suspicion of being a thief, 'Do not tie your shoelaces in a melon patch or touch your hat under a pear tree.'

- Koreans have often needed guts and determination to overcome defeats and disasters: 'After the house is burnt, pick up the nails.'

A BANG LIFESTYLE

In every city and town you can find plenty of *bang* (rooms) which play a large role in the modern Korean lifestyle They always charge reasonable prices, so why not join the locals as they enjoy their varied leisure activities. Some of the different types of *bang*:

Bideobang Grubby rooms with a sofa and a screen that show your video choice.

Board game bang A large room where you can play board games. Mainly found in Seoul but spreading fast.

Da bang Old-fashioned teashops where the 'coffee girls' deliver more than their name suggests.

DVD bang Smart small rooms with a sofa and a big screen that show your choice of DVD film in English or with English subtitles. Popular with courting couples.

Jjimjilbang Sweating in these smart and sultry saunas is part of the Korean way of life.

Noraebang Small rooms full of happy groups of all ages singing along to their favourite songs. English songs and soft drinks are available.

PC bang Big rooms that are full of young male computer game addicts and the occasional emailer.

expect to receive W1.9 million a month as well as free accommodation, return flights, health insurance and a bonus at the end of a one-year contract. An office worker with a degree starts on about W1.7 million a month, but W2 million in a big company, while doctors, lawyers and pilots are up in the W4 million to W6 million a month bracket. In contrast bar staff jobs are advertised at W600,000 a month and fast-food outlets pay only W2350 an hour.

Marriage is changing and the traditional pattern of arranged marriages at a young age organised by parents and with the wife forced to stay home and be subservient to her husband and in-laws is disappearing fast; divorce is on the increase. Over 40% of university graduates are female and the balance of power between the genders is shifting.

In the future, not all young Korean men will be able to marry Korean brides, as South Korea is facing a shortage of marriageable women. In 2002, 109 boys were born for every 100 girls, and by the year 2010 it is estimated that there will be 128 single men at 'peak marriageable age' (27 to 30 years old) for every 100 single eligible women (24 to 27 years old). And those numbers get worse every year.

What is going wrong? Most young Korean families these days want only two children, and one of each gender is seen as ideal – two sons are acceptable but two daughters less so. Ultrasound scans can be used to discover the sex of any foetus and if female she will sometimes be aborted. It is illegal in South Korea for doctors to inform prospective parents of the sex of their foetus, but it does happen in some cases.

So why don't some Korean parents want just daughters? The answer mostly stems from the strong residual Confucianism in their social mores. It remains all-important that a man's family name be passed on to future generations and only males can properly perform the ancestor rituals that are still practised. Economic security in the golden years is another concern and some parents want a son to continue their family business. Parents traditionally tend to think of their daughters as given away to her husband's family and lost to her birth family when she gets married. Importing brides would ease the female baby shortage but other Asian countries have the same problem.

POPULATION

South Korea's population is 47.6 million, of whom 10 million live in the capital Seoul, and 12.5 million live in nearby Incheon and Gyeonggi-do. The population density of 480 per sq km is one of the highest

DID YOU KNOW?

International marriages are increasing and in 2002 5% of Korean weddings involved foreigners. Over 7000 Korean men chose a Chinese bride, while 959 slipped a ring on a Japanese finger and 859 married Filipinas. On the other hand 2377 Korean females married their Japanese sweethearts, 1200 said 'I do' to Americans, and 272 walked down the aisle with a Chinese groom.

in the world – 82% of the population is crammed into urban areas. Farming and fishing villages are in terminal decline as older people die and young people leave for a more alluring life in the cities. Villages are losing 3% of their population every year, and only 4% of the rural population is under 40 years old. Local and central governments are doing their best to halt rural decline but despite the traffic jams, crowded streets and polluted air in the cities, no one wants to give up the educational facilities, health services, entertainment venues and job opportunities that

TRADITIONAL COSTUMES

The striking traditional clothing that used to be worn all the time by Koreans is known as *hanbok* and was as much part of the local culture as *hangeul* and *kimchi*. Traditionally women wore a loose-fitting short blouse with long sleeves and a voluminous long skirt, while men wore a jacket and baggy trousers. Both sexes wore socks. Cotton replaced hemp as the main clothing material during the Joseon era. In winter, overcoats were worn over the top of padded clothes and people piled on lots of undergarments to keep out the freezing cold. Men sometimes wore a wide waistcoat. The exact designs have varied over the centuries, especially female *hanbok*, but the clothes have maintained their basic pattern of simple lines without any pockets or buttons.

Hanbok style followed the Confucian principle of unadorned modesty. Natural dyes were used to create plain colours, although some parts of clothing could be embroidered, and the very rich could afford silk *hanbok*. In the Joseon period clothing was strictly regulated and poorer people generally had to wear white. In those days you could tell a person's occupation and status from the *hanbok* they wore. For instance, only *yangban* (aristocrats) could wear the black horse-hair hats that were a badge of their rank, while a fancy hairpin *(pinyo)* in a big wig was a female status symbol. Scholars (invariably male in those days) wore a plain white gown with wide sleeves. At court, government officials wore special black hats and *heungbae* – embroidered insignia on the back and front of their gowns. Peasants and slaves wore white hemp or cotton clothes and straw sandals.

High-class women hardly ever left their home during the day and if they did they had to wear a headscarf as a veil and were often carried about in a curtained palanquin by their slaves. Women of lower rank were not veiled and in some respects had more freedom than their wealthier sisters.

In the summer, lightweight, almost transparent *ramie*, made from pounded bark, provided cool and comfortable clothing for those who could afford it. *Ramie* clothing with its unique texture and look is making a come-back in the fashion world.

The problem with *hanbok* is that hardly anyone wears it. Up until the 1960s it was common but urbanisation and Westernisation have made it seem old-fashioned and backward. The only horsehair hats you are likely to see are in dusty folk museums or on the heads of actors in historical TV dramas. *Hanbok* is usually only worn at weddings, festivals or other special occasions, except for waitresses in some traditional restaurants and residents in touristic folk villages. Men prefer Western suits or casual wear, and most women find *hanbok* uncomfortable and unflattering. It restricts their movements, has no pockets and is difficult to clean.

However fashion designers are reforming *hanbok* and reinventing it for the modern world. In markets and shops you can buy modern or traditional *hanbok*. The everyday kind of *hanbok* is reasonably priced, but the formal styles, made of silk and intricately embroidered, are objects of wonder and cost an arm and a leg.

Waistcoats are still popular but only among hikers. Elderly men sometimes wear trilby hats which are akin to modern *hanbok* and *ajumma* (market women) sport brightly-coloured baggy trousers with clashing multi-coloured patterned blouses. Men used to have long hair tied in a topknot but King Gojong had his cut off in 1895 and yet another custom gradually died out.

Hanbok: The Art of Korean Clothing by Sunny Yang (Hollym, 1997) gives a comprehensive history of traditional clothing with masses of pictures.

are available there. Young people see rural life as backward and boring rather than relaxing and friendly, and it's difficult to see how government campaigns can change this attitude.

Population trends mirror those of other developed nations. People are living longer (life expectancy is 80 years for women, 72 years for men), and women are having fewer and fewer children – the very low fertility rate of 1.17 means that the population will decline quite drastically in the future. Korea faces a general shortage of babies, not just female babies, and the government is unlikely to be able to do anything about it. This means a shortage of workers if the economy remains strong, so more and more foreign workers will be needed. Persuading Korean families to adopt Korean orphans and abandoned children would reduce the number adopted by foreigners.

SPORT

Baseball

South Korea won a bronze medal for baseball at the Sydney Olympics in 2000 and has had a professional league since 1982, with teams sponsored by local *jaebol* (giant, family-run companies). General admission to matches is W5000 and the season runs from April to July and from August to October. View http://kbo.hyperboards2.com for match schedules and other information.

Basketball

Ten teams play in the Korean basketball league and matches are played from November to April. Two foreign players (usually Americans) are allowed in each team.

Soccer

Soccer has become much more popular due to the heroic efforts of the South Korean team in the 2002 FIFA World Cup finals, which were co-hosted by South Korea and Japan. Ten new stadiums were built to host the matches. The South Korean team reached the semifinals and defeated Poland, Portugal, Spain and Italy along the way. Cities around the nation became a sea of red on the days that the Korean team was playing, as soccer fans, sporting 'Be the Reds' T-shirts, watched the matches on giant outdoor screens. The cheering and chanting started hours before the matches began and continued late into the night whenever the team won, which was quite often. Keeping ahead of their Asian neighbours and rivals, Japan and China, is South Korea's aim in the future – and not just on the soccer field

Ssireum

Ssireum is Korean-style wrestling, which bears more resemblance to Mongolian wrestling than Japanese sumo wrestling. Wrestlers start off kneeling, then grab their opponent's piece of cloth, called *satba*, which is tied around the waist and thighs, and try to throw each other to the ground.

Taekwondo

Taekwondo is an increasingly popular Korean martial art with millions of followers world-wide. In Korea all young men are taught taekwondo as part of their compulsory two years' military training. The headquarters and main hall for taekwondo competitions is at the World Taekwondo Federation Complex (p92).

DID YOU KNOW?

Winners of *ssireum* tournaments were given the title of *changsa* – the strongest man in the world – and they were given a live bull as a prize.

RELIGION

These days half the population claims to have no religion while 25% are Buddhist and 25% are Christian, mainly Protestant. There are four broad streams of influence in the Korean spiritual and ethical outlook: shamanism, which originated in central Asia; Buddhism, which entered Korea from China in the 4th century AD; Confucianism, a system of ethics of Chinese origin; and Christianity, which first made inroads into Korea in the 18th century.

Buddhism

Buddhism in Korea belongs to the Mahayana school and, since its arrival in AD 370, has split into a number of schools of thought, the most famous of which is Seon, better known to the outside world by its Japanese name, Zen.

About 90% of Korean Buddhists belong to the Jogye sect, which claims to have 8000 monks and 5000 nuns and is an amalgamation of two Korean schools of Buddhism: the Seon school, which relies on meditation and the contemplation of paradoxes to achieve sudden enlightenment; and the Gyo school, which concentrates on extensive scriptural study.

Buddhism is a remarkably adaptable faith and has always coexisted with shamanism. Many Buddhist temples have a *samseonggak* (three-spirit hall) on their grounds, which houses shamanist deities such as the Mountain God and the seven stars of the Big Dipper.

A Little Monk (2003), directed by Ju Gyeong-jung, is an intriguing and original Buddhist fable. Beautifully photographed, every scene offers insights into the Buddhist philosophy of life and the universal themes of a child longing for his mother and the human search for wisdom and happiness.

Buddhism was persecuted throughout the Joseon period and monasteries and temples were only tolerated in remote mountains. It suffered another sharp decline after WWII as Koreans pursued worldly goals. But ironically, South Korea's success in achieving developed-nation status, coupled with a growing concern about spiritual values and the environment, is encouraging a revival of Buddhism. Visits to temples have increased and a huge amount of money is flowing into temple repairs and reconstruction.

Visiting historic temples in the mountains or staying with the monks on a temple stay programme provide lasting memories. An annual highlight is the Buddha's Birthday Parade in Seoul (p96).

Chondogyo

This home-grown Korean religion contains Buddhist, Confucian and Christian elements and was started in 1860 by Cheoe Suun. Born the son of an aristocratic family in 1824, Cheoe experienced a religious revelation and put his egalitarian ideas into practice by freeing a couple of his family's female slaves. The church was originally part of the Donghak (Eastern Learning) reform movement and embraced the idea of equality of all human beings, a revolutionary concept in the Neo-Confucian order of the time. The church headquarters, Suun Hall, was built in 1921 near Insadong.

Christianity

Korea's first exposure to Christianity was via the Jesuits from the Chinese imperial court in the late 18th century. A Korean aristocrat was baptised in Beijing in 1784. When it was introduced to Korea, the Catholic faith took hold and spread quickly; so quickly, in fact, that it was perceived as a threat by the Confucian government and was vigorously suppressed, creating thousands of Christian martyrs. The Christian ideal of human equality clashed with the ethos of a rigidly-stratified society. Christianity got a second chance in the 1880s, with the arrival of American Protestant missionaries who founded schools and hospitals and gained many followers. Nowhere else in Asia, with the exception of the Philippines, have the efforts of Christian missionaries been so successful.

The Catholic cathedral in Myeong-dong (p88) was a refuge for protestors against the military rulers of the recent past, and is still a national symbol of democracy and human rights. Churches of all designs can be seen throughout the country, and their red neon crosses shine out at night.

Confucianism

Confucianism is a system of ethics rather than a religion. Confucius (555–479 BC) lived in China during a time of chaos and feudal rivalry known as the Warring States period. He emphasised devotion to parents and family, loyalty to friends, justice, peace, education, reform and humanitarianism. He also urged that respect and deference should be given to those in positions of authority and firmly believed that men are superior to women and that a woman's place was in the home.

His ideas led to the system of civil-service examinations, where one gains position through ability and merit, rather than from noble birth and connections. Confucius preached against corruption, war, torture and excessive taxation. He was the first teacher to open his school to all students on the basis of their willingness to learn rather than their noble birth and their ability to pay for tuition.

As Confucianism trickled into Korea, it evolved into Neo-Confucianism, which combined the sage's original ethical and political ideas with the quasi-religious practice of ancestor worship and the idea of the eldest male as spiritual head of the family.

Confucianism was viewed as being enlightened and radical when it first gained popularity, but during its 500 years as the state religion in Korea, it became authoritarian and ultraconservative. It still lives on as a kind of ethical bedrock (at least subconsciously) in the minds of most Koreans, although some of the younger generation follow quite different ideas. For an account of how Confucianism underpins modern Korean values, see p35.

The main Confucian shrine is on the campus of Seoul's Sungkyunkwan University (Map p73) where traditional rites are occasionally held. Local Confucian school buildings called *hanggyo* can be seen all over the country but they are invariably locked. Other Confucian ceremonies are re-enacted in Seoul at Jongmyo shrine, Seonnong altar and Sajik altar (p96).

'Female shamans act as intermediaries between the living and the spirit world.'

Shamanism

There are few shamanist shrines and the religion lacks a body of scriptures or written texts. Nevertheless, shamanism is still an important part of the Korean religious outlook. *Mudang* (female shamans) act as intermediaries between the living and the spirit world, and shamanist ceremonies are held for a variety of reasons: to cure illness, before setting out on a journey, to ward off financial problems, to guide a deceased family member safely into the spirit world. A ceremony might be held by a village on a regular basis to ensure the safety and harmony of its members and a good harvest of rice or fish.

These *gut* (ceremonies) take place indoors or outdoors and involve contacting departed spirits who are attracted by the lavish offerings of food and drink. Drums beat and the *mudang* dances herself into a frenzied state that allows her to communicate with the spirits and be

DID YOU KNOW?

40,000 women in South Korea are registered as *mudang* (female shamans).

possessed by them. Resentments felt by the dead can haunt and plague the living and cause them all sorts of misfortune, so their spirits need placating. For shamanists, death does not end relationships, they simply take another form.

On Inwangsan, a wooded hillside in northwestern Seoul, *gut* ceremonies take place in or near the historic shrine called Guksadang, and the offerings of food made to the hungry spirits often include a pig's head (p93).

Dano day is the main shamanist festival – for details, see p370.

ARTS
Architecture

The best examples of Korean traditional architecture are found in Seoul's palaces and the Buddhist temples scattered throughout the country. Their style is characterised by massive wooden beams set on stone foundations, often built with notches instead of nails. Roofs are usually made from heavy clay tiles. The strikingly bold and colourful painted design under the eaves is called *dancheong*.

Examples of traditional *yangban* architecture can be seen at Seoul's Namsangol Traditional Village (p88) and in Jeonju (p279) while a range of traditional houses can be seen in the ten major folk villages that have sprouted up around the country.

Cinema

The Korean film industry (www.koreanfilm.org) produces around 50 films a year and, protected by a quota system that forces every cinema to show Korean films on at least 146 days of the year, commercial success has been achieved with a string of gangster and comedy films.

Korea's film culture is strong. The Pusan International Film Festival (PIFF) has grown quickly after being launched in 1996 to become the most respected festival in Asia, and attracts crowds of film enthusiasts.

Visit a DVD *bang* and you can watch Korean movies with English subtitles in the comfort of your own minicinema.

Oasis (2002) is a challenging, dramatic and brilliantly acted film by ace director Lee Chang-dong (now Minister of Culture) about an irresponsible, simple-minded but good-hearted man who becomes involved with a seriously handicapped woman who suffers from cerebral palsy.

Peppermint Candy (2000) is also written and directed by Lee Chang-dong. Although bleak and sometimes brutal, this thought-provoking film begins with a man's suicide and then goes back in time to reveal his tragic life. Ultimately it's the portrait of a romantic young man corrupted by his years in the army and police force.

JSA (2001) is a taut thriller directed by Park Chan-wook about a friendship that develops between soldiers on opposite sides of the Demilitarized Zone that separates North and South Korea.

My Sassy Girl (2001), directed by Kwak Jae-young, is a role reversal comedy about a girlish guy and his aggressive, bossy girlfriend. Based on a true story that was posted on the Internet, hilarious scenes and film parodies give the film a wide appeal.

Christmas in August (1998) is a modern-day classic that rewrote the rules of melodrama, providing a down-to-earth and heartbreakingly simple tale of love and loss.

In the action stakes, *Sympathy for Mr Vengeance* (2002) is a bleak, gut-wrenching film about a kidnapping gone horribly wrong.

Nowhere to Hide (1999) is a stylish and ceaselessly inventive film about a detective's pursuit of a silent killer.

Waikiki Brothers, a film by Im Soon-rye, takes a nostalgic look back at the 1980s. It is about a rock band trying to live life as they choose. Sharp editing gives the film a distinctive style, and the early scenes about youthful dreams and disappointments in small-town Korea are excellent. As the band members age, the film loses its panache but it's still worth seeing.

Crazy Marriage (2002) is an amusing film with a message that is directed by Yu Ha, a well-known poet. Gam Woo-sung plays an unemo-
ional university lecturer who meets up with sexy Uhm Jung-hwa. The
ilm focuses on their ups and downs in and out of bed. She marries a
loctor, but their relationship continues. In one scene Gam refuses to eat
a fancy birthday cake that Uhm has given him and eats a small tomato
nstead. That sums up his character and their relationship, which is a
kind of 'crazy marriage'.

DID YOU KNOW?

In 2002 Korean films
attracted almost as
many paying customers
as imported Hollywood
ones.

Literature

In the 12th century, the monk Illyeon wrote *Samgukyusa* (Myths and
Legends of the Three Kingdoms), the most important work of early Korean literature. During the Joseon dynasty, three-line *sijo* poems based
on Chinese models continued to be written in Chinese characters even
after the invention of *hangeul* in the 15th century. The usual theme was
love of nature and the joys of a hermit lifestyle. In 1945 there was a sharp
turn away from Chinese and Japanese influence of any kind, Western
influence increased dramatically and existentialism became the guiding
cultural philosophy.

Playing With Fire by Lee Chong-rae (Cornell University, 1997) is
a complex and melodramatic saga of family revenge that spans generations, and is written from the viewpoints of the family members who
are caught up in the cycle of violence. It grips you from the first to the
final line.

Appointment With My Brother by Yi Mun-yol (Jimoondang, 2002) is a
brilliant novella about a man from the South who meets his half-brother
from the North secretly in China. It's an emotional and stressful meeting for both of them, a collision of two completely different worlds. But
they overcome their awkwardness and misunderstandings and achieve a
reconciliation of sorts.

A Dwarf Launches a Little Ball by Cho Se-hui (Jimoondang, 1976)
is a passionate and poetic novella about a family made homeless by
urban redevelopment. The story is memorable in spite of the inferior
translation.

KOREAN LITERATURE ON THE WEB

English translations of short stories written by leading contemporary Korean writers are available
free of charge on the Web. Poetry, folk tales, legends and even short novels can also be down-
loaded. Visit www.korea.net and click on 'Culture' for access to eight short stories that provide
a good introduction to modern Korean literature. Written in a variety of styles, the stories reflect
many aspects of life in Korea. Most of the stories are about love, friendship, alienation from society
and the meaning of life, and the characters include an earnest rural schoolteacher, a student
protester, an insect collector, a schizophrenic, a lesbian and a bored housewife.

Where the Red Moon Rises by Bak Sang-u is an existentialist love story about two nameless
writers, with a twist at the end.

The Longhorn Beetle by Lee Oe-su is a long short story, set during the Japanese occupation,
that contrasts two brothers – one a Zen Buddhist man of the mountains and the other a professional insect collector who loses his girlfriend and lands up in prison.

The Old Well by O Jeung-hui is a well-written but uneventful story about a bored middle-aged
housewife looking back over her unfulfilled life.

By the Sea by Kim In-suk is about a diffident female writer and student protester who remin-
isces about her brittle, on-off friendship with a very different kind of woman who is focussed
on boyfriends and fashion.

Faint Shadow of Love by Kim Kwang-kyu (2002) and translated by Brother Anthony, contains poems that are protests about ecological degradation and the sadness of the middle-aged who have lost the dreams and idealism of their youth.

The Silence of Love by Han Yongun (1926) is an original and unusual book of poems based on traditional Buddhist and pastoral themes but with a modernist twist.

Music

Gayageum Masterpieces by Chimhyang-moo is a CD which comes with a booklet in English. The quiet and relaxing sounds resemble raindrops falling on a lake.

Beautiful Things in Life by Jeong Soo-nyun is a CD that blends the unique sound of the *haegum* (a two-stringed fiddle) with other Korean and Western instruments to produce beautiful and haunting melodies.

Korean traditional music *(gugak)* is played on stringed instruments most notably the *gayageum* (12-stringed zither) and *haegum* (two-stringed fiddle), and on chimes, gongs, cymbals, drums, horns and flutes. Traditional musical instruments can be seen in a Seoul museum (p111). View www.ncktpa.go.kr for information on 50 Korean musical instruments. Radio Gugak broadcasts traditional Korean music to the Seoul area (p363).

Traditional music can be subdivided into three categories: Firstly the slow and sonorous court music *(jeongak)*, which, together with elegant court dances, is performed in front of Jongmyo every year on the first Sunday in May as part of the ceremony honouring the Joseon dynasty kings (p96).

A second musical style, *bulgyo eumak*, is played and chanted in Buddhist temples. Cassettes and CDs of this music are on sale inside major temples and in shops outside.

Last is *samulnori*, a fast and lively style of music and dance that was played by entertainers who went from village to village and was enjoyed by peasant farmers. It died out during Japanese rule but was reinvented in the 1970s by four musicians playing four traditional Korean percussion instruments, the *kkwaenggwari* (small gong), *ching* (large gong), *changgu* (hour-glass drum) and *puk* (large barrel drum).

Painting & Sculpture

Seumusalui Eumakjyeonji is a sampler of modern Korean popular music and includes rock anthems, punk rock, rap and ballads among the 16 tracks.

Chinese influence is paramount in traditional Korean painting, as with other arts. The brush line, which varies in thickness and tone, is the most important feature, and the function of traditional landscape painting was to be a substitute for nature. The painting is meant to surround the viewer and there is no fixed viewpoint as in classical Western painting. Court ceremonies, portraits, flowers, birds, insects and everyday scenes were also painted.

Zen-style Buddhist art can be seen inside and on the outside walls of hundreds of temples scattered around remote areas all over the country. Murals usually depict scenes from Buddha's life or stories and images that aid spiritual enlightenment.

Modern Korean artists tend to follow Western trends but with a Korean twist. Gwangju hosts a two-month modern art festival every two years (p237).

Stone Buddhist statues and pagodas are the most common examples of ancient sculpture. Cast bronze was also common for Buddhas and some marvellous examples can be seen in the National Museum (p85). Stone and wooden shamanist guardian posts are common and Jejudo has its own unique *harubang* or 'grandfather stones' (p257).

Many towns have sculpture gardens – see them at Seoul's Olympic Park (p90), Chuncheon (p142), Buyeo (p303) and all over Jeju-do. Many tall buildings have a sculpture out the front to beautify the streets and mystify passers-by. Check out Hammering Man in Seoul (p86).

Pottery

Archaeologists have unearthed Korean pottery made some 10,000 years ago, although it wasn't until the early 12th century that Korean pottery-making reached its peak as amazingly skilled potters turned out wonderful celadon pottery with a characteristic green tinge. Nowadays original Korean celadon is much sought after and fetches millions of dollars at auction. Pottery fans shouldn't miss out on visiting Icheon Ceramic Village (p127) near Seoul and two pottery villages in Jeollanam-do (p249 and p245).

Theatre & Dance

DANCE

Popular folk dances include *samulnori* (drum dances), *talchum* (mask dances) and solo improvisational *salpuri* (shamanist dances).

The *samulnori* dancers perform in brightly-coloured traditional clothing, twirling a very long tassel from a special cap on their heads. Good coordination is required to dance, twirl and play a drum at the same time. These dancers appear at every festival.

Talchum dance-dramas were a folk art performed by low-class travelling performers on market days. They usually satirised the *yangban* class from the point of view of the peasants and slaves. The masks indicated the status of the character – a *yangban*, a monk, a shaman, a grandmother, a concubine, a butcher or a servant – but also served the purpose of hiding the identity of the performer. These mask dance-dramas are characterised by vigorous leaping, comedy and big gestures, together with shouting, singing and reciting. The performers usually mingle with the audience once their part is over. Masks are usually made of wood and every souvenir shop sells them. Different localities have different masks and dances, some of which have been performed since the Three Kingdoms period.

View www.korea.net and follow the link from the Culture section for an overview of modern dance in Seoul, which is very active with an annual dance festival in Daehangno.

KOREAN OPERA

Somewhat similar to Western opera is *changgeuk*, which can involve a large cast of characters. Another type of opera is *pansori*, which features a solo storyteller (usually female) singing in a strained voice to the beat of a male drummer, while emphasising dramatic moments with a flick of her fan. For details on Seoul's traditional theatres that stage these shows, see p110.

Environment

South Korea's helter-skelter economic growth since 1960 has transformed the country from a rural to an urban society. Sprawling apartment-block cities, dams and huge industrial complexes have been constructed, and wide freeways have been bulldozed through the countryside. Authoritarian governments stamped on any opposition to development projects and the environmental impacts were ignored.

But the situation is very different nowadays. Governments are more democratic and many large projects face fierce local opposition. The government has been searching for a nuclear waste site since 1986 without success. Environmental groups are no longer ignored by the media. Fortunately 70% of Korea is mountainous and these areas are generally unspoilt as are many of the offshore islands where only fishermen and their families live.

THE LAND

South Korea's land area is 99,538 sq km, making it about the same size as Portugal and almost as large as North Korea. Its overall length from north to south is 500km, while at its narrowest point it is 216km wide. Seventy percent of the land is forest-covered mountains although they are not very high – Hallasan (1950m) on Jejudo is the highest peak. Many mountains are granite with dramatic cliffs and pinnacles, but there are also some impressive limestone caves to visit and Jejudo is volcanic with craters and lava caves. Increasing numbers of well-equipped ski resorts lure winter-sports enthusiasts into the mountainous regions in the colder northern half of the country.

The plains and shallow valleys are still dominated by irrigated rice fields, interspersed with small orchards, plastic greenhouses growing vegetables, and barns housing cows, pigs and chickens. In the south are a few green tea plantations and on Jejudo citrus fruit is grown. Despite large government subsidies and protection from imports, the rural population is greying and shrinking every year. Few young people want to be farmers and fewer still want to marry a farmer. Most large rivers have been dammed but the upside is that there are a number of scenic inland lakes that were never there before.

Also worth visiting are some of the thousands of sparsely populated islands scattered around the western and southern coasts of the peninsula. The west coast mudflats are a vast outdoor larder of shellfish and crabs that not only support thousands of migrating water birds but also supply seafood markets and restaurants. Reclaiming the mudflats has become a highly emotive and divisive issue – see Environmental Issues (p49).

WILDLIFE

Korea's forested mountains used to be crowded with Siberian tigers, leopards, bears, deer, goral antelopes, wolves and foxes. Unfortunately these animals are extinct or rare and hikers generally see only cute little Asiatic chipmunks, squirrels and birds. Magpies, pigeons and sparrows account for most of the birds in the towns and cities, but egrets and herons are common in the countryside and raptors, woodpeckers and pheasants can also be glimpsed if you are lucky. In fact over 500 bird species have been sighted, although most are visiting migrants, and Korea has a growing reputation among birders keen to see Steller's sea eagles, black eagles, black vultures, red-crowned cranes and black-faced spoonbills. *Field Guide to the Birds of Korea* by Lee, Koo & Park is the standard bird guide, but doesn't include everything.

Animals

Han Sang-hoon, director of the Jirisan bear project (see 'Half-moon Bears' p48), is an expert on the animals that live or used to live in the park:

The last Siberian tiger in Jirisan was captured in 1944. Of course there are people who claim to have seen a tiger here since then, or a footprint or whatever. But there is no definite evidence. Siberian tigers are critically endangered as less than 500 survive in the wild, mostly in east Russia or northeast China but they are occasionally reported in North Korea. Amur leopards used to be common in Korea but now they are extinct here, and there are less than 50 in the wild world-wide.

The grey wolf is probably extinct in the wild in South Korea, as there has been no confirmed sighting of one for over 10 years. However there are a few in North Korea near Paekdusan. I know that because I was lucky enough to see one when I was there on a joint project.

I estimate that there are 20 to 30 red foxes living in the wild in the South. I've seen red foxes three times – in 1993, 1995 and 1997 – twice in Jirisan and once on Namhae island. There are perhaps less than 10 in Jirisan but they've never been photographed or videoed. If any visitor sees a fox please photograph it and send me a copy!

Sika deer died out in the 1940s. Unhappily musk deer are also on the verge of extinction in Korea despite government protection. However the number of water deer is increasing, which is good news because they are a special sub-species that is only found in China and Korea. Roe deer can also be found in higher elevations in Jirisan. Hallasan on Jejudo is famous for roe deer – they come up to you to be fed. That's a bad idea.

River otter numbers are decreasing due to dam and road construction disturbing their habitat. Badger numbers are increasing in Jirisan but illegal hunting is reducing their numbers elsewhere. Badgers are still a popular food for women after they've given birth. Racoon dogs were doing well but recently they've been hit by some kind of virus. Leopard cats, martens and wild boars also live in the park.

If you want to see any of these animals, dusk or dawn is the best time. Find a little-used trail and just stand still, they will come out if they are around.

Han Sang-hoon

Plants

Northern parts of South Korea are the coldest and the flora is alpine – beech, birch, fir, larch and pine. Further south deciduous trees are more common. The south coast and Jejudo are the warmest and wettest areas, so the vegetation is lush. Cherry trees blossom in spring and azaleas and camellias come in to bloom as well. Korea's mountainsides are a pharmacy and salad bar of health-giving edible leaves, ferns, acorns, roots, nuts, mushrooms and other fungi. Many of these wild mountain vegetables end up in side dishes and *sanchaebibimbap* (rice, egg, noodles and mountain vegetables in hot sauce). Wild ginseng is the most sought after.

TOP BIRDING WEBSITES

www.wbkenglish.com has wonderful photos of Korean birds and loads of useful information for bird lovers.

www.knto.or.kr (click on 'sightseeing', 'theme tours' and then 'bird-watching') is also useful.

http://home.megapass .co.kr/~skua is run by an enthusiastic local birder and features photos.

DID YOU KNOW?

Goral antelopes have been reintroduced to Woraksan National Park and half-moon bears have been released in Jirisan National Park. Keep a look-out for them when you visit.

HALF-MOON BEARS

Manchurian black bears (called half-moon bears because of the crescent moon of white fur on their chests) were thought to be extinct in South Korea. But in 2001 video camera footage proved that a few bears were living in Jirisan National Park, perhaps six of them. Later that year four baby bears from bear farms were released to boost their numbers. One female baby bear died during the winter and a second female kept pestering hikers for food and had to be removed. However the two male bears survived. Pandol is shy but Jangun is bolder and gets into trouble. In 2003 he hit the headlines when he started raiding farmers' beehives and had to be trapped and moved to another area.

The lifespan of the bears is 20 to 30 years. Bears hibernate in winter, eat leaves, bamboo shoots, wild strawberries, chestnuts, acorns, ants and honey, and make comfortable nests for themselves by weaving bamboo and tree branches together. The Korean bears are bigger, with a wider face and shaggier hair than the Manchurian black bears that are common in Japan. They are nocturnal and shy so hikers rarely see them. If you're lucky enough to see one, stand still so as not to frighten it, and give way.

There are 20,000 Manchurian black bears in Russia and China, and the plan is to introduce more into Jirisan to build up a self-sustaining group of 50. However, importing live bears is a complicated bureaucratic process. Releasing some of the 2000 bears on farms or the 20 to 50 in zoos in South Korea is another option, but they would have to be trained to fend for themselves in the wild.

Unfortunately numerous bear products are still sold by the traditional medicine industry. A bear produces around 2kg of bile a year which sells for US$10,000 per kilogram.

NATIONAL & PROVINCIAL PARKS

Korea has 20 national parks (www.npa.or.kr) that cover 38,240 sq km of land or 6.5% of the country. Jirisan established in 1967 was the first national park and is the third most-visited park with 2.6 million paying customers a year. Only Seoraksan (2.8 million) and Bukhansan (4 million) have more visitors. There are also 22 provincial parks (747 sq km) and 29 county parks (307 sq km) that cover smaller areas but are also worth visiting. Entrance fees to the parks vary but most cost W2600/1500 for adults/children. All the parks have well-marked hiking trails but their popularity means that some trails have to be closed in rotation to protect them from serious erosion.

The parks can be enjoyed at any time of the year. In spring cherry blossoms, azaleas and other flowers are a delight; in summer the hillsides and river valleys provide a cool escape from the heat and humidity of the cities and the monsoon rains make the waterfalls particularly impressive; in autumn red-coloured leaves and clear blue skies provide a fantastic sight; and in winter snow and ice turn the parks into a white wonderland, although crampons and proper clothing are needed for any serious hikes. Gaily painted wooden temples and hermitages grace nearly every mountain, and river valleys, waterfalls and rocky outcrops abound. It's not surprising that many visitors rate the parks as the country's top attraction.

A pressure group with practical ideas is Green Korea (www.greenkorea.org), which organises Buy Nothing Day, Car Free Day and Save Paper Day.

Koreans are the world's most enthusiastic hikers and most parks are crowded at weekends, particularly in summer and autumn. Many hikers dress up in smart hiking gear (red waistcoats with plenty of pockets are a long-standing fashion favourite), and take a bottle of *soju* and a picnic along. All the parks have tourist villages near the main entrances with restaurants, market stalls, souvenir and food shops, and budget accommodation, where a big group can squeeze into a small room. Camping grounds (W3000 for a three-person tent) and mountain shelters (W3000 to W5000 for a bunk) are cheap, but provide only basic facilities.

Top national parks include:

Park	Area	Features & Activities
Bukhansan	78 sq km	Great hiking and subway access from Seoul (p119)
Dadohae Haesang	2344 sq km	A marine park full of unspoilt small islands (p248) (2004 sq km marine)
Gyeogyusan	219 sq km	A ski resort, a fortress and a magical valley walk (p284)
Gyeongju	138 sq km	Strewn with ancient Silla and Buddhist relics (p176)
Hallasan	149 sq km	This extinct volcano is Korea's highest peak and is on Jejudo (p275)
Jirisan	440 sq km	A giant park with high peaks that is popular with serious hikers (p229)
Seoraksan	373 sq km	Korea's most popular and beautiful park (p151)
Sobaeksan	320 sq km	Three limestone caves and Guinsa – an impressive temple complex (p322)

Top provincial parks include:

Park	Area	Features & Activities
Maedunsan	38 sq km	Granite cliffs, great views and a hot-spring bath (p283)
Najisan	104 sq km	Scenic views and two famous temples, Tongdosa and Seongnamsa (p222)
Mudeungsan	30 sq km	Near Gwangju with an art gallery and a temple surrounded by a tea plantation (p235)
Namhansanseong	36 sq km	Subway access from Seoul. Hike round the fortress wall and eat in the restaurant village (p123)
Taebaeksan	17 sq km	Visit the Coal Museum and hike up to Dangun's altar (162)

ENVIRONMENTAL ISSUES

Long-running environmental controversies concern where to store nuclear waste and the reclamation of mudflats at Saemangeum in Jeollabuk-do.

South Korea relies on nuclear power to generate one-third of the country's electricity, but the government has failed to find a permanent storage site for the radioactive waste that continues to be produced. Many sites have been proposed since 1986 but they have always provoked fierce local opposition despite the billions of *won* in compensation offered to the local communities. In 2003 Wido (a small island off Jeollabuk-do) was chosen but local protestors could spike this proposal as they have all the others. For information on this and other environmental issues see http://kfem.or.kr.

For more information on the Saemangeum wetlands issue view http://kfem.or.kr.

The huge Saemangeum land reclamation project involves constructing a 33km sea wall that will reclaim 40,000 hectares of mudflats, mainly for agricultural use. The campaigners believe that the mudflats are important for migrating birds and as a fish and shellfish breeding area. However some civic groups and leaders in Jeollabuk-do support the project and most of the sea wall has already been built.

A uniquely Korean protest took place in spring 2003 when hundreds took part in a 'Three Steps, One Bow' campaign. The protestors took three steps and then prostrated themselves on the ground before taking another three steps and prostrating themselves again. They did this for 65 days to cover the 300km from the Saemangeum project in Jeollabuk-do to Seoul. Organised by environmental, Buddhist and Christian leaders, it mobilised opposition to the project and a Seoul court ordered work on the project to be suspended, which led to the resignation of the agriculture minister.

Food & Drink

Korea has one of Asia's richest culinary traditions, and although man visitors find it foreign at first, once the switch has been flipped it stay on for good.

A typical Korean meal is dizzying in its variety and copious in it volume. It's based around rice, soup and Korea's national dish, *kimc* (pickled or fermented vegetables), but you might find as many as a doze small plates, called *banchan*, around the table.

Garlic, ginger, green onion, black pepper, sesame oil, soy sauce and vir egar abound. But the big spice is the chilli pepper, which usually takes th form of *gochujang*, red pepper paste. A good general rule: red = spicy.

STAPLES & SPECIALITIES
Barbecued & Grilled Dishes

'If there's any food for which Korea is famous worldwide, it's barbecue.'

If there's any food for which Korea is famous worldwide, it's barbecu Barbecue restaurants typically have a grill set into the table, on whic you cook beef ribs (*galbi*), pork (*dwaejigalbi* or *samgyeopsal)* or, in son places, chicken (*dak*), seafood or vegetables. Often your server will g you started by putting the meat on the grill; after that, generally you' on your own to remove the meat when it's cooked. All are delicious, b *samgyeopsal* is marbled like bacon and can be fatty.

Galbi and *samgyeopsal* are served with leaves of lettuce and oth greens such as fan-shaped sesame leaves. Take a leaf in one hand (combine two leaves for different flavours), and with your other hand u your utensils to load it with rice, *banchan* and sauces to taste. Then r it up into a little package and eat it. The size of the package should small enough to fit into your mouth whole.

Barbecue dishes are also served with raw garlic, which you can e plain or roast on the grill.

Many of these restaurants also serve *bulgogi*, thin slices of marinate beef that are cooked with vegetables; it's popular food while drinking.

Barbecue dishes are usually available only in servings of two or more.

Bibimbap

Bibimbap is a tasty mixture of vegetables, meat and a fried egg on top rice. Mix it all together with your spoon before digging in. *Bibimbap* is us ally served with a generous dollop of *gochujang* (red pepper paste) – if yc don't want it so hot, remove some of this paste before you begin mixin *Bibimbap* is also usually served with soup but don't mix that in too! The

---

TOP KOREAN FOOD

In a recent Korean National Tourism Organisation survey, tourists voted the following as their favourite Korean meals:

- *bibimbap* (rice, egg, meat and vegetables in hot sauce)
- *bulgogi* (barbecue beef and vegetables)
- *dolsot bibimbap* (*bibimbap* in stone hotpot)
- *galbi* (beef ribs)
- *mandu* (dumplings)

WE DARE YOU

Some dishes for the more adventurous:

Beondegi (번데기) Silkworm larvae; you'll often find them sold near schools – kids love the stuff.

Bosintang (보신탕) Dogmeat soup (see 'Rough!' p53).

Godung (고둥) Roll shells, usually stewed by street vendors.

Mettugi (메뚜기) Fried grasshoppers. Some say they taste like bits of fried egg.

Nakjiboggeum (낙지볶음) Stir-fried baby octopus.

Sannakji (산낙지) Live baby octopus, cut into small bits. Warning: the suction cups still work, and people have choked, especially while drinking.

---

are many varieties, but two common styles are *sanchae bibimbap* (made with mountain greens) and *dolsot bibimbap* (served in a hot stone pot). Both can be ordered without meat and/or egg.

Breakfast

While Western-style breakfast is available in the cities, traditional Korean breakfast is centred on soup, rice and *kimchi*. If that sounds like lunch or dinner, it is, except with fewer *banchan*. The soup bowls tend to be larger than at other meals.

Chicken

Samgyetang is a small whole chicken stuffed with glutinous rice, red dates, garlic and ginseng and boiled in broth. It's commonly eaten in summer, often accompanied by ginseng wine. *Dakgalbi* is pieces of boneless chicken, cabbage, other vegetables and finger-sized pressed rice cakes, which are all grilled at your table. They're mildly spicy. Very much zingier is fashionable *jjimdak*, a spicy mixture of chicken pieces, transparent noodles, potatoes and other vegetables. Korea abounds with informal places serving barbecued or fried chicken, and beer.

Desserts

As in many other Asian nations, sweet desserts are not traditional in Korea, although Western-style bakeries are fairly common in residential areas and busy commercial districts.

At the end of the meal at barbecue restaurants, you'll probably be served *sujeonggwa*, a drink made from cinnamon and ginger, served cold and very refreshing, followed by a stick of chewing gum. In some Western restaurants, the 'dessert' course can be coffee, a soft drink or ice cream.

Otherwise, sweets are generally saved for special occasions such as weddings and milestone birthdays. Commonly they're made from pounded sticky rice and do not approach the sweetness of Western confections.

> 'Traditional Korean breakfast is centred on soup, rice and *kimchi*.'

Gimbap

This inexpensive dish consists mostly of rice rolled in dried seaweed. For this reason, it's sometimes called Korean sushi, but unlike Japanese sushi it doesn't contain raw fish – if there's any fish at all it will be cooked, processed or in a paste form. Rather, *gimbap* usually contains strips of vegetables, egg or meat in the centre. Often, the rice is flavoured beforehand with sesame oil.

Hanjeongsik

A banquet that includes fish, meat, soup, *dubujjigae* (tofu stew), rice, noodles, steamed egg, shellfish and lots of cold vegetable *banchan*. It's a good way to sample a wide range of Korean food at one sitting. Like barbecue dishes, *hanjeongsik* almost always needs to be ordered for two or more people.

Hoetjip (Fish & Seafood)

Seafood *(haemul)* and fish *(seongseon)* are generally served stewed broiled or grilled. When fish is served sushi-style (raw over rice) it's called *chobap*. Sashimi (without the rice) is called *saengseonhoe*. Another popular preparation is *hoedeupbap*, which is like *bibimbap* except that it contains raw fish and/or seafood and vegetables. Note that unlike Japanese sushi, Korean-style raw fish is often eaten with generous dollops of chilli sauce (you add them yourself to taste).

Jjigae

These stews are thicker than soups and served in a stone hot pot with generally, lots of spice. Popular versions are made with tofu *(dubujjigae)* and *kimchi*. They're steaming hot so let them cool before eating them!

Kimchi

One could write an entire chapter on this national dish that's served at every Korean meal.

If you're familiar with any variety of *kimchi*, it's probably *tongbaechu kimchi*, made from Chinese cabbage. However, that's just one of hundreds of varieties. *Kimchi* can be made from cucumbers, radishes and just about any other vegetable. Some varieties are aged for hours, others for years. Some are meant to be eaten in individual strips, tiny morsels or wrapped around rice; others, such as *bossam kimchi*, are gorgeous little packages containing vegetables and seafood. Many regions (and families) have their own distinctive style of *kimchi*. See p59 for some common varieties.

'Traditionally, *kimchi* was made to preserve vegetables and ensure proper nutrition during harsh winters.'

Traditionally, *kimchi* was made to preserve vegetables and ensure proper nutrition during harsh winters. Even now, late-November to early December is the season for *gimjang*, or putting up *kimchi*. But *kimchi* isn't just for winter anymore – it's now eaten year-round to add zest to any meal.

Bonus: *kimchi* is said to have many health benefits, including antibiotic properties, neutralising stomach acid, and prevention of high blood pressure, obesity and cancer of the digestive tract.

Mandu

Another inexpensive favourite, these small dumplings are filled with meat, vegetables and herbs. Fried, boiled or steamed, they make a tasty

---

FOR THE THOROUGHLY MODERN COUPLE...

Kimchi is the one thing that no Korean kitchen can be without.

However, *kimchi* storage can be problematic. The temperature must be kept just so – if it's too warm, the *kimchi* can over-ferment; too cold, and it will freeze. That's to say nothing of the odour it can impart to more delicate foods in the fridge.

In these go-go days of apartment living, who has the time, much less the land or wherewithal, to bury the *kimchi* jar in the yard, as much of the country did even a generation ago? (Incidentally, this remains an excellent method for pickling and fermenting, and geothermal insulation means that *kimchi* doesn't freeze.)

Modern kitchen science's answer: the *kimchi* refrigerator! Some *kimchi* refrigerators are separate temperature-controlled compartments within larger refrigerators, while others are stand-alone units.

In the market for a unique wedding gift? Say it with a *kimchi*-fridge.

ROUGH!

Korea is famous – or perhaps infamous – for the tradition of eating dogmeat. If the thought of it makes you squeamish, it's a sensitive topic for many Koreans too.

Prior to big international events here, there's usually a wave of protests from abroad about the practice, as well as local animal rights activists, followed by reports of domestic authorities clamping down on and diverting attention from dogmeat establishments. For decades even the word for dogmeat soup, *bosintang*, was considered somewhat taboo. Still, many Koreans remain enthusiastic – and unapologetic – about the tradition.

A few things you should know: first, the dogs used are a special breed, meaning that you needn't worry about your pets. Second, dogmeat is only served in speciality restaurants, so it won't find its way onto your table unless you really want it there. Koreans favour it because it's reputed to be very low in fat and good for virility and general nutrition. In summer, the 'heat' of the meat is supposed to cool the body.

And how does it taste? Kind of like your grandmother's brisket, if a little stringier. Two popular ways to serve it are *suyuk* (boiled, an assortment of small pieces of meat and skin, which you can wrap in leaves as you would with *galbi*) and *bosintang* (in a spicy soup, like the beef varieties).

snack or light meal for under W4000. Even *kimchi* has been known to make its way into *mandu. Manduguk* is *mandu* in soup.

Noodles

By far the most popular noodle dish is *naengmyeon*, also called *mul naengmyeon* (water noodles); it's buckwheat noodles in an icy beef broth, garnished with chopped vegetables and half an egg – add red pepper paste or *gyeoja* (mustard), to taste. It's especially popular in warm weather, and is often eaten after a meat dish as a kind of dessert.

Another popular preparation is *bibim naengmyeon*, which pairs the noodles (still cold but not in soup) with vegetables and other ingredients found in *bibimbap*.

Japchae are clear noodles made from sweet potatoes, stir-fried in sesame oil with strips of egg, meat, mushrooms, carrots and other vegetables.

Ramyeon is noodles served in hot soup, like Chinese-style *ramen*.

Soups

Soups (*tang* or *guk*) are a Korean speciality and they vary from spicy seafood and crab soups to bland broths such as *galbitang* (beef short-ribs and vegetable soup with rice) or *seolleontang* (slices of beef with spring onions and rice in a cloudy broth). *Haejangguk* (bean sprout soup) is said to be good for hangovers. Soup is a main component of Korean breakfasts – see p59 for some common soups. Hint: If a soup is too spicy for you, add some rice.

'*Haejangguk* (bean sprout soup) is said to be good for hangovers.'

DRINKS

Let's start with that most basic of drinks, good old H_2O (*mul*). Even if some visitors may find Korea less clean than their home countries, Koreans are fastidious about their drinking water.

Virtually every restaurant has a powerful water filtration machine or receives bottled water to dispense from a water cooler. Usually each diner is presented with a cup of water at the beginning of the meal, or the waiter will leave a container of water. Often the water dispensers are right in the dining room, and Korea is informal enough that visitors feel welcome to fill up their own portable bottles before leaving the restaurant.

THE GEOGRAPHY OF DRINKING

A night out with Koreans usually involves three stops, which they call 'first stop' 'second stop' and 'third stop' (il cha, ee cha, sam cha). First is dinner, then to the next place for booze, followed by a round in a karaoke room.

Why? To change the mood when the first place becomes a little stale, to give different people a chance to pay the bill (a different person pays at each stop) and to provide a convenient opportunity to leave – it's best to part company when the gang is on the street between stops. But with food ordered at each place, your night out drinking may leave you feeling a bit full.

Tea is also popular. *Nokcha* (green tea) is grown in great quantities (you can visit tea plantations in Jeju-do and Jeollanam-do). Other teas not made from the tea plant include *boricha* (barley tea) and *oksu-sucha* (roast corn tea; often served cold in place of water), or *insamcha* (ginseng tea). Another popular, sweet and very tasty variety is *yujacha* (citron tea).

For a country with a tea tradition, Korea has taken to coffee in a big way. In addition to coffee shops, there are vending machines nearly everywhere people congregate (about W300 per cup), and in some restaurants you can serve yourself from a self-service coffee machine. Sorry, decaf drinkers, you're probably out of luck but it never hurts to ask.

Multinational soft drinks are everywhere in Korea, and you'll also find some unique Korean choices alongside them, like *sikhye*, rice punch with grains of rice inside.

Health tonics are available in shops and pharmacies. Many are made with fibre blends, ginseng and other medicinal herbs. They're usually sold in small (100ml) glass bottles. Popular brands are usually labelled in English (eg Fibe-Mini).

If you're looking for something stronger, Korean beers are popular, although drinkers from Oz, Britain, Belgium or Ireland might find them a bit watery. The most popular brands are Cass, Hite, and O.B. – the latter derives from 'Oriental Brewery' and not anything medical. The newest from O.B. is a brew called Cafri.

Finally, no discussion of Korean drinks can be complete without *soju*. Dating back to the 13th century, this distilled spirit is often likened to vodka in that it's clear, nearly flavourless and cheap to produce. Also like vodka, it can be made from different ingredients, but mostly these days it's mass-produced from sweet potatoes. Some find it not unlike what a nurse rubs on your arm before giving you an injection. The good news: *soju* generally has an alcohol content of 20% to 25%.

Its cousin *dongdongju* is fermented from rice or corn, and in its unrefined state has a brownish, cloudy appearance. It has a lower alcohol content than *soju* and is served cold in summer.

> **DID YOU KNOW?**
>
> Most Koreans consider it unhealthy to drink on an empty stomach, so most bars serve bar snacks. *Hofs* (pubs) and other nightspots also have menus of plates known as *anju*, which can be large and are meant for sharing. Some places charge for these as a sort of cover.

WHERE TO EAT
Restaurants

The general word for 'restaurant' in Korean is *sikdang*, and you'll see that many restaurants feature their specialities in their names (eg *samgyetang, galbi, ssambap, hanjeongsik, hoetjip*). A restaurant serving inexpensive dishes is sometimes called *bunsik*. If the word *yaksu* appears in the name, the place offers meals that are somehow medicinal (herb-raised beef, etc). Raw fish restaurants feature the character *hoe* (회, raw) marked prominently outside – these are easily spotted along virtually any coastline.

Many cities in Korea are famous for local or regional specialities and often entire streets or districts have nothing but speciality restaurants. Some examples are:

Busan (Gyeongsangnam-do) Raw fish.

Chuncheon (Gangwon-do) *Dakgalbi* (chicken grilled with vegetables and rice cakes).

Danyang (Chungcheongbuk-do) Garlic.

Gwangju (Jeollanam-do) *Oritang* (duck soup), *tteokgalbi* (grilled cakes of ground beef).

Jeju-do Seafood of any variety, mushrooms, oranges.

Jeongdongjin (Gangwon-do) *sundubu* (tofu stew).

Sokcho (Gangwon-do) Squid, especially prepared *sundae* (sausage) style.

Suwon (Gyeonggi-do) *Galbi*.

Tongyeong (Gyeongsangnam-do) *Chungmu gimbap* (rice, dried seaweed, pickled radish and *kimchi*).

Yeosu (Jeollanam-do) *Gakkimchi* (leafy *kimchi*).

In most cases a meal like *bibimbap* or *dwaejigalbi* (pork ribs) will cost under W7000, while *galbi* might be W13,000. Soups and stews are generally around W5000. *Banchan* will automatically be included in the price and will generally be refilled for free. If rice is not included, it's usually W1000.

If you see a dish for W20,000 or up, chances are it's meant for sharing, like a whole fish, or a seafood stew.

NATIONAL CHAINS

We strongly suggest sampling the local colour and cuisine, but when you need a quick, easy choice, there are some highly regarded national chains:

Type of cuisine	Restaurant name	
Chicken (barbecue)	BBQ	비비큐
	Pelicana	페리카나
Jjigae	Nolboo	놀부
Mandu	Teolbo	털보
	Myeongdong Gyoja	명동 교자
Naengmyeon	Hamheung	함흥
	Pyeongyang	평양
Spaghetti	Sorrento	쏘렌토
Udong & Gimbap	Jang Udong	장 우동
	Yong Udong	용 우동

Markets

Markets are usually loaded with character – and characters – making them great for browsing even if you're not shopping. You'll find butchers, sellers of vegetables and *kimchi*, noodles, drinks and the staples, alongside stalls and small restaurants. It's perhaps the most Korean way to shop.

Street stalls

At tourist sites, commercial districts and residential areas there are almost always feasting opportunities aplenty.

Common street foods are *sundae* (sausage made from, among other things, vegetables and noodles inside a pork-intestine casing), *tteokbokgi* (spicy rice cakes), *dakkochi* (skewers of grilled chicken marinated in chilli, ginger and soy sauce) and the more challenging *godung* (roll shells) and *beondegi* (silkworms). Another easy-to-find street food is *odeng* (boiled cakes of pressed fish and seafood in a fish broth).

If you're in the mood for something sweet, try *hodeok* (sweet fried dough) or the more familiar *aiseukeurim* (sure sounds like ice cream!).

DID YOU KNOW?

Raw fish and seafood is Korea's most expensive category of food, even at restaurants in fishing harbours. Typically, diners choose a live fish from a tank, for the chef to prepare. Fish are market price, so if you're on a budget, state how much you want to spend before you order.

Convenience Stores

Korean convenience stores are clean, popular and, yes, convenient. With names like Mini-Stop, Family Mart, LG25 and 7-Eleven, some cities have them on seemingly every corner. They're great places to pick up drinks, snacks and small meals, as well as everyday needs. Many even have stand-up counters or simple seating where you can eat.

Staples include instant noodles, *gimbap*, sandwiches, soft drinks, ice cream and chocolate, all at reasonable prices, although fruit can be expensive. Some even sell beer and *soju*.

Student Hangouts

Your typical student hangout serves meals for W2000-4000, with selections such as *mandu*, *gimbap* and *naengmyeon* (see p50). The commercial area in front of the main gate of a university is ripe ground for inexpensive food and bars.

Fast Food Outlets

Let's face it, after a week in Korea nothing will look as good to some visitors as the golden arches. Not to worry, you're covered. Korea's large towns abound with international fast-food restaurants – with the usual fare and some Koreanised additions. But you might check out Korea's contribution to the industry, Lotteria. Here you can get a *kimchi* burger, *bulgogi* burger, shrimp burger or even rice burger (served on a bun made of pressed rice). The multinationals may have their own versions of these, but to Lotteria this is home cookin'.

VEGETARIANS & VEGANS

As in many countries in Asia, Koreans don't have many rules when it comes to food. While they respect the idea of people from other cultures abstaining from certain foods for religious or moral reasons, the concept doesn't completely gel.

Fortunately, despite Korean cuisine's meat-heavy reputation, there's enough variety that vegetarians can usually find something. Rice is served with virtually any meal, and many *banchan* are vegan, though some are made with fish, seafood or their extracts. The same goes for *kimchi*. If you're veg-aquarian you'll have fewer problems.

If all else fails, you can order *bibimbap* minus any ingredients you don't eat.

A singularly good option for vegetarians is Buddhist temple meals, which are made according to Buddhist precepts, meaning vegan. Certain sects avoid spices said to hinder meditation (eg garlic), but generally temple meals are as flavourful as the rest of Korean cuisine. The best part: temple meals are often free! In exchange for your free meal, you'll be expected to respect the Buddhist custom of not wasting food, and you may be asked to help wash your dishes afterwards.

Watch out for stews and soups. These are a staple of Korean cuisine and are often made with beef or seafood stock. Soups made from seaweed or tofu are generally safe, but it's always good to ask if you have a particular need.

The KNTO publishes an excellent booklet, *The Wonderful World of Korean Food*, with descriptions and photos, recipes and lists of specialty restaurants in well-visited cities. The website www.tour2korea.com has an extensive food section, also with recipes of regional dishes.

HABITS & CUSTOMS

The Korean concept of a meal has evolved differently from in other countries. Whereas in the West, rice, soup or pickles might be side dishes, in Korea the reverse is true. The soup, rice and *kimchi* are the centre of the meal, and everything else accompanies them. Typically, you'll order a main course, and it will automatically come with rice, soup, *kimchi* and an assortment of *banchan* selected to create balance on the table in terms of saltiness, temperature and colour combinations.

The level of formality of a meal is determined by the number of *banchan*, starting at three and ascending in odd numbers (sauces and condiments are not counted). For example a five-dish table *(5-cheop bansang)* might include some stewed fish, grilled meat and a few vegetable or tofu dishes, each served in its own plate or shallow bowl. The most elaborate meal, 12-dishes *(surasang)*, was historically reserved for royalty.

Even in an everyday restaurant, a Korean meal is always served with a collection of *banchan*. To many Koreans, the Western system of a single plate with many different foods on it looks rather lonely.

DINING DOS & DON'TS

Dos

- Do try to sit on the floor. You may sit with your legs crossed or to the side. If you need a seatback, try to find a table near the wall so you can back up against it.
- Do pour drinks for others if you notice that their glasses are empty. It is polite to use both hands when pouring.
- Do use the most appropriate utensil for the job. Communal dishes can be eaten with either chopsticks or your spoon. While in other countries it's considered rude to eat rice with a spoon, in Korea it's standard practice.
- Between bites, use a chopstick or spoon rest if one has been provided. If there's no rest, place your chopsticks and your spoon on the table and not over or in a bowl (placing them on a napkin is OK).
- If you need to set a bit of food somewhere before eating it, try on top of your rice. If there's no rice, ask for an empty bowl. Although most Koreans don't eat this way, hosts and restaurants are generally happy to accommodate foreign visitors.
- Knives are not used at the table, so if you're trying to cut something and your spoon won't work, ask for scissors. Sometimes your server will do the cutting for you, but don't be shy about doing it yourself.
- When drinking in front of elders, it is polite to turn your torso slightly (perhaps 20 degrees).

Don'ts

- If you're dining in front of elders, it's considered rude for you to start or finish your meal before they do. It's considered rude to even pick up your chopsticks until the most senior person at the table does.
- Don't touch food with your fingers (exceptions: when handling leaves for wrapping other foods, or when filleting a fish).
- Don't pick up bowls and plates from the table to eat from them. It's considered impolite, and when they're made of stainless steel, they can be hot!
- Don't leave your chopsticks or spoon sticking up from your rice bowl. This is done only in food 'presented' to one's deceased ancestors.
- Don't blow your nose at the table, even if the food is spicy. If you need to blow your nose, excuse yourself and head to a private place such as a washroom.
- Don't put used napkins in dishes, but rather on the table with your utensils.
- Don't tip in a restaurant. If you would like to give special thanks, the manager and staff will probably be thrilled with a note.

WHY METAL BOWLS?

Given that Korea has one of the world's great ceramic-making traditions and is surrounded by nations which use bowls of porcelain and ceramic, and chopsticks of plastic or wood, many visitors find it surprising that Korea uses stainless steel bowls, dishes and utensils.

As with many Korean customs, there are many interpretations, but the most common dates back to the Joseon dynasty. It is said that the kings, ever vigilant about security, would insist on using silver chopsticks as silver would tarnish in the presence of toxins. The tradition caught on and was passed down to the common people.

There's probably also something to the fact that metal is relatively easy to clean and disinfect, and that it stores easily and is hard to break. Downside for those not adept at chopsticks: the thin metal strips can be difficult to use compared with their bulkier wooden or plastic cousins.

Diners traditionally sit on a raised floor (the *ondol* heating system is beneath), usually on cushions. Before stepping up, always remove your shoes – use shoe racks or boxes if provided – otherwise just leave them on the floor. You needn't worry about your shoes being stolen, though in some fancier restaurants the management may store them for you.

Upon sitting down, you may receive a wet washcloth; in hotter months, these are refreshingly cool.

If the table is not set, there will be an oblong box containing chopsticks and long-handled spoons. The person seated next to the box should pass the utensils around the table. Many fancier restaurants have adopted the Western concept of a napkin, but in other places don't be surprised to receive a roll of toilet paper.

Meals are eaten communally, so all dishes are placed in the centre, except for foods like rice and soup – it is said that eating together helps establish good relations. Although we've never looked, we can imagine that from above a full Korean table looks like a fast-paced game of checkers – diners eat a bit from one dish, a bite from another, a little rice, a sip of soup, from all around the table. If you eat in this style, your Korean companions may remark that you eat like a Korean!

EAT YOUR WORDS
Useful Words & Phrases
EATING OUT
We'd like non-smoking/smoking, please.
geumyeonseogeuro/heupyeonseogeuro juseyo   금연석으로/ 흡연석으로 주세요
Do you have an English menu?
yeong-eoro doen menyu isseoyo?   영어로 된 메뉴 있어요?
Do you have seating with tables and chairs?
taeibeul issoyo?   테이블 있어요?
I want to eat spicy food.
maepge hae juseyo   맵게 해 주세요
I can't eat spicy food.
maeun eumsigeun meokji mothamnida   매운 음식은 먹지 못합니다
Is this dish spicy?
i eumsing maeweoyo?   이 음식 매워요?
Can you make it less spicy?
teol maepge haejusilsu isseoyo?   덜 맵게 해 주실 수 있어요?
Could you recommend something?
mweo chucheon haejusillaeyo?   뭐 추천해 주실래요?
I'll have what they're having.
jeobundeurirang gateun menyuro juseyo   저분들이랑 같은 메뉴로 주세요

Excuse me! (please come here)
  yeogiyo!   여기요!
Please bring...
  ...juseyo   ...주세요
Water, please.
  mul juseyo   물 주세요
The menu, please.
  menyureul boyeo juseyo   메뉴를 보여 주세요
The bill/check, please.
  gyesanseo juseyo   계산서 주세요
Bon apetit.
  masikke deuseyo   맛있게 드세요
Thank you.
  gamsahamnida   감사합니다
Thank you. (lit. 'It was delicious')
  masipseoyo   맛있어요
Our compliments to the chef.
  daedanhan yori somssieyo   대단한 요리 솜씨예요
I'm a vegetarian.
  chaesikjuuija imnida jeon chaesikjuuijaeyo   채식주의자입니다 전 채식주의자예요
I don't eat meat.
  jeon gogireul anmeogeoyo   전 고기를 안 먹어요
I can't eat dairy products.
  jeon yujepumeul anmeogeoyo   전 유제품을 안 먹어요
Do you have any vegetarian dishes?
  gogi andeureogan eumshik isseoyo?   고기 안 들어간 음식 있어요?
Does this dish have meat?
  i eumshige gogiga deureogayo?   이 음식에 고기가 들어가요?
Can I get this without meat?
  gogi bbaego haejushilsu isseoyo?   고기 빼고 해 주실 수 있어요?
Does it contain eggs?
  gyerani deureogayo?   계란이 들어가요?
I'm allergic to (peanuts).
  jeon (ddangkong)eallereugiga isseoyo   전 (땅콩)에 알레르기가 있어요
Is there a kosher restaurant here?
  juwie yutaeinsik sikdang isseoyo?   주위에 유태인식 식당 있어요?

Menu Decoder
FISH & SEAFOOD

chobap	초밥	sushi-style raw fish
garibi	가리비	scallops
gwangeo	광어	popular raw fish
hoedeupbap	회덮밥	rice, egg & vegetables with raw seafood in hot sauce
kijogae	키조개	razor clam
nakji	낙지	octopus
odeng	오뎅	pressed fish & seafood cakes in broth
saengseonhoe	생선회	sashimi without the rice
ureok	우럭	popular raw fish

GIMBAP 김밥

chamchi gimbap	참치김밥	tuna *gimbap*
chijeu gimbap	치즈김밥	cheese *gimbap*
kimchi gimbap	김치김밥	*gimbap* containing *kimchi*
modeum gimbap	모듬김밥	assorted *gimbap*
sogogi gimbap	쇠고기김밥	beef *gimbap*

KIMCHI 김치

baechukimchi	배추김치	cabbage *kimchi*; the spicy classic version
baekkimchi	백김치	white cabbage *kimchi*; less spicy than 'regular' *kimchi*, with a sour taste
chonggak kimchi	총각김치	pickled radish *kimchi*
ggakdugi	깍두기	cubed radish *kimchi*
mulkimchi	물김치	cold *kimchi* soup
oisobagi	오이소박이	stuffed cucumber *kimchi*

KOREAN-STYLE CHINESE DISHES

boggeumbap	볶음밥	fried rice
jjajangmyeon	자짱면	egg noodles in black bean sauce
jjambbong	짬봉	noodles & vegetables in broth
tangsuyuk	탕수육	sweet & sour pork
udong	우동	Chinese-style *udong* (thick wheat noodles in thick broth)

MEATS & BARBECUE DISHES

bulgalbi	불갈비	grilled ribs
bulgogi	불고기	barbecued beef & vegetables/marinated beef or pork
dakgalbi	닭갈비	diced grilled chicken
dakgangjeong	닭강정	skewered boneless chicken
dakkochi	닥고치	skewers of grilled marinated chicken
dwaejigalbi	돼지갈비	grilled barbecued pork ribs
galbi	갈비	beef ribs
galbi gui	갈비구이	grilled barbecued beef ribs
hanbang oribaeksuk	한방 오리백숙	duck in medicinal soup
hunjejeongsik	훈제정식	roast duck meal
jjimdak	찜닥	spicy chicken pieces with noodles
metdwaejigogi	멧돼지고기	wild pig
moksalsogeumgui	목살 소금구이	barbecued pork
neobiani	너비아니	large minced patty
ogolgye	오골계	black chicken
samgyeopsal	삼겹살	barbecued bacon-type pork
sogeum gui	소금구이	salted beef ribs
tongdakgui	통닭구이	roasted chicken

NOODLES

bamnaengmyeon	밤냉면	cold chestnut noodles
bibim naengmyeon	비빔냉면	spicy cold noodles without soup
bibimguksu	비빔국수	cold noodles with vegetables in hot sauce
japchae	잡채	mixed vegetables & beef with soybean noodles
kalguksu	칼국수	thick hand-made noodles
kongguksu	콩국수	noodle dish & soy milk broth
makguksu	막국수	vegetables, meat, noodles & chicken broth
mul naengmyeon	물냉면	cold noodle soup
Pyeongyang naengmyeon	평양냉면	North Korean cold noodles
ramyeon	라면	soup ramen noodles
ramyeon bokki	라면북이	fried ramen noodles
yeolmu naengmyeon	열무냉면	cold noodle *kimchi* soup

RICE DISHES

bap	밥	rice (general term)
beoseotssambap	버섯쌈밥	mushroom, rice & vegetable wraps

jibimbap	비빔밥	rice, egg, meat & vegetables in hot sauce
boribap	보리밥	steamed rice with steamed barley mixed in
doenjang bibimbap	된장비빔밥	*bibimbap* with soy sauce
dolsot bibimbap	돌솥비빔밥	*bibimbap* in stone hotpot
dolsotbap	돌솥밥	hotpot rice
dolssambap	돌쌈밥	rice & lettuce wraps
gonggibap	공기밥	steamed rice
gulbap	굴밥	oyster rice
hoedeopbap	회덮밥	seafood rice
honghapbap	홍합밥	mussel rice
kimchi bokkeumbap	김치볶음밥	fried *kimchi* rice
ojingeodeopbap	오징어덮밥	squid rice
pyogodeopbap	표고덮밥	mushroom rice
sanchae bibimbap	산채비빔밥	*bibimbap* made with mountain vegetables
sinseonlo	신선로	meat, fish & vegetables broth cooked at table

SNACKS

beondegi	번데기	boiled silkworm larvae
bungeoppang	붕어빵	fish-shaped cake with red bean filling
hotteok	호떡	sweet pitta bread snack
mettugi	메뚜기	fried grasshoppers
nurungji	누룽지	crunchy burnt-rice globe
odeng	오뎅	processed seafood
susubukkumi	수수부꾸미	red bean pancake
tteok	떡	rice cake
tteokbokgi	떡볶이	spicy rice cakes

SOUPS

bosintang	보신탕	dogmeat soup
bugeoguk	북어국	pollack (seafood) soup
chueotang	추어탕	mudfish soup
dak baeksuk	닭백숙	soft boiled stuffed chicken soup
doganitang	도가니탕	ox leg soup
galbitang	갈비탕	beef ribs soup
gamjatang	감자탕	meaty bones & potato soup
gomtang	곰탕	beef soup
haejangguk	해장국	bean sprout soup
haemultang	해물탕	spicy assorted seafood soup
heukyeomsotang	흑염소탕	goat soup
kkorigomtang	꼬리곰탕	ox tail soup
maeuntang	매운탕	spicy fish soup
manduguk	만두국	soup with meat-filled dumplings
miyeokguk	미역국	brown seaweed soup
oritang	오리탕	duck soup
samgyetang	삼계탕	ginseng chicken soup
seolleongtang	설렁탕	beef & rice soup
seonjigukbap	선지국밥	rice with ox blood soup
tokkitang	토끼탕	rabbit soup
tokidoritang	토끼도리탕	thick rabbit soup
ureongtang	우렁탕	snail soup
yukgaejang	육개장	spicy beef soup

STEWS

| *budae jjigae* | 부대찌개 | ham-&-everything stew |
| *dakjjim* | 닭찜 | chicken stew |

doenjang jjigae	된장찌개	soybean paste stew
dubu jjigae	두부찌개	tofu stew
galbi jjim	갈비찜	barbecued beef ribs stew
gopchang jeongol	곱창전골	tripe hotpot
jjigae	찌개	stew
kimchi jjigae	김치찌개	*kimchi* stew
nakji jeongol	낙지전골	octopus hotpot
sundubu jjigae	순두부찌개	tofu & clam stew

OTHER KOREAN DISHES

agutchim	아구찜	steamed spicy angler fish
bindaetteok	빈대떡	mung bean pancake
bossam	보쌈	steamed pork & cabbage
bulgogijeongsik	불고기정식	*bulgogi* with side dishes
dongchimi	동치미	pickled daikon radish
donkkaseu	돈까스	pork cutlet with rice & vegetables (like Japanese tonkatsu)
dotorimuk	도토리묵	acorn jelly
galbijeongsik	갈비정식	beef ribs with side dishes
gamjabuchim	감자부침	potato pancake
gujeolpan	구절판	eight wrapped snacks
hanjeongsik	한정식	Korean-style banquet
honghapbapdosirak	홍합밥 도시락	mussel rice with side dishes
jang-eo gui	장어구이	grilled eel
jeonbokjuk	전복죽	abalone porridge
jjinppang	찐빵	giant steamed bun with sweet bean paste
jokbal	족발	steamed pork hocks
kimchimandu	김치만두	*kimchi* dumpling
kkotgejjim	꽃게찜	steamed blue crab
kongnamulgukbap	콩나물국밥	spicy rice bean sprout porridge
kwongdoritang	꿩도리탕	pheasant stew
mandu	만두	dumplings
mandugukjeongsik	만두국정식	dumpling soup with side dishes
mandukalguksu	만두칼국수	dumpling & noodle soup
modeumhoe	모듬회	mixed raw fish platter
muk muchim	묵무침	jellied acorn puree
ojingeosundae	오징어순대	stuffed squid
oksusu	옥수수	corn on the cob
omeuraiseu	오므라이스	omelette with rice
pajeon	파전	green onion pancake
ppyeohaejangguk	뼈해장국	meaty bones hotpot
saengseongui	생선구이	fried fish
saengseonjeongsik	생선정식	meat & fish banquet
saeugui	새우구이	grilled prawns
samchigui	삼치구이	barbecued fish
sanchaebaekban	산채백반	rice with mountain vegetable side dishes
sanchaejeongsik	산채정식	modest banquet of mountain vegetables
sangcharim	상차림	banquet of meat, seafood & vegetables
shabu shabu	샤브샤브	beef & noodle casserole
sigol babsang	시골밥상	vegetarian banquet
siksa	식사	budget-priced banquet
ssambap	쌈밥	assorted ingredients with rice & leaves
ssambapjeongsik	쌈밥정식	rice with side dishes & leaf wraps
sujebi	수제비	dough flakes in shellfish broth
sundae	순대	pork sausage

sundubu	순두부	uncurdled tofu with spicy sauce
tteokbokgi	떡볶이	spicy rice rolls
twigim	튀김	seafood & vegetables fried in batter
ureongmuchim	우렁무침	seasoned river snails with mixed vegetables
wangmandu	왕만두	large steamed buns
yukhoe	육회	seasoned raw beef

English–Korean Glossary
AROUND THE TABLE

bowl	*geureut*	그릇
chair (chair seating)	*uija*	의자
chopsticks	*jeokkarak*	젓가락
cup	*keop*	컵
dish	*jeopsi*	접시
floor (floor seating)	*bang*	방
fork	*pokku*	포크
knife	*naipeu*	나이프
ladle	*gukja*	국자
low table	*sang*	상
napkin (often facial tissue or toilet paper)	*naepkin*	냅킨
scissors	*gawi*	가위
spoon	*sutgarak*	숟가락
table	*taeibeul*	테이블

CONDIMENTS

butter	*beoteo*	버터
jam	*jaem*	잼
ketchup	*kechap*	케첩
mayonnaise	*mayonejeu*	마요네즈
mustard	*gyeoja*	겨자
pepper (black)	*huchu*	후추
red pepper (ground)	*gochuggaru*	고춧가루
red pepper paste	*gochujang*	고추장
salt	*sogeum*	소금
soy sauce	*ganjang*	간장
soybean paste	*doenjang*	된장
sugar	*seoltang*	설탕
vinegar	*sikcho*	식초

DESSERTS

cake	*keikeu*	케이크
fried dough	*hodeok*	호떡
ice cream	*aiseukeurim*	아이스크림
pastry	*gwaja*	과자
pie	*pai*	파이
red bean parfait	*patbingsu*	팥빙수
waffles	*wapeul/pulppang*	와플/풀빵

WESTERN STAPLES

bread	*bbang*	빵
butter	*beoteo*	버터
cereal	*sirieol*	시리얼
cheese	*chijeu*	치즈
chocolate	*chokollit*	초콜릿
eggs	*gyeran*	계란

fruit	*gwail*	과일
ham	*haem*	햄
honey	*kkul*	꿀
margarine	*magarin*	마가린
marmalade	*mameolleideu*	마멀레이드
yogurt	*yogureuteu/yogeoteu*	요구르트/요거트

DRINKS
Nonalcoholic

cup of...	*hanjan...*	한 잔...
cinnamon/ginger punch	*sujeonggwa*	수정과
coffee	*keopi*	커피
decaffeinated coffee	*mukapein keopi*	무카페인 커피
cola	*kolla*	콜라
juice	*juseu*	주스
apple	*sagwa*	사과
grape	*podo*	포도
orange	*orenji*	오렌지
lemonade	*remoneideu*	레모네이드
milk	*uyu*	우유
mineral spring water	*saengsu*	생수
rice punch	*shikye*	식혜
seaweed drink	*haeryonggak*	해룡각
tea	*cha*	차
with/without milk	*...uyu neo-eoseo/baego*	우유 넣어서/빼고
with/without sugar	*...seoltang neo-eoseo/baego*	설탕 넣어서/빼고
black tea	*hongcha*	홍차
citron tea	*yujacha*	유자차
date tea	*daechucha*	대추차
ginger tea	*saenggangcha*	생강차
green tea	*nokcha*	녹차
water	*mul*	물
boiled water	*ggeurin mul*	끓인 물

Alcoholic

beer	*maekchu*	맥주
brandy	*beuraendi*	브랜디
champagne	*shampein*	샴페인
cocktail	*kagteil*	칵테일
liquors		
flavoured with		
buckwheat flowers	*memilkkotsul makgeolli*	메밀꽃술
pine needle, chestnut		
& ginseng liquor	*albaminsamsul*	알밤인삼술
red date liquor	*daechusul*	대추술
rice wine	*sansachun*	산사춘
rice wine fermented	*dongdongju*	동동주
rice wine unstrained	*maggeolli*	막걸리
rum	*reom*	럼
soju	*soju*	소주
corn *soju*	*dongdongju*	동동주
whisky	*wiseuki*	위스키
shot of whisky	*wiseuki hanjan*	위스키 한 잔
wine	*wain*	와인
glass of wine	*wain hanjan*	와인 한 잔
green plum wine	*maeshilchu*	매실주

GREATER SEOUL

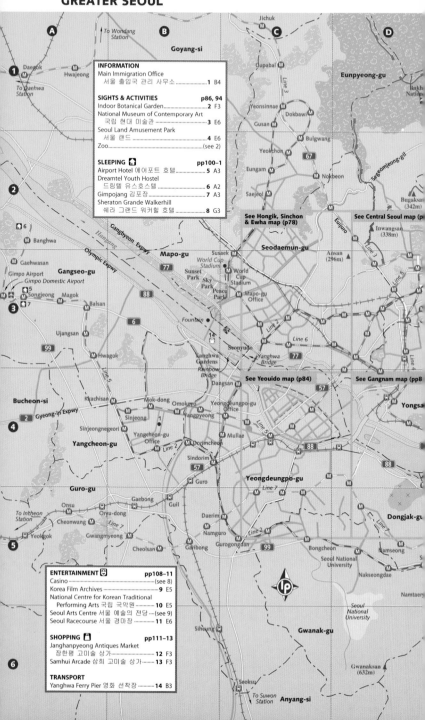

SEOUL RAIL NETWORK

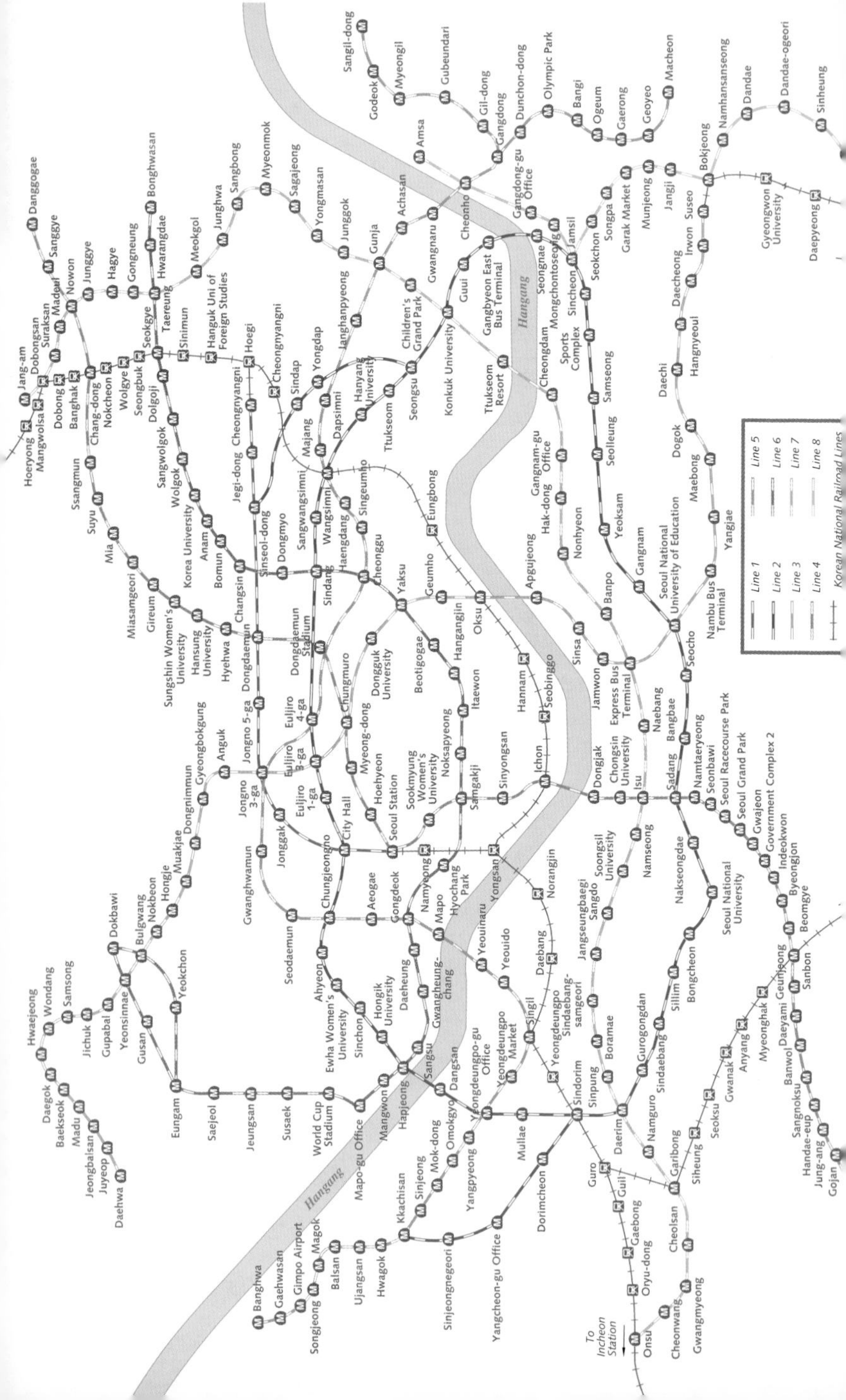

Seoul 서울

No other Korean city approaches the size and importance of Seoul. It is the political, financial, educational and cultural hub of the country, a buzzing and modern Asian city with a high standard of living. Seoul's busy streets are lined with smart shops, markets of all kinds, unusual cafés, reasonably priced restaurants, lively bars, luxury cinemas and dazzling high-rise shopping malls laden with the latest electronic and clothing gear. Entertainment districts are packed with Internet rooms, billiard halls, bowling alleys, live jazz clubs, raging nightclubs and private rooms where you can sing and dance to karaoke.

Yet reminders of Seoul's traditional aristocratic society remain – five ancient palaces where re-enactments of court ceremonies are held; fortress walls and gates; royal shrines and tombs; and one-storey wooden houses with tiled roofs called *hanok*. Cultural performances, folk villages and folk museums allow visitors to experience the historical rural lifestyle. Sit on floor cushions in a traditional restaurant and enjoy the truly diverse Korean food, teas and folk liquors.

Public transport is a dream come true and despite being home to over 10 million residents, Seoul is a safe and friendly city with a low crime rate. Seoulites work long hours but also enjoy socialising and often go out of their way to help foreigners.

Seoul is the 600-year-old capital of a world-class economic powerhouse. In every aspect of life and culture – architecture, religion, politics, film, literature, art, music, dance, food and fashion – it is a fascinating Asian kaleidoscope.

HIGHLIGHTS

- Step back in time inside Seoul's feudal **Confucian palaces** (p85)
- Rub shoulders with the locals in Seoul's boisterous **traditional markets** (p112)
- Go arty crafty in **Insadong** (p87)
- Eat, drink and be merry in the buzzing entertainment districts of **Itaewon** (p106), **Hongik** (p106) and **Daehangno** (p107)
- Be captivated by a traditional **music and dance show** (p111)
- Get out and about – **cycle** along the Han river (p91), **cable car** up Namsan (p88) and **walk** through Inwangsan (p93)

Inwangsan ★   ★ Daehangno
★ Insadong
★ Hongik   ★ Namsan
Itaewon ★

Hangang Cycleway

| ▪ TELEPHONE CODE: 061 | ▪ POPULATION: 10.3 MILLION | ▪ AREA: 605 SQ KM |

HISTORY

Seoul became the capital of Korea following the establishment of the Joseon dynasty by General Yi Seong-gye in 1392. Some of the palaces, shrines, fortress walls and gates that still stand were originally built at that time. Within 10 years Seoul had a population of 100,000.

Neo-Confucianism was the ruling philosophy of the dynasty, Buddhism was banished to the mountains, and in the 19th century Korean Catholics were persecuted and executed. The rigid feudal system of kings, aristocrats, peasants, slaves and outcasts was little changed until 1910 when Japanese colonial rule began and Seoul had a population of 190,000. Over the next 35 years Seoul's palaces were destroyed, and Korean culture and national pride nearly suffered a similar fate as the country was caught up in Japan's ambitious bid for Asian domination.

Since 1948 Seoul has been the capital of South Korea and was fought over four times during the Korean War (1950–53). The city then led the South's rapid transformation into an urban, modern and technologically advanced society as high-rise buildings mushroomed and the streets filled up with made-in-Korea cars and trucks. Only 9% of the population lived in Seoul in 1960, but the figure reached 24% by 1990. Seoul's staging of the 1988 Olympics was a milestone for the country's developed-nation status, and the city is now one of Asia's great cities, packed with cultural events, both traditional and modern.

ORIENTATION

The main historical, sightseeing and accommodation part of Seoul is the downtown area of Gwanghwamun, Insadong and Tapgol Park, with Myeong-dong, Namsan and Seoul Tower forming the southern perimeter.

SEOUL IN...

Four Days

Start at **Gyeongbokgung** (p85), a grand palace with two top museums. Lunch in **Insadong** (p87) and look round the art galleries, craft shops and cafés. Pop into Buddhist **Jogyesa** (p87) before strolling to **Tapgol Park** (p88) and the *tteok* shops (p88). Spend the evening in **Daehangno** – eat at **Nolbu** (p102) then go to a theatre, go to **Ssitipad Noraebang** or **Opera House Noraebang**, or go bar hopping (p106).

Next day buy clothing at bustling **Dongdaemun market** (p112) and health foods and traditional medicines at **Gyeongdong market** (p112) before visiting the massive **War Memorial Museum** (p89) and the ethnic restaurants, expat bars and nightclubs of **Itaewon** (p109).

Day three is the **Between the Palaces Walk** (p93) followed by **Deoksugung** (p85), a palace with museums and art galleries inside and outside its walls. In the evening enjoy a show at **Nanta Theatre** (p110) or **Cheongdong Theatre** (p110).

Next day explore traditional **Namdaemun market** (p112) followed by **Myeong-dong's** fashion boutiques and the **Catholic Cathedral**. Look round **Namsangol Folk Village** (p88) and climb up **Namsan** (p88). Then hang out in funky **Hongik** (p109) where you can enjoy live music and club until dawn.

One Week

Follow the four-day schedule above and on day five start at a **market** – antiques (p112), secondhand goods (p112), electronics (p112) or fish (p112) and then visit chilling **Seodaemun Prison** (p88) and hike up **Inwangsan** (p93) to a shamanist shrine. At nightfall, head to the **casino** (p108), a DVD *bang* or a traditional culture theatre.

Next day tour **Changdeokgung** (p87) and its World Heritage secret garden, followed by a **cycle ride** (p91) along and across the Han river to the World Cup stadium and parks. In the evening try a **river cruise** (p91) and a buffet dinner in the **63 Building** (p91) on Yeouido.

Spend day seven south of the Han river at **Olympic Park** (p90), the **COEX Mall** (p89), **Bongeunsa** (p90) and the **royal tombs** (p90). And the evening in **Lotte World** (p90), or listen to live jazz or rock in smart **Apgujeong** (p109).

Also see p15 for highly recommended day trips from Seoul.

The tourist shopping and entertainment area of Itaewon is south of Namsan. Further south, the Han river winds through the city and mid-river is the island of Yeouido, an important administrative centre. South of the river is the modern Gangnam district, containing department stores, brand-name boutiques and mid-range hotels; and Jamsil, home to the giant COEX Mall, Lotte World and Olympic Park.

Maps
The Korean National Tourism Organisation (KNTO) and Seoul Metropolitan Council publish numerous free maps of Seoul. There is even a map showing the public toilets.

INFORMATION
Bookshops
Bandi & Luni's (Map pp82-3; ☎ 6002 6002; ⊗ 10.30am-9pm) In the COEX Mall; has the best selection of English-language books and magazines.
Kyobo Bookshop (Map pp72-4; ☎ 3973 5100) Has a good selection of English-language books and CDs in its downtown megastore.
Royal Asiatic Society (RAS; Map pp72-4; ☎ 765 9483; www.raskorea.org; Room 611 Korean Christian Bldg; ⊗ 10am-noon, 2-5pm Mon-Fri) Can help with hard-to-find English-language books on Korea.
Seoul Selection Bookshop (Map pp72-4; ☎ 734 9565) Has books on every aspect of Korean culture in English as well as CDs, DVDs and second-hand books.

Emergency
Ambulance (☎ 119)
Fire Brigade (☎ 119)
Helpline for Foreigners (☎ 790 6783)
Police (☎ 112)

Note that emergency services operators are unlikely to be able to understand or speak any English, but the police should have an interpreter available (8am to 11pm Monday to Friday; 8am to 6pm Saturday and Sunday). Phone ☎ 1330 (24 hours) to contact an English-language speaker in a tourist information centre. There are plenty of neighbourhood police boxes where police have an English phrase book and telephone access to an interpreter.

Internet Access
Internet rooms charge W1000 or W1500 per hour and can be found on almost every street – look for their 'PC 방' signs. They

are popular with Internet gaming fans an some are open 24 hours and only charg W500 per hour from 10pm to 8am. Unfor tunately they can be full of cigarette smok even though half the room is supposed t be smoke-free.

As well as the following, many back packer guesthouses, top-end hotels, café and even some fashion boutiques offer fre Internet access.
City Hall (Map pp76-7)
Gimpo domestic airport (Map btwn pp64 & 65)
Incheon international airport (Map p119)
Itaewon subway station tourist information centre (Map p75)
KNTO (Map pp72-4)
Megaweb (Map pp82-3; COEX Mall)

Internet Resources
www.adventurekorea.com For anyone wanting to hik or do adventure sports – the club also has its own pub.
www.clickkorea.org Information on current and upcoming arts and culture events in Seoul.
www.knto.or.kr Excellent site with masses of tourism info on Seoul and Korea.
www.lifeinkorea.com Covers every topic.
www.seoulnow.net Information on all aspects of livin in Seoul.
www.seoulselection.co.kr Excellent weekly newslette about what's on in Seoul.
www.theseoultimes.com Roommate and homestay offers and details about Korean-language classes.
www.visitseoul.net The Seoul Metropolitan Govern ment website for foreign tourists.

Laundry
Backpacker guesthouses usually provid free use of a washing machine and ex pensive hotels provide a laundry service Laundrettes do exist but there are very fe and hard to find. If you stay in a *yeogwa* (motels with small, well-equipped en suit rooms) you may have to do your washin in the bathroom and dry it on the hot *ondo* floor. Midokeompyuteosetak (Map p75 will do a load for W10,000. Dry-cleanin shops are more common so you could dry clean everything.

Left Luggage
Nearly every subway station and bus termin al has a stack of lockers that cost W1000 day, though large ones cost W1500.

To store luggage press the red butto then enter the number of the locker yo want to use and insert the money. To retrieve luggage, press the green button and then the number of your locker. You'll have to pay any extra money owing before you can unlock it.

Medical Services

Seoul is a healthy city with standards of sanitation and medical care that are equal to that of Western countries. Top hospitals have international clinics where the staff speak English, while oriental medicine hospitals adhere to more holistic practices such as acupuncture.

Asan Hospital (Map pp82-3; ☎ 222 5001, emergencies ☎ 2224 5001; ⏰ 9am-4pm Mon-Fri, 9-11am Sat) A top international clinic – the nearest subway station is Seongnae (Line 2, Exit 1).

Dr Park's Dental Clinic (Map p75; ☎ 794 0551; fax 794 0551; above Seoul Pub; ⏰ 10am-5.30pm Mon-Fri, 10am-2pm Sat) Dr Park speaks English. A check-up is W20,000.

International Clinic (Map p75; ☎ 790 0857; www.internationalclinic.co.kr; Hannam Bldg, Itaewonno; ⏰ 9am-noon & 2-6pm Mon-Fri, 9am-noon & 2-3pm Sat) A consultation costs W30,000 to W50,000, X-rays are W25,000 and a blood test is W150,000.

Kyunghee Oriental Hospital (Map p120; ☎ 958 8111; www.khmc.or.kr) A famous oriental medicine hospital.

Severance Hospital (Map p78; ☎ 361 6540; www.severance.or.kr; ⏰ 9.30am-noon & 2.30-5pm Mon-Fri, 9.30am-noon Sat) Part of Yonsei University, which also has a College of Dentistry.

Money

The banks are open 9.30am to 4pm Monday to Friday and most offer foreign exchange services, but there are licensed moneychangers in Itaewon, who keep longer hours and provide a much faster service. However, as with shops and hotels that exchange money, compare their rates and commissions with the banks before using their services.

Post

Main post office (Map pp76-7; ⏰ 9am-6pm Mon-Fri Mar-Oct, 9am-5pm Nov-Feb) It's also open once a fortnight on Saturday from 9am to 1pm, and it has some night counters open until 10pm Monday to Friday and until 6pm on Saturday. There is free Internet access and the poste restante counter is on the 3rd floor.

Toilets

Seoul is one of the few cities in the world with plenty of clean, modern and clearly signposted public toilets. Virtually all toilets are free of charge and some are decorated with flowers and pictures. The cleaning staff do an excellent job. All the tourist attractions, parks, subway stations, train stations and bus terminals have public toilets. Carry tissues around with you as not all the rest rooms supply toilet paper.

Tourist Information

Gwanghwamun Tourist Information Centre
(Map pp72-4; ☎ 731 6337; ⏰ 9am-10pm) Convenient and helpful.

Itaewon Tourist Information Centre (Map p75;
☎ 3785 2514; www.enjoy.itaewon.com; ⏰ 7am-10pm) In Itaewon subway station, it has free Internet access. Another centre is on the main Itaewon road opposite McDonald's.

KNTO (Map pp72-4; ☎ 757 0086; www.knto.or.kr;
⏰ 9am-8pm) Operates an excellent tourist information centre, that covers Seoul as well as the rest of the country. It has stacks of brochures as well as well-informed and helpful staff. Free Internet access, a café, a travel agent and a souvenir shop are also available. The auditorium shows Korean films with English subtitles free of charge at 4pm Tuesday.

Seoul Tourist Information Centre (Map pp76-7;
☎ 731 6671; City Hall; ⏰ 9am-6pm Mon-Fri, 9am-5pm Sat) Offers free Internet access.

Other tourist information centres include a couple at Incheon international airport, Itaewon and Insadong and one at Gimpo domestic airport, Korea City Air Terminal (KCAT), Deoksugung, Namdaemun market and Dongdaemun market.

Travel Agencies

Apple Tours & Travel (Map pp70-1; ☎ 793 3478; fax 798 0698; USO Bldg) Has flights and cheap package tours and the staff can speak English.

KISES (Map pp72-4; ☎ 733 9494; fax 732 9568; YMCA Bldg) The STA Travel agent in Seoul.

Shoestring Travel (Map p78; ☎ 333 4151; fax 336 0258; ⏰ 9am-6pm Mon-Fri, 9am-3pm Sat) A youth-oriented travel agent in Hongik with some English-speaking staff. It also sells Lonely Planet books.

Top Travel (Map pp72-4; ☎ 720 8056; fax 722 0329; 5th fl, YMCA Bldg) Has been recommended by travellers. Look for the English-speaking section.

Other travel agents advertise fares in the English-language newspapers so check these before visiting a travel agent.

[Continued on p85]

A
B
C
D

1
2
3
4
5
6

See Gwanghwamun, Tapgol Park & Insadong map (p72-3)

Inwangsan (338m)

Inwangsangil

Seoul

Fortress

Wall

3

5

2

Sajik Park

Jongno-gu

Gyeongbokgung

Changdeokgung

Changgye

Unhyeongung

Jongn

Jong

6

Dongnimmun Park

Dongnimmun

Line 3

Line 5

Samilro

Line 5

Gumhwa Tunnel

Line 5

See Namdaemun & Myeong-dong map (p76-7)

Sejongno

Line 5

Line 1

Jongno

Gyeonghuigung

Saemunangil

Cheonggyejeonno

Line 3

Ujeongukno

Seodaemun

Deoksugung

Line 2

Euljiro

Seosomunno

Banpo

Chungjeongno

1

Namdaemun

Line 4

To Sinchon

Line 1

Daepyeongno

Doegyero

Banpo

Ahyeon

Seoul

Banpo

Namsan Park

Aeogae

Mapo

Maliljaegil

Jung-gu

Namsan (262m)

Namsa

See Itaewon map (p75)

Hyochang Park

Sookmyung Women's University

Namyeong

Baekbeomno

Line 6

Hyochang Park

10

11

Yongsan US Military Base

37

Samgakji

Line 4

0 — 1 km
0 — 0.5 miles

Daehangno map (p79)

E · Hangsung University
F
G
H · Korea University

Anam · Line 6

Bomun

Gyeongdong Market

Changsin

Jegi-dong · Line 1

Sinseol-dong

Dongdaemun
4 · 9
Dongdaemun Market
Dongmyo
Hwanghak-dong Flea Market
Jungang Market
Sangwangsimni

14
15 · 16
13
Dongdaemun Stadium
8
Dongdaemun Stadium
Sindang

Line 2

Wangsimni

Cheonggu

Dasamno

Haengdang

Jangchung Park
12

Singuemho

Yaksu
Gumhodonggil

Beotigogae

Geumho

Geumho Tunnel

Oksu · 77

Hanganjin

Dongho Bridge

Line 6

Daehangno
Line 4
Line 6
Line 1
Line 3
Changgungdangil
Haewoanno
Donghoro

INFORMATION
French Embassy 프랑스 대사관............**1** B4

SIGHTS & ACTIVITIES **pp85–93**
Bongwonsa 봉원 사...........................**2** A2
Dangun Shrine.................................**3** B2
Dongdaemun 동대문.......................**4** E3
Guksadang 국사당...........................**5** A2
Seodaemun Prison
독립 공원 서대문 형무소 역사관....**6** A2
Seonnongdan 선농단......................**7** H2

SLEEPING **pp96–101**
Busanjang 부산장............................**8** E3
Dongdaemun Hotel 동대문 호텔.......**9** F3
Kaya Hotel 가야 호텔......................**10** B6

EATING **pp101–6**
Dongdaemun Hotel Restaurant.........(see 9)
United Services Organization Canteen
주한미연합 봉사기구.....................**11** B6

ENTERTAINMENT **pp108–11**
Jangchung Gymnasium 장충 체육관..**12** E4

SHOPPING **pp111–13**
APM Mall 에이피엠 몰......................**13** E3
Doosan Tower (Doota) Mall 두산 타워**14** F3
Freya Town Mall & Multiplex
프레야 타운...................................**15** E3
Migliore Mall 밀리오레 몰................**16** F3

A   B   C   D

1

2

3

4

5

6

85

Samcheong Park

79

View Point

🏛 21

● 20

Hyangwonjeong

🏛 26

69 🍴 71 63

56 🍴

Samjeongdong-gil

Bukchonhanok-gil

Jongno-gu

Gyeongbokgung

Gyeonghoeru Pavilion

32 🏛
18 ●

Geunjeongjeon

P

27 🏛

Line 3

Gyeongbokgung

23 ● ● 3

22 🍴 84

86 1

Yulgokno

Ar

● 5

6

25

15
72

57
40 76
60 🍴 77
80
78

Ins

Naejadonggil

16

48

83

Gwanghwamun

Line 5

55

7 ●

45

51

39
61

41

17

2

59 🍴 74

10 ●

Line 1

73 58
Jongno Underground Arcade
8

Gyeonghuigung

29

30

Saemunangil

13

87

4

Jonggak

19

Gyeonghuigung Park

24

11

75

9

28

82

44 43

Namdaemunno

Cheonggy

Sejongno

Hyoja-ro

Ujeongukno

Insadonggil

Jusaro

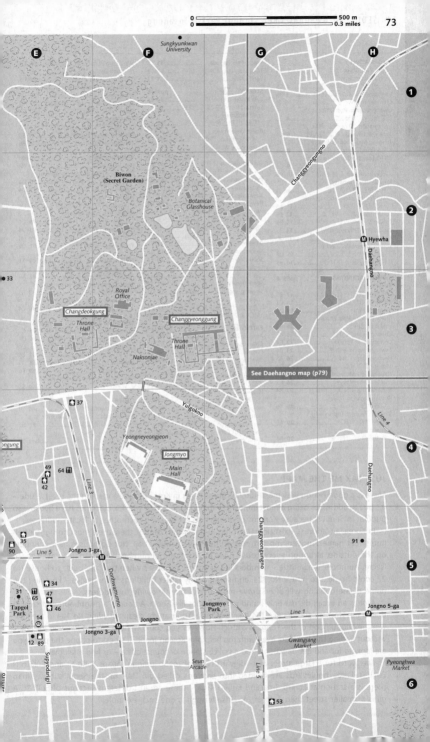

0 ⎯⎯⎯⎯⎯ 500 m
0 ⎯⎯⎯⎯⎯ 0.3 miles

Sungkyunkwan University

Biwon (Secret Garden)

Botanical Glasshouse

Hyewha

Daehangno

Changgyeongungno

● 33

Royal Office

Changdeokgung

Throne Hall

Changgyeonggung

Throne Hall

Naksonjae

See Daehangno map (p79)

Yulgokno

Line 4

Daehangno

37

Yeongneyeongjeon

Jongmyo

Main Hall

49
64
42

Line 3

35

90

Line 5

Jongno 3-ga

Donhwamunno

91 ●

34

31
65

47

Tapgol Park

14

46

Jongmyo Park

Jongno 5-ga

12
89

Jongno 3-ga

Jongno

Line 1

Gwangjang Market

Seun Arcade

Supyodarigil

Pyeonghwa Market

Line 5

53

JUST FAX ME THE MAP!

There is a good reason why most hotel business cards in Korea include a map on the reverse side – it's due to addresses being almost impossible to find. One reason why fax machines have become so popular in Seoul is because Koreans often have to fax maps to each other to locate addresses.

In Korea, an 'address' exists in name only. In the entire country, there are almost no signs labelling street names. Indeed, most streets do not have names at all. Nor do houses have numbers on the outside, although every house does have an official number. Unfortunately, even these 'secret numbers' mean little – numbers are assigned to houses when they are built, so house No 27 could be next to house No 324, and so on. Many larger buildings have names – knowing the name of the building will often prove more useful than knowing the address.

A *gu* is an urban district only found in large cities like Seoul. A *dong* is a neighbourhood smaller than a *gu*. Thus, an address like 104 Itaewon-dong, Yongsan-gu means building No 104 in the Itaewon neighbourhood of the Yongsan district. However you could wander around Itaewon for hours without finding this building, even with the help of a Korean friend. It's best to phone the place you are looking for and get directions, find a police station or tourist office – or find a fax machine.

The word for a large street or boulevard is *no* or *ro*. So Jongno means Jong St and Euljiro is Eulji St. Large boulevards are divided into sections called *ga*. Thus on the Seoul subway map there is a station at Euljiro 3-ga and Euljiro 4-ga – these are just different sections of Eulji St. A *gil* is a smaller street than a *no* or *ro* – Insadonggil is one such example.

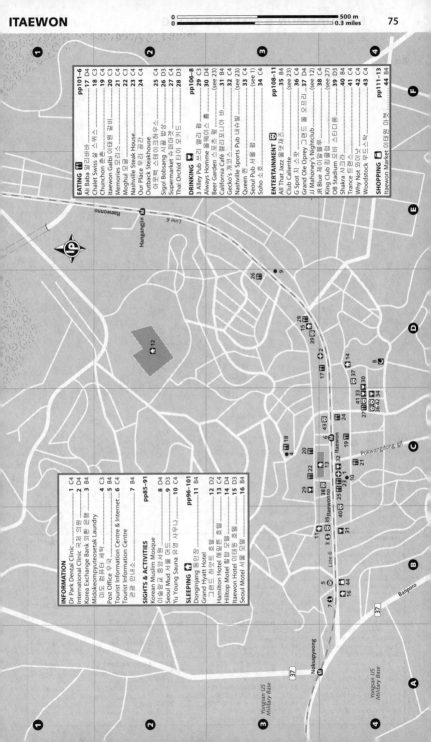

0 — 500 m
0 — 0.3 miles

INFORMATION	
Dr Park Dental Clinic 닥터박치과의원	1 C4
International Clinic 국제 의원	2 D4
Korea Exchange Bank 외환은행	3 B4
Midokeompyuteosetak Laundry 미도 컴퓨터 세탁	4 C3
Post Office 우체국	5 B4
Tourist Information Centre & Internet 관광안내소	6 C4
Tourist Information Centre 관광 안내소	7 B4

SIGHTS & ACTIVITIES	pp85–91
Korean Muslim Mosque 이슬람교 중앙사원	8 D4
Seoul Mud 서울 머드	9 D3
Yu Young Sauna 유 영 사우나	10 C4

SLEEPING 🛏	pp96–101
Donginjang 동인장	11 B4
Grand Hyatt Hotel 그랜드 하야트 호텔	12 D2
Hamilton Hotel 해밀튼 호텔	13 C4
Hilltop Motel 힐탑 모텔	14 D4
Itaewon Hotel 이태원 호텔	15 D3
Seoul Motel 서울 모텔	16 B4

EATING 🍴	pp101–6
Ali Baba 알리바바	17 D4
Chalet Swiss 샬 스위스	18 C3
Chunchon 춘촌	19 C4
Itaewon Galbi 이태원 갈비	20 C4
Memories 모리스	21 C4
Moghul 모굴	22 C3
Nashville Steak House	23 C4
Our Place 우리 꿈간	24 C4
Outback Steakhouse 아웃백 스테이크하우스	25 C4
Sigol Bobsang 시골 밥상	26 C3
Supermarket 슈퍼마켓	27 C4
Thai Orchid 타이 오키드	28 D3

DRINKING 🍸	pp106–8
3 Alley Pub 쓰리 엘리 펍	29 C3
Always Homme 올웨이스 홈	30 D4
Beer Garden 스포츠 펍	31 B4
California Café 캘리포니아 바	32 C4
Gecko's 게코스	33 C4
Nashville Sports Pub 내쉬빌	(see 23)
Queen 퀸	34 C4
Seoul Pub 서울 펍	(see 1)
Soho 소호	

ENTERTAINMENT 🎭	pp108–11
All That Jazz 올댓재즈	35 B4
Club Caliente	(see 23)
G Spot 지 스팟	36 C4
Grand Ole Oprey 그랜드 오프리	37 D4
JJ Mahoney's Nightclub	(see 12)
JR Blue 제이알블루	38 C4
King Club 킹클럽	(see 27)
OB Stadium 오비 스타디움	39 D3
Shakra 샤크라	40 B4
Trance 트랜스	41 C4
Why Not 와이낫	42 C4
Woodstock 우드스탁	43 C4

SHOPPING 🛍	pp111–13
Itaewon Market 이태원 마켓	44 B4

0 ————————— 500 m
0 ————————— 0.3 miles

E

F

G

H

Taerim
Arcade

Euljiro

Euljiro Underground Arcade

Euljiro 3-ga Ⓜ

Ⓜ Euljiro 4-ga

1

Jungbu Market

Sampung
Arcade

Line 5

Donghwamuro

Mareunnaegil

Line 3

Shinseong
Arcade

Line 4

2

🏠 30
🏠 41

Chungmuro Ⓜ

🍴 34
🍴 35

Dongguk
University

🏠 21

Line 3

Ⓜ **3**

16

Dongguk University

Jangchung
Park

Time Capsule
Square

Namsangong-Wongil

4

🏠 24

Namsan Park

🏠 42

Jung-gu

SHOPPING 🛍	pp111–13
Cats Mall 캣츠	**43** D2
Good & Good Mall 굿 앤 굿	**44** C3
Lotte Department Store 롯데 백화점	**45** C1
Mesa Mall 메사	**46** C3
Metro Midopa Department Store 미도파 백화점	**47** C2
Migliore Mall 밀리오레	**48** D2
Shinsegae Department Store 신세계 백화점	**49** C2
Utoozone Mall 유투존	**50** D2

5

● 12

Namsan
(262m)

2nd Namsan Tunnel

1st Namsan Tunnel

Changjungdangil

6

Beotigogae
Ⓜ

0　　　　　　　1
0　　　　　　　0.5 miles

INFORMATION
Post Office 우체국 **1** D4
Severance Hospital 세브란스 병원 **2** D4
Shoestring Travel 신발끈 여행사 **3** B5

SIGHTS & ACTIVITIES pp85–91
Jeoldusan Martyrs' Shrine & Museum
　절두산 순교성지 **4** A5
Seoul Foreigner's Cemetery
　서울 외국인 묘지 **5** A5
Yonsei International Taekwondo Centre
　연세 태권도 협회 **6** C4

SLEEPING pp96–101
Guesthouse Korea
　게스트하우스 코리아 **7** B3
Kims' Guesthouse
　킴스 게스트하우스 **8** A5
Mirabeau Hotel 미라보 호텔 **9** D4
Prince Hotel 프린스 호텔 **10** D4
Seogyo Hotel 서교 호텔 **11** B4
WOW Guesthouse
　와우 게스트하우스 **12** C3

EATING pp101–6
Gio 지오 **13** B5
Haejeodon 해저돈 **14** B5
Huedeura Ramyeon 웨드라 라면 **15** C4
idame 이염 **16** D4
Nolbu 놀부 **17** B4
Pizza Hut 피자헛 **18** B4
Zen Zen 젠젠 **19** C4

Baengnyeonsan
(216m)

DRINKING pp106–8
Bagdad Magic Café
　바그다드 매직 카페 **20** C4
Beatles 비틀즈 **21** C4
Free Crocodiles 악어를 풀어놔봐 **22** C4
Gold 골드바 **23** B5
Labris 라브리스 **24** B5
Woodstock 우드스탁 **25** C4

ENTERTAINMENT pp108–11
Bahia 바이아 **26** B4
Be Bop Jazz Club 비밥 재즈 클럽 **27** B4
DVD Bang 21 DVD방 21 .... **28** B4
Free Bird 프리버드 **29** B5
Haeyeolje 해열제 **30** C4
Hodge Podge 호지부지 **31** B5
Macondo 마콘도 **32** B4
Rolling Stones 롤링스톤스 **33** C4
Sk@ 스카 **34** B5
SLUG.er 슬러거 **35** B5
Water Cock 워터콕 **36** B5

SHOPPING pp111–13
Ahyeon-dong Wedding Street
　아현동 웨딩거리 **37** D4
E'Claire (Grand Mart & Cinema)
　이끌레엣 그랜드마트 **38** C4
Hyundai Department Store
　현대 백화점 **39** C4
Indoor Market 신촌 시장 **40** C4

TRANSPORT
Sinchon Bus Terminal
　신촌 시외 버스 터미널 **41** C5

To World Cup
Stadium

Mangwondonggil

Seogyoro

Hapgeumno

Line 6

Line 2

Dongyoro

Mangwon

Hongik University

Hapjeong

Line 2

Picasso St

Sangsu

Line 6

Line 6

Daeheungno

Gwangheungchang

Daeheung

Wausan-gil

Hongik
University

Yonsei University

Ewha Women'
University

Seongsanno

Ansan
(296m)

Ewha Women's
University

Line 3

Sinchon

Sogang
University

To Centra

To Dow

16

Yanghwa
Bridge

Gangbyeon Expwy

77

Seogang
Bridge

Hangang

Bamseom Island
Bird Sanctuary

To Yeouido

Tochonggil

Taehungno

Gangbyeon Expwy

Mapo

Seogang

Hongje

Euljuro

Hangang Cycleway

DAEHANGNO

INFORMATION
Hyehwa Post Office 혜화 우체국 **1** B2
International House **2** C4
Seoul National University Hospital
  서울대 병원 **3** A6

SLEEPING 🏠 **p100**
Daeseong Yeogwan 대성 여관 **4** B4
Friends House 프렌즈하우스 **5** A2

EATING 🍴 **p105**
Beer Oak 비어 오크 **6** B6
Bongchu Jjimdak 봉추 찜닭 **7** C5
El Paso 엘파소 **8** C5
Nolbu 놀부 **9** B3
Obseoye 옵서예 **10** C5
Sale e Pepe 싸레에페페 **11** C5

DRINKING 🍷 **p107**
Bier Halle 비어 할레 **12** C5
Boogie Boogie Bar 부기부기 **13** C4
Chicago Sports Bar 시카고 **14** C5
Funny Funny Café 파니파니 **15** C4
Mindeulreyeongto Café 1
  민들레영토 본관 **16** C5
Santana 산타나 **17** C5
World Village 월드 빌리지 .... (see 2)

ENTERTAINMENT 🎭 **pp108–11**
Hakjeon Green Theatre 학전 그린 **18** C4
Live Jazz Club 라이브 재즈 **19** C4
Munye Theatre 문예 회관 **20** C5
Opera House Noraebang
  오페라 하우스 **21** C4
Ssitipab Noraebang 씨티팝 노래방 **22** C4

OTHER
Outdoor Covered Stage **23** C6

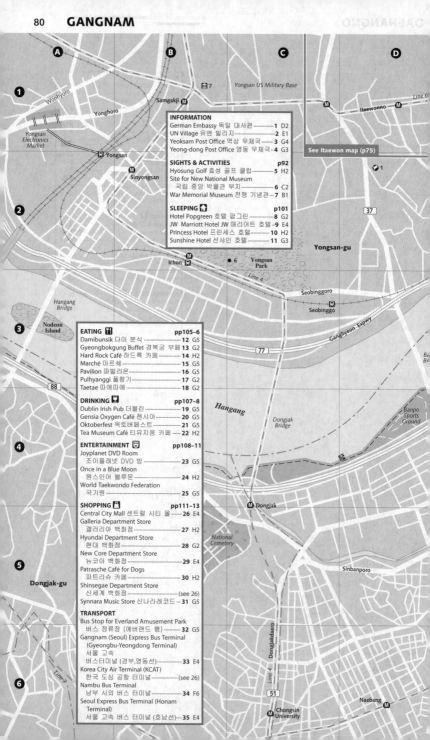

INFORMATION

German Embassy 독일 대사관 **1** D2
UN Village 유엔 빌리지 **2** E1
Yeoksam Post Office 역삼 우체국 **3** G4
Yeong-dong Post Office 영동 우체국 ..**4** G3

SIGHTS & ACTIVITIES   p92

Hyosung Golf 효성 골프 클럽 **5** H2
Site for New National Museum
국립 중앙 박물관 부지 **6** C2
War Memorial Museum 전쟁 기념관 ..**7** B1

SLEEPING 🏠   p101

Hotel Popgreen 호텔 팝그린 **8** G2
JW Marriott Hotel JW 매리어트 호텔 ..**9** E4
Princess Hotel 프린세스 호텔 **10** H2
Sunshine Hotel 선샤인 호텔 **11** G3

See Itaewon map (p75)

Yongsan-gu

EATING 🍴   pp105–6

Damibunsik 다미 분식 **12** G5
Gyeongbokgung Buffet 경복궁 부페 ..**13** G2
Hard Rock Café 하드록 카페 **14** H2
Marché 마르쉐 **15** G5
Pavilion 파빌리온 **16** G5
Pulhyanggi 풀향기 **17** G2
Taetae 따에따에 **18** G2

DRINKING 🍸   pp107–8

Dublin Irish Pub 더블린 **19** G5
Gensia Oxygen Café 젠시아 **20** G5
Oktoberfest 옥토버페스트 **21** G5
Tea Museum Café 티뮤지엄 카페 **22** H2

ENTERTAINMENT 🎭   pp108–11

Joyplanet DVD Room
조이플래넷 DVD 방 **23** G5
Once in a Blue Moon
원스인어 블루문 **24** H2
World Taekwondo Federation
국기원 **25** H2

SHOPPING 🛍   pp111–13

Central City Mall 센트럴 시티 몰 **26** E4
Galleria Department Store
갤러리아 백화점 **27** H2
Hyundai Department Store
현대 백화점 **28** G2
New Core Department Store
뉴코아 백화점 **29** E4
Patrasche Café for Dogs
파트라슈 카페 **30** H2
Shinsegae Department Store
신세계 백화점 ....(see 26)
Synnara Music Store 신나라레코드 ...**31** G5

TRANSPORT

Bus Stop for Everland Amusement Park
버스 정류장 (에버랜드 행) **32** G5
Gangnam (Seoul) Express Bus Terminal
(Gyeongbu-Yeongdong Terminal)
서울 고속
버스터미널 (경부,영동선) **33** E4
Korea City Air Terminal (KCAT)
한국 도심 공항 터미널 ....(see 26)
Nambu Bus Terminal
남부 시외 버스 터미널 **34** F6
Seoul Express Bus Terminal (Honam
Terminal)
서울 고속 버스 터미널 (호남선) **35** E4

0 _____ 1 km
0 _____ 0.5 miles

E **F** **G** **H** **1**

Seongsu Bridge

Dongho Bridge

Olympic Expwy

88

Line 3

Apgujeong

18 🍴

28 🏢 Ⓜ 🏢 8

🍴 13

17 🍴

Dosan Park

22 🖥

27 🏢 Brand Name St

10 🏢

30 🏢

24 📷

🍴 14

5 •

2

Apgujeongno

Rodeo St

Hannam Bridge

Hannam 🚉

77

2

Hangang

Jamwon Riverside Park

⬛ — Hangang Cycleway

11 🏢

Dosandaero

88

Olympic Expwy

Jamwonno

Ⓜ Sinsa

Hokdong Park

Hak-dong

Ⓜ 📷
4

Hakdongno

Ⓜ Gangnam-gu Office

3

Jamwon Ⓜ

Line 3

Nonhyeon Ⓜ

Gangnamdaero

Bongeunsaro

Nonhyeonno

4

Banpo Ⓜ

Sinbanporo

29 🏢

35 🏢
9 🏢 Ⓜ
26 🏢

Express Bus Terminal

📷 33

Sabyeongro

🏢 32

📷
3

🏢 19

16 🍴 23
32 🏢 📷 25
31 🍴
12 🍴

Yeoksam Ⓜ

50

37 Ⓜ

1

21 🏢 📷 20
15 🍴 Ⓜ Gangnam

5

Bamboro

Line 2

Seochoro

Ⓜ Seoul National University of Education

Seocho Ⓜ

Saimdang-gil

Gyeongbu Expwy

Dogokdong-gil

6

Nambu Bus Terminal

34 🏢 Ⓜ

Maebong Ⓜ

0 _____ 1 km
0 _____ 0.5 miles

0   1
0   0.5 miles

INFORMATION
Yeouido Post Office 여의도 우체국 **1** C2

SIGHTS & ACTIVITIES   **p91–3**
63 Building 빌딩 **2** D3
Korea Stock Exchange 증권 거래소 **3** C2
LG Twin Towers 엘지 트윈 타워 **4** C2
National Assembly 국회 의사당 **5** A1
Swimming Pool 수영장 **6** C1

SLEEPING 🏠   **p101**
Yeouido Hotel 여의도 호텔 **7** B2

EATING 🍴   **pp105–6**
Noryangjin Fish Market Restaurants
  노량진 수산 시장 **8** D3
Plaza Fountain Buffet .... (see 2)

SHOPPING 🛍   **p111–13**
Kyeongbang Phill Department Store
  경방필 백화점 **9** A3
Lotte Department Store 롯데 백화점 **10** A3
Shinsegae Department Store
  신세계 백화점 **11** A3
Shopping Mall 쇼핑몰 **12** C3
Yeouido Shopping Centre
  여의도 쇼핑 센터 **13** C2

TRANSPORT
Bicycle Hire 자전거 대여 **14** C2
Bicycle Hire 자전거 대여 **15** C2
Yeouido Ferry Pier 여의도 선착장 **16** D2

Continued from p69]

SIGHTS

Gwanghwamun 광화문

GYEONGBOKGUNG 경복궁

Originally built by King Taejo, this **palace** (Map pp72-4; ☎ 762 8262; adult/youth W1000/500; � 9am-6pm Wed-Mon Mar-Oct, to 5pm Wed-Mon Nov-Feb) served as the principal palace until 1592 when it was burnt down during the Japanese invasions. The grandest palace in Seoul, it lay in ruins for nearly 300 years until Heungseon Daewongun, regent and father of King Gojong, began to rebuild it in 1865, and King Gojong moved in during 1868. Nearly 30 years later, on 8 October 1895, his wife, Queen Myeongseong (Queen Min), was killed in her bedroom by Japanese assassins. King Gojong fled from the palace to the sanctuary of the Russian legation, smuggled out in a curtained palanquin by a eunuch and a maid.

During Japanese colonial rule nearly all the 330 buildings in the palace were either destroyed or moved. Two large-scale models in the National Museum show the palace before and after Japanese rule. However the palace is being restored to some of its former glory. The outstanding 48-columned **Gyeonghoeru** pavilion and the imposing **Genjeongjeon**, with its spacious flagstone courtyard and surrounding corridors, illustrate the splendour of the Joseon dynasty. The attractive lily pond, the island pavilion of **Hyangwonjeong**, the rock garden and the decorative brickwork of the residential quarters show the more relaxed side of life in those feudal, Confucian times.

Inside the grounds is the **National Folk Museum** (www.nfm.go.kr; admission free with entry to Gyeongbokgung). Outside are shamanist stone statues and wooden posts that used to guard the entrances to villages. Inside the clothing, games, rituals, handicrafts, food, housing and occupations of the Joseon era are displayed to illustrate life in the days when aristocratic women wore exquisitely embroidered silk shoes, while peasant women and slave girls wore wooden clogs, straw sandals or went barefoot. Aristocratic men wore black horsehair hats that ordinary folk were not allowed to wear. An English-language audio guide costs W3000 and provides brief but helpful comments. The museum also runs classes that teach foreigners how to make fans, pottery, *hanji* boxes and *kimchi*.

TOP FIVE SITES

Travellers recently voted the following as their favourite places to visit in Seoul:

- Dongdaemun market (p112)
- Gyeongbokgung (p85)
- Insadong (p87)
- Namdaemun market (p112)
- Namsan (p88)

The **National Museum** (www.museum.go.kr; adult/youth W700/300; � 9am-6pm Tue-Sun Mar-Oct, to 5pm Tue-Sun Nov-Feb) focuses on pre-Joseon artefacts. A highlight is the collection of ancient Goryeo celadon with its classical yet varied designs. It is more refined than the Buncheong pottery that came later and has rougher designs that look more like folk art. The giant metal Buddhas are also impressive. Interesting videos (with English subtitles) are shown on the hour, and English-speaking guides lead tours at 10am, 1pm and 3pm from Tuesday to Friday. There are plans to move the National Museum in 2005 to a huge new building being constructed in **Yongsan Park** (Map pp80–1) – take subway Line 4 or 1 to Ichon. When that happens the current National Museum building will become the Joseon Palace Museum.

From March to November the **changing of the guard** takes place at 10am, noon, 2pm and 4pm daily except Tuesday.

DEOKSUGUNG 덕수궁

In 1593 King Seojo moved into this **palace** (Map pp76-7; ☎ 771 9952; adult/youth/child W1000/500/free; � 9am-6pm Tue-Sun Mar-Oct, to 5.30pm Tue-Sun Nov-Feb) because all the other ones were destroyed during the Japanese invasion. Despite two kings being crowned here, it became a secondary palace. Then in 1897 King Gojong moved in after leaving the nearby Russian legation. Although he was forced to abdicate in 1907 by the Japanese, he carried on living there in some style until he died in 1919. He'd lost his kingdom but he kept his harem, and his son, Sunjong, reigned as a puppet emperor with his Japanese wife until 1910 when he too was forced to abdicate. The Joseon dynasty was finally ended after more than 500 years.

The palace contains gardens and ponds and a mixture of architectural structures that include an audience hall in traditional Korean style, a tea pavilion, and two 20th-century neoclassical buildings. The unusual stone animals are *haetae* – mythical creatures that were believed to eat and protect against fire.

The **Royal Museum** (admission free with entry to Deoksugung) is housed in one of the neoclassical buildings. The 1st floor used to be occupied by palace staff and servants, the 2nd floor was for used official meetings and the 3rd floor was the private apartment of the king and queen. Many royal items are on display including clothing, food, kitchenware, furniture and works of art. Highlights include pocket-sized sundials, an eight-section screen showing King Jeongjo's procession to his father's tomb, and a *choheon* – a one-wheeled sedan chair used by government officials that was pushed by up to nine servants.

The **National Museum of Contemporary Art (Annexe)** (Map pp76-7; ☎ 779 5310; adult/youth/child W1000/500/free) is in the other neoclassical building. With four large galleries on two levels, the exhibitions vary but concentrate on pre-1960 modern art.

From March to December the colourful and musical **changing of the guard** takes place outside Daehanmun, Deoksugung's impressive entrance gate. It brings to life the pageantry of the Joseon dynasty. The initial ceremony starts at 2pm and the guards are changed at 2.15pm, 2.45pm and 3.15pm daily except Monday.

CHEONGWADAE 청와대
Known as the **Blue House** (Map pp72-4; ☎ 737 5800; www.president.go.kr), the president's office is white but has blue tiles on the roof. To visit you must join a free Korean-language guided tour that lasts 80 minutes and covers the palatial grounds but doesn't take you inside any important buildings. Tours are available in April, May, September and October on Friday and Saturday starting at 10am and 1.20pm. Also included in the tour is **Chilgung** – small locked shrines that contain the spirit tablets of seven royal concubines whose sons became Joseon kings. Back in 1968 a squad of 31 North Korean commandos was caught just 500m from the Blue House – their mission was to assassinate President Park Jung-hee. The threat

from the North has diminished but sti remains, so security is tight.

The **ticket booth** (⏱ 9am-3pm tour days) is b Gwanghwamun, Gyeongbokgung's mai gate. You need to show your passport to re ceive your free tour ticket. A tour bus take you the short distance from the nearby ca park to Cheongwadae.

SEOUL MUSEUM OF ART 서울 시립 미술관
This brand new **art gallery** (Map pp76-7; ☎ 212 8800; adult/stu●nt W2000/1000; ⏱ 10am-7pm Tue-St Mar-Oct, to 6pm Tue-Sun Nov-Feb) opened in 200 and puts on adventurous exhibitions tha reflect every style of modern art. Its ultra modern and bright galleries hide behind th brick-and-stone facade of the 1927 Suprem Court Building.

SEOUL MUSEUM OF HISTORY
서울 역사박물관
This **museum** (Map pp72-4; ☎ 724 0114; ww .museum.seoul.kr; adult/youth/child W700/250/fre ⏱ 9am-9pm Tue-Sun Mar-Oct, to 8pm Tue-Sun Nov-Fe was opened in 2002. It focuses on Seo during the Joseon period, and the styl of presentation encourages individual ex ploration. Only brief descriptions of item are given, so the English-language tour a 2.30pm is a good idea. The museum als organises special exhibitions that chang regularly.

Nearby is the 22m-high moving scuptu known as Hammering Man.

GYEONGHUIGUNG 경희궁
Originally built between 1617 and 162 this **palace** (Map pp72-4; ☎ 724 0274; admission fre ⏱ 9am-6pm Tue-Sun Mar-Oct, to 5pm Tue-Sun Nov-Fe used to consist of 100 buildings surrounde by courtyards, walls and gardens, but it wa completely dismantled by the Japanese du ing their colonial rule. The area is a now park where a few buildings – Sungjeongjeo the audience hall, and behind it Jujeongjeo the private living quarters – have been re constructed. **Heunghwamun**, the impressiv entrance gate, was moved around Seou including a spell outside Hotel Shilla, befor it was returned here in 1988.

ANGLICAN CHURCH 대한 성공회 대성당
This imposing Renaissance-style churc (Map pp76–7), built in the shape of a cros with Korean-style tiles on the roof, is

fine example of architectural fusion. Work began in 1922 but the full design wasn't completed until 1996.

BOSINGAK 보신각

Situated in Jongno (Bell street), Seoul's main street during the Joseon period, this **pavilion** (Map pp72–4) houses a modern version of the city bell that was originally forged in 1468. The bell is only rung at New Year, when crowds gather to celebrate, but in Joseon times it was struck 33 times at dawn (for the 33 heavens in Buddhism) and 28 times at sunset (for the 28 stars that determine human destiny). This signalled the opening and closing of the city gates.

Insadong 인사동

CHANGDEOKGUNG 창덕궁

This World Heritage **palace** (Map pp72–4; ☎ 762 9531; adult/youth W2500/1300) can only be visited on a tour. English-speaking guides run tours which take 90 minutes from Tuesday to Sunday at 11.30am, 1.30pm and 3.30pm. Originally constructed between 1405 and 1412, it was Korea's centre of power from 1618 to 1896. Seoul's oldest stone bridge (built in 1411) is there along with a throne hall, a blue-tiled royal office, and **Naksonjae** (originally built by King Honjong for one of his concubines), which was home to descendants of the royal family until 1989. Cadillac and Daimler cars, used by the last Joseon king, Sunjong, are on display. But the highlight is the wonderful **Biwon** (Secret Garden), where the library, poem-writing pavilions, square lily ponds and park-like setting create a perfectly tranquil rural atmosphere.

From March to December the **changing of the guard** takes place outside from 2pm to 3.30pm daily except Monday.

CHANGGYEONGGUNG & JONGMYO 창경궁, 종묘

Originally built in the early 15th century, the buildings of **Changgyeonggung** (Map pp72–4; ☎ 762 4868; adult/youth W1000/500; 9am-5pm Wed-Mon Mar-Oct, to 4.30pm Wed-Mon Nov-Feb) are modest in size. The oldest structure, which is the throne hall, dates from 1616, while the splendid botanical garden glasshouse is almost a century old. In olden days Joseon kings used to plant and harvest rice at the location of today's scenic pond. They did

this to keep in touch with the nation's agricultural roots. During the Japanese occupation Changgyeonggung suffered the ultimate indignity of being turned into a zoo. In October the Joseon government exam *gwageo* is re-enacted here.

Walk over the footbridge to **Jongmyo**, the shrine where the spirit tablets of all the Joseon kings and queens are kept. They are housed in small locked rooms in two long buildings surrounded by woodland. The **main hall** was originally built in 1395, while **Yeongneyeongjeon** dates from 1421.

If you visit both places at the same time and use the footbridge between them, you only pay one admission fee.

INSADONG-GIL 인사동길

Insadong (Map pp72–4) has retained an atmosphere of the past despite all the recent rebuilding. The narrow alleyways are packed with art galleries, traditional teashops and small restaurants, including vegetarian ones. Craft shops sell fans, handmade paper boxes, masks, lacquer ware, pottery and antiques. Munch on traditional snacks bought from street stalls, and buy a *tojang* (name seal), handmade pottery or a second-hand book – the choice is endless. This fascinating shopping street is traffic-free on Saturday from 2pm to 10pm and on Sunday from 10am to 10pm.

JOGYESA 조계사

The largest **Buddhist temple** (Map pp72–4) in Seoul was built here in 1938, but the design followed the Joseon-dynasty style. Murals of scenes from Buddha's life and the carved floral latticework doors are two attractive features. Jogyesa is the headquarters of the Jogye sect, the largest in Korea, which emphasizes Zen-style meditation and the study of Buddhist scriptures to achieve enlightenment. The temple sometimes runs programmes where visitors can join the monks for a typical vegetarian meal, meditation, tea ceremony and other activities.

UNHYEONGUNG 운현궁

This modest **palace** (Map pp72–4; ☎ 766 9098; adult/youth/child W700/300/free; 9am-7pm Tue-Sun Mar-Oct, to 5pm Tue-Sun Nov-Feb) was the home of Heungseon Daewongun, the stern and conservative father of King Gojong, whose policies included closing Confucian schools, massacring Korean Catholics and excluding foreigners. King Gojong was born and raised there until he ascended the throne in 1863 at the age of 12. Unhyeongung's buildings are smaller than the other palaces but are well preserved and the small but charming rooms are furnished in *yangban* style.

An hour-long re-enactment of the marriage of King Gojong to Queen Myeong-seong (Queen Min), with authentic music and costumes, is held here in October, where the actual event took place in 1867. He was 15 and she was 16.

TAPGOL PARK 탑골 공원

Tap means 'pagoda' and this **park** (Map pp72–4) is named after its 10-tier, 12m-high **marble pagoda** that was constructed in the 1470s and is decorated with beautiful Buddhist carvings. Sadly it has been encased in a protective metal and glass structure.

On 1 March 1919, Son Pyong-hui (1861–1922) and 32 other Korean nationalists drew up a declaration of independence, which was read aloud in this park two days later. National protests, known as the *sam-il* (March 1st) movement, against Japanese rule broke out but were ruthlessly suppressed.

North of the park are some *tteok* shops selling traditional homemade rice cakes of all shapes and colours.

East Seoul

Seoul's other surviving fortress gate, **Dong-daemun** (Heunginjimun; Map pp70–1), dates back to the 14th century, but the existing structure was built in 1869 and renovated after being severely damaged during the Korean War. It marks the start of the massive market.

Myeong-dong & Namsan 남산

SEOUL TOWER & NAMSAN 서울 타워, 남산

The views from the top of Namsan are memorable – this is where you'll get the best views of Seoul, and a romantic view at night. Tourists regularly vote it a top spot. **Seoul Tower** (Map pp76-7) has a range of restaurants, shops and tourist attractions. Take the lift to the **observation deck** (adult/youth/child W5000/3500/2500; 9-1am) for the highest view.

The **Global Folk Museum** (☎ 773 9590; adult/youth/child W3000/2500/2000; 9am-10pm) is full of curiosities such as African masks, chastity belts and the world's largest silver coin. Nearby are two attractions for children – **Fairy Land** and a **3-D Animation Cinema** – which cost the same as the Global Folk Museum and have the same opening hours. Restaurants include the well-known semivegetarian **Pulhyanggi** (set lunch/dinner from W20,000/32,000).

The **signal beacons** are replicas of those that were built on Namsan during the Joseon period so that messages could be sent from the capital to all parts of the country via a series of hill-top beacons.

The **cable car** (adult/child one-way W4500/2800, return W5800/3500; 10am-11pm Tue-Sun) is a fast and easy way up and down.

NAMSANGOL TRADITIONAL VILLAGE
남산골 한옥 마을

This small **village** (Map pp76-7; www.fpcp.or.kr; admission free; 9am-7pm Wed-Mon May-Sep, to 6pm Wed-Mon Oct-Apr), situated at the foot of Namsan, contains five different *yangban* houses from the Joseon era, which are furnished in period style. The architecture and furniture are austere and plain, reflecting the Confucian tastes of the aristocracy.

NAMDAEMUN 남대문

The **Great South Gate** (Sungnyemun; Map pp76-7) of Seoul fortress was originally constructed in 1398, rebuilt in 1447 and has often been renovated since then. Designated as National Treasure No 1, it's an impressive sight, especially when floodlit at night, and marks the beginning of the sprawling market.

MYEONG-DONG CATHOLIC CATHEDRAL
명동 성당

This **cathedral** (Map pp76-7) is an elegant brick Renaissance-style building that was completed in 1898. It provided a sanctuary for student and trade-union protestors during the long period of military rule after the Korean War, and is an important national symbol of democracy and human rights. English-language worship occurs at 9am on Sunday.

West Seoul
SEODAEMUN PRISON
독립 공원 서대문형무소 역사관

This historical **prison** (Map pp70-1; ☎ 363 9750; adult/youth/child W1100/550/220; 9.30am-6pm Tue-Sun Mar-Oct, to 5pm Tue-Sun Nov-Feb) is a stark

MARTIN VINCENT ROBINSON

View from fortress wall (p93), Seoul

MARTIN VINCENT ROBINSON

Traditional drumming, Seoul
Norimadang (p111)

War Memorial Museum (p89), Seoul

PATRICK HORTON

Gyeonghoeru pavilion, Gyeongbokgung (p85), Seoul

Ice skating at Lotte World (p90), Seoul

Namdaemun Market (p112), Seoul

reminder of the sufferings of Korean independence fighters who challenged Japanese colonial rule between 1910 and 1945. The entrance gate and watchtower, the execution room, punishment cells and seven of the original 15 buildings are on view. You can walk between long lines of cells where the prisoners were held, and see photographs and videos of the harsh life inside the high brick walls. Overcrowding, poor food, beatings, torture and interrogation caused many deaths. The interrogation rooms are nightmarish.

Next to the prison is **Dongnimmun Park** and **Independence Gate**, which is a Western-style granite archway built by the Independence Club in 1898. It stands where envoys from Chinese emperors used to be officially welcomed to Seoul, a ritual that symbolised Chinese suzerainty over Korea, but was ended when King Gojong declared himself an emperor in 1897.

WORLD CUP STADIUM & PARKS
월드컵주경기장

Costing US$151 million, the 64,000-seat **World Cup Stadium** (Map btwn pp64 & 65) was built on a landfill site. The impressive stadium has a Teflon-covered roof shaped like a traditional Korean kite and staged the opening ceremony of the 2002 World Cup soccer finals. Cinemas, shops, an indoor market, attractive parks, ponds, wind turbines and a 202m fountain surround the stadium.

The best way to explore the stadium and the surrounding area is by bicycle (p91). However it is also easily accessible by subway – take subway Line 6 to World Cup Stadium station.

JEOLDUSAN MARTYRS' SHRINE & MUSEUM 절두산 순교 성지

Jeoldusan (Map p78) means 'Beheading Hill' and is the place where up to 2000 Korean Catholics, some of them as young as 13, were executed in 1866 following a decree signed by Regent Heungseon Daewongun, King Gojong's father, to kill all Catholics. The victims' bodies were thrown into the river and only 40 of their names are known. The small **museum** (☎ 3142 4434; admission W1000; ⌚ 9am-5pm Tue-Sun) has relics of early Catholic converts and martyrs who faced waves of government persecution.

The chapel is open every day with Mass at 10am and 3pm. A volunteer guide may be available.

Take subway Line 2 or 6 to Hapjeong station and leave by exit 7. Go left at the second turning and walk along the covered railway line, following the small brown signs – it's a 10-minute walk.

SAJIK PARK 사직 공원

A small **park** (Map pp70–1) surrounds Sajikdan where Joseon kings performed sacrificial rites for a good harvest. Up the granite steps is a simple shrine to Dangun, Korea's mythical founder.

Itaewon 이태원

WAR MEMORIAL MUSEUM 전쟁 기념관

This large and interesting **museum** (Map pp80-1; ☎ 709 3139; www.warmemo.co.kr; adult/child W3000/2000; ⌚ 9.30am-6pm Tue-Sun Mar-Oct, to 5pm Tue-Sun Nov-Feb) documents the many attacks on Korea by Mongols, Chinese and Japanese among others. Korea has a turbulent and tragic history and it's a miracle that the country has survived. Upstairs are exhibits giving a detailed description of the Korean War using newsreels, photographs, maps and artefacts of the period. Also covered is Korea's involvement in the Vietnam War where 4000 Koreans died. The Combat Experience Room shows the reality of modern warfare. Outside are 150 large items of military hardware ranging from artillery to aircraft.

Every Friday from March to November at 2pm a performance by a military band and a marching parade culminate in an awesome display of military precision and weapon twirling by the honour guard of the army, navy and air force. Try to visit on a Friday.

YONGSAN PARK 용산 가족 공원

This **park** (Map pp80–1), south of Itaewon, is a quiet, natural area of ponds and trees ideal for family picnics, but the new National Museum being built here is due to open in 2005.

South of the Han River

COEX MALL 코엑스 몰

This huge underground **mall** (Map pp82-3; www.coexmall.com) includes numerous shops, four food courts, the Hyundai Department

Store, the COEX Conference Centre & Exhibition Hall, two luxury hotels and a multiplex cinema.

COEX Aquarium (☎ 6002 6200; www.coexaqua .co.kr; adult/child/secondary student W14,500/9500/12,000; 🕙 10am-8pm Sun-Fri, closes 9pm Sat), with live coral and evil-looking piranhas, is one of Korea's best. Sharks, turtles and rays swim around a huge tank, but don't miss the exquisitely beautiful small creatures such as sea horses, glass fish and pulsating jellyfish.

Megaweb (🕙 10am-11pm) has a free fun zone funded by Korea Telecom (KT). Besides playing computer and video arcade games, watching DVDs and using the one-hour Internet service, you can beat the hell out of a drum kit in a sound-proof room, and even record your own CD – all for free. In XBox you can play 60 different computer games for free, including the very latest ones.

The **Kimchi Museum** (B2; adult/child W3000/1000; 🕙 10am-5pm Tue-Sat, 1-5pm Sun) is only for real fans of this peppery pickled cabbage.

BONGEUNSA 봉은사

North of the COEX Mall, this **temple** (Map pp82–3) was originally founded in AD 794, but was rebuilt in 1498 when restrictions on Buddhists were eased. The oldest building still standing, constructed in 1856, is a library that has 150-year-old woodblocks carved with Buddhist scriptures and art. Ask at the entrance gate if an English-speaking volunteer guide is available. Bongeunsa also runs temple-stay programmes where visitors experience at first hand different aspects of a monk's life (p91).

ROYAL TOMBS 왕릉

The spirit tablets of the Joseon kings and queens are in Jongmyo, but their impressive tombs are scattered all over Seoul. The tomb of King Seonjeong (r 1469–94), his second wife, Queen Jeonghyeonwanghu, and his second son, King Jungjeong (r 1506–44), are in wooded **Samneung Park** (Map pp82-3; admission W400; 🕙 9am-5.30pm Tue-Sun Mar-Oct, to 4.30pm Tue-Sun Nov-Feb), a 15-minute walk from the COEX Mall. King Seonjeong is remembered as a prolific father – he had 28 children by 10 concubines – while King Jungjeong ruled for a long time but was a weak king. The tombs follow the Chinese fashion and are guarded by stone statues of warriors, horses, tigers and imaginary animals that look like sheep.

To get there, take subway Line 2 to Seolleung station and leave by Exit 8. Turn left at the first road and left again at the park fence – it's a 10-minute walk.

LOTTE WORLD AMUSEMENT PARK 롯데월드

Lotte World (Map pp82-3; www.lotteworld.com) is a huge complex that includes Lotte World hotel, Lotte department store, a shopping mall, a five-cinema multiplex, a billiard hall, an art gallery and numerous restaurants and fast food outlets.

Enjoy yourself on the **indoor ice-skating rink** (☎ 411 2000; adult/child under 14 yr before 7pm W9500/ 8500, after 7pm W8000/7000; 🕙 10.30am-10.30pm) where skates can be hired for W3500. Have a game at the 26-lane **bowling alley** (adult/child under 14 yr W2900/2700; 🕙 9am-midnight) where shoe rental is W1200. Then cool off in the large indoor **swimming pool** (adult/child under 14 yr Sep-Jun W7000/6000, Jul-Aug W9000/7000; 🕙 1-7pm Mon-Fri, 6am-8pm Sat & Sun). The big slide is W500 a go (W1000 in July and August).

The **Folk Museum** (adult/youth/child W4500/3000/ 2000; 🕙 9.30am-11pm) is on the 3rd floor. Using imaginative techniques like moving waxworks, dioramas and scale models, it brings to life how ordinary Koreans used to live.

The main attraction is **Lotte World Adventure & Magic Island** (adult/child 13-18 yr/child 4-12 yr W18,000/15,000/12,000, Big-5 ticket W28,000/24,000/ 20,000; after 5pm W12,000/10,000/8000, Big-5 ticket W24,000/20,000/17,000; 🕙 9.30am-11pm). This Korean version of Disneyland has a monorail train, live musical entertainment, 3-D films, and a laser show at 9pm. You can swing in the Viking Ship, ride in simulators, whiz through water, and go round and round and up and down on other thrill rides. On the Gyro Drop you fall 70m in two seconds – but the scarier the ride, the longer the queue will be. The main Lotte World Adventure section is indoors, while Magic Island is outside in the middle of a lake.

OLYMPIC PARK 올림픽 공원

This **park** (Map pp82–3) has a large open green area with a lake that is home to pheasants, herons, ducks and geese. An early Baekje-dynasty earth fortification **Mongchontoseong** has been reconstructed, and the cosy **Mongchontoseong Museum** (admission free; 🕙 10am-5pm Tue-Sun Mar-Oct, to 4pm Tue-Sun Nov-Feb) displays Baekje golden crowns, jewellery and a ceremonial seven-pronged sword.

The Seoul **Olympic Museum** (☎ 410 1052; www.seoulolympicmuseum.com; adult/youth/child W3000/2000/1000; ☺ 10am-5.30pm Tue-Sun Mar-Oct, to 4.30pm Tue-Sun Nov-Feb) is full of screens showing action from the 1988 Seoul Olympics. Take a simulated ride and test your skills on the do-it-yourself sports equipment downstairs (W500 coins needed).

The park contains the stadiums used during the Seoul Olympics. The **velodrome** (www.cyclerace.or.kr; admission W400; ☺ 11am-6pm Fri-Sun Mar-Oct) puts on six-lap, 2km cycle races and you can bet on which of the seven riders will win. Nearby is the **indoor olympic swimming pool** (☎ 410 1696; adult/child W4500/3500; ☺ 12.15-9pm Mon-Fri).

Most of the two hundred outdoor **modern sculptures** are puzzling even after you have read the artists' descriptions of their work. On warm evenings and weekends hundreds of young people visit the park to roller blade around the plaza, play roller blade hockey and do skateboard tricks, while the older generation play badminton, jog, eat ice cream, picnic under the trees or exercise tiny dogs.

YEOUIDO 여의도

This **island** (Map p84) in Hangang, 3km long and 2km wide, is a mixture of pleasant parks and high-rise buildings that house the headquarters of many media, finance and insurance companies, the stock exchange and the National Assembly.

The **Hangang parks** are popular places on warm weekends with cyclists and rollerbladers. Families come for a picnic and take advantage of the outdoor **swimming pool** (adult/child W2500/1500; ☺ swimming 9am-6pm Jul-Aug, ice skating Dec-Feb) and other sports facilities. Bicycles can be hired, see p91.

At the eastern tip of the island is the gold-tinted **63 Building** (www.63city.co.kr). On B1 floor is an **aquarium** (☎ 789-5663; adult/child 13-18 yr/child W9500/9000/8500), which features fish feeding and seal and sea-lion shows, and an **Imax large screen cinema** (☎ 789 5663; adult/student/child W7000/6500/6000) with headphones that provide a commentary in English. The **observation deck** (adult/student/child W6000/5500/5000) is on the 60th floor. All three attractions cost W18,000 (adult), W16,500 (student) and W15,000 (child).

The 56th to 59th floors have Western, Chinese and Japanese restaurants with a view, while down on the 4th floor is a Korean restaurant and lower still are the fast-food franchises. Also in the basement is Plaza Fountain Buffet, famous for its sumptuous buffet and 'dancing' fountain (p101).

The **Hangang Pleasure Boats** (☎ 785 4411) provide enjoyable one-hour trips along the river – one-way and return trips both cost W7000 (adult) and W3500 (child). There are four ferry piers – Yeouido (Map p84), Yanghwa (Map btwn pp64 & 65), Ttukseom (Map pp82–3) and Jamsil (Map pp82–3). One option is to take the 15km cruise from Yeouido pier to Jamsil pier and then walk the 15 minutes to Sincheon subway station (Line 2). Alternatively, you can come back on the ferry for the same price. The boats operate all year round, and run every hour from 11am to 8pm in July and August, and every one to two hours in other months.

ACTIVITIES
Buddhist Temple Programmes

Bongeunsa (Map pp82–3) offers a four-hour programme (W20,000). It starts with a typical temple four-bowl lunch of rice, soup, vegetables and water. No talk is allowed and not even a scrap of food should be discarded – Buddhists are strict. A guided tour of the beautiful temple buildings is followed by Seon meditation. Everyone sits cross-legged and a monk tells participants to concentrate their minds on their breathing. After this a monk prepares organic green tea, which must be served at exactly the right temperature and should be drunk in three sips. Tea calms the mind and the body and if Korean monks have a disagreement they settle it over a cup of organic green tea.

Cycling

Cycle paths line both banks of the Han river and bicycles can be rented in many of the parks along it. In summer, swimming pools, paddle boats, windsurfing, jet-skiing and water-skiing can all be enjoyed. Hire a bike on Yeouido from a **rental hut** (Map p84; bicycles/tandems per hr W2000/5000; ☺ 9am-7pm May-Aug, 9am-6pm Mar-Apr & Sep-Oct, 9am-5pm Nov-Feb) near the swimming pool in Hangang Park, or near the ferry boat terminal in Yeouido Park. Padlocks and bicycle helmets are not supplied and some form of ID is required.

YEOUIDO TO THE WORLD CUP STADIUM

This trip (Map btwn pp64 & 65) is 7km return and takes 90 minutes to cycle, but longer if you spend time at the stadium and its surrounding parks.

From Yeouido cycle past the National Assembly and after 1km you reach Yanghwa gardens and then Yanghwa Bridge, which you can use to cross the river. Walk up the steps of the bridge pushing your bike up the little path. Have a look round Seonyudo in mid-river – it was a water treatment plant but is now an attractive park. Wheel your bike down the narrow path on the right of the steps on the other side of the bridge, and continue right along the cycleway that runs along the northern side of the river. After 10 minutes, turn right at the orange bridge, ride over a small bridge and then turn right again, following the green signs. After another 10 minutes you should arrive in the large attractive park that surrounds the World Cup Stadium.

YEOUIDO TO OLYMPIC PARK

This is a long route (Map btwn pp64 & 65), 38km return, and takes four hours cycling, but nearly all of it is on a cycleway and there are no hills.

Along the way are parks, sports fields and lots of bridges and fishermen. Herons, geese and other birds can be seen. Near the 18km distance marker from Yeouido, turn right (no sign), ride under a couple of bridges and follow the left side of a dry riverbed. At the road, turn left, cross over the minor road, and then cross the major road using the pedestrian crossing. Then turn right, go over the bridge and Olympic Park is on your left, with its museums, stadiums, ponds and outdoor sculptures (p90).

Golf

Golf courses near Seoul are usually expensive and members-only, so it's probably best to stick to the driving ranges, which you can find all over Seoul as well as in some top-end hotels. **Hyosung Golf** (Map pp80-1; per hr W14,000; ☼ 5am-10.30pm) in Apgujeong is a typical one.

Saunas & Bathhouses

A swelter in a sauna like **Yu Young Sauna** (Map p75; Itaewon; ☼ 24hr) costs only W3500. Many are open 24 hours a day, but they are segregated and some only have facilities for men. More luxurious male-only saunas are available downtown at the New Seoul Hotel (W10,000) and the Koreana Hotel (W13,000).

Health and beauty tours in Seoul are popular with Japanese tourists, but these upmarket facilities are expensive. **Seoul Mud** (Map p75; ☎ 749 8012; ☼ 9am-midnight) in Itaewon charges W82,000 for a two-hour stay, which includes bathing in a mud pool, a milk pool, a ginseng pool and an orange pool, followed by a sauna. It's a cheap price to pay for skin-deep beauty if it works.

A less-expensive option is offered at **Dreamtel Youth Hostel** (p100; Map btwn pp64 & 65) which is a 45-minute subway ride west of the city centre. It has a sauna, exercise room and indoor swimming pool that cost W7000 a day.

For further information on Hot Spring Baths, see p366.

Swimming

The best places for swimming are the sandy beaches of the unspoilt islands scattered off Incheon in the West Sea (p132). In the hot humid months of July and August, outdoor swimming pools open in the parks along Hangang. **Yeouido Pool** (Map p84; admission W2500) is near Yeouinaru subway station on Line 5.

Large indoor pools are available at **Lotte World** (p90) and **Olympic Park** (p90–1) and are usually open to the public in the afternoons. Most luxury hotels have 25m indoor pools and some are available to non-guests. Prices start at W8000 but are reasonable considering the facilities provided.

Caribbean Bay is the best aquatic centre and part of Everland (p126). Icheon Miranda Spa has a pool and other great facilities (p127).

Taekwondo

The headquarters of the **World Taekwondo Federation** (Map pp80-1; ☎ 566 2505), northeast of Gangnam subway station, has a tournament hall. For information on tournament dates log on to www.koreataekwondo.org or www.wtf.org.

Hoki Taekwondo (☎ 336 6014; www.taekwontou .com) organises a 1½-hour (W30,000) or a 3-hour (W65,000) introductory taekwondo programme at the War Memorial Museum gymnasium. Participants get the chance to break a 2cm-thick wooden board. Contact Hoki Taekwondo before turning up at the gymnasium.

Yonsei International Taekwondo Centre (Map p78; ☎ 738 8397) provides four training sessions in a week for W20,000.

WALKING TOURS
Inwangsan Shamanist Hillside Walk

On this short but uphill walk you can see Seoul's most famous shamanist shrine, visit small Buddhist temples and see part of the Seoul fortress wall. The walk only takes an hour if you just want a quick look but it's sensible to take longer and soak up the unique atmosphere.

Take subway Line 3 to Dongnimmun station, leave by Exit 2 and turn down the first winding alley on your left. Walk uphill past the golf driving range and grocery shops for 10 minutes, and you'll see a temple gateway on your left. Walk through it to the notice board. Turn left to walk around the village where **Buddhist temples** and traditional houses cling to the rocky hillside. The temples have colourful murals on the outside that illustrate the Buddhist philosophy of life.

Back on the main path, a bronze bell marks the **Bongwonsa** entrance, the largest of the temples. The paintings on the entrance gate doors depict the guardian kings of heaven who protect Buddhists from evil. The shrine hall has five golden Buddha statues and a side shrine for the shamanist deities: Sanshin (the mountain god), Doksung (the river god) and Chilsung (the seven stars of the Big Dipper). Buddhism and shamanism have always coexisted peacefully in Korea.

Carry on up the steps to see the shamanist shrine, **Guksadang**. It was originally built on Namsan but was demolished by the Japanese in 1925 and Korean shamanists secretly rebuilt it on Inwangsan. The shrine is small but the altar inside is often loaded down with food offerings – rice cakes, fruit, meat and a pig's head – as shamanists believe that spirits still need food and drink. Walk left and up some steps to the extraordinary **Zen rocks** that look like a Salvador Dali painting – two large rocks have been eroded into a semi-human shape. Women come here to pray for a son.

The hillside above is full of eroded rocks that create an uncanny atmosphere. In front of small crevices are candles, incense sticks and offerings of sweets. Climb up the hill for

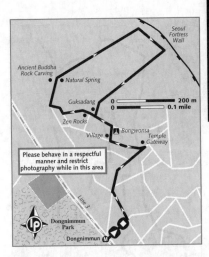

10 minutes and you reach an altar where an **ancient Buddha** is carved on a rock. Shamanists perform their ceremonies under the shade of the trees – an old lady is bowing and waving five different coloured flags to attract the spirits, and a young girl is drumming and meditating. **Natural springs** in the area provide fresh water and you can easily walk to part of the **Seoul fortress wall**, which dates back to 1396 and is being renovated.

All visitors should treat the area and the people with respect and remember that taking a photograph could interfere with an important ceremony.

Between the Palaces Walk

This walk (Map p94) takes as little as one hour, but allow another hour or two to explore the park and the interesting shops, art galleries and teashops. The walk is shaded by trees most of the way and avoids crossing major roads.

Take subway Line 3 to Anguk station, leave by Exit 1 and turn right along the main road until you reach **Dongsipjagak**, an old watchtower. Turn right past **Seoul Selection Bookshop** which is worth a visit. Further on are lots of **art galleries** to look around.

Fork right and walk past a **hanbok shop** to a couple of **traditional restaurants** opposite the prime minister's residence, which has large white gates and guards outside. Continue past **Seomulseoduljae Teashop**, which specialises in medicinal teas and *danpatjuk* (red

SEOUL

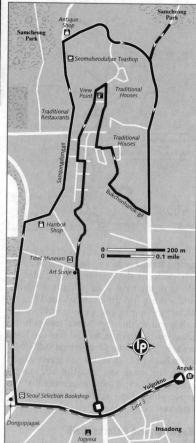

On your right is the **Tibet Museum** (adult/student W5000/2000; ☺ 10am-7pm) which has a small but interesting collection of Tibetan items. Admission includes a cup of tea.

At the crossroads is **Art Sonje** (admission varies; ☺ 11am-7pm Tue-Sun), which accommodates an art gallery, a café, a cinema that shows international films, and a posh Indian restaurant. At the main road, turn left for Anguk subway station or cross over the road to visit Insadong or Jogyesa temple.

COURSES
Cooking

The **Yoo Family** (Map pp72-4; ☎ 3673 0323; www.korea-family.com; per hr W45,000) will teach you how to make *kimchi*. The **Institute of Traditional Korean Food** (Map pp72-4; ☎ 741 5414; fax 741 5415; 3hr course W70,000) operates Jilsiru Tteok Cafe and upstairs runs a course on making Korean rice cakes.

Language

World Village (Map p79; ☎ 018-239 9981; www.ih.or.kr) offers Korean-language lessons held in a casual atmosphere that cost a nominal W10,000 for three months (see also p107). There are six levels of classes, run on Tuesday and Thursday evenings and Saturday afternoons. Other language classes (Japanese, Chinese, Russian and Spanish) are organised, as well as Latin dance classes and computer classes.

Sisa Institute (Map pp72-4; ☎ 2278 0509; www.ybmedu.com) is opposite Tapgol Park and offers month-long language courses (six levels are available) for W190,000 a month with a maximum class size of 15.

Yonsei University (Map p78) runs both part-time and full-time Korean-language classes for serious students.

Click on www.metro.seoul.kr for a long list of universities and institutes that offer Korean-language courses

SEOUL FOR CHILDREN

Log on to www.travelwithyourkids.com for advice on visiting Seoul with children.

Children's Grand Park (Map btwn pp64 & 65; adult/youth/child Jul-Aug & Nov-Mar W1500/1000/free, Apr-Jun & Sep-Oct W900/W500/free; ☺ 9am-7pm, closes 8pm Jun-Aug) includes, among many other things, a large zoo and an indoor botanical garden. The natural surroundings make it ideal for a picnic although there is no shortage of

bean porridge), turn right and further on cross over the road to **Samcheong Park**. A short loop walk takes you past natural springs and through dense woodland.

Cross back over the road and Seoul Tower appears in the distance. Walk down the hill to Bukchonhanok-gil on your right. Follow this alley through a quiet neighbourhood of **traditional houses**. At the end of the alley (building No 2 faces you) turn left and walk uphill. At the top, is a splendid view of tiled rooftops that hasn't changed much in the past 100 years. The Joseon-dynasty aristocrats used to live here close to the palaces.

At the next junction turn right, and then turn left at the red-brick public bath chimney. Turn left again at the end of this alley.

restaurants and food stalls. A seal show, a circus (May only), an outdoor swimming pool (July and August only) and funfair thrill rides cost extra.

The **Children's Puppet Theatre** (Map pp82-3; ☎ 420 0360; adult/child W7000/4500) in Olympic Park puts on fun shows but all the puppets speak Korean.

There are **aquariums** (☎ 6002 6200; www .coexaqua.co.kr; adult/child/secondary student W14,500/9500/12,000; ✆ 10am-8pm Sun-Fri, closes 9pm Sat) at the COEX Mall (see p89) and at the 63 Building (see p91) on Yeouido, which are worth visiting.

Seoul Grand Park (☎ 500 7114; www.grandpark .seoul.go.kr; adult/youth/child W1500/1200/700; ✆ 9am-7pm, 9am-6pm Oct-Mar) can be reached by subway. It has a large zoo (see p122), and Seoul Land Amusement Park (Map btwn pp64 & 65).

Everland (☎ 759 1408; www.everland.com), an hour from Seoul by bus, has a world-class aquatic centre as well as a popular Disney-style amusement and safari park (see p126).

Lotte World (www.lotteworld.com) is a Disney-style amusement park (mostly indoors) next to an ice-skating rink, a swimming pool, cinemas, and ten-pin bowling (see p90). Next door is Lotte World hotel which is, not surprisingly, kid friendly (p101).

An International Children's Theatre Festival is held in Daehangno in late July –

contact **KNTO** (Map pp72-4; ☎ 757 0086; www .knto.or.kr) for details.

In winter there is skiing, snowboarding and sledding at ski resorts near Seoul. In summer head for swimming pools in the parks along the Han river, where bikes are for hire too. At any time head for a cinema where films are shown in their original languages. For further information on travelling with children, see p367.

TOURS

The **Royal Asiatic Society – Korea Branch** (☎ 763 9483) arranges tours all over Korea each weekend that cost from W6000 to W60,000. Non-members can join in and tours are led by English speakers who are field experts.

United Services Organization (USO; Map pp70-1; ☎ 724 7003; www.uso.org/korea) runs tours for American troops but civilians are welcome to join in. Twice a week the USO runs excellent tours to Panmunjeom, the Demilitarized Zone (DMZ) and an Infiltration Tunnel for US$40, not including lunch. The tours start at 7.30am and finish at 3pm (p137). The USO also runs day tours to Icheon Ceramic Village (US$43) and Ganghwado (US$24) as well as white-water rafting tours (US$43). In winter it organises ski trips.

DMZ Tour with a Defector (Map pp76-7; ☎ 771 5593; www.koreadmztour.com; 2nd fl, Lotte Hotel) offers a

---

CITY ESCAPES – TOP 10 DAY TRIPS FROM SEOUL

- Tour the DMZ and **Panmunjeom** (p137)
- Visit **Ganghwado** to tour the island's cycleway and hike up **Manisan** (p135)
- Take a subway to **Incheon** for a historical walk and **Wolmido promenade** (p130)
- Hike around **Bukhansan National Park** (p119) or **Namhansanseong Provincial Park** (p123)
- Spend half a day at the atmospheric **Korean Folk Village** (p126)
- Walk around the **World Heritage fortress** in **Suwon** (p124) and eat *galbi*
- Explore the ceramic pottery village in **Icheon** (p127) and take a dip in the luxurious hot spring spa
- Relax on one of the **West Sea** island beaches (p132)
- Cycle along a lake in **Chuncheon** (p142) and take a ferry to a temple (p146)
- Take a train to **Gangchon** and cycle to the waterfall and bungee jump (p145)

once-in-a-lifetime chance to meet and question a defector from North Korea through an interpreter. The tour costs W70,000 but doesn't include Panmunjeom.

TrekKorea (☎ 540 0840; www.trekkorea.com) runs rafting, mountain-biking, horse-riding, caving, camping and hiking tours that last one or two days and cost around W60,000.

Exciting Korea (☎ 725 1237; www.excitingkorea.com) runs small-group minibus tours around Korea that cost W30,000 to W50,000. For information on its hostel, see p100.

Visit KNTO (Map pp72–4) or view www.startravel.co.kr for information on the many tours available, or log on to www.adventurekorea.com for something adventurous.

Seoul City Tour Bus

Especially designed for tourists, these comfortable buses tour Seoul's top tourist attractions north of the Han river. Buses run every 30 minutes between 9am and 7pm. Ticket holders are also entitled to discounts on some tourist attractions. View www.seoulcitytourbus.com for more details. The Tour Bus is excellent if you want to see the main sights as quickly as possible. A one-day ticket (buy it on the bus) costs a very reasonable W10,000 while a two-day ticket is only W15,000. One stop is outside Deoksugung (Map pp76–7).

FESTIVALS & EVENTS

Festivals of all kinds have proliferated in Seoul in recent years. There is a flower festival, animated film festival, fringe theatre festival, video film festival, dance festival and drum festival. View www.knto.or.kr or www.visitseoul.net for the location and dates of these festivals which tend to vary from year to year.

April

Seonnong-je For centuries the Joseon kings went to the altar Seonnongdan (Map pp70-1) to pray for a good harvest. The re-enactment begins with a royal procession, then musicians in red robes play traditional instruments and a singer chants the words used in the original Confucian ritual. After the ceremony everyone tucks into *seolleongtang* (beef soup) and *makgeolli* (milky-white fermented rice wine) free of charge. To get there, take subway Line 1 to Jegi-dong station, leave by Exit 1 and walk to the information board where you turn right. Then fork right along the tree-lined street, and the altar is a few minutes walk up the hill on the right.

May

Jongmyodaeje At Jongmyo shrine (Map pp72-4) on the first Sunday in May after the royal procession comes a seven-hour Confucian ritual performed by the many living descendants of the Joseon royal family, who pay homage to their august ancestors. The royal spirits are welcomed and praised, fed with offerings of cooked meat and rice wine, entertained with solemn music and dance, and then respectfully farewelled.

Buddha's Birthday On the Sunday before Buddha's birthday, a huge parade is held from Tapgol Park to Jogyesa (Map pp72-4) starting at 7pm.

September

Seokjeondaeje This ceremony is staged in the courtyard of the Confucian shrine at Sungkyunkwan University (Map pp72-4).

October

Sajikdaeje A re-enactment of a royal thanksgiving ceremony at the altar in Sajik Park (Map pp70-1).

Seoul Citizen's Day The Seoul metropolitan government organises a programme of cultural and sporting events, some especially for foreigners.

SLEEPING
Gwanghwamun
BUDGET

Gwanghwajang (Map pp72-4; ☎ 738 0751; r W38,000; 🞨) This *yeogwan* has rooms with fancy furniture and décor, a table and chairs, cable TV and video. It's like a mini version of Lotte Hotel, but a lot cheaper.

Inn Daewon (Map pp72-4; ☎ 738 4308; dm/s/d W15,000/20,000/25,000; 🖳) This long-established guesthouse, owned by a helpful elderly couple who speak some English, is in a rundown building in the downtown area. The living conditions are cramped, the kitchen is tiny, some rooms have no window, and guests share two toilets and a shower. But it offers a TV lounge, free breakfasts, a washing machine (W1000) and Internet (W1000 per hour).

See also the boxed text on the next page for more recommendations.

MID-RANGE

New Kukje Hotel (Map pp72-4; ☎ 732 0161, 732 1774; r W150,000; 🞨 🖳) Akin to New Seoul, it has restaurants, a good W11,000 buffet breakfast, a karaoke lounge with hostesses, and a 24-hour men's sauna (W11,000 for non-guests).

New Seoul Hotel (Map pp72-4; ☎ 735 9071; www.bestwesternnewseoul.com; s & d/tw/ste W140,000/160,000/

AUTHOR'S CHOICES

Free M Hotel (Map pp76-7; ☎ 771 9111; s/tw incl tax & service W121,000/154,000; ❄ 🖳) A unique new hotel in Myeong-dong for women only. Rooms are small, with *yo* or bed options, have traditional furniture, and the toilet is separate from the shower. Hotel facilities include an 8th-floor sky bar, a business centre, coffee shop, karaoke, hair and nail treatments, foot and face massages and even plastic surgery. The sauna and breakfasts are free.

Lotte Hotel (Map pp77-7; ☎ 771 1000; www.hotel.lotte.co.kr; s/d W340,000/370,000; ❄ 🖳 🏊) With over 1300 rooms and a classical palatial style, this excellent luxury hotel has every facility and is close to a department store, a duty-free shop, underground shopping arcades and the fashionable boutiques in Myeong-dong. There's the English-style **Bobby London Bar** and the **Vine Restaurant** (meals W27,000-38,000; ✆ 10.30am-2pm) which does a Sunday brunch buffet. Stay here or the Shilla for Korean-style luxury.

Ritz Hotel (Map pp72-4; ☎ 764 0353; r W40,000, Sat & Sun W50,000; ❄ 🖳) A modern love motel near Tapgol Park with a space-age metallic exterior, an elevator, and rooms with big TVs, circular beds and starry skies painted on the ceilings.

Seoul Guesthouse (Map pp72-4; ☎ 745 0057, 011-9134 7741; www.seoul110.com; s/d/f W30,000/40,000/100,000; 🖳) This delightful *hanok* down a quiet alley is built around an attractive courtyard. You sleep on a *yo* on an *ondol* floor in a bare room with no en suite facilities except in the family room. Guests can use the TV lounge, kitchen, free Internet and washing machine – the facilities are ultramodern even though the house is a century old. Mrs Lee the owner speaks English and is very helpful.

Seoul Backpackers (Map pp72-4; ☎ 3672 1972; www.seoulbackpackers.com; dm/s/d W17,000/27,000/37,000; ❄ 🖳) A good location near Insadong, smart, modern facilities and helpful staff who speak English make this a budget option that gets rave reviews. The dorms have two or three double bunks and every room has its own toilet and shower. The guesthouse has *ondol* underfloor heating, a lounge with TV (11 channels), kitchen, outside area, free washing machine, free breakfast and free Internet.

290,000; ❄ 🖳) This quality hotel, popular with Japanese tourists, has a perfect downtown location with a porridge restaurant, coffee shop and a 24-hour men's sauna (W11,000 for non-guests).

TOP END

Radisson Seoul Plaza Hotel (Map pp76-7; ☎ 771 2200; www.seoulplaza.co.kr; s/d/ste W320,000/360,000/660,000; ❄ 🖳 🏊) Opposite City Hall, the luxury facilities include six restaurants, a pub which has live music, a sauna (men as well as women), fitness club, Jacuzzi and free baby cots.

Westin Chosun Hotel (Map pp767; ☎ 771 0500; www.westinchosun.com; s/d W372,000/392,000; ❄ 🖳 🏊) Seoul's first Western-style hotel opened in 1914 but has kept up-to-date and houses the popular O'Kim's bar. 'It may not be the plushest hotel,' according to one guest, 'but it has good atmosphere and staff.' In the garden is the renovated **Altar of Heaven Pavilion** originally built when King Gojong proclaimed himself an emperor and gave thanks to heaven at an altar here.

Tapgol Park Area
BUDGET

Cala Motel (Map pp72-4; ☎ 741 4455; r Sun-Fri W32,000-35,000, Sat W40,000; ❄) A modern almost luxurious motel with a receptionist who speaks some English.

Emerald Hotel (Map pp72-4; ☎ 743 2001; r Mon-Fri W28,000, Sat & Sun W30,000; ❄) Located in a quiet alley just north of Nakwon Arcade, this large pink motel offers clean and tidy rooms with cable TV, video, a table and chairs and a bath as well as a shower.

Guesthouse Korea (Map pp72-4; ☎ 3675 2205; www.guesthouseinkorea.com; dm/s/d W15,000/25,000/35,000; ❄ 🖳) Not to be confused with the Guesthouse Korea in Hongik, the building, located behind Hyundai Oilbank petrol station, is old and rundown and some rooms have no windows. However facilities include four showers and toilets, a kitchen, TV lounge (cable TV and video), free Internet, free washing machine, free breakfast and the staff are helpful and friendly.

Motel Jongnowon (Map pp72-4; ☎ 763 4249; www.jongnowon.com; s/d W25,000/30,000; ❄ 🖳)

This popular and newly-decorated motel is behind Seoul Backpackers and offers free laundry, free breakfasts and free Internet as well as cable TV and all other facilities in the *yeogwan*-style en suite rooms.

Paradise Motel (Jongno; Map pp72-4; ☎ 730 6244; r Sun-Fri W35,000, Sat W40,000; ✗) Rooms are small but this is one of the best downtown *yeogwan* although hard to find as it's hidden away down a back alley.

MID-RANGE

Paradise Motel (Tapgol Park; Map pp72-4; ☎ 763 3000; r Mon-Fri W40,000, Sat & Sun W45,000; ✗) Another large modern motel but not as flash as the Ritz.

Seoul Hotel (Map pp72-4; ☎ 735 9001; fax 733 0101; s/d/tw/ondol incl tax & service W80,000/85,000/90,000/ 100,000; ✗) This modestly-priced hotel has Korean and Western restaurants, a coffee shop and sauna.

YMCA (Map pp72-4; ☎ 734 6884; www.ymca.or.kr/ hotel; s/d/tw W40,000/55,000/60,000; ✗) Open to everyone, the YMCA has a good Jongno location but the building is old and due for demolition. The rooms have TV, fridge and a table and chairs but are old-fashioned. Western-style breakfasts cost W4000 to W10,000, while lunch and dinner cost from W6000 to W25,000. The reception desk is on the 6th floor – take the lift.

Insadong
BUDGET

Gwanhunjang (Map pp72-4; ☎ 732 1682; s, d & ondol W35,000; ✗) This typical but newly-renovated *yeogwan* is in an alley off Insadong 4-gil.

Singungjang (Map pp72-4; ☎ 733 1355; s, d & ondol Sun-Fri W30,000, Sat W35,000; ✗ 🖳) The rooms are small but clean and tidy, the owner speaks a little English, and one foreigner stayed here a year which must mean something.

MID-RANGE & TOP END

Guesthouse Woorichip (Map pp72-4; ☎ 744 0536; woorichip@hanmail.net; s & d/f W50,000/100,000; ✗) Sleep on a *yo* and share a traditional *hanok* with the Park family, their rabbit and two cute dogs.

Saerim Hotel (Map pp72-4; ☎ 739 3377; fax 735 3355; s, d & ondol W45,000; ✗) Modern and clean rooms are available in this smart hotel with an elevator. The electronic bidets are impressive but confusing, and some rooms have a water bed.

Fraser Apartments (Map pp72-4; ☎ 6262 8888; www.fraserhospitality.com; 1-/2-/3-/4-bedroom apartment W8.8m/10m/12m/14m; ✗ 🖳 ♨) The 200 luxury apartments, rented on a monthly basis, offer more space and privacy than a hotel room and share a baby-sitting service, restaurant, bar, coffee shop, sauna, gym and indoor pool.

Myeong-dong

Astoria Hotel (Map pp76-7; ☎ 2268 7111; fax 2274 3187; d/tw W82,500/91,700 incl tax & service; ✗) Another business hotel with a karaoke bar, restaurant and good views of Namsan and Seoul Tower from some rooms.

New Oriental Hotel (Map pp76-7; ☎ 753 0701; fax 755 9346; s/d/tw W55,000/68,000/83,000; ✗) A reasonably priced hotel with a bar and coffee shop.

Prince Hotel (Map pp76-7; ☎ 752 7111; fax 752 7119; s/d/tw/ste incl tax & service W75,000/85,000/95,000/ 122,000; ✗) This business hotel has a good location in Myeong-dong and a karaoke bar but no restaurant although the coffee shop provides American-style breakfasts.

Savoy Hotel (Map pp76-7; ☎ 776 2641; www .savoy.co.kr; s/d/tw/ste W110,000/130,000/160,000/240,000; ✗ 🖳) Facilities in this more luxurious hotel include a Mexican restaurant and a bar with live jazz from 8pm to midnight on Sunday.

See the Author's Choice boxed text (p97) for more recommendations.

Dongdaemun
BUDGET & MID-RANGE

Busanjang (Map pp70-1; ☎ 2269 1051; r Sun-Fri W30,000, Sat W40,000; ✗) The best option among the *yeogwan* in the alleys around Dongdaemun market.

Dongdaemun Hotel (Map pp70-1; ☎ 741 7811; fax 744 1274; d/tw & ondol incl tax & service W110,000/ 130,000; ✗) This Best Western hotel overlooks Dongdaemun gate, which looks beautiful when lit up at night. It has a karaoke lounge and a sauna (admission W6000) and the restaurant offers good value multicourse steak meals for W25,000.

Travelers A Motel (Map pp72-4; ☎ 2285 5511; www.travelersa.com; dm/r W12,000/30,000; ✗ 🖳) Also near Dongdaemun down an alley of sewing machine shops, it is cheap but needs renovating. The dorms have two or three bunks in a room and the toilets and showers open onto the TV lounge. The double rooms are similar to facility-filled *yeogwan* rooms. It offers free Internet, but the kitchen facilities are very poor. To get there, take subway Line 2 or 5 to Euljiro 4-ga station, leave by Exit 4, turn right down the second alley and then take the first left.

TOP END

Hilton Hotel (Map pp76-7; ☎ 317 3114; www.hilton.com; s/d/ste W360,000/380,000/490,000; ✖ 🖳 ☎) You can eat in a different restaurant every night for a week. Rooms have high speed Internet, a safe and views of Namsan. The lobby has a 1982 Henry Moore bronze sculpture and the revamped nightclub, Arenos, has a foreign DJ every night and no cover charge.

Sejong Hotel (Map pp76-7; ☎ 773 6000; www .sejong.co.kr; s/d/tw/ste W160,000/220,000/230,000/ 400,000; ✖ 🖳 ☎) This Korean-style hotel has had a recent facelift and has a luxurious fitness club with a men's **sauna** (✋ 24 hr). The Eunhasu buffet (p104) is popular.

Namsan

Hotel Shilla (Map pp76-7; ☎ 2233 3131; www .shilla.net; s/d, tw & ondol from W360,000/390,000, ste W500,000-7m; ✖ 🖳 ☎) A huge hotel with spacious rooms situated at the foot of Namsan, it is run by Samsung, one of Korea's mighty *jaebol* and no expense is spared on its flagship hotel. It has a duty-free shop, six restaurants, indoor and outdoor swimming pools, a fitness centre, tennis courts, a golf driving range, sculpture garden, sauna and a 24-hour massage service – you can opt for a blind masseur.

Itaewon
BUDGET

Donginjang (Map p75; ☎ 795 6707; r Mon-Thu W25,000, Fri-Sun W30,000; ✖) Rooms are small but clean and tidy.

Hilltop Motel (Map p75; ☎ 793 4972; r Sun-Thu W25,000, Fri & Sat W30,000; ✖) In the middle of the hostess bar area, the rooms are small and a bit tatty as is usual at this price.

MID-RANGE & TOP END

Hamilton Hotel (Map p75; ☎ 794 0171; www .hamilton.co.kr; s/d, tw & ondol W100,000/135,000; ✖ 🖳 ☎) This Itaewon landmark has a large shopping mall on four levels that contains 100 stores. Every room has Internet and satellite TV and there is an outdoor swimming pool (open July and August). Buffet breakfasts are W11,000.

Itaewon Hotel (Map p75; ☎ 792 3111; fax 795 3126; r W140,000; ✖) On the main street, it offers comfort at a reasonable cost, as well as a restaurant and a nightclub.

Kaya Hotel (Map pp70-1; ☎ 798 5101; fax 798 5900; ondol/d & tw incl tax & service W53,000/63,000; ✖) A 'no-frills' but very reasonably priced mid-range hotel, popular with American GIs as it is near the Yongsan base. It has a pleasant restaurant (Korean or American food) and coffee shop. To get there, take subway Line 1 to Namyeong station, turn right at the exit and right again at the main road.

Seoul Motel (Map p75; ☎ 795 2266; fax 797 0300; r Sun-Thu W40,000, Fri & Sat W45,000; ✖) Located on the 3rd floor above McDonald's this new and clean motel is the best in Itaewon. The rooms are small but the bathrooms are large. Stay here and you can enjoy the nightlife without worrying about getting a taxi home.

Grand Hyatt Hotel (Map p75; ☎ 797 1234; www .seoul.grand.hyatt.com; r from W220,000; ✖ 🖳 ☎) The exact price depends on the occupancy rate. All rooms have high-speed Internet connection and an electronic safe. Situated on a hill overlooking Itaewon the décor is functional but stylish and the facilities include six restaurants, a popular nightclub with a foreign resident band, outdoor and indoor swimming pools, and tennis and squash courts.

Hongik, Sinchon & Ewha
BUDGET

Guesthouse Korea (Map p78; ☎ 3142 0683; www.guesthousekorea.com; dm/s/tw W15,000/25,000/ 35,000; 🖳) Don't confuse it with the Guesthouse Korea near Insadong. This is a comfortable guesthouse with modern facilities in a quiet neighbourhood, but within walking distance of the Hongik nightclubs. It has a TV room, kitchen and free Internet, breakfast, washing machine and pick-up service. One dormitory has two double bunks and the other has three double bunks. It's a 15-minute walk to Hongik University subway station (Line 2) and the nearest Incheon airport bus stop is at Seogyo Hotel (bus No 601 or 602). Telephone from there and someone will pick you up.

Kims' Guesthouse (Map p78; ☎ 337 9894; www .kimsguesthouse.com; dm/s/d & tw W17,000/27,000/ 37,000; 🖳) This modern guesthouse is one of the best and is like a homestay. The dorm has two double bunks and guests share two toilets and showers. It has cable TV in the lounge, a kitchen, large balcony, small garden, free breakfast, and free use of the washing machine and Internet. The resident owners speak English and are friendly and helpful. It's located in a quiet area, a 12-minute walk from Hapjeong subway station (Line 2 or 6).

WOW Guesthouse (Map p78; ☎ 322 8644; www .wowgh.co.kr; dm/r W15,000/20,000, r with en suite W25,000; ☒ ▣) The dorms in this rather run-down guesthouse have eight, six and four beds. Guests share a kitchen, TV lounge and a nice balcony. Free use of washing machine and Internet.

MID-RANGE & TOP END

Mirabeau Hotel (Map p78; ☎ 392 9511; www.hotel mirabeau.co.kr; d/ste incl tax & service W89,000/137,000; ☒) Prices rise 30% on Saturday and this French-style hotel near Ewha Women's University has a grill restaurant and coffee shop.

Prince Hotel (Map p78; ☎ 363 4700; r W40,000, Sat W50,000; ☒ ▣) A reasonably-priced hotel with an elevator among a cluster of motels southwest of Sinchon subway station.

Seogyo Hotel (Map p78; ☎ 333 7771; www.hotel seokyo.co.kr; d & tw/ste W242,000/302,500 incl tax & service; ☒ ▣ ☒) The only luxury accommodation in Hongik, it has four restaurants (lunch/dinner buffet W18,000/30,000), a business and fitness centre and a men's sauna. It could be getting a new name to go with the recent renovations.

Daehangno

Daeseong Yeogwan (Map p79; ☎ 3673 2028; r W30,000; ☒) A reasonable *yeogwan* in this popular entertainment area famous for its numerous small theatres, bars and restaurants.

Friends House (Map p79; ☎ 3673 1515; www.friends-house.com; s/d W30,000/40,000; ▣) This traditional *hanok* house is modern inside. Guests sleep on a *yo* on the floor in a small room, and facilities include a TV lounge and kitchen. There's free breakfast, Internet access and washing machine. To get there, take subway Line 4 to Hyehwa station and leave by Exit 4. Walk north up the main road to the roundabout and turn left at the post office. Then turn left again at Yun Hyun Pharmacy and it's down the second turning on the right, altogether a 10-minute walk from the station. Make a reservation before turning up.

Other Areas North of the Han River

Exciting Korea Guesthouse (Map btwn pp64 & 65; ☎ 3217 8231; www.excitingkorea.com; dm W14,000 ☒ ▣) Only dorm beds are offered (two or three double bunks per room), and guests share two toilets and showers. Popular with long-termers (W11,000 a night if you stay a month) it offers a kitchen, TV lounge and small garden and free Internet, washing machine, breakfast and a free T-shirt if you stay long enough. But the location is inconvenient – take subway Line 3 to Gyeongbokgung station, leave by Exit 3 and walk to the bus stop. Take any bus to the Boam Art Hall stop (5 minutes). Walk up Baeksasil-gil, go left and it's on your right. It's easier to telephone if you've just arrived from Incheon airport and someone will pick you up from the nearest airport bus stop. The owners also run inexpensive tours (p95).

Sheraton Grande Walkerhill Hotel (Map pp82-3; ☎ 453 0121; www.walkerhill.co.kr; r W340,000; ☒ ▣ ☒) The hotel is way out east but provides free shuttle buses to Itaewon and Dongdaemun market. Rooms overlook the Han river and facilities include tennis courts, a golf driving range, health club, spa pool, sauna and in summer three big outdoor swimming pools (adult/child W45,000/W31,000). Its 24-hour casino (p108), cabaret dance show (p108) and duty-free shop are all well known.

Gimpo Domestic Airport

Airport Hotel (Map btwn pp64 & 65; ☎ 2662 1113; www.hotel airport.com; r/ste W101,000/220,000; ☒ ▣) Located 100m from Songjeong subway station (Line 5) or a five-minute shuttle bus ride from Gimpo airport, rooms vary and are somewhat drab but facilities include two restaurants, a coffee shop and karaoke.

Dreamtel Youth Hostel (Map btwn pp64 & 65; ☎ 2667 0535; www.hostelbooking.com; dm/f W20,000/70,000; ☒) Although far from downtown, the facilities are modern and more like a resort hotel than a youth hostel. Most rooms have three double bunks but the four-person family rooms have a double bunk and two single beds. All the rooms have their own toilet, shower, TV and fridge. The hostel has a shop, café, restaurant, sauna, exercise room (W4000), indoor swimming pool (W4000) and a woodland park behind. To get there take subway Line 5 to Banghwa station (the end of the line, and 45 minutes from the city centre) and leave by Exit 4. Go straight, turn left at the end of the road and then turn left again at the end of the next road; altogether it's a five-minute walk from the subway station.

Gimpojang (Map btwn pp64 & 65; ☎ 2663 1311; s, d & ondol W33,000; 🏠) The staff speak some English in this *yeogwan* located south of Songjeong subway station (Line 5).

South of the Han River
BUDGET & MID-RANGE
Hotel Popgreen (Map pp80-1; ☎ 544 6623; fax 514 1810; d/tw incl tax & service W157,000/169,000; 🏠 🖥) Smart and modern rooms with white décor are available at this hotel in Apgujeong which has a restaurant, coffee shop and men's sauna (W5000).

Olympic Parktel (Map pp82-3; ☎ 421 2111; www.parktel.co.kr; r incl tax & service W180,000; 🏠 🖥) Overlooking Olympic Park, this hotel has a sauna, exercise room and pool as well as a buffet restaurant on the top floor and a business centre.

Olympic Parktel Youth Hostel (Map pp82-3; ☎ 421 2111; www.hostelbooking.com; dm W22,000; 🏠 🖥 🍴) This unusual hostel is part of a luxury hotel that overlooks Olympic Park. The rooms have two double bunks and two *yo* mattresses on the floor which are rolled up when not in use. Each room has its own small toilet, shower, air-con, heater, fridge, cable TV (55 channels), telephone and excellent view – all the hostel rooms are on the 7th, 8th and 9th floors. There is a kitchen and laundromat. You can use the hotel swimming pool, exercise room and sauna for W6500 a day and eat a hotel breakfast for W9900 (half-price). On the 2nd floor is a YHA Office (☎ 2202 2585; fax 2202 7772; 🕙 9.30am-5.30pm Mon-Fri, 9.30am-1.30pm Sat).

Princess Hotel (Map pp80-1; ☎ 544 0366; fax 544 0322; r/ste incl tax & service W80,000/120,000; 🏠) This metal-clad, ultramodern love hotel in the upmarket Apgujeong shopping area has rooms with 10 different styles. Short-term rates are W35,000 for three hours.

Sunshine Hotel (Map pp80-1; ☎ 541 1818; fax 547 0777; s/d/tw incl tax & service W96,000/139,000/153,000; 🏠 🖥) This hotel has a business centre, a sauna, a karaoke lounge and a popular nightclub, Boss.

Yeouido Hotel (Map p84; ☎ 782 0121; fax 785 2510; r W97,000; 🏠 🖥) One of the few accommodation options on Yeouido, facilities

include a business centre, two restaurants, a karaoke lounge and a nightclub.

TOP END
Grand Inter-Continental Hotel (Map pp82-3; ☎ 555 5656; www.seoul.intercontinental.com; s/d & tw W300,000/320,000; 🏠 🖥 🍴) This luxury hotel has seven restaurants (one with singing waiters), a disco, beauty salon, health club and a business floor.

JW Marriott Hotel (Map pp80-1; ☎ 6282 6262; www.marriott.com; r from W360,000; 🏠 🖥 🍴) Opened in 2000 and located inside Central City Mall it has large rooms, four restaurants and excellent health club facilities.

Lotte World Hotel (Map pp82-3; ☎ 419 7000; www.lottehotel.co.kr; s & d/tw W340,000/360,000; 🏠 🖥 🍴) Stay here if you have youngsters with you, if possible. A baby-sitting service costs US$9 an hour. Next door is Lotte World and three subway stations away is the COEX Mall. Facilities include a business centre, five restaurants, a sauna, exercise room and duty-free shop.

EATING
Gwanghwamun
BUDGET
Goryeo Supermarket Food Court (Map pp72-4; meals under W5000) Three cheap food stalls – try the *gamjatang* (감자탕). The supermarket is also useful for self-caterers or anyone looking for something for a picnic lunch.

Gwasai Restaurant (Map pp76-7; meals under W5000) A no-frills eatery near Deoksugung that offers a wide range of Korean food at budget prices. Try the *dolsotbibimbap* or the excellent 'nude *gimbap*' with a dozen fillings, which has the dried seaweed wrapped inside the rice, not outside.

Witch's Table (Map pp72-4; drinks & snacks W1400-5500; 🕙 8am-10pm) A small New York-style sandwich bar which has plain bagels, large filled bagels, sandwiches and salad. Tea and coffee are W3000 while juice and beer are W5000.

MID-RANGE & TOP END
Hoejeonchobap (Map pp72-4; meals W10,000-12,500) Japanese-style sushi is served on a conveyor belt.

Yongsusan (Map pp72-4; lunch W22,000-48,000, dinner W36,000-100,000) A posh restaurant with *hanbok*-clad waitresses that serves royal cuisine meals. The décor is simple and

AUTHOR'S CHOICES

Baekje Samgyetang (Map pp76-7; meals W9000-10,000) This well-known restaurant in Myeong-dong is on the 2nd floor, but the restaurant sign is only in Chinese characters. It specialises in *samgyetang*, which is a whole small chicken stuffed with rice and ginseng, cooked in broth and served with side dishes and a small glass of *insamju*, ginseng liquor. Dip the chicken in a mixture of salt and pepper. Roast chicken is another option.

Nolbu (Map p79; banquet W12,000) Don't miss this excellent basement restaurant which puts on a twice-daily traditional music concert from noon to 2pm and from 6.30pm to 9pm. The music, the food and the price are hard to beat. You sit on floor cushions and the *sangcharim* (상차림) banquet is brought to you on a low table – 20 dishes including steamed egg, *pajeon*, octopus, fish, chicken, *galbi*, soup, *japchae* noodles, potato salad, quail's eggs and burnt rice tea. Other Nolbu restaurants are not like this one. Otherwise *bulgogi* is W8000 and smoked duck or *galbi* are W15,000.

Seoul Moemaeul (Map pp72-4; meals W7000-22,000) This restaurant north of Insadong offers an English menu and excellent food in a rural décor. You sit on floor cushions with classical music in the background. Order the *moejeongsik* for a sumptuous banquet. The pork is excellent, the broths and sauces are tasty, the salad is fiery, the *gujeolpan* is interesting (eight types of shredded vegetables, which you wrap in thin slices of white radish) and the jujube tea finishes the meal off perfectly.

Sigol Bobsang (Map p75; meals W7000-12,000; ⊙ 24hr) This 'countryside food' restaurant in Itaewon has an incredibly rustic décor and soothing traditional Korean music plays in the background. Order *sigol bobsang* (시골밥상) – 20 mainly vegetarian side dishes, including some unusual ones, with spicy tofu soup and rice. If you want meat order the plate of *bulgogi*.

Techno Mart Food Court (Map pp82-3; meals W3000-8000) Forty stalls offer everything from raw fish to pizza and from *samgyetang* to *tteokbokki*. Many offer huge platters of food with all kinds of fun fusion concoctions that you share – a W10,000 platter feeds three hungry people. It's an eat-as-much-as-you-can global fusion buffet on a large platter. The stalls compete to pile more on your platter than anyone else. See the world's largest *bibimbap* bowls! Giant fruit and ice-cream desserts are also available as is yoghurt ice cream. All the stalls display plastic replicas of the food they offer so it's choosing rather than ordering that is the problem.

Zen-style. Interesting dishes include dragon firepot (meat, fish and vegetable soup), five-grain rice cooked in bamboo, ginseng and rice porridge, and pink *omija* tea.

See also the boxed text above.

Tapgol Park Area
BUDGET

Gamjatangjip (Map pp72-4; meals W5000) This cheap joint behind Pizza Hut serves typical Pimatgol peasant fare. The *gamjatang* (감자탕) has big meaty bones and a lump of potato in a spicy soup, while the *samchigui* (삼치구이) is a tasty barbecued fish served whole. Wash it down with *sansachun* (산사춘) rice wine, although it costs more than the food at W7000 a bottle.

Jilsiru Tteok Café (Map pp72-4; set lunch W5000) serves unusual and colourful *tteok* rice cakes – try tropical fruit, coffee, *kimchi* or pumpkin ones – and traditional teas. Upstairs is a *tteok* museum and *tteok*-making

classes are available (W70,000). To get there take Exit 6 of Jongno 3-ga subway station (Lines 1, 3 & 5).

Mangogangsan (Map pp72-4; meals W5000) The speciality here is North Korean-style Pyongyang *naengmyeon* – thin chewy noodles garnished with half a boiled egg, a segment of nashi pear and strips of cucumber and meat in a sweetish cold broth seasoned with roasted sesame seeds. It's definitely worth trying this version of North Korea's national dish.

MID-RANGE & TOP END

Nutrition Centre (Map pp72-4; meals W5900-8900) A no-frills restaurant that offers a menu of *samgyetang*, roast chicken or chicken lunches.

Top Cloud Restaurant (Map pp72-4; ☎ 2230 3000; set lunch W40,000-47,000, set dinner W70,000-130,000; ⊙ noon-2.30pm, 6-10pm) Perched on the 33rd floor of Jongno Tower, Seoul's most striking skyscraper, it's a place to go for special occasions as long as you don't suffer from vertigo. The seven-course dinners feature items such as *foie gras,* crab ravioli, lobster, rack of lamb or king prawns and the food has French, Italian and Asian influences. You can also go à la carte. The views are spectacular, some of the smartly dressed staff speak English and there is live classical and jazz music every evening.

Insadong
BUDGET & MID-RANGE

Anjip (Map pp72-4; meals W6000-20,000) You can eat in your own private room in this traditional restaurant, hidden away down an alley. Order *siksa* (식사) for a bargain banquet of 20 dishes that include *bulgogi,* spicy cockles and steamed egg, with fruit and cinnamon tea for a rare dessert. The *hanjeongsik* offers a couple of extra dishes.

Chilgabsan (Map pp72-4; meals W5000-12,000) A popular traditional restaurant serving *neobiani* (너비아니), a giant beef patty which is meant for sharing. With it, you could try *pajeon* or *doenjang bibimbap.*

Dimibang (Map pp72-4; meals W6000-30,000) A vegetarian restaurant well-known for its use of *hamcho* (함초) root and other medicinal herbs and roots. It also serves herbal alcohol and teas. You can order dishes like *doenjang jjigae* and *bibimbap* or set meals. You sit on bamboo mats and eat with wooden spoons and chopsticks.

Hayangim Pureunnae (Map pp72-4; meals W7000-10,000) This typical Insadong restaurant has a relaxing atmosphere and you sit on floor cushions. The mushroom hotpot is a good deal and comes with side dishes such as mashed potato and egg. Also recommended is the meat, vegetable and mushroom soup that is cooked at your table.

Sadongmyeonok (Map pp72-4; meals W5000-8,000) A cosy restaurant that serves up the best *mandugukjeongsik* (만두국정식) in Seoul – four big meat-and-vegetable dumplings in soup with side dishes. Other meals include *bulgogijeongsik* served in a hotpot but very sweet, or grilled oysters.

Sosin (Map pp72-4; meals W10,000-15,000) A small home-cooking restaurant that serves up some vegetarian meals. Set meals vary with the seasons but include organic rice and unusual side dishes like boiled peanuts. Three types of grilled fish are available – salmon, mackerel or pollack.

TOP END

Min's Club (Map pp72-4; lunch W15,000-32,000, dinner W30,000-60,000) Housed in a beautifully restored 1930s *hanok* this classy restaurant is filled with antiques. Despite its name it is a restaurant open to all. It offers a wide choice of wines and the food is Asian/European, with items such as crab *roulade,* steaks, pumpkin chowder, or pork with ginseng, chestnuts and seared sesame leaves.

Sanchon (Map pp72-4; set lunch/dinner meals W18,700/32,000) This famous vegetarian restaurant serves up Buddhist temple food but the prices are not very Buddhist. You sit on floor cushions in a soothing atmosphere with art on the wall and candles on the tables. It offers the same set meal for lunch and dinner – 16 small dishes including sesame and rice soup, soya bean soup, *pajeon,* mountain vegetables and medicinal tea. The marinades, glaze, sauces and seasoning are good. A traditional dancer performs at 8.15pm.

North Of Insadong
BUDGET

Chongsujong (Map pp72-4; meals W5000) Order *honghapbapdosirak* (홍합밥도시락), which is rice and mussels served with side dishes and soup, or s*anchaebibimbap.* Unusual drinks include cucumber *soju* and bamboo leaf wine.

Hyangnamusegeuru (Map pp72-4; meals W5000-12,000) This restaurant has three trees outside. No English is spoken but just ask for *moksalsogeumgui* (목살소금구이), which is pork barbecued at your table that you eat like *bulgogi* wrapped in lettuce with sauces and spicy vegetables. You can cut some of the fat off the pork with the scissors provided. Also recommended is the earthy *doenjang jjigae.*

Samcheongdongjip (Map pp72-4; meals W5000) A no-frills restaurant that serves Seoul's best *sujebi* (수제비) – big dough flakes in a shellfish and vegetable broth.

BUDGET & MID-RANGE

Nakwon Garden (Map pp76-7; meals W5500) The main attraction is the salad and fruit bar that costs W1100 for 100g. The *tteokbokki* is spicy.

Nutrition Centre (Map pp76-7; meals W5900-8900) A no-frills restaurant offering a simple menu of *samgyetang* or roast chicken and chicken lunches.

Seochogol (Map pp76-7; meals W4000-12,000) Located behind Popeye's, it specialises in *galbi* that is charcoal-grilled at your table, giving the whole restaurant a smoky atmosphere. It comes with side dishes for two, or try the *naengmyeon* and *soju*.

Eunhasu Buffet Dinner (Map pp76-7; lunch/dinner buffets W33,000/36,000) This buffet in Sejong Hotel offers more than 70 different types of food. It's generally Western-style but there are plenty of Korean dishes to sample such as *galbi,* pork hocks, spicy crab soup, pumpkin porridge, rice cakes, rice punch, raw seafood, deliciously sweet raw meat, sea ginseng and cow cartilage soup. The buffet menu varies with the season.

See the boxed text on p102 for more options.

Dongdaemun

Dongdaemun Hotel Restaurant (Map pp70-1; meals W15,000-30,000) Conveniently situated on the edge of Dongdaemun Market. Its six-course steak or prawn meals are a good deal.

Itaewon
BUDGET
Chunchon (Map p75; meals W6000-8000; ☺ 10am-7am) In a street full of cheap restaurants, this one has some seats outside and offers *dakgalbi, bulgogi* and seafood pancakes.

United Services Organization (USO) Canteen (Map pp70-1; breakfast US$2, lunch $2-5, coffee/tea 50c; ☺ 7am-2.15pm Mon-Fri) This typical American diner has red and blue plastic seats, a juke box, real breakfasts and you can pay in US dollars. There are muffins, sandwiches, burgers and salads, lunch platters, apple pie.

See the boxed text on p102 for more choices.

MID-RANGE
Ali Baba (Map p75; meals W12,000-20,000) On the main street, this authentic Egyptian restaurant has a tiled floor, comfortable chairs and plays Arabic music. Enjoy soup, salad, hummus and *babaganesh,* or falafel and mixed grills. Portions are small but the food is good, especially the freshly-made pitta bread.

Itaewon Galbi (Map p75; meals W6000-25,000) Fairy lights give this restaurant a festive atmosphere. It specialises in *galbi,* or try the *galbitang, samgyetang,* the tasty mushroom and meat *bulgogi* hotpot or a vegetarian *bibimbap.*

Nashville Steak House (Map p75; meals W5000-26,000; ☺ 7am-11pm) In the basement of the Nashville Sports Pub, this restaurant has action movies on a big screen, plus vegetarian meals, burger meals, salads, pasta and steaks. American breakfasts are served from 7am to 11am.

Our Place (Map p75; lunch W6000-8000, dinner W8000-16,000; ☺ 11.30am-2am) On the 6th and 7th floors with a nice balcony, this new fusion food and wine bar run by Hong Seok-cheon has hummus with tortilla, chicken meals and cheesecakes, as well as sandwiches and coffee. Beer is W3500.

Outback Steakhouse (Map p75; meals W13,000-25,000) Offers salads, steaks, desserts, beer and set lunches.

TOP END
Chalet Swiss (Map p75; meals W15,000-30,000) With a homely décor and yodelling music, it has been an Itaewon institution since 1983 and serves soups, entrees and salads, *roesti,* fondues and grills. Desserts are W5000.

Memories (Map p75; lunch/dinner meals W10,000/25,000) This Deutschland oasis offers real German food like bratwurst, schnitzel and steaks cooked by a real German chef. Substantial set dinners are washed down with German beers (W7000).

Moghul (Map p75; meals W15,000-25,000) This Indian restaurant has a garden section that is popular on summer evenings, and weekend buffets.

Thai Orchid (Map p75; set lunch meals W18,000-26,000, set dinner meals W36,000-48,000) With over 100 items on the menu, not everything can be excellent, but this is another Itaewon institution. Vegetarian meals are W9000 and desserts are W4000. It's on the 3rd floor – not the 2nd floor which has a Thai steamboat restaurant.

Hongik, Sinchon & Ewha
Gio (Map p78; meals for 2 people W9000) This shack serves only two dishes which are both cooked at your table. First is a bowl of mushrooms and home-made noodles, the widest in Seoul. Take out some of the red pepper paste and cook it for 15 minutes. Next is a rice, seaweed and herb mixture cooked in the same pot. You may have to queue.

Haejeodon (Map p78; meals W4000-8000) This restaurant with an outdoor area specialises in *samgyeopsal* marinated in wine or ginseng.

Traditional changing of the guard outside Deoksugung (p85), Seoul

Women selling kimchi, Korea's famous pickled vegetables (p52)

Watchtower at Seodaemun Prison (p88), Seoul

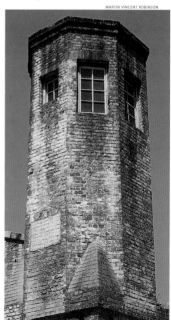

PATRICK HORTON

Man practising calligraphy, Tapgol Park (p88), Seoul

MARTIN VINCEN

Independence Gate, Dongnimmun Pa[r Seoul

Traditional dancing at Korean Folk Village (p126), Gyeonggi-do

Galbi is also on the menu, and *bibimguksu* – cold noodles garnished with vegetables and a hot sauce, which you mix up as you do with its more famous brother, *bibimbap*.

Huedeura Ramyeon (Map p78; meals W3000-5000) This tiny dungeon serves unforgettable food – probably the hottest *ramyeon* in Seoul with a big ladle of green chillies added to every bowl. Take up the challenge.

idame (Map p78; meals W5000-12,000; ✆ closed Mon) This vegetarian restaurant tries to be organic and offers 18 unusual meals, an English menu and a soothing white décor. It's on the 2nd floor down an alley near the entrance of Ewha Women's University. Service is slow but the food is unique.

Nolbu (Map p78; meals W4000-8000) Try the ham, sausages, vegetables, beans, tofu, noodles and anything-else-hanging-around that is all thrown into a big wok and cooked at your table. This meal, which some people call *johnson-tang*, is said to have originated after the Korean War when just about the only meat available in Seoul was 'black market' tins of ham and sausages that were smuggled out of the US army base at Yongsan.

Zen Zen (Map p78; meals W6000-8000; ✆ noon-2am) With a beer-hall atmosphere this large restaurant serves up *samgyeopsal* marinated in wine in a bamboo container. It's served with *doenjang jjigae* and as much salad wrapping as you want. Try the pungent sesame leaf with the serrated edges.

Daehangno

Beer Oak (Map p79; meals W5000-10,000) A whole chicken barbecued on a spit over a wood fire is the speciality. Draught beer costs W2000.

Bongchu (Map p79; meals W10,000) A popular *jimdak* restaurant that offers the usual big platter of freshly cooked chicken pieces, potatoes, carrots and onion on a bed of noodles, with a sweet and spicy soy sauce covering everything. There are no side dishes and you need a minimum of two mouths for this party food.

El Paso (Map p79; meals W7500-13,000) The owner of this Mexican restaurant in Korea used to own a Korean restaurant in Mexico. The food is authentic and the décor is Mexican artworks and souvenirs. An **African Museum** (admission W3000; ✆ 11.30am-7.30pm) is upstairs.

Obseoye (Map p79; meals W9000-18,000) This rural-retreat restaurant has a thatched roof and a small garden, and you can eat outside. *Shabu shabu*, beef and noodle casserole and *bulgogi* with mushrooms are all tasty with good side dishes, and the dark *chikcha* (arrowroot tea) is special too.

Sale e Pepe (Map p79; meals W7000-24,000; ✆ 11am-2am) This café/bar/restaurant has various zones – outdoors under the smart canvas awning is the best option if the weather is warm. Despite the Spanish-style broken-mosaic designs, the food is Italian – salads, pasta, pizzas, fish and meat dishes. A 700cc beer is W3500.

See the boxed text on p102 for more options.

Other Areas North of the Han River

Hankook (Map pp76-7; meals W4000) Located outside Korea House, it's a good place for a cheap lunch of *galbitang, seolleongtang* (설렁탕) or *bibimbap*.

Korea House (Map pp76-7; set menus W30,000-80,000) Enjoy a buffet of traditional Korean royal court food and drink in a Joseon-era *yangban* house near Namsangol Traditional Village. Every evening top-class performers put on one-hour folk music and dance shows, which cost W29,000. The performances start at 7pm and 8.50pm, except on Sunday when there is only one show at 8pm.

South of the Han River
BUDGET & MID-RANGE

Damibunsik (Map pp80-1; meals up to W4000) Everything is a bargain here including a *sundubu* (순두부) set or *dolsotbibimbap*.

Gyeongbokgung Buffet (Map pp80-1; lunch/dinner buffets Mon-Fri W12,000/19,000, buffets Sat & Sun W21,000) A rather grand Korean-style buffet in a traditional-style house.

Hard Rock Café (Map pp80-1; meals W8000-24,000; ✆ 5pm-2am Mon-Thu, noon-3am Fri & Sat, noon-midnight Sun) Dine, drink and dance amid rock memorabilia. Steaks, chicken meals, burgers, salads and rock bands that start nightly at 10pm.

Marché (Map pp82-3; meals W15,000) Inside the COEX Mall, it offers continental European food served from counters in an informal market-like atmosphere. The food is fresh, and organic salads, muffins and other culinary delights are available.

Pavilion (Map pp80-1; meals W5000-22,000; ✆ 11.30am-midnight) A large popular fusion restaurant but the food can be bland. Avoid the shrimp gratin. Lunch specials are a good deal, otherwise the rice and pasta meals or steak sets. Desserts are W3500.

Pulhyanggi (Map pp80-1; lunch specials W6000-8000, dinner sets W18,000-50,000) This well-known restaurant in Apgujeong offers mainly vegetarian food. The dinner sets offer 12 to 18 items including sesame or soya-bean soup, sweet-and-sour mushrooms, acorn jelly, rice cakes and traditional tea.

Taetae (Map pp80-1; meals W10,000-15,000) An unusual menu of Chinese *dim sum* and the Japanese *shabu shabu* with small portions of food that you cook at your table, like fried rice served in half a hollowed-out pineapple, or roast duck.

N-zle (Map pp82-3; meals W5500) Located opposite the COEX Aquarium, this place offers quick, cheap meals such as Mongolian orange noodles.

See the boxed text on p102 for other options.

TOP END
Noryangjin Fish Market Restaurants (Map p84; meals from W25,000) A handful of identical restaurants are on the first floor of the fish market. They specialise in raw fish that is guaranteed to have been swimming around a few minutes before you eat it. Raw fish meals are meant for sharing and include side dishes, and the bones are cooked up into a spicy soup. There are no English menus and no English-speaking staff, so take this book along and use the Food & Drink chapter to help you order.

Plaza Fountain Buffet (Map p84; meals W35,000-40,000) This famous restaurant in the basement of Yeouido's 63 Building offers a classy cosmopolitan buffet on tables grouped around a 'dancing' fountain.

Deep Blue (Map pp82-3; ☎ 6002 6199; lunch sets W20,000-32,000, dinner sets W57,000-107,000) Located next door to the COEX Aquarium in the COEX Mall is this classy Western-style restaurant. One wall is taken up by a huge aquarium tank so diners can watch sea creatures float by. It creates a special atmosphere and the prices reflect this, but you can also just order tea and cake.

DRINKING
Downtown
Baesangmyeon (Map pp72-4; B1, Seoul Finance Centre) Try some of Korea's folk liquor health drinks such as Hwalin (W10,000) which is flavoured with 18 herbs.

Top Cloud Café (Map pp72-4; drinks W3000-14,000) This smart modern café has expensive views – draught beer costs W3000/8500 before/after 6pm, coffee is W7,000, juice, wine and cocktails are W13,000, and half a bottle of champagne is W62,000.

Itaewon
Gecko's (Map p75; meals W8500-22,000; ⏱ 10am-2am) This popular bar and eatery has a party atmosphere and loud music. Draught beers start at W2500 and a bottle of Murphy's is W7500. Salads, chicken meals and grills, or daily specials such as tequila and lime chicken are worth a try.

Nashville Sports Pub (Map p75; ⏱ noon-2am, closes 4am Fri & Sat) has pool, darts, bar football and local beers at W2500. The **Beer Garden** (⏱ 11am-midnight Apr-Oct) on the roof is the perfect place to catch the breeze on a humid summer evening. **Club Caliente** (admission free; ⏱ 6pm-2am Fri-Sun) is for South American dance fans. Free dancing lessons are available.

Seoul Pub (Map p75; ⏱ 3pm-2am Mon-Fri, noon-3am Sat & Sun) A relaxed and friendly place with a jukebox, pool, darts and meals such as German sausages and *bulgogi*. Draught local beer is W2500, a pint of draught Guinness is W9000 and cocktails with rude names are W5000. Pitchers are cheaper during happy hour (before 7pm).

3 Alley Pub (Map p75; meals W12,000; ⏱ 4pm-midnight Wed-Mon) An English-style pub run by a German that has darts and pool and offers eight draught beers from W2500 and Strongbow cider. It's a popular and friendly watering hole with bar meals such as homemade sausages, sauerkraut and Irish stew.

Hostess Bars can be found all over Itaewon, but many are concentrated on the hill across from the Hamilton Hotel, known locally as Hooker's Hill. Their future is uncertain because American GIs are moving out of Seoul to new bases further south. The bars have signs including 'Sweetheart Club – Drink Food Woman', 'Woman & Cocktails' or 'For Gentlemen'.

Hongik & Sinchon
Bagdad Magic Café (Map p78; meals W5000-10,000; ⏱ 1pm-1am) A fun café where youthful magicians do magic tricks at your table involving coins, cards, straws and rubber bands. Free stage magic shows happen at 7pm and 9pm on Friday, Saturday and Sunday.

UNUSUAL TEASHOPS THAT SERVE UNUSUAL TEAS

Insadong (Map pp72-4) has many small teashops that serve traditional hot and cold teas made from fruit, leaves, herbs and roots. Many of the teas are delicious and the teashop owners make a big effort to create memorable décor. Some are so full of old junk and antiques that there is hardly room for the customers. A cup of tea costs from W4000 to W6000 but it's a quality product usually served with rice-cake snacks. Birdsong, running water and ethereal music add to the atmosphere.

Dalsaeneun Dalman Saeng Gakhanda (Moon Bird Thinks Only of the Moon) is packed with plants and rustic artefacts. Among the 14 teas on offer are *gamipcha* (persimmon-leaf tea) and *yeongjicha* (mushroom tea). The *saenggangcha* (ginger tea) has a peppery but sweet taste and is recommended. The teas in the big jars take a year to make.

Dawon is opposite Kyongin Gallery and you can sit in the pleasant courtyard under the trees or on floor cushions inside a 19th-century building. The *omijacha* is a delicious, cold, pink tea made from schisandra berries – it's said to have five flavours. The *nokcha* (green tea) is unusual, as it's served with milk and syrup.

Hakgyo Jongi Ttaeng Ttaeng Ttaeng (School Bell Goes Ding, Ding, Ding!) is furnished like an old school classroom with small wooden tables and chairs. The menu is written in chalk on a blackboard. The *mogwacha* is excellent and has lots of real fruit.

Sinyetchatjip (New Old Teashop) has a junk shop décor and a peacock, rabbit and monkey to entertain its customers who sit on floor cushions. The *maesilcha* (plum tea) is deliciously sweet and sour.

Yetchatjip (Old Teashop) is located up some stairs, and has a candle-lit, bric-a-brac décor but the major attraction are the little birds that fly freely around the teashop. It offers nine hot teas and seven cold ones – the hot *mogwacha* (quince tea) has a subtle fruity flavour and the cold nashi-pear tea used to be enjoyed by Joseon kings and queens.

Beatles (Map p78) is a basement bar that plays '60s and '70s music, has a log cabin décor and over 1000 LPs. A beer costs W3000, a pitcher W7000.

Free Crocodiles (Map p78; meals W7000-10,000) This bar has free Internet access, its own microbrewery which produces brown ale, stout and porter (all W2500) and meals like sausages or smoked chicken.

Gold (Map p78; ☯ 5pm-6am) A popular bar with an English-speaking owner, wood cabin décor, bar food and best of all – draught beer or a shot of tequila for only W1500.

Woodstock (Map p78) is a dark den (scribbles on the walls and rough-hewn tables and chairs) that plays loud rock music. Beer is W3000 and a pitcher is W7000. Another Woodstock is located in Itaewon.

Daehangno

Bier Halle (Map p79; meals W12,000) Youthful customers are attracted by bare brick archways and Mediterranean murals, 2.7L pitchers of draught beer for W11,500, and a menu that includes German sausages and smoked chicken.

Other bars include Chicago Sports Bar (cosy sofas and a pool table), Boogie Boogie Bar (1950s America décor and music), and Santana (wide range of dark beers).

Funny Funny Café (Map p79; ☯ 1pm-2am) Pay W4000 and play your choice of 200 board games with free soft drinks.

Mindeulreyeongto Café 1 (Map p79; meals W11,000) This amazing café (its name means Dandelionland) has 12 themed areas with different furniture, decoration and atmosphere with drinks and fusion meals. Free films are shown downstairs.

World Village (Map p79) has beers from 10 countries that cost around W6000. Upstairs the owner Mr Moon runs International House which provides almost-free Korean-language lessons (see p94).

South of the Han River

Dublin Irish Pub (Map pp80-1; ☯ 4pm-3am) A Guinness is W5000, Newcastle Brown is W10,000 and Irish stew is W12,000 in this Irish pub with an outdoor area.

Gensia Oxygen Café (Map pp80-1) is a clean and smart café that offers a free oxygen blast when you buy a drink (W4500 to W7000), but avoid the smoking area.

Oktoberfest (Map pp80-1; meals W11,000; ☯ 11-3am) This stylish new beer hall and microbrewery has it all; it has three German-style home-brews with genuine flavour (weissbier, pils and dunklesbier) as well as home-made sausages.

Tea Museum Café (Map pp80-1; ⊙ 10.30am-9pm) This is a shop, café and exhibition room for tea lovers which stocks 80 teas with unusual names like Gunpowder, Snow and Rooibos Royal, from a dozen countries. A cup of special tea costs from W6000.

O'Kim's Brauhaus (Map pp82-3; meals W5000-8000, platters W18,000-32,000; ⊙ 11.30am-midnight) This classy microbrewery near the east gate of the COEX Conference Centre has dark home-brew for W6000, wheat beer for W5200 and a yard of ale for W13,700.

ENTERTAINMENT
Casino

The only **casino** (Map btwn pp64 & 65; ☎ 456 2121) in Seoul is at the Sheraton Grande Walker-hill Hotel. Open 24 hours a day, it offers the usual ways of losing money. Snacks are free and free drinks are available at the gaming tables. There is no dress code and Korean nationals are not allowed. To get there, take subway Line 5 to Gwangnaru station, leave by Exit 2 and find a shuttle bus or take a taxi (W2000) as it's a 1km, 20-minute uphill walk.

Cinemas

Luxurious new multiplex cinemas with large screens and the latest sound equipment are opening all over Seoul. Cinema tickets cost W7000 and films usually run from 11am to 11pm, although the Freya Town Multiplex (Map pp70-1) in Dongdaemun shows films 24 hours a day and the COEX Mall Multi-plex (Map pp82-3) has some midnight films. English-language films are shown in cinemas in their original language with Korean subtitles.

Korea Film Archives (Map btwn pp64 & 65) at the Seoul Arts Centre, it screens classic Korean films with English subtitles during programmes that run every spring and autumn. These Korean films are free and are not available on DVD.

KNTO (Map pp72-4; ☎ 757 0086; www.knto.or.kr) Screens Korean films with English subtitles for free at 4pm on Tuesday.

Seoul Selection Bookshop (Map pp72-4; ☎ 734 9565; www.seoulselection.com) Shows Korean films with English subtitles – telephone or log on to the website for details.

Megabox (Map pp82-3; ⊙ 9am-midnight) Lo-cated in the COEX Mall is this popular 17-screen multiplex cinema with over 4000 seats. It shows films on large screens and uses the latest digital sound system.

DVD Rooms

DVD *bang* (rooms) are all over Seoul and can show Korean films with English sub-titles. Watch a film in your own private room sitting on a comfortable sofa. The usual cost is W7000 per person (the same as a cinema ticket) and they are popular with dating couples. A DVD *bang* is a lot smarter than a *bideobang* (video room). Joyplanet (Map pp80-1) is typical.

Gay & Lesbian Venues

Itaewon has the only gay and lesbian bar and club scene in Seoul that attracts foreigners and English-speaking Koreans. Most venues huddle together in an alley near Hooker's Hill. The staff often speak English and they welcome everyone. Not much happens until 9.30pm or later, even on Friday and Saturday.

California Café (Map p75; ⊙ 6pm-late) Down some steps from the main road, this long-running gay venue has a quiet and relaxing atmosphere and beers are W4000.

Labris (Map p78; meals W4500; ⊙ 3pm-2am) This low-key women-only lesbian bar has comfortable sofas, a big screen and beers for W4500. Saturday night is party night with dancing.

Shakra (Map p75; ⊙ 9pm-4am) Beers cost W3000 in this gay karaoke bar. Saturday night is the time to visit.

Soho (Map p75; ⊙ 8pm-4am, 6pm-7am Fri & Sat) This smart bar has friendly staff and beers cost W4000.

Trance (Map p75; ⊙ admission free Sun-Fri, Sat W10,000; ⊙ 9pm-6am) This hip-hop and techno dance club in the basement of Queen has a drag show on Saturday that starts at 3am. Leave at 6am and you can take the subway home.

Why Not (Map p75; admission free Sun-Thu, Fri & Sat incl a drink W15,000) is a small dance club, while the set-up at the underground **G Spot** (admission free Sun-Thu, Fri & Sat incl 2 drinks W15,000) is more of an actual disco.

Always Homme (Map p75) is a large bar with a bric-a-brac décor while Queen (Map p75) is another bar option.

Live Music

DOWNTOWN

Buck Mulligan's (Map pp72-4; B2, Seoul Finance Centre; meals W27,000) A smart Irish bar that offers darts and pool, Guinness or Guinness pie. Local beers are W3000 and live music starts at 9pm.

Feel (Map pp76-7; admission incl drink W5000) This double-decker den looks like a junkshop but Mr Shin and his friends play rock and folk music amid the incredible clutter. To get here, take subway Line 4 to Myeong-dong station, leave by Exit 10, walk to the elevated expressway, turn left and it's on the left past the school.

O'Kim's (Map pp76-7; Westin Chosun Hotel; meals W20,000-40,000; ☻ 11.30-2am) This well-known bar with green décor has darts, pool, bar football, free Internet and an Irish band that plays at 8.30pm every night except Sunday. Draught local beer is W8000, a pint of Guinness is a record-breaking W22,000.

ITAEWON

All That Jazz (Map p75; admission W3000) Live jazz music in an intimate atmosphere can be enjoyed every evening between 9pm and midnight. Try to catch the jazz fusion group 'Wave'. Beers are W6000, cocktails W7000 and food is available.

JR Blue (Map p75; admission free) This funky cellar is an informal venue with candles on the table and offers live jazz, soul or rock at 10pm Friday and Saturday. On other nights the staff have a choice of 6000 LPs as well as numerous CDs.

Woodstock (Map p75; admission free) A resident rock band plays every evening, starting around 9pm Sunday to Thursday and at 10pm Friday and Saturday. There's another Woodstock in Hongik but it doesn't have live music.

HONGIK

Live indie concerts run from around 7pm until 10pm. Entry is usually W5000 to W10,000 and includes a drink, but W15,000 or W20,000 for popular bands or special events.

Be Bop Jazz Club (Map p78; admission free) This smart lounge has live jazz at 8pm and 10pm Friday to Monday. Beers cost W5000.

Free Bird (Map p78; admission free) A rough-looking venue that puts on mainly rock bands every evening. Beers are W5000.

Rolling Stones (Map p78; admission W7000-10,000) Live rock, hardcore and punk bands blast out their music in this tiny cellar furnished with only a few benches. No alcohol available, but admission includes a soft drink.

SLUG.er (Map p78; admission free Mon-Thu, Fri-Sun W10,000) Indie bands (mainly rock and hip-hop) perform from 8pm to 10.30pm, but it stays open until 2am. Try to catch a band called 815. Beers cost W4000.

Water Cock (Map p78; admission free) Run by a real jazz lover with live jazz from 9pm to midnight and a jam session on Sunday nights. Drinks are W5000.

DAEHANGNO

Live Jazz Club (Map p79; admission W5000; meals W18,000-25,000; ☻ noon-3am) A serious venue with black décor which puts on three different live bands every evening, starting at 6.50pm Monday to Thursday, 6pm Friday, 5pm Saturday and 3.30pm Sunday and serving beer (W6000), wine (W7500 a glass) and Western-style meals.

SOUTH OF THE HAN RIVER

Hard Rock Café (Map pp80-1) has live rock music every night (p105).

Once In a Blue Moon (Map pp80-1; admission free, snacks W22,000; ☻ 5pm-2am) A beer in this classy jazz club costs W10,000 and a glass of wine W12,000 but different jazz bands play every evening – from 7pm to 8pm and then from 8.30pm until 12.30am Monday to Saturday and until 11pm Sunday. Try to catch Taste of Jazz.

Nightclubs

ITAEWON

Grand Ole Oprey (Map p75; ☻ 6pm-2am, 6pm-5am Fri & Sat) This country-and-western dance hall has been running since 1975. The American DJ (9pm to 1am Friday and Saturday) has 1000 LPs and current hits to choose from. Beers are W2300 and saluting the American flag is at midnight.

JJ Mahoney's (Map p75; Grand Hyatt Hotel; ☻ 6pm-2am) This smart nightclub has cosy zones and local beers are W12,000. Live rock music (NZ or Canadian bands) starts at 10pm every night except Sunday.

King Club (Map p75; ☻ 6pm-5am) A large and popular club above a supermarket, with a good sound system, a bunch of screens and Russian dancing girls. Beers cost W4000

SEOUL

and spirits are W5000 to W7000. Try the infamous kettle of *soju*.

OB Stadium (Map p75; 🕑 7-11pm Mon-Thu, 11.30am-10pm Fri & Sat) Pay just W17,000 and you can eat as much *bulgogi, galbi* and chicken as you can and drink as much beer as you can. Pay W12,000 if you just want to drink. A three-hour limit applies and any left-over food or drink results in a W2000 donation to charity. A dance floor and karaoke add to the fun.

HONGIK

Samba, techno, trance, house, hip-hop, rap and whatever else comes along is played in this clubbing area. Entry usually costs W5000 but increases on Friday and Saturday if the club has hired a special guest DJ. Hongik Club Day happens once a month. W15,000 entitles you to free entrance to 11 dance clubs (Hodge Podge, Hooper, matamata, mi, nb, dd, SAAB, Sk@, Old Rock, Joker Red and Myeongwongwan). It's the best night out in Asia but expect them to be packed.

Bahia (Map p78; admission W8000; 🕑 6pm-midnight Tue-Thu, 6pm-3am Fri & Sat) A Latin American dance club larger than Macondo (see below). Dancing lessons are available.

Hodge Podge (Map p78; admission Tue-Thu & Sun W7000, Fri & Sat W10,000; 🕑 7pm-4am) A popular, colourful place with a varied trancey music policy.

Macondo (Map p78; admission free Sun-Thu, Fri & Sat W5000; 🕑 7pm-midnight Sun-Thu, 7pm-2am Fri & Sat) A Latin American dance club with tables and chairs and a homely décor. The cover charge includes a drink.

Sk@ (Map p78; admission Sun-Thur W5000, Fri & Sat W10,000; 🕑 7pm-5am) This typically tiny, cellar-like dance club plays rap and other dance music. The admission price includes a beer.

SINCHON

Haeyeolje (Map p78; admission W8000; 🕑 6pm-3am) The admission price to this unusual club includes a fancy dress costume, a wig and make-up. You can be a witch, soldier, monkey, rabbit, Count Dracula or whatever you want. The cave-like club has benches and sofas, disco lights, a screen, and a DJ who plays techno and hip-hop. To get there, turn left at Domino's Pizza and it's on the third alley on the left.

Sport

South Korea's number one sport is baseball with teams sponsored by local *jaebol* corporations. Matches are held during the summer at Jamsil Baseball Stadium (Map pp82–3).

Soccer has become more popular due to the success of the South Korean team in the 2002 FIFA World Cup finals. Watching the Korean national team play at the World Cup Stadium (Map btwn pp64 & 65) is an opportunity to experience the fervour of the Red Devil supporters.

Ten league teams play basketball between November and April usually at Jamsil Gymnasium (Map pp82–3). Two foreign players are allowed in each team.

Korean-style wrestling is called *ssireum* and occasional tournaments take place at Jangchung Gymnasium (Map pp70–1).

Taekwondo competitions are held in the main hall of the World Taekwondo Federation (Map pp80–1).

Theatres

Cheongdong Theatre (Map pp76-7; ☎ 751 1500; www.chongdong.com; ticket W30,000-40,000; 🕑 Tue-Sun) This theatre stages 1½-hour performances of traditional music, singing and dancing at 8pm (April to September) and at 4pm (October to March). English subtitles appear on a screen and explain the meaning of the songs.

Nanta Theatre (Map pp72-4; ☎ 1588 7890; ticket W20,000-60,000) Set in a kitchen, this long-running, high-energy show mixes together varied ingredients – magic, circus tricks, drumming with kitchen utensils, slapstick comedy, dancing, martial arts and audience participation – to produce a clever and enjoyable musical pantomime. It plays at 4pm and 8pm (Monday to Saturday) and 3pm and 6pm (Sunday).

National Centre for Korean Traditional Performing Arts (Map pp64 & 65; ☎ 580 3300; www.ncktpa.go.kr) Next door to the Seoul Arts Centre, it includes two theatres and a **museum** (☎ 580 3333; admission free; 🕑 9am-6pm Tue-Sun Mar-Oct, to 5pm Tue-Sun Nov-Feb) that displays traditional musical instruments. Every Saturday at 5pm (March to December) traditional music, singing and dancing programmes are performed – tickets cost W10,000 and W8000 (students half-price).

National Theatre (Map pp76-7; ☎ 2274 3507; www.ntok.go.kr) This splendid theatre stages mainly traditional shows. To get there, take subway Line 3 to Dongguk University station, leave by Exit 6 and walk for 20 minutes up the hill past Hotel Shilla. Alternatively, you can take a taxi (W2000) or hop on to bus No 17 at the subway station.

Sejong Centre for the Performing Arts (Map pp72-4; ☎ 399 1700; www.sejongpac.or.kr) A lively arts complex that puts on lavish drama and music shows, including an annual drum festival.

Seoul Arts Centre (Map btwn pp64 & 65; ☎ 580 1300; www.sac.or.kr) This huge cultural complex has a circular opera house, two theatres, and a concert hall. To get there, take subway Line 3 to Nambu Bus Terminal station and leave by Exit 5. Take the frequent shuttle bus (W400), or walk to the end of the bus station building, turn left and the centre is at the end of the road – a 15-minute walk.

Seoul Norimadang (Map pp82-3; ☎ 414 1985; admission free) This outdoor circular arena for traditional performances stages excellent two-hour shows that start at 3pm Saturday and Sunday in April, May, September and October, but start at 5pm from June to August.

Seoul has a very lively small theatre scene mainly based in Daehangno (Map p79). Admission prices are generally W8000 to W25,000. The performances are in Korean, but Hakjeon Green Theatre (www.hakchon.co.kr) sometimes uses a screen that shows English subtitles. Munye Theatre hosts an annual dance festival. Free performances take place on the covered stage or anywhere in Marronnier Park on warm weekends.

Theatre Restaurants

Korea House (Map pp76-7; ☎ 2266 9101; www.koreahouse.or.kr; ☽ noon-2pm, 5.30-7pm & 7.30-8.50pm Mon-Sat, 6.30-8pm Sun; lunch/dinner buffets W30,000/33,000) This beautifully restored, palatial *hanok* offers a sumptuous buffet of traditional food and drink. Set menus of court food cost W50,000 to W80,000. Every evening top performers put on a one-hour folk music and dance show, which costs W29,000. The shows start at 7pm and 8.50pm every day, except Sunday when only one show is put on at 8pm.

Sheraton Grande Walkerhill Hotel (Map btwn pp64 & 65; ☎ 455 5000; www.walkerhill.co.kr) A 1½-hour show is put on twice nightly at 5.20pm and 7.30pm that usually includes

traditional Korean music and dance and a Western-style glitzy cabaret revue. The two shows and dinner cost around W80,000.

SHOPPING
Ahyeon-dong Wedding Street

This street (Map p78) of romantic dreams contains 200 wedding outfitters with expensive *hanbok* and Western-style wedding gowns displayed in their windows – it's a free fashion show.

Apgujeong

This posh area (Map pp76-7) has deluxe department stores, foreign brand boutiques, high-class hairdressers, beauty salons and cosmetic surgery clinics. Even dogs have their own beauty parlours, surgeons and cafés here.

Department Stores

Seoul has plenty of classy, retail-therapy establishments with supermarkets and food courts in their basements. Near Yeongdeungpo Market (Map p84) is a cluster of three department stores. You can find the Galleria Department Store in Apgujeong

---

DOG MANIA IN APGUJEONG

Koreans are more famous for eating dogs than loving them but this is changing. Dogs, the smaller the better, are fast becoming a must-have fashion accessory in the streets of Apgujeong.

Patrasche (Map pp80-1; ☽ noon-midnight) is a dog café and home to 15 dogs such as a golden retriever, a dachshund, a spaniel and a husky. Customers bring their own dogs to add to the doggie noise and excitement. The hamburger, chicken and strawberry yogurt on the menu is for dogs not humans. Coffee, beer and cake for humans are W6000.

Pet shops in Apgujeong add a new dimension to the phrase 'pampered pets'. They sell long-handled dog toothbrushes, poultry-flavoured toothpaste and mints to reduce doggie bad breath. Dog shoes cost W15,000 but you do get four of them, while pet jewellery costs W20,000 and dog nail clippers cost W13,000. Also on sale is dog shampoo and dog hair dye – why not dye your pet's ears pink or give it a fashionable green tail?

TOP MARKETS

Dongdaemun Market

This huge wholesale and retail shopping area (Map pp70–1) combines traditional markets and street stalls with modern high-rise shopping malls. The area is buzzing with activity all day and night and it never completely closes, as different parts have different days off. Clothing, leather jackets, local fashion brands and shoes are reasonably priced and a complete new kit of trousers, a shirt, socks, underwear and backpacker sandals can cost less than W40,000 if you bargain. Doosan Tower (Doota), Migliore, Freya Town and APM are four high-rise shopping malls with food courts and entertainment areas that are open from 10.30am to 5am every day except Monday, so insomniacs can shop all night.

Gyeongdong Market

This interesting market (Map pp70–1) specialises in traditional Asian herbal medicines, ginseng and dried food. Leaves, bark, herbs, seeds, roots, flowers, mushrooms, seaweed, fruit, prawns, fish and frogs are all dried and put on sale here. Bark is sold to be made into medicinal soup, while *gine* is a millipede that is boiled to make a soup or eaten dry. Said to be good for backache, a handful costs W6000. Prickly pear fruit is sold as a remedy for coughs and colds, aloe leaves are good for your skin and stomach, dried fungus lowers blood pressure and hundreds of products claim to be more effective than Viagara.

Hwanghak-dong Flea Market

Dubbed Dokkaebi (Goblin Market; Map pp70–1), thousands of second-hand LPs, cassettes, CDs, videos and DVDs are for sale on pavement stalls and in small shops. Second-hand clothes, sporting equipment, tools, brass Buddhas, musical instruments, paintings, books, pottery and bric-a-brac turn the market into a giant car-boot sale. The area is being redeveloped and could change.

Janghanpyeong Antique Market

This market (Map btwn pp64 & 65) consists of Samhui, Woosung and Songwha Arcades which house small, dusty shops crammed from floor to ceiling with wood and stone carvings, paintings, embroidery, furniture, books, musical instruments, swords, celadon pottery and teapots. Some shops specialise in old clocks, radios, telephones, cameras and other collectables.

Namdaemun Market

Another traditional day-and-night retail and wholesale market (Map pp76–7), which is mixed in with underground arcades, new fashion malls and Shinsegae, a classy department store with a supermarket in the basement. You can find good deals on backpacking equipment, *hanbok*, children's clothes, ginseng, dried seaweed, fresh food and flowers, imported and household goods, spectacles, watches and handicrafts. Food stalls and restaurant alleys in the market offer cheap meals for the adventurous.

Noryangjin Fish Market

At Noryangjin (Map p84) every kind of marine life is swimming around in tanks, buckets and bowls – it's a free aquarium show that is well worth a visit. Giant octopuses, prawns, mussels and crabs are on view and on sale. A take-away large plate of raw fish on salad costs from W15,000, which is a good deal considering what you normally have to pay in a restaurant.

Yongsan Electronics Market & Techno Mart

This is the largest electronics market (Map pp80–1) in Asia, with thousands of small shops spread around a dozen buildings. The very latest mobile phones, digital cameras, video cameras, DVD players, music, wide-screen digital TVs, computers and computer accessories are temptingly laid out. If you can plug it in, you can find it here. A LAN card (W50,000 elsewhere) costs W30,000. Techno Mart (Map pp82–3) is another electronic wonderland.

(Map pp80–1) and Hyundai Department Stores also in Apgujeong (Map pp80–1) as well as next to the COEX Mall (Map p82–3) and in Sinchon (Map p84).

Duty-Free Shops

Large duty-free shops are scattered around Seoul and stock the usual perfumes, cameras, watches, clothing and accessories, alcoholic drinks, cigarettes and souvenirs. Donghwa (Map pp72–4) is a duty-free shop with a wide choice of luxury items, located in a central position.

Insadong

This fascinating shopping area (Map pp72–4) is traffic-free on Saturday afternoon and Sunday. Over 50 small art galleries display paintings, while art-and-craft shops sell pottery, antiques, calligraphy brushes and knick-knacks. Stalls sell traditional snacks like *hotteok* (W500) or gingery toffee on a stick (W1000). Buddhist items such as cassettes of monks chanting, incense sticks, candles and monk's and nun's clothing can be bought in shops around Jogyesa. The winding back alleys are home to traditional teashops and restaurants. Close to Anguk subway station is **Beautiful Store** (🕙 10.30am-8pm Mon-Sat), a charity shop with heaps of second-hand bargains.

Itaewon

Most of the retailers in this district (Map p75) speak some English, and custommade suits, shirts and shoes are a specialty – suits start at W180,000. Go there for skateboarder baggies too. Cow-skin leather jackets cost W50,000 but the soft lambskin ones start at W200,000. Shops will embroider any garment with any design for around W3500. Spectacles (W50,000) and contact lenses are good quality and reasonably priced.

Myeong-dong

The traffic-quiet narrow streets of Myeong-dong (Map p76–7) are leading fashion centres. Every evening crowds of young people come here to shop in boutiques, high-rise malls and department stores such as Lotte for local and imported clothes, shoes, bags, accessories, cosmetics and CDs, and to relax in the cafés, restaurants and cinemas.

Nakwon Arcade & Rice-Cake Shops

On the 2nd floor of this elevated arcade (Map pp72–4) are small shops selling musical instruments. Locally-made guitars and flutes are a good buy. Around the arcade are shops selling home-made *tteok*, which are flavoured with nuts, red beans, sesame, honey and other ingredients. Eat them on the day you buy them.

Underground Arcades

Exploring underground shops is a particularly good idea if the weather above ground is too hot, too cold or too wet.

GETTING THERE & AWAY
Air

For details of airline companies and flights in and out of Seoul, see p376.

INCHEON INTERNATIONAL AIRPORT

Spacious modern **Incheon international airport** (Map p119; ☎ 032-741 0114; www.airport.co.kr), 52km west of Seoul, opened in March 2001 and relegated Gimpo airport to handling domestic flights. However there are a few domestic flights from Incheon airport to Jejudo, Busan and Daegu. The airport has been built on reclaimed land between two islands in the West Sea off Incheon city and is connected by a road bridge to the mainland. The subway train link to Seoul won't be completed until at least 2006.

The 1st floor is for arrivals. There are car-rental counters, a **convenience store** (🕙 24hr), two helpful **tourist information centres** (🕙 7am-10pm), plenty of Global ATMs and 20 **foreign currency exchanges** (🕙 6am-10pm) offering similar rates. Mobile phones can be rented at the **KT office** (🕙 6.30am-9.30pm) and **LG Telecom** (🕙 6.30am-10pm) – hire rates are W2000 to W4000 a day, but don't lose the phone as that could cost you up to W400,000. Frequent buses leave for destinations in Seoul and elsewhere from just outside the airport building.

The 2nd floor has a business centre and next to the post office is **KT Plaza** (☻ 7am-7.30pm), which offers free Internet access.

The 3rd floor is for departures and has plenty of retail therapy opportunities. Restaurants, fast-food outlets, cafés and bars charge reasonable prices. The **left-luggage counter** (☻ 7am-9.30pm) stores backpacks for W3000 a day. Go to the **lost & found office** (Gate L; ☎ 032-741 3114; find119@airport.or.kr; ☻ 7am-10pm) if you mislay something. Banks in the shopping area beyond immigration control allow you to exchange your won before leaving the country.

To obtain a tax refund on goods you bought at a shop that participates in a tax refund scheme, you must show the goods and receipts to one of the customs officers behind the check-in counters. After you've gone through immigration control, show the stamped receipt at the refund counter to receive your money.

The 4th floor is hard to find but has Korean and Japanese restaurants. **Panarama** (meals W6000-18,000; ☻ 7am-9pm) serves breakfasts, *bulgogi* sets, fancy desserts and a good view of the planes.

The basement contains an ice-cream parlour, supermarket, laundry, beauty and hairdressing salons and restaurants that offer a range of meals including pizzas for under W10,000. The **Medical Centre** (☎ 032-743 3115, emergency ☎ 743 3119; ☻ 24hr) charges W30,000 to W40,000 for a consultation, and can take X-rays and blood and urine tests. A **dentist** (min fee W20,000-30,000; ☻ 9am-5pm Mon-Fri, 9am-noon Sat) is also available.

Air Garden Transit Hotel (☎ 032-743 3000; www.airgardenhotel.com; 6-hr r/deluxe/ste W42,000/53,000/75,000; 🍴 💻) Inside the airport and only available to transit passengers. Rooms (non-smoking) are rented on a short-term basis, but add 21% for tax and service and W12,000 for double occupancy. Facilities include lounges, snacks, a business centre, a DVD room and a video games room.

GIMPO DOMESTIC AIRPORT

Reasonably-priced direct flights link **Gimpo domestic airport** (Map btwn pp64 & 65; gimpo.airport.co.kr), 18km west of the city centre, with a dozen Korean cities. The 1st floor is for arrivals, the 2nd floor is for checking

in, the 3rd floor is for departures, and the **Sejong Restaurant** (meals W12,000) is on the 4th floor. The **tourist information centre** (☻ 9am-9pm) offers free Internet access. Shopping facilities include a nearby E-Mart discount store, souvenir shops, a convenience store and the Sky City shopping centre. There are banks, car-hire counters, a food court, fast-food outlets, a traditional teashop and a bar. The **Biz Café** (snacks W5000) provides Internet, fax, printing and photocopying services. The **First Aid Centre** (☻ 6am-10pm) has a doctor available or on call, and a **pharmacy** (☻ 7am-8pm) is nearby. The **left-luggage counter** (☎ 666 1054; ☻ 6.10am-10pm) on the 1st floor charges W3400 per day for a big backpack.

KOREA CITY AIR TERMINAL

You can check in your luggage and go through customs and immigration procedures at the **Korea City Air Terminal** (KCAT; www.kcat.co.kr; ☻ approx 5.30am-6.30pm). The service is only available for Korean Air and Asiana passengers. The terminal has a post office, a bank and a tourist information centre. Non-stop limousine buses run every 10 minutes to Incheon international airport (W12,000) or Gimpo domestic airport (W6000) although these prices are sometimes discounted. Allow 90 minutes to get from KCAT to Incheon airport and 60 minutes to get to Gimpo airport. There are two locations – the main one is at the **COEX Mall** (Map pp82-3; ☎ 551 0077) while the one at the **Central City Mall** (Map pp80-1; www.centralcityseoul.co.kr) only serves Korean Air's international passengers.

Bus

Around 2 million Seoulites leave the city every Saturday, many by bus and train, for destinations around the country only to return on Sunday evening. It's like a tidal wave that flows out and back in again, and the surge is even greater on public holidays, especially at New Year and Chuseok. So try to avoid travelling at peak times.

All Seoul's bus terminals can be reached by subway.

Dong-Seoul bus terminal (Map pp82-3) Serves the eastern provinces.

Gangnam (Seoul) express bus terminal (Map pp80-1) The largest and is divided into two sections.

Honam terminal Part of the brand-new Central City Mall, which includes a Korea City Air Terminal (KCAT),

Shinsegae department store and the JW Marriott Hotel. Buses depart from here en route to the southwestern Jeolla provinces.

Gyeongbu-Yeongdong terminal In an old building with flower, clothing and linen shops on the floors above. Buses leave from here for cities and towns in the eastern provinces.

Nambu bus terminal (Map pp80-1) Serves towns southwest of Seoul and in the south central region.

Sinchon bus terminal (Map p78) Serves Ganghwado, a historical island northwest of Seoul.

Sample bus schedules from Gangnam/ Honam terminal:

Destination	Price (W)	Duration	Frequency
Cheongju	5600	1¾hr	every 30min
Gwangju	13,000	4hr	every 10min
Jeonju	9400	3¼hr	every 10min
Mokpo	15,100	5hr	every 40min

Sample bus schedules from Gangnam/ Gyeongbu-Yeongdong terminal:

Destination	Price (W)	Duration	Frequency
Busan	18,400	5¼hr	every 10min
Daegu	13,100	4hr	every 10min
Daejeon	7000	2hr	every 10min
Icheon	3300	1hr	every 30min
Sokcho	12,800	4½hr	every 30min

Train

Nearly all trains leave from Seoul Station (Map pp76–7) but trains heading east on the line that ends at Chuncheon and trains for Wonju, Jecheon, Danyang, Andong and Gyeongju leave from Cheongnyangni Station (Map btwn pp64 & 65). Change at Jecheon for the east coast. Both train stations can be reached by subway. The following are sample train fares from Seoul:

Destination	Saemaeul (W)	Mugunghwa (W)	Tongil (W)
Busan	33,600	22,900	12,800
Daecheon	14,500	9900	5500
Daegu	24,500	16,700	9300
Daejeon	12,600	8600	4800
Gwangju	27,300	18,600	10,400
Gyeongju	30,600	20,800	11,600
Jeonju	20,900	14,200	8000
Mokpo	31,400	21,400	12,000

GETTING AROUND
To/From the Airport

There are two types of buses that run from **Incheon international airport** (☎ 032-741 0114; www.airport.or.kr) to Seoul: the City limousine buses (W7000) run along various routes from around 5am to 11pm. The KAL limousine 25-seat buses (W12,000) run along several routes and take passengers to 18 major hotels in Seoul. Buses usually run every 15 minutes and take up to 90 minutes to the city centre, depending on traffic conditions.

Regular taxis charge around W40,000 to Seoul while a deluxe taxi could cost W60,000.

Buses also run to Gimpo airport (W4500, 30 minutes, every 10 minutes) along a special road. If your accommodation in Seoul is nearer a subway station than an airport bus stop, you can take a bus to Gimpo airport and then transfer.

The best way to travel between Gimpo domestic airport and downtown Seoul is to walk (10 minutes) to subway Line 5 (W800, 50 minutes to downtown). But many buses from Incheon airport drop into Gimpo airport on their way into Seoul so the bus service is excellent too. City buses cost W700 or W1300 while limousine buses cost W3000 or W6000.

A regular taxi ride to the city centre costs W15,000 while a deluxe taxi could set you back W28,000.

CITY LIMOUSINE BUS ROUTES

600 (Jamsil) Gonghangno, Heukseok-dong, Seoul express bus terminal, Bongeunsaro, Samseong station, Lotte World.

601 (Dongdaemun) Yanghwa Bridge, Hapjeong-dong, Sinchon, City Hall, Jongno, Dongdaemun.

602 (Cheongnyangni) Hapjeong station, Seogyo Hotel, Sinchon station, Gwanghwamun, Dongdaemun, Cheongnyangni.

603 (Guro) Mokdong Ogeori, Jinmyeong school, Galsan school, Guro station.

604 (Geumcheon-gu Office) Nambu cargo terminal, Gaerong station, Novotel Hotel, Geumcheon-gu office.

605 (City Hall) Gangbyeon expressway, Mapo, Gongdeok-dong, Seoul station, City Hall, Gwanghwamun, Chungjeongno.

606 (Jamsil) Olympic expressway, Seoul express bus terminal, Apgujeong-dong, Samseong station, Lotte World, Olympic Park.

607 (Songjeong station) Songjeong station.

608 (Yeongdeungpo station) Dangsan station, Yeongdeungpo station.

609 (Daechi station) Seoul express bus terminal, Gang-nam station, Yangjae station, Dogok-dong, Daechi-dong.

KAL LIMOUSINE BUS ROUTES
KAL1 (City Hall) KAL Building, Chosun Hotel, Lotte Hotel, Plaza Hotel, Koreana Hotel.
KAL2 (Namsan) Seoul Station, Hilton Hotel, Tower Hotel, Shilla Hotel, Hyatt Hotel, Seoul Station, Holiday Inn.
KAL3 (Gangnam) Renaissance Hotel, Grand Inter-Continental Hotel, COEX Inter-Continental Hotel, Novotel Hotel, Ritz Carlton Hotel, Palace Hotel.
KAL4 (Jamsil) Sheraton Grande Walkerhill Hotel, Dong-Seoul bus terminal, Lotte World.
Direct (KCAT) Korea City Air Terminal.
Direct (Seoul express bus terminal) Seoul express bus terminal.
Direct (Seoul station) Seoul station.
Itaewon 63 Building, Itaewon Hotel, Crown Hotel.
Dobong & Nowon Naebu expressway, Gireum station, Dongduk Women's University, Taereung station, Hagye station, Junggye station, Nowon station, Chang-dong station, Sofia, Banghak Sageori.

Public Transport
BUS
It is usually more convenient to travel by subway, but Seoul also has a comprehensive and cheap city bus system (http://bus.seoul.go.kr) that operates from around 5am to midnight and beyond. Buses have their major destinations written in English on the outside and they usually have a taped announcement of the names of each stop in English, but most bus drivers don't understand any English. The *Seoul Bus Guide Map* shows major bus routes.

The fare on ordinary buses (*ilban*) is W700 (irrespective of how far you travel); express buses (*jwaseok*) cost W1300, and deluxe express buses (*jikhaeng jwaseok*) cost W1400 as do night buses (*simya jwaseok*) which run on 12 routes from midnight until around 2am. Neighbourhood buses (*maeul*) and the small short-distance buses cost W350. Buy a bus and subway card, *gyotongkadeu*, at a kiosk near major bus stops (you must pay a W1500 deposit on the card) if you plan to travel frequently on the buses.

SUBWAY
Seoul's **subway system** (www.seoulsubway.co.kr, www.smrt.co.kr) is modern, fast, frequent, clean, safe and cheap, but try to avoid rush hour. Trains run every few minutes from around 5.30am to around midnight.

In central Seoul the average time between stations is two minutes, so it takes about 20 minutes to go 10 stops. Virtually every tourist sight is near a subway station.

Many subway stations have lifts or stair lifts for wheelchairs. Neighbourhood maps help you to decide which of the many exits to take. The stations have clean modern toilets, but you need to carry around your own toilet paper. Luggage lockers are available although most are too small to take a full-size backpack. Every station is well signed in English and the whole system is very user friendly.

Hawkers walk up and down the carriages selling a variety of small goods such as rubber gloves, torches, razors, CD players and CD carrying bags. The occasional handicapped beggar also wanders down the aisle with a begging bowl and a cassette playing hymns.

The basic one-way subway fare is only W700 and this covers most of the Seoul area. Hour-long trips cost up to W1000. The best plan is to buy a W10,000 stored-value card (*jeongaekgwon*) which gives you W11,000 worth of travel. You can't share a card so everyone needs to buy a separate card. Another type of travel card called *gyotongkadeu* can be used on buses as well as the subway – see the previous Bus section.

The **Korea Pass Card** (☎ 1566-7331; koreapasscard .com) is a handy prepaid card that can be used on the subway and buses. It also works as a telephone card and credit card and offers discounts on some tourist attractions and services. You can buy the cards in denominations from W50,000 to W500,000.

Taxi
Regular taxis (*ilban*) are a good deal and are cheaper than the bus or subway for three people who want to make a short trip. Regular taxis cost W1600 for the first 2km and then W100 for every 168m or 41 seconds after that. A 20% surcharge is payable between midnight and 4am. Deluxe taxis (*mobeom*) are black with a yellow stripe, cost W4000 for the first 3km and then W200 for every 205m or 50 seconds and don't have a late-night surcharge.

Few drivers can speak English, but some taxis have a free interpretation service – whereby an interpreter talks to the taxi driver and you by phone. All taxis are metered. Tipping is not required.

Gyeonggi-do
경기도

CONTENTS

GYEONGGI-DO

The province of Gyeonggi-do surrounds Seoul, and even pokes into North Korea. You have about as much chance of visiting the moon as you do of crossing the DMZ (of course this could change) but you can visit it on a tour to Panmunjeom. The West Sea islands and excellent hiking destinations such as Bukhansan National Park and Namhansanseong Provincial Park offer fresh air and an escape from the stresses of city life. Tourist highlights include the World Heritage Suwon Fortress, the Korean Folk Village and Icheon Ceramic Village and Spa. For children there's Seoul Grand Park (a giant zoo and amusement park) and the Everland and Caribbean Bay complexes. In winter the province's ski resorts lure skiers, and all parts of the province can be reached from Seoul in a day trip – one of the bonuses of Gyeonggi-do. The Incheon metropolitan area has its own local government and telephone code and is the port for ferries to nearby islands, and further afield to Jejudo and China. Ganghwado is a relatively unspoilt island with *dolmen* (ancient tombs), a mountain-top altar, fortifications and an interesting history, which makes it well worth a visit.

HIGHLIGHTS

- Hike up to granite peaks and an ancient fortress in **Bukhansan National Park** (p119)
- Feel the chill of the Cold War at **Panmunjeom** (p137) in the DMZ
- Spend a day among the rustic charms of the laid-back **Korean Folk Village** (p126)
- Stroll around **Suwon's World Heritage fortress** (p124)
- Head to **Icheon** (p127) if you're a pottery and hot spa bath fan
- Take the kids to **Seoul Grand Park Zoo** (p122) or **Everland Amusement Park** (p126)

★ Panmunjeom (DMZ)

Bukhansan National Park ★

Seoul Grand Park Zoo ★

Everland Amusement Park ★ ★ Icheon

Suwon's World Heritage Fortress ★ ★ Korean Folk Village

| ■ TELEPHONE CODE: 031 | ■ POPULATION: 10 MILLION | ■ AREA: 10.189 SQ KM |

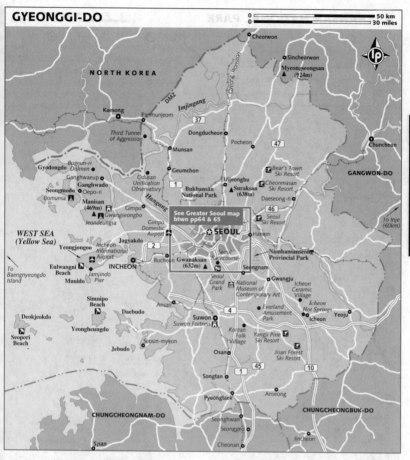

GYEONGGI-DO

BUKHANSAN NATIONAL PARK
북한산 국립공원

Just north of Seoul is **Bukhansan** (☎ 909 0497; www.npa.or.kr; adult/child W1300/300; ☼ sunrise-sunset); the ticket booths sell a hiking map (mostly in Korean) for W1000. This national park has impressive granite peaks, forests, temples, an 18th-century fortress and tremendous views. Many peaks are over 500m and rock climbers particularly enjoy Insubong (810m), which is a free-climber's dream, with some of the best multipitch climbing in Asia and routes of all grades.

Bukhansan receives five million visitors a year and to reduce environmental damage, footpaths are closed in rotation, so don't ignore 'track closed' signs. Try to avoid hiking at weekends or you might find yourself standing in a long queue to reach the summit. Every year rescue teams are called out to help over 100 hikers, mainly for leg and ankle injuries, so take care, especially in winter.

Camping is possible in summer or you can stay in basic mountain huts but they are not usually open in winter. During peak periods (10 July to 20 August and 1 October to 14 November), on public holidays and weekends, some huts and camping grounds have an online reservation system (see earlier for the website).

The following two hikes are highly recommended, the first in the south of the park and the second in the northern section. Both are all-day hikes so you need to be reasonably

GYEONGGI-DO

BUKHANSAN NATIONAL PARK

0 ___ 3 km
0 ___ 2 miles

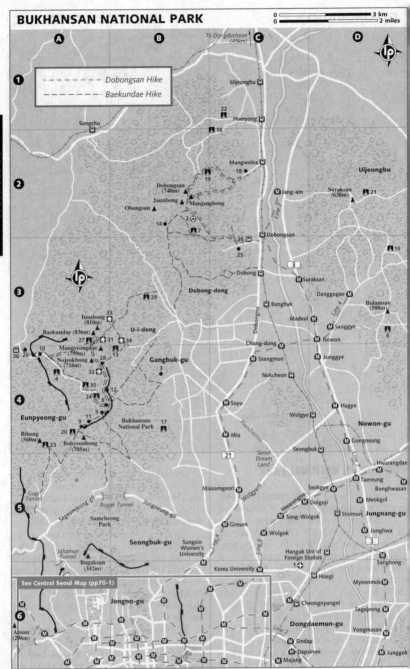

+ + + + + + + Dobongsan Hike
– – – – – – – Baekundae Hike

To Dongducheon
(45km)

Songchu

Uijeongbu

22
16
Hoeryong

Mangwolsa
18
19
Jang-am

Dobongsan
(740m)
Jaunbong ▲ Manjangbong
Obongsan ▲
14
2
7
35
25
Dobongsan

Suraksan
(638m)
21

Uijeongbu

15

Dobong

29

Dobong-dong

Suraksan

Banghak
Danggogae

Madeul

Bulamsan
(508m)
6

Insubong
(810m)
33
Baekundae (836m)
27
31
34
U-i-dong
Mangyeongdae
(799m)
Nojeokbong
(716m)
28
13
32
30
24
8
12
5
Gangbuk-gu
3

Sanggye

Nowon

Chang-dong

Ssangmun

Junggye

Nokcheon

Hagye

Suyu

Wolgye

Eunpyeong-gu
11
9
Bukhansan
National Park
17

Bibong
(560m)
20
23
Bohyeonbong
(705m)

Mia
Gongneung

Nowon-gu

Seongbuk

Hwarangdae
Taereung
Bonghwasan

Miasamgeori

Seodream
Land

Seokgye
Dolgoji
Meokgol

Gugi
Tunnel

Bugak Tunnel
Jongneung-gil

Segeomjeong-gil

Samcheong
Park

Gireum

Wolgyero

Sang-Wolgok
Sinimun
Jungnang-gu

Junghwa

Wolgok

Jahamun
Tunnel
Bugaksan
(342m)

Seongbuk-gu
Sungsin
Women's
University

Hanguk Uni of
Foreign Studies
1

Sangbong

Hoegi

Myeonmok

See Central Seoul Map (pp70–1)

Cheongnyangni

Sagajeong

Yongmasan

Ansan
(296m)

Jongno-gu

Dongdaemun-gu

Junggok

Sindap

Dapsimni

Majang

fit to complete the full course. If your energy begins to flag consider taking a shot of the Korean hiker's friend – pine-needle *soju*. One mouthful should be enough to help you make it to the top.

Baekundae Hike 백운대

This is a moderate to strenuous hike that takes six hours, including short breaks.

Take subway Line 5 to Gwanghwamun station, leave by Exit 1 and walk round to the front of the Sejong Cultural Centre. Get on bus No 156 (W800) and tell the driver 'Bukhansan'. The journey takes 35 minutes in normal traffic conditions and will drop you at a bus stop at the western edge of the park.

Follow the other hikers as they walk to the end of the small village, turn right and walk to the ticket booth. The park's highest peak, Baekundae (836m), is 4km or two hours away. A five-minute walk brings you to the fortress wall and Daeseomun gate. The wall is 9.5km long and was made of earth in the Baekje dynasty. It was rebuilt with 13 gates and stone blocks in 1711 during the reign of King Sukchong and encircled 12 temples and numerous wells.

Fifteen minutes after leaving the gate the road crosses a bridge. Fork left following the sign to Baekundae and keep a look out for little striped squirrels. Spring water is available at Yaksu-am, a hermitage that you reach 45 minutes after leaving the road. Past Yaksu-am there are stairs up to another fortress gate and then you use metal cables to haul yourself up Baekundae peak. Surrounded by granite cliffs and with a 360-degree view, it's a top-of-the-world feeling.

The easiest option is to return the same way, but it's more interesting to turn left on the stairs and walk along a scenic, rocky route to Yongammun, another fortress gate 35 minutes away. Then walk along the

remains of the wall to Dongjangdae, a command post, and on to Daedongmun, which is 40 minutes from Yongammun.

At Daedongmun, walk down to the toilets and take the path that follows the river bed. There is no sign but the track is reasonably clear. The path goes through an attractive valley and passes three small temples: Taegosa, Yonghaksa and Beopyongsa, to the beginning of the road, which you reach after 45 minutes. From here it's another 40 minutes back to the bus stop.

Dobongsan Hike 도봉산

Dobongsan is a mountain with three rocky peaks and this cool shady 10km-hike takes about five hours, but add time for a picnic lunch. Moderate fitness is required but if Korean grandmothers can do it, so can you.

Take subway Line 1 north to Dobongsan station (W800). It takes 45 minutes from City Hall if your train goes all the way (not all do). Exit the station and follow the other hikers across the road, through the market and food stalls and past a bus terminal to the ticket booth.

Keep on the main path, following the sign to Jaunbong, one of Dobongsan's peaks, which is 2.7km away. Five minutes past the spring, turn right, following the sign to Manjangbong (another Dobongsan peak). Keep a look out for woodpeckers and squirrels.

About an hour from the subway station, you arrive at Dobong Hut. Bear right following the sign to Mangwolsa. Then follow signs to Jaunbong, go past the police rescue post and up the final steep and rocky stretch to the top which is between two rocky peaks. Here the adventure begins as you scramble down a ravine helped by metal cables, then up and along a rocky ridge and through narrow crevices.

Follow the signs and descend via Mangwolsa, or turn right at the sign marked 'Wondobong Ticket Box' for a less-used short cut down the hillside past a small spring. Half an hour from the right turn you join the main track down to the car park. Follow the road, bearing left as you enter the town, to Mangwolsa subway station (Line 1).

SURAKSAN 수락산

To the east of Bukhansan National Park is Suraksan (638m), another attractive climbing and hiking area. It's not a national or provincial park, but expect crowds at the weekends. One relatively easy hike is to take subway Line 4 to Danggogae station and hike up past Heungguksa to Suraksan peak and then descend to Jang-am subway station. A shorter hike from Danggogae station is up to the top of Bulamsan (508m) and then on to Bulamsa and down to Sang-gye station.

SEOUL GRAND PARK 서울대공원

This excellent **zoo** (☎ 500 7114; www.grandpark.seoul.go.kr; adult/youth/child W1500/1200/700; 🕑 9am-7pm, 9am-6pm Oct-Mar) is set among the forested hillsides south of Seoul. A river runs through the park and families picnic along its shady banks. You can hike along a number of marked trails which are 2km to 6km long.

The zoo is home to a long list of exotic creatures including the popular African ones. A huge aviary contains cranes, swans, pelicans and other large birds, and an indoor botanic garden houses a forest of cacti, numerous orchids and carnivorous pitcher plants. Ants and swimming beetles are on display in a 'miniature creature' exhibit. An entertaining dolphin and seal show costs only W500 and starts at 11.30am, 1.30pm and 3pm.

The huge globe-shaped structure on the right is **IT World** (www.itworld.org.kr; adult/youth/child W3000/2000/1500; 🕑 10am-6pm Tue-Sun, 9am-5pm Nov-Feb). Designed for computer-crazy kids, it has a 17m dome screen, 3-D computer graphics, virtual reality games and a hyperspace ride.

Next door is **Seoul Land** (☎ 504 0011; adult/youth/child W9000/7000/4000, all-inclusive ticket W25,000/20,000/16,000; 🕑 9am-7pm, 9am-6pm Oct-Mar), a large amusement park with rides for all ages, with a roller coaster, shot drop, and bungee swing among the many adrenalin rides.

Next to Seoul Land, the large and striking **National Museum of Contemporary Art** (☎ 218-6000; www.moca.go.kr; adult/youth/child W700/300/free 🕑 9am-6pm Tue-Sun, to 5pm Nov-Feb) is spread over three floors and also has sculptures in the garden. You are unlikely to miss one exhibit - a huge pagoda-shaped video installation that is 18m high and uses 1000 flickering screens to make a comment on our increasingly electronic universe. It's the work of Paik Nam-jun, a video artist with an international reputation, and is entitled *The More the Better*. Decide for yourself if the title is ironic. Free films are shown on Saturday during August, concerts are held in July, and music and dance performances are put on in October. To get there, walk up to the entrance of Seoul Grand Park and bear left.

Getting There & Away

Take subway Line 4 to Seoul Grand Park station (W800), which is 45 minutes from City Hall. Leave by Exit 2 and then either walk (10 minutes) or take a **mini-train** (adult/child W600/500) to the entrance of the park. Another option is to take the **cable car** (adult/child W4000/2000). A free shuttle bus runs every 20 minutes from the subway station (outside Exit 4) to the National Museum of Contemporary Art, or it's a 20-minute walk.

SEOUL RACECOURSE 서울 경마장

The **racecourse** (Map btwn pp64 & 65; ☎ 509 2337; fax 509 2309; admission W800; 🕑 11am-5.30pm Sat & Sun, but closed 5 weekends of the year) has an area in the new grandstand on the left for foreigners - take a lift to the 4th floor, turn right and it's near Block A. Foreign currency exchange and English-speaking betting clerks are available. A booklet in English gives the form of the horses and lots of other information. Two giant outdoor screens on the course (as well as numerous small screens in the suite) show close-ups of the racing action. Short races over 1km or 2km take place every half-hour between 11am and 5.30pm at the weekend. There are plenty of canteens and fast-food outlets. The small **Equine Museum** (admission free) has traditional items relating to horses. The only other horse-racing track is far away on Jejudo and options for gamblers in Seoul are limited, so race days are crowded with some 30,000 mainly male punters. But everything is well organised and convenient - the only problem is picking the winners.

Getting There & Away

To get there, take subway Line 4 to Seoul Racecourse station (W800) and leave by Exit 2. Turn right and you can arrive in style by taking the free horse and carriage ride, or you can walk down the covered walkway to the entrance.

NAMHANSANSEONG PROVINCIAL PARK 남한산성 도립공원

Completed in 1626, Namhansanseong, 20km southeast of downtown Seoul, guarded the city's southern entrance, while Bukhansanseong guarded the northern approaches. It was garrisoned by tough Buddhist monks who were soldiers rather than pacifists in those days.

In 1636 King Injo fled to this fortress when the Manchus from China invaded and occupied Seoul. After a siege of 45 days, the king surrendered and was forced to accept Manchu suzerainty. To ensure that he did, his son was kept hostage in China for eight years.

This easy hike in Namhansanseong Provincial Park takes less than two hours and follows part of the ancient fortress wall, which is 3m to 7.5m high and stretches for 9.6km (although the inner circle is only 6.5km).

To reach Namhansanseong, take subway Line 8 to Namhansanseong station and leave by Exit 1. Then take any bus the short way up the road to the park entrance. From the park entrance, walk for 30 minutes along the road past freshwater springs, exercise

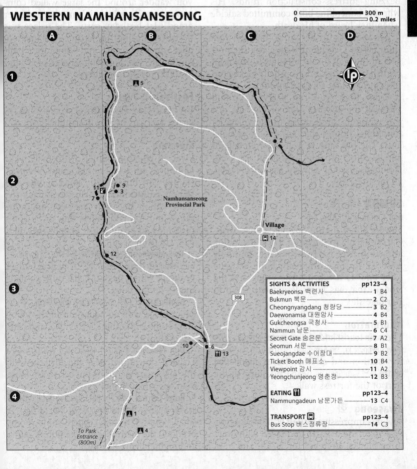

WESTERN NAMHANSANSEONG

0 — 300 m
0 — 0.2 miles

Namhansanseong Provincial Park

Village

308

To Park Entrance (800m)

SIGHTS & ACTIVITIES	pp123–4
Baekryeonsa 백련사	1 B4
Bukmun 북문	2 C2
Cheongnyangdang 청량당	3 B2
Daewonamsa 대원암사	4 B4
Gukcheongsa 국청사	5 B1
Nammun 남문	6 C4
Secret Gate 숨은문	7 A2
Seomun 서문	8 B1
Sueojangdae 수어장대	9 B2
Ticket Booth 매표소	10 B4
Viewpoint 감시	11 A2
Yeongchunjeong 영춘정	12 B3

EATING	pp123–4
Nammungadeun 남문가든	13 C4

TRANSPORT	pp123–4
Bus Stop 버스정류장	14 C3

GYEONGGI-DO

equipment and temples up to Nammun, the southern fortress gate. Pay the W1000 entry fee at the ticket booth and ask for the free map. Near the gate is Nammungadeun restaurant where you can eat *gamjajeon* (감자전, potato pancake), which is pizza-sized and costs W6000. Nearby a stall sells *makgeolli* bread, another cheap but filling food that's popular with hikers.

Turn left and walk along the wall which has extensive views of Seoul and the Han River – look out for big butterflies and golden dragonflies. Pass Yeongchunjeong pavilion and a secret gate before reaching Sueojangdae command post and Cheongnyangdang, Yi Hoe's shrine. Yi Hoe was executed after being falsely accused of embezzling fortress-construction funds. His wife and concubine both committed suicide when they heard of his death.

Ten minutes further on, go through Seomun (West Gate) and walk along the outside of the wall for 30 minutes to Bukmun (North Gate); Bukmun is usually locked but most people can squeeze through.

From there you can carry on round the wall for another 4km or else it's just a five-minute stroll down to the village of traditional houses that are mainly restaurants. The bus stop is near the roundabout and bus No 9 provides a frequent service to Namhansanseong subway station (W1000, 20 minutes).

SUWON 수원
pop 1 million / 120 sq km

Suwon, 48km south of Seoul, is the provincial capital of Gyeonggi-do. The outstanding attraction here is Hwaseong, the faithfully restored fortress originally built between 1794 and 1796 during the reign of King Jeongjo that has been designated a World Heritage site.

Information

The **main tourist information centre** (☎ 228 2785; www.suwon.ne.kr; ⏰ 6am-8pm) is outside the railway station and another **tourist information centre** (⏰ 9am-6pm) is near Paldalmun at the start of the fortress walk.

Hwaseong 화성

Suwon's impressive **fortress wall** (admission free; ⏰ 24hr), made of earth and faced with large stone blocks, stretches for 5.7km and 95%

of it has been restored. Hiking round the wall with its command posts, observation towers, entrance gates and fire beacon platform makes for a fascinating two-hour historical walk. Start at **Paldalmun**, also known as Nammun (the South Gate), and follow the sign. Walk along the wall up to the top of **Paldalsan** (143m), a good viewpoint, where you might hear and see cuckoos.

Hwaseonghaenggung 화성행궁

Before setting off around the fortress wall you can visit the newly restored **palace** (admission free; ⏰ 9am-5pm) that was also originally built by King Jeongjo, a much-loved king due to his filial piety and concern for ordinary people. Courtyard follows courtyard as you wander around the large walled complex where King Jeongjo's mother held her grand 61st birthday party. The palace was destroyed during the Japanese occupation, after which a hospital and school were built on the site. An admission charge of around W1000 may be introduced.

Festivals & Events

Every October a grand royal procession is re-enacted as part of Suwon's annual festival.

Sleeping

Over 30 *yeogwan* (motels with small, well-equipped en suite rooms) and *yeoinsuk* (family-run hotels with small rooms and shared bathroom) are clustered near the train station but there are very few mid-range and top-end hotels due to Suwon's proximity to Seoul. Most people visit on a day trip from Seoul.

Gwangmyeong Yeoinsuk (☎ 2543701; s & d without/ with en suite W15,000/20,000; 🗶) A typical budget *yeoinsuk* which has no beds, only *yo* mattresses on the floor.

Sambo Motel (☎ 242 5776; s & d W30,000; 🗶) A smart place with an aquarium in the lobby and rooms with cable TV, a video, and beds rather than *yo*.

Ujin Yeogwan (☎ 254 4673; s & d W30,000; 🗶) Located downtown near the fortress wall this has smart *yo* rooms but ask to see more than one room as they vary.

Hotel Central (☎ 246 0011; fax 246 0018; d/tw/ste incl tax & service W88,000/99,000/180,000; 🗶 🖵) A small hotel (32 rooms) where some rooms overlook the fortress wall. The hotel's sauna and nightclub are nearby.

SUWON

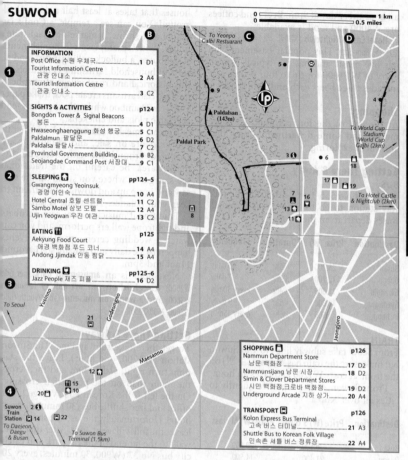

INFORMATION
Post Office 수원 우체국................................1 D1
Tourist Information Centre
관광 안내소...2 A4
Tourist Information Centre
관광 안내소...3 C2

SIGHTS & ACTIVITIES   p124
Bongdon Tower & Signal Beacons
봉돈..4 D1
Hwaseonghaenggung 화성 행궁...................5 C1
Paldalmun 팔달문...................................6 D2
Paldalsa 팔달사......................................7 C2
Provincial Government Building...................8 B2
Seojangdae Command Post 서장대..............9 C1

SLEEPING   pp124–5
Gwangmyeong Yeoinsuk
광명 여인숙..10 A4
Hotel Central 호텔 센트럴..........................11 C2
Sambo Motel 삼보 모텔.............................12 A4
Ujin Yeogwan 우진 여관...........................13 C2

EATING   p125
Aekyung Food Court
애경 백화점 푸드 코너...............................14 A4
Andong Jjimdak 안동 찜닭.........................15 A4

DRINKING   pp125–6
Jazz People 재즈 피플...............................16 D2

SHOPPING   p126
Nammun Department Store
남문 백화점...17 D2
Nammunsijang 남문 시장...........................18 D2
Simin & Clover Department Stores
시민 백화점,크로바 백화점.........................19 D2
Underground Arcade 지하 상가...................20 A4

TRANSPORT   p126
Kolon Express Bus Terminal
고속 버스 터미널.....................................21 A3
Shuttle Bus to Korean Folk Village
민속촌 셔틀 버스 정류장............................22 A4

Hotel Castle (호텔 캐슬; ☎ 211 6666; d/tw/ste incl tax & service W225,000/275,000/350,000; ※ ▣) The top-range choice with helpful staff – rooms have Internet access and the hotel has a business centre, men's sauna and a popular nightclub.

Eating & Drinking

Aekyung Food Court (meals up to W5000) On the 2nd floor of the railway station, this smart and clean food court has 17 outlets that cook up more than 60 different dishes.

Andong Jjimdak (half/whole chicken W12,000/18,000; ※ 11am-midnight) This spicy and fashionable chicken spot has many young fans.

Yeonpo (연포; meals W6000-25,000) Halfway round the fortress-walk at Hwahongmun, walk down the steps to this popular restaurant, serving *galbi* (beef ribs) and the famous Suwon version of *galbitang* – big serve of beef ribs in a broth served with spicy side dishes.

World Cup Galbi (월드컵 갈비; meals W5000-25,000) Overlooking the superb World Cup Stadium, the best lunch deal is *galbijeong-sik*, a banquet with excellent side dishes or *galbi* (with more meat). Try the *galbitang* and *naengmyeon* (buckwheat noodles in an icy beef broth, garnished with chopped vegetables and half an egg) .

Entertainment

Jazz People (※ 11.30am-2am, to 4am Sat) With a bird's-eye view of Suwon, this comfortable 8th floor hang-out has live music for half an hour every day at 9pm. Beers and coffees are W4000 and food is available.

Hotel Castle Nightclub (호텔 캐슬나이트클럽; ☺ 6pm-5am) This popular basement club has live music and has the typical Korean entry of W40,000 for up to four people and includes three beers each and *anju* snacks.

Shopping

At the end of the fortress-walk is a large market and some department stores that are worth exploring.

Getting There & Away

BUS

Catch bus No 5, 5-1 or 7-1 outside the railway station to go to Suwon bus terminal. Buses depart from there for:

Destination	Price (W)	Duration	Frequency
Busan	25,200	5hr	10 daily
Daegu	12,200	3½hr	7 daily
Gwangju	11,800	4hr	every 30min
Gyeongju	18,000	5hr	9 daily
Incheon	3600	1½hr	every 15min

TRAIN

From Seoul take subway line No 1 to Suwon but make sure the train has 'Suwon' (수원) on the front. It costs W1200 and takes an hour.

From Suwon, trains depart frequently to cities all over Korea:

Destination	Price (W) S class	Price (W) M class
Busan	30,500	20,800
Daegu	21,400	14,500
Daejeon	9500	6400
Jeonju	17,700	12,100
Mokpo	28,200	34,700

Getting Around

Outside the railway station on the left bus Nos 11, 13, 36, 38 and 39 go to Paldalmun (W700) for the 'round-the-fortress' walk. A taxi costs W3000 (the same cost to go from Paldalmun to the World Cup Stadium).

KOREAN FOLK VILLAGE
한국 민속촌

This splendid **folk village** (☎ 286 2111; www .koreanfolk.co.kr; adult/youth/child W11,000/8000/7000; ☺ 9am-6pm, 9am-5pm Nov-Feb) has a very large collection of thatched and tiled traditional houses that takes at least half a day to look around. You can see a temple, a Confucian school and shrine, a market, a magistrate's house with examples of punishments, storehouses, a bullock pulling a cart, and all sorts of household furnishings and tools. In this historical and rural village atmosphere, *hanbok*-clad artisans create pots, make paper and weave bamboo while other workers tend vegetable plots and chickens.

Korean meals, snacks and handicraft souvenirs are on sale, and restaurants are clustered around the entrance and the market area. Be careful on the traditional see-saw game, where you stand on the see-saw and jump up and down – it's difficult to keep your balance. The swing is safer.

Traditional musicians, dancers, acrobats and tightrope walkers perform, and you can watch a wedding ceremony. These events happen twice daily and usually start around 11am and 3pm.

Next door is an **amusement park** (per ride W2500) for children, an **art gallery** (admission W3000) and a **world folk museum** (adult/youth/child W3000/2500/2000).

Getting There & Away

To get there take subway Line 1 to Suwon station (W1200, one hour). Leave the station, turn right, walk 150m and then cross the main road on the pedestrian crossing. On the left is the Korean Folk Village ticket office and free shuttle bus (30 minutes, every hour). Unfortunately, the last free shuttle bus leaves the folk village at 4pm. After that time, walk to the far end of the car park and catch city bus No 37 (W900, 30 minutes, every 20 minutes) back to Suwon station.

EVERLAND 에버랜드

An excellent amusement park, **Everland** (☎ 759 1408; www.everland.com), an hour southeast of Seoul, is divided into four separate parts.

Caribbean Bay (adult/child W45,000/35,000 Jun & Sep, W55,000/45,000 Jul & Aug; ☺ 9.30am-6pm, closes later Jul & Aug) is a world-class water park. The **outdoor section** (☺ 1 Jun-15 Sep) has a wave pool, sandy beach, tube rides, body slides, spa pools, a surf pool, lazy pool, an adventure pool and a scuba diving pool. The **indoor section** (adult/child W25,000/18,000; ☺ year-round) is all that is open from September to May. It is similar to the outdoor section but smaller in scale. The advantage is that it is cheaper.

Festival World (adult/child day-pass W28,000/20,000; ☾ 9.30am-6pm, closes later Jul & Aug) follows the Disneyland formula with fantasy buildings, thrill rides, impressive gardens and parades, live-music entertainment and lots of restaurants and fast-food outlets. One novelty feature is the African safari where lions and tigers live together.

Speedway is a motor racing track that is close to the other two sections. You can watch races for free from the grass bank. Sometimes visitors can drive a racing car – the cost depends on the car's horsepower.

The **Hoam Art Museum** (☎ 031-320 1801; www hoammuseum.org; adult/child W3000/2000; ☾ 10am-6pm Tue-Sun) is one of Korea's major art collections with 91 Korean national treasures, foreign 20th-century art and a sculpture garden. A free shuttle bus runs on the hour from outside Festival World Entrance B, which is near the buses to Seoul.

Getting There & Away

To get to Everland: take subway Line 2 to Gangnam station, leave by Exit 6 and walk to the Everland bus stop (Map pp80–1) and take bus No 5002 (W1400, one hour, every 15 minutes). Other buses go to Everland from outside Suwon's train station – bus Nos 66 and 6000 (W1400, one hour, every 30 minutes). Check the Everland website for up-to-date transport details.

ICHEON 이천
pop 190,000

Just 60km southeast of Seoul is the small city of Icheon (not to be confused with Incheon on the west coast). Its two main attractions are a hot spring resort and Icheon Ceramic Village.

Miranda Hot Spring Spa 미란다 온천

The splendid **Spa Plus** (스파 플러스; ☎ 633 2001; www.mirandahotel.com; adult/child W10,000/8000, Sat & Sun W14,000/11,000; ☾ 6am-10pm) is a large complex that has ultramodern facilities including saunas, outdoor hot pools (great in winter when it's snowing), an indoor swimming pool, slide and wave pool, an exercise room, a DVD room and a food court. Treat yourself to hot, warm and cold baths, a waterfall bath and rice wine, herbal, pinewood and fruit baths. Use of the swimming pool, slide and wave pool cost extra. The spa is next to the Miranda Hotel, which is just a five-minute walk from Icheon bus terminal.

Icheon Ceramic Village 이천 도예촌

The name Icheon Ceramic Village (Icheon Doyechon) conjures up images of wispy-bearded artisans working in a rural idyll, but this village is a busy town with a main street full of traffic. The many potteries are spread out over a wide area. You can see potters at work and try your hand at making pots – but only on a tour (see p95).

Catch a taxi (W5000) or local bus No 114 (W1300) from outside the bus terminal and get off after 15 minutes near the large traditional building with blue/green tiles, Songpa Pottery (송파 도예 명품관). Inside is unusual crystalline pottery with fern-like designs as well as traditional inlaid celadon and *buncheong*-style pottery. Don't break anything – it could cost you W1 million. Some household items are W10,000 but a tea set is W60,000.

Walk along the main road and over the bridge to the town and you will come to a sign in *hangeul* indicating a right turn to

---

THE REDISCOVERY OF GORYEO DYNASTY CERAMICS

Yoo Kun-hyung was a potter who worked under the name of Haegang. He became fascinated by the elegant lines, subtle colours and soft shine of classic Goryeo dynasty ceramics – particularly the flying crane and willow patterns which he felt had a 'mysterious beauty'. The art of making Goryeo pottery had been lost for centuries, but in 1911 Haegang began experiments with shaping, inlaying, kiln design and using different clays to try and recreate Goryeo ceramics.

In 1926 he set up a Goryeo-style kiln, and in 1928 he won a gold prize in a pottery exhibition in Japan. Unfortunately everything he had spent a lifetime building up was destroyed during the Korean War, but he set to work again after the war, and was named a living national treasure in 1960. His son, Yoo Gwang-yeol (born in 1942), has continued his father's work. Without Haegang's pioneering work, there wouldn't be thousands of Goryeo-style pots for sale in the souvenir shops in Icheon and the rest of the country.

Haegang Museum (a 20-minute walk from Songpa Pottery showroom). **Haegang Ceramics Museum** (해강 도자 미술관; ☎ 634 2266; adult/child W2000/1500; ☼ 9.30am-5.30pm Tue-Sun) has some interesting old kilns outside which are still used – see the boxed text (p127) on the rediscovery of Goryeo dynasty pottery-making methods. Inside the downstairs section are details (no English but lots of pictures) about where the kilns were and the development of pottery styles in Korea. Comb-patterned pottery dates back 7000 years. Upstairs are examples of the most famous styles – Goryeo celadon, and Joseon-era white porcelain and *buncheong*. The 12th century was the Golden Age of Korean ceramics with a great variety of shapes, colours and designs and the development of inlaid motifs. The royal pottery in Gwangju started in 1467, employed 380 workers and continued until 1883 when it was privatised.

Back to the main road, cross over and you might be able to see potters at work in the small Hancheong Pottery (한청 도예 명품관).

Festivals & Events
Icheon hosts a World Ceramics Biennale in the autumn of odd-numbered years.

Sleeping
Jeongeonpark Motel (정언 파크 모텔; ☎ 635 1661; s & d W30,000; ✖) A good place to stay and the nearest accommodation to the bus terminal, which is a one-minute walk away.

Miranda Hotel (미란다 호텔; ☎ 633 2001; www .mirandahotel.com; s & d incl tax & service W127,000; ✖ ▢) Next to Spa Plus (guests receive a 20% discount) and overlooking a small lake with a pavilion on an island, this is the best hotel in Icheon. It has a small business centre and a **bowling alley** (W2400, shoes W1000; ☼ 8pm-1am).

Other motels can be found around Icheon bus station and in Icheon Ceramic Village.

Eating
Yetnalssalbapjip (옛날 쌀밥집; meals W8000-15,000) Near to Songpa Pottery showroom, you sit on cushions on the floor and eat a banquet of over 20 dishes such as *pajeon* – steamed egg, raw seafood, spicy tofu soup, barbecued fish, lettuce and dried seaweed wraps plus the famous shiny Icheon rice.

Cold plum tea rounds off an excellent feast. The more expensive options include additional steak, crab and fish dishes.

Getting There & Away
Buses run from Seoul's Gangnam bus terminal (Map pp80–1) and Dong-Seoul bus terminal (Map pp82–3) to Icheon (W3300, one hour, every 30 minutes).

INCHEON 인천
☎ 032 / pop 2.5 million / 958 sq km
Incheon is a major port 36km west of Seoul with the international airport on an offshore island. If you are in Seoul don't go to Incheon to get to the international airport – take a direct bus from Seoul. Incheon became briefly famous in 1950 when the American General Douglas MacArthur led UN forces in a daring landing there behind enemy lines. Military experts doubted that such a tactic could succeed, but it did and within a month the North Koreans were all but defeated. Unfortunately for the allies, the tide turned again in November of the same year when large numbers of Chinese troops stormed across the border.

Today, the Chinese are crossing the sea to South Korea, though now they have tourist or business visas. There are sailors from Russia and elsewhere – Incheon is a cosmopolitan city with docks full of container ships and giant cranes. With a subway system, historical buildings, a reborn Chinatown, new shopping malls and underground shopping arcades, the city is worth a visit.

Incheon has its own metropolitan government, is not part of Gyeonggi-do and has its own telephone code number. Ganghwado and other West Sea islands are also part of the Incheon municipality.

Information
The principal **tourist information centre** (☎ 430 7257; ☼ 10am-noon & 1-6pm) is outside Incheon subway station and the staff are very helpful. Smaller ones are in the bus terminal and on **Wolmido promenade** (☎ 765 4169; ☼ 10am-noon & 1-6pm).

Sights
Songdo Resort (☎ 832 0011; admission W3000) has a fairground with thrill rides, paddle boats, a water slide and swimming in a large saltwater lake that is popular in summer.

A Big Three ticket is W10,000, a Big Five ticket W15,000.

Also in Songdo is the **Incheon Landing Memorial Monument Hall** (☎ 832 0915; admission free; ⏰ 9am-6.30pm Tue-Sun, to 5pm Nov-Feb). Old newsreel films of the Korean War reveal the ugly reality of modern warfare. Sixteen countries sent troops or medical units to

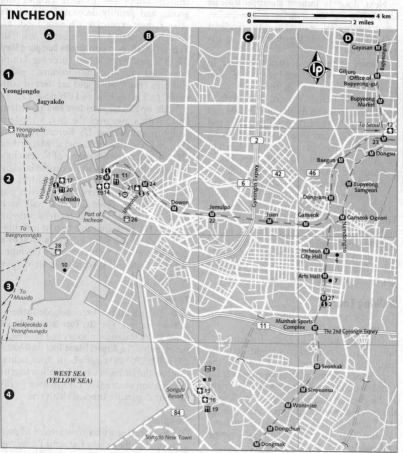

INCHEON

help South Korea, and 70,000 UN and South Korean troops took part in the surprise landing in Incheon in 1950, supported by 260 warships.

Next door is **Incheon Municipal Museum** (☎ 832 2570; adult/child W400/free; ☯ 9am-6pm Tue-Sun, to 5pm Nov-Feb), which has an excellent collection of celadon pottery that spans 19 centuries.

Wolmido is the most attractive place in Incheon and enjoys sea breezes. A wide promenade along the seafront with views of boats and islands is lined with seafood restaurants (raw fish meals are W50,000 and are meant to be shared), bars, smart cafés and an outdoor concert area. In summer young people gather here in the evening to listen to music, drink alcohol and let off fireworks.

An amusement park has the usual rides for around W3000 each. The *Harmony* and *Cosmos* pleasure boats (W10,000; hourly from 11am to 7pm) leave from the promenade. They are popular with middle-aged Koreans, and offer a 1½-hour cruise with live music and Bulgarian dancing girls. Frequent ferries leave from here to Yeongjongdo, the airport island (see Tours later) which has a popular spa, beach and seafood restaurants.

Walking Tour
The walk is only 2km and takes an hour, but more if you linger and explore.

Take the subway to Dong-Incheon station (**1**), come out and go straight along the main road, Uhyeonno. Head down to the huge **Sinpo underground shopping arcade** (**2**) for a look around but don't get lost. Turn right at the pop art archway (**4**), and walk past the covered market and fashionable shops (**5**). Turn right again at Korea First bank (**6**) and walk past three **historical Japanese bank buildings** (**7**, **8**, **9**), which date back to the 1890s when Korea was opened up to foreign companies.

At the end of the road is **Chinatown**, which is being improved with a grand Chinese entrance gate, lamp posts and murals. It dates back to 1883 and has a Chinese school and church. Shops sell Chinese clothes and goods, and gaudily decorated restaurants offer rather expensive Chinese food, although set meals provide a better deal. For a cheap snack, pop into **Wonbo Dumpling Shop** (**10**; 원보; meals W3000-10,000). Three big dumplings filled with meat, mushrooms, noodles and tofu cost W3000 and are served with sauce, pickled onions and Chinese tea.

Walk up the steps to **Jayu Park** (Freedom Park) with views over the city, a modern sculpture celebrating US-Korean relations (**11**) and a statue of General MacArthur (**12**), who changed the course of Korean history with his daring and successful landing at Incheon in 1950 which resulted in the North Korean invaders being driven out of South Korea. From the park, walk back down to Chinatown and Incheon subway station (**13**), next door to a tourist information office. If you want a drink, a meal or a gamble, pop over to the Paradise Olympos Hotel & Casino (**14**) which has views over the busy port.

Tours
You can pick up two tours outside Incheon subway station. The **City Tour** (adult/youth/child W1000/500/300) takes four hours and runs eight times daily. The **Airport Island Tour** (adult/youth/child W4000/3000/1300) takes about three hours. Contact the Incheon subway station tourist information centre (see Information p128) for tour departure times which vary.

Sleeping
Old-fashioned *yeogwan* are scattered all over Incheon, but they cluster around Bupyeong subway station (take Exit 6 and walk towards the golf driving range) and in Wolmido and Songdo.

NEAR INCHEON SUBWAY STATION
Paradise Olympos Hotel (☎ 762 5181; fax 763 581; d/tw incl tax & service W205,000/216,000; ☒ ▢) Built on a hill overlooking the port, this long-established hotel, a short walk from Incheon subway station, has a small **casino** (admission free; ☯ 24hr), which is for foreigners only. Steak meals cost W36,000 in the Western-style restaurant.

Hongkong Motel (☎ 777 9001; s & d W25,000; ❄)
One of the best budget options, with an elevator and smartish rooms with cable TV, it faces the Paradise Olympos Hotel.

NEAR BUPYEONG SUBWAY STATION
Plaza Motel (☎ 522 5855; s & d W35,000, Fri & Sat W45,000; ❄) This has the best rooms but is a love hotel, and the staff are not very helpful or friendly.

Bando Yeoinsuk (☎ 522 1767; ondol W20,000; ❄)
It has en suite rooms with *yeogwan*-style facilities.

WOLMIDO
A number of motels are dotted around Wolmido, including **Utopia Motel** (☎ 434 4351; s & d W30,000, Fri & Sat W35,000; ❄) and **Sopia Motel** (☎ 773 1783; s & d W25,000; ❄).

SONGDO
Hilltop Hotel (☎ 834 3500; s & d W40,000; ❄) A good budget option.

Songdo Beach Hotel (☎ 830 2200; www.songdo beach.co.kr; s, d & tw W190,000; ❄) The luxury choice with three restaurants, a sauna and gym, business centre and an Internet line in every room. Prices may rise in summer.

Eating
WOLMIDO
The waterfront is decked out with raw fish and seafood restaurants that boast a sea view from the second floor. Your selection of cuisine here is limited only by the size of your wallet. Prices are high but dishes are meant for sharing and you can order *gongibap* (steamed rice) to cut down on the number of seafood dishes.

SONGDO
Restaurants in this touristy neighbourhood tend to be more Western than Korean but by Songdo Beach Hotel is **Multeombeong** (meals W20,000), which offers fish and crab meals.

Getting There & Away
BOAT
Yeon-an Pier and International Ferry Terminal 2 are the departure points for regular international ferries to a number of Chinese cities – see p379. Yeon-an pier also has a domestic ferry terminal where boats leave for Jeju-do (W46,000 to W90,000) and 14 of the larger inhabited islands in the West Sea,

which cost from W5500 to W24,700 depending on the distance and the speed of the ferry. A more frequent service is provided in summer when many holidaymakers head out to the beaches and seafood restaurants on these attractive and relaxing islands. A regular ferry (W1500, 25 minutes, every 20 minutes from 6am to 9.30pm) runs from Wolmido promenade to Yeongjongdo (p134).

BUS
From Seoul, it's faster, cheaper and easier to take the subway to Incheon. But from other cities it is not necessary to go to Seoul first, as there are direct buses to Incheon. From Incheon you can get a bus to:

Destination	Price (W)	Duration	Frequency
Cheonan	6000	1½hr	every 30min
Cheongju	8300	2hr	every 30min
Chuncheon	9900	3hr	hourly
Gongju	9500	2½hr	every 1½hr
Incheon Int'l Airport	5000	1hr	every 30min
Jeonju	10,300	3hr	hourly
Suwon	3400	1hr	every 20min

The bus terminal has a Shinsegae department store, chemist shop, post office, cinema and a tourist information centre.

TRAIN
Take subway Line 1 from Seoul (W1100) which takes around 70 minutes. Incheon has its own subway system, which doesn't cover the tourist areas, but does go to the bus terminal.

Getting Around
BUS & TAXI
Buses (W700) and taxis leave from outside Dong-Incheon and Incheon subway stations.

To get to Songdo, hop on bus No 6, 9 or 16, or take a taxi (W5000).

To get to Wolmido, it's a 20-minute walk from Incheon subway station or a W1500 taxi ride.

To get to Yeon-an Pier, take bus No 12, 24 or 28, or hail a taxi (W4500).

To get to International Ferry Terminal No 2, take bus No 23 or a taxi (W1600). If you go to the wrong ferry terminal a taxi between the two costs W5000.

Bus No 306 goes to Yeongjongdo (W3600, every 20 minutes), the airport island, where Yeongjongdo market and Eulwangni Beach are worth a visit – see p132.

SUBWAY

Incheon has one subway line, running in a north–south direction. It intersects with the KNR line at Bupyeong station, where there is Lotte Mart, an underground shopping arcade, a budget food court, cinemas and a cluster of older-style *yeogwan*. If you arrive at Incheon bus terminal, you can walk down to the subway station. The basic subway fare is W700 and Seoul subway cards can be used on the Incheon line.

ISLAND HOPPING IN THE WEST SEA

Sandy beaches, sea views, rural scenery, vineyards, fresh air and fresh seafood – the West Sea islands are a different world to Seoul. There are dozens of islands that are technically part of the Incheon municipality, even though it can take hours to reach them by boat. The islands are mostly rocky, though there are a few excellent sandy beaches hidden in coves. On some islands are rare smooth-stone beaches. The stones are called *mongdol*, and it takes centuries of tidal action to produce them. It is illegal to collect these stones, so don't try to take any home with you.

For the Koreans, a major reason to visit the islands is to indulge in a raw fish (*saengseonhoe*) culinary safari. Island restaurant menus typically include vinegared rice with raw fish (*saengseonchobap*), broiled fish (*saengseongui*) and spicy fish soup (*maeuntang*). If seafood appeals to you, be sure to ask the price first – the species of fish as well as the season and the cooking (or noncooking) method greatly influence the price, which can vary from reasonable to outrageous.

Before embarking for the islands, stock up with sufficient cash – money-changing facilities and ATMs are next to nonexistent in this far-flung corner of Korea.

Minbak (private homes with rooms for rent) and *yeogwan* cost W20,000 to W30,000 but prices double in July and August when the island beaches become crowded. However at other times (even warm weekends in June and September) you'll probably have the beach to yourself.

Yeongjongdo & Muuido
영종도, 무의도

Although Yeongjongdo is home to Korea's busiest international airport, the western beaches are not disturbed by the air traffic. The seafood market at Yeongjongdo Wharf and a flashy seawater hot spa are other popular attractions. In the north of the island Airport Town Square has been developed with half a dozen new mid-range hotels, a guesthouse and apartments for airport workers.

At **Yeongjongdo Wharf Market** they sell fish, shellfish, crabs and other seafood, which nearby restaurants will cook and serve for you – see Eating p134.

Behind the market, take bus No 202 (W1200, 20 minutes, hourly) and ask the bus driver to drop you near Jamjindo if you want to visit Muuido. From the bus stop walk over the causeway from Yeongjongdo to the islet of **Jamjindo** (잠진도), and enjoy the sea and island views. A 15-minute walk brings you to the small ferry to Muuido, which costs W1000 and leaves at least every hour.

On **Muuido Wharf**, try a delicious fresh shellfish barbecue – a big bowl costs W25,000 (feeds three or four people) and octopus *pajeon* (green-onion pancake) is W4000. Then it's a 10-minute walk to the fishing village, where you can turn right and walk over the hill past cherry trees and grapevines for 15 minutes to **Keunmuri Resort** (큰무리 리조트, admission Jun & Sep/Jul & Aug W1000/2000, huts W30,000/42,000) where there are camp sites, pine trees, a sandy beach and a swimming pool. At low tide you can walk across to the unspoilt and uninhabited islet of **Silmido** (실미도).

Return the same way you came, and on Yeongjongdo you can catch a bus or hitch a lift to the popular western beaches. **Eulwangni Beach** (을왕리 해수욕장) is 10 minutes from the Jamjindo drop-off point by bus, and has new motels, *minbak*, *noraebang* (karaoke rooms) and many restaurants. This beach is the most popular because the sea doesn't recede at low tide leaving behind huge mud flats, as it does along most of the west coast. For a quieter beach, walk north to **Wangsan Beach** (왕산 해수욕장). The western beaches, set among rice fields and vineyards, are attractive (nearby Incheon International Airport doesn't affect them). Bus No 306 (W1300, 15 minutes, every 30 minutes) runs between Eulwangni and the airport.

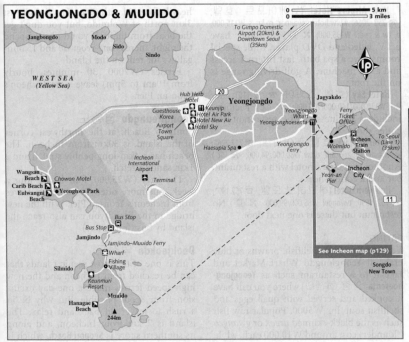

GYEONGGI-DO

Haesupia Spa (해수피아 스파; ☎ 886 5800; adult/child W6000/4000; ✆ 6am-8pm) is a luxury seawater hot spa with nice views and restaurants, located on the road between Yeongjongdo Wharf and Jamjindo. Shuttle buses run there from Yeongjongdo Wharf.

SLEEPING
Eulwangni Beach
A wide range of accommodation is available by Eulwangni Beach – everything from small bare rooms to luxury suites with a balcony.

Yeonghwa Park (영화 파크; ☎ 746 1118; s & d W30,000; ✖) This reasonably priced option has a friendly owner and is behind the beachside camping ground and pine trees. Prices double in July and August and balcony rooms are W10,000 extra.

Chowon Motel (초원 모텔; ☎ 746 3369; s & d W30,000; ✖) This has small but modern rooms right on the beach, but prices double in summer.

Carib Beach (카리브 모텔; ☎ 751 5455; s & d W40,000-80,000, 50% more Fri & Sat) This brand new ship-shape luxury hotel has a range of high quality, light rooms with great views.

Airport Town Square
Airport Town Square is a new town that has been built on Yeongjongdo a few kilometres from the airport. It has restaurants, hotels and shops, and is surrounded by apartment blocks. All the accommodation is brand new. Bus Nos 223 (W700, 10 minutes, every 30 minutes) and 203 (W1200, 10 minutes, every 30 minutes) run between Airport Town Square and Incheon International Airport. There is also a free shuttle bus service (10 daily). Some hotels provide a free pick-up or drop-off service to and from the airport, but others charge up to W20,000. Bus No 111-1 runs between Town Square and Incheon city.

Guesthouse Korea (게스트하우스코리아; ☎ 747 1872; www.guesthousekorea.co.kr; dm/s/d W20,000/35,000/45,000; ✖ ▣) This unusual and luxurious guesthouse has large, light, modern motel-style rooms on the 10th floor of a high-rise building opposite Hub Herb Hotel. Rooms have en suite facilities, cable TV and fully-equipped kitchens. Free Internet and a free pick-up from the airport are also provided.

New Airport Hotel (뉴에어포트 호텔; ☎ 752 2066; www.hotelnewairport.co.kr; s W115,000, d, tw & ondol W135,000; ⊠ ⬚) All rooms have a TV, video and DVD player, while special rooms have a spa bath, fast Internet access and a fax machine. A golf driving range is on the roof.

Hotel Sky (호텔 스카이; ☎ 752 1101; d/tw/ ste W130,000/140,000/200,000; ⊠ ⬚) Facilities include a business centre, restaurant and coffee shop.

Hotel Air Park (호텔 에어파크; ☎ 752 2266; www.hotel.airpark.com; d/tw W80,000/94,000; ⊠ ⬚) Another brand new hotel with a restaurant, bar and a coffee shop.

Hub Herb Hotel (허브허브 모텔; ☎ 752 1991; fax 752 1990; tw/ondol W88,000/99,000; ⊠ ⬚) No restaurant but there is one next door.

EATING

You can buy fish, shellfish, prawns or blue crabs at Yeongjongdo Wharf Market and take it to a restaurant such as **Yeongjong-hoesenta** (영종 회센타) where you can have it cooked and served with quail eggs and shellfish soup for W5000. Popular raw fish such as the black-skinned *ureok* or *gwangeo* (flounder) cost around W10,000 each, while prawns or blue crab are around W20,000 per kg. It's a much better deal than you get in Wolmido.

Keunjip (큰집; meals W5000-10,000) This restaurant in Airport Town Square cooks up a tasty *ppyeohaejangguk*, a hotpot of big meaty bones served with rice.

GETTING THERE & AWAY

To visit Yeongjongdo and Muuido, take subway Line 1 to Incheon station and then a taxi (W1500) to Wolmido. On the promenade is the ticket office for the car ferry to Yeongjongdo. The adult fare is W1500 for the 20-minute trip and ferries run every half hour from 7am to 9.30pm daily. An alternative way to or from Muuido is by a high-speed ferry (W8900, 20 minutes, 10.30am) or regular ferry (W5650, one hour, 8am and 5pm) which travel between Incheon's Yeon-an Pier and the port on the south of Muuido island.

Jagyakdo 작약도

In summer the landscape of this tiny island is decked out with peonies (*jagyak*), thus the island's name. The island is also heavily forested with pines. Jagyakdo is just 3km north of Wolmido, but you don't get the boat from there. If you'd like to spend the night, there is one *yeogwan* and 15 bungalows for rent on the island.

Ferries (W7000, 30 minutes, hourly from 10am to 5pm) leave from Incheon's Yeon-an Pier.

Yeongheungdo 영흥도

Simnipo Beach, at the northwest corner of the island, is 30km from Incheon. The beach has a 4km-long pebbly stretch and a 1km sandy stretch.

The ferry (W25,000, four hours, four a week, but more often in summer) leaves from Incheon's Yeon-an Pier. With the new bridge to the island you can also reach the island by bus (four a day).

Deokjeokdo 덕적도

This is one of the most scenic islands that can be reached from Incheon and the new high-speed ferries make a one-day excursion from Seoul possible. But why be in a rush to leave? Sit back and relax. The island is 77km from Incheon, and along its southern shore is **Seopori Beach**, which is 2km long and lined with a thick grove of 200-year-old pine trees. The beach is spectacular, and easily the most popular on the island. The island also has many unusual rock formations, and it's worth climbing the highest peak, Bijobong (292m) for the grand view. There are plenty of *yeogwan* and *minbak* as well as a camping ground at Seopori Beach.

No matter which ferry you take, you will be dropped off at Jinri Pier on Deokjeokdo. From there, it's a 20-minute bus ride to Seopori Beach. The high-speed ferry (W17,500, 50 minutes, 9.30am and 3pm) is the best option, although there is a cheaper regular ferry (W12,000, 2½ hours, 1.30pm and 7.30pm).

Baengnyeongdo 백령도

Far to the northwest of Incheon and within a stone's throw of North Korea is Baengnyeongdo, a scenic island that is attracting an increasing number of tourists. The island is South Korea's westernmost point and is notable for its remoteness and dramatic coastal **rock formations** – taking a tour around the island by boat to view these unusual rock shapes is a 'must do'. Baengnyeongdo is 12km long and about 7km wide. There is a significant military presence on the island, a necessity with North Korea only 11km away, but this shouldn't interfere with your enjoyment of the place – just don't climb over any barbed-wire fences.

Sagot Beach is one of Baengnyeongdo's unexpected sights. The beach is 3km long and consists of sand packed so hard that people can (and do) drive cars on it. In contrast, some of the other beaches in the area are pebble. The Koreans like to walk barefoot on the pebbles or even lie down on them because they believe that the resulting 'acupressure' is good for their health.

Aside from seafood, the island produces buckwheat, which is used to make buckwheat noodles, and fields of buckwheat flowers blooming in springtime are a fantastic sight.

Yeogwan, yeoinsuk and *minbak* are easy to find – you should have some offers upon arrival at the ferry pier.

The island is served by a high-speed ferry (W43,700, four hours, twice daily) and a regular ferry (W29,500, eight hours, once daily). They both leave from Incheon's Yeon-an Pier.

GANGHWADO 강화도

☎ 032 / pop 67,000 / 319 sq km

Part of the Incheon municipality, Ganghwado is still a rural island of rice fields and forested hills despite being connected to the mainland by two bridges. The island, strategically placed at the mouth of the Han River, has played a major role in Korean history. When the Mongols invaded Korea in 1232, the Goryeo king and court fled here, and stayed nearly 40 years until 1270. In the 1860s and 1870s French, American and Japanese warships separately attacked and invaded the island.

Attractions include numerous small fortifications, one of Korea's largest dolmen (a prehistoric burial chamber) which is a World Heritage monument, Manisan with an ancient stone altar on its summit, and a 10km coastal bicycle track. A short ferry trip away on Seongmodo is one of the country's most important temples, Bomunsa.

Only 100 minutes from Seoul by bus, the island is a laid-back rural retreat with numerous seafood restaurants.

Ganghwa-eup 강화읍

The main town, Ganghwa-eup, is just 2km beyond the northern bridge and is a good base for visiting the island's attractions.

The **tourist information centre** (☎ 930 3515; www.ganghwa.incheon.kr; ☺ 9am-6pm) in the bus terminal has helpful English-speaking staff.

A palace surrounded by an 18km **fortress wall** was built in 1231, and 2km of walls and three major gates have been renovated. The fortress was destroyed in 1866 by French troops who invaded Korea in response to the execution of nine French Catholic missionaries. The French army burnt many priceless books and took 300 back to France where they still remain.

The **market** near the bus terminal sells locally grown ginseng and *hwamunseok* (화문석), which are large reed mats with floral designs that are beautiful but very expensive. Woven baskets are cheaper, easier to transport and have similar designs.

The accommodation nearest the bus terminal, **Hyatt Hotel** (하얏트 호텔; ☎ 932 4422; fax 934 3078; s & d W30,000, Sat & Sun W35,000; ✵) has large comfortable rooms and a friendly owner. Turn left outside the bus terminal and it's a 10-minute walk along the main road.

Namsan Youth Hostel (남산 유스호스텔; ☎ 934 7777; dm/f W12,000/40,000) offers a cheap bed for solo travellers but is a 20-minute, 2km walk southwest of the bus terminal, so you might want to take a taxi.

Other *yeogwan* are scattered around the town centre.

Hwangganehotteok (황가네 호떡; meals W2000-6000), in the bus terminal, sells a box of *dakgangjeong* (boneless chicken pieces in a tangy sauce), red-bean *hotteok* (pitta bread), *odeng* (processed seafood stick, W500) and *sundae*.

GETTING THERE & AWAY

Buses to Ganghwa-eup (W3900, 1½ hours, every 10 minutes from 5.25am to 9.45pm) leave from Sinchon bus terminal (see Map p78) in Seoul.

Around Ganghwa-eup

GANGHWA HISTORY HALL 황가네 호떡

A small but modern **museum** (☎ 933 2178; adult/youth & child W1300/700; ☺ 9am-6pm, 9am-5pm Nov-Feb) reveals the island's interesting history and is located near a fortification

(Gapgot Dondae) close to the northern bridge. If you want to visit ask the bus driver to drop you off there rather than in Ganghwa-eup bus terminal.

A new cycle path starts here and goes to Gwangseongbo, 10km away along the coast (see next). Mountain bikes can be hired from the **bicycle rental shop** (☎ 933 3692; mountain bike/tandem W2000/4000 per hour, W8000/16,000 per day) but must be returned by 6pm. There are some eel restaurants along the way.

Buses (W700, five minutes, every 1½ hours from 6.20am to 7.45pm) go from the museum to Ganghwa-eup bus terminal, which is 2km away. Otherwise hitching a lift into town should not be a problem.

Gwangseongbo 광성보

There are numerous small fortifications dotted around the coast but **Gwangseongbo** (☎ 937 4480; adult/child W1100/800; ⏰ 9am-6pm) is the largest. Located in the southeast, it was built in 1658 and has been recently renovated. Attacked by the French in 1866, the Americans in 1871 and the Japanese in 1875, it has seen plenty of action.

Buses go from Ganghwa-eup to Gwangseongbo and other nearby fortifications (W3000, 30 minutes, every 1½ hours from 6.20am to 7.45pm). However the best way to visit is to cycle along the coast from Ganghwa History Hall (see previous entry).

Manisan 마니산

This **park** (☎ 937 1624; adult/youth/child W1500/800/ 500; ⏰ 6am-6pm) is in the southwest of the island, 14km from Ganghwa-eup. On the 468m summit is **Chamseongdan** (참성단), a large stone altar said to have been originally built and used by Dangun, the mythical first Korean, who was born in 2333 BC. Every 3 October, National Foundation Day which is a public holiday, a colourful shamanist ceremony is held there. The 3km walk to the top from the bus stop includes over 900 steps, takes an hour and on a fine day the views are splendid.

Buses from Ganghwa-eup run to Manisan (W1300, 30 minutes, every 50 minutes from 6.50am to 7.30pm).

Jeondeungsa 전등사

This **temple** (☎ 937 0125; adult/youth/child W1800/ 1300/1000; ⏰ 6am-sunset) built inside a fortress

is famous for the wooden blocks of Buddhist scriptures, the Tripitaka Koreana, that were carved here between 1235 and 1251 and later moved to Haeinsa Temple (see p175).

Bugeun-ri Dolmen 부근리 고인돌

The biggest **dolmen** (admission free; ⏰ 24hr) on Ganghwado is an impressive sight and has a top stone weighing more than 50 tonnes. Replicas of other ancient relics such as Stonehenge and the Easter Island statues can be seen there too. The site can be visited by bus (W700, 15 minutes, hourly from 6.20am to 8pm).

Oepo-ri 외포리

Oepo-ri, a fishing village on the west coast 13km from Ganghwa-eup, has reasonable prices in its seafood market and there are plenty of restaurants and *yeogwan*. It's also the terminal for the ferry to Seongmodo (석모도), where the main attraction is the temple Bomunsa.

Oepo Park Motel (외포 파크 모텔; ☎ 932 8086; s & d W30,000, Sat W40,000; ❄) This is the nearest accommodation to the port with smart rooms and seaviews from the top floors.

Ganghwa Youth Hostel (강화 유스호스텔; ☎ 933 8891; fax 933 9335; dm/f W12,000/55,000) Recommended for budget solo travellers.

Buses from Ganghwa-eup (W1100, 30 minutes, every 30 minutes from 6.40am to 6.40pm) take a scenic cross-island route.

Bomunsa 보문사

Situated high in the forested hills of Seongmodo island, this **temple** (☎ 933 8271; adult/youth/child W1500/1200/800; ⏰ 7am-7pm) has some superbly ornate painting on the eaves of its various buildings. The grotto and 10m rock carving are stand-out features. Korean women come here to pray for sons and the Korean grandmothers you see are not praying for sons for themselves but for their daughters. Resorts and restaurants are dotted around the island's coastline.

Ferries (☎ 932 6007) depart Oepo-ri for Seongmodo (adult/child W600/300, 10 minutes, every 30 minutes) between 7am and 8.30pm. The ferry also transports cars (W14,000 return). On Seongmodo a bus (W1000) takes you to near the temple but it's a steep climb up.

PANMUNJEOM & THE DMZ TOUR
판문점

Situated 55km north of Seoul, the truce village of Panmunjeom is the only place in the Demilitarized Zone (DMZ) where visitors are permitted. This is the village established on the ceasefire line at the end of the Korean War in 1953. In the blue UN buildings in Panmunjeom, peace discussions still take place.

There's nowhere else in South Korea where you can get so close to North Korea and North Korean soldiers without being arrested or shot, and the tension is palpable. Occasionally gun battles erupt in this frontier village – the last one was in 1984 when a Russian defector escaped from the North to the South. But more recent shots have been fired in other parts of the DMZ – in November 2001 and as recently as July 2003.

Other chilling incidents have occurred here and are described by the US military personnel who conduct the tour within the DMZ, a strip of land 4km wide and 240km long, that divides the two Koreas and is one of the most heavily fortified borders in the world. High fences topped with barbed wire, watchtowers, antitank obstacles and minefields line both sides of the DMZ.

More than 5000 US and South Korean troops live in Camp Bonifas which is 'In Front of Them All' and would face the brunt of any surprise attack from the North. However there are plans to pull the American troops back to a base further south.

There are only two villages in the DMZ, and they're both near Panmunjeom – and within hailing distance of each other if you

---

DMZ NATIONAL PARK?

The DMZ separates North and South Korea. It is 4km wide and 248km long, surrounded by tanks and electrified fences, and is virtually sealed off to all people. Ironically, this has made it something of an environmental haven. No other place in the world with a temperate zone climate has been so well preserved. This has been a great boon to wildlife – for example, the DMZ is home to large flocks of Manchurian cranes. Environmentalists hope that the day the two Koreas cease hostilities, the DMZ will be kept as a nature reserve.

---

have a big enough loudspeaker. On the south side is Daesong, a subsidised village with a church and high tax-free incomes. Each family there lives in a modern house with a high-speed Internet connection and each farms seven hectares. All 230 residents must be at home by the 11pm curfew, and soldiers stand guard while the villagers work in the rice fields or tend their ginseng plants.

The North Korean village, Gijong, is even more unusual because all the buildings are empty and always have been. It's a ghost town whose only function is to broadcast propaganda to anyone around for six to 12 hours a day, using ultrapowerful loudspeakers as big as a house that any rock band would love to own.

The village also has an Eiffel Tower-like structure, 160m high, flying a flag that weighs nearly 300kg. The North Korean flag is larger than the one on the South Korean side. Giant *hangeul* letters on the northern hillsides spell out slogans such as 'Follow the way of the Leader', while on the South Korean side the message 'Freedom, Abundance and Happiness' is lit up at night.

Panmunjeom is where important diplomatic talks are still held. On the South Korean side is a pagoda-style building, from where you can look down on the three blue UN buildings that straddle the border. On the North Korean side is a large concrete building, guarded by soldiers, and some watchtowers.

The tour includes a visit inside one of the UN buildings, which looks like a temporary classroom with simple tables and chairs. Both sides constantly monitor the rooms so everything you say can be overheard. On the ceasefire line soldiers from the North and South stand only centimetres apart. The South Korean soldiers stand guard in an unusual 'taekwondo' stance. Despite the South's 'sunshine policy' this is still a dangerous and frightening front line and visiting it is a sobering experience that will give you a lot to think about. See the excellent film *JSA* for a dramatic story set in the DMZ about what happens when ordinary soldiers from both sides meet by accident.

Getting There & Away
Access to Panmunjeom is permitted for tour groups only – this is not a do-it-yourself trip. You must have your passport or

---

THE UNDERGROUND WAR

A brass plaque in Panmunjeom gives the following account of the North Koreans' tunnelling activities; since it was put up, a fourth tunnel extending 1km into South Korean territory was discovered in 1990.

On 15 November 1974, members of a Republic of Korea Army (ROKA) patrol inside the southern sector of the DMZ spotted vapour rising from the ground. When they began to dig into the ground to investigate, they were fired upon by North Korean snipers. ROKA units secured the site and subsequently uncovered a tunnel dug by the North Koreans which extended 1.2km into the Republic of Korea. On 20 November, two members of the United Nations Command (UNC) investigation team were killed inside the tunnel when dynamite planted by the North Koreans exploded. The briefing hall at Camp Kitty Hawk is named after one of the officers killed, Lieutenant Commander Robert N Ballinger.

In March 1975, a second North Korean tunnel was discovered by a UNC tunnel detection team. In September of 1975, a North Korean engineer escaped and provided valuable intelligence concerning the communist tunnelling activities. Acting on the information, a tunnel-detection team successfully intercepted a third tunnel in October 1978, less than 2km from Panmunjeom.

Today the North Koreans continue to dig tunnels beneath the DMZ. The UN and ROKA have fielded tunnel-detection teams, which drill around the clock in hope of intercepting these tunnels of aggression.

---

you won't be allowed to board the tour bus. There's also a dress and behaviour code, and before you enter the DMZ all visitors must sign a document absolving the UN and the South Korean government of responsibility in case of any injuries due to 'enemy action' while on the tour.

The **United Services Organization** (USO; ☎ 724 7003; www.uso.org/korea), the US army's social and entertainment organisation at the Yongsan base, runs twice-weekly tours that cost US$40 and include the Third Tunnel, but not lunch. They start early at 7.30am and finish at 3pm. To reach the USO take subway Line 1 to Namyeong station.

Half-day tours with Korean companies cost around W40,000 and full-day tours cost around W60,000. Ensure they include Panmunjeom. On these tours your Korean guide will accompany you to Camp Bonifas on the southern side of the DMZ, where your group will eat lunch. You are then given a slide show and briefing by an American soldier, who will accompany your group on a military bus into the Joint Security Area of Panmunjeom.

Not all the tours are the same. Some include a visit to the Third Tunnel which was dug by the North Koreans. Visiting the tunnel is worthwhile and you should make sure it's included in the tour before handing

over the cash. A tour with a difference is one that doesn't include Panmunjeom but is accompanied by a North Korean defector. You can ask him any question you want through an interpreter. See p95 or visit KNTO (Map pp72–4) for brochures and details on the different tour options, but most foreigners take the USO tour.

ODUSAN UNIFICATION OBSERVATORY
오두산 통일 공원

The **Unification Observatory** (Tongil Jeonmangdae ☎ 945 3171; adult/student & senior W1500/1000 ⏱ 9am-7.30pm, 9am-6pm Nov-Feb) at Odusan is as close as most Korean civilians can get to the DMZ. Panmunjeom, north of Seoul, is actually inside the DMZ and can be visited by foreigners, but Korean civilians are not normally allowed there.

Since the Unification Observatory does offer South Koreans a rare peek at the forbidden North, tourists by the bus load turn up there daily throughout the summer months. It isn't quite the same as going to Panmunjeom – there's little of the palpable tension evident at Panmunjeom's 'Truce Village', since the Unification Observatory isn't actually in the DMZ but a few kilometres away. If you want to see anything at all (such as the UN post, the North Korean post – only just – and the North's propaganda signs) you have to use the available pay telescopes for viewing. It's essentially a non-event but it's a pleasant day out, the government lays on a free slide show and there is a shop selling goods made in North Korea (goods which the average North Korean cannot buy).

Getting There & Away

From Seoul's Seobu bus terminal in Bulgwang-dong, take a bus (50 minutes, every 40 minutes) to Geumchon (buses to Munsan stop in Geumchon). Or from Seoul station, take a train to Geumchon (one hour, hourly). From Geumchon bus station, take a local bus (30 minutes, every 40 minutes) to the Unification Observatory (these buses are marked Songdong-ri).

SKI RESORTS

Gyeonggi-do has a handful of ski resorts within easy reach of Seoul (an hour or less by bus) and they all provide shuttle buses (around W12,000 return) to and from the capital during the ski season from December to February. Travel agents sell package deals that include transport, accommodation, ski equipment hire and lift passes. Some Koreans ski and snowboard like they drive, so expect a few bumps. The resorts' telephone numbers and the numbers of their Seoul offices:

Bears Town Resort (☎ 02-594 8188, 031-532 2534; www.bearstown.com) 50 minutes northeast of Seoul, has 11 slopes, two sledding hills and nine lifts. Accommodation includes a youth hostel and a condominium; facilities include a supermarket, heated pool, sauna, bowling alley and tennis courts. English-speaking instructors, snowboarding and night skiing are available. USO, the American troops' activities organisation, runs ski tours to this resort which anyone is welcome to join. The resort also has its own golf course to attract visitors outside the winter period.

Cheonmasan Ski Resort (☎ 02-2233 5311, 346-594 1211; www.chonmaski.com) 40 minutes northeast of Seoul, has five slopes and seven lifts. The hotel has a heated pool and English-speaking instructors are available.

Jisan Forest Ski Resort (☎ 02-3442 0322, 031-638 8460; www.jisan.resort.co.kr) 60 minutes southeast of Seoul, has nine slopes, snowboarding slopes and four lifts. English-speaking instructors are available.

Seoul Ski Resort (☎ 02-959 0864, 031-592 1220) 40 minutes east of Seoul, has four slopes, three lifts, a sledding hill, and hotel accommodation (66 rooms).

Yangji Pine Ski Resort (☎ 02-542 8700, 033-5338 2001; www.pineresort.com) 50 minutes southeast of Seoul, has seven slopes, one sledding hill and six lifts. Accommodation is in a hotel or condominium and the latter has a heated pool and bowling alley.

Gangwon-do
강원도

CONTENTS

The northeast province of Gangwon-do (www.gangwon.to) is one of the least populated, most mountainous and scenic in South Korea. Historically, the province has been isolated due to its rugged terrain, and during the Korean War it was the site of many fierce battles for strategic mountain tops. After the war, the area's rich natural resources, including coal and timber, were industrialised, bringing road and rail links. With the closure of many of the coal mines during the 1990s, the province was forced to create alternative employment opportunities. Tourism was the solution.

Outdoor activities reign supreme here, with spectacular mountain and valley hiking, swimming at beautiful white-sand beaches, down-hill and cross-country skiing, white-water rafting, and plenty of peaceful fishing spots, all of which are accessible by bus. Public transport is good and the roads are probably the quietest in the country except in July and August when crowds flock to the east-coast beaches, and accommodation prices double. Most of the more beautiful parts of the province are found in obscure valleys with dramatic gorges, raging rivers and dense forests, although the sandy coves and rocky headlands south of Samcheok provide alternatives that include sea views. Seoraksan is the most outstanding of the province's three national parks, but popular areas can be overrun with visitors.

GANGWON-DO

HIGHLIGHTS

- Hike around the splendours of **Seoraksan National Park** (p151)
- Tour the presidential summer houses and relax on the beach at **Hwajinpo** (p150)
- Marvel at the limestone formations in **Hwanseondonggul** (p161), a cave near Samcheok
- Tour unusual marine attractions in **Jeongdongjin** (p157)
- Cycle along the lakeside at **Chuncheon** (p142) as the sun sets behind the hills
- Explore the Coal Museum and Dangun's mountain-top altar in **Taebaeksan Provincial Park** (p162)
- View the artistic Buddhist treasures at **Woljeongsa** (p155) and **Sangwonsa** (p155) in Odaesan National Park

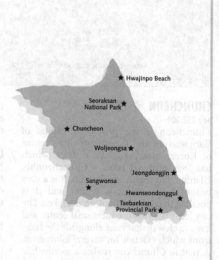

■ TELEPHONE CODE: 033　　■ POPULATION: 1.6 MILLION　　■ AREA: 16,874 SQ KM

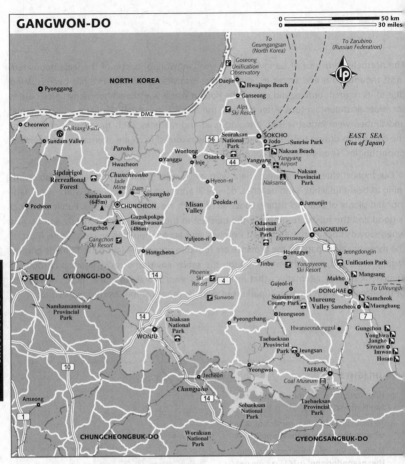

GANGWON-DO

CHUNCHEON 춘천

pop 252,000

Chuncheon is the provincial capital of Gangwon-do and the metropolitan centre of Korea's northern lake district, which has four artificial lakes – Chuncheonho, Uiamho, Soyangho and Paroho. It is a very beautiful mountainous region and it is possible to take boat trips on the lakes. The city itself is a major educational centre and has a cycleway that runs alongside the lakefront which extends for several kilometres. A visit to Chuncheon makes a worthwhile stopover en route to Sokcho and Seoraksan National Park, especially if you prefer the boat and bus combination to taking a bus for the entire way. Every May the Interna-

tional Mime Festival comes to town an diverse troupes of entertainers transcen the language barrier.

Orientation

Nam (South) Chuncheon train station i the main station, but it is located som distance from the town centre and the bu terminal.

Information

A large and helpful **tourist information centr** (☎ 244 0088; www.iccn.co.kr; ☺ 9am-6pm, 9am-5p Nov-Feb) is near the bus terminal and ha brochures on the whole of Gangwon-d and free Internet access. A smaller office near the lake, Uiamho.

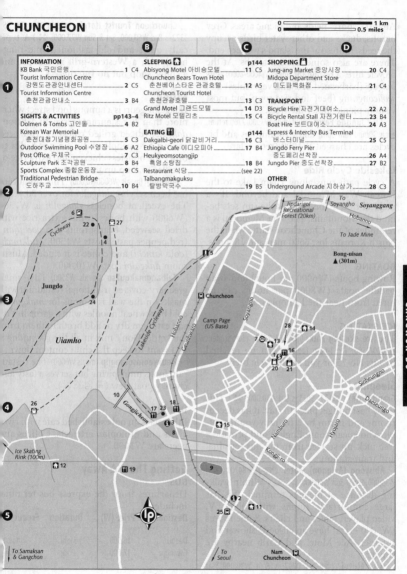

CHUNCHEON

| 0 | 1 km |
| 0 | 0.5 miles |

INFORMATION
KB Bank 국민은행 1 C4
Tourist Information Centre
강원도관광안내센터 2 C5
Tourist Information Centre
춘천관광안내소 3 B4

SIGHTS & ACTIVITIES pp143–4
Dolmen & Tombs 고인돌 4 B2
Korean War Memorial
춘천대첩기념평화공원 5 C3
Outdoor Swimming Pool 수영장 6 A2
Post Office 우체국 7 C3
Sculpture Park 조각공원 8 B4
Sports Complex 종합운동장 9 C5
Traditional Pedestrian Bridge
도하주교 10 B4

SLEEPING p144
Abisyong Motel 아비숑모텔 11 C5
Chuncheon Bears Town Hotel
춘천베어스타운 관광호텔 12 A5
Chuncheon Tourist Hotel
춘천관광호텔 13 C3
Grand Motel 그랜드모텔 14 D3
Ritz Motel 모텔리츠 15 C4

EATING p144
Dakgalbi-geori 닭갈비거리 16 C3
Ethiopia Cafe 이디오피아 17 B4
Heukyeomsotangjip
흑염소탕집 18 B4
Restaurant 식당 .... (see 22)
Talbangmakguksu
탈방막국수 19 B5

SHOPPING
Jung-ang Market 중앙시장 20 C4
Midopa Department Store
미도파백화점 21 C4

TRANSPORT
Bicycle Hire 자전거여소 22 A2
Bicycle Rental Stall 자전거렌터 ... 23 B4
Boat Hire 보트대여소 24 A3
Express & Intercity Bus Terminal
버스터미널 25 C5
Jungdo Ferry Pier
중도페리선착장 26 A4
Jungdo Pier 중도선착장 27 B2

OTHER
Underground Arcade 지하상가 28 C3

Activities

BICYCLE TOURS

Jungdo Cycle Ride

Hire a bicycle from the **bicycle rental stall** (W3000/5000 per hr/day; ⊙9am-7pm), near the lakeside tourist information centre. You will need to leave some form of ID. Cycle to Talbangmakguksu for lunch (see Eating p144) and then pedal to the ferry pier for Jungdo (중도). Alternatively catch bus No 74 (W800, 10 minutes, 20 daily).

This pretty little lake island has horse-and-carriage rides (per person W5000 for 10 minutes), water skiing (W30,000 for 10 minutes), rowing boats (W5000 per hour), an outdoor swimming pool (open in July and

August), sports fields and picnic areas. Grey herons, ducks and other water birds occupy the reeds, moreso at the island's western end. There are also some ancient tombs. At the bicycle hire, a **restaurant** (meals W4000-8000) sells *bulgogi* (barbecued beef and vegetables) and *seolleongtang* (beef and rice soup) but most visitors picnic under the trees.

The **Jungdo Ferry** (adult/child W3900/2200 return, every 30min, 9am-6pm) takes 10 minutes and bicycles are charged W1000 (return fare).

Lakeside Cycle Ride

A cycle path runs along Uiam Lake to the Korean War Memorial and beyond. It's a magical ride if you do it as the sun sets behind the mountains. The War Memorial is a reminder of the Chuncheon battle when the North Koreans lost 6600 men and 18 tanks.

BOATING

Rowing boats (W6000 per hour) and swan paddle boats (W8000 per hour) can be hired from near the Ethiopia Cafe.

ICE SKATING

The **ice skating rink** (☎ 263 7302; adult/student W3000/2500; ⏰ 1-6pm Tue-Sun) can be reached by bus No 75 or you could cycle there.

Sleeping

Grand Motel (☎ 243 5021; s & d W30,000; 🔀) This is the best budget place to stay; it has decent rooms and is run by a friendly young couple who speak some English and provide a free pick-up service from the bus terminal and train station.

Abisyong (Avignon) Motel (☎ 255 8470; s & d W35,000, Sat & Sun W50,000; 🔀 🖳) Within walking distance of the bus terminal, this has large comfortable rooms with cable TV, video player, tables and chairs. Some rooms (W5000 extra) have an all-body shower and Internet. Ace Motel and Carib nearby are similar.

Ritz Motel (☎ 241 0797; s & d W30,000, Sat W40,000; 🔀 🖳) Opened in 2003, this motel has small but ultramodern rooms. The sheets have the motel's name embroidered on them in gold.

Chuncheon Bears Town Hotel (☎ 256 2525; fax 256 2530; d, tw & ondol W64,000, Sat W80,000; 🔀 🖳) It has a restaurant, coffee shop, 24-hour men's sauna but best of all are the sunset views over the lake.

Chuncheon Tourist Hotel (☎ 255 3300; fax 25 3372; s & d W50,000, Sat & Sun W77,000; 🔀) A typically quiet and old-fashioned mid-range hotel with a Western-grill restaurant and a coffee shop but no Internet.

Eating

Dakgalbi-geori is a famous food street where more than 20 restaurants serve up delicious *dakgalbi* (diced grilled chicken). You need at least two people and it's a good idea to order the boneless chicken and extra rice o noodles to mop up the leftover sauce.

Abisong (meals W6000-10,000) This restaurant has been serving *dakgalbi* for over 30 years The excellent boneless *dakgalbi* is W7500 (W6000 with bones) while extra rice with dried seaweed, beansprouts and *gochujang* (red pepper paste) costs W1500. *Mulkimchi* (cold *kimchi*) and coffee is included. Mushroom *dakgalbi* costs W10,000.

Talbangmakguksu (meals W3500) This small greenery-covered traditional restaurant with masks on the wall is famous for *makguksu* cold buckwheat noodles with a garnish. You can eat them dry or add broth to them from the kettle. Don't mix in all the *gochujang* i you want to keep the chilli content down.

Heukyeomsotangjip (meals W6000) The restaurant looks uninspiring but serves a tasty and chunky goat stew (흑염소탕).

Drinking

Ethiopia is an old established café with river views and Ethiopian artefacts. Coffees and beers are W3000.

Getting There & Away

BUS

Departures from the express bus terminal include:

Destination	Price (W)	Duration	Frequency
Daegu	16,500	3½hr	hourly
Gwangju	17,500	4½hr	4 daily

From the intercity bus terminal:

Destination	Price (W)	Duration	Frequency
Cheongju	12,300	3½hr	hourly
Cheorwon	8000	2½hr	every 20min
Dong-Seoul	6400	1¾hr	every 30min
Gangneung	10,100	3½hr	every 20min
Sokcho	13,300	3½hr	hourly
Wonju	5500	1½hr	every 15min

RAIN

rains to Chuncheon depart from Seoul's
heongnyangni Station (W5200, 1¾ hours,
ourly) which can be reached by subway
ine 1. Unfortunately, Chuncheon's two
ain stations are both inconveniently lo-
ted, so you'll need to deal with the city
uses, take a taxi or walk about 1.5km.

ROUND CHUNCHEON

undam Valley 순담 계곡

his valley, 8km from Cheorwon, which is
p near the DMZ, is the base for **adventure
orts companies** (☎ 452 8006; fax 452 6011 to contact
e of them) that organise kayaking, canoeing
r rafting on the Hantang River. The season
ins from mid-April to October. There are a
w rapids but they are not scary except after
e summer monsoon season. A 1½-hour
fting trip (9km) along a scenic ravine costs
/30,000, and a longer 18km, eight-hour trip
sts W60,000. Kayaking and canoeing cost
bout the same and mountain bikes can be
red (W5000 to W15,000). A survival game
n be played by a group of people – W25,000
r three games and 90 paintballs.

About 5km away near Chiktang falls is a
ew bungee jump, **Taebang Daekyo** (W30,000;
 9am-noon & 1-6pm) where you drop 52m
om a bright-orange bridge to the river.

To get there, catch a bus to Cheorwon
r Sincheorwon (www.cheorwon.gang
on.kr) from Dong-Seoul bus terminal
W6500, two hours, every 30 minutes).
ou can then ring a **rafting company** (☎ 452
78) to pick you up – but they only speak
orean, so it might be easier to log on to
ww.adventurekorea.com and go on one
 their tours from Seoul.

pdarigol Recreational Forest
갑다리골 자연 휴양림

his peaceful **forest** (☎ 243 1442; adult/youth/child
2000/1500/1000; 1 May-30 Nov) 23km northwest
f Chuncheon is a great escape from the city.
ccommodation includes **camping** (per tent
'3000) and basic **log cabins** (per cabin W25,000, Fri &
t W40,000). In addition to the nearby streams,
aterfalls and dense forest, there are **hiking
ails** into the surrounding mountains. A cou-
le of restaurants and shops are nearby.

Transport is a problem as most people
rive there, but local bus No 38 (W800,
ne hour, four daily) runs there from
huncheon.

Jade Mine 옥 채석장

The **Jade Mine** (☎ 242 1042; admission free; 9am-
5pm) is difficult to get to, so check with the
tourist information centre before you go.
The jade is a very pale green, almost white.
The water that trickles through the jade
rock is said to be good for your health and
bottles of it are for sale. Apparently onions
grow well when watered with it! Some people believe that jade 'radiation' is good for
their health, and the mine has mattresses on
the floor so you can take a health-giving rest
inside. Outside are some big jade boulders
waiting to be hugged. A small shop sells jade
items – prayer beads for W10,000, rings for
W45,000 and necklaces for W250,000.

A taxi from Chuncheon to the jade mine
and back with half-an-hour waiting time at
the mine costs W28,000. Bus No 65 (W800,
40 minutes) runs to the mine but only four
times daily.

Samaksan 삼악산

This **park** (☎ 262 2215; adult/youth/child W1600/
1000/600; sunrise-sunset) has panoramic views
from Samaksan peak (654m), two temples,
a narrow gorge and a waterfall, Deungseon-
pokpo.

Catch local bus No 81 or 82 (W800) to
the park entrance, and another local bus
(W800) back to Chuncheon from near the
waterfall.

GANGCHON 강촌

Gangchon is a popular resort village, well
known for the 'membership training' by
university students who come to have a
good time in the picturesque mountains.
A small funfair, DVD rooms, bars, *dakgalbi*
restaurants and quad bikes add to the student fun. There are more bicycles than residents and everywhere you look are *minbak*
(private homes with rooms for rent) signs.
It's a much prettier place to stay than nearby
Chuncheon city.

Hire a **bicycle** (W2000/5000 per hr/day) and ride
along the cycleway towards Gugokpokpo.
On the way you can experience a 21m
bungee jump (번지 점프; adult/student W12,000/
10,000; 10am-6pm except rainy days) but only if
you weigh less than 90kg. It must be the
world's cheapest bungee.

Park your bike at the entrance to **Gugokpokpo** (구곡 폭포; ☎ 261 0088; adult/youth/child
W1600/1000/600; 8am-sunset), which is 6km

GANGWON-DO

from the train station. Market ladies sell black rice, dried apricots, sweet potatoes, *omijacha* (five flavours tea), pumpkin jelly sweets and *dongdongju* (rice wine) home-brew. Walk for 15 minutes and you come to the delightful waterfall, which cascades down a 50m cliff. In winter it's a popular spot for ice climbing (*bingbyeok* 빙벽). From near the waterfall you can also hike up **Bonghwasan** (봉화산; 486m), which takes around 30 minutes. Bus No 50 (W800, 30 minutes, hourly) makes trips from Gangchon to the waterfall entrance.

The **Gangchon Ski Resort** (☎ 02-449 6660, 033-260 2000) opened in 2002, has 10 slopes and six lifts, and there is a shuttle bus from Gangchon train station in the ski season.

Sleeping

The best place to stay in Gangchon is the new **White Bell Minbak** (화이트벨 민박; ☎ 262 0083; www.whitebell.co.kr; s & d W30,000, Fri & Sat W60,000; 🅿), which has charming rooms with pot plants and a balcony.

Gangchon Youth Hostel (강촌 유스호스텔; ☎ 262 1201; fax 262 1204; dm/f W15,000/55,000) is out of town, opposite the bungee jump, with a very rural ambience.

Getting There & Away

Gangchon is a short bus ride away from Chuncheon (W800). The bus stop is outside Gangchon train station. Trains from there go to Seoul's Cheongnyangni station (W5200, 1½ hours, hourly).

SOYANG LAKE 소양호

The most interesting way to travel from Chuncheon west across Gangwon-do is to start via a short ferry ride across Soyang lake, a large artificial lake created by one of Korea's largest dams. Catch bus No 11 (W800, 30 minutes, hourly) from Chuncheon's intercity bus terminal to Soyhang Dam, and walk 1km past the market stalls (some of which sell *mettugi*, fried grasshopper, for W2000 a cup) to the ferry pier. There are **hydrofoil trips** (adult/child W5000/2500) which run hourly from 8.30am to 4.30pm and at 6pm to Yanggu Pier. Dense pristine forests reach down to the lake and provide a scenic background to the speedy 30-minute ride.

There are also **boat rides** (adult/child return W4000/2000) from the pier to a nearby scenic temple, **Cheongpyeongsa** (adult/child W2000/1000).

At Yanggu Pier, a bus (W940, 15 minute runs to Yanggu, from where you catch a b for a winding ride through the mountai to Wontong (W2700, 30 minutes) and the another bus (W750, 10 minutes) to Inje b terminal.

INJE 인제
pop 33,000

Inje (www.inje.gangwon.kr) is a small tow and an adventure sports centre – white-wat rafting, kayaking and bungee jumping a becoming increasingly popular with you Koreans.

Bungee Vic (W30,000; 🕙 8.30am-sunset; closed Nc Mar & windy & wet days) operates a 60m bunge jump from an orange tower above the riv on the edge of the town. It even has an elev tor so you don't have to climb up any stair

White-Water Rafting (☎ 461 5859; 🕙 May-O is organised by more than 20 rafting con panies who provide a pick-up service fro Inje. The rafting takes place on the Nae incheon, which flows peacefully or energet cally depending on the recent rainfall lev A 6km, 2½-hour course costs W30,000 whi the longer 19km, five-hour course cos more. There are buses along the river vall but they are infrequent (every 1½ hours).

Next to Inje bus terminal is a *gamjata* (meaty bones and potato soup) restaura where a delicious and meaty pork bo soup is W5000.

Getting There & Away

Buses from Inje to Sokcho (W6100, every 3 minutes) go via Osaek in Seoraksan Nation Park's southern part and Yangyang. Bus also run to Chuncheon (W6600, every 1 hours) and Dong-Seoul (W11,300, hourly

SOKCHO 속초
pop 90,000

Sokcho is a sprawling port city that is th gateway to nearby Seoraksan National Par Fishing is still a major industry and Dongm eong Port is worth a wander round with i sea views, fishing boats, seafood restauran and a lighthouse. Ferries leave from here f the tours round Geumgangsan in Nor Korea, and for Russia and tours of Paekdusa on the Chinese border with North Korea.

There is a small **tourist information cent** (☎ 635 2003; 🕙 9am-5pm) outside the expre bus terminal.

Sleeping

Room rates go up 50% in July and August. Good quality motels surround the express bus terminal and are within easy walking distance of the beach. In July and August you can camp on the beach (W6000 per night) or rent a tent (W12,000 per night). A shower costs W1300.

Samsung Motel (☎ 636 0069; s & d W30,000, Sat W40,000; ❄) This fairyland castle has good, comfortable rooms.

Rocustel (☎ 633 4959; s & d W40,000, Sat W60,000; ❄) A more expensive fairyland castle with fancier rooms.

Motel Royal Beach (☎ 633 5599; fax 635 5588; s & d W30,000, Sat W40,000; ❄) and **Namgyeong Motel** (☎ 637 6810; r W25,000; ❄) are also recommended.

Other accommodation is around the intercity bus terminal in the north of the city near the port:

Jongkyeong Motel (☎ 631 644; s & d W30,000; ❄) This large motel is the best option here.

Jingwangjang (☎ 635 5177; s & d W20,000; ❄) Cheaper but facilities are shared.

Eating

On the harbour side of Dongmyeong raw fish market are small stalls serving *mo-eumhoe* (a large platter of mixed raw fish) for W80,000 which includes side dishes, sauce and spicy fish soup. The meal can be shared by four people. A small plate of sliced raw fish costs W20,000, while spider crabs go for W9000 to W20,000. You can sit outside on the seawall and look at the fishing boats while you eat.

Ieodo (meals W5000-10,000) A small restaurant that serves the local speciality, squid *sundae* (pork sausage), that two people can share. The squid is stuffed with minced-up noodles, tofu, onion, carrot, seaweed and seasoning, which is then sliced and fried in egg – an unusual but tasty dish. *Saeng-seongui* (fried fish), *ojingeodeopbap* (squid rice) and spicy squid *bibimbap* (rice, meat, egg and vegetables in hot sauce) are other options.

Pungnyeon (meals W4000) Sample *sundubu*, another local speciality, which is uncurdled tofu in a shellfish broth with a spicy sauce that you blend into the broth. The meal is healthy and delicious – Koreans are so proficient at serving up unusual but tasty soups.

Abaimaeul (meals W5000-10,000) Another small restaurant that serves squid *sundae* (오징 어순대).

Hanyanggol (meals W5000) Try *wangmandu* (large steam buns filled with meat and vegetables) or *kalguksu* (thick noodles).

Getting There & Away

AIR

Flights from Seoul (Gimpo) to the new Yangyang International Airport cost W53,500 one-way, and the airport is well serviced by buses that run north to Sokcho and Goseong Unification Observatory and south to Gangneung.

BOAT

Hyundai Asan operates tours by boat from Sokcho port to Geumgangsan in North Korea (see p374). Dongchun runs a ferry to Zarubino in Russia (see p379) with onward travel to China and Paekdusan, a mountain that straddles the border between China and North Korea.

BUS

Buses leave Sokcho express bus terminal for Seoul Gangnam (W12,800, 4½ hours, every 30 minutes).

Departures from Sokcho intercity bus terminal include:

Destination	Price (W)	Duration	Frequency
Busan	30,800	7½hr	hourly
Chuncheon	13,300	3½hr	hourly
Chungju	16,400	3¾hr	3 daily
Daegu	16,600	3½hr	7 daily
Dong-Seoul	12,800	4hr	every 30min
Gangneung	5300	1½hr	every 20min
Yanggu	8100	2 ¼hr	7 daily

Buses also leave the intercity bus terminal for Jinburyeong (W4100, eight daily from 6.10am to 3.50pm), which stop at Baekdamsa and Yondae-ri on the way. From Jinburyeong shuttle buses go to the Alps Ski Resort.

Local buses leave from outside the intercity bus terminal in the north of Sokcho, but bus No 7 (W750, 25 minutes, every 15 minutes) that goes south to Seorak-dong, and bus No 9 (W750, 15 minutes, every 15 minutes) to Naksan can both be picked up along its route which includes the express bus terminal.

GANGWON-DO

GANGWON-DO

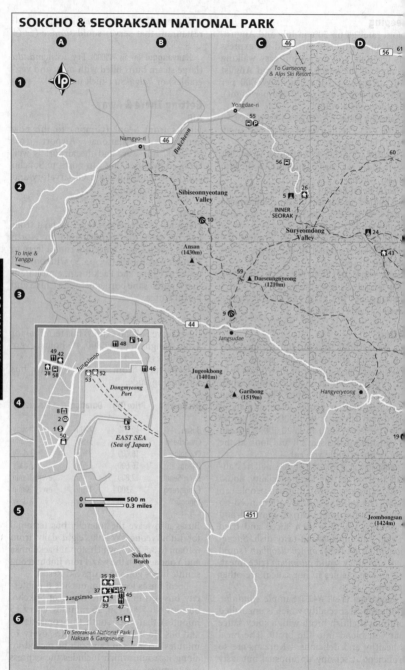

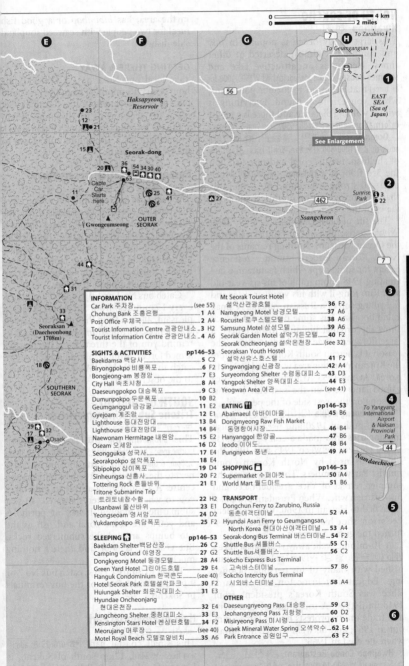

INFORMATION

Car Park 주차장	(see 55)
Chohung Bank 조흥은행	**1** A4
Post Office 우체국	**2** A4
Tourist Information Centre 관광안내소	**3** H2
Tourist Information Centre 관광안내소	**4** A6

SIGHTS & ACTIVITIES pp146–53

Baekdamsa 백담사	**5** C2
Biryongpokpo 비룡폭포	**6** F2
Bongjeong-am 봉정암	**7** E3
City Hall 속초시청	**8** A4
Daeseungpokpo 대승폭포	**9** C3
Dumunpokpo 두문폭포	**10** B2
Geumgangul 금강굴	**11** E2
Gyejoam 계조암	**12** E1
Lighthouse 등대전망대	**13** B4
Lighthouse 등대전망대	**14** B4
Naewonam Hermitage 내원암	**15** E2
Oseam 오세암	**16** D2
Seongguksa 성국사	**17** E4
Seorakpokpo 설악폭포	**18** E4
Sibipokpo 십이폭포	**19** D4
Sinheungsa 신흥사	**20** F2
Tottering Rock 흔들바위	**21** E1
Tritone Submarine Trip 트리토네잠수함	**22** H2
Ulsanbawi 울산바위	**23** E1
Yeongseoam 영서암	**24** D2
Yukdampokpo 육담폭포	**25** F2

SLEEPING pp146–53

Baekdam Shelter백담산장	**26** C2
Camping Ground 야영장	**27** G2
Dongkyeong Motel 동경모텔	**28** A4
Green Yard Hotel 그린야드호텔	**29** E4
Hanguk Condominium 한국콘도	(see 40)
Hotel Seorak Park 호텔설악파크	**30** F2
Huiungak Shelter 희운각대피소	**31** E3
Hyundae Oncheonjang 현대온천장	**32** E4
Jungcheong Shelter 중청대피소	**33** E3
Kensington Stars Hotel 켄싱턴호텔	**34** F2
Meourujang 머루장	(see 40)
Motel Royal Beach 모텔로얄비치	**35** A6
Mt Seorak Tourist Hotel 설악산관광호텔	**36** F2
Namgyeong Motel 남경모텔	**37** A6
Rocustel 로쿠스텔모텔	**38** A6
Samsung Motel 삼성모텔	**39** A6
Seorak Garden Motel 설악가든모텔	**40** F2
Seorak Oncheonjang 설악온천장	(see 32)
Seoraksan Youth Hostel 설악산유스호스텔	**41** F2
Singwangjang 신광장	**42** A4
Suryeomdong Shelter 수렴동대피소	**43** D3
Yangpok Shelter 양폭대피소	**44** E3
Yeogwan Area 여관	(see 41)

EATING pp146–53

Abaimaeul 아바이마을	**45** B6
Dongmyeong Raw Fish Market 동명항어시장	**46** B4
Hanyanggol 한양골	**47** B4
Ieodo 이어도	**48** B4
Pungnyeon 풍년	**49** B4

SHOPPING pp146–53

Supermarket 수퍼마켓	**50** A4
World Mart 월드마트	**51** B6

TRANSPORT

Dongchun Ferry to Zarubino, Russia 동춘여객터미널	**52** A4
Hyundai Asan Ferry to Geumgangsan, North Korea 현대아산여객터미널	**53** A4
Seorak-dong Bus Terminal 버스터미널	**54** F2
Shuttle Bus 셔틀버스	**55** C1
Shuttle Bus 셔틀버스	**56** C2
Sokcho Express Bus Terminal 고속버스터미널	**57** B6
Sokcho Intercity Bus Terminal 시외버스터미널	**58** A4

OTHER

Daeseungnyeong Pass 대승령	**59** C3
Jeohangnyeong Pass 저항령	**60** D2
Misiryeong Pass 미시령	**61** D1
Osaek Mineral Water Spring 오색약수	**62** E4
Park Entrance 공원입구	**63** F2

NORTH OF SOKCHO
Hwajinpo 화진포
This large sandy beach is popular in July and August but almost deserted at other times. Nearby is an attractive lake and **summer houses** (admission adult/child W1500/1000 for all three) that belonged to former politicians, which you can look round. Everything is within walking distance and there is a **tourist information centre** (☎ 682 0500; ☼ 9am-5.20pm).

Ocean Museum (해양 박물관; ☎ 682 7300; adult/child W1000/800; ☼ 9am-5pm) has displays of shellfish, fossils, coral and rare fish. On the 3rd floor is a **teashop** (teas W2000) which offers 10 strongly flavoured medicinal teas that are brewed on the premises, and great views of the beach and lake.

The site of **Kim Il-sung's Villa** (김일성 별장; ☼ 9am-6pm) is a pleasant 20-minute walk from the Ocean Museum. Nothing remains of the North Korean leader's summer residence except for some steps which feature in a fascinating 1948 photograph of his six-year-old son, Kim Jong-il with his younger sister and the young son of a Russian general. A small exhibition hall has some old photos, which show the original building to have been a large European-style villa built of stone. The reason it is here in South Korea is that before the Korean War, this area was ruled by North Korea. At the 1953 Armistice, South Korea gained land here on the east side but lost Kaesong on the west side of the peninsula.

Lee Ki-boong's Villa (이기붕 별장; ☼ 9am-6pm) was built in 1920 and used by English missionaries who made a crazy golf course in the garden. Between 1945 and 1953 the house was used by North Korean Communist Party members. Then it became the summer retreat of Vice President Lee and his Austrian wife. When President Syngman Rhee fled to Hawaii in 1960, Vice President Lee's son shot his parents dead and then turned the gun on himself.

A 10-minute walk away is **Syngman Rhee's Villa** (이승만 별장; ☼ 9am-6pm) which is furnished with many of his personal belongings. Educated at Princeton and Harvard, Rhee was South Korea's president from 1948 until 1960. A tough autocrat, student and trade union protests finally forced him out in 1960, and he went to live in Hawaii where he died in 1965.

Hwajinpo Condo Restaurant (화진포 콘도 식당; meals W4000-10,000), the only restaurant in the area, has *bibimbap* or a good fish meal for two people with seaweed soup and side dishes.

GETTING THERE & AWAY
Take local bus No 1 or 1-1 (W3300, one hour, every 15 minutes) from the bus stand outside Sokcho intercity bus terminal. Get off at the access road to Hwajinpo (15km south of Goseong Unification Observatory). From there it's a 10-minute walk down to the Ocean Museum.

Goseong Unification Observatory
고성 통일 전망대
The **Unification Hall** is to your left as you enter the **complex** (☎ 682 0088; adult/child W2000/1000, ☼ 9am-4.30pm Mar-Jun & Sep-Oct, 9am-5.30pm Jul & Aug, 9am-3.30pm Nov-Feb) which is surrounded by souvenir shops and restaurants. Binoculars are available to take a closer look at the forbidden North and you should be able to see the Geumgang mountain range.

Catch bus No 1 or 1-1 (W3400, 1½ hours, every 15 minutes) from Sokcho to Daejin, a pleasant 50km ride up the coast with barbed wire fences, fortifications and tank traps to remind you of the threat from the North's armed forces. From Daejin education centre catch the shuttle bus (W2000, 20 minutes) to the observatory.

SOUTH OF SOKCHO
Tritone Submarine Experience
트리토네 잠수함
This **submarine trip** (☎ 636 3736; www.tritone marine.com; adult/child W49,500/29,700; ☼ 9.30am-5.30pm, 6 tours per day) starts at Sunrise Park, next to the national park tourist information centre. A 15-minute boat ride to Jodo takes you to where the battery-powered, 40-seat submarine is moored. It has big portholes and you'll see some coral and fish as the sub bumps around the submerged rocks. But visibility is poor and there's nothing much to see.

To get to Sunrise Park, catch bus No 7 or 9 from outside either of the bus terminals in Sokcho.

Naksan Provincial Park
낙산 도립공원
This small coastal **park** (☎ 670 2518; admission free; ☼ 24hr), 12km south of Sokcho, is famous for the temple **Naksansa** (☎ 672 2448;

adult/youth/child W2500/1500/1000; 🕙 5am-7pm). A 15m white statue of Gwaneum, the Goddess of Mercy, completed in 1977, looks out over the East Sea from atop a small, pine-covered rocky outcrop. Overnight temple stays are possible but must be pre-booked (see p363). The pavilion, Ulsangdae, is a popular spot to watch the sunrise.

Down below the temple is **Naksan Beach** which is very popular in summer and has a tourist town of motels, *minbak* and restaurants. Beach **camping** (W2000-4000) is possible in July and August. The **Naksan Youth Hostel** (☎ 672 3416; fax 672 3418; dm/f W15,000/50,000) is next to the temple but is a bit run-down. **Naksan Beach Hotel** (☎ 672 4000; s & d from W80,000; 🔀) offers upmarket accommodation with restaurants, a nightclub and a seawater sauna.

GETTING THERE & AWAY

Catch bus No 9 (W750, 15 minutes, every 15 minutes) from outside either of Sokcho's bus terminals. It runs between Sokcho and Yangyang.

There are direct buses from Naksan to Dong-Seoul bus terminal (W13,700, 4½ hours).

SEORAKSAN NATIONAL PARK
설악산 국립공원

Top of the charts in the Korean national park scene, Seoraksan (Snowy Crags Mountain) is spectacular. It's a region of high peaks, granite cliffs, lush forests, tremendous waterfalls, hot springs, boulder-strewn rivers, and temples whose roots go back to the Silla era. The park is at its picturesque best in mid-October, when the leaves begin to change hue and the mountainsides are transformed into a riot of colour, but a visit at any time of year is rewarding. The nearby coast has some of Korea's best sandy beaches.

Ironically, Seoraksan's beauty is its biggest problem. The peak season is July and August, though the mid-October leaf-changing show attracts coach loads of visitors. Prices for accommodation more than double at these times and can become completely full, so reservations are essential. Avoiding weekends is best although you could still bump into thousands of noisy school students on spring and autumn excursions.

Despite all this, persevere! After an hour of hiking up the trails, the terrain gets rough and most of the day-trippers disappear.

Orientation

The **park** (☎ 636 7700; adult/youth/child W2800/1300/700; 🕙 5am-sunset) is divided into three sections:

Outer Seorak is the most accessible and popular area of the park and is nearest to Sokcho and the sea. Seorak-dong has hotels, motels, restaurants, bars, *noraebang* and a 24-hour supermarket. The left luggage facility by the ticket office costs W1000 for most items and W2000 for a big backpack.

Inner Seorak at the western end of the park is the least commercialised area. It has three entrance points – from Hwy 46 at Yongdae-ri to Baekdamsa; at Namgyo-ri where a hiking trail goes through Sibiseonnyeotang Valley; and from the south (Hwy 44) a trail goes north from Jangsudae.

South Seorak is the name given to the Osaek (Five Colours) area which is famous for its cold mineral spring for drinking, and hot mineral springs for bathing and soothing those aching muscles after a long day's hike.

Information

A helpful **tourist information centre** (☎ 635 2003; 🕙 9am-6pm, 9am-5pm Nov-Feb) is located rather inconveniently at Sunrise Park, where the Seorak-dong access road joins the main coast road.

Outer Seorak
GWONGEUMSEONG 권금성

A 1.1km **cable car** (W3000/5000 one way/return) runs every 20 minutes and the views (and queues!) on a nice day are amazing. It drops you just a 10-minute walk away from the fortress remains and summit.

HEUNDEULBAWI (TOTTERING ROCK) & ULSANBAWI 흔들바위, 울산바위

This massive 16-tonne boulder can be rocked to and fro by a small group of people, and half the Korean population has played at being Superman here! Other boulders have Chinese characters carved on them. Nearby is **Gyejoam** with a prayer hall inside a cave. Wild grape booze, cold mountain tea, and waffles and ice cream are on sale. It's a 40-minute, 3km walk from Sinheungsa and the impressive Unification Buddha near the Seorak-dong park entrance.

From Heundeulbawi you should carry on and scale the imposing granite cliff known as Ulsanbawi. To reach the 873m summit you have to climb up an 808-step staircase. It takes 45 minutes and is hard-going but the reward is a spectacular view from the top.

TWO WATERFALLS HIKE 쌍폭포
A 45-minute hike from Seorak-dong brings you to a couple of impressive waterfalls, Yukdampokpo and Biryongpokpo. This relatively easy 2km hike starts at the stone bridge beyond the cable car station.

DAECHEONGBONG 대청봉
This is the highest peak in the park at 1708m, and since it is a strenuous 10km, eight-hour hike from Seorak-dong there are four mountain shelters around it – see Sleeping later.

Southern Seorak
It's easier to hike up Daecheonbong from **Osaek Hot Springs** in the south. The hike is steep and difficult but is reckoned to take four hours up and three hours down, after which you can soak your aching body in the hot spring pools (adults W8000). Alternatively you could continue and descend to Seorak-dong (six hours down).

Inner Seorak
BAEKDAMSA 백담사
In the relatively uncrowded northwestern section of the park lies **Baekdamsa** (☎ 462 2554; adult/youth/child W2000/1200/600; ☼ sunrise-sunset). Its name means Hundred Pools Temple, which aptly reflects the abundance of beautiful rocky pools scattered along the river valley. Founded in the Silla period, former president Chun Doo-hwan and his wife spent two years of exile and penance there. Shaven-headed, he did cleaning and other jobs around the temple grounds.

Shuttle buses run from the car park 4km up the valley (W800, every 20 minutes). It's another 3km hike to the temple (50 minutes). The hike beyond the temple along Suryeomdong Valley (another two hours) is highly recommended.

SIBISEONNYEOTANG VALLEY
십이선녀탕 계곡
This is another legendary Seoraksan valley strewn with waterfalls, cascades, pools and large boulders. The 2½-hour hike to Dumunpokpo is a real treat and after another

two hours uphill you can turn right for a 30-minute hike up Anson (1430m) or turn left for Daeseungnyeong (1210m), which take the same length of time. Then you can head south down to Jangsudae (two hours from Ansan or 1½ hours from Daeseungnyeong). From Jangsudae you can do the above cours in reverse or follow a shorter course up to Daeseungnyeong and Ansan. Another option is to cross the park from south to north entering at Jangsudae and leaving via Baek damsa (allow six hours).

Sleeping
During the peak season (July, August and mid-October) you need to reserve accommo dation, as many places are full even though prices double or more. Out-of-season or on weekdays you may be able to bargain th price down. *Yeogwan* (motels with small well-equipped en suite rooms) tend to charge W30,000, but W50,000 on busy weekend and even more in peak season.

Camping sites are available in Seorak dong, Jangsudae and Osaek for around W5000 but don't expect any fancy facilities

There are mountain shelters – Jungcheong Huiungak, Yangpok, Suryeomdong and Baekdam – which are basic, cost W500 and can be reserved (☎ 672 7700 – Korean speaking).

SEORAK-DONG 설악동
The first big section of *yeogwan*, shops and restaurants is on the left. Expect to pay W30,000 a room off-peak and W50,000 when it's busy.

Seoraksan Youth Hostel (☎ 636 7115; fax 63 7107; dm/f W20,000/50,000) is the cheapest option for solo travellers.

Further on is another bunch of facilitie on the right.

Seorak Garden Motel (☎ 636 7474; d & ondo W30,000; ☼) Rooms are reasonable and som have a kitchen.

Meorujang (☎ 636 7077; fax 636 7680; s & d W30,000 ☼) Like all these *yeogwan* it can be overrun with noisy tour groups.

Hanguk Condominium (☎ 636 7661; fax 636 8274 2-bedroom apt W120,000; ☼) The apartments have a kitchen and two bedrooms – one Western style and one *ondol*-style. Discounts of 60% are possible on off-peak weekdays.

Kensington Stars Hotel (☎ 635 4001; www.ke sington.co.kr; d & ondol/tw W149,000/179,000 incl ta

& service; ⊠ ▣) The off-season price is
W129,000 including breakfast. With English-style décor and more than a touch of
class, this hotel has the best view and is
very near the park entrance. Some rooms
are shrines to Korean film stars.

Hotel Seorak Park (☎ 636 7711; www.hotel
sorakpark.com; tw & ondol W150,000; ⊠ ▣) Discounts
of 20% are possible on off-season weekdays.
The hotel features balconies, mountain
views and is within walking distance of the
park entrance. Facilities include a casino,
karaoke lounge, restaurants and men's and
women's **saunas** (guests/nonguests W4000/8000).

Mt Seorak Tourist Hotel (☎ 636 7101; www.seorak
hotel.co.kr; d, tw & ondol W90,000; ⊠) This simply
furnished hotel is the only one inside the
national park. It normally offers 20% weekday discounts, but charges 30% extra at peak
season in summer and autumn.

SOUTHERN SEORAK

Accommodation clusters around the Osaek
hot spring pools.

Hyundai Oncheonjang (☎ 672 4088; s & d W30,000,
Sat & Sun W35,000 or W40,000; ⊠) No *oncheon* but
hot spring water in the bathrooms.

Seorak Oncheonjang (☎ 672 4111; s & d W30,000,
Fri & Sat W40,000) The *oncheon* is free for
guests.

Green Yard Hotel (☎ 672 8500; s & tw W60,000,
Fri & Sat W85,000; Jul, Aug & Oct W180,000; ⊠ ▣)
The top accommodation with an *oncheon*
(W5000), nightclub, billiards and restau-
rants. Rooms have balconies.

INNER SEORAK

Access to Baekdamsa is by way of Yongdae-ri
where you can find *minbak* and restaurants.

Eating

Seoraksan is not noted for its food but popular meals are *sanchaebibimbap* (W5000) and
sanchaejeongsik (W8000), which feature
mountain vegetables. Trailside stalls sell
snacks such as roast potatoes (W2000) and
potato starch cakes with red bean filling
(W1000).

Getting There & Away

The access road to Outer Seorak branches
off the main coast road half-way between
Sokcho and Naksan. Bus Nos 7 and 7-1
run every 10 minutes between Sokcho and
Seorak-dong and cost W750.

Buses from Sokcho intercity bus terminal
run every 30 minutes to Osaek Hot Springs
(W3000) and Jangsudae (W4400).

Baekdamsa and Namgyo-ri can be accessed by buses that go from Sokcho intercity bus terminal to Jinburyeong (eight daily
from 6.10am to 3.50pm).

ALPS SKI RESORT
알프스 스키 리조트

This **resort** (☎ 681 5030; fax 681 2788) was
opened in 1984 and is nowhere near as
large as the nearby Yongpyeong Ski Resort (see p157) but it receives the heaviest
snow falls of any resort in Korea and has
some of the most spectacular scenery, due
to its proximity to Seoraksan National
Park. There are eight slopes, five lifts and
English-speaking instructors are available.
Facilities include a pool and a nightclub;
accommodation is in a hotel, condominium or *yeogwan*. The season runs from late
November to March.

The resort can be reached by buses that
go from Sokcho intercity bus terminal to
Jinburyeong (eight daily from 6.10am to
3.50pm) or from Yangyang International
Airport.

GANGNEUNG 강릉
pop 234,000

Gangneung is the largest city on the northeast coast of Korea and hosts an annual
Dano Festival, which has been held for the
past 400 years. It is the gateway to Jeongdongjin beach, Odaesan National Park and
Korea's top ski resort, Yongpyeong.

The main **tourist office** (☎ 640 4414; www.ga
ngneung.gangwon.kr; ⏰ 9am-5pm) is near the bus
terminal and there is a smaller booth in
front of the train station.

Sights
OJUKHEON 오죽헌

This **complex** (☎ 648 4271; adult/youth/child
W1000/500/300; ⏰ 9am-6pm Wed-Mon, to 5pm Nov-
Feb), 4km from downtown, is the place to
experience the strange world of Confucian
yangban scholars. Sin Saimdang (1504–51)
was born here as was her son Yi Yul-gok
(1536–84) whose pen name was Yi-yi. Sim
Saimdang is regarded as a model daughter,
wife and mother, and was an accomplished
poet and artist who liked to paint detailed
studies of plants and insects. Her son was

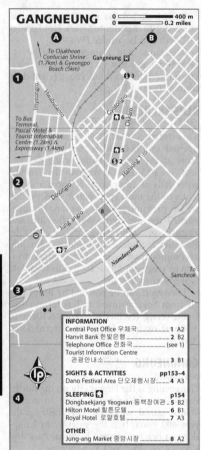

GANGNEUNG

0 _____ 400 m
0 _____ 0.2 miles

INFORMATION
Central Post Office 우체국.................1 A2
Hanvit Bank 한빛은행.......................2 B2
Telephone Office 전화국.............(see 1)
Tourist Information Centre
관광안내소.......................................3 B1

SIGHTS & ACTIVITIES   pp153-4
Dano Festival Area 단오제행사장.......4 A3

SLEEPING   p154
Dongbaekjang Yeogwan 동백장여관...5 B2
Hilton Motel 힐튼모텔.......................6 B1
Royal Hotel 로얄호텔.........................7 A3

OTHER
Jung-ang Market 중앙시장.................8 A2

an outstanding Confucian philosopher and scholar. He could read at three years old and learned the Chinese Confucian classics from his mother at a very young age. In 1564 he won first prize in the state examination for prospective government officials. He served in various government posts including minister of war. Unfortunately his advice to the king to raise an army of 100,000 to prepare against a possible invasion by Japan was ignored – with disastrous consequences in 1592, eight years after his death, when the Japanese did invade.

To get there, take bus No 202 or 300 (W800, 10 minutes, every 10 minutes) from outside the express bus terminal.

GYEONGPO BEACH 경포 해수욕장

Gyeongpo is Gangneung's best beach, 1.8km long with the usual *minbak* and restaurants. In July and August tents can be rented for W8000 a night or a beach hut for W15,000, and showers cost W2000. A giant swimming tube and a beach umbrella can be hired for W5000 each. Bungee jumping (W30,000) and banana boat rides (W15,000) are just two of the fun activities in the peak season.

Festivals

The shamanist Dano Festival overtakes the city for a week on the 5th day of the 5th lunar month (for exact dates, see p370). People flock to Gangneung and a tent city rises to house them. There are circus and carnival acts, shamanist rituals, mask dramas (one of them had been performed by government slaves), folk operas, farmers' bands, *ssireum* wrestling and assorted stalls and hawkers. There is an air of a medieval fair, which provides a rare chance to see Korea's original shamanist religion. During the festival, an information stall staffed with multilingual guides is set up in the market centre.

The Yulgokje Festival is held annually at Ojukheon on 25 and 26 October when traditional rites of respect are enacted and classical Korean music is played.

Sleeping & Eating

In 1996 Gangneung's bus terminal moved to a new facility far from the city centre but only one motel has been built nearby:

Pascal Motel (파스칼 모텔; ☎ 646 9933; s & d W45,000, Sat W55,000; 🅿) It's modern, and hence better than average.

Other motels are near the now-defunct bus terminals, which are not far from the train station.

Dongbaek-jang Yeogwan (동백장여관; ☎ 647 7758; s & d W25,000, Sat W30,000; 🅿) Clean and well-kept rooms.

Hilton Motel (힐튼 모텔; ☎ 647 3357; s & d W30,000, Sat W40,000; 🅿) A bit newer and more upmarket.

Royal Hotel (로얄 호텔; ☎ 646 1295; s, d & ondol W38,000, Sat W40,000; 🅿) Within walking distance of the Dano Festival action.

Getting There & Away
BUS

Gangneung's express and intercity bus terminals share the same building, a shiny new facility near the expressway entrance.

Express bus departures include:

Destination	Price (W)	Duration	Frequency
Dong-Seoul	10,100	3hr	every 30min
Seoul Gangnam	10,700	3hr	every 15min

Intercity departures include:

Destination	Price (W)	Duration	Frequency
Chuncheon	10,100	3½hr	every 20min
Daejeon	12,800	3½hr	hourly
Donghae	2500	½hr	every 10min
Hoenggye*	2000	½hr	every 20min
Jinbu**	3100	¾hr	every 10min
Samcheok	3600	1hr	every 10min
Sokcho	5300	1½hr	every 20min
Wonju	6200	1½hr	every 30min

* get off here for the shuttle bus to Yongpyeong Ski Resort

** get off here for the hourly bus to Odaesan National Park

TRAIN

Six daily *mugunghwa* trains connect Gangneung (W15,800, 6½ hours) with Seoul's Cheongnyangni station via Wonju.

Getting Around

Bus Nos 202 and 303 (every 15 minutes) connect the bus terminal with the train station.

ODAESAN NATIONAL PARK 오대산 국립공원

Like Seoraksan, Odaesan (Five Peaks Mountain) is a high-altitude massif. The **park** (☎ 332 6417; adult/youth/child W2800/1300/700; ⌚ 9am-7pm) has great hiking possibilities, superb views and two prominent Buddhist temples, Woljeongsa and Sangwonsa. Near the southern entrance, the **Korea Botanical Garden** (adult W3000) is 1.7km down a lane and has over 1000 native plants, orchids and a café.

Birobong (1563m) is the highest peak in the park. From Sangwonsa you can hike it (it's steep and not for the faint-hearted) and continue along a ridge to Sangwangbong (1493m) and back down to the road and along to the temple (five hours). If you have the stamina you can continue along the ridge to Durobong (1422m) and Dongdaesan (1433m) before heading down to Hwy 446.

As with Seoraksan, the best times to visit are late spring and early to mid-autumn when the hillside colours are prettiest.

Woljeongsa 월정사

The temple was founded in AD 645 by the Zen Master Jajang during the reign of Queen Seondeok of the Silla dynasty to enshrine relics of the historical Buddha. Over the next 1350 years the temple was often destroyed by fire and rebuilt. During the Korean War it was completely flattened. Yet today you would never suspect these disasters had ever occurred.

A nine-storey octagonal **stone pagoda** is an impressive relic of the early Goryeo period and is a symbol of the dynasty's artistic talent. A kneeling **Bodhisattva** statue has a smile as enigmatic as Mona Lisa and is another unique national treasure. Bodhisattvas are followers of Buddha who have chosen not to enter paradise in order to help ordinary people to become enlightened.

The **paintings** inside the main hall are masterpieces of religious art. Not even in Tibet will you find anything so colourful, imaginative and intricate. One of them could be compared to Hieronymus Bosch.

The temple has a **teashop** (W3000 or W4000 a mug) and a **museum** (adult/child W1000/500; ⌚ 9am-5pm Wed-Mon) of Joseon-era Buddhist art.

Sangwonsa 상원사

A further 10km beyond Woljeongsa is Sangwonsa where the hiking trails begin. The intricately decorated bronze bell, one of the oldest and largest in Korea, was cast in AD 663, one year after construction of the temple commenced. Check out the graceful features and hairstyle of the famous statue of a Buddhist saint, Munsu the Bodhisattva of Wisdom. Not much has survived in Korea that reveals the artistic talent of its people from over a millennium ago, so it is a prized possession, a symbol of an advanced Buddhist culture.

Sogeumgang 소금강

Sogeumgang means 'small Geumgang' and suggests that this area, with its granite pinnacles and numerous pools and waterfalls, is a smaller version of the Geumgang mountains in North Korea, which are said to be the most beautiful in the peninsula.

Almost an hour's walk from the bus stop brings you to a small temple, Geumgangsa. A further two hours' walk along a picturesque valley provides stunning landscapes. Energy permitting, it's two hours of hard

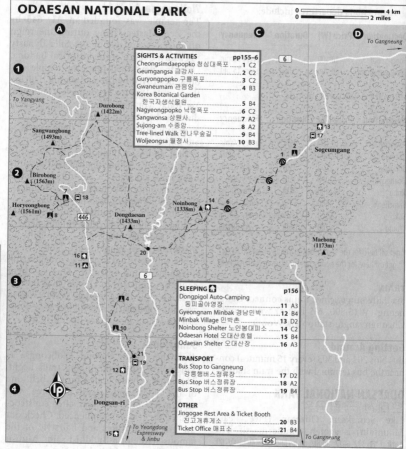

ODAESAN NATIONAL PARK

SIGHTS & ACTIVITIES	pp155–6
Cheongsimdaepopko 청심대폭포 1	C2
Geumgangsa 금강사......................2	C2
Guryongpopko 구룡폭포..................3	C2
Gwaneumam 관음암.......................4	B3
Korea Botanical Garden	
한국자생식물원..........................5	B4
Nagyeongpopko 낙영폭포...............6	C2
Sangwonsa 상원사........................7	A2
Sujong-am 수종암.........................8	A2
Tree-lined Walk 전나무숲길.............9	B4
Woljeongsa 월정사.......................10	B3

SLEEPING	p156
Dongpigol Auto-Camping	
동피골야영장...........................11	A3
Gyeongnam Minbak 경남민박.........12	B4
Minbak Village 민박촌..................13	D2
Noinbong Shelter 노인봉대피소.......14	C2
Odaesan Hotel 오대산호텔.............15	B4
Odaesan Shelter 오대산장.............16	A3

TRANSPORT	
Bus Stop to Gangneung	
강릉행버스정류장.......................17	D2
Bus Stop 버스정류장....................18	A2
Bus Stop 버스정류장....................19	B4

OTHER	
Jingogae Rest Area & Ticket Booth	
진고개휴게소............................20	B3
Ticket Office 매표소....................21	B4

climbing up to the summit of **Noinbong** (1338m), which is 12km from the park entrance. There's shelter for an overnight stay (water only available for drinking). The next day, enjoy a gentle walk to Sangwonsa, and then take the bus to Woljeongsa and Jinbu.

Sleeping & Eating

A small village of *minbak* and restaurants is on the left side of the access road, a 40-minute walk south of Woljeongsa.

Gyeongnam Minbak (☎ 332 6587; ondol W20,000) offers mattresses in small rooms furnished with a mirror and a TV on a woodblock. Toilets and showers are communal. The **restaurant** (meals W5000-10,000) serves tasty *sanchaebibimbap*, *sanchaebaekban* and huge *gamjabuchim* (감자부침). Order a bottle of delicious *memilkkotsul* (메밀꽃술, W3000), which is *makgeolli* flavoured with buckwheat flowers, and finally a free coffee.

If you want more comfort there are two *yeogwan* near the ticket office.

Odaesan Hotel (☎ 330 5000; fax 330 5123; s & d from W160,000 incl tax & service;) This is the only deluxe option and offers a 40% discount on off-peak weekdays, and a 20% discount on off-peak weekends.

Halfway between the temples is Dongpigol Auto-camping and Odaesan Shelter which both cost W5000.

A large camping ground and numerous *minbak* are also available at the entrance to Sogeumgang.

Getting There & Away

Take an intercity bus from Gangneung to Jinbu (W3100, 45 minutes, every 10 minutes). From Jinbu, local buses (12 per day) run from outside the bus terminal to Woljeongsa (W1200) and Sangwonsa (W2000) in Odaesan National Park.

Take local bus No 303 or 7-7 (W800, one hour, 12 daily) from outside Gangneung bus terminal to Sogeumgang.

YONGPYEONG SKI RESORT
용평 스키 리조트

With world-class facilities and lots of trees, **Yongpyeong** (☎ 033-335 5757; www.yongpyong.co.kr) is one of Asia's best ski resorts. It only missed out on hosting the 2010 Winter Olympics to Vancouver by 56 votes to 53. The season runs from December to March and there are 18 slopes for skiers and snowboarders, mogul bumps and a 15km cross-country trail.

A lifts-and-gondola day pass costs W55,000/40,000 for adults/children while a day's ski equipment rental is W22,000/16,000 for adults/children. Snowboards cost W25,000 for a half-day hire, while cross-country skiing costs W15,000 and sledding is W10,000. Ski classes (in English) for beginners are W33,000/24,000 for adults/children, but you need a group of 10. Package deals including transport and accommodation are offered with discounts outside the peak season.

A swimming pool (W9500), sauna and health club (W10,000), bowling (W2500), pool, darts, golf driving range (W8000 for a box of balls), Internet room, disco, supermarket, and baby-sitting service are all available.

In summer: golf, pitch-and-putt (W8000), gondola rides (W10,000), bicycle hire (W8000 for three hours) and hiking are available, as well as some indoor facilities.

Sleeping

Dragon Valley Hotel (☎ 335 5757; tw & ondol/d W190,000/210,000 incl tax & service; 🛇 🖳) You can get 50% discounts March to October.

Condominiums (☎ 335 5757; fax 335 0160; W190,000-480,000; 🛇) Also discounted 50% March to October.

Youth Hostel (☎ 335 5757; fax 335 0160; dm/f W6500/60,000) It's closed except for group bookings from March to October.

Getting There & Away

Buses leave from Gangneung intercity bus terminal to Hoenggye (W2000, ½ hour, every 20 minutes). From Hoenggye a free shuttle bus leaves for Yongpyeong (10 minutes, 12 daily from 5.30am to 11.30pm). It's more frequent during the ski season.

Direct buses run to the resort from Seoul, Incheon, Busan, Daejeon and other cities.

JEONGDONGJIN 정동진

Twenty kilometres south of Gangneung is a holiday resort with novel tourist attractions, including a North Korean submarine. The town is famed for having a train station on the beach and swifts nest in its eaves. The sand-timer hourglasses in the souvenir stalls relate to a popular Korean TV soap opera *Hourglass*, which used the station in some scenes. On a hilltop you can see a giant cruise ship and a sailing ship – a surreal sight. The town attracts young couples who wake up early and hold hands while watching the sunrise from the sandy beach.

Unification Park 통일 공원

In this **park** (☎ 640 4469; adult/child W2000/1000; 🕙 9am-5.30pm, 9am-4.30pm Nov-Feb) you can venture inside a small North Korean spy submarine and a large American warship. There is also a tourist information centre.

The **North Korean submarine** weighs 325 tonnes, is 35m long and had a top speed of 13km an hour. The conditions must have been unbearably cramped for the 11 crew, 15 soldiers and agents inside. On 17 September 1996 the submarine got stuck on some nearby underwater rocks. The commander burnt important documents (the fire-blackened compartment is still visible), shot the crew members, then landed with the soldiers and agents to attempt returning to the North. None succeeded, but it took 49 days to capture or kill them, and 17 South Korean civilians and soldiers were killed, and 22 injured.

The large **warship** has a less dramatic story to tell, having been built in America in 1945 and donated to the South Korean government in 1972.

To get there, take bus No 11-1 (W800, 15 minutes, every 30 minutes) from Jeongdongjin train station or Gangneung. Taxis charge W8000 for the 5km-drive south along the coast from Jeongdongjin.

GANGWON-DO

Two Ships on a Hill
참소리 축음기 박물관

North of Jeongdongjin are **two ships** (☎ 610 7000; adult/child W5000/3000; ⊙ 9am-5pm). The bigger of the two buildings that are shaped like ships is a luxury hotel surrounded by palm trees and a sculpture garden. The other has a sailing ship design and houses an interesting **gramophone museum** that includes musical instruments and even a veteran car. The whole set-up on the hill is very odd, but the museum is worth seeing. The ships are a 20-minute walk from Jeongdongjin train station. Otherwise there is a bus or you can take a taxi.

Sleeping & Eating
Numerous motels (with names like Paradise and Sun Lovehouse) offer comfortable modern rooms from W25,000 (but double that in July and August). Try to find a room with a balcony overlooking the sea and the sunrise.

Jijunghae Motel (지중해 모텔; ☎ 642 1518; s & d W25,000; 🛜) Clean rooms with a balcony and an almost palatial en suite toilet and shower.

Beachside tent restaurants serve up crab, raw fish and squid *sundae*. Some offer a bowl of exotic-looking shellfish, which are barbecued at your table for W30,000 and make a delicious hors d'oeuvre for three people.

Halmeonichodang (할머니 초당; meals W4000-15,000) Try the *sundubu* (순두부) – a bowl of unset tofu that you mix with seasoning and eat with rice and vegetable side dishes.

Getting There & Away
BUS
Bus Nos 109 (W1100, six daily) and 112 (W700, every 30 minutes) leave from outside Gangneung bus terminal for Jeongdongjin. Other buses leave from near Gangneung train station.

TRAIN
Trains leave Gangneung station for Jeongdongjin 12 times daily and cost W2100. The same service operates to and from Donghae and costs W5200.

Getting Around
The attractions are spread out, so seeing them involves some leg-work, working out the bus routes and times, or taking a taxi.

DONGHAE 동해
pop 104,000

This sprawling east-coast city has popular beaches, a ferry service to Ulleungdo (daily between March and October), buses to nearby Mureung Valley, and a small cave in the downtown area.

A useful **tourist information centre** (☎ 530 2868; ⊙ 9am-6pm) is outside the Cheongok-donggul entrance.

Sights & Activities
CHEONGOKDONGGUL 천곡 동굴
This **cave** (☎ 422 2972; adult/youth/child W2000/1100/700; ⊙ 9am-6pm, 9am-5pm Nov-Feb) was only discovered in 1991 and is in the centre of town. While it's not that big (700m long) it is well-lit and the many different kinds of calcified formations make it a worthwhile visit. Keep an eye out for cave insects with incredibly long feelers. There are bats but you probably won't see any. Upstairs is a museum and a cinema which shows a film about the cave and other local attractions. A taxi from the intercity bus terminal to the cave costs W2000, or it's a 20-minute walk.

BEACHES
Mangsang Beach (망상 해수욕장) is a large, popular stretch of sand north of Donghae with shallow water and many amusements and accommodation in July and August.

Chuam Beach (추암 해수욕장) to the south is an attractive sandy cove with rocky headlands.

BOWLING
Indoor bowling (game W2300, shoe hire W1000; ⊙ 10am-midnight) is near the intercity bus terminal.

Festivals
A three-day cuttlefish festival at Mangsang Beach every July includes a cuttlefish-slicing contest, a catching-cuttlefish-by-hand competition and a cuttlefish quiz.

Sleeping
There are some good options next to Donghae intercity bus terminal:

Dongcheonjang (☎ 535 2486; s & d W30,000; 🛜) This older-style *yeogwan* is the cheapest but the owner is keen that you turn off the lights when you go out, and you have to put W200 into the slot to use the hairdryer.

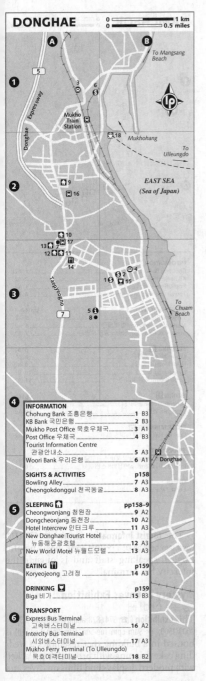

DONGHAE

New World Motel (☎ 532 1212; fax 532 8844; s & d W35,000) A better-than-average motel.

New Donghae Tourist Hotel (☎ 533 9215; s & d/ tw W51,000/67,000; ❄ ⬜ 💪) This has a sauna and is a good deal at this price.

Hotel Intercrew (☎ 533 7722; fax 531 7371; d & ondol/tw W70,000/90,000 incl tax & service; ❄ ⬜ 💪) Another good-quality hotel at a reasonable price – except in July and August when prices rise to W120,000/150,000.

Cheongwonjang (☎ 533 4429; s & d W30,000; ❄) A reasonable option next to the express bus terminal but there is a bunch of similar ones around it.

Eating & Drinking

Koryeojeong (meals W5000-25,000) Sit on the floor in your own private room with paper-windowed sliding doors. Order *saengseon-jeongsik* (생선정식) for 15 dishes of a high standard, with divine pork, jellyfish salad, honeyed sweet potatoes and more fish than you can eat. It's behind Domino's Pizza.

Biga (admission free; food W8000-10,000; ☯ 3pm-midnight) Go there for a drink (draught beer W2500 for 500cc) and listen to live music every evening at 9pm.

Getting There & Away
BOAT

The **Ulleungdo ferry** (☎ 531 5891; W42,000 one way) sails at 10am daily from March to October, but times can vary. From November to February there may be weekend sailings. Ask a Korean speaker to ring for details.

BUS

From Donghae express bus terminal, buses leave for Seoul's Gangnam bus terminal (every 30 minutes) and Dong-Seoul (10 daily). The standard bus fare is W12,500, deluxe buses cost W18,400, night buses are W20,200 and the journey takes around 3 hours 20 minutes.

Intercity bus destinations include:

Destination	Price (W)	Duration	Frequency
Busan	22,900	5hr	18 daily
Daegu	22,600	6½hr	every 30min
Gangneung	2500	40min	every 10min
Samcheok	1100	20min	every 10min
Sokcho	7800	2½hr	8 daily
Taebaek	5400	2hr	every 30min
Yangyang Airport	9200	2¼hr	4 daily

GANGWON-DO

GANGWON-DO

Local buses leave from outside the intercity bus terminal next to the SK gas station.

TRAIN

Mukho station is nearer the town centre than Donghae station, but you need to take a local bus (W750) or a taxi (W2300) to go downtown or to the bus terminals. Seven trains a day run to Seoul's Cheongnyangni station (W16,200/24,200 on *mugunghwa/saemaeul* class). There are trains to Busan, Danyang, Jecheon, Taebaek and Gangneung.

MUREUNG VALLEY 무릉 계곡

This valley southwest of Donghae is considered by locals to be one of the prettiest in the country.

Suinunsan County Park (쉰음산 군립공관; ☎ 534 7306; admission W2000; ⊙ 9am-6pm) features a couple of temples (Gwaneumsa is the most notable), a slab of rock adorned with Chinese characters that were carved centuries ago by Joseon poets and calligraphers, curiously shaped rocks, and the Twin and Yongchu waterfalls, which are 2km from the park entrance. From there you can carry on up Cheongoksan (1403m) or go back and take the trail up Dutasan (1352m) past a fortress. With so much to see it's not surprising that hikers rave about this easily accessible park.

Accommodation is available at **Mureung Plaza Motel** (무릉 프라자 모텔; ☎ 534 8855; s & d W30,000, Jul-Aug & Oct W60,000; ⊠). Many restaurants double up as *minbak* and charge around W20,000.

Getting There & Away

Bus Nos 12-1, 12-2, 12-3, 12-4, and 12-5 (W750, 25 minutes, every 10 minutes) go to Mureung via the local bus stops outside both bus terminals.

SAMCHEOK 삼척

pop 84,000

Samcheok is more compact than other larger east-coast cities, which makes it more convenient to sightsee. It is the gateway to Hwanseongul, a huge cave complex under green-clad mountains, and is promoting itself as the City of Caves with plenty of cave exhibitions. Sandy beaches, coves, rocky headlands and cliffs can be seen along the coastline that stretches south of Samcheok. If you are there in July, you might want to check out the Penis Sculpture Festival.

The **tourist information centre** (☎ 575 1330; www.samcheok.go.kr; ⊙ 9am-6pm) has helpful English-speaking staff and is outside the intercity bus terminal.

Mystery of Caves Exhibition
동굴 신비관

This **exhibition** (☎ 574 6828; adult/youth/child W3000/2000/1500; ⊙ 9am-6pm Tue-Sun, 9am-5pm Nov-Feb) is housed in a building that resembles a wedding cake dripping with brown icing. Packed with modern displays and films on caves and cave creatures it will amuse you for an hour or so. An **IMAX film** (adult/youth/child W3000/2000/1000) is shown at 11.30am and 2pm.

A building with a bat-shaped roof of solar panels houses another exhibition of cave mock-ups that is due to open in 2004.

Municipal Museum 시립 박물관

A **museum** (☎ 575 0768; adult/youth/child W2000/1500/1000; ☯ 9am-6pm Tue-Sun, to 5pm Nov-Feb) with the usual collection of local historical and folk items.

Jukseoru 죽서루

This **pavilion** (adult/youth/child W550/330/220; ☯ 9am-6pm, 9am-5pm Nov-Feb) is just an old building in a small park perched on a cliff overlooking the river.

Festivals

Every July Samcheok hosts a Penis Sculpture Festival when penis enthusiasts gather to have a good time.

Sleeping & Eating

It's a more-pleasant environment staying near a beach, but the usual motels can be found around Samcheok's bus terminals.

Samil Yeoinsuk (☎ 573 2038; s & d W20,000) This is the cheapest, has en-suite rooms and the ancient owner speaks some English but everything is tatty.

Hanil Motel (☎ 574 8277; s & d W40,000; ☒) is the best option although others are slightly cheaper. Also recommended are **Hwasinjang** (☎ 574 7571; s & d W35,000; ☒) and **Crown Motel** (☎ 574 8831; s & d W35,000; ☒).

Opposite the hospital is **Yeongbin** (meals W5000-12,000) which serves up *samgyetang* (ginseng chicken soup) and *galbitang*.

Getting There & Away

BUS

Bus departures from Samcheok's express bus terminal include Seoul Gangnam (W13,100, four hours, every 1½ hours) and Taebaek (W4300, 70 minutes, every 15 minutes).

The intercity bus schedule almost mirrors the Donghae schedule. See p159 for details.

TRAIN

The schedule is the same as the Donghae schedule, although trains from Seoul arrive in Samcheok about 15 minutes earlier than in Donghae.

AROUND SAMCHEOK
Hwanseondonggul 환선 동굴

This immense limestone **cave** (☎ 570 3255; adult/youth/child W4300/3000/2100; ☯ 8.30am-5pm, 8.30am-4pm Nov-Feb) is one of the largest in Asia. Inside are cathedral-sized caverns, waterfalls, cascades and pools. Nearly 2km of steel stairways inside the cave allow visitors to get a good look at the many features. Some formations have fanciful names like Palace of Dreams, the Summit of Hope, the Fountain of Life and the Demon's Claw, and there are English-language information boards. It's cool inside (10°C to 14°C), so take a jacket.

The cave is located in a majestic valley and it's a steep 35-minute uphill climb from the ticket office. A few restaurants offer the usual countryside fare such as *sanchae-bibimbap*, *gamjabuchim*; *makguksu* and *dotorimuk* (acorn jelly) for very reasonable prices (W3000-5000). Otherwise stalls sell bright-yellow corn bread (W1000), and big discs of teeth-challenging toffee and nuts for W2000.

Near the ticket office are a couple of **bark shingle houses** (*gulpijip*) that are typical of the style that used to be common in the mountains. The roofs were made of bark and had to be replaced every three years, and farm animals shared the houses.

Hiking up to the mountain peaks above the caves is usually possible but at the time of writing the trails were closed.

Bus No 50 (W2000, 50 minutes, nine times a day between 6.30am and 5.10pm) leaves Samcheok intercity bus terminal for the cave. The last bus back leaves at 6.40pm.

South of Samcheok

The coast becomes rocky with high cliffs south of Samcheok but the sandy coves make the area a picturesque getaway. Small harbours and fishing villages mean plenty of seafood, seaweed and barbecued fish is available, and *minbak* cluster around every stretch of sand. Basic rooms cost W20,000 out of season but increase to W30,000 to W50,000 in July and August. The new coastal expressway is having an adverse effect on the landscape, but it's still worth a visit.

MAENGBANG BEACH 맹방 해수욕장

About 12km down the coast from Samcheok is Maengbang Beach, one of the more popular spots. The water is very shallow, making

GANGWON-DO

it a big hit with families with young children. A small freshwater creek runs nearby which is OK for swimming.

YONGHWA BEACH 용화 해수욕장
This beach, 25km south of Samcheok, has pine trees and is an attractive sandy cove between two rocky headlands. There are plenty of *minbak* and restaurants.

JANGHO BEACH 장호 해수욕장
Next to Yonghwa is this sandy beach with a fishing village and harbour at the end of it.

SINNAM 신남 해수욕장
This small fishing village is home to the new **Fishing Village Folk Museum** (어촌 민속 전시관; ☎ 570 3568; adult/youth/child W3000/2000/1500; ⏰ 9am-6pm Tue-Sun, to 5pm Nov-Feb). Displays include shamanist rituals to ensure a good catch, and taboos observed by local fishermen such as not eating eggs before going on board. It seems local fishermen are still staunch shamanists and are keen on phallic symbols. Outside the museum is **Penis Park** (해신당 공원), which is full of giant wooden penis carvings. Sinnam is 20km south of Samcheok and the bus ride takes 50 minutes.

IMWON BEACH 임원 해수욕장
Only 200m long, this beach has a dramatic setting in a cliff-lined cove. Nearby is a sea cave and a freshwater creek.

HOSAN BEACH 호산 해수욕장
The southernmost beach in Gangwon-do, Hosan is 1km in length and has good white sand. There is a pine tree grove next to the beach where camping is popular.

Getting There & Away
Bus Nos 20, 30, 70, 90 and 90-1 go to Maengbang Beach. Bus No 20 continues to Jangho Beach, bus No 30 goes as far as Geundeok Beach, bus No 70 goes to Yongeunsa, bus No 90 (nine daily) turns round at Imwon Beach, and bus No 90-1 (five daily) continues to the end of the line at Hosan Beach. The standard buses charge W800 and deluxe buses charge W1200 whatever the length of the journey.

TAEBAEK 태백
pop 57,000
The train station, bus terminal, information centre and *yeogwan* are all conven-

iently within sight of each other in the town centre.

The **tourist information centre** (☎ 550 2828; www.seecomes.com; ⏰ 9am-5pm) has kind English-speaking staff.

The Taebaeksan Snow Festival takes place at the end of January with giant ice sculptures, sledding, igloo restaurants and other winter fun.

Getting There & Away
Buses connect Taebaek to various destinations:

Destination	Price (W)	Duration	Frequency
Dong-Seoul	15,900	5½hr	every 30min
Samcheok	4300	1¼hr	every 15min
Taebaeksan	1000	25min	every 45min

TRAIN
Trains depart for Seoul train station (W12,900, 11 daily) and Gangneung (11 daily).

TAEBAEKSAN PROVINCIAL PARK 태백산 도립공원
Taebaeksan (☎ 550 2740; adult/youth/child W2000/1500/700 ⏰ sunrise-sunset) means Big White Mountain and is the sixth-highest mountain in South Korea. The mountain actually consists of twin peaks, Janggunbong (1568m) and its neighbour, Munsubong (1546m). The mountain is one of the three most sacred for shamanists and on the summit is **Cheonjedan** (천제단), an altar connected with Dangun, Korea's mythical founder, where ceremonies are still occasionally performed (3 October to 5 October, and on 1 January). A rare outdoor **Statue of Dangun** (단군상) is in front of the Dangun shrine near the entrance to the park. The shrine is a simple bare wooden hall with Dangun's portrait and some food offerings in brass bowls.

Two shamanist guard posts, one male ('The Sky is Big' is written on the post) and one female ('The Earth is Woman' is written on this post), have big ears, perhaps to listen in to loose-tongued talk. Most people hike up to Cheonjedan, 4.4km from the entrance, which takes about two hours.

The Taebaek region was once South Korea's main coal mining area and the **Coal Museum** (태백 석탄 박물관; ☎ 550 2743; adult/youth/child W2000/1500/700; ⏰ 9am-5.30pm Tue-Sun, to 4.30pm Nov-Feb) by the park entrance is well worth a visit. You can't miss the building, which has a mine-head contraption at one end. Anyone interested in social history should plan to spend half a day in the museum – there are so many photos and films of the miners, as well as a full-scale replica mine downstairs. Don't miss the simulated roof collapse. Miners' art, sports, housing and community life are all covered. Miners, like fishermen, had their superstitions – they always had to have three ladles of rice in their lunchbox, which had to be wrapped in a red or blue cloth. Accidents and deaths were common, and more than 200 miners were killed between 1970 and 1996. At some mines in the remote mountains, tigers were another hazard and miners killed by tigers were given a special gravestone.

In 1988 there were 347 coal mines in the area, but by 1999 there were only 11, and the number of miners was reduced from 62,000 to 8000. Miners went on protest rallies to Seoul, but their jobs still disappeared. Some effort has been made to create alternative jobs by promoting tourism.

In front of the park entrance is a 'tourist village' of identical two-storey houses and there are plenty of restaurants as well.

Getting There & Away
Buses from Taebaek bus terminal (W1000, 25 minutes, every 45 minutes) provide a good service to the park.

Jeongseon 정선
pop 50,600
This mountain-locked, remote town can be visited on a one-carriage, gaily decorated train. Catch a train from Taebaek to Jeungsan (증산; W4400, 35 minutes, 11 daily) and change to the Jeongseon line, which goes to Jeongseon (35 minutes) and on to the end of the line at Gujeol-ri (one hour). It's one of the prettiest routes in Korea with classic Gangwon-do scenes of densely wooded mountains and rivers bordered by terraced rice fields, vegetable gardens and orchards. Very occasionally there'll be an ox pulling a plough: a scene from a previous era.

Jeongseon train station is 2km from the town centre and the nearest yeogwan, so you may need to take a taxi (W1500) as there are not many buses. It's another 2km from the town centre to the express bus terminal. Daewangjang (대왕장) is a typical old-fashioned yeogwan but a reasonable deal at W30,000.

Getting There & Away
BUS
Buses leave Jeongseon for a number of destinations:

Destination	Price (W)	Duration	Frequency
Dong-Seoul	14,600	4hr	7 daily
Gangneung	7000	1¾hr	13 daily
Jecheon	5900	2hr	6 daily
Taebaek	4700	1¼hr	7 daily

MARKET WATCHING
The food section of Jeongseon's five-day market is what catches the eye. Middle-aged ladies are frying up vegetable pancakes, putting red beans into small doughnuts, and stirring big cauldrons of bubbling brown soup. Maemilmuk are thick strips of noodle that are put into the brown soup and garnished with dried seaweed. Heaped up at the market traders' feet are pile after pile of different mountain vegetables and fern fronds, and to pass the time in between customers, the ladies peel the skin off various roots. A small boxful of dried omija tea is half the price it is in Seoul. Under a multicoloured golf umbrella, a lady is making green rice cakes that look like strips of plasticine. The inevitable kimchi sellers guard tables groaning under the weight of 20kg jars of fiery, glowing kimchi – some of them containing small whole kimchi-pickled crabs. Nearby, strips of pungent but tasty dried squid are being heated up and passed through a small mangle. Next up are containers of soy bean paste – the basis of millions of soups that are enjoyed every day throughout Korea. An ajumma (an older woman) with a towel wrapped round her head is selling homebrew, but what's in it she won't say. The next stall has a monstrous octopus laid out on a bed of ice, and further on table-sized slabs of white tofu are for sale – something bland at last – together with grey intestines that are steaming in a big metal pot. Finally there is the 'popping man' with his ancient machine – he puts a handful of grain into a metal cup, there's a puff of steam, and hey presto a rice cracker pops out. Now that's real magic. No wonder a gang of small kids is watching him intently.

WONJU 원주

pop 275,000

Wonju is a big city with a large Korean army base, but the main reason for going there is to catch a bus to Chiaksan National Park.

Getting There & Away

BUS

Destination	Price (W)	Duration	Frequency
Cheongju	7900	1½hr	hourly
Gangneung	6200	1½hr	every 30min
Seoul Gangnam	5400	1½hr	every 15min

TRAIN

Trains (W4800, nine *mugunghwa* a day) run between Wonju and Seoul's Cheongnyangni station.

CHIAKSAN NATIONAL PARK
치악산 국립공원

Chiaksan means 'Magpie Crags Mountain' and this **park** (☎ 732 5231; adult/youth/child W2600/ 1300/700; �) sunrise-sunset) is 20km northeast of Wonju. The highest peak is Birobong (1288m), but there are a number of other peaks over 1000m, such as Hyangnobong and Namdaebong which are lined up along a north–south axis. Hiking all of them is impractical, and the most popular hike starts from Guryongsa and goes up to Birobong (three hours) and then either back down again to Guryongsa or down to Hwanggol. The hike down takes about two hours whichever route you take. The hikes are quite tough and there are no mountain shelters in the park.

In the southern part of the park is Sangwonsa which must be the highest temple in Korea as it's located not far below the peak Namdaebong (1181m). Perched on top of a 50m cliff, the temple commands a mind-liberating view across the valley. It's a three-hour hike up from Seongnam-ri and then another 20 minutes up to the peak from the temple.

Sleeping & Eating

The main *minbak* and restaurant area is outside the Guryongsa entrance. There is even an amusement park – Chiaksan Dreamland.

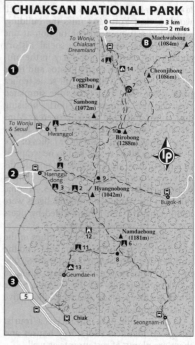

CHIAKSAN NATIONAL PARK

SIGHTS & ACTIVITIES	p164
Beommunsa 범문사	1 A2
Bomunsa 보문사	2 A2
Gukhyangsa 국향사	3 A2
Guryongsa 구룡사	4 B1
Gwaneumsa 관음사	5 A2
Sangwonsa 상원사	6 B3
Seryeompokpo 세렴폭포	7 B1
Spring 쌍룡수	8 B3
Spring 쌍룡수	9 A2
Spring 쌍룡수	10 B2
Yeongwonsa 영원사	11 A3
Yeongwonseong 영원성	12 A3

SLEEPING	p164
Geumdae-ri Camping Ground 금대리야영장	13 A3
Guryongsa Camping Ground 구룡사야영장	14 B1

Camping is possible at Geumdae-ri (W3000 to W5000 depending on the tent size).

Getting There & Away

From Wonju, you can catch bus No 41 or 41-1 (W800, 40 minutes, every 30 minutes) to Guryongsa. Bus No 82 or 82-1 run to Hwanggol, while bus Nos 21 to 25 run to Geumdae-ri and Seongnam-ri.

Gyeongsangbuk-do
경상북도

A province endowed with more than just scenic attractions, Gyeongsangbuk-do is home to some of the most fascinating reminders of Korea's cultural, historical, scientific and religious heritage.

The province's most famous and popular destination is definitely Gyeongju. The capital of the Silla dynasty (57 BC–AD 935), it is a treasure trove of historical relics. North of Gyeongju is Andong, another city surrounded by interesting cultural and historical sites. Over 130km out to sea, towards Japan, is the rugged island of Ulleungdo, another popular destination.

Gyeongsangbuk-do was one of the first provinces to reap the benefits of Korea's rapid post-war development and growth. A large proportion of the country's wealth and industry is based here, and the province is well represented in Seoul. Due to its strong historical and political links, the province evokes a strong sense of regionalism.

HIGHLIGHTS

- Delve into the history of **Gyeongju** (p176), the ancient Silla capital

- Be inspired by the 80,000-plus wooden tablets of the Buddhist sutras at the temple **Haeinsa** (p174)

- Experience the Confucian academies, **Oksan Seowon** (p189) and **Dosan Seowon** (p194)

- Escape it all on the rugged island of **Ulleungdo** (p200), 135km offshore

- Step back in time at the folk villages of **Hahoe** (p194) and **Andong** (p191)

| ■ TELEPHONE CODE: 054 | ■ POPULATION: 5.6 MILLION | ■ AREA: 20,023 SQ KM |

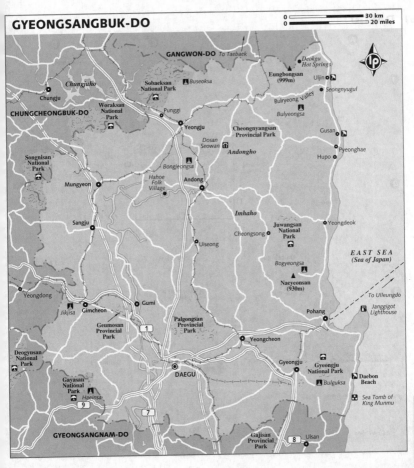

GYEONGSANGBUK-DO

DAEGU 대구

☎ 053 / pop 2.53 million

While many visitors give Daegu a pass en route to Gyeongju, as the nation's third-largest city it has plenty to offer, and some scenic attractions as easy day trips. Many visitors come here for conventions, sporting events and for the two US military bases near the city centre.

Daegu has long been an important industrial and commercial centre, and today it is famous for the quality of its textiles, which can be seen in the city's many markets; other market streets cover everything from herbal medicines to motorcycles. Daegu also boasts some worthwhile dining and nightlife, and it is a staging point for reaching the scenery of Palgongsan Provincial Park and Haeinsa, one of the country's most famous temple-monasteries.

Note that Daegu, while surrounded by Gyeongsangbuk-do, is its own administrative district and has its own telephone area code.

Orientation

At 885 sq km, Daegu covers a larger area than Seoul. Most of the action is in the central shopping district and near Dongdaegu station, the main station for intercity trains. EXCO, the city's new convention centre, is north of town, though there's little reason for tourists to visit it. The city centre is quite lively and fun, with some pedestrian streets,

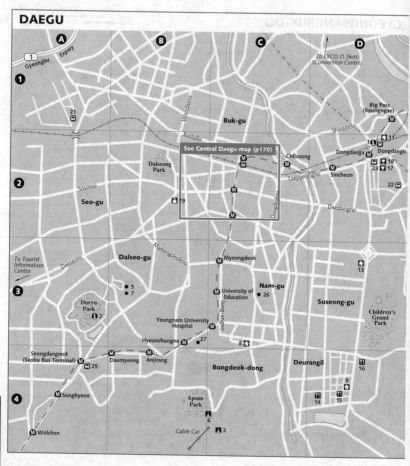

DAEGU

while south of the centre is Deurangil, a newer district with hundreds of restaurants.

The most efficient way to get through the city is via subway, although the subway system brought the city unwanted world attention when a horrific fire ripped through the centre of the line on 18 February 2003, killing 198 people. Planners have taken the lesson very much to heart; flaws have been corrected, a proper memorial was in the works during our visit, and a second line is due to open in 2005.

Information

Daegu has tourist offices at all major transit points and destinations, including the airport, outside Dongdaegu station, inside Seomun Market, in the central shopping district and by the Herbal Medicine Market. They have comprehensive local maps in English, reams of pamphlets and, at some, free Internet terminals.

Kyobo Books (Map p170; ☎ 425 3501) is a good place for English-language books. It's on the 2nd floor of Kyobo Books, near Jungangno subway station.

Sights & Activities
MARKETS & SHOPPING STREETS

These are where Daegu shows its stuff, literally and figuratively. You might start at the **Seomun Market** (Map pp168-9; ☑ 9am-6pm Mar-Oct, to 5pm Nov-Feb, closed 2nd & 4th Sun of month), a hulking, multi-storey complex with over 4000 shops

in six sections. Bustling yet orderly, it's been one of Korea's big-three markets since opening in 1669, even if the current buildings have little of that historic character. Good buys include anything made of fabric (from casual clothing to tailor-made suits), house wares, trinkets and food: endless *kimchi* and *panchan*, rabbits, ducks, chickens, dogs (for pets or meat) and all manner of seafood. Bargaining is expected.

Commerce is also intense on several streets in the city centre, lined with shop after shop specialising in a single type of product. Among the most interesting, **Motorcycle Street** (Map p170) is a great place to see the latest in mostly Korean and Japanese two-wheeled, internal-combustion transportation, along with some four-wheelers (ATVs), helmets, parts and accessories. Koreans often commemorate events such as weddings or school trips by giving out printed towels, which you will find made and sold on **Towel Street** (Map p170). Northwest of Dong-A Department Store, **Rice Cake Street** (Map p170) has about a half-dozen shops with colourful displays of traditional Korean sweets served at weddings and milestone birthdays – some cakes are works of art in their own right.

There's even a market for pleasures of the night. **Jagalmadang** (Map p170) red-light district is one of Korea's 'big three'; the other two are in Busan and Seoul. Although it caters to domestic business, it can be interesting for foreigners, even women. Each brothel fronts the street with huge plate-glass windows behind which, under intense lighting, sit up to two dozen women in everything from evening gowns to bikinis to schoolgirl uniforms, waiting for clients to choose them. Nevertheless, this is no bawdy environment – you might see women embroidering, slurping noodles or text-messaging on their mobile phones as they wait.

YASIGOLMOK 야시 골목
Yasigolmok (Map p170) is the heart of Daegu's shopping district, a hive of clothing and fashion outlets catering to Daegu's youth; bustling day and night. The main streets are pedestrianised.

HERBAL MEDICINE MARKET 한약 시장
This market (Map p107), west of the central shopping district has a history as vast as its scope. It dates from 1658, making it Korea's oldest and still one of its largest. Begin at the **Yangnyeong Exhibition Hall** (☎ 257 4729; admission free; ☉ 9am-6pm Mon-Fri, to 5pm Sat, holidays & Mon-Fri Nov-Feb), for an introduction to *insam* (ginseng), reindeer horns and the people who popularised them – there's usually someone who speaks English at the tourist booth outside who'll show you around. Then head out to the street to stock up on everything from lizard's tails to magic mushrooms (the latter with a prescription, of course); you might also catch a glimpse

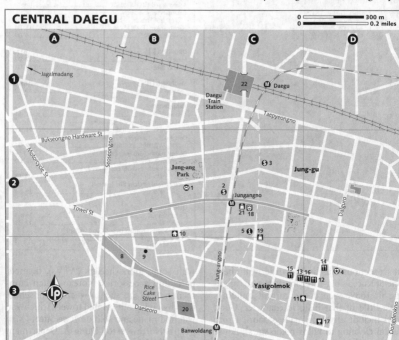

CENTRAL DAEGU

0 — 300 m
0 — 0.2 miles

of someone receiving acupuncture. On the days ending with 1 or 6 (except the 31st), a wholesale market (*yangnyeong sijang*) takes place downstairs in the exhibition hall.

DAEGU NATIONAL MUSEUM
국립 대구 박물관

This **museum** (Map pp168-9; ☎ 768 6051; http://daegu.museum.go.kr/; adults W400; ☑ 9am-6pm Mar-Oct, to 5pm Nov-Feb, closed Mon year-round) houses a fine collection of pottery, Buddhist icons and dioramas showing local history. An exhibit in the Traditional Folk Life gallery examines the life of *seonbi* – the Confucian literati who rivalled the Joseon kings for power – their ceremonies, clothing and customs. The English-language signage is quite good.

Another exhibition room often presents works by current local artists, making for a sharp contrast to the historical exhibits. Children can often play with traditional toys on the entry plaza. On special occasions, pottery classes are held here as well – contact the museum for more details.

The museum is well served by bus lines. From Central Daegu take bus No 242 or 427 to Daegu National Museum and from Dong Daegu Station take bus No 814 or 514.

WOOBANG TOWER LAND 우방 타워랜드
Visitors with kids will want to head to this **amusement park** (Map pp168-9; ☎ 620 0100; www.woobangland.co.kr/english; adult/teen/child W6500/4300/3000, attraction tickets or packages extra; ☑ hours vary monthly), in the huge Duryu Park west of the city centre. There are over 30 rides, plus games, shows, gardens and restaurants. The namesake needle-shaped tower (also known as Daegu Tower) has a revolving restaurant and bars, all quite high-end (pun intended).

BULLO-DONG TUMULI PARK
불로동 고분 공원
North of town, not far from Daegu airport, Bullo-Dong Tumuli Park (☎ 940 1224; admission free; ☑ 9am-6pm) covers some 330,000 sq metres. The grassy hillocks rising like bumps across the valley are tumuli (burial mounds, similar to those in Gyeongju). Dating from the 2nd to the 6th century AD the tumuli are for both nobles and commoners – the higher the location on the hill, the higher the status of the person. Larger tumuli are said to have entombed nobles and their entire families. You can't enter the tumuli

and there's only limited signage, but it's a nice place for a stroll or picnic.

Tours
The city **tourist information centre** (☎ 627 8900; ☑ 9am-6pm, to 7pm summer) offers a series of seven tours that are free for foreigners (not including admission, meals etc). Tour programmes change weekly and include some of the above sights and others that are hard to reach and out of town. Even if the tour on offer during your visit doesn't match your schedule, many of the tour brochures are full of useful info.

Sleeping
As always, ask about discounts in more expensive hotels. Travel agencies can often help.

BUDGET
Just to the north of Dongdaegu station are a number of *yeogwan* (motels with small, well-equipped en suite rooms), though nice ones are difficult to find.

Motel Milano (Map pp168-9; ☎ 942 7789; d Sun-Thu W25,000, Fri & Sat W30,000; ☐) An exception in the station area, it's clean and has Internet service available.

Silla-jang Yeogwan (Map p170; ☎ 424 4220; d W25,000) In the middle of central shopping and nightlife area – look for the alley with the large Kenzo billboard. Clean rooms are both Western and *ondol*. Downside: it's a bit noisy.

And if you find yourself stuck in Deurangil after dinner, this restaurant district is also known as Daegu's love motel paradise.

MID-RANGE
Central Tourist Hotel (Map p170; ☎ 257 7111; central-hotel@hanmail.net; d/t from W53,000/60,000; ☒) It may feel a bit old (especially the bathrooms), but it's priced well for the convenient location between the central shopping district and herbal medicine market.

Hotel Ariana (Map pp168-9; ☎ 765 7776; www.ariana.co.kr; d/tw from W88,000/98,000; ☒) A great deal on new, crisp rooms. It's near the Deurangil restaurant district.

Garden Hotel (Map pp168-9; ☎ 471 9911; www.gardenhotel.co.kr; d/tw W95,800/103,800; ☒) Near the US military camps and used to catering to English-speaking guests. Cosy, up-to-date rooms have minibars and hair dryers.

TOP END

Taegu Grand Hotel (Map pp168-9; ☎ 742 0001; www
.taegugrand.co.kr; d/tw from W137,500/144,100; ✖ ☐)
A kilometre or two south of Dongdaegu
station, renovated in mid-century modern
style. Amenities include a business centre,
health club and saunas, and rooms have
computers for Internet access.

Hotel Inter-Burgo (Map pp168-9; ☎ 952 0088;
www.hotel.inter-burgo.com; s/d & tw from W130,000/
180,000; ✖) Opened in 2001, it's tops in town.
It boasts a park-like setting, contemporary
lines, river views, pool, sauna, putting green
and Spanish touches – courtesy of its Spanish owners. You can also book here for Park
Hotel – the two share facilities.

Park Hotel (Map pp168-9; d/tw from W175,000/
186,000; ✖) Slightly less glamorous than the
neighbouring Hotel Inter Burgo.

Eating

Around the Yasigolmok district (Map
p170) are literally hundreds of cafés, bars
and nightclubs.

Gaejeong (dishes W5000-7500) A popular and
respected place specialising in chewy and
very tasty *naengmyeon* (cold noodles), as
well as *mandu* (dumplings) and varieties
of *bibimbap* (rice with vegetables and hot
sauce). An English menu is available.

Gimbapjang (dishes W2000-4000) Nearly across
the street from Gaejeong, with *naengmyeon*
and *mandu* at rock-bottom prices.

Gangsan Myeonok (dishes W5000-9000) One of
Daegu's oldest establishments, this eatery
is well-regarded for *naengmyeon*, *bulgogi*
and *galbi*.

Into (dishes W4000-12000) This offers a break
from Yasigolmok's bustle and Korean cuisine. Into bills itself as a European café and
serves fine pastas and salads. There are just
four tables, but sister restaurant Dijon (next
door) is larger and Euro as well.

The massive Deurangil restaurant district
(Map pp168–9) makes up with variety what
it lacks in streetside charm. Many of its
hundreds of restaurants (and their car parks)
front a wide avenue. With so many choices,
it's best just to follow the crowd. Two of the
best-loved are:

Geumsan Samgyetang (Keumsan Samgyetang;
meals W6000-10,000; ☯ 24hr) A favourite in this
district, it serves a tasty bowl of ginseng
chicken. Look for the big yellow chick on
the billboard.

Hantibullak (meals W8000-12,000) Famous for
its fish and seafood stews including baby
octopus.

Seokryujip (meals from W7000) For an only-in-
Korea adventure, come here for dog meat.
Try yours *su yuk* (boiled; W25,000, meant
for sharing) or in *bosintang* (spicy dog-meat
soup; W7000).

Ariana Bräu (dishes W9000-35,000) Downstairs
at the Hotel Ariana, it's both an eating
and drinking establishment with Bavarian-
goes-modern décor, house-brewed beer
from German ingredients and German
(and Korean) dishes. Food prices may seem
steep, but plates are meant for sharing.

Entertainment

The central shopping district is teeming
with hofs, karaoke bars and cafés. There
is a huge Xn Milano (Map p170) complex
which houses the Hanil Gukjang cinema,
where there are often English-language
movies. Across the district, **Gypsy Rock** (Map
p170; ☎ 423 9501) is part Western bar and
part 'heavy-crazy'.

Ariana Bräu (see Eating earlier) turns
into a pub after 8pm, often with live music.
Morrison (☎ 783 4010) is another pub with
music, popular with foreigners. It's southeast of the city centre, near the Dong-A
department store.

Being Korea's third-largest city, Daegu
has a gay district (Map pp168–9) with
many bars near the express bus terminal.
Foreign visitors might start at tiny **Tombo**
(☎ 745 5425) or the 20-something karaoke
bar **Mask** (☎ 756 1040).

Getting There & Away

AIR

Asiana and Korean Air connect Daegu with
Seoul and Jeju. International destinations
include Shanghai and Bangkok.

BUS

There are five bus terminals (Map pp168–
9): an express bus terminal (by Dongdaegu
train station), plus Dongbu, Seobu, Nambu
and Bukbu (east, west, south and north)
intercity terminals. This list is not meant
to be comprehensive, and note that buses
to some destinations leave from multiple
terminals, so it's best to inquire which is
most convenient. Some are connected by
Daegu's subway system.

From the express bus terminal:

Destination	Price (W)	Duration	Frequency
Andong	6000-6500	1½hr	every 20min
Busan	6200	1¾hr	every 30min
Daejeon	6800	2hr	every 30min
Dong Seoul	13,600	3¾hr	every 30min
Gwangju	9900	3¾hr	every 30min
Gyeongju	3000	50min	every 20min
Jinju	6600	2¼hr	hourly
Seoul	13,100	3¾hr	every 10min

From Dongbu intercity bus terminal:

Destination	Price (W)	Duration	Frequency
Gyeongju	3000	1¾hr	every 25min
Pohang	5500	1¾hr	every 45min

From Seobu intercity bus terminal:

Destination	Price (W)	Duration	Frequency
Busan	8300	1½hr	9 daily
Haeinsa	3900	1hr	every 20min

From Bukbu intercity bus terminal:

Destination	Price (W)	Duration	Frequency
Andong			
(nonstop/express)	6000	1½/2¼hr	every 20/30min
Chuncheon	16,500	3½hr	10 daily

TRAIN

Dongdaegu station (Map pp168–9), on the eastern side of the city, is the main station for long-distance trains. It's also next door to the express bus station.

You'll find that there are good connections to Busan and Seoul. *Mugunghwa* (limited express) trains run every 30 minutes to Seoul (W14,200 to W16,700, 3½ to four hours) and Busan (W5300 to W6200, 1½ hours).

Getting Around
TO/FROM AIRPORT

Daegu's airport is northeast of the city, about 2km from the express bus terminal. Bus No 401 (W700) winds a circuitous route to the airport and can take 45 minutes. Bus No 104 (W1300) is a bit better. A taxi from the airport to the centre will cost around W2500 and takes about 20 minutes.

BUS

Local bus fares are W700/1300 (standing/seated). To get to Deurangil from Central Daegu or Dong Daegu station take bus No 401.

TRAIN

The line runs through the city centre. Important stops include Dongdaegu station and Jungangno (city centre). A second line is due to open 2005. Tickets cost W700.

AROUND DAEGU
Palgongsan Provincial Park
팔공산 도립공원

Just 20km north of Daegu, this park is sprawling, mountainous and well visited. Its highest peak, **Palgongsan** (1192m; 'mountain of the eight meritorious officers') received its name around the end of the Silla period, after eight generals saved Wang-Geon, the founding king of the Goryeo kingdom.

The park's most popular destination is **Donghwasa** (☎ 982 0101; admission W2500; ☻ 8am-7pm Apr-Nov, to 6pm Dec-Mar), the province's leading temple, with a history stretching back to 493. There are plenty of ancient sights here, but the most noticeable feature is the 33m-high **Tong-il Daebul** (Reunification Buddha, erected 1992), in the medicinal Buddha style. The same, contemporary, plaza also contains two 17m stone pagodas; their respective plain and elaborate decorations suggest the balance central to Korean culture. There is an park information booth at Donghwasa.

Another major – and to our mind, more moving – pilgrimage is to **Gatbawi** (☎ 983 8586; admission free), a medicinal Buddha and national treasure, some 850m above sea level and said to date back to 638. This Buddha is famed for the flat stone 'hat' hovering over its head, 15cm thick. Given that this Buddha is said to hear one prayer from each visitor, there's often quite a crowd praying before him on the open plaza, even early in the morning and especially on the first of the month and at university entrance-exam time. It takes about 45 minutes to walk up the stone steps to Gatbawi from the tourist village.

The **Palgongsan Skyline Cable Car** (☎ 982 8801; return W5500; ☻ 9.45am-sunset) is the quickest way to ascend Palgongsan. The 1.2km-long ride drops you at the observatory (820m), which affords a panoramic view of Daegu. There's

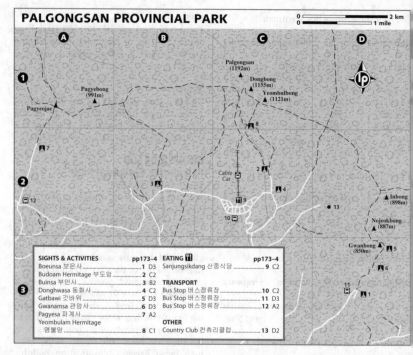

PALGONGSAN PROVINCIAL PARK

SIGHTS & ACTIVITIES	pp173–4
Boeunsa 보은사	1 D3
Budoam Hermitage 부도암	2 C2
Buinsa 부인사	3 B2
Donghwasa 동화사	4 C2
Gatbawi 갓바위	5 D3
Gwanamsa 관암사	6 D3
Pagyesa 파계사	7 A2
Yeombulam Hermitage 염불암	8 C1

EATING	pp173–4
Sanjungsikdang 산중식당	9 C2

TRANSPORT	
Bus Stop 버스정류장	10 C2
Bus Stop 버스정류장	11 D3
Bus Stop 버스정류장	12 A2

OTHER	
Country Club 컨츄리클럽	13 D2

a tourist village at the base of the cable car that has many restaurants – **Sanjungsikdang** (meals W5500-18,000) is known for mushroom cuisine, including tasty mushroom *pajeon* (pancakes).

There's also an 18-hole golf course in the park.

GETTING THERE & AWAY
Bus No 104 (W1300) runs between Dongdaegu station and the tourist village below Gatbawi. Bus No 105 (W1300) connects Donghwasa and the bus stop near Dongdaegu station. These buses run at least once every 12 minutes and take 50 minutes to complete the journey.

Haeinsa 해인사
This Unesco World Heritage **temple** (☎ 055-931 1001; admission W2800; ☼ 9am-9pm) pulls out all the stops. It's in Gayasan National Park (part of the Sobaek range) and, although Haeinsa is actually in Gyeongsamnam-do, easiest access is from Daegu.

Haeinsa is one of the 10 great temples of the Hwaom (Avatamsaka) sect, but the reason for its fame is that it is the repository of the **Tripitaka Koreana** – 81,340 carved woodblocks, on which are the complete Buddhist scriptures, as well as many illustrations remarkably like those in Nepal. The blocks are housed in four enormous buildings at the temple's upper reaches, complete with simple but effective ventilation to prevent deterioration. Also housed here are an additional 2835 blocks from the Goryeo period containing more Buddhist scriptures, literary works and an illustration of Avatamsaka Sutra.

Although the buildings are normally locked, the blocks are easily visible through slatted windows.

The woodblocks you see today are actually the second set. The first set was created from 1011 to 1087 and destroyed by invaders in 1232. This second set was begun shortly thereafter and completed 1251. The Tripitaka has been kept at Haeinsa since the early years of the Joseon dynasty.

Haeinsa itself was founded at the beginning of the 9th century by two monks, Suneung and Ijong, following many years of study in China. It was not until the early days of the Goryeo dynasty (mid-10th century) that it attained its present size.

As well as being one of Korea's most significant temples, Haeinsa is also one of the most beautiful. Part of its beauty lies in the natural setting of mixed deciduous and coniferous forest. It's a romantic's paradise in wet weather, when wisps of cloud drift at various levels through the forest. At prayer times (3.30am, 10am and 6.30pm) the place can feel otherworldly (try listening with your eyes closed), and on our visit we were able to create our own print from an actual woodblock in the **exhibition hall**.

The main hall, **Daegwangjeon** was burnt down during the Japanese invasion of 1592 and again (accidentally) in 1817, though, miraculously, the Tripitaka escaped destruction. The hall was reconstructed again in 1971. More reconstruction has been undertaken since then – all of it, naturally, along traditional lines.

A new **Haeinsa museum** (☎ 055-934 0988; admission W2000; ⏲ 10am-6pm Mar-Oct, to 5pm Nov-Feb, closed Tue), built in 2002, showcases some of the temple's treasures and has a reverie on Haeinsa in contemporary art upstairs. It's a short walk from the main road, and the temple is another 15 minutes' walk.

Hikers will want to challenge **Gayasan** (1430m), the main peak in the national park and a pretty one, though the 1100m up from Haeinsa are known to be tough.

SLEEPING & EATING

Haeinsa is a popular day trip from Daegu, but there are options to spend the night. Probably the most interesting is **Haeinsa**, offering free room and board provided that you don't abuse the privilege (ie no more than two nights, respect monastic customs, and observe the temple's schedules for wakeup, lights out and meals). Don't expect luxury (men and women sleep in separate *ondol*-style dorms), but it's a worthwhile option to experience the 3.30am service. Groups of 20 or more can reserve a more intensive temple stay (W30,000 per person per night).

Camping is available, 500m from the bus terminal.

There are other options in the tourist village, about five minutes' walk uphill from the temple entrance.

Munhwa Jang (☎ 055-932 7237; r from W30,000; ✖) A swell little *yeogwan* in the tourist village, with renovated doubles, *ondol* rooms and a balcony for socializing.

TRIPITAKA KOREANA

The **Tripitaka Koreana**, also known as the Goryeo Buddhist canon, is one of the world's most significant complete Buddhist sacred texts. Tripitaka literally means 'three baskets', representing the three divisions of Buddhism: the Sutra (scriptures), Vinaya (laws) and the Abhidharma (treatises).

The Tripitaka Koreana has been preserved on more than 80,000 beautifully carved woodblocks, their extraordinary workmanship further emphasising their importance. The carving took 16 years to complete. Every stage of the process was carried out to ensure their continued preservation. From carefully selecting appropriate birch wood, then soaking it in brine and boiling it in salt before drying it, to locating and constructing a sophisticated repository, the techniques involved were so complex and the artwork so intricate that they remain an inspiration today. The woodblocks are housed and preserved in the 15th-century hall, **Janggyong Pango**, a masterpiece of ingenuity in its own right; among its techniques: charcoal beneath the clay floor. Despite the ravages of Japanese invasion and fires that destroyed the rest of the temple complex, the repository remained standing, with the woodblocks preserved intact.

During the 1970s, President Pak Chung-hee ordered the construction of a modern storage facility for the woodblocks. The facility was equipped with advanced ventilation, temperature and humidity control. However, after some test woodblocks began to grow mildew the whole scheme was scrapped. Today, the four storage halls and woodblocks are inscribed on the Unesco World Heritage List to ensure their continued preservation. In a bold attempt to ensure accessibility to more people, Haeinsa's monks have completely transcribed the complete works onto a single CD-ROM and translated the classical Chinese text into modern-day Korean – the 20-plus-volume set costs about W3,000,000 – if you can afford to buy it!

For more, check out the website at www.ocp.go.kr/english/treasure/dom_hae.html.

Sanjangbyeol-jang Yeogwan (☎ 055-932 7245; r W30,000-60,000) There's a traditional feel here, although *ondol* rooms are modern. It's up the hill in the tourist village. Price varies with season and room size.

Haeinsa Tourist Hotel (☎ 055-933 2000; www .haeinsahotel.co.kr; d/tw W78,650/84,700, 20% weekday discount; ✍) The top-end option, comfort at the top of the hill, even if it's showing its age a bit. The website has lots of helpful local information.

Gorau (meals W9000) The menu totals one dish, *sanchae jongsik* (rice with many assorted side dishes). Try for a table in the back room, where windows look out over a stream and trees. The former Japanese prime minister ate here, and if it was good enough for him…

GETTING THERE & AWAY
Daegu (Seobu terminal) offers the most convenient bus access to Haeinsa (W3900, one hour, every 20 minutes).

GYEONGJU 경주
pop 287,000
Gyeongju is one of Korea's most popular tourist destinations, with good reason.

In 57 BC, around when Julius Caesar was subduing Gaul, Gyeongju became the capital of the Silla dynasty (see the Timeline p21), and it remained so for nearly 1000 years. In the 7th century AD, under King Munmu, Silla conquered the neighbouring kingdoms of Goguryeo and Baekje, and Gyeongju became capital of the whole peninsula. The city's population eventually peaked at around one million, but as empires do, Silla eventually fell victim to division from within and invasion from without.

Following Silla's conquest by Goryeo in 927, the capital of Korea was moved far to the north, and Gyeongju began a prolonged period of obscurity. It was pillaged and ransacked by the Mongols in the early 13th century and by the Japanese in the late 16th century. The city began a cultural revival in the early 20th century – with much preservation and restoration work thanks to the dictator Park Chung-hee in the 1970s – which continues today. Many sights have been restored, close to original specifications, and almost every year archaeologists uncover precious relics which help throw light on life during the Silla period.

Today, central Gyeongju is essentially an open-air museum. Walk in any direction, and you will come across tombs, temples, rock carvings, pagodas, Buddhist statuary and the ruins of palaces, pleasure gardens and castles. Tumuli (grass-covered burial mounds) are only the most conspicuous and accessible of the sights.

However, one can't truly know Gyeongju's charms without visiting its outlying districts. Gyeongju covers a vast 1323 sq km, and you should allow several days to take it all in. Round a ridge on Namsan, the mountain south of town, and you may come face-to-face with an ancient Buddha statue or a very-much-alive monk. Towards the east are Unesco World Heritage temples, a martial-arts monastery and the world's only sea tomb. To the north are the well-preserved village of Yangdong and the former Oksan Confucian Academy. Even further afield are literally thousands of Silla relics, not to mention reminders of later dynasties.

The entire region is a hiker's dream and, with nearly 300 designated cultural assets here, if you're not charmed by one monument, another is probably just around the bend.

Orientation & Information
Central Gyeongju is fairly compact, encompassing the bus and train terminals (under 20 minutes' walk apart) and, between them, sights, lodgings and dining.

About 5km east of the centre is Bomunho, a lakeside resort with a golf course, luxury hotels and posh restaurants. A 16km drive southeast brings you to Bulguksa, one of Korea's most famous temples and a major tourist drawcard. From here's it's a quick ride to Seokguram, a mountain grotto with a historic Buddha.

Many of the region's noteworthy sights are in Gyeongju National Park. It's not one contiguous park, but numerous separate districts surrounding the city centre.

There are tourist information kiosks outside the express bus terminal and train station and in the car park near Bulguksa, all with English-speaking staff and a comprehensive English-language map with everything from sights to bike trails.

For the legends, the detailed history and current archaeological debate surrounding the Silla remains, read *Korea's Golden Age*

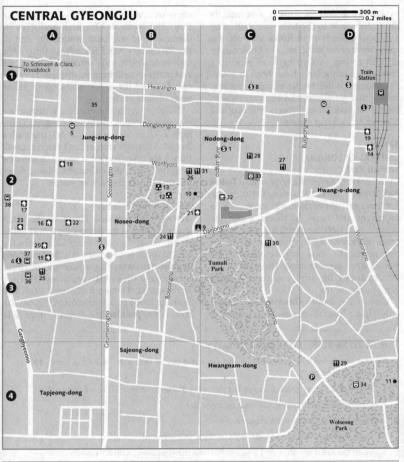

CENTRAL GYEONGJU

by Edward B Adams. This is a beautifully illustrated guide to the Silla sites written by a man who was born in Korea and who has spent most of his life there. The book can be difficult to buy in Gyeongju, so pick up a copy at one of the large bookshops in Seoul.

Gyeongju is deservedly popular, but that means that some sites can be overrun with tourists at peak times (especially spring and autumn school-trip season).

Sights

CENTRAL GYEONGJU

Tumuli Park

In the heart of town, the huge walled **Tumuli Park** (Map p177; ☎ 746 6020; admission W1500; ☯ 9am-9pm, 9am-sunset colder months) has 23 tombs of Silla monarchs and famiy members. From the outside, they look like grassy hillocks – much more subtle than the Egyptian pyramids, but they served the same purpose; many of the tumuli have been excavated to yield fabulous treasures, on display at the Gyeongju National Museum.

One of the tombs, **Cheonmachong** (Heavenly Horse Tomb), is open to visitors. A cross-section display shows its construction. The tomb is 13m high and 47m in diameter, and was built around the end of the 5th century AD. Facsimiles of the golden crown, bracelets, jade ornaments, weapons and pottery found here are displayed in glass cases around the inside of the tomb; other finds include ancient eggs.

Nearby, across the pond, is a distinctive two-part tumulus, **Hwangnamdaechong** (25m high x 120m long x 80m wide), the park's largest. Although visitors can't enter, excavations have revealed that it was the tomb of a king and queen and contained, among other treasures, five glasses from Rome.

Noseo-dong Tombs

Across the street and closer to the main shopping area is the **Noseo-dong district** (Map p170), where there are other Silla tombs for which there is no entry fee. **Seobongchong** and **Geumgwanchong** are adjacent tombs built between the 4th and 5th centuries AD. They were excavated between 1921 and 1946. The finds included two gold crowns. Across the road is **Bonghwadae**, the largest extant Silla

---

HOW TO BE BURIED LIKE SILLA ROYALTY

If you're impressed by the Silla tumuli and you'd like one of your own, here's our handy 10-step guide to making one:

1. Dig up and flatten ground; suggested size: 47m diameter (to match Cheonmachong)

2. Cover ground with gravel, followed by stone slabs

3. Place a layer of stone slabs atop the gravel

4. Place a wooden chamber atop the stone slabs, in the centre

5. Insert deceased in coffin, and insert coffin into chamber along with deceased's crown, sword, jewels, food for the afterlife and other artefacts to fascinate future generations (we're partial to the DVD of the movie *Airplane!*)

6. Seal chamber

7. Pile stones around and on top of chamber, forming a large mound. In Korea, the guideline for stone size is 'as big as your head'

8. Cover mound with clay and let dry

9. Cover clay with dirt

10. Plant with grass

Sorry, do-it-yourselfers: you can't build your own tumulus. Unlike with the Egyptian pyramids, construction of Silla tumuli didn't begin until after the person passed on, so the task will fall to your loved ones, subjects, slaves or acolytes. On the positive side, once the piled-stone structure is constructed, it's very difficult to loot; as potential crooks dig towards the centre, the stones will collapse around them. Excavations have to be done with great care and from the top, from where they're sure to be noticed.

tomb at 22m high and with a circumference of 250m. Adjoining Bonghwadae is **Geum-nyeongchong**. Houses covered much of this area until 1984, when they were removed; more are due for demolition. It's tempting to climb to the top of these tombs, but if you do you'll have park guardians chasing you and blowing whistles!

Wolseong Park
This park, southeast of Tumuli Park, houses the Far East's oldest astrological observatory, **Cheomseongdae** (Map p170; ☎ 772 5134; admission W300; ☼ 8am-6pm, 9am-6pm in winter), constructed between 632 and 646. Its apparently simple design conceals amazing sophistication: the 12 stones of its base symbolise the months of the year. From top to bottom there are 30 layers – one for each day of the month – and a total of 366 stones were used in its construction, corresponding to the days of the year (OK, so time was calculated a little differently back then!). Numerous other technical details relate, for example, to the tower's position in relation to certain stars.

A few minutes' walk south from Cheomseongdae is the site of **Banwolseong** (Castle of the Crescent Moon; Map p170; admission free), once a fabled fortress. Now it's attractive parkland, with some walls and ruins. The only intact building is Seokbinggo or 'Stone Ice House' (early 18th Century, restored 1973), which was once used as a food store; it's in the far corner of the site.

Anapji Pond
Across the main road, Wolseongno, on the left-hand side, is **Anapji Pond** (Map pp180-1; ☎ 772 4041; admission W1000; ☼ 8am-sunset, 7.30am-7pm in summer), constructed by King Munmu in 674 as a pleasure garden to commemorate the unification of the Korean peninsula under Silla. The buildings here burned in 935, and many relics ended up in the pond itself, to be rediscovered only when it was drained for repair in 1975. Thousands of well-preserved relics were found, including wooden objects, a die used in drinking games, scissors and a royal barge – you can see them in the Gyeongju National Museum.

Nowadays the buildings are still gone, but the pond has been refilled and is a popular spot for couples to take pre-wedding photos.

Gyeongju National Museum
Continuing along Wolseongno, you come to the **Gyeongju National Museum** (Map pp180-1; ☎ 740 7518; http://gyeongju.museum.go.kr; admission W400; ☼ 9am-5pm, closed Mon), several buildings housing the best collection of historical artefacts of any museum in Korea. In addition to the main hall, whose design is based on classical Korean architecture, you'll find an entire building devoted to the findings at Anapji Pond and a new art hall focusing on Buddhist works.

The hall of ancient tombs includes many original, glimmering pieces excavated from the Tumuli Park site, in materials including gold, glass and jade. Just one example: the crown from Cheonmachong is 97% pure gold, with shapes meant to evoke deer antlers and mountains.

Outside the main hall, in its own pavilion, hangs the **Emille Bell**, one of the largest and most beautifully resonant bells ever made in Asia. It's said that its ringing can be heard over a 3km radius when struck only lightly with the fist. Unfortunately, you won't be allowed to test this claim!

An English-language audio guide to the museum is available for W3000.

Bunhwangsa 분황사
Completing this circuit is the large pagoda of **Bunhwangsa** (Map pp180-1; ☎ 742 9922; admission W1000; ☼ sunrise-sunset). It was built in the mid-7th century during Queen Seondeok's reign, making it the oldest datable pagoda in Korea. It's a rare example of one made from brick. Based on the size of the foundation, experts estimate that the pagoda originally had nine storeys, but only three are left today. The magnificently carved Buddhist guardians and stone lions are a main feature of the pagoda; it is unique in that each entrance is guarded by two guardians. Bunhwangsa is in an intimate courtyard.

To get there follow the willow-lined road across from the National Museum until you reach the first intersection. Turn right at the intersection and then take the first lane on the right. The walk will take about 20 to 25 minutes.

EASTERN GYEONGJU
Bomunho Resort 보문 단지
This newer district (Map pp180–1), around an artificial lake some 5km east of central

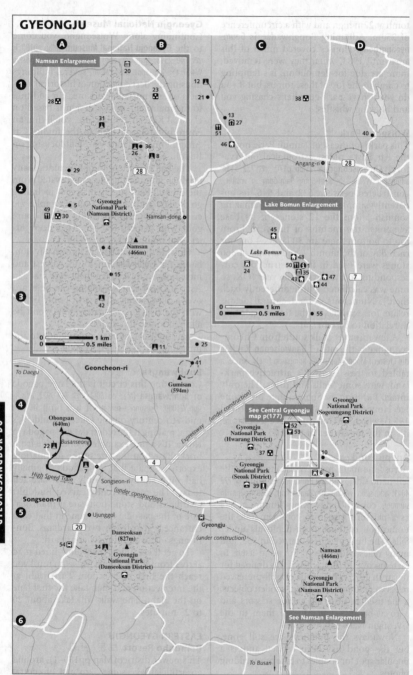

GYEONGJU

Namsan Enlargement

20

23

28

31

26 36
8

29

28

49 5
30

Gyeongju
National Park
(Namsan District)

Namsan-dong

4

Namsan
(466m)

15

42

0   1 km
0   0.5 miles

11   25

Geoncheon-ri

41

Gumisan
(594m)

To Daegu

12
21

13
27
51
46

38

40

Angang-ri   28

Lake Bomun Enlargement

45

Lake Bomun

24

48
50 1
35
43   44
47

0   1 km
0   0.5 miles   55

Gyeongju
National Park
(Sogeumgang District)

See Central Gyeongju
map p(177)

52
53

Gyeongju
National Park
(Hwarang District)

37

Gyeongju
National Park
(Seoak District)

39

10

6   3

7

Expressway
(under construction)

Obongsan
(640m)

22   Busanseong

7

High Speed Train

Songseon-ri

(under construction)

Songseon-ri

To Busan

Ujunggol

20

54   34

Danseoksan
(827m)

Gyeongju
National Park
(Danseoksan District)

Gyeongju

(under construction)

Namsan
(466m)

Gyeongju
National Park
(Namsan District)

See Namsan Enlargement

GYEONGSANGBUK-DO

0   5 km
0   3 miles

See Pohang map (p199)

31

INFORMATION
Information Centre 관광안내센터 **1** C3
Tourist Information 관광안내센터 **2** E5

SIGHTS & ACTIVITIES   **pp178–86**
Anapji Pond **3** D5
Badukbawi 바둑바위 **4** A3
Baerisamjonseokbul 배리삼존석불 **5** A2
Banwolseong 반월성 **6** D5
Bokduam Hermitage 복두암 **7** A5
Borisa 보리사 **8** B2
Bulguksa 불국사 **9** E5
Bunhwangsa 분황사 **10** D4
Chilbulam 칠불암 **11** B3
Dodeokam 도덕암 **12** B1
Dongnakdang 동낙당 **13** C1
Gameunsa Site 감은사지 **14** H6
Geumsan 금오산 **15** A3
Girimsa 기림사 **16** F4
Golgulsa 골굴사 **17** F5
Gwaeneung Tomb 괘릉 **18** E6
Gyeongju Folk Handicraft Village
  경주민속공예촌 **19** E5
Gyeongju National Museum **20** B1
Jeonghyesa 정혜사지13층석탑 **21** B1
Jusaam 주사암 **22** A4

Mangdeoksa Site 망덕사지 **23** B1
Myeonghwal Fortress Site 명활산성 **24** C3
Namsarisa 남사리사지3층석탑 **25** B3
Okryongam 옥룡암 **26** B2
Oksan Seowon 옥산서원 **27** C1
Oreung Tombs 오릉 **28** A1
Poseokjeongji 포석정지 **29** A2
Samneung Tombs 삼릉 **30** A2
Sangseonam Hermitage 상성암 **31** A1
Sea Tomb of King Munmu
  대왕암(문무대왕릉) **32** H6
Seokguram 석굴암 **33** F5
Sinseonsa 신선사 **34** A5
Sonje Museum of Contemporary Art
  선재미술관 **35** C3
Tapgol (Pagoda Valley) 탑골 **36** B2
Tomb of General Kim Yu-sin
  김유신장군묘 **37** C4
Tomb of King Heundeok **38** C1
Tomb of King Muyeol 무열왕릉 **39** C5
Yangdong Folk Village 양동민속맛? **40** D1
Yongdamjeong Pavilion 용담정 **41** B4
Yongjangsaji 용장사지 **42** A3

SLEEPING   **pp186–7**
Gyeongju Hilton 힐튼호텔 **43** C3

Hansol-jang 한솔장 **44** D3
Hotel Hyundai 현대호텔 **45** C2
Oksan Motel 옥산모텔 **46** C2
Swiss Rosen Hotel 스이스로젠호텔 **47** D3
Wellich Chosun Hotel
  웰리치조선호텔 **48** C3

EATING   **p187**
Galibi Haemul 가리비해물 **49** A2
Halim Restaurant **50** C3
Sanjang Sikdang 산장식당 **51** C1

DRINKING
Schumann & Clara **52** C4
Woodstock **53** C4

ENTERTAINMENT   **p187**
Bomun Outdoor Performance
  Theatre .... (see 1)

TRANSPORT
Bus Stop for Sinseonsa **54** A5

OTHER
Gyeongju Expo Site 경주엑스포장 .. **55** D3

**See Lake Bomun
Enlargement**

**Gyeongju National Park
(Tohamsan District)**   16

Yangbuk-myeon

● 19
Tohamsan
(745m)

17

Oryu
Beach

31

Gampo-ri

Gampo-eup

● Andongsamgeo-ri

4

9
2

● 33

Najeong Beach

Bulguk-dong

7

Bulguksa

18

*EAST SEA
(Sea of Japan)*

To Ulsan

14

32

● Daebon

Bonggil Beach

Gyeongju, has become a popular resort and conference destination and is home to Gyeongju's top-end lodgings (as well as some mid-range options). What Bomunho lacks in history, it makes up for in polish. The lake and extensive parklands are great for strolling or bike-riding.

There are also a couple of cultural sites. The **Sonje Museum of Contemporary Art** (☎ 745 7075; admission W3000; ⊙ 10am-6pm, closed Mon) is just in front of the Hilton Hotel. Its three cavernous exhibition spaces host a diverse range of exhibitions – shows change every two to three months. The permanent collection contains paintings, sculpture and mixed-media from overseas and Korea.

Traditional dancing and musical performances are held on a regular basis throughout the year at **Bomun Outdoor Performance Theater**, below the information centre by the lake. If you're lucky enough to be in Gyeongju during a festival, many of the main events take place in and around Bomunho and down at the expo site.

Bulguksa 불국사

On a series of stone terraces about 16km southeast of Gyeongju, this **temple** (Map pp180-1; ☎ 746 9913; ⊙ 6.30am-6pm, 7am-5pm colder months) is the crowning glory of Silla temple architecture, and is on the Unesco World Cultural Heritage List. The excellence of its carpentry, the incredible skill of its painters (particularly the interior woodwork and the eaves of the roofs) and the subtlety of its landscapes all contribute to its magnificence.

Originally built in 528 during the reign of King Beop-heung, and enlarged in 751, it survived intact until destroyed by the Japanese in 1593. It subsequently languished in ruin and, though a few structures were rebuilt, Bulguksa didn't regain its former glory until 1969–73, when the late President Park Chung-hee had it reconstructed along the original lines.

The approach to the temple leads you to two national treasure '**bridges**' (now closed for preservation), actually stairways to the main hall. One of these bridges has 33 steps, representing the 33 stages to enlightenment. Two more national treasures are the pagodas that stand in the courtyard of the first set of buildings and that somehow survived Japanese vandalism. The first, **Dabotap**, is of plain design and typical Silla artistry, while the other, **Seokgatap**, is much more ornate and typical of the neighbouring Baekje kingdom. The pagodas are so revered that replicas appear on the grounds of the Gyeongju National Museum.

Ascending to the top level, outside the **Gwaneumjeon** hall, look down and you'll be presented with a rolling sea of tiles formed by one sloping roof after another.

The downside: Bulguksa can be crowded, and as we went to press a museum was under construction on the grounds. If it's all a bit overwhelming, at the quiet, far left corner of the complex is a simple but moving garden of 'wishing stones' placed by visitors.

You can reach Bulguksa from central Gyeongju via buses No 10 or 11 (W1150). There's a tourist information booth in the car park, near the bus stop.

Seokguram Grotto 석굴암

In the mountains above Bulguksa is the famous grotto of **Seokguram** (Map pp180-1; ☎ 746 9933; admission W3000; ⊙ 6am-6pm, 7am-5.30pm colder months), also on the Unesco World Cultural Heritage List. In an intimate rotunda inside the grotto sits an image of the Sakyamuni Buddha, surrounded by over three-dozen guardians and lesser deities. All are considered masterpieces. This Buddha's position looking out over the East Sea (visible in clear weather) has long made him regarded as a protector of his country. He also bears striking resemblance to similar figures found in China and India, especially those at Badami, north of Mysore.

Seokguram was quite a feat of engineering when it was constructed (mid-8th century). Huge blocks of granite were quarried far to the north at a time when the only access to the Seokguram site (740m above sea level) was a narrow mountain path.

Subsequent centuries were not so kind. When the Goryeo dynasty was overthrown and Buddhism was suppressed during the Joseon dynasty, Seokguram gradually fell into disrepair, and shoddy 'restoration work' under Japanese occupation may have done more harm than good, destroying age-old ventilation patterns and stonework (some of the detritus of this past lines the temple's pathways). It was not until 1961–64 that a more thorough restoration took place under the auspices of Unesco. For protection, the rotunda is now behind glass.

All that aside, Seokguram can be a magical place, especially at quiet times. Like Bulguksa, Seokguram is often well-touristed.

Buses run hourly between the car parks for Bulguksa and Seokguram (W1150, 15 minutes). From the Seokguram car park, it's a 400m walk along a shaded gravel track and up the stairs to the grotto. Alternatively, there's a hiking trail between Seokguram ticket office and Bulguksa (about 3.2km).

Girimsa 기림사

Once you've descended through the pass in the eastern district of Gyeongju National Park, you will reach the turn-off to **Girimsa** (Map pp180-1; ☎ 744 2922; admission W2500; 8am-6pm), one of the largest complexes in the vicinity of the Silla capital. Its size (14 buildings in all) compares with that of Bulguksa, yet it receives a fraction of the visitors because of its location. While you'll see all the usual temple elements (gates, heavenly kings, musical instruments, Buddhas in various forms), the relative peace and quiet may help you feel somehow closer to them here than elsewhere. Girimsa is also noted for **Geonchilbosal**, a seated Buddha made from paper, sawdust and fabric, and then lacquered. The temple's natural setting, surrounded by mountains and alongside a stream, plus a 500-year-old Bodhi tree near the entrance, only adds to the experience.

The temple originated in early Silla times, when a monk named Gwangyu arrived from India and acquired a following of some 500 devotees. Known originally as Imjongsa, its name was changed to the present one in 643 when the temple was enlarged. The present buildings date from 1786 when Girimsa was rebuilt. The temple was renovated in 1997.

There is a small tourist village at the entrance to the temple; *minbak* rooms (rooms available for rent in private homes) are available. If you visit around noon, you may partake in the vegetarian lunch in the temple's dining hall. It's free, but leaving food behind is severely frowned upon, so please don't take more than you can eat. You'll probably also have to wash your own dishes.

Getting to Girimsa requires a degree of perseverance since there are no direct buses. From Gyeongju intercity bus terminal, take a bus towards Gampo-ri or Yangbuk-myeon (No 100 or 150) and ask the driver to drop you off at Andongsamgeo-ri, where the turn-off to the temple goes off to the left. From there you'll either have to walk, hitch or take a taxi the 4.5km (along a paved road).

Golgulsa 골굴사

This **temple** (Golgulam; Map pp180-1; ☎ 744 1689; www.sunmudo.com; admission free) with a kick features a cliffside Buddha carved out of solid rock in the 6th century, part of an interesting cave hermitage. Guardrails are designed to keep you from falling off precipices, but visitors afraid of heights may still wish to stay down below.

Visitors come here to study *sunmudo*, a Korean martial art which has *taekwondo* characteristics and involves principles of the Buddhist eight-fold path and four noble truths. Demonstrations (1½ hours) occur at 8.30am and 7pm daily at Sunmudo University, on the temple grounds. To join morning or evening training sessions, the cost is W15,000, and two-day, one-night training sessions are also available (US$50, including meals). Reservations are needed for all training; English translation may be arranged.

To reach Golgulsa, take the bus to the same stop as for Girimsa. From the bus stop it's a 15-minute walk, or someone may be able to pick you up if you ring the temple.

Gameunsa Site 감은사지

About 1km before the coast, along the main road to Gyeongju, stand the remains of this large **Silla-era temple** (Map pp180-1; admission free; 24hr). A diagram by the entrance shows the one-time layout, but for now all that remain are two three-storey pagodas – among the largest in Korea – and foundation stones. The pagodas are prototypes of those constructed following the unification of Silla. A huge bell, some four times larger than the Emille Bell in the Gyeongju National Museum, once hung in Gameunsa but was stolen by the Japanese during their 1592 invasion, who tried to take it back to their homeland. They didn't get far and the bell was lost in the sea nearby. A team from Gyeongju National Museum searched for the bell several years ago but was unsuccessful. There are reportedly plans to try again.

Sea Tomb of King Munmu
대왕암(문무대왕릉)
A group of small, rocky islets 200m off the coast is the setting for the famous tomb of the

Silla king, Munmu (r 661–81; Map pp180–1), who unified the peninsula in 668. It is billed as the world's only underwater tomb.

Munmu had made it known that on his death he wished to be cremated and his ashes buried at sea close to Gameunsa. The idea was that his spirit would become a dragon and protect the eastern shores of the Silla kingdom from Japanese pirates. His wishes were carried out by his son, Sinmun, who became the next Silla king.

The rock visible in the pool at the centre of the islets is presumed to cover Munmu's ashes, though no investigations have been carried out and some experts dismiss it as a flight of fantasy. Don't plan on researching it yourself, however; the islets are off-limits, and even if visits were permitted, strong tides can make them dangerous to reach.

The tomb sits off **Bonggil Beach**. Both it and **Daebon Beach** (a cove to the north) are popular with Koreans, especially during the summer holiday period, but there's nothing special about this stretch of coastline. There are plenty of *minbak* and seafood restaurants in the area.

From Gyeongju, take bus No 150 toward Yangnam (W2700, one hour, every 15 minutes) and get off at Bonggil.

SOUTHERN GYEONGJU (NAMSAN)

This mountain south of the city centre is one of the region's most rewarding areas to explore, a place where you can easily combine the athletic with the spiritual.

It's beautiful, and strewn with relics, active temples, monasteries and sites for impromptu religious observance. Among the relics found (so far) are 122 temple sites, 64 stone pagodas, 57 stone Buddhas, and many royal tombs, rock-cut figures, pavilions and the remains of fortresses, temples and palaces. You can choose from hundreds of paths, many of which run alongside streams that tumble down the mountain.

Paths and tracks are well-trodden, though at times you will need to head off the main trails to scout for relics which are not immediately visible, since only a few of them are signposted. Or, you may just stumble across a thousand-year-old-plus monument – talk about adventure travel! See boxed text Namsan Day Hiking Routes following for some day-hike suggestions. Tourist offices can help with more and provide maps.

BOTTOMS UP

Legend has it that the Silla king, in the company of his concubines and courtiers, would sit beside the Poseokjeongji waterway while dancers performed in the centre. The king would recite a line of poetry and command one of his guests to respond with a matching line, at the same time placing a cup of wine on the water. If the guest couldn't come up with a matching line by the time the cup reached him, the guest was required to drink the entire cup.

Bus Nos 11, 500, 501, 503, 505, 506, 507 and 591 all pass by Namsan.

Oreung Tombs 오릉

South from the city over the first bridge, these **tombs** (Map pp180-1; ☎ 772 6903; admission W300; ◷ 8am-6pm) are five of the region's most ancient, including the 2000-year-old tomb of the kingdom's founder, King Hyeokgeose.

Poseokjeongji 포석정지

Quite a walk down the road is this **former banquet garden** (Map pp180-1; ☎ 745 8484; admission W500; ◷ 9am-6pm Mar-Nov, to 5pm Dec-Feb) in a glade of shade trees. The site is known for one symbol of Silla elegance: a thin, shallow, abalone-shaped granite waterway, several metres in diameter, through which a stream once flowed (see boxed text 'Bottoms Up' above). It's now dry, and contemporary visitors may find the history more interesting than the site.

Baerisamjonseokbul 배리삼존석불

Less than 1km down the road from Poseokjeongji, peaceful **Baerisamjonseokbul** (Map pp180-1; admission free; ◷ 24hr) gets few visitors, but there are **three Buddha images** said to display the style of the early Silla period.

Samneung 삼릉

This **pine grove** (Map pp180-1; admission free; ◷ 24hr) has the tumuli of three Silla kings, mostly thought to be one of the earliest (Adalla, r 154–84) and two of the last (r 912–27). Another tomb, located away from the others, is said to contain King Gyeongae, who was killed when robbers raided Poseokjeongji during an elaborate banquet, setting the stage for the dynasty's collapse.

PATRICK HORTON

JOHN BORTHWICK

Cheomseongdae (p179), in Wolseong Park

Seonunsa (p287), Seonunsan Provincial Park

Tapsa (p284), Maisan Provincial Park

MARTIN MOOS

Hahoe Folk Village (p194), near Andong

Beomeosa (p209), Busan

Bulguksa (p182), Gyeongju

Samneung is also a good place to start your hike up Namsan. See Namsan Day Hiking Routes boxed text below.

WESTERN GYEONGJU
Tomb of King Muyeol
The main tomb of the Muyeol group is that of **King Muyeol** (Map pp180-1; ☎ 772 4531; admission W500; ☉ 9am-6pm, to 5pm winter). In the mid-7th century he paved the way for the unification of Korea by conquering the rival Baekje kingdom; the peninsula was fully unified by his son, King Munmu. An interesting monument to his exploits (and national treasure) sits near the entrance to the tomb compound: a tortoise carrying a capstone finely carved with intertwined dragons, symbolising his power.

Tomb of General Kim Yu-sin
Back towards town and along a branch road which initially follows the river, the **tomb of General Kim Yu-sin** (Map pp180-1; ☎ 749 6713; admission W500; ☉ 9am-6pm, to 5pm winter) commemorates one of Korea's greatest military heroes, leader of the armies of Kings Muyeol and Munmu, in the 7th-century campaigns which resulted in the unification of the

---

NAMSAN DAY HIKING ROUTES

Central Namsan
There are numerous trails through Namsan, but perhaps the most convenient of them start at Samneung – you can arrive here by way of other sights on the west side of the mountain, or just take a bus.

Whichever route you take, be sure to include detours – necessary to hunt for relics off track. There's virtually no English signage, but with some *hangeul* skill you should do fine. As long as the weather's clear, you can be assured of fine views and reasonable trails.

Three-hour course: Head up from Samneung, breaking to take in several relief carvings and statues along the way, to the hermitage **Sangseonam** (상선암), where you'll find lovely views across the valley and maybe a monk chanting. Continue up past the rock formation **Badukbawi** (바둑바위) and along the ridge to **Sangsabawi** (상사바위). Then walk back the way you came.

Five-hour course: Instead of doubling back from Sangsabawi, continue on to the summit of **Geumsan** (금오산, 468m), to **Yongjangsaji** (용장사지, Yongjang temple site), where you can break to look at the seated Buddha image carved in stone and the three-storey stone pagoda. Descend to Yongjang-ri (용장리, Yongjang village), from where you can catch a bus back to central Gyeongju.

Eight-hour course: Follow the route as far as Yongjangsaji, but instead of heading down towards Yongjang-ri head across the ridge to **Chilbulam** (칠불암, 'hermitage of seven Buddhas'), Namsan's largest relic with images carved in natural rocks and stone pillars. From here, it's mostly downhill towards the road, and about another 1km to **Namsan-ri** (남산리, Namsan village) on the eastern side of the park, from where it's an easy bus ride back to town.

Northeastern Namsan
Take local bus No 11 from Gyeongju, and get off as soon as the bus crosses the river, about 2.5km past the National Museum. Off the main road is a fork – take the left branch, and you can wind your way to **Borisa** (보리사), a beautifully reconstructed nunnery set amid old-growth trees and ancient images. It is possible to head over the hill behind Borisa to **Tapgol** (탑골, Pagoda Valley), but it's a rough climb. It's perhaps easier to backtrack down to the fork and take the other branch. Follow the river for several hundred metres until you come to a small village. Turn left here and head up the road through Tapgol, and you'll reach the secluded, streamside hermitage **Okryongam** (옥룡암) – in the upper corner are ponderous boulders covered with Korea's greatest collection of **relief carvings**.

Returning to the bridge and looking towards the main road, you will see two stone **pillars** standing in a thicket of trees amid rice paddies. These pillars are all that remain standing of **Mangdeoksa**, a huge Silla-era temple complex. From there it's an easy trip back towards the National Museum, about 20 minutes.

Depending on your route, this itinerary might take you a half-day.

country. Though smaller in scale than the tomb of King Muyeol, the tomb of General Kim is much more elaborate and surrounded by finely carved figures of the eastern zodiac.

Tours

Public tour buses (☎ 743 6001; W10,000) access all the sights and depart from the intercity bus terminal at 8.30am and 10am The tours take seven hours and lunch and admissions are excluded from the price.

Sleeping

Lodgings in the city centre are clustered near the bus terminal; only the cheapest are near the train station, some 20 minutes away on foot. Most restaurants are between the two. Higher-end lodgings and restaurants are at Bomunho, with some less expensive options a short hop east from the lake.

BUDGET

Je-il Yeoinsuk (Map p177; ☎ 772 2792; r from W13,000) Down the block from the train station, it's really bare bones (eg exposed concrete, no private facilities), but rooms have traditional wood-and-paper doors.

Arirang-jang Yeoinsuk (Map p177; ☎ 772 2460; r with/without private facilities W15,000/10,000) Slightly newer, it has tiny, odd-shaped *ondol* rooms and is also close to the station.

Sarangchae (Map p177; ☎ 773 4868; www.kjstay.com/eng.htm; s/d & tw from W20,000/25,000; 💻) For a little more cost, this place has lots of character. It's in a traditional Korean house offering rooms with *ondol* or beds (no private facilities), well-decorated, courtyard, kitchen, Internet, laundry machines and friendly owners. Bookings are essential. It's behind a small temple, Peopchangsa, but may move location; check the website for updates.

Hanjin Hostel (Hanjin-jang Yeogwan; ☎ 771 4097; http://hanjinkorea.wo.to; s/d/t W20,000/24,000/29,000, with private facilities W25,000/26,000/30,000; 💻) People don't stay here for the rooms; many are rather grotty. However, the kitchen, courtyard, meeting room and roof deck are great places to commune and plan forays with fellow travellers. The owner speaks English and Japanese, hands out free maps and is knowledgeable about local sights.

There are several very decent lodgings northeast (Map p177) of the bus terminals, all with private facilities:

Motel Seorim-jang (☎ 772 7676; r from W25,000; 🌐) Opened in 2003; quite clean and good value.

Taeyang-jang Yeogwan (☎ 773 6889; r from W25,000; 🌐) Twenty metres from Hanjin Hostel, this place has pleasant rooms and an owner with a perma-smile.

Yeongbin-jang Yeogwan (☎ 772-6303; r from W30,000; 🌐) Bed and *ondol* rooms have been decorated thoughtfully. Plus, there are free video rentals.

MID-RANGE

Two nice choices are in Bomunho (Map pp180–1).

Hansol-jang (☎ 748 3800; fax 748 3799; r from W40,000; 🌐) Rooms here, both *ondol* and bed, each have a tiny balcony. Free video rentals are also available.

Swiss Rosen Hotel (☎ 748 4848; fax 748 0094; www.swissrosen.co.kr; r from W48,000; 🌐) Across from Hansol-jang, the Swiss Rosen is a nice deal even if the rooms are not enormous. Rates can rise steeply on weekends and during peak season.

There are other options near the bus terminals.

Hilltop Motel (Map p177; ☎ 743 1900; r from W40,000; 🌐) This opened 2002 and has well-kept, somewhat frilly rooms with nice bathrooms. However, you may want to avert the kiddies' eyes from the 'adult' vending machines.

Inns Tourist Hotel (Map p177; ☎ 741 3335; fax 741 3340; d/tw W49,000/69,000; 🌐 💻) This has modern décor in both *ondol* and Western rooms (*ondol* rooms have nicer decoration), all with bathtub. There's web access in the lobby.

Gyeongju Park Tourist Hotel (Map p177; ☎ 742 8804; fax 742 8808; d/tw W65,000/76,000; 🌐 💻) This friendly place was renovated in 2003. Some rooms on the 2nd floor are above a nightclub, but these have in-room Internet terminals to compensate. Ask about seasonal discounts.

TOP END

Gyeongju's top lodgings sit along the lake at Bomunho (Map pp180–1). Discount packages may be available (try travel agents).

Wellich Chosun Hotel (☎ 745 7701; www.chosunhotel.com; d & tw from W170,000; 🌐) This hotel was renovated in 2002 and is already getting Korean celebs as guests. There's nice woodwork in the rooms, Gyeongju green and terracotta-coloured motifs downstairs, and one of the city's favourite spas.

Hotel Hyundai (☎ 748-2233; www.hyundaihotel.com; r from W200,000; ❌ 🖳 🗷) Marble everywhere, gardens by the lake, balconies and Internet connections in each room, plus fitness club.

Gyeongju Hilton (☎ 745 7788, toll-free ☎ 00798-651 1818; www.hilton.com; r from W210,000; ❌ 🗷) This hotel of the chain has sauna, squash courts, gym and a World Cup floor, where the German and Danish teams stayed. We also like the Miró in the lobby.

Eating

Gyeongju's greatest concentration (and diversity) of choices is in the city centre (Map p177).

Jang Udong (dishes W2500-4000) Covering your basic noodles, *gimbap* and Korean snacks, near the bus terminal.

Pyeongyang (meals W5000-13,000) Don't be put off by the sign out front reading 'tourist restaurant'; plenty of locals love it too for *bulgogi* and other Korean faves.

Nolboo (meals W5000-10,000) A *cheolpan* (hot-plate dish) restaurant serving a variety of hot-plate beef, pork and chicken dishes in a rich, spicy sauce and vegetables.

Sukyong Sikdang (meals W5000-10,000) A local favourite for *bori-bap* (rice and barley with vegetables), and for its intimate courtyard setting. Some English is spoken.

Donghaegwan (course menus from W10,000) This handsome place serves *hanjeongsik* (Korean table d'hôte), or *bibimbap* for W7000.

Terrace (meals W8300-27,000) This clean and contemporary chain offers Korean and Western food, and outdoor seating next to a tumulus (more pleasant than it sounds).

Kisoya (meals W3500-23,000) This is right next door to Terrace, with a similar setting and decent menu of Japanese standards (with Korean touches).

Southeast of Tumuli Park is a street full of *ssambap* restaurants – *ssambap* is lots of tasty side dishes, which you wrap up in lettuce and other leaves.

For dessert, Gyeongju *bang* are baked wheat dumplings filled to bursting with red-bean paste. Shops throughout the city centre sell them and, if you're lucky, yours will be fresh out of the oven.

In Bomunho is **Halim** (Map pp180-1; meals W7000-15,000), where mushrooms are the specialty. Order *beoseot jeongol*, assorted mushrooms stewed at your table with vegetables and beef.

Bomunho's deluxe hotels all have deluxe restaurants (Italian, Chinese, international buffet etc) at deluxe prices. At the other end of the spectrum, those who are self-catering will find no shortage of convenience stores or bakeries in Bomunho and the city centre.

Near Namsan, **Galibi Haemul** (Map pp180-1; meals W3000-10,000) is across from the car park at Samneung and serves seafood *pajeon* and *haemul galgaksu*, wondrous homemade noodles with seafood – the noodles are greenish because they contain seaweed.

Drinking

Mahayeon (Map p177) doesn't look like much from outside, but if you're after traditional tea in a traditional setting, you'll hardly do better; it's on the second floor.

Schumann & Clara (coffee W3500-10,000) Coffee drinkers will definitely like this place. It offers coffees from all around the world, and has classy classical music and understated contemporary décor. It's northwest of the centre, on the student-populated street east of the bridge that heads to Dongguk University.

Woodstock (☎ 773-2431) A bar across the street from Mahayeon and a short walk east of Schumann & Clara, Woodstock is a hangout for expat teachers and students.

Entertainment

There are outdoor traditional dance and music performances every Saturday during April, May, September and October (3pm to 5pm) on the stage in Wolseong Park (Map pp180-1). More regular traditional performances are held at Bomunho between April and November. In April and November, these performances are held at 2.30pm and during summer are held in the evenings at 8.30pm. Check with **KNTO** (☎ 1330) for more details (p374).

For more contemporary fare, there's a cluster of cinemas in central Gyeongju.

Getting There & Away

AIR

There is no airport at Gyeongju itself, but the airports at Busan (Gimhae) and Ulsan are readily accessible. Ulsan's airport is closer, but Gimhae has more flights. For information on airport transport, see Getting Around following.

BUS

Gyeongju's express bus terminal (Map p177) and intercity bus terminal are adjacent to one other. Buses from the express bus terminal:

Destination	Price (W)	Duration
Busan	4900	1hr
Daegu	2800	1hr
Daejeon	13,200	3hr
Seoul	21,700	4½hr

Buses from the intercity bus terminal:

Destination	Price (W)	Duration
Busan	3300	1hr
Gangneung	19,300	6hr
Uljin	10,800	4hr
Ulsan	3100	1hr

TRAIN

Gyeongju–Seoul *mugunghwa* services run twice daily (W17,000 to W20,000). There are four daily *saemaeul* (luxury express) from Seoul (W26,000 to W30,600). There are more services on weekends and holidays. Trains also connect Busan and Gyeongju, but buses are more frequent.

Getting Around

TO/FROM THE AIRPORT

Several daily direct buses link Gyeongju with both the Ulsan airport (W4500, four daily) and Busan's Gimhae airport (W9000, 12 daily).

BICYCLE

Hiring a bicycle for a day or two is a great way of reaching the sites in the close vicinity of Gyeongju. There are some bike trails around Namsan (but it's rather hilly) and Bomunho. Most of the roads are quite safe.

There are bicycle-rental shops everywhere, and the rates are standard. A mountain bike costs about W3000 per hour or W10,000 per day.

BUS

Many local buses (W800 regular, W1150 deluxe) terminate just outside the intercity bus terminal, alongside the river. For shorter routes (eg, to Bulguksa), buses can be picked up along Sosongno and Daejeongno.

Bus Nos 10 (which runs clockwise) and 11 (counterclockwise) run a circuit of most of the major sights, including Bulguksa, Namsan, Bomunho, as well as the bus terminals and Gyeongju train station (every 15 minutes). Bus No 150 departs from the train station to the eastern sights, via the Bomunho Expo arena (every 30 minutes).

TAXI

If your time is limited and you want to cover a lot of ground in a short time, taxis are often available for day-hires outside the train and bus stations. Rates are negotiable but hover around W70,000 for five hours or W100,000 for seven hours. Do not expect the driver to speak much English.

NORTH OF GYEONGJU

This district contains outstanding examples of traditional Korean architecture, in drop-dead gorgeous settings. While it's possible to visit on a day-trip from Gyeongju, there's enough to do here that you could easily consider spending the night.

Yangdong Folk Village

Having steeped yourself in Silla history, you can move on to the Joseon period. This beautiful and peaceful, hillside Joseon-dynasty village (Map pp180–1) is full of superb mansions and traditional wooden houses. It's been designated as a preservation area.

The village was established in the 15th and 16th centuries and consists of around 150 houses typical of the *yangban* class – a largely hereditary class based on scholarship and official position. Yangdong was the birthplace of Son-so (1433–84), a scholar-official who was one of the key figures in quashing the revolt against King Sejo in 1467. His grandson, the great Confucian scholar Yi Eon-jeok (pseudonym: Hoejae; 1491–1553), was born in the same house. Much of the area around Oksan Seowon (p189) is devoted to him.

Highlights among the larger buildings include the Yi Hui-tae (1733; with its many outbuildings), Simsujeong (1560; the village's largest structure) and Hyangdam (1543; known for tight-knit spaces) houses. Most of the houses here are still lived in, so you need to observe the usual courtesies when looking around; some of the larger mansions stand empty and are open to the public. There are descriptive plaques with English explanations outside some of the more important structures. If buildings are locked, you may be able to ask for a key nearby. The people who live here tend to be very friendly. There are no entry fees to any of the buildings.

You should plan on spending several hours here.

Uhyangdasil (dishes W4000-13,000), just behind the church, is a friendly café in a traditional building, serving tea, wine, snacks and small meals. There are also some simple restaurants and shops for snacks and drinks.

GETTING THERE & AWAY

From Gyeongju, bus Nos 200, 201, 202, 203 and 206 (all toward Angang-ri) will get you to within 1.5km of Yangdong. From the bus stop, follow the train line and then go under it. There's only one road into the village.

It's easy to catch buses back to Gyeongju or, if you prefer, continue on to Angang-ri and from there to Oksan Seowon.

OKSAN SEOWON & AROUND
옥산 서원

A *seowon* is a Confucian academy, and Oksan Seowon (Map pp180–1) was one of the most important. It was established in 1572 in honour of Yi Eon-jeok (1491–1553) by another famous Confucian scholar, Toe-gye (see p194). Oksan Seowon was enlarged in 1772 and was one of the few *seowon* to escape destruction in the 1860s. However, an early 20th-century fire destroyed some of the buildings here; today only 14 structures remain.

Today it looks ramshackle-handsome, and the sublime setting, surrounded by shade trees and overlooking a stream with a waterfall and rock pools, must have made it an ideal place for contemplation and study. The main gate is usually unlocked, so you can wander at will through the walled compound. Chinese characters on a plaque over the gate facing the river are a quote from an ancient text describing the pleasure of a visit from friends.

During the summer holiday period the banks of the stream are a popular camping spot, and swimming is possible in the rock pools below the waterfall. It's also a great place for a picnic.

Sights
DONGNAKDANG 독락당
A 10-minute walk beyond Oksan Seowon along the road up the valley will bring you to **Dongnakdang** (Map pp180-1; ☎ 752 7712; admission free; ☒ by appointment), a beautiful collection of well-preserved buildings, constructed in 1515 and expanded in 1532 as the residence of Yi Eon-jeok after he left government service. Like the *seowon*, it has a timeless and relaxing atmosphere, as well as a beautiful pavilion which overlooks the stream. The walled compound is partly occupied by descendants of Master Yi himself. A library of his manuscripts was under construction as we went to press.

Due to past vandalism, the family requests visitors to book appointments in advance (ask at tourist offices). They will open up the inner rooms and answer any questions (in Korean). Even if you don't speak Korean, a visit feels like a private tour of someplace special.

JEONGHYESA 정혜사지13층석탑
Just 400m beyond Dongnakdang and off to the left, surrounded by rice fields, the site of **Jeonghyesa** (Map pp180-1; admission free) is now marked by a 5.9m, 13-storey stone pagoda, framed by mountains. Its origins are somewhat obscure, but it's generally agreed that Jeonghyesa dates from the unified Silla period. Unfortunately, the pagoda is all that's left; the rest of the temple was destroyed during the Japanese invasion of 1592.

DODEOKAM 도덕암
About 1.75km beyond Dongnakdang, up in the forested mountains near the end of the valley, is this tiny, intimate **hermitage** (Map pp180-1; ☎ 762 9314; admission free). It's a rustic place perched on a rock outcrop from which two springs emerge. The views, both above and below, are magnificent.

Dodeokam is a steep walk up from the road, meaning that it's about as far as you can get from the madding crowd. Barely any Koreans even know about it. To get here, take the main road through the valley past Dongnakdang and Jeonghyesa. Follow the stream for another 600m and you'll see a rusty sign on the left. Turn left and follow the zigzag path up the mountain. It's about 900m from here to the temple.

Sleeping & Eating

Home stays and general info on this area can be arranged by phoning ☎ 017-533 2196. Otherwise, near the sights, the late-1990s **Oksan Motel** (Map pp180–1; ☎ 762 9500; fax 762 9510; d W30,000; ☒) has *ondol* or bedrooms with shower and an attractive setting. **Sanjang Sikdang** (Map pp180–1; ☎ 762 3716; chicken/duck stew for 2-4 people W25,000/30,000) specialises in free range duck and chicken. *Tojongdak baeksuk* and *orihanbang baeksuk* are chicken and duck stews served with rice porridge. Note: stews will take up to 40 to 50 minutes to prepare, so you can take it easy (there's outdoor seating if the weather's nice), or have a Korean speaker phone before you arrive. It's not far from Dongnakdang.

Getting There & Away

Bus No 203 (every 30 to 40 minutes) to Angang-ri connects Gyeongju train station and Oksan Seowon.

TOMB OF KING HEUNDEOK

The farthest of the royal tombs (Map pp180–1) from central Gyeongju, this was also one of the last ones constructed during the Silla dynasty. It's one of the most complete tombs and has a pretty setting among the trees.

The tomb is 4km north of Angang-ri, about halfway between Oksan Seowon and Yangdong Folk Village.

SONGSEON-RI 송선리

Close to the summit of the thickly forested mountain Obongsan (640m), Bokduam hermitage (Map pp180–1) features a huge rock face out of which 19 niches have been carved. The three central niches hold a figure of the historical Buddha flanked by two *bodhisattva* (Munsu and Bohyeon); the remainder house the 16 *arhat* monks who have attained Nirvana. The carving is recent and although there's an unoccupied house up here, the actual hermitage was burned down in 1988 after an electrical fault started a blaze. There is also a recently erected statue of Gwanseeum, the Goddess of Mercy, just beyond the rock face. Just below the hermitage is a stunning viewpoint from the top of a couple of massive boulders. It's a great place for a picnic lunch.

The trail is well maintained and easy to follow, but bring water as there are no springs along the way. The walk up will take around an hour. From the bus stop in Songseon-ri, follow the creek up along the narrow road about 500m to a small temple (Seongamsa). The trail starts just to the left of this temple and is well marked with *hangeul*.

Not far away is **Jusaam**, a temple founded some 1300 years ago by monk Uisang and has since provided a home for a number of famous monks. To reach it, follow the same directions as you would for Bokduam, but instead of turning off at the concrete causeway, continue on over it and up the other side of the valley.

A further 3.8km up the road from the bus stop for Bokduam and Jusaam, remote **Sinseonsa** temple near the top of Danseoksan (827m) was used as a base by General Kim Yu-shin in the 7th century. It has seen a bit of renovation work since then. About 50m to the right as you face the temple are some ancient rock carvings in a small grotto – it's believed to be one of the oldest cave temples in Korea. It's about a 1½- to two-hour circuit walk from the bus stop. There's a little village along the way, about 2.5km from the bus stop.

En route to Sinseonsa, Danseok Sanjang sells drinks and light meals.

Getting There & Away

Bus No 350 (W1050, every 40 minutes) from Gyeongju passes Songseon-ri, for Bokduam and Jusaam. If you're continuing on to Sinseonsa, tell the driver that's where you'd like to get off the bus.

JIKJISA 직지사

Jikjisa (☎ 436 6174; admission W2500; ⏰ 7am-7pm Mar-Oct, to 5.30pm Nov-Feb) is one of Korea's largest and most famous temples. Situated in the foothills of Hwang-aksan, it was first constructed during the reign of the 19th Silla king, Nul-ji (AD 417–58), which makes it one of the very first Buddhist temples built in Korea. It was rebuilt in AD 645 by priest Jajang, who had spent many years studying in China and brought back to Korea the first complete set of the Tripitaka Buddhist scriptures. Further reconstruction was done in the 10th century but the temple was completely destroyed during the Japanese invasion of 1592 and reconstructed in 1602.

These days Jikjisa is a sprawling and polished complex. Of the 40 original buildings, about 20 still exist, the oldest dating from the 1602 reconstruction. Highlights include the **Daeungjong**, with stunning Buddhist triad paintings on silk (1774), which are national treasures, and the rotating collection in the temple's **Buddhist art museum** (admission W1000; 9.30am-5.30pm, 10am-5pm Nov-Feb, closed Mon).

Jikjisa's most famous monk was called Samyeong (aka Son-gun or Yujeong), a militant monk who spent many years in Geumgangsan (the Diamond Mountains, in North Korea). He organised troops to fight against the Japanese in 1592 and later became the chief Korean delegate to the Japanese court when a peace treaty was negotiated in 1604. Following the completion of the treaty, Sa-myeong returned to Korea with over 3000 released prisoners of war.

Sleeping & Eating

Many visitors day-trip to Jikjisa, and the temple participates in **Temple Stay Korea** (Jikjisa ☎ 436 2773; www.templestaykorea.net; per night W30,000); programmes are arranged on a one-on-one basis. Otherwise, there's a well-established tourist village by the bus stop with a range of *minbak, yeogwan* and restaurants.

Getting There & Away

Jikjisa is reached via Gimcheon (pop 152,000), about 20 minutes by bus. Local buses No 11 (W800) and 111 (W1150) depart every 10 minutes from Gimcheon's intercity bus terminal via the train station. The temple complex is a pleasant 15-minute walk from the bus stop.

Gimcheon can be reached by train, on the line connecting Daegu (50 minutes) and Seoul. By bus:

Destination	Price (W)	Duration	Distance
Andong	9100	3hr	125km
Daegu	4200	1¼hr	88km
Daejeon	5200	1¼hr	88km
Gochang*	5100	1¼hr	65km

*for Haeinsa & Gayasan National Park

ANDONG 안동

pop 180,000

The whole area surrounding Andong, roughly in the middle of Gyeongsangbuk-do, is peaceful, rural and notable for having preserved much of its traditional character. While Andong makes a good base, sights are outside the city – some of them a considerable distance away – and getting to them requires a series of bus rides. Having your own transport, either a bike or car, would simplify matters considerably.

Information

By the time you read this, the tourist office should have opened its new location, to the left as you exit the train station.

Sights & Activities

ANDONG FOLK VILLAGE & FOLKLORE MUSEUM 안동 민속 마을, 박물관

On a hillside 40 minutes' walk from the centre of town, **Andong Folk Village** serves as a repository for homes moved to prevent them from being submerged by the construction of Andong Dam in 1976. Relocated and partially reconstructed traditional-style buildings range from simple thatched peasant farmhouses to the more elaborate mansions of government officials and the like, with their multiple courtyards.

The village may not have the size (or English signage) of its counterparts elsewhere, but it looks so authentic that the television network KBS has used it as sets for historical dramas.

The village also stands out for the quality of the restaurants at the top of the hill. Many are based around re-creations of traditional homes (with lots of less-formal tent seating outside), serving local specialities at very decent prices. Owners are friendly, as are the locals who frequent the restaurants on weekdays (there are often tourists on weekends). Typical is **Yetgoeul** (☎ 821 0972) serving *gangodeung-eo* (broiled mackerel; W7000) and *hoetje sabap* (a precursor to *bibimbap*; W5000).

Just next door to the folk village is **Andong Folklore Museum** (Andong Minsok Bangmulgwan; ☎ 821 0649; admission W550; 9am-6pm Mar-Oct, to 5pm Nov-Feb). It offers clear and fascinating displays of Korea's folk traditions from birth through to death. One large model is of an outdoor gathering including local folk games and traditions like *dongchaessaum* (in which teams balance players on planks over their heads while the other team tries to knock the opposing players off), *notdari palgi* (bridge-crossing play), *Hahoe byeolsingut talnori* (Hahoe mask dance), *uiseonggamassaum* (sedan-chair game) and *hwajeonnori* (picnic day for ladies).

The village is about 3km east of Andong, close to the dam wall on the opposite side of the river from the road alongside the train track. To get there catch bus No 3 (every 35 minutes) and hop off at *minsokchon* (folk village). A taxi will cost around W2500.

If you're walking (about 40 minutes) or have your own transport, stop off at the seven-storey Silla period **brick pagoda**, which is the largest and oldest brick pagoda in Korea.

SOJU MUSEUM 소주 박물관

The heady *soju* of Andong may not be to your taste, but its significance has been preserved with its designation as a provincial intangible cultural property. A few cups of this wicked brew (made with rice, yam or tapioca) and you will start to understand. With 45% alcohol content you will need to keep the lid on tight to avoid evaporation. On the grounds of the Andong Soju Brewery, this **museum** (☎ 858 4541; admission free; 🕑 9am-5pm, closed Sun) houses a couple of displays that detail the distilling process, the drinking ceremony and a history of *soju* labels.

The museum is in the south of Andong, across the Nakdonggang, and best reached by taxi (W2000).

JEBIWON 제비원

The huge rock-carved Amitaba Buddha known as **Jebiwon** (Icheon-dong Seokbulsang; admission free; 🕑 24hr) is some 5km north of Andong. The body and robes of this Buddha are carved on a boulder over 12m high, on top of which are the head and hair – carved out of two separate pieces of rock. Interestingly, the head was actually added at a later date.

Catch bus No 54 (every 30 minutes). Ask the driver to drop you off at Jebiwon. Local buses to Yeongju can also drop you off at Jebiwon.

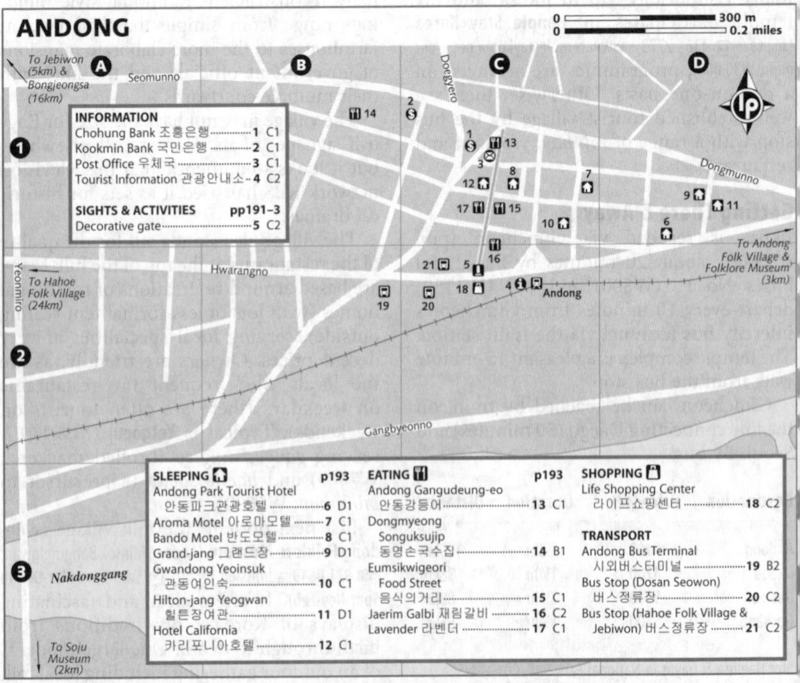
ANDONG
0 300 m
0 0.2 miles
To Jebiwon (5km) & Bongjeongsa (16km)
Seomunno
Doegyero
Dongmunno
Hwarangno
Yeonmiro
Gangbyeonno
Nakdonggang
Andong
To Hahoe Folk Village (24km)
To Andong Folk Village & Folklore Museum (3km)
To Soju Museum (2km)
INFORMATION
Chohung Bank 조흥은행 1 C1
Kookmin Bank 국민은행 2 C1
Post Office 우체국 3 C1
Tourist Information 관광안내소 4 C2
SIGHTS & ACTIVITIES pp191–3
Decorative gate 5 C2
SLEEPING p193
Andong Park Tourist Hotel 안동파크관광호텔 6 D1
Aroma Motel 아로마모텔 7 C1
Bando Motel 반도모텔 8 C1
Grand-jang 그랜드장 9 D1
Gwandong Yeoinsuk 관동여인숙 10 C1
Hilton-jang Yeogwan 힐튼장여관 11 D1
Hotel California 카리포니아호텔 12 C1
EATING p193
Andong Gangudeung-eo 안동강등어 13 C1
Dongmyeong Songuksujip 동명손국수집 14 B1
Eumsikwigeori Food Street 음식의거리 15 C1
Jaerim Galbi 재림갈비 16 C2
Lavender 라벤더 17 C1
SHOPPING
Life Shopping Center 라이프쇼핑센터 18 C2
TRANSPORT
Andong Bus Terminal 시외버스터미널 19 B2
Bus Stop (Dosan Seowon) 버스정류장 20 C2
Bus Stop (Hahoe Folk Village & Jebiwon) 버스정류장 21 C2

BONGJEONGSA 봉정사
This Silla-period **temple** (☎ 853 4181; admission W1300; ◷ 7am-7pm summer, 8am-sunset rest of year), 16km northwest of Andong, has the ornately decorated **Geungnakjeon** (Paradise Hall), seen as the oldest wooden structure in Korea. Repair work on the Daeungjeon (main sanctuary) has revealed a Goryeo-era mural.

From bus No 51 (W800, seven daily), it's a 500m walk to the temple.

Festivals & Events
Andong Mask Dance Festival (held end September to early October) is a great time to visit Andong. It brings together a colourful array of national and international mask dance troupes. It is usually held in tandem with Andong's folk festival, showcasing many traditional performances of music and dance. Check with **KNTO** (☎ 1330) for details.

Sleeping
There are plenty of inexpensive *yeoinsuk* (family-run hotels with small rooms and shared bathroom) around the bus terminal, although most are pretty grotty affairs.

Gwandong Yeoinsuk (☎ 859 2487; d W10,000) Your best deal on a tight budget, set around a courtyard on a quiet side street east of the train station.

Hilton-jang Yeogwan (☎ 857 6878; d Sun-Thu W25,000, Fri & Sat W30,000; 🌂) No relation to those other Hiltons, this is your basic no-frills *yeogwan* but it has clean doubles and *ondol* rooms.

Grand-jang (☎ 859 0014; d Sun-Thu W25,000, Fri & Sat W30,000; 🌂) Opposite Hilton-Jang, it has similar prices and standard.

Bando Motel (☎ 841 3563; d W30,000) Pretty basic but gets points for its city-centre location. Enter through the undercover carpark; the reception is on the 3rd floor.

Aroma Motel (☎ 856 6644; d from W40,000; 🌂) O*ndol* rooms (which are nicer) or rooms with beds are available. Renovated 2003.

Hotel California (☎ 854 0622; d from W40,000; 🌂) Neat, sweet and central. Rooms come with water coolers, hair dryers, shower doors (your author obsesses about neat showers) and a bit of contemporary style.

Andong Park Tourist Hotel (☎ 859 1500; www .andonghotel.com; d & tw from W60,000) Andong's establishment choice; rooms are clean, up-to-date and comfortable, if a bit charmless, and there are restaurants on site.

Eating
You could eat each meal in Andong on Eumsikwigeori, the restaurant row in the town centre, marked by the decorative gate off the main street. Among its many choices:

Jaerim Galbi (☎ 857 6352; meals W4000-12,000) Locals swear it's Andong's best.

Andong Gangudeung-eo (☎ 852 7308; meals W5000-15,000) The enormous model fish hanging out front preps you for the broiled salted mackerel, plus side dishes, served inside.

Lavender (☎ 855 8550; meals W5000-8000) A very civilized pasta and salad place – pastas come with garlic bread, salad and a drink.

The streets around Eumsikwigeori are packed with bakeries, fast food, convenience stores and *hofs* (pubs).

Dongmyeong Songuksujip (☎ 853 3068; dishes W2500-4800) Popular with students and budget travellers, west of the centre (look for the yellow-and-green sign) and featuring tasty dishes like *bibim naengmyeon* (assorted vegetables and cold noodles; W4000), *dolsot bibimbap* (stone pot mixed vegetables; W4000) and *mandu* (W2500). Pay first and staff will bring your food to you.

For self-caterers, Life Shopping Center is conveniently located between the bus terminal and the train station.

Getting There & Away
BUS
The bus terminal serves both express and regular buses.

Destination	Price (W)	Duration	Frequency
Busan	17,800	3¾hr	6 daily
Cheongsong*	4200	1hr	6 daily
Daegu	6700	2¼hr	frequently
Daejeon	14,800	4hr	frequently
Pohang	10,900	2½hr	10 daily
Seoul	14,900	5¼hr	frequently

*for Juwangsan National Park

TRAIN

Destination	Price (W)	Type	Duration	Freq.
Busan	10,800-12,700	*mugunghwa*	4hr	2 daily
Gyeongju	5800-6800	*mugunghwa*	2hr	2 daily
Daegu	5400-6300	*mugunghwa*	2hr	4 daily
Seoul	11,200-13,200	*mugunghwa*	4½hr	5 daily
Seoul	16,500-19,400	*saemaeul*	4hr	2 daily

GYEONGSANGBUK-DO

Getting Around
The tourist office hands out a very helpful
local bus timetable with English explanations. The town is small enough to get
around on foot, and the local buses serve
all the sights.

HAHOE FOLK VILLAGE
하회 민속 마을
Hahoe Folk Village (Hahoe Minsok Maeul; ☎ 854 3669;
admission W1600; ⊙ 9am-6pm Mar-Oct, to 5pm Nov-Feb)
is 24km west of Andong and centuries back
in time. While other Korean folk villages can
be tourist productions, this one has residents
maintaining old ways, and the government
helps with preservation and restoration.
Some locals run tourist shops too, but
there's nothing quite as earthy, traditional
or authentic elsewhere; it goes back around
600 years. There are about 130 traditional
houses here, and although there are better
roads, computers (this is Korea, after all) and
the occasional satellite dish, the farm-and-
mud-wall atmosphere still dominates.

There is a tourist information booth at
the entrance to the village. Various houses
are open to the public, while others are private homes, so remember to respect people's
privacy if you step beyond the entrance
gates. The most important houses usually
have signs outside describing their history.
Highlights include **Chunghyodang**, where a
museum displays artefacts pertaining to the
talented scholar and military strategist Ryu
Seong-ryong, who was prime minister in the
late-16th to early-17th century.

Two kilometres back in the direction of
Andong, **Hahoe Mask Museum** (☎ 853 2288; www
.maskmuseum.com; admission W700; ⊙ 9.30am-6pm)
houses a remarkable collection of traditional
Korean masks, plus masks from across Asia
and countries as diverse as Nigeria, Italy and
Mexico. The English signage is excellent.

If you're lucky, you can catch one of
two daily buses to Hahoe that stop at
Byeongsan Seowon (☎ 853 2172; admission free;
⊙ 9am-6pm, to 5pm in winter), a riverside former
Confucian academy dating from 1572 and
renamed in honour of Ryu Seong-ryong.
This spot, boasting some original buildings
(with impressively bowed support posts),
is way off the tourist map except during
summer – then the river bank is busy
with young people picnicking and enjoying
the relaxing atmosphere. There are a couple
places to buy snacks by the river.

Hahoe has a number of *minbak* (W20,000
to W25,000). Some prove the theory that
'traditional' is next-door neighbours with
'spartan', but you came here for the old-
style atmosphere, right? Mostly, though, you
should stay here in order to have the place
to yourself once the tourists clear out, and
to experience the architecture from inside.
Meals can usually be provided on request.

Getting There & Away
Bus No 46 (regular/deluxe W900/1280, 50
minutes, eight daily) runs out to Hahoe
from Andong. Two buses daily stop by
Byeongsan Seowon and stay about 20 minutes to allow you to look around.

DOSAN SEOWON 도산 서원
If the sloping setting and attractive buildings of **Dosan Seowon** (☎ 856 1073; admission
W1100; ⊙ 9am-6pm Mar-Oct, to 5pm Nov-Feb) give you
a feeling of *déjà vu*, open your wallet – you'll
find an image of this revered Confucian
academy on the back of the W1000 note.

HAHOE FOLK DANCE

Hahoe is renowned throughout Korea for **Byeolsingut Talnori**, a traditional dance style created
by the common folk for the common folk to satirize the establishment. Characters wear masks
representing social classes including corrupt monks and the rich, some with bulging eyes and
crooked mouths. The conflicts among them are portrayed in amusing combinations of popular
entertainment and shamanism. Accompanying the dance are the sounds of *nong-ak*, a traditional
farmers' musical percussion quartet.

Every weekend at 3pm from May to October (as well as Sunday at 3pm in March, April and
November), Byeolsingut Talnori performances take place in a small stadium near Hahoe's car
park. These shows are a must-see; plus, they're free, although donations are demanded by hardworking *halmeoni* (grandmas). If you can't make it to a performance, you can view many masks
at the Hahoe Mask Museum.

Some 28km to the north of Andong, Dosan Seowon was founded in 1574 in honour of Yi Hwang (aka Toegye 1501–70, see also p189), Korea's foremost Confucian scholar – he's on the *front* of the W1000 banknote. For centuries during the mid-Joseon dynasty, this was the most prestigious school for those who aspired to high office, and qualifying examinations for the civil service took place here – with the mountains on one side and farm fields below.

Toegye was also a prolific writer, publishing dozens of volumes summarising and explaining the Chinese classics. Some of his most famous expressions: 'When you are alone, behave decently' and 'In practicing virtue one should perform it with perseverance, suppressing one's desires'. The buildings are beautifully preserved (and are often used by Korean filmmakers) and an exhibition hall gives clues about Toegye's life and work.

Continuing along Route 35 you'll find the **Ocheon-ri Traditional Houses** (Ocheon-ri Yujeokji; admission free; ☼ 9am-6pm), rescued from destruction before the building of the Andong dam. These buildings (12th to 18th centuries) housed the local Kim clan, which included scholars and government officials. The hillside setting is relaxing, relatively unvisited and excellent for picnicking.

Getting There & Away
Bus No 67 (W900, 40 minutes) runs along the main road, dropping you off about 2km from the *seowon*; four buses daily continue the last 2km.

CHEONGNYANGSAN PROVINCIAL PARK
청량산 도립공원
Beyond Dosan Seowon, this **park** (☎ 679 6321; admission W800; ☼ 8.30am-6pm) boasts some spectacular views and tracks wandering along cliff precipices. In addition to the mountain Cheongnyangsan, the summit of which is **Changinbong** (870m), there are 11 scenic peaks, eight caves and a waterfall, **Gwanchanpokpo**. A spider web of tracks radiates out from Cheongnyangsa – most are well signposted and marked. The largest temple in the park is **Cheongnyangsa**, and there are a number of small hermitages. Built in AD 663, the temple is quite scenic, sitting in a steep valley below the cliffs. **Ansimdang**, at the base of the temple, is a pleasant teahouse. By the time you read this, a folk museum should have opened near the bus stop.

It takes about five hours to complete a round trip of the peaks and return to the bus stop; or about 90 minutes to the temple and back again.

Sanseong Sikdang (☎ 672 1133; r W20,000) is a restaurant and *minbak*. Try washing your meal down with some of the local *dongdongju* (W5000). There is also a small store near the restaurant.

It's a 1.5km walk from the bus stop to the restaurant and first trail. Bus No 67 (W1300; one hour, six daily) continues past Dosan Seowon to the park; note that not all buses stop here.

BUSEOKSA 부석사
This **'temple of the floating stone'** (☎ 633-3258; admission W1200; ☼ 6am-9pm Apr-Sep, 7am-6pm Oct-Mar) is small, worthy and way-out-of-the-way, about 60km north of Andong. It was established in 676 by the monk Uisang after he had returned from China, bringing with him the teachings of Hwaeom Buddhism. Though burnt to the ground in the early 14th century by invaders, it was reconstructed in 1358 and escaped destruction during the late-16th-century Japanese invasions.

This stroke of good fortune has resulted in the preservation of the beautiful main hall **Muryangsujeon**, making it one of the oldest wooden structures in Korea. It also has what are considered to be the Korea's oldest Buddhist wall paintings, as well as a unique gilded-clay sitting Buddha. The small exhibition room houses some of Korea's oldest paintings of Indra, Brahmadeva and four Deva kings.

There is a small tourist village below the entrance with restaurants and *minbak*.

Transport to Buseoksa is from Yeongju or Punggi, in either case taking about one hour (city bus/express/deluxe W880/2470/3200, one hour, hourly).

JUWANGSAN NATIONAL PARK
주왕산 국립공원
Far to the east of Andong and reaching almost to the coast, this is 106-sq-km **park** (information centre ☎ 873 0014; admission W2600; ☼ sunrise-1hr before sunset) is dominated by impressive limestone pinnacles that seem to appear from nowhere. Beautiful gorges,

JUWANGSAN NATIONAL PARK

0 — 2 km
0 — 1 mile

INFORMATION
Park Information Centre
공원 안내 센터 ....(see 15)
Ticket Office 매표소 **1** A2

SIGHTS & ACTIVITIES pp195–6
Daejeonsa 대전사 **2** A2
Gwangamsa 광암사 **3** A2
Hurimaegi 후리매기 **4** C2
Jeilpokpo (1st Waterfall) 제일 폭포 **5** B2
Jeipokpo (2nd Waterfall) 제이 폭포 **6** B2
Jesampokpo (3rd Waterfall) 제삼 폭포 **7** B2
Juwang-am 주왕암터 **8** B2
Juwanggul Cave 주왕굴 **9** B3
Mujanggul Cave 무장굴 **10** B3
Yeonhwagul Cave 연화굴 **11** A2

SLEEPING pp195–6
Bangalo Minbak 방갈로민박 **12** A3
Camping Ground 야영장 **13** A3
Minbak Village (Minbakchon)
주왕산 민박 **14** A3

TRANSPORT
Bus Terminal 버스 터미널 **15** A3

OTHER
Picnic Ground **16** A2
Shelter 대피소 **17** B2

waterfalls and cliff-face walks also feature strongly, and with any luck you'll glimpse an otter or protected Eurasian flying squirrel, among 900-plus species of wildlife here.

Most visitors are content to see the waterfalls and caves, but for a more rigorous experience try hiking up from Daejeonsa to Juwangsan (once known as Seokbyeongsan or 'Stone Screen Mountain', 1¼ hours), along the ridge to **Kaldeunggogae** (15 minutes) and then down to Hurimaegi (50 minutes), before following the valley back to Daejeonsa (1¾ hours). On the way back down take the side trip to **Juwanggul**: the track first passes Juwang-am Hermitage, from where a steel walkway takes you through a narrow gorge to the modest cave.

Also within the park is **Naewonmaeul**, a tiny village where craftspeople do woodworking.

There is a **national park information centre** (2nd floor, bus terminal) with English-language park maps (W1000). *Dubu* (tofu) lovers will appreciate the several restaurants making their own tofu in the busy tourist

village between the bus terminal and the park entrance.

The main gateway to the park is the town of Cheongsong, about 15km away.

Sleeping & Eating

There is a **camping ground** (☎ 873 0014; sites W3000) on the other side of the stream and a minbak village *(minbakchon)* opposite the Juwangsan bus terminal. A bit nicer, **Bangalo Minbak/Restaurant** (☎ 874 5200; r low/high season W30,000/40,000) has a log-cabin exterior with central courtyard, and rooms have *ondol* or beds; some have a space for you to bring your own camping stove. It's just outside the parking lot on the way back to town. The region's most upmarket hotel in the region is in Cheongsong, **Juwangsan Spa Tourist Hotel** (☎ 872 6801; d low/high season W55,000/80,000; ❄) lives up to its name with hot-spring baths.

Getting There & Away

Virtually all buses to Juwangsan stop in Cheongsong (W1300, 20 minutes, every 30 minutes).

Destination	Price (W)	Duration
Andong	5500	1hr
Busan	13,000	3¾hr
Dongdaegu	10,700	3hr
Dong Seoul	21,200	5hr

ULJIN 울진

pop 67,000

There's not much to see in this sea-coast town – its big claim to fame is as the home of four of Korea's nuclear power plants. However, some regional attractions (see below) are well worth a look.

The bus terminal is in the south of town with the main shopping area at least 1km away, across a bridge. If you need to cash up, the Nonghyeup Bank in the shopping district handles foreign exchange.

Sleeping

A stay near the bus terminal is convenient for quick getaways, but the atmosphere is typical bus-terminal grim. The shopping district, a quick taxi ride away (W1600), is a nicer setting at similar prices. Rates all over town can climb steeply in summer. Just north of the bus terminal is **Daerim-jang** (☎ 783 2131; d W25,000; ✕), a decent, basic *yeogwan*. At the northern end of town, **Yongkkum-jang** (☎ 783 8844; d W30,000; ✕) is slightly better kept (rooms have bathtubs) and near restaurants, shopping and bakeries.

Getting There & Away

You can catch intercity express buses from Uljin to:

Destination	Price (W)	Duration
Busan	16,4000	4hr
Daegu	15,700	4hr
Seoul	23,600	5hr
Gangneung	9100	2½hr
Gyeongju	11,700	2½hr
Pohang	9500	2hr

AROUND ULJIN

Seongnyugul 석류굴

To spot the Buddha, the Virgin Mary, a Roman palace and a wild boar all in one place, head for this 470m-long cave (☎ 782 4006; admission W2200; ✆ 8am-6pm Apr-Oct, to 5pm Nov-Mar). Impressive stalactites, stalagmites and rock formations are said to resemble images of these and dozens more, alongside a number of large caverns and pools. It was Korea's first cave to be developed for tourism. Although there are walkways and bridges inside, larger visitors (height and/or girth) may find some passages a tight squeeze – hard hats are provided.

Spooky legend has it that human bones have turned up here over the years, said to date from the 1592 Japanese invasion, when locals holed up inside only to be sealed in.

The easiest way to get there is by taxi (W5500) from Uljin. Otherwise five buses a day depart from Uljin.

Bulyeongsa 불영사

It's a pretty forest- and river-lined road through the Bulyeong Valley, but you may wonder 'is it worth the 15km drive?' Emphatically yes.

At the end of the canyon, and another 15 minutes' walk from the car park, **Bulyeongsa** (admission W2000; ✆ 6.30am-6.30pm) is an idyllic spot. The temple is a centre for ascetic practice for some 50 Buddhist nuns, set around a pond and ringed by mountains. It is said that one of the boulders topping one mountainside is a natural representation of the Buddha and, in the right light, the boulder casts its image onto the pond; hence 'Bulyeongsa' means 'Temple of the Buddha's Shadow'. The atmosphere is as harmonious as the name suggests, with well-maintained buildings, groomed grounds, pagodas and Buddhist paintings.

Buses connect Uljin with the temple (W2100, 35 minutes, hourly) but the best way to get around is independently: riding a bike (note that there's a rather long uphill through the valley) or driving a car.

Deokgu Hot Springs 덕구 온천

The chief attraction here is the waters at **Deokgu Hot Springs Hotel** (☎ 782 0677; fax 785 5169; r from W121,000, spa admission W6000; ✕ ☎), said to cure digestive and skin ailments. Separate men's and women's baths are large and attractive, while the hotel's new, outdoor Spa World is mixed bathing (requiring a swimsuit). Although well maintained, the hotel's a notch or two below luxurious. However, its restaurants are better than they need to be, and discounted rooms are often available (inquire through a travel agency).

Deokgu has some good walks further up the valley. One walk takes you 4km to Yongsopokpo, the original hot springs (no bathing facilities) – there are plans to build a series of replicas of famous bridges of the world along the route. A much more strenuous hike (about five hours) takes in the mountain Eungbongsan (999m), returning via Minssimyo (five hours).

There are a couple of other *yeogwan* below the Hot Springs Hotel, which charge W30,000 a night but don't have mineral springs on tap.

Buses connect Uljin and the hot springs (W2350, one hour, hourly).

Beaches

Running north and south from Uljin are a number of pleasant sandy beaches, some of them developed, with attendant restaurants and *minbak*, while others remain fishing villages. Mangyang, Gusan and Bongpyeong are three of the most popular. Local buses run along the coast but are few and far between.

POHANG 포항
pop 514,000

Pohang is the largest city on Korea's east coast and an important industrial centre, but most travellers are most likely to come here in transit to Ulleungdo or Bogyeongsa. The city and its coastline are dominated by Posco (Pohang Iron and Steel Company), the world's second-largest steel maker. That said, the city centre is quite lively, and Bukbu Beach on the north side of town is popular with both visitors and locals. The two central intersections, Ogeori and Yukgeori, ('5-road' and '6-road' junctions) brim with cafés, clothing stores, *hofs*, restaurants and games parlours. Another lodging, dining and entertainment strip faces lively Bukbu Beach.

Orientation & Information

There are information booths by the bus and ferry terminals, which are about 3km apart. However, little English is spoken, and local maps are not detailed enough to be of much help. Bukbu beach, adjacent to the ferry terminal, is 1.7km long, making it one of the longest sandy beaches on Korea's east coast. Bus Nos 105 and 200 go to Bukbu Beach from the intercity bus terminal.

Sights
BOGYEONGSA 보경사

This **temple** (☎ 262 1117; admission W2000; ⊙ 6am-7pm, to 6pm winter), 30km north of Pohang, is a gateway to a beautiful valley boasting 12 splendid waterfalls, gorges spanned by bridges, hermitages, stupas and the temple itself. There are a number of good hikes, including ascending **Naeyeonsan** (930m). The summit itself is called Hyangnobong, and the return trip from Bogyeongsa is about 20km (around six hours).

The temple is 15 minutes' walk from where the buses from Pohang terminate, and there's a tourist village with a collection of souvenir shops, restaurants, *minbak* and *yeogwan*.

The trail to the gorge and waterfalls branches off from the tourist village and is well maintained. It's about 1.5km to the first waterfall, **Ssangsaengpokpo**, which is 5m high. The sixth waterfall, **Gwaneumpokpo**, is an impressive 72m and has two columns of water with a cave behind it. The seventh waterfall is called **Yeonsanpokpo**, and is a respectable 30m high.

As you head farther up the trails, the going gets difficult and the ascent of Hyangnobong should only be attempted if the day is young.

Buses run between Pohang's intercity bus terminal and the temple (W2350, 25 minutes, hourly).

HOMIGOT 호미곶

This district, on a natural cape that protects Pohang's harbour, is a popular spot at sunrise, especially 1 January. The **Jonggigot lighthouse museum** (☎ 284 4857; admission W700; ⊙ 10am-6pm, to 5pm winter) has a large collection of memorabilia relating to lighthouses in Korea and overseas.

Catch either bus No 200 or 200-1 from the bus terminal. Hop off at Guryongpo (W1400, every 12 minutes), then catch a bus going to Daebo (W1150, every 40 minutes).

Sleeping

There are about two dozen *yeogwan* around the intercity bus terminal with rooms from W25,000. Note that rates in all categories may go up in peak times.

Ibeu-jang Motel (☎ 283 2253; d from W25,000) This is hardly fancy but is well-kept.

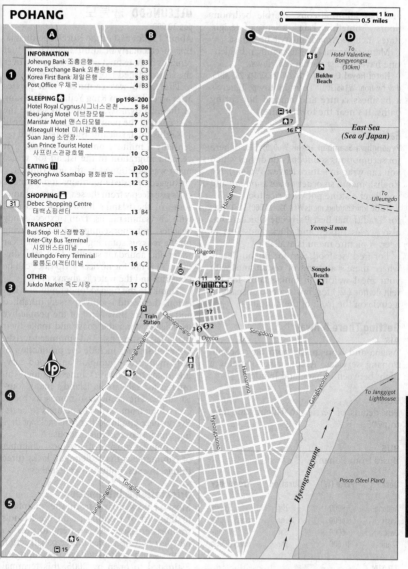

POHANG

0	1 km
0	0.5 miles

INFORMATION
Joheung Bank 조흥은행 1 B3
Korea Exchange Bank 외환은행 2 C3
Korea First Bank 제일은행 3 B3
Post Office 우체국 4 B3

SLEEPING pp198–200
Hotel Royal Cygnus 시그너스온천 5 B4
Ibeu-jang Motel 이브장모텔 6 A5
Manstar Motel 맨스타모텔 7 C1
Miseagull Hotel 미시갈호텔 8 D1
Suan Jang 소안장 9 C3
Sun Prince Tourist Hotel
  사프린스관광호텔 10 C3

EATING p200
Pyeonghwa Ssambap 평화쌈밥 11 C3
TBBC 12 C3

SHOPPING
Debec Shopping Centre
  태백쇼핑센터 13 B4

TRANSPORT
Bus Stop 버스정류장 14 C1
Inter-City Bus Terminal
  시외버스터미널 15 A5
Ulleungdo Ferry Terminal
  울릉도여객터미널 16 C2

OTHER
Jukdo Market 죽도시장 17 C3

East Sea (Sea of Japan)

To Hotel Valentine; Bongyeongsa (30km)

Bukbu Beach

To Ulleungdo

Yeong-il man

Yukgeori

Songdo Beach

Cheongnyongno

Ogeon

To Janggigot Lighthouse

Hyeongsangang

Posco (Steel Plant)

The nightlife district in the town centre has similar options.

Suan-jang Motel (☎ 241 3111; d from W25,000) Good rooms on a quiet block.

Sun Prince Tourist Hotel (☎ 242 2800; fax 242 6006; d from W35,000) It's worn but well-priced.

For better scenery and more choice, head up to Bukbu Beach.

Manstar Motel (☎ /fax 244 0225; r W30,000) Down a street off the main drag, it has nice rooms and the owner speaks basic English.

Miseagull Hotel (☎ 242 8400; fax 248 1818; d/tw from W50,000/70,000) Looking out over Bukbu Beach, it's quite nicely managed.

Hotel Valentine (☎ 251 1600; fax 251 9089; d from W80,000) Up the beach road, it opened in 2002 and has all mod-cons, marble bedroom floors – something rare – a sense of design. Rates include American-style breakfast.

Many rooms at the Miseagull and Valentine have at least partial sea views.

Hotel Royal Cygnus (☎ 275 2000; fax 283 4075; d & tw from W145,200) Tops in town. There's a business centre and natural hot-spring baths. It's near the town centre.

Eating

Pyeonghwa Ssambap (meals W6000) Head here for scrumptious *ssambap* (side dishes which you can wrap in lettuce leaves; W6000). No English menu, so order *dolsot ssambap* and you'll get a stone pot with rice too.

TBBC (chicken/duck meals W10,000/12,000) It stands for Traditional Best Barbecue Chicken, but also serves turkey and duck, plus lots of beer. A picture menu is available.

For fresh seafood, aim for Bukbu Beach, where there's a string of restaurants with your meal waiting in tanks. Look for the telltale *hoe* (회) for 'raw seafood', usually in a circle on the front of the building.

Getting There & Away
AIR
Asiana and Korean Air both have Seoul–Pohang services. Asiana also operates a flight between Pohang and Jejudo.

BOAT
For details of ferries to Ulleungdo, refer to p205.

BUS
Buses from Pohang:

Dest.	Price (W)	Duration	Frequency
Andong	9900	2hr	5 daily
Busan	6000	1½hr	every 10min
Daegu	6000	2hr	30 daily
Seoul	16,600	5hr	every 20min

TRAIN
There are a few trains from Pohang, including to Seoul (*saemaeul*; W27,700 to W32,600, five hours, four daily).

Getting Around
Local buses cost W700 (regular) or W1150 (deluxe). Bus No 200 runs between the airport and the intercity bus terminal.

ULLEUNGDO 울릉도
pop 10,000

About 135km east of the Korean peninsula, this spectacularly beautiful island is all that remains of an extinct volcano towering over the storm-lashed Donghae (East Sea).

The island was captured from pirates after an order from King Yeji, the 22nd king of the Silla dynasty, in order to secure the east coast of the peninsula. From then until 1884 this small volcanic island remained essentially a military outpost, but from that year on migration to the island for settlement was sanctioned by the government.

Rugged, forested mountains and dramatic cliffs rise steeply from the sea, and in autumn, some of the island's hillsides are covered with chrysanthemums. Don't expect sandy beaches, but snorkelling and scuba diving off the rocks is stunning, thanks to the clear water and abundant sea life. That said, diving here is not for novices – rip tides can be powerful and the water is always cold.

Thanks to the rugged topography and isolation, the island is only sparsely inhabited and farms are tiny. Most of the people live in villages along the coast and make their living harvesting fish and summer tourists. Other industries include the production of taffy made from pumpkin and wood carvings made from native Chinese juniper – all offered for sale at the island's many tourist shops. The island also names its rocks, everything from turtles to helmets to bears. Everywhere you look there are racks of drying squid, seaweed and octopus.

A popular slogan of the local chamber of commerce is that Ulleungdo lacks three things: thieves, pollution and snakes.

Orientation & Information
Most visitors arrive from the mainland to the port of Dodong-ri, on the island's southeastern side. As we went to press, a new ferry terminal was under construction in the south-central village of Sadong-ri. Estimated to open by 2005, this terminal is set to take over most traffic to the mainland. On the coast north of Dodong-ri is the busy village of Jeodong-ri, which retains a traditional fishing-village feel. The other main point of interest to tourists is Naribunji, a basin in the north of the island.

Although the island is basically round, the road around it is C-shaped. The last

MARTIN MOOS

Namsan (p184), near Gyeongju

BILL WASSMAN

Dabotap at Bulguksa (p182), Gyeongju

The rugged peaks of Wolchulsan National Park (p249)

MARTIN MOOS

Baekje-dynasty tomb mounds (p185), western Gyeongju

Hwa-eomsa's famous three-tiered pagoda (p239)

Beopjusa and its huge bronze standing Buddha (p315), Songnisan National Park

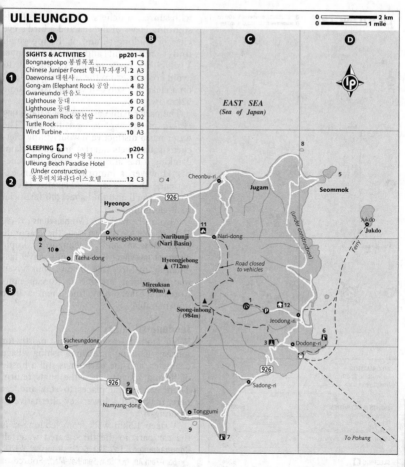

ULLEUNGDO

SIGHTS & ACTIVITIES	pp201–4
Bongnaepokpo 봉래폭포	1 C3
Chinese Juniper Forest 향나무자생지	2 A3
Daewonsa 대원사	3 C3
Gong-am (Elephant Rock) 공암	4 B2
Gwaneumdo 관음도	5 D2
Lighthouse 등대	6 D3
Lighthouse 등대	7 C4
Samseonam Rock 삼선암	8 D2
Turtle Rock	9 B4
Wind Turbine	10 A3

SLEEPING	p204
Camping Ground 야영장	11 C2
Ulleung Beach Paradise Hotel (Under construction) 울릉비치파라다이스호텔	12 C3

EAST SEA (Sea of Japan)

---

section, along the east coast, has been under construction for years, and nobody's sure when/if it will open. Spurs detour to sights on the island's interior.

There is no English spoken at the information booth by the Dodong-ri ferry terminal; however, there are some bilingual maps of the island, as well as bus schedules in Korean. More-detailed maps of the island can be purchased from tourist shops. You can change money at Nonghyeop Bank in Dodong-ri.

Sights
DODONG-RI 도동리

Dodong-ri is the island's administrative centre and largest town. Like a pirate outpost, its very narrow harbour is almost

hidden away in a narrow valley between two craggy, forested mountains, making it visible only when approached directly. It's also the island's main tourist hub, meaning the greatest selection of lodging and dining, but for some the number of tourists can become a little overwhelming.

By the ferry terminal, a staircase leads around the base of the cliffs to a lighthouse (allow one hour to walk).

Mineral Spring Park 약수 공원
The highlight of this park, a 350m climb above Dodong-ri, is the **cable car** (☎ 791 7160; return W6500; ☼ approx ½hr before sunrise-when last visitor leaves) across a steep valley to **Manghyangbong** (316m), a peak popular

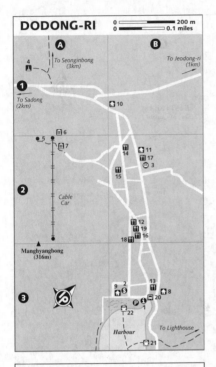

DODONG-RI

0 — 200 m
0 — 0.1 miles

Ⓐ   Ⓑ

❶ 4   ↑ To Seonginbong
            (3km)   To Jeodong-ri
                                         (1km)
To Sadong
(2km)   🏠 10

      ● 5   🏛 6
              🏛 7   🏠 11
                         🍴 14 🍴 17
                                ◎ 3
                         🍴 15
❷   Cable
        Car
                         🍴 12   🍴 19
                         🍴 16
              18 🏠 🍴   🍴
▲
Manghyangbong
  (316m)
                    9 2   13
❸   🏠 🚩   🍴   🏠 8
         ✴   🅿 🚩 20
                         1
                    🚩 22
              Harbour   To Lighthouse
                    🚩 21

with sunrise-watchers. The ride up affords stunning views of the sea and a bird's-eye view of Dodong-ri, and at the top you'll find a restaurant and karaoke lounge. Visit either early or late in the day to avoid crowds. From the observation deck, on a clear day you can view Dokdo, some 92km away.

The park's namesake **mineral-water spring** (*yaksu gwangjang*) is near the top. The water has a distinctive flavour (think diet-citrus-soda-meets-quartz) and some claim drinking it has all sorts of medicinal benefits. However, a minority of travellers experience, shall we say, mild laxative effects. Nearby, you'll also find a **rack cliff** (artificial rock-climbing wall).

Also in the park are two **museums** (☎ 790 6421; admission free; ⏰ 9am-6pm), the elaborate **Dokdo Museum** and Ulleungdo's simple **historical museum**. Both islands have fascinating history (see below), but given that the exhibits are only in Korean, non-Korean-speakers may find them a little impenetrable.

Jeodong-ri 저동리

While Dodong-ri seems to exist mostly for tourism, Jeodong-ri retains a fishing-village character, and the harbour is still a bustle of fishing activity when the boats return. There are several places to stay and eat here, making it a lower-key alternative to Dodong-ri.

A steep 1.5km walk from Jeodong-ri is the car park to the three-tiered waterfall **Bongnaepokpo** (☎ 790 6422; admission W1200; ⏰ 6am-7pm Apr-Oct, 8am-5pm Nov-Mar). Source of the island's drinking water, it's 25m high and quite spectacular during the summer. From the car park, a stone and concrete path (about 720m, 20 minutes) takes you up to the lookout, and if you need to cool off on the walk, duck into the little glass booth along the way, where a sort of natural air conditioning blows from inside the mountain. Hourly buses serve the car park from Dodong-ri via Jeodong-ri (W1500, mid-spring to mid-autumn).

Namyang-dong 남양

Half the fun of this small fishing village on the south coast is just getting there. The road from Dodong-ri follows a tortuous path along spectacular coastal cliffs, passing rock formations (one is said to resemble a turtle) and ocean cliffs covered with Chinese juniper. The journey can be made by public bus or taxi. **Sunset Point Pavilion** (Ilmoljeon Mangdae) is a steep 15-minute walk above the town, commanding great views of the ocean and, yes, of the sunset. Follow the western creek out of town and cross the bridge after the school. A small trail continues up to the pavilion.

Nari-bunji 나리 분지

Nari Basin is on the northern slope of **Seonginbong** (984m), the island's highest peak and the summit of a dormant volcano. Nari is the only place on the island that's reasonably flat, so there are several farms here and a couple of reconstructed traditional thatched-roof houses made from timber, straw and mud. Plus, it's encircled by thickly-forested slopes, making for a very photogenic sight. It's a popular place to start or conclude a hiking expedition (p204).

Minbak, camping and restaurants are available. At the restaurants by the campground, you might try *hanjeongsik* (Korean banquet; W5000), *gamja buchim* (potato pancake; W5000) or *sanchae deodeokjeon* (mountain vegetable pancake; W5000) and wash it down with some local *dondongju* (rice wine; W5000).

Activities
BOAT TRIPS
A **round-island tour** (W13,000) is a great way to admire Ulleungdo's dramatic landscape. Tours depart from Dodong-ri terminal and last around two hours. They run up to four per day, depending on demand, with more tours possible during summer.

Other sightseeing boats serve the island of Jukdo, a nature preserve just 4km from Ulleungdo. Boats (W10,000; up to four daily, depending on demand) offer more excellent views of Ulleungdo as well as Jukdo's own cliffs. Visitors are welcome to take a picnic to eat on the island. It takes about 1½ hours, including walk or picnic time.

On Saturday in summer, boats offer trips around Dokdo, with a reservation and sufficient demand (three hours return).

At both Dodong-ri and Jeodong-ri, you'll see plenty of squid-fishing boats docked during the daytime. They work at night – bright lights draw the squid to their doom, like moths to flame. During the annual squid festival (three days in mid-August), you may be able to board boats and even ride a vessel out to sea. The rest of the year it is interesting to watch them in the evening when they head out to sea with their brilliant lanterns glaring.

WAITING FOR DOKDO

Imagine a tree near your house. It never bore fruit, and you never planned on using it for anything. In fact, it was a pretty useless tree, so you never much thought about it…

…until your neighbour declared it his, and suddenly it mattered greatly to you.

That, in essence, has been the Korean experience with Dokdo, two tiny, rugged islands and several rocky outcroppings some 92km southeast of Ulleungdo.

In 1905, during the Japanese occupation, Japan annexed Dokdo and renamed it Takeshima. Korea protested, but as a colony did not have much say. Following WWII, US general Douglas MacArthur designated the island part of Korea, and US forces erected a monument there to Korean fishermen accidentally killed nearby by American ordinance. However, Japan destroyed the monument in 1952, prompting Korea to send a defence unit and Japan to put the island under surveillance. It remains disputed territory to this day, despite close ties between Japan and Korea.

Most Japanese have probably never heard of Takeshima, but Dokdo is still a sore point for many Koreans, especially on Ulleungdo. Much of the Dokdo Museum is devoted to maps backing up Korea's historical claim to Dokdo. And as recently as the 1980s, elementary school children were taught a song about Dokdo; a portion of the lyrics translates approximately thus:

There is Dokdo, southeast of Ulleungdo,
Home to many birds,
Whoever insists this land is theirs:
Know that it is ours.

CAR TRIPS

Another popular way to see the island is by hire-taxi. Fees are negotiable, but you can expect to spend about W80,000 per day. Some of the drivers are excellent and know many hidden places around the island, though you're unlikely to find one who speaks English. It takes about one hour from Nari-bunji to Dodong-ri.

HIKING

Various pathways lead to the summit of **Seong-inbong**, but the two main routes run from Dodong-ri (about five hours return) or Nari-bunji (four to five hours return).

From Dodong-ri, take the main road towards the temple Daewonsa. Just before you reach the temple there is a fork in the trail and a sign (in Korean only) pointing the way to Seong-inbong (a steep 4.1km).

From Nari-dong, enter the forest, adhering to the right-hand path, and you will arrive at sign-boarded fields of chrysanthemum and thyme. Farther on you'll pass some traditional homes. Finally, at the entrance to the virgin forest area and picnic ground, the steep ascent of Seong-inbong takes you (one hour) through a forest of Korean beech, Korean hemlock and Korean lime.

Just below the peak as you descend to Dodong-ri is a trail off to the right, down to Namyang-dong (1½ hours).

Sleeping

Ulleungdo has loads of choices (from around W20,000), although luxury travellers will be disappointed. Room rates rise steeply in peak season (July, August and holidays), so it's wise to book ahead.

Camping is available on the beach at Namyang-dong, Naessujeon and Sadong-ri. Toilets and showers are available at the latter two during summer. Camping (free) is also available at Nari-dong.

DODONG-RI

Paldo-jang Yeogwan (☎ 791 3207; d W30,000) Pretty basic and a little noisy, but it's just above the harbour. Rooms are all *ondol*-style.

Hanil-jang Yeogwan (☎ 791 5515; d W30,000) This is nicer than Paldo-jang; *ondol* rooms are fairly large.

Sanchang-jang Yeogwan (☎ 791 0552; d W30,000) It's hardly fancy, but it has good, clean *ondol* rooms and is in the centre of town.

Ulleung Hotel (☎ 791 6611; fax 791 5577; d W45,000) Aging but comfy, not unlike the typical guest. Some of the rooms are large (extra charge). One advantage: it's quiet, set back from the street. Don't confuse it with the grotty Ulleung Beach Hotel near the harbour.

Pension Skyhill (☎ 791 1040; fax 791 0203; d with ondol/bed W50,000/60,000; 💽) This new place (opened 2003), near the top of town, has a shared kitchen, rooftop BBQ facilities, VCRs and videos to borrow.

JEODONG-RI

Many lodgings in town offer free pick-up from Dodong ferry terminal with advance notice.

Jamsil-jang Yeogwan (☎ 791 3261; r W20,000) Budget travellers will find this their best option (no Dodong-ri pick-up available).

Cheong-il Minbak (☎ 791 0336; r from W25,000; 💽) All *ondol* rooms, with decent bathrooms.

Nakwon-jang Yeogwan (☎ 791 0580; r W25,000; 💽 W5000 extra) Decent standard rooms; very central and close to the bus stop.

Sejin Minbak (☎ 791 2576; r from W25,000) Rooms are small and simple, though each has a bathroom, and almost all have harbour and sunrise views from above town.

On the way to Bongnaepokpo, Ulleung Beach Paradise Hotel has been under construction for years. If it ever opens, it will be an enormous top-end resort.

Eating & Drinking

Outdoor seafood stalls are so ubiquitous in Ulleungdo that you have to be careful not to trip over a squid; October is peak season.

DODONG-RI

99 Sikdang (dishes W5000-20,000) A friendly place that's received press throughout Korea for its *ojing-eo bulgogi* (squid grilled at table with vegetables and hot pepper sauce; W8000). *Taggaebibap* (shellfish with rice; W13,000) is also a favourite, and adventurous eaters can try *buk-eo* (blowfish; from W20,000).

Sanrok Sikdang (meals W5000-12,000) The speciality is mixed seafood including *honghapbap* (mussel rice porridge; W10,000) and *ttaggaebibap* (W10,000).

Ulleung Hoet-town (meals W6000-10,000) Serves mainly seafood stews, or raw fish for sharing (raw fish prices vary).

Sutbul Garden (meals W5000-13,000) is known for organic beef from 'medicinal cows' raised on medicinal herbs.

Sanchang-hoe Sikdang, downstairs from Sanchang-jang Yeogwan, specialises in *hongeapbap* (W10,000) and *mulhoe* (W10,000).

There are also a few scattered *mandu/naengmyeon/gimbap* shops where you can eat for as little as W2000, and some casual outdoor restaurants by the harbour allow you to watch the boats unload squid for the women to clean and sell.

Koreaned-out? **Jeil Jegwa** is a comfy bakery with a table for you to enjoy your treats. Self-caterers will find numerous tiny groceries, and the larger **Hannam Chain Supermarket** just up from the ferry terminal.

Janbieosu (☎ 791 3122) A pleasant café to relax or enjoy a drink; it's on the 2nd level above Soul clothing shop. It means 'my glass is empty' (implication: please refill it). Otherwise, there's loads of karaoke during the summer months.

EODONG-RI

Gyeongju Sigyuk Sikdang (dishes W5000-13,000) serves tasty *yaksu bulgogi* (medicinal herb-marinated beef; W13,000), but you have to order a minimum of three serves. The mixed-vegetable dishes and *sanchae bibimbap* are just as tasty. Across the street, **Byeoljang Garden** (dishes W5000-13,000) has a similar menu and covered outdoor bench seating.

Getting There & Away

You should carry your passport; you'll need the number in order to board the ferry, and you may need it to register your arrival on Ulleungdo.

FERRY

You can get to Ulleungdo by ferry from Pohang (ordinary/1st class W51,100/56,200, three hours, one to three daily), but ferries are subject to cancellation in poor weather. The departure timetable varies month to month. Other ferries from Hupo and Sokcho may only run during July and August.

It is best to reserve all your tickets to and from the island, especially during summer. Otherwise you can buy your ticket at the boat terminal first thing in the morning, but you may go on a waiting list. Advance bookings and news about cancelled ferries can be obtained in Seoul (☎ 02-514 6766), Ulleungdo (☎ 791 0801) and Pohang (☎ 242 5111). Ring **KNTO** (☎ 1330) for more details.

Some travel agents make reservations and sell tickets.

Getting Around

BUS

Buses run between Dodong-ri and Jeodong-ri every 30 minutes (W900, 10 minutes). Eleven daily buses go from Dodong-ri via Namyang (25 minutes) to Cheonbu (50 minutes), where you can transfer to Nari-bunji (10 minutes, eight daily). For an up-to-date timetable, ask at the tourist information booth.

4WD TAXI

Taxis regularly ply between Dodong-ri and Jeodong-ri – wave them down if a seat is empty (per person W2400).

Gyeongsangnam-do
경상남도

CONTENTS

Gyeongsangnam province is a study in contrasts. Busan, the economic powerhouse endowed with big city diversions and aspirations of becoming an international logistics hub, lies in the southeastern part of the province.

Busan's brash urban panache is a world away from the genteel pace of life that manages to survive in the cities, towns and fishing villages dotting the countryside. Those willing to move beyond Busan and explore rural Gyeongsangnam-do, in addition to finding beautiful temples, rugged coastlines and scenic mountains, will discover a more sedate and pleasantly surprising side to the province's inhabitants.

Another delightful aspect of Gyeongsangnam-do is the ease of getting around. Many sites, such as Jinju's fortress and magnificent Seongnam temple, are an easy day trip from Busan while the furthest corners of the province can be reached in about three hours or less. For travellers with limited time, destinations such as Burilpokpo (Buril Falls) on Jirisan or Geoje Island make for terrific overnight adventures.

HIGHLIGHTS

- Take a trip through time strolling **Busan's traditional markets** (p220)
- Visit a Korean War POW museum on **Geoje Island** (p226)
- Rejuvenate your body at **Heosimcheong** (p211), one of the world's largest hot spas
- Board a replica of Admiral Yi's **Turtle Warship** (p228)
- Hike the striking trails of **Jirisan National Park** (p229)

| ■ TELEPHONE CODE: 055 | ■ POPULATION: 7.9 MILLION | ■ AREA: 12,3333 SQ KM |

GYEONGSANGNAM-DO

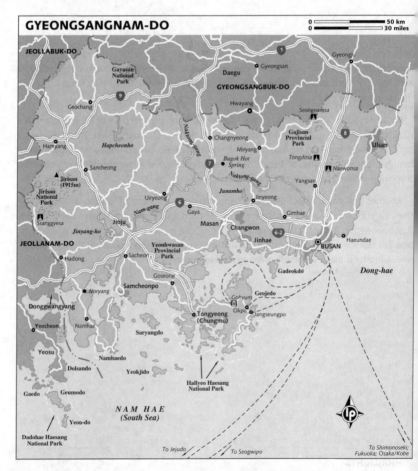

GYEONGSANGNAM-DO

0 ——— 50 km
0 ——— 30 miles

JEOLLABUK-DO

Gayasan National Park

Geochang

Daegu • Gyeongsan

Gyeongju

GYEONGSANGBUK-DO

Hwayang

Seongnamsa

Hamyang

Hapcheonho

Sancheong

Changnyeong

Miryang

Bugok Hot Spring

Gajisan Provincial Park

Tongdosa

Ulsan

Naewonsa

Jirisan (1915m)

Jirisan National Park

Uiryeong

Gaya

Nam-gang

Junamho

Jinyeong

Yangsan

Gimhae

Ssanggyesa

Jinju

Masan

Changwon

JEOLLANAM-DO

Yeonhwasan Provincial Park

Jinhae

6-2

BUSAN

Haeundae

Hadong

Sacheon

Goseong

Gadeokdo

Dong-hae

Donggwangyang

Noryang

Samcheonpo

Gohyum

Geojedo

Yeocheon

Namhae

Tongyeong (Chungmu)

Okpo

Jangseungpo

Yeosu

Saryangdo

Dolsando

Namhaedo

Yeokjido

Gaedo

Geumodo

Yeon-do

Hallyeo Haesang National Park

NAM HAE (South Sea)

Dadohae Haesang National Park

To Jejudo

To Seogwipo

To Shimonoseki; Fukuoka; Osaka/Kobe

Getting Around

Most tourists coming by train stop at Busan train station, a newly renovated facility close to the city's heart. Train travel in the province is possible but the destinations and frequency of trips are not always convenient. The well-developed bus system covers the whole province. Travellers exploring Gyeongsangnam might consider Jinju as a transport hub because its great connections and short travel times (usually two hours or less by bus) to mountains, islands and temples. Miryang, Eonyang and Hadong are also good transfer points though there isn't much activity in those places. By air, most travellers land at Gimhae International Airport, about 30 minutes west of Busan.

BUSAN 부산

☎ 051 / pop 3.8 million / 761 sq km

Although it's the country's second-largest city and the world's fourth-busiest container port, Busan has a cosmopolitan city-in-waiting feel manifest in its populace's gauche urban temperament and a quirky custom of banging into strangers in public places. Like any rogue, however, there's a charming and likeable element to Busan that can best be appreciated by eating and drinking with the locals. Underneath the somewhat drab urban landscape created by an unimaginative use of concrete, there are enough sites to keep travellers busy for more than a few days exploring mountains, temples, fun beaches and a spectacular array of eating and entertainment ptions. As seaports go, it's a relatively safe place, but you should exercise caution in the central area at night.

Orientation

Hurly burly Nampodong is the downtown movie and shopping district with a mishmash of back alleys. Weekend afternoons and early evenings are ideal times to experience an Asian wall-to-wall people feel. One subway stop north in Jungangdong, there are the city's two passenger ferry terminals, immigration office and financial district plus some budget yeogwan (motels with small, well-equipped en suite rooms) placed among the draggletailed buildings that serve as a living museum of Busan 40 years past. Seomyeon, the city centre, is a lively restaurant and shopping area with a lane of street vendors and bars, called Youth St. Asia's largest hot spa, must-see Beomeo temple and good nightlife in front of Pusan National University are in the city's north end. To the east, Haeundae is known for beachfront hotels and upscale bars. The west end has the Gimhae International Airport.

Information

EMERGENCY
Fire & Rescue ☎ 119
Police ☎ 112

INTERNET RESOURCES
www.museum.busan.kr This English-language site has basic information about city museums.
www.provin.gyeongnam.kr/eng Operated by the provincial government, the English version provides information about the region's sites and geography.
www.pusanweb.com A useful site to find teaching employment.

LEFT LUGGAGE
Lockers are available in many subway stations including Seomyeon and Busan train station.

MEDICAL SERVICES
Dr Seo (Map p210; ☎ 755 0920) For general medical maladies. Dr Seo speaks English well. His clinic is at a major intersection beside a large pharmacy in Milakdong, 10 minutes on foot from Gwangalli train station. Take Exit 1, turn right at the second corner and walk about 600m; look for the yellow sign that says 'Jun Clinic'.
Dong-Eui Medical Centre (Map p210; ☎ 850 8523) Marie Kim is an American RN who can help travellers.

Dr Hyun (Map p210; ☎ 897 2283) For dental problems. His 2nd-floor office is at Gaya train station; take Exit 2 to the street and walk 40m; look for the yellow sign on the left.

MONEY
Gimhae International Airport has currency exchange kiosks at the **domestic terminal** (🕙 9:30am-4:30pm) and the **international terminal** (🕙 8:30am-9pm). Most city banks exchange currency, though the level of service varies; your chances of finding reasonably efficient service are greatest at the Korea Exchange Bank (KEB). There's a black market for US dollars in Jungangdong and Nampodong; look for women sitting on chairs clutching black purses and whispering, 'changee'.

POST
Central post office (Map p212; 🕙 8am-6pm Mon-Fri, 8am-1pm Sat) Take Exit 9 at Jungangdong train station; it's the building on the corner. The packaging service prepares custom-made boxes, and there's free Internet access on the 1st floor.

TOURIST INFORMATION
Busan Train Station (Map p210; ☎ 441 6565; 🕙 9am-9pm Tue-Sat, 9am-6pm Sun-Mon) The city's most comprehensive tourist office is in the public square outside the station.
Busan Metropolitan City Hall (Map p210; ☎ 888 3527; 🕙 9am-6pm Mon-Fri, 9am-1pm Sat) On the main floor beside a post office, it's easily accessed from City Hall train station.
Haeundae (Map p219; ☎ 749 4335; 🕙 9am-6pm, 9am-8pm Jul-Aug) Beside the Busan Aquarium on Haeundae Beach.
Gimhae International Airport Domestic terminal (☎ 970 2800; 🕙 9am-9pm); International terminal (☎ 973 4537; 🕙 7am-9pm) A great resource when searching for the correct bus into the city.
Gukje Market (Map p212; ☎ 241 4942; 🕙 9am-7pm Mon-Fri, 9am-2pm Sat) Provides maps and free Internet access; 100m north of the Millennium Statue in Nampodong.

Sights
BEOMEOSA 범어사
A magnificent Buddhist **temple** (Map p214; adult/student/child W1000/700/500; 🕙 7am-7pm, 8am-6pm Nov-Feb), Beomeosa is perhaps the best sight in Busan. Founded in AD 678, all of the original buildings have been destroyed and rebuilt at some point during Korea's history of invasions and conquests. Despite its city location, Beomeosa is a world away

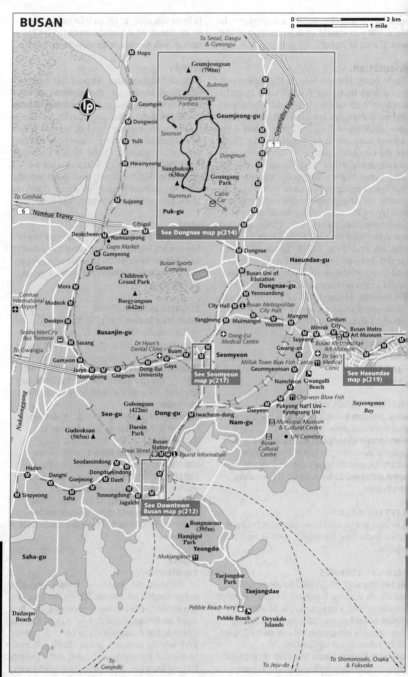

BUSAN

See Dongnae map p(214)

See Seomyeon map p(217)

See Haeundae map p(219)

See Downtown Busan map p(212)

GYEONGSANGNAM-DO

om the urban jungle, with beautiful archiecture neatly set against an extraordinary
nountain setting. It's a busy place, as the
path leading to the temple serves as the
northern starting point for trails across
Geumjeongsan (Mt Geumjeong). Before
leading back to the city, visit the restaurants near the bus stop to enjoy tasty *pajeon*
green onion pancake) for W6000. Take the
subway to Beomeosa train station (Exit 5);
t street level look back and take the first
left, then walk 200m to a small terminus and
atch bus No 90 (W700, 15 minutes, every
5 minutes).

GEUMJEONG FORTRESS 금정산성
Sitting high atop Geumjeongsan, hiking
rails provide views of the city and an
up-close look at what may have been an
mpressive fortress (Map p214). Today,
Geumjeong Fortress consists of stone walls
occasionally covered with shrubbery, and a
handful of gates and watchtowers. Although
a disappointment for those coming with expectations as to what constitutes a fortress
ie there's a fort), your efforts to reach the
mountaintop will be rewarded with occasionally challenging trails, fresh air and
the opportunity to encounter the Korean
custom of yodelling 'Yaho' from mountain
peaks. Outdoor enthusiasts seeking an intimate nature experience should avoid the
mountain on holidays and late Sunday
mornings – peak times for maddening
crowds of fashionable hikers.

The journey to Geumjeongsan, in Zen
fashion, is better than the destination. The
least arduous and most picturesque route
is by **cable car** (Map p214; adult one-way/return
W3000/5000, child W2000/2500; ☼ 9am-6pm, 9am-5pm
Nov-Feb) inside Geumgang Park (Map p214),
which is located at the southern base of
the mountain. Climbing 540m, the ride
provides a splendid view of the city's valley
development. Hiking from the cable car to
Beomeosa takes three to four hours. Just off
the trails, look for middle-aged women selling food and beverages, including duck and
black goat – a W30,000 serving is normally
sufficient for two people.

From Oncheonchang train station, take
Exit 1 and walk left towards the overhead
pedestrian crosswalk. After crossing the
crosswalk, walk down the left staircase and
turn right at the first corner. At the next cor

ner, turn left and you'll see a sign pointing
to **Geumgang Park** (Map p214; adult/child W600/300;
☼ 9am-6pm, 9am-5pm Nov-Feb). Once through
the park's gate take the middle paved road
to the cable car.

At the north end of the trail, hiking starts
left of the temple and runs up to Bukmun,
or North Gate (북문). If you're heading
down, continue past the temple to the restaurants and car park for the No 90 bus to
Beomeo train station.

HEOSIMCHEONG SPA 허심청
Reportedly the largest hot spa in Asia,
Heosimcheong (Map p214; adult/child W8000/5000,
before 9am W7000/4000; ☼ 5.30am-9pm, last entry
8pm) is packed with soaking tubs and saunas
on the 4th floor, with a capacity of 2000
people. Massages and a scrubbing service
that removes dead skin are available for
an additional fee. Guests are welcome to
stay as long as they like and take a break
in the 3rd floor snack bar (use one of the
spa's robes). It's located 15 minutes from
Oncheonjang train station and the base of
the cable car.

BEACHES
Haeundae (Map p219) is the most popular
beach in Korea and the favoured housing
district of corporate expats. During the peak
travel season, umbrellas mushroom across
the 2km beach while frolickers fill the water
with truck size inner tubes rented from the
booths behind the beach. It's a fun place for
families and 500,000 of your closest friends,
though the marketing bumph portraying
it as a world-class facility is more fiction
than fact. Crowds cram the beach every
day in August. Take Exit 3 from Haeundae
train station, turn left at the first corner and
walk about 250m.

Among the city's seven other beaches,
Gwangalli is the best option for access and
relative quality (the other beaches are
Dadaepo, Songdo, Songjeong, Ilgwang,
Imnang and Pebble Beach). Although the
crowded feel created by an ugly wall of
commercial development right behind the
beach diminishes the daytime experience,
in the evenings Gwangalli really shines.
The multicoloured light show illuminating the bridge is grand. Take the subway to
Geumnyeonsan (not Gwangalli) station.
From Exit 1 turn left at the first corner.

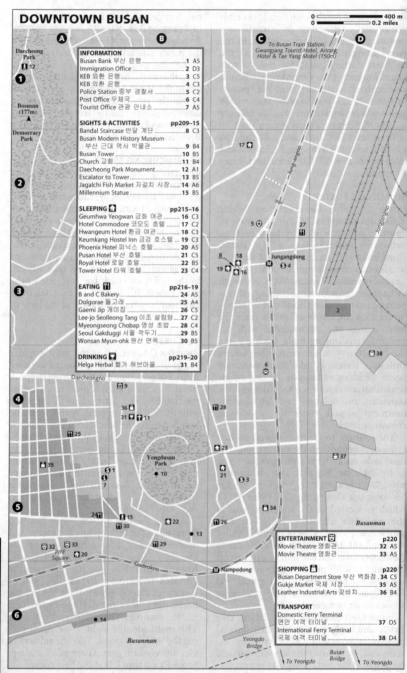

DOWNTOWN BUSAN

| 0 | 400 m |
| 0 | 0.2 miles |

INFORMATION
Busan Bank 부산 은행......................1 A5
Immigration Office........................2 D3
KEB 외환 은행...............................3 C5
KEB 외환 은행...............................4 C3
Police Station 중부 경찰서.............5 C2
Post Office 우체국.........................6 C4
Tourist Office 관광 안내소.............7 A5

SIGHTS & ACTIVITIES pp209–15
Bandal Staircase 반달 계단.............8 C3
Busan Modern History Museum
 부산 근대 역사 박물관.................9 B4
Busan Tower..................................10 B5
Church 교회...................................11 B4
Daecheong Park Monument............12 A1
Escalator to Tower.........................13 B5
Jagalchi Fish Market 자갈치 시장...14 A6
Millennium Statue..........................15 B5

SLEEPING 🏠
Geumhwa Yeogwan 금화 여관.......16 C3
Hotel Commodore 코모도 호텔......17 C2
Hwangeum Hotel 황금 여관...........18 C3
Keumkang Hostel Inn 금강 호스텔..19 C3
Phoenix Hotel 피닉스 호텔............20 A5
Pusan Hotel 부산 호텔..................21 C5
Royal Hotel 로얄 호텔...................22 B5
Tower Hotel 타워 호텔..................23 C4

EATING 🍴 pp216–19
B and C Bakery..............................24 A5
Dolgorae 돌고래............................25 A4
Gaemi Jip 개미집...........................26 C5
Lee-jo Seolleong Tang 이조 설렁탕..27 C2
Myeongseong Chobap 명성 초밥....28 C4
Seoul Gakduggi 서울 깍두기..........29 B5
Wonsan Myun-ohk 원산 면옥........30 B5

DRINKING 🍸 pp219–20
Helga Herbal 헬가 허브마을..........31 B4

To Busan Train Station,
Gwangjang Tourist Hotel, Arirang
Hotel & Tae Yang Motel (150m)

Daecheong
Park

Bosusan
(177m)

Democracy
Park

Daecheongno

Jungangno

Jungangno

Jungangdong

Yongdusan
Park

Busanman

Daecheongno

Gudeokno

Nampodong

PIFF
Square

ENTERTAINMENT 📺 p220
Movie Theatre 영화관....................32 A5
Movie Theatre 영화관....................33 A5

SHOPPING 🛍 p220
Busan Department Store 부산 백화점.34 C5
Gukje Market 국제 시장................35 A5
Leather Industrial Arts 갖바치........36 B4

TRANSPORT
Domestic Ferry Terminal
 연안 여객 터미널.........................37 D5
International Ferry Terminal
 국제 여객 터미널.........................38 D4

Busanman

Yeongdo
Bridge

Busan
Bridge

To Yeongdo

To Yeongdo

GYEONGSANGNAM-DO

YONGDUSAN PARK 용두산 공원

In the centre of this humble mountain park stands the 118m **Busan Tower** (Map p212; adult/teen/child W3000/2500/2000; ☼ 9.30am-10pm Oct-Mar, 8.30am-10pm Apr-Sep). If the haze is not too thick, daytime views of container ship traffic in the harbour provide a sense of the port's scale of operations. There's a modest aquarium and arcade for children at the base of the tower, though parents should inspect the rickety rides for jagged edges before letting their kids jump on. In the outdoor plaza, visitors can buy corn from a small kiosk and watch the undulating flock of pigeons swoop down for food. The park and tower are a 10-minute walk from Nampodong train station.

DAECHEONG PARK 대청 공원

From Nampodong, look northwest and you'll see a mountaintop memorial for Koreans who died fighting for their country. Up close, the **Daecheong Park monument** (Map p212; admission free; ☼ 9am-6pm) is an attractive piece of work that by itself is worth the effort to get there. The best part however is the panoramic view from **Democracy Park**, immediately opposite the monument. Climb the stairs leading to the top of the building with a piece of art that looks like mangled scaffolding to get a superlative view of the harbour and a picture of housing development reminiscent of a Pete Seeger song: there's a green one, a pink one, a blue one and they're all made out of ticky-tacky. From the street opposite Busan train station, bus No 38 or 43 drives right up to the park. From the movie theatre–side of the street in Nampodong, catch bus No 70 or 86 to the end of the line and follow the paved road left up the hill.

JAGALCHI FISH MARKET 자갈치 시장

Anyone with a love of seafood, and a tolerance for powerful fish odours, could easily spend a couple of hours exploring the country's largest **fish market** (Map p212). Waterfront warehouses, tiny shops and elderly women perched on street corners process and sell an incredible variety of seafood, which unfortunately includes whale meat. Walk along the pier and you may be approached by sea-weathered sailors offering a 20-minute boat tour of the harbour; if interested make sure you bargain down from the asking price of W10,000 per person. Jagalchi is opposite Nampodong's theatres.

BUSAN IN FILM

Chingu begins in the 1970s with four boys running behind a truck spewing a thick cloud of insect repellent, a powerful image underscoring this gangster film's theme of blindly chasing after something without considering the reasons or consequences. By the 1990s, the boys are men and their lives have taken radically different directions with two friends ending up as leaders in rival gangs, which leads to a compelling courtroom scene. Artfully directed and skilfully acted, the semi-autobiographical story based on director Kwak Kyung-taek's life is set in Busan, with local sites such as Jagalchi fish market and a gang fight inside a movie theatre – which today sits as an underutilised skin-flick venue. *Chingu*, which is Korean for friend, is the highest grossing movie in the country, and attracted 8 million viewers. The DVD version has English subtitles.

TAEJONGDAE PARK 태종대

This downtown **park** (Map p210; adult/child W600/300, car W4000, van W4000-7000, admission free before 9am & after 6pm; ☼ 4am-midnight) cum fresh air oasis is on Yeongdo (영도, Yeong Island) linked to Nampodong by two bridges. The park is unremarkable and, as some travellers have noted, an unwarranted trip if time is limited. The main attraction is **Pebble Beach**, a rugged cove at the south end of the park. Tent restaurants dominate the beach during the hot summer months, so if you're looking for shade and don't plan on buying anything, avoid the tables or you'll be swatted away by the proprietor. From Nampodong's theatres, cross the street via the underground passage and take bus No 30 to the end of the line.

MUSEUMS & EXHIBITIONS

The **Busan Metropolitan Art Museum** (시립 미술관; adult/teen/child W700/300/free; ☼ 10am-6pm Tue-Sun, 10am-5pm Nov-Feb, closed 1 Jan & national holidays) houses traditional works along with a modest collection of outdoor sculptures. Take Exit 5 from Metro Art Museum train station and walk straight for 100m.

In Haeundae, the **Busan Aquarium** (Map p219-000; adult/student/child W14,000/11,500/9000; ☼ 10am-7pm Mon-Fri; 9am-9pm Sat, Sun & holidays; 9am-11pm Jul-Aug) is a large underground fish tank with 50,000 sea creatures. It's on the beach

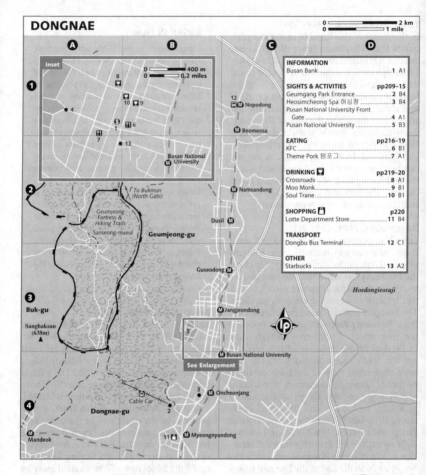

DONGNAE

INFORMATION	
Busan Bank	1 A1

SIGHTS & ACTIVITIES	pp209–15
Geumgang Park Entrance	2 B4
Heosimcheong Spa 허심청	3 B4
Pusan National University Front Gate	4 A1
Pusan National University	5 B3

EATING	pp216–19
KFC	6 B1
Theme Pork 템포ㄱ	7 A1

DRINKING	pp219–20
Crossroads	8 A1
Moo Monk	9 B1
Soul Trane	10 B1

SHOPPING	p220
Lotte Department Store	11 B4

TRANSPORT	
Dongbu Bus Terminal	12 C1

OTHER	
Starbucks	13 A2

and a 10-minute walk from Haeundae train station (Exit 3).

In Jungangdong, the **Busan Modern History Museum** (Map p212; admission free; 9am-6pm Tue-Sun, 9am-5pm Nov-Feb; closed 1 Jan) contains photos, videos and maps with English signboards recounting the city's history and Japanese occupation. It's north of Yongdusan Park in what used to be the American Cultural Centre, 300m from the Jungangdong post office.

In Uamdong, the **Busan Municipal Museum** (Map p210; adult/teen/child W500/300/free; 9am-6pm Tue-Sun, 9am-5pm Nov-Feb, last entry 1hr before closing, closed 1 Jan) has a modest collection of artefacts plus photos and video footage from the Korean War. It's opposite the **UN**

Cemetery (Map p210; admission free; 9am-5pm, last entry 4.30pm), the only cemetery in the world managed by the UN. Hardly a must-see site, it may appeal to history enthusiasts, though some regard the photo exhibition as an embarrassingly modest tribute. English-speaking tour guides are inside a kiosk next to the cemetery's main gate. Beside the museum, the **Busan Cultural Centre** (www.bsculture.busan.kr) has regular music performances, including free Korean culture shows in the **Small Hall** (Map p210; 4pm Sat). Although the centre's website has no English links, programme information may be translated in the future. To get there, take Exit 5 at Daeyon train station; at street level look behind you to see a sign pointing to the UN Cemetery.

Tours

Mi Wharf (Map p219; adult/child W9900/6000), at the most easterly point along Haeundae beach's promenade, is the home base for one-hour ferry tours around the islets of Oryukdo. Tours depart hourly from 8.30am to 10pm in July and August, and there are between five and seven daily departures from 8.30am to 5pm September to June.

Taejeongdae Pebble Beach Ferry (Map p210; adult/child W5000/3500) provides a nice look at the cliffs and nearby Korea Maritime University. The occasionally rocky but pleasant tour (40 minutes, hourly) runs from 8am to 8pm; the ear-cracking music coming out of the speakers can be grating. Catch the ferry on the right side of Pebble Beach in Taejeongdae Park.

Festivals & Events

The Pusan International Film Festival (PIFF; www.piff.org) is the city's largest and most significant festival. First launched in 1996, the seventh version in 2002 screened 226 films from 57 countries. The festival is held sometime between September and October. Check the website for details.

In August, special events are held on each of the city's six beaches as part of the Busan Sea Festival, including the Busan International Rock Festival. Limited information is online at www.festival.busan.kr. Several local events celebrate Busan's affinity with the ocean including the Jalgalchi Festival (www.chagalchi.co.kr) in October and the Gijang Anchovy Festival (www.anchovy festival.or.kr) in May.

Sleeping

BUDGET

Keumkang Hostel Inn (Map p212; ☎ 469 3600; ondol W11,000) Perhaps the city's cheapest joint and smallest rooms. Commensurate with the fare, there's a shared toilet and shower with hot water available 8pm to midnight. It's located at the top of the Bandal staircase in Jungang-dong; take Exit 17 from the station and the first left at the top of the stairs.

Geumhwa Yeogwan (Map p212; ☎ 469 1769; d/ondol W25,000/20,000) Tiny, clean rooms are good value for bargain hunters who want to be close to the subway. Located at the base of the Bandal staircase.

Hwangeum Hotel (Map p212; ☎ 463 3851; d/ondol W25,000/20,000) The grandmother who runs this small inn doesn't speak English but certainly knows the colour of money. Almost identical to the Geumhwa Yeogwan, there's great value here for budget travellers who want to keep costs down but want the convenience of a private bathroom. Located opposite Gumhwa Yeogwan.

Tae Yang Motel (Map p212; ☎ 464 3608; d & ondol W30,000; 🏠) From the outside, it looks like a shady *yeogwan*, and it probably is, but the rooms in this love motel are clean, attractive and come with large queen size beds. Exit Busan train station and walk left; it's behind the Arirang Hotel. If full, there are many similarly priced *yeogwan* down the street.

MID-RANGE

Gwangjang Tourist Hotel (광장 관광 호텔; ☎ 464 3141; d, tw & ondol W48,000; 🏠) An attractive hotel with updated rooms, it's popular with female travellers. Located outside Busan train station; look right as you leave the station.

Tower Hotel (Map p212; ☎ 241 5151; d/tw/ste W50,000/65,000/100,000; 🏠) Don't be put off by the building's bilious green exterior or the rumpled red carpets lining the corridors. The bright rooms are clean and the suite option comes with two sofas and a pair of beds. While clean and functional, the bathrooms have the same industrial appearance found in public restrooms.

Pusan Hotel (Map p212; ☎ 241 4301; d, tw & ondol W85,000; 🏠) Unlike some of the cosmetically refurbished hotels in Nampodong, these rooms have new bedding, a good supply of wardrobe space and newly tiled bathrooms.

Phoenix Hotel (Map p212; ☎ 245 8061; www.hotel phoenix.net; d/tw W68,000/73,000; 🏠) The best feature of this simple, clean hotel is its central Nampodong location close to theatres, shopping and the subway. Peeling wallpaper in the hallways and an unusual selection of carpet colours suggest recent renovation efforts lacked both budget and sincerity.

Riviera Hotel (Map p219; ☎ 740 2111; d/ste W60,000/230,000; 🏠) Located in Haeundae on top of a department store bearing the same name, attractive rooms come with nonpeak-season rates that reflect the hotel's distance from the beach and less than stunning views. The luxuriously appointed Royal Suite boasting two large bedrooms and separate bathroom is good value for the area.

Angel Hotel (Map p217; ☎ 802 8223; d/tw W44,000/50,000; ☒) This recently renovated hotel offers clean though compact rooms located in the heart of Seomyeon close to restaurants and Bohemian nightlife. Most rooms come with a stand-up shower; inquire about rooms with tubs.

Royal Hotel (Map p212; ☎ 241 1051; d/ste W48,000/77,000; ☒) In central Nampodong, standard rooms are small, so ask for a larger one. Suites come with two beds, 1960s retro furniture in the living room and two toilets in the bathroom.

Arirang Hotel (☎ 463 5001; d, tw & ondol W57,000; ☒ ☐) A popular choice for businessmen and Russian tourists, the large rooms come with renovated bathrooms. Many downtown area hotels charging mid-range rates, like this one, share the same mystery: why can't wallpaper be hung properly? The décor is occasionally off-putting, so inspect the room before paying. Exit Busan train station and look for the large brown building to the left.

Hotel Commodore (Map p212; ☎ 466 9101; d W98,000-145,000; ☒) This place boasts a colourful temple-like exterior, and the steady flow of businessmen and evening companions suggests this may not be an ideal family hotel.

TOP END

Lotte Hotel (Map p217; ☎ 810 1100; www.lottehotel.co.kr; d & tw W240,000; ☒ ☐ ☒) An impressive, full service hotel with attractive standard rooms. Services include a health club and pool, banquet rooms and an evening Las Vegas style song and dance revue. Next to Lotte department store in Seomyeon.

Westin Chosun Beach Hotel (Map p219; www .chosunbeach.co.kr; ☎ 749 7201; d & tw W193,000; ☒ ☐ ☒) Busan's first international hotel, established in 1978, the Chosun usually has the cheapest off-season rates among beachfront hotels. For a number of Busan expats, the Westin Chosun is a sentimental favourite because of the friendly service, panoramic views and an illusion of seclusion created by the beach and ocean in front of the hotel, and a small forest to the rear. When booking into this or any other Haeundae hotel ask about special discount packages.

Paradise Hotel and Casino (Map p219; ☎ 749 2111; www.paradisehotel.co.kr; d W240,000; ☒ ☒) With 521 rooms, the Paradise is the grand-daddy of beachfront hotels in Haeundae.

On-site services include a heated outdoor pool, indoor driving range and outdoor jogging track. It's also famous in Busan as home to the city's only casino. Like all beachfront hotels, rooms with an ocean view cost more. If you have the means, go the full nine yards with the W1.2 million per night Diamond Suite.

Marriott Hotel (Map p219; ☎ 743 1234; www .busanmarriott.co.kr; d & tw W155,000; ☒ ☐ ☒) Located on the beach near the Busan Aquarium, the Marriott will satisfy guests who demand corporate efficiency in their lodgings. Sometimes, however, efficiency can be rather dull. In addition to the standard range of facilities that international clientele tend to expect, such as a pool, exercise centre and 24-hour access to business services, this hotel can arrange for childcare. Like all of the beachfront hotels, there are multilingual staff who can provide assistance in English.

Eating

The food in Busan is salty, spicy and raw, just like the people of this fair metropolis. The local speciality is raw fish, an expensive delicacy that attracts people from across the country.

Myeongseong Chobap (☎ 246 1225; sushi sets from W12,000; raw fish sets per person W30,000-60,000) is a popular Japanese-style restaurant serving saengseon chobap (생선초밥, Japanese sushi) and saengseonhoe koseo (생선회 코스, Korean raw fish). Located in Jungang-dong, it's 100m north of the Tower Hotel with 'sushi' written on the signboard.

For a more authentic Korean atmosphere, try the Millak Town Raw Fish Centre (밀락타운 외 센터) at the northeast end of Gwangalli beach. Purchase a fish for W15,000 to W25,000 from one of the pushy vendors on the 1st floor and take the elevator up to another floor where the food is sliced and served for an additional W10,000 per person. If you don't need to pick a fish, walk up to the 2nd floor to find **Haryu** (☎ 753 1126; raw fish meals per person from W20,000), a cosy restaurant run by the English-speaking owner, Mr Jeon. Ride the subway to Gwangan station and take Exit 5. At the top of the stairs, turn 180 degrees and then right at the first street. Walk 600m and turn left at the beach. The raw fish centre is the large brown building 300m down the road.

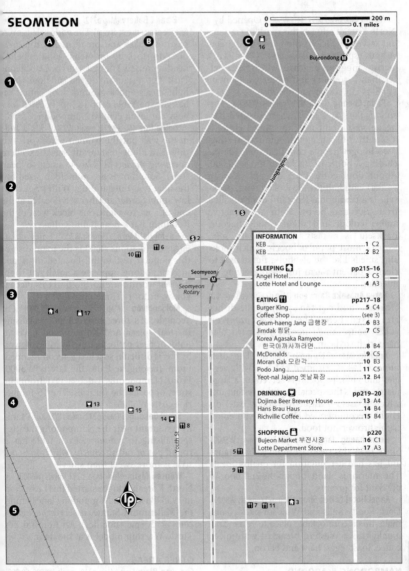

SEOMYEON

Map

0 ———— 200 m
0 ———— 0.1 miles

Bujeondong Ⓜ

Jungangno

Seomyeon Ⓜ
Seomyeon Rotary

Youth St.

INFORMATION
KEB 1 C2
KEB 2 B2

SLEEPING 🏠 **pp215–16**
Angel Hotel..................................3 C5
Lotte Hotel and Lounge 4 A3

EATING 🍴 **pp217–18**
Burger King..................................5 C4
Coffee Shop ....(see 3)
Geum-haeng Jang 금행장 6 B3
Jimdak 찜닭 7 C5
Korea Agasaka Ramyeon
  한국아까사까라면 8 B4
McDonalds 9 C5
Moran Gak 모란각 10 B3
Podo Jang 11 C5
Yeot-nal Jajang 옛날짜장 12 B4

DRINKING 🍷 **pp219–20**
Dojima Beer Brewery House 13 A4
Hans Brau Haus 14 B4
Richville Coffee 15 B4

SHOPPING 🛍 **p220**
Bujeon Market 부전시장 16 C1
Lotte Department Store 17 A3

SEOMYEON

Yeot-nal Jajang (Map p217; sets W3500) There is a superstition in the restaurant industry that successful shops avoid remodelling. Consequently, there are some shoddy-looking restaurants that serve great food. This is one of those places. The *jiambbong* (짬뽕, spicy seafood soup), *jjajangmyeon* (자장면, noodles with black bean sauce), *gun mandu* (군만두, fried *mandu*) and *tangsuyuk* (탕수육, sweet-and-sour fried pork) are excellent. It's a busy restaurant where guests are expected to eat and run, which is not a problem as the constant noise created by cooks whacking dough on the counter is irritating.

Moran Gak (Map p217; sets W5000) Opened by a North Korean refugee, this sparkling restaurant serves a delicious though limited menu. A house specialty is *nokdujijim* (녹두지짐), a crispy mugwart pancake (which tastes better than it sounds) and *bibim naengmyeon* (비빔냉면), a spicy noodle dish.

Podo Cheong (Map p217; dishes W5000) This *sutbulgalbi* (숯불갈비, charcoal-fired barbecue) restaurant near the Angel Hotel is a rare treat because of the outdoor seating. Two hungry people could eat their fill, including a bottle of Baekseju, for W30,000. About double the cost of *soju* (Korean vodka) with half the alcohol content, Baekseju is a traditional Korean liquor distilled from rice and herbs. With an attractive amber colour and slight woody flavour, Baekseju is a tasty alternative to *soju*, Korea's most popular hooch, which looks and smells like the alcohol a nurse uses to clean a patient's arm just before giving an injection.

Korea Agasaka Ramyeon (Map p217; meals W4000) Delicious and not too spicy noodle dishes are served here. The Agasaka *ramyeon* (라면, soup ramen noodles) in particular has a rich soybean flavour.

Jimdak (Map p217; meals W18,000) The dish *jjimdak* (찜닭, steamed chicken with veggies and chilli peppers) is served on a large platter and is the speciality of this restaurant, which boasts an attractive woody exterior. Highly recommended by people who enjoy flamethrower-hot food.

Geum-haeng Jang (Map p217; servings W5000) Since 1953, this steadfast *sutbulgalbi* restaurant has had a reputation for quality meat. The interior is bland though the 2nd floor is pleasant for groups.

Angel Hotel Coffee Shop (Map p217; meals W8000) Dark woody walls and Windsor-back chairs make this a comfortable place to relax. The highlight is a Western breakfast with juice, coffee, toast, eggs, ham and bacon.

NAMPODONG & AROUND
Lee-jo Seolleong Tang (Map p212; meals W5000; Mon-Sat) Lunch time is busy as the suits from nearby banks and law offices come to enjoy hearty *gomtang* (곰탕, beef broth soup). Add a spoonful of rock salt to enjoy the full flavour. If you're really hungry ask for the big size with noodles (특설렁탕, *teuk seolleong tang*) for W6000.

B and C Bakery (Map p212; daily Jul & Aug, close first Tue of month rest of year) The wide selection o pastries, cakes and bread makes it a grea place to stock up on picnic goodies before heading out to Young Island or Daecheon Park. The restaurant on the 2nd floor serve light meals and a ground floor coffee ba has very passable cappuccino. Located on a busy corner in central Nampodong.

Dolgo Rae (Map p212; meals W2500) It's a hole in the wall but the women who work this tiny 2nd floor restaurant serve excellent *doenjang jjigae* (된장찌개, spicy soybean stew). Soup bowls are munchkin sized but the quality is outstanding. With prices this low simply order another set. Located at the end of a narrow lane one block west of the Kookmin Bank near B and C Bakery.

Gaemi Jip (Map p212; meals W7000) Spicy *nakji-boggeum* (octopus stew) is the main dish o this popular restaurant. Located on a lane in Nampodong opposite a small hat shop, it's well worth the effort to find this place if you want to try something different.

Mokjangwon (Map p210; meals W10,000) On Yeongdo, it's three restaurants specialising in steak, pizza and Korean food have an outdoor beer patio. Getting to Mokjangwon by bus is difficult, so a taxi is recommended. From Taejongdae Park, the fare is W3000. From Nampodong, catch a taxi from the street opposite the theatres. The 15-minute ride costs W5000.

Seoul Gakduggi (Map p212; meals W5800) A family restaurant near the Nampodong theatres specialising in *gomtang*. Each table has a round pot of radish *kimchi*, which in Seoul style is more sweet than spicy.

Wonsan Myun-ohk (Map p212; meals W6000) A North Korean refugee started this busy shop in 1953. Based in a Nampodong lane behind the Millennium Statue, it serves *naengmyeon* (냉면, spicy noodles). An Admiral Yi's Turtle Warship model is at the door.

OTHER AREAS
Cho-won Blow Fish (Map p210; meals W8000-50,000) Anyone with a taste for blowfish should make the effort to find this off-the-beaten-track restaurant. The *bokmaeuntang* (복매운탕, spicy blowfish soup) is excellent, as are the *boktwaygim* (복튀김, fried blowfish) and *bokshabushabu* (복샤브샤브, par-boiled blowfish). Take Exit 3 from Namcheon train station and walk to the

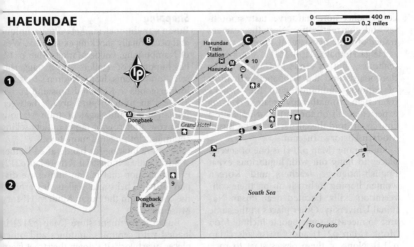

HAEUNDAE

second corner. Turn left and continue 300m to the overhead crosswalk. Cross over and descend to the bottom of the stairs, then turn left at the first corner. The restaurant is about 60m down the street on your right.

Theme Pork (Map p214; servings W1500) A lively meat-and-*soju* restaurant favoured by students who appreciate high quality and low prices, and don't mind the no-frills interior. Two hungry people can eat their fill including a couple of bottles of *soju* for W30,000. It's on a small lane with loads of other *samgyeopsal* (삼겹살, pork restaurants) near the front gate of Pusan National University.

Drinking

There are literally thousands, perhaps hundreds of thousands, of places to drink ranging from sophisticated hotel bars to plastic tables on the street in front of a convenience store.

Dojima Beer Brewery House (Map p217) is Busan's first microbrewery and is a popular destination that serves meals, though most customers prefer drinking. With a 550cc mug starting at W5500 you'll run up a substantial tab if you plan on tipping back more than a few pints. Located one block behind Lotte department store.

Hans Brau Haus (Map p217; 🕑 12.30pm–4am) The quality and prices at Busan's second microbrewery are similar to Dojima, though the opening hours are longer and

the interior is more elaborate. On the 2nd floor of a corner building on Seomyeon's Youth St.

Mi Wharf (Map p219) is located at the most easterly point alongside the Haeundae beach promenade. It's a rustic outdoor drinking area, in a plastic table and chair kind of way, has a great sunset view of the beach.

Lotte Hotel Lobby Lounge (Map p217) is a large, upscale lounge which has palm trees, comfy chairs and live lizard-lounge muzak. These, combined with a passable though pricey Irish coffee, make this a pleasant place to impress a date. In the basement level of Lotte Hotel.

Richville Coffee (Map p217) is a take-out stand carved into the corner of a 24-hour convenience store that serves tasty smooth-ies and gourmet coffee. Near the rear en-trance of Lotte department store.

Helga Herbal (Map p212) is not a great teahouse, but it's good. Dark wooden floorboards and tan wallpaper with hints of bamboo combined with the owner's interest in aromatherapy create a relaxing experience. It's on the 2nd floor opposite a church, around the corner from the Busan Modern History Museum.

Soul Trane (Map p214) is one of several places to hang out with lugubrious expat English-language teachers and Korean women hoping to brush up on their con-versation skills. Located near Pusan Na-tional University. Other places in the same area to meet the same people include Moo Monk (Map p214) and Crossroads (Map p214). None of these places start to rock until after 10pm.

In Busan's Russian district, across the street from Busan train station, Texas Street has a handful of late-night bars with heav-ily made-up, mini-skirted women pushing overpriced hooch. A small number of im-bibed visitors have reported late night credit card fraud and robbery while patronising this area.

Entertainment

There are four large multiscreen cinemas in Nampodong within a two-block radius of PIFF Square. The 10th floor of Lotte department store in Seomyeon holds 12 screens that show first-run English-language movies; advance purchases are required on weekends. There are two theatres in Haeundae: the 10-screen facil-ity in the Megabox building (Map p219), 100m from Haeundae station Exit 1, with a ticket booth on the 1st floor and screens on the 6th floor. There's also one screen in the Grand Hotel.

Anyone with a talent for the science of gambling may wish to test his or her skills at the **Paradise Casino** (☎ 742-2110; ☽ 24hr) in Haeundae. Open only to foreign patrons, visitors can play blackjack, roulette, bac-carat, slots and tai-sai, a Chinese game that is like betting on the dice game Yahtzee. The casino caters mostly to the Japanese market (read: big spenders) though most of the staff speak English. Note that there is a dress code.

Shopping

Busan's traditional markets offer a unique and occasionally shocking experience. West of Nampodong, Gukje Market (Map p212) has hundreds of retailers with a staggering selection of items, from children's toys and leather goods to Korean drums and gongs. There's an underground arcade between Jungangdong and Jagalchi train stations with row after row of junky outlets selling ceramics, clothing and more toys.

If you're looking for handcrafted leather goods, Leather Industrial Arts (Map p212) is a small shop that has an impressive dis-play of bags, belts and wallets. It's around the corner from the Busan Modern History Museum.

Busan department store (Map p212) is loaded with ceramics, antiques and other pieces of artwork. It's down the street from Exit 5 of Nampodong train station.

Bujeon Market (Map p217) is a chaotic de-light and a great place to buy cheap in-season fruit and vegetables. Teeming walkways are often impassable as vendors nonchalantly wheel pushcarts loaded with fruit and dried anchovies. The market is easily accessible from Bujeondong train station (Exit 5).

Gupo Market (Map p210) has a large selection of clothing, pungent Korean food and butcher shops specialising in fowl and dogmeat. Whatever one's take on the an-cient practice of using man's best friend for human nourishment, images of an eviscer-ated canine carcass are bound to produce lasting memories. Take Exit 1 from De-okcheon train station, turn right at the first street, then take the first left and continue 100m. There are more vendors one block behind these shops.

Modern department stores are definitely worth a look, if for no other reason than to experience the custom of saturating the sales floor with clerks. All have grocery stores with ready to eat food and some Western goods. The biggest is Lotte department store (Map p217), adjacent to the hotel bearing the same name in Seomyeon. There's also a smaller version outside Exit 1 of Myeongnyundong train station (Map p214). Hyundai depart-ment store is slightly down-market com-pared to Lotte, which usually means lower prices. It stocks hard-to-find plain yogurt. To get there, take Exit 7 from Beomildong train station.

Getting There & Around
Air
Korean Air Lines (KAL) runs two airport limousine services from Gimhae International Airport (Map p210), one each to the major hotels in Haeundae and Nampodong (W4500, one hour, every 30 minutes). A taxi from the airport to Seomyeon takes 30 minutes and costs W15,000, depending on traffic. The most economical link between the airport and city is bus No 307 to Deokcheon train station or bus No 310 to Sasang station (Map p210); the W1000 bus takes 15 minutes while taxis to either station cost W7000. There are also buses from the airport to cities in the area including Gyeongju (W9000, see p187), Changwon (W4500), Masan (W4700), Eonyang (W5000), Ulsan (W6700), Yangsan (W3600) and Jinhae (W5200).

International flights are mostly to Japan (Tokyo, Nagoya, Osaka and Fukuoka), with less frequent links to Beijing, Shanghai, Bangkok, Manila and Vladivostock. Some carriers with international flights to Busan:

Asiana (☎ 972 4004)
China Air (☎ 463 6888)
China Eastern (☎ 973 8254)
JAL (☎ 469 1215)
Korean Air (☎ 970 3238)

On the domestic routes, the Busan–Seoul run (W65,000, one hour, every 30 minutes) usually requires reservations for weekend and holiday travel. There are also flights to Jeju Island (W60,000, one hour).

Boat
Both ferry terminals are near the Immigration office (Map p212). From Jungangdong train station, take Exit 12 and walk straight before crossing the street at the light. On the other side of the street, turn left and walk past the Immigration office to a fenced path leading to the international ferry terminal (Map p212). To find the domestic ferry terminal, instead of turning left, walk straight 300m. See p379 for ferry details to Japan. For ferry details to Jeju, see p258. See Geoje Island (p228) for the ferry service to Gohyun, Jangseungpo and Okpo.

Bus
Dongbu bus terminal (Map p214) is located at Nopodong station. Intercity buses travelling to Dongbu allow passengers to get off at Duhil station, a great time saver if you don't need to go to the terminal. Departures from Dongbu include:

Destination	Price (W)	Duration	Frequency
Daegu	9000	2hr	every 30-60min
Gwangju	18,700	4½hr	every 20-60min
Gyeongju	5300	1¼hr	every 8min
Seoul	27,500	5¼hr	every 10-20min
Ulsan	3000	1hr	every 10min

Seobu intercity bus terminal (Map p210) is located just outside Sasang station and can be accessed at the street level by walking through a department store. Departures include:

Destination	Price (W)	Duration	Frequency
Daewonsa	9500	1½hr	7 times per day
Hadong	9500	2½hr	every 30-60min
Namhae	9800	2½hr	every 20min
Ssanggyaesa	11,400	3½hr	every 2hr

Subway
Subway fares use a two-zone system: either W700 or W800. Consider buying a Hanaro card (W2000, available at ticket booths) if you're staying in the city for some time to get a discount on bus and train fares. It can also be used in taxis sporting a flash seagull on the roof. There are two subway lines with a third planned for 2007. See p222 for the map.

Train
Trains depart from and arrive at Busan's newly renovated train station. Between Busan and Seoul, there are two trains: the *saemaeul* (adult/child W28,600/14,300, 4½ hours, every 30 to 60 minutes) and the *mugunghwa* (adult/child W19,500/9800, 5½ hours, every 30 to 60 minutes). It's best to visit the Korea Rail website (www.korail.go.kr) for detailed schedules. If you're heading to Japan, a Korea–Japan Through Ticket provides discounted travel between the two countries. It covers travel by train to Busan, the ferry crossing between Busan and Shimonoseki and a train to your destination in Japan. Contact Korea Rail at Busan train station for details.

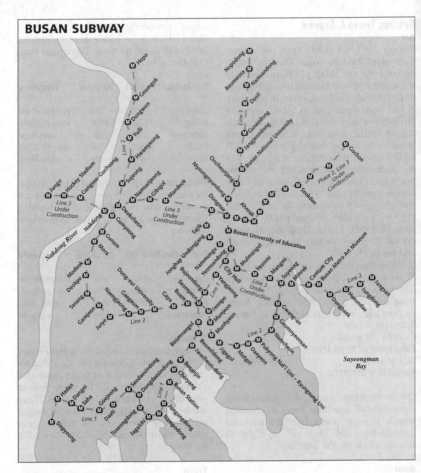

BUSAN SUBWAY

GAJISAN PROVINCIAL PARK
가지산 도립공원
This park has three separate sections. The northernmost section, not far from Gyeongju, is known for its rocky terrain. This is where you'll find **Gajisan** (1240m), the park's highest peak. Most hikers start their ascent to Gajisan from Seongnamsa.

Seongnamsa 석남사
This must-see **temple** (adult/teen/child W1500/1300/ 1000; ♥ 3am-8pm) is a visual masterpiece. The 800-metre walk along an interlocking stone path from the park entrance to the temple cuts through a heavily wooded forest where patches of sunlight struggle to break through the thick canopy of foliage. Typical

of less touristed temples, the crisp clean air is lightly scented with burning incense and fresh garden fertiliser. At the temple's main gate, pause half way up the stairs and take in the image of a multistoreyed pagoda and a stand of bamboo trees juxtaposed against the horizontal spread of a hip roof and sprawling green mountain.

Just before the temple, the path forks right over a bridge to a Korean-only map and a stone monument. The trail to the right is the starting point for a 6.4km hike to Gajisan.

Limited accommodation options are a 15-minute walk from the main gate. Walk down the paved road and take the first left turn to find a pocket of motels. The best of the bunch is the **Motel Alps** (알프스 모텔;

☎ 254 5666; ondol & d W30,000; ❷), with beautiful rooms decorated in rich earthy colours, and whirlpool or steam sauna options. There are few restaurants within walking distance, so bring your own supply of nourishment or stock up on snacks at the convenience store near the park entrance.

Getting There & Away

The most scenic route leaves Miryang bus terminal (W4100, 40 minutes, every 30 to 60 minutes). During the second half of the trip, the bus climbs a steep, winding road carved into the mountainside with stunning views of peaks and valleys smothered in a green forest. Be sure to sit on the right side of the bus to get the best view. Originating from points east of the temple, buses depart Ulsan via Eonyang (언양; W1300, one hour, every 30 minutes). From Busan's Dongbu terminal, catch an express bus to Eonyang (W2800, 40 minutes, every 20 minutes) and buy a ticket for Seongnamsa (W1300, 30 minutes, every 30 minutes). Buses to Seongnamsa terminate near the park entrance in front of a convenience store, which doubles as a ticket booth.

TONGDOSA 통도사

Seen as one of the three jewels of Korea's temples, **Tongdosa** (adult/teen/child/toddler W2000/1500/1000/free; ❷ 3.30am-8pm) is important due to it having a *sari*, a crystal-like substance thought to develop inside the body of a monk who leads a pure life. A *sari* was recovered from a monk after his body was cremated and brought here. Although visitors cannot see the *sari*, it is apparently located in a fenced area outside the main hall. It is a focal point for Buddhist devotion, which is why Tongdo does not have a Buddha statue in the main hall, a rarity in Korea.

Just outside the temple, the **Tongdosa Museum** (adult/child W2000/1000; ❷ 9am-5pm Wed-Mon, 9am-6pm Mar-Oct) houses what is reported to be the world's largest collection of Buddhist temple paintings, as well as 30,000 artefacts including gongs, roof tiles and wooden blocks used to print Buddhist scriptures. Before entering the museum, take off your shoes and put them in a bag at the front door.

Although the forest, creek and surrounding mountains are pleasant, yakkity bus tour crowds detract from the natural ambience. If you do come, pack a lunch and enjoy a creek-side picnic. If time is short, take a pass on Tongdosa (a half-day trip from Busan) and visit Seongnamsa via Miryang (a day trip from Busan).

Getting There & Away

From Dongbu terminal, buses run to a village called Shinpyeong (신평; W2200, 50 minutes, every 20 minutes). From the terminal, walk to the street and turn right, then turn left at the second street and walk five minutes to the main gate. Buses connect Shinpyeong and Ulsan (W2200, 35 minutes, four times daily) and there are frequent buses to Eonyang (W780, 30 minutes) about every 20 minutes.

BUGOK HOT SPRINGS 부곡 온천

The only attraction here is **Bugok Hawaii** (☎ 536 6331; ondol, d & tw weekdays W96,000, Sat & holidays W108,000, daily Jul & Aug W120,000; ❷ park hours 8.30am-7.30pm; ❷ ❷), a resort with indoor and outdoor pools, a zoo, botanical garden and amusement rides. For family outings, it's a terrific alternative to Lotte World (see p90) and Everland (see p126), which gets rave reviews from kids.

There are plenty of accommodation options though the total cost for a family is unlikely to be significantly less than the resort's package deal, which includes unlimited access to the amusement park. Judging by the number of stains, rips and scuffs on the walls and carpets, it's a popular hotel for families with young children. Reservations are recommended.

From Busan's Seobu terminal, buses run to Bugok (W5700, 1½ hours, every 30 minutes). Buses also connect with Miryang (W1700, 40 minutes, hourly), Daegu (W4200, one hour, hourly) and Masan (W3000, 50 minutes, every 40 minutes).

TONGYEONG 통영
pop 136,000 / 235 sq km

On the southern tip of Goseong Peninsula, Tongyeong is a coastal city wedged between Namhae and Geoje Islands. There are enough sights to fill a half-day exploring Gangguan (강구안), a quaint fishing harbour several kilometres from the bus terminal apocryphally called 'the Naples of Korea'.

On the northeast side of the harbour, Nammang Mountain (남망산) is an easy climb with views of the city and access to the **International Sculpture Park** (Nammangsan Gukje

Jogak Gongwon; 남망산 국제 조각 공원), a grassy plot with outdoor artwork.

Near the top of the mountain just beyond the imposing cultural centre, there's an earthy teahouse called **Jangseong Baek Ee** (장승백이; light meals W3500; ☻ 6am-noon) operated by a friendly grandmother. Along the western side of the harbour, a string of 24-hour restaurants sell *chungmu gimbap* (충무김밥) – a rice, seaweed, squid and radish dish made famous in Tongyeong – for W3000. Look for the restaurant signboards with large spooky pictures of someone's grandmother that for some travellers might serve to eliminate rather than stimulate an appetite. Just behind these restaurants, Jungangdong is a commercial district with attractive lanes and small shops.

From the bus terminal, cross the street and catch any city bus (W800) in series Nos 10 to 29 or Nos 40 to 79 for a 15-minute ride to the harbour. Express buses connect Seoul (W16,100, 5½ hours, hourly), Jinju (W4300, 1½ hours, hourly), Busan (W7100, two hours, every 30 minutes) and Gohyun (W1900, 30 minutes, every 20 minutes). During the summer, a tourist booth is erected in front of the bus terminal providing one English-language map.

JINJU 진주
pop 342,000 / 713 sq km

Jinju's quiet and litter-free downtown is ideal for a half day of exploring the sites, smell and taste of Korea past. Worthwhile places like Jinju's fortress are 10 to 15 minutes on foot from the intercity bus terminal located on the north side of the Nam River. Jinju is a convenient base from which to explore the province's western region and the eastern side of Jirisan National Park. For information on visiting the western side of the park, see Hwa-Eomsa (see p239).

Sights & Activities

The most interesting place to visit is **Jinju-seong** (진주성, Jinju's Fortress; adult/child W1000/500; ☻ 9am-10pm). Local street signs call it a castle, but it's actually a well-preserved fortress built during the Goryeo dynasty that was partially destroyed during the Japanese invasion of 1592. It was here that one of the major battles of the campaign was fought, in which 70,000 Koreans lost their lives. Inside the fortress walls, traditional gates, shrines and temples

dot the grassy knolls of this heavily wooded oval park. Enter the fortress from the North Gate, not far from a large E-Mart department store, or the East Gate beside a tourist office, which doubles as a ticket booth.

Inside the fortress, the **Jinju National Museum** (진주 국립 박물관; ☎ 742 5951; adult/child W400/free; ☻ 9am-5pm Tue-Sun, 9am-4pm Nov-Feb; closed 1 Jan) is a modern structure built in traditional style with exquisite stonework. Specialising in artefacts from the 1592 Japanese invasion, it houses a small though impressive collection of calligraphy, paintings and crafts from the Goryeo dynasty that were donated by Kim Yong-doo, an ethnic Korea, who lived in Japan. One of the more interesting pieces in the **Doo-am Collection** is a large folding screen with a red, white and blue painting depicting a naval battle that looks like a Where's Waldo picture.

Sleeping
BUDGET

Hite Motel (☎ 748 6606; d W35,000; 🚭) The friendly couple running the Hite are eager to help foreign tourists. Basic rooms come with a small, though functional bath. For the price, it's one of the better budget options.

Byeoksan Hwang Tobang Motel (☎ 741 7738; d W30,000; 🚭) It's the William Shatner of Korean *yeogwan*: it's clean, decent and has a style that hasn't changed in 30 years.

Geumwha Yeoinsuk (☎ 746 4787; ondol W10,000) Modestly appointed matchbox-size rooms come with a thin mattress, a fan, flimsy doors and common showers. If you're in the market for budget accommodation, this is the place. If full, the area east of the tourist office is packed with *yeoinsuk* (family-run hotels with small rooms and shared bathroom) in the W10,000 to W15,000 range.

MID-RANGE

Lotte Motel (☎ 741 4888; d W40,000; 🚭 🖳) Three things set this motel apart from most others: it's new, clean and has an elevator. If you don't need a room with a river view, ask for a discount. An additional W5000 gets you a room with a computer (of some vintage) and Internet connection.

Hyundai Motel (☎ 743 9791; d W40,000; 🚭) A clone of the next door Lotte Motel, right down to the red brick facade. Although they share the same lot, different people apparently own them.

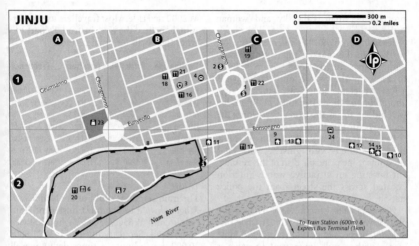

JINJU

Greece Motel (☎ 741 6723; d W40,000; ☒) The dingy hallways of this elevator-challenged motel create a poor first impression though the clean rooms are comfortable and come equipped with a water cooler.

TOP END

Dong Bang Tourist Hotel (☎ 743 0131; www.hotel dongbang.com; d & tw W140,000; ☒) At the eastern end of the river road, it's an oasis of quality with pleasant rooms overlooking the Nam River. Most of the friendly front desk staff speak English, so getting what you need won't be a challenge. Reservations are recommended.

Eating & Drinking

Jinju is well known for *bibimbap* and there's no shortage of restaurants serving this rice and veggie mix, especially around the bus terminal and fortress. For a meal of more substantial portions, the area around the downtown police station is a good spot to start hunting. For something different,

there's a line of fresh water eel restaurants along the waterfront near the fortress. They're all the same quality and price (W13,000 per person); look for a plume of smoke that smells like a tyre fire. Travellers looking forward to an evening of tippling will be disappointed as Jinju's nightlife is inexplicably quiet, save the ever-present *da bang* (다방). *Da bang* are a traditional Korean shop where patrons socialise over a cup of tea or coffee. A relic of years gone past, *da bang* are virtually extinct in big cities but continue to thrive in small towns where patrons are asked to buy their conversation partners a drink. Female staff sometimes provide more than companionship, hence the *da bang's* reputation for seediness.

Kwan Nam-gaek Sik Dang (sets W5000) This air-con restaurant and coffee shop behind the Jinju National Museum is a welcome pit stop before completing the fortress tour. It serves light meals, including *bibimbap*. If you ask nicely, you can have your drink outside under the trees next to the carved totems proclaiming, 'man is the sky' and 'woman is the earth'.

Jeil Sik Dang (sets W5000) Frequented by people working in the market, this is a tiny shop with simple, hearty food. From 4.30am to 11.30am they serve only *haejangguk*, a leafy vegetable soup with ham and rice, and *bibimbap* thereafter until 11.30pm. It's well hidden so ask the women crowding the walkways for directions.

Dae Samgyetang (meals W7500) *Samgyetang*, chicken stuffed with ginseng, rice and chestnuts is the principle dish of this restaurant boasting an attractive woody interior. Located across the street from the police station.

Won-kung Galbi (servings W6000) This is the place if you're looking for Korean-style *sut-bulgalbi*, barbecued pork or beef. Each table comes with a pull-down vent to exhaust smoke that looks a lot like the Cone of Silence. Around the corner from the police station, it's one block north on the east side of the street.

Zio Ricco (sets W8000) A dimly lit eatery with low chairs, rustic brick behind the bar and folksy classical music popular with the university crowd. Pasta and chicken are on the menu if you're looking for a break from *bibimbap* or want a cosy place to enjoy a drink.

Hanguksidae (servings W20,000) Small cities always seem to have one up-market restaurant blending high prices with an impersonal, banquet hall–like interior. This meat restaurant is like that. Two hungry people could easily munch their way to a bill in excess of W100,000, which is not unreasonable if the restaurant cries out 'great dining experience'. Here, however, there is only a whimper.

Getting There & Around
AIR
Jinju's airport is in Sacheon, 28km from the city centre. Seven daily flights connect with Seoul via Korean Air and Asiana (W70,000, one hour). Korean Air also has two daily flights to Jeju Island (W61,000). Local buses connect Jinju's north bus terminal to Sacheon airport (W700, 30 minutes) or take a 20-minute taxi ride for W12,000.

BUS
There's an express bus terminal south of the river, a 1.5km walk from the city centre or

W2000 taxi ride. Most travellers use the terminal north of the river instead. Departures from the north terminal include:

Destination	Price (W)	Duration	Frequency
Busan	6000	1½hr	every 10-20min
Daewonsa	3400	1hr	every 1-2hr
Gohyun	7000	2hr	every ½-1hr
Hadong	3800	1¼hr	every 20-30min
Haeinsa	7900	2½hr	every ½-2hr
Namhae	4100	1½hr	every 10-20min
Ssangyesa	5800	1½hr	every 1-1½hr

TRAIN
The train station is south of the Nam River. *Mugunghwa* trains connect Busan and Jinju (adult/child W6500/3300, 2½ hours, twice daily) and Seoul (adult/child W21,800/10,900, seven hours, 4 times daily) as well as one *saemaul* departure for the capital (adult/child W37,000/16,000, six hours).

GEOJE ISLAND 거제도
pop 170,000 / 399 sq km
Rugged, mountainous Geoje Island (Geojedo) has awe-inspiring coastal scenery that on occasion compares with Nova Scotia's Cabot Trail. It's the country's second largest island, birthplace of Kim Young-sam, Korea's first sort of freely elected president, and home for two shipyards, Daewoo in Okpo and Samsung in Gohyun, which together build 30% of the world's container ships. With a few exceptions, easy access to the island's treasures requires a car; local and express buses cover parts of the island, though the routes and schedules are not always convenient. One accessible route providing a taste of the island's history starts in Gohyun, one of three towns with a ferry link to Busan.

The island's website (www.geoje.go.kr) has a map and basic information about the island.

Sights & Activities
POW CAMP 거제 포로 수용소
During the Korean War, prisoner of war camps that housed 175,000 North Korean and Chinese soldiers were established on Geoje Island, with the largest facility in Gohyun. The newly renovated and expanded **POW Camp Museum** (adult/teen/child W3000/2000/1000; 9am-6pm, 9am-5pm Nov-Feb) is a significant improvement over lacklustre efforts of the

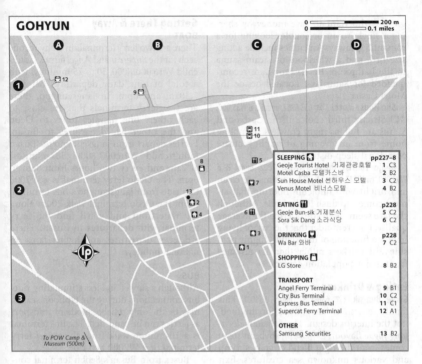

GOHYUN

0   200 m
0   0.1 miles

To POW Camp & Museum (500m)

SLEEPING 🏠	pp227–8
Geoje Tourist Hotel 거제관광호텔	1 C3
Motel Casba 모텔카스바	2 B2
Sun House Motel 썬하우스 모텔	3 C2
Venus Motel 비너스모텔	4 B2

EATING 🍴	p228
Geoje Bun-sik 거제분식	5 C2
Sora Sik Dang 소라식당	6 C2

DRINKING 🍸	p228
Wa Bar 와바	7 C2

SHOPPING 🛍	
LG Store	8 B2

TRANSPORT	
Angel Ferry Terminal	9 B1
City Bus Terminal	10 C2
Express Bus Terminal	11 C1
Supercat Ferry Terminal	12 A1

OTHER	
Samsung Securities	13 B2

past. Although most information boards describing photos, memorabilia and sometimes kitsch displays are in Korean, it's a rare opportunity to learn about the war. Exit Gohyun's city/express bus terminal and you'll see a sign pointing the way to the camp. Walk a couple of kilometres or catch a W2000 taxi.

OE ISLAND 외도 해상 공원

Oe Island (Oedo; pronounced 'way-dough') is a private 145-sq-km botanical garden off the coast of Haegeumgang in the southeastern part of the island. Over the past four decades, a couple from Seoul plus 40 gardeners have transformed the island into a Garden of Eden money machine drawing 2 million visitors annually. You'll need plenty of cash plus patience and humour to navigate the pushy crowds that weave single-file through the manicured path, a surreal experience that feels like an assembly line simulation straight out of Aldous Huxley's *Brave New World*.

Before de-ferrying, passengers are given a medallion indicating which ferry to board on the return trip. As ferries are usually full, it's imperative to get back to the terminal on time. Tours depart from Jangseungpo (adult/child W13,000/6500, three hours, every three hours) as well as Haegeumgang, Wahyeon and Hakdong. From Gohyun take the express bus to Jangseungpo (W1900, 30 minutes, every 20 minutes) and a W2000 taxi from the bus terminal to the Oedo ferry terminal.

Sleeping

Each town on the island has a decent supply of *yeogwan* accommodation though Gohyun is a better option for those who want to make an early morning departure.

Motel Casba (☎ 638 1075; ondol & d Sun-Fri W40,000, Sat W50,000; ✴) This newly constructed motel with clean rooms is run by a friendly husband and wife team. Exit the front of the bus terminal, turn at the first right, walk up a couple of blocks then turn left at the lane behind the Samsung building.

Venus Motel (☎ 637 9586; basic ondol/d Sun-Fri W35,000/40,000, Sat W40,000/50,000, large ondol & d W50,000, special amenities W50,000; ✴) A rarity among many *yeogwan*, Venus has a variety of room sizes and amenities well suited for groups who want to save money by sharing a single room or couples looking for a romantic getaway. Amenities include a king size bed, and a whirlpool or steam sauna in the bathroom. Reservations are recommended for Saturdays. Located beside the Motel Casba.

Sun House Motel (☎ 633 6262; ondol & d W35,000; ✂) Strictly third choice if the Casba and Venus are full, as night crawlers stumbling home from an evening of tippling create occasional sleep disturbances.

Geoje Tourist Hotel (☎ 632 7002; ondol & d W93,000, tw W113,000; ✂) The rooms are clean and bright with linoleum flooring that almost comes up flush to the walls. Although the fare seems high considering the average quality, it's a reminder that the cost of living here is a function of the island's highly paid shipyard workers rather than its distance from major population centres.

Eating & Drinking

Geoje Bun-sik (☎ 636-3987; meals W3500) This family restaurant has patrons for the food, not the interior design. The delicious *doenjang jjigae* flavour(된장찌개, soybean stew) comes from the right blend of crab, shrimp and various unknown sea creatures. Exit right from Gohyun's bus terminal then turn right at the first corner; it's a few doors up and close to several other restaurants.

Sora Shik Dang (☎ 632 9229; meals W4000) Run by a mother and daughter team, it's one of the few restaurants around the Gohyun terminal that serves relatively cheap and not too spicy food well suited for breakfast. The *galbitang* (갈비탕, beef ribs soup) tastes better with a dash of salt and pepper.

Wa Bar (☎ 637 7676; ☾ 3pm-4am) A smart-looking tavern with woody walls and photos of jazz greats; too bad they don't play any of that music. At W4000 for a tiny bottle, the beer is expensive.

Si-in Ui Ma-eum (시인의 마음; ☎ 633 0260; sets W5000) Car travellers should make the effort to find this delightfully cosy restaurant on the western side of the island near Oh-song (오송). Take in the graceful sunset while enjoying country-fresh *pajeon* (green onion pancake) and a bowl of *dongdongju* (동동주), a traditional rice wine that packs a punch. In Korean culture, a superlative place provides harmony between man and nature. This restaurant is one of those places.

Getting There & Away
BOAT

There are two ferry terminals in Gohyun, one each for the *Supercat* and *Angel* ferries (adult/child W16,000/8000, 50 to 75 minutes) with a total of nine daily departures between 7.30am and 6pm. In Jangseungpo, there are two ferry terminals that are close to each other: one handles tours to Oedo and the other has departures to Busan. Ferries depart from Jangseungpo for Busan (adult/child W16,000/8000, 50 minutes) at 7am and every two hours from 8am to 6pm. The Oedo ferry terminal is a W2000 taxi ride from Jangseungpo's bus terminal. From the Oedo terminal walk 200m along the waterfront and you'll find the ferry terminal with departures to Busan. There are fewer departures and higher fares on national holidays.

BUS

Although a slower and less stimulating ride, bus connections during the typhoon season may be the only reliable mode of transport as ferries can be cancelled. The bus terminal is a 10-minute walk from the *Angel* ferry terminal or a W2000 taxi ride.

Buses from Busan's Seobu terminal connect Gohyun (W11,800, 2½ hours, every two to three hours); more frequent buses run from Busan to Tongyeong (W8500, 2½ hours, every 15 minutes) at which point you can jump on a city bus to Gohyun. Standing in front of the Gohyun terminal ticket booth, city buses are on the left, express buses on the right.

NAMHAE ISLAND 남해도
pop 67,000 / 357 sq km

The country's third largest island is Namhae Island (Namhaedo) a terrific place for travellers to stretch their legs and explore a slower pace of life, so clearly evident in the countryside where some farmers continue to use oxen to plough rice paddies.

The island's only unique sight is a replica of Admiral Yi's **Turtle Warship** (adult/teen/child W1000/800/500; ☾ 9am-7pm). For history buffs it's a worthwhile trip as tourists can board the vessel and visualise how a crew of 40 to 50 men survived in such cramped quarters. The original ship was built in 1591 and is a source of considerable pride for Koreans as a symbol of military ingenuity that defeated

---

ACCORDING TO SUPERSTITION, DID YOU KNOW...

■ a pig's head is placed in front of new businesses to bring good luck

■ at a Korean wedding, the groom's mother tosses dates and chestnuts to the bride. The number of caught pieces indicates the number of children the bride will have.

■ you'll die if you leave a fan on in a room with the window and door closed

■ children who loose a tooth throw it on the roof for good luck

■ a person will die if you write their name in red ink

■ new car buyers hire a shaman to perform rituals for good luck

---

the Japanese in several important battles. The current version was built in 1980.

The ship is moored in Noryang (노량), a village at the foot of the Namhae Island bridge. Six daily buses connect Noryang (on route to Namhae) and Hadong (W3000, 30 minutes). More frequent connections link Jinju and Noryang (W4100, 1½ hours, every 20 minutes). In both cases, be sure to tell the driver you're going to Noryang otherwise you might end up further down the highway in Namhae.

JIRISAN NATIONAL PARK
지리산 국립공원
Jirisan National Park (adult/teen/child W2800/1300/700) offers some of Korea's best hiking opportunities with many peaks over 1500m high, including **Cheonwangbong** (1915m), the country's second highest mountain. If you plan to hike here, the Jirisan National Park map (W1000, available at the park entrance) lists topographical information as well as road-heads, trails, campsites, springs, shelters, temples and other points of interest. There are three principal park entrances, each with its own temple. Two of the three temples, Ssanggyesa and Daewonsa, are in Gyeongsangnam province. Another temple, Hwa-eomsa, is accessible from Gurye (see p239).

Ssanggyesa 쌍계사
One of the principal temples of the Jogye Order of Korean Buddhism, this magnificent **temple** (adult/teen/child W2800/1300/700; ⏰ dawn-dusk) was originally built in AD 722 to enshrine a portrait of monk Yukjo that was brought back from China. The visual imagery is a feast for the eyes, and like any exquisite dinner, should be consumed with deliberation and contemplation in order to enjoy every

morsel. Stone walls supporting multiple levels of buildings neatly notched into the mountainside combined with mature trees and the trickling sound of a creek in the background create a pleasant sensory experience. Like all great temples, there are three gates along the path to the main hall; take the time to read the English-language signs to appreciate the symbolism of your visit.

Hiking
It's impossible to describe the myriad of trails within this great park. The most challenging course runs east to west (Daewonsa to Hwa-eomsa), which experienced Korean hikers say requires three days. There are also half-day hikes along incredible valleys that channel into the mountain, including Daeseong-gol, Jungsanni, Daewonsa, Baekmudong, Baemsagol and Hwa-eomsa.

Travellers with less ambitious plans who want to experience Jiri Mountain's beauty should consider the trail to **Buril Pokpo** (불일폭포, Buril Falls). Beginning at the rear of Ssanggyesa, the trail (2.3km each way, three hours return including breaks) winds through the forest alongside a rippling creek. The trail is dotted with rocky pools, which hikers use to take a break and wash their feet (so make sure you bring bottled water). About two-thirds along the way, just when you've noticed the sound of the creek has disappeared, the trail bursts onto an open field. Down the path, there's a pit stop which is home to a mountain hermit who sells beverages and chocolate bars. The final 300m requires some delicate footwork along a steep, slippery path, which can be managed by most inexperienced hikers thanks to a steel cable fence. At the foot of the falls, there's a large rocky pool where meditators regain their chi.

GYEONGSANGNAM-DO

JIRISAN NATIONAL PARK

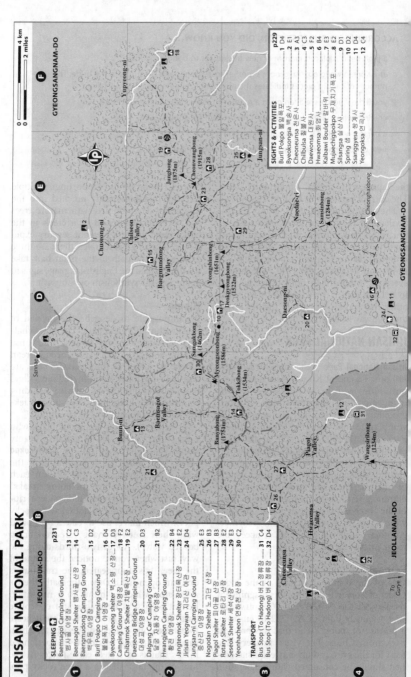

SLEEPING 🏠   p231
Baemsagol Camping Ground
  범사골 야영장 13 C2
Baemsagol Shelter 범사골 산장 14 C3
Baengmudong Camping Ground
  백무동 야영장 15 D2
Buril Pokpo Camping Ground
  불일폭포 야영장 16 D4
Byeoksoryeong shelter 벽소령 산장 17 D3
Camping Ground 야영장 18 F2
Chibatmok Shelter 치밭목산장 19 E2
Daeseong Bridge Camping Ground
  대성교 야영장 20 D3
Daigung Car Camping Ground
  대굴 자동차 야영장 21 B2
Hwangjeon Camping Ground
  황전 야영장 22 B4
Jangteomok Shelter 장터목산장 23 E2
Jirisan Yeogwan 지리산 여관 24 D4
Jungsan-ni Camping Ground
  중산리 야영장 25 E3
Nogodan Shelter 노고단 산장 26 B3
Piagol Shelter 피아골 산장 27 C4
Rotary Shelter 로타리 산장 28 E2
Seseok Shelter 세석산장 29 E3
Yeonhacheon 연하천 산장 30 C2

TRANSPORT
Bus Stop (To Hadong) 버스정류장 31 C4
Bus Stop (To Hadong) 버스정류장 32 D4

SIGHTS & ACTIVITIES   p229
Buril Pokpo 불일폭포 1 D4
Byeoksongsa 벽송사 2 E1
Cheoneunsa 천은사 3 A3
Chilbulsa 칠불사 4 C3
Daewonsa 대원사 5 F2
Hwaeomsa 화엄사 6 B4
Kalbawi Boulder 칼바위 7 E3
Mujaechigipokpo 무재치기폭포 8 E2
Silsangsa 실상사 9 D1
Spring 샘 10 D2
Ssanggyesa 쌍계사 11 D4
Yeongoksa 연곡사 12 C4

Sleeping

CAMPING

Camping (W3000 to W6000) is available at Daewonsa, Dalgung, Hwangjeon, Baemsagol, Buril Falls, Jungsan-ni, Baengmudong and Daeseong Bridge. Facilities are basic.

SHELTERS

There are nine **shelters** (W2000-5000) along Jiri Mountain's ridge where hikers crash for the night. From west to east, they are: Nogodan, Piagol, Baemsagol, Yeonhacheon, Byeoksoryeong, Saeseok, Jangteomok, Chibalmok and the Rotary shelter. Jangteomok has enough space for 250 bodies, and sells film, torches, noodles and drinks. Seseok is the largest shelter, with spots for 300 people. For overnight hikes bring bedding, food and tea/coffee, as most shelters have limited supplies. Bookings are essential on weekends and holidays. See the park's website www.npa.or.kr) for details.

MINBAK & YEOGWAN

The path leading to Ssanggyesa is lined with restaurants, people selling energy drinks and a few places to sleep. About 25m from the second signboard, **Jirisan Yeogwan** (지리산 여관; ☎ 883 1668; ondol W20,000; 🔀) has basic rooms overlooking a swiftly flowing creek. For something more secluded, continue up the path and turn right at the road past the first water wheel to find three *minbak* (private homes with rooms for rent) with identical rooms and prices.

Getting There & Away

All buses to Ssanggyesa connect via Hadong (W1900, 30 to 60 minutes, 17 times daily), a good transfer point for other places in the area. On route to Ssanggyesa from Hadong, the bus passes a large orange and blue bridge and shortly thereafter makes a quick stop in Hwagae; don't get off there. Further down the road (usually the next stop) the bus stops near a concrete bridge. Cross the bridge, turn left at the second signboard and follow the winding road to the temple. Bus tickets are purchased from the restaurant beside the concrete bridge. The signboard outside the restaurant lists times for other destinations, though most travellers are best served by making connections from Hadong.

Jeollanam-do
전 라 남 도

For Koreans, this region has an air of the exotic. Located at the peninsula's southwest corner, Jeollanam-do is known for dramatic rocky coastlines, thousands of islands, unique Buddhist sites, its craft heritage and its fine food. Jeollanam-do is also known for its politics – political dissent has a long history here.

Just as a one-time radical can become part of the establishment, Jeollanam-do is slowly but surely becoming more like the rest of Korea. Former President Kim Dae-Jung is the region's favourite son and is credited with bringing recent investment to the region. New transit links – notably the Seohaean Gosokdoro (West Coast expressway, 2001) – have shortened travel times dramatically, and major islands are connected to the mainland via bridges. Despite this, things remain more easygoing than elsewhere on the peninsula.

Many destinations in this chapter can be visited as day trips from Gwangju or Mokpo.

HIGHLIGHTS

- Taking in the arts – and political radicalism – in **Gwangju** (p234)
- Becoming one with the clay at the ancient ceramic centres of **Gangjin** (p244) and **Yeong-am** (p249)
- Taking time away in the islands of **Dadohae Haesang National Park** (p248), especially **Heuksando** (p248) and the fabled **Hongdo** (p248)
- Savouring the flavour – and the mountain-side location – of the **tea plantation** (p244) at Boseong
- Losing yourself in the rugged, rustic coastal scenery of **Yeosu** (p241), **Wando** (p250) and **Jindo** (p252)

| ■ TELEPHONE CODE: 061 | ■ POPULATION: 3.5 MILLION | ■ AREA: 12, 400 SQ KM |

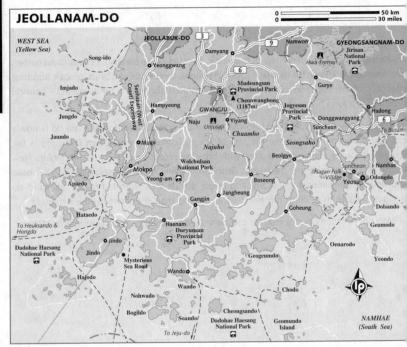

GWANGJU 광주

☎ 062 / pop 1.4 million

Gwangju, Korea's fifth largest city, may look like any other with its shop-filled central area, an attractive riverside, busy restaurants, pubs and bars, and encircled by apartment blocks, but within this everyday exterior reside the heart of an artist and the soul of a revolutionary. This city emphasizes the arts well beyond its size, and it has an important place in the history of Korean political dissent and the advancement of human rights. Some quite decent hotels and restaurants help you enjoy the experience.

Gwangju sits in the centre of Jeollanam-do and is the seat of the provincial government, although it is technically a separate governmental entity. Note that its telephone area code is different from that of the surrounding province.

Information

Tourist information office (☎ 942 6160; Gwangju airport; ☺ 9am-6pm)

Tourist information office (☎ 360 8733; bus terminal; ☺ 9am-6pm)

Tourist information office (☎ 522-5147; train station ☺ 9am-6pm)

Sights

GWANGJU NATIONAL MUSEUM

광주 국립 박물관

This **museum** (☎ 570 7014; admission W400, free first Sun each month; ☺ 9am-6pm Tue-Sun Mar-Oct, to 5pm Tue-Sun Nov-Feb) is part of a large art park also containing the Folk Museum. The National Museum specialises in the ceramics that are Jeollanam-do's claim to fame. It was built after a Chinese Yuan dynasty junk, believed to have sunk off the Korean coast in 1323, was rediscovered in 1975 with a full load of immaculately preserved pieces of celadon (the 'Sinan Relics'), from elegant vases to homey mortars and pestles. Also exhibited are Goryeo dynasty (early-12th-Century) works found in a separate shipwreck, and works from other kilns; the official kilns of the Joseon dynasty were here in Gwangju. There's decent English signage throughout. Interestingly, ceramics preserved above sea level didn't fare as well as those below, due to breakage. Other galleries house 11th- to

14th-century Buddhist relics, scroll paintings and white porcelain.

GWANGJU MUNICIPAL FOLK MUSEUM
민속 박물관

The **Gwangju Municipal Folk Museum** (☎ 521 9041; admission W550; ☺ 9am-6pm Mar-Oct, to 5pm Nov-Feb, closed day after national holidays) is connected to the National Museum via a tunnel under the expressway. Like many such museums, this one uses dioramas to show life rites from birth until death and beyond, as well as festivals, clothing and folk paintings. Bonus: an entire section of plastic models of Jeollanam-do's unique cuisine.

The museums are to the north of the city centre. From Gwangju station, catch bus No 1, 16, 19, 26 or 101, and from Gwangju bus terminal hop on bus No 23 or 25 to the Folk Museum.

MAY 18TH NATIONAL CEMETERY
국립 5.18 묘지

It's hard for Koreans to hear the word 'Gwangju' without thinking of the massacre of May 18, 1980 and its brutal aftermath (see the boxed text below). This new **memorial park** (☎ 266 5187; admission free; ☺ 8am-7pm Mar-Oct, to 5pm Nov-Feb), opened in 2002, contains an impressive burial site and a moving museum. The memorial hall features photos of those killed – middle-school students to grandmothers – and an exhibit recounts the events in painful detail, though much of it is in Korean. The remains were buried elsewhere before being interred here; others who participated in the uprising – but did not perish – are welcome to be buried here when they pass on.

Bus No 25 departs the bus terminal for the memorial approximately every 40 minutes (W700, 40 minutes).

MUDEUNGSAN PROVINCIAL PARK
무등산 도립공원

Overlooking Gwangju, **Mudeungsan Provincial Park** (☎ 265 0761; admission free) is an undulating mountain range with a spider's web of trails leading to the peak, Cheonwangbong (1187m). About 1km up from the park entrance is a **tea plantation** established by the Joseon dynasty scholar-painter, Heo Baek-ryeon (1891–1977; pseudonym 'Uijae'). Uijae believed that expressing poetry through calligraphy was the consummation of three great arts: painting, poetry and calligraphy. He used this area as a retreat, and chief among several buildings related to him is the contemporary museum **Uijae Misulgwan** (☎ 222 3040; admission W1000; ☺ 10am-5.30pm Tue-Sun Mar-Oct, to 5pm Nov-Feb) which houses his and others' work; there's little English signage, but the works have their own voices.

MAY 18TH

What the Kent State Riots were to 1960s America and the Tiananmen Massacre to 1989 China, the Gwangju Massacre was to South Korea: a mass demonstration with deadly consequences that became an icon for its time.

A series of events in 1980 led to large-scale student protests against the government. On 18 May, the military moved into Gwangju. The soldiers had no bullets, but they used bayonets to murder dozens of protesters. Outraged residents broke into armouries and police stations, and used the seized weapons and ammunition to drive the military forces out of the city. The brutal military response came nine days later: on 27 May, soldiers armed with loaded M16 rifles retook the city, and most of the protest leaders were summarily shot. One hundred and fifty four people were killed during the uprising, 70 are still listed as missing, and an additional 4089 were arrested or wounded.

The chief culprits behind these tragic events were two generals, Chun Doo-hwan and Roh Tae-woo, both of whom later became president. A longstanding movement sought to prosecute them, but in 1998 president (cum democracy activist, Nobel Peace Prize laureate and native son of Jeollanam-do) Kim Dae-jung pardoned Chun Doo-hwan and Roh Tae-woo in a widespread amnesty to political prisoners.

Gwangju, for its part, has turned the lessons of 1980 into useful activism. It was here that the Asian Human Rights Charter was proclaimed in 1998, and every May busloads of Koreans young and old come to the city to pay tribute to the fallen fighters and demonstrate for the causes of the day.

JEOLLANAM-DO

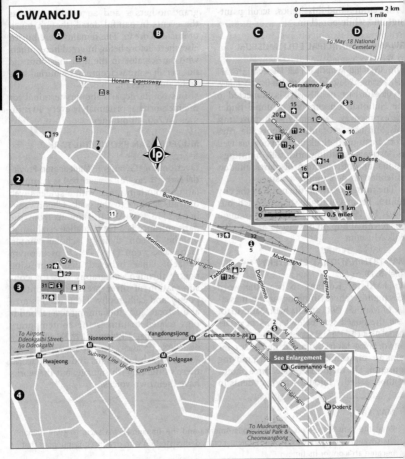

GWANGJU

The plantation extends to **Jeungsimsa**, a Buddhist temple with a rare iron Buddha sculpture and two highly-regarded curved-edged pagodas. Another 1km takes you to **Yaksasa**, a small Buddhist temple dating from the late Silla period, with a famous three-storey pagoda. In the northern, less developed part of the park is **Wonhyosa**, a mountain-ringed temple with a lovely pavilion where you can sit (rare for a Korean temple) overlooking the valley.

Mudeungsan's thick forests offer a splendid display of colours during autumn. There are plenty of streams, and it's popular hiking country.

To get to the park entrance, take local bus No 15, 23, 27, 52, 106, 555 or 771; ask the driver for Jeungsimsa. For Wonhyosa take bus No 18 or 777. Buses cost W700.

Festivals & Events

The Gwangju Biennale (http://gwangju biennale.org) is an international contemporary art festival, held over two months biannually (next held 10 September to 13 November 2004). The inaugural mid-1990s festival declared 'globalisation rather than Westernisation; diversity rather than conformity' and that 'art must reject conflict, confrontation, violence and discrimination'. Each biennale is themed and venues alter. The city fills with colourful and thought-provoking performances, displays, lectures, exhibitions and music, across media from traditional to experimental.

Every October, Gwangju hosts a six-day Kimchi Festival, perhaps your best opportunity to make, taste, purchase or just enjoy the visual sensation of Korea's most famous dish in all its varieties. Venues change from year to year, but shuttle buses connect the venue and major transit points. Contact **KNTO** (Korean National Tourism Organisation; www.knto.or.kr) for more details.

Sleeping

As a 2002 World Cup host city, Gwangju boasts some nice new inns and restaurants, but it may appear that much of the new construction was love hotels, which are known to rent by the hour or overnight for couples with 'specific' needs. For that reason we've not gone out of our way to recommend any, but if you want to try one they're easy to spot thanks to their garish exteriors.

Lodgings are concentrated around the bus and train stations and Chungjangro.

Garden Jang (☎ 524 7282; r W20,000; 😮) Plain but spotless, this older *yeogwan* (motels with small, well-equipped en suite rooms) is an excellent deal near the train station – and the only lodging for blocks that's explicitly *not* a love hotel.

Eunhasu (☎ 367 0510; r W25,000; 😮) Among a plethora of oldish *yeogwan* in the alleys north of the bus terminal, this one is the newest and arguably the best. Ignore the round beds.

Lawrence Motel (☎ 366 1900; W30,000; 😮 💻) In a love-hotel galaxy south of the bus terminal, this spanking new inn is a sane choice with nice TVs and in-room water coolers. Some rooms have Internet connections (per day W5000).

Riverside Tourist Hotel (☎ 223 9111; fax 223 9112; r W35,000; 😮) For a little more money, you can stay in the centre of dining and nightlife, although you're paying for location, not room quality.

Phoenix Motel (☎ 226 5007; d W40,000; 😮) On a quiet block by the river, this brand new place offers large rooms with free Internet connections. Video rentals available.

Gwangju Grand Hotel (☎ 224 6111; fax 224 8933; d from W90,000; 😮) Try here for spacious rooms, mid-80s construction, very professional staff and a cake shop in the lobby. Ask about off-peak discounts.

Gwangju Palace Tourist Hotel (☎ 222 2525; www .hotelpalace.co.kr; d from W99,000; 😮 💻) Here you'll find marble bathrooms, spiffy linens and a can't-beat-it central location. Ask about discounts.

Hotel Hiddink Continental (☎ 227 8500; www.hotel -continental.co.kr; d & tw from W121,000; 😮) Named for the Dutch coach of the Korean 2002 World Cup team – now a national hero – this comfy place has some rooms named for Korean players (yes, they slept here). There are also saunas, in-room water coolers and VCRs. Ask about discounts.

Prince Hotel (☎ 524 0025; www.prince-hotel.co.kr; d/tw W127,000/169,400; 😮 💻) Near the national museum, with some *ondol* rooms, free in-room Internet access and nice city views.

Eating

Gwangju is blessed with a couple of streets where several restaurants serve the same style dish – and compete for your business.

Yeongyang Duck Center (☎ 524 6687; half/full duck stews W20,000/25,000) On what the locals call 'duck street' this place serves the local specialty *yeongyang oritang*, a glorious duck stew, filled with vegetables and so thick the staff give you aprons when you eat it. Even if you're just coming in from the airport, stop on Ddeokgeori for *tteokgalbi*, rectangular patties of grilled beef.

Ijo Ddeokgalbi (tteokgalbi meals W7000) This establishment is so popular it's been on TV.

Minsokchon (meals W5800-11,000) Two locations in the Chungjangro shopping district, with an updated folksy appearance. Barbecues usually sizzle on tables, especially *dwaeji galbi* (barbecued pork) and *so galbi* (barbecued beef).

Moojinjoo (meals W6000-12,500) A contemporary, architecturally adventurous place, specialising in a special type of *bossam* (steamed pork and cabbage), in which the pork was prepared with medicinal herbs. Most dishes are for sharing, including *kimchi bossam* (pork which you wrap in *kimchi*) and *geumbaechu bossam* (pork wrapped in cabbage). Some seats have garden views.

Songjukheon (meals from W35,000) This is one of Gwangju's most expensive and well-known establishments and it occupies a setting like a traditional home. Korean banquet is its specialty, with elaborate displays of food. It's very popular – book ahead.

Choon Chun Jip (meals W6000) An informal place where the staff cook for you at your table. *Dak galbi* (stir-fried chicken fillet with vegetables and hot sauce, W5000) is the specialty. *Maek ban seok cchimdak* (W14,500) is made from a whole chicken.

There's no shortage of cheap eats in Chungjangro, and the Lotte, Hyundai and Shinsegae department stores have all sorts of restaurants upstairs and food floors in the basements.

Shopping

Yesului-geori (Art Street) has art galleries, and antique, souvenir (with traditional handicrafts) and framing shops. It has no traffic on weekends for an open-air art market.

Chungjangro is Gwangju's trendy shopping district, with popular clothing and accessory shops, plus bars, restaurants and nightclubs, a couple of bookshops and all of the fast-food giants. The street bustles nightly with young hipsters.

Getting There & Away

AIR

Both Asiana and Korean Air offer Gwangju–Seoul and Gwangju–Jeju flights.

BUS

Gwangju's bus terminal is a monolithic structure housing both express and inter-city buses, an information desk and easily a dozen restaurants.

The terminal is in the west end of town; city bus Nos 7, 9, 13, 17, 36 and 101 connect the terminal with the train station area.

Express bus destinations include:

Destination	Price (W)	Duration
Busan	12,700	4hr
Daegu	9900	3¾hr
Daejeon	8200	3hr
Dong Seoul	14,500	4hr
Jeonju	4800	1¼hr
Seoul	13,000	3½hr

Intercity buses departing Gwangju include:

Destination	Price (W)	Duration
Baegyangsa*	3300	1hr
Haenam**	7300	1½hr
Mokpo	5700	1¾hr
Suncheon***	5200	1½hr
Wando	10,600	2½hr
Yeosu	8200	2½hr

*for Naejangsan National Park
**for Duryunsan Provincial Park
***for Nagan and Seonamsa (Sogyesan National Park)

TRAIN

Trains to Seoul include *saemaeul* (W27,300, four hours, five daily) and *mugunghwa* (W18,600, 4½ hours, eight daily).

Getting Around

TO/FROM THE AIRPORT

Bus Nos 50 and 999 from the train station and bus terminal regularly run to the airport (40 minutes). A taxi between the airport and the centre costs about W7500 and takes 20 minutes.

TRAIN

A subway line was under construction as this book went to press. The first stage was due

o open in 2004, with eventual service from
ust north of the airport, just south of the bus
erminal and throughout the city centre.

AROUND GWANGJU
Unjusa 운주사

This fascinating **temple** (☎ 374 0660; admission
W1300; 8am-6pm Mar-Oct, 9am-5pm Nov-Feb), occupies a river valley and its hillsides in Hwasun-
gun, 40km south of Gwangju. Legend has it
that the site originally housed 1000 Buddhas
and 1000 pagodas, although the remaining
23 pagodas and some 100 Buddhas are still
the greatest numbers of any Korean temple.
According to legend they were all built in
one night by stone masons sent down from
heaven; another theory is that Unjusa was
the site of a school for stone masons.

Whatever their origins, many works are
unique, and some are national treasures.
Back-to-back twin Buddhas (Seokbulgam
sangbaebul Jwasang) face their own pagodas. Another pair of Buddhas lying on their
backs are said to have been the last works
sculpted that evening; work was interrupted
when one mason, tired after all-night toil,
imitated a rooster call while it was still
dark – the others returned back to heaven
before the Buddhas could be stood upright.

To reach Unjusa catch bus No 218 or
218 from Gwangju bus terminal (W2300,
½ hours, twice hourly); the temple is a
10-minute walk from the bus stop. Check
with the driver as some buses do not go
all the way to Unjusa. The last bus back to
Gwangju passes around 7.50pm.

Damyang Bamboo Crafts Museum
담양 죽공예 박물관

North of Gwangju is the town of Damyang,
famous for its abundant bamboo forests
and crafts.

At the **Bamboo Crafts Museum** (☎ 381 4111;
admission W500; 9am-6pm Mar-Oct, to 5pm Nov-Feb)
there are baskets, furniture, fans, scoops
and sculpture (but little English signage).
The best visiting time is during the bamboo
products market, the second, 7th, 12th, 17th,
22nd and 27th of each month. An annual
Bamboo Crafts Festival is held in May. At
other times, you can view the rows of shops
lining the plaza in front of the museum.

Daenamu Tongbap (meals W10,000) serves a
meal of over a dozen dishes, but the spe-
ialty is bamboo kimchi and rice steamed

in a bamboo stalk. It's above the shops to
the right as you exit the museum.

Local bus No 311 to Damyang runs from
Gwangju's bus terminal (W1700, 50 minutes, every 20 minutes).

HWA-EOMSA 화엄사

One the three famous temples in Jirisan
National Park, **Hwa-eomsa** (☎ 783 9105; admission W3000; 6am-7pm, 7am-6pm Nov-Feb) was
founded by priest Yon-gi in AD 544 after
his return from China. It is dedicated to
the Birojana Buddha. The temple has suffered five major devastations, including the
Japanese invasion of 1592, but luckily much
remained despite the various cataclysms. It
was last rebuilt in 1636.

On the main plaza is **Gakgwangjeon**, a huge
two-storey hall. There are some massive pillars and striking scroll paintings inside,
but there are paintings which are national
treasures nearly 12m long and 7.75m wide,
and feature Buddhas, disciples and assorted
holies. These are displayed outdoors only on
special occasions. Korea's oldest and largest
stone lantern fronts Gakgwangjeon, which
was once surrounded by stone tablets of the
Tripitaka Sutra (made during the Silla era).
These were ruined during the Japanese invasion. Many pieces are now preserved in the
temple's **museum**.

Up many further flights of stairs is Hwa-
eomsa's most famous structure, a unique
three-storey pagoda supported by four
stone lions. The female figure beneath the
pagoda is said to be Yon-gi's mother; her
dutiful son offers her tea from another lantern facing her.

The temple is about 15 minutes' walk from
the ticket office. It is possible to continue
from the temple and along the valley. After
about 2½ to three hours the trail begins to
ascend to a shelter, Nogodan Sanjang (four
hours). From the shelter the trail continues
to rise until you are finally on the spine of
the Jirisan ridge. For more hiking details
see p229.

Sleeping & Eating

Jirisan Prince (☎ 782 0740; fax 782 0741; r Sun-Thu from
W30,000, Fri & Sat from W35,000;) Common areas
are in better shape than the rooms (bed or
ondol), but upstairs rooms have ondol lofts
above the main bedrooms. It's the log-
cabin-like building behind the car park.

Jirisan Swiss Tourist Hotel (☎ 783 0700; fax 782 1571; d W85,000; ✄) It's about 20 minutes' walk down the main road before the temple ticket office. Well maintained with valley views, shower curtains in the bathrooms, and a restaurant. There are off-season discounts.

Ttukbaegi Sikdang (☎ 782 7390; per person W6000-12,000) A cut above usual tourist village restaurants, with generous and tasty side dishes. Try *sanchaejeongsik* (mixed vegetables set meal, W9000), *dolsotbibimbap* (mixed vegetables and rice in a stone pot, W6000) or *doenjang jjigae* (bean curd stew, W6000). The restaurant is up the stairs directly opposite the police box.

Getting There & Away

Direct buses to/from Hwa-eomsa include:

Destination	Price (W)	Duration
Busan	12,600	3¼hr
Gwangju	5900	1½hr
Jeonju	6700	2hr
Yeosu	5900	2hr

Other long-distance buses must be reached via Gurye (W700, 20 minutes), including Seoul Nambu (W20,000, 4½ hours).

JOGYESAN PROVINCIAL PARK
조계산 도립공원

This park centres around two noteworthy temples, their beauty complemented by the attractive surrounding forest.

To the west, **Songgwangsa** (☎ 755 0107; fax 75 0408; admission W2300; ☺ 7am-7pm Mar-Oct, 8am-6pm Nov-Feb) is considered one of the three jewels of Korean Buddhism (along with Tongdosa and Haeinsa, in Gyeongsangnam-do). It is the main temple of the Jogye sect, by far the largest in Korean Buddhism. It is also one of the oldest Zen temples in Korea, originally founded in AD 867 although most of the buildings date from the 17th century. Songgwangsa is known for having produced many prominent Zen masters over the years, and today the temple is home to a community of monks.

On the eastern side of the mountain is **Seonamsa** (☎ 754 6160; admission W2300; ☺ 8am-7pm Mar-Oct, 8.30am-6pm Nov-Feb), a quieter hermitage dating back to AD 529, where some 50 monks study and try to preserve the old ways. Below Seonamsa is **Seungseongyo**, one of Korea's most exquisite ancient granite bridges, with a dragon's head hanging from the top of the arch.

A spectacular hike over the peak of **Janggunbong** (884m) connects the two temples. The walk takes six hours if you go over the peak, or four hours if you go around it. Either route is fantastic.

Accommodation and restaurants are available by the car park at Songgwangsa. Lodgings here range from W20,000 to W25,000. There's also a tourist village near Seonamsa where one nice option is **Seonam Garden** (☎ 754 5233; d W15,000-20,000) a *minbak* (private homes with rooms for rent)/restaurant in

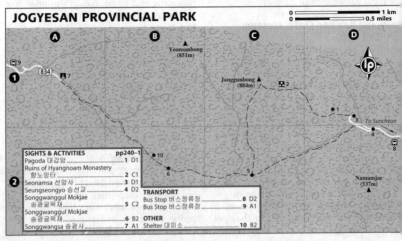

JOGYESAN PROVINCIAL PARK

0 — 1 km
0 — 0.5 miles

SIGHTS & ACTIVITIES	pp240-1
Pagoda 대갑암	1 D1
Ruins of Hyangnoam Monastery 향노암터	2 C1
Seonamsa 선암사	3 D1
Seungseongyo 승선교	4 D2
Songgwanggul Mokjae 송광굴목재	5 C2
Songgwanggul Mokjae 송광굴목재	6 B2
Songgwangsa 송광사	7 A1

TRANSPORT	
Bus Stop 버스정류장	8 D2
Bus Stop 버스정류장	9 A1

OTHER	
Shelter 대피소	10 B2

Yeonsanbong (851m)

Janggunbong (884m)

To Suncheon

Namamjae (537m)

traditional-style Korean home with large rooms and *bibimbap* for W5000.

Getting There & Away

From Gwangju there are direct buses to Songgwangsa (W5200, 1½ hours, hourly) or less frequent connections to Seonamsa via Suncheon (W6000).

Buses depart from Yeosu for Songgwangsa every 40 minutes. For Seonamsa, change buses at Suncheon (W790, 50 minutes, twice hourly).

NAGAN FOLK VILLAGE
낙안 민속 마을

Among Korea's several folk villages **Nagan** (☎ 749 3893; admission W1100; ☻ 9am-6pm) is unique for its setting: within 1410m of Joseon-period fortress walls. It's also Korea's only fortress built on a plain.

No fort remains, but some 90 households now live in a variety of traditional homes within the old walls, alongside agricultural plots. Some points of interest are labelled in English. There is also a **folk museum** housing a variety of tools and exhibits detailing traditional customs, practices and rites.

Although residents receive a government subsidy, incomes can still be sparse, so many of the homes double as shops, restaurants and *minbak* (W25,000 – inquire directly or contact the office to reserve). However, many are private homes, and you should ask permission before entering. You may walk on the fortress walls for attractive rooftop views, and imagine spotting invaders descending the surrounding mountains.

Festivals are held here on the 15th day of the lunar new year and around 5 May. The huge Namdo Food Festival (which receives 200,000-plus attendees) is usually held here early in October. It features about 300 Korean dishes, plus eating contests and traditional cultural events. Check with KNTO (www.knto.or.kr) for dates and details.

Nagan Spa (☎ 753 0035; admission W5000; ☻ 6am-10pm), a few kilometres away, is a new, unprepossessing facility overlooking the valley. Its waters are said to soften skin and help burn fat. Steam, sauna and tubs are available, as is a shuttle service to/from Nagan Folk Village.

Catch bus No 63 or 68 from Suncheon (W790, 40 minutes, hourly) to the Folk Village.

YEOSU 여수
pop 327,000

The municipality of Yeosu covers a vast area about halfway along Korea's steep, island-pocked and deeply-indented southern coast. By the time you reach Yeosu you will have seen comparable city centres, but its shoreline, peppered with cliffs, islands and peninsulas, is spectacularly beautiful.

Orientation & Information

On a map, Yeosu is shaped like a molar. The two roots (mountainous, dramatic island coastlines) straddle a bay, crowned by the city centre. The island of Odongdo sits east of town, and the much larger Dolsando is to the southeast. The bus terminal is about 3.5km north of the town centre, reachable by local bus or taxi.

There is a **tourist information booth** (☎ 664 8978; ☻ 9am-6pm) by the entrance to Odongdo bridge.

Sights & Activities
HARBOUR CRUISES

The best way to see Yeosu's coastal scenery is from the water. Several companies depart from different piers, on alternate routes. Among them, **Hallyosudo** (☎ 662 9068) offers a quick cruise across the central harbour from Dolsan Daegyo (Dolsan Bridge) to Odongo boat terminal (W3500, 30 minutes), or a trip around Dolsando with a possible stop at Hyang-il-am (see following p243; W13,600, time varies). **Odongo Yuramseon** (☎ 663 4424) is based on the pier on the mainland side of Odongdo Bridge and offers short cruises to or around Odongo (W2000 to W4000) as well as its own Hyang-il-am cruise (W13,000, no stopover). Note that sailings are subject to sufficient demand.

ODONGDO 오동도

This craggy, tree- and bamboo-covered **island** (☎ 690 7301; admission W1300; ☻ 6am-10pm Mar-Nov, to 9pm Dec-Feb) is a favourite destination among locals for its lighthouse, gardens, picnic spots and walking trails. It's linked to the mainland by a 730m-long causeway. Among its many paths, you may climb (barefoot) up the 'health foot-pressure walkway' between the island's boat terminal and lighthouse. It's several hundred metres of alternating stones, wood blocks, discs and triangles. Ouch. Whichever path you choose, walk

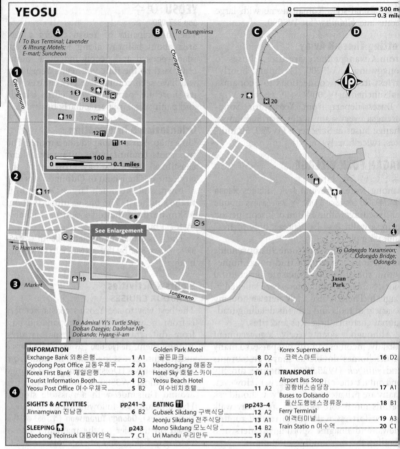

YEOSU

around the lighthouse and down the stairs for a nice harbour view.

HANSANSA 한산사

For a more substantial trek, try this **temple** (admission free; 24hr) high up on wooded mountain slopes west of central Yeosu. It was first built in 1194 by a high priest named Bojo during the reign of the Goryeo king, Myeongjong, but the reason to go is the views.

You can take a taxi to the temple, or bus No 1, 2 or 10 to Beoksugol, from where it's about 20 steep minutes to the temple, then another 10 minutes to the summit. Facing the temple from the plaza with the large bell, head to the right, take the footpath and (mostly) descend to a small platform where

the local people have been known do their washing. Continue to your left, up the stair behind the path lined with gym equipment and on to the highest point – a grassy cliff top. The views are practically 180°.

ADMIRAL YI'S TURTLE SHIP 거북선

Yeosu's historical claim to fame is in connection with Admiral Yi, who defeated the Japanese navy on several occasions in the 16th century (p29). Here you'll find a full-size re-creation of a *geobukseon* or **turtle ship** (644 1411; admission W1200; 8am-6.30pm Mar-Aug, 9am-5.30pm Sep-Feb), one of the admiral's famous iron-clad war vessels.

The ship moors at the passenger boat pier just across the Dolsan Bridge on Dolsando aboard, costumed mannequins demonstrate techniques for rowing, shooting, sleeping in crowded bunks and receiving torture. Some find the exhibits a little simple, but it's a unique experience.

HYANG-IL-AM 향일암

This **hermitage** (☎ 644 3650; admission W1200; ☼ 7am-7pm Mar-Sep, 8am-6pm Nov-Feb), part of Dadohae National Park, is perched above the cliffs on the southern tip of Dolsando, some 40 minutes from the town centre by bus. It is famous among sunrise-watchers, with superb views over the clear blue seas. The hermitage sits in a forest of old camellia trees that usually bloom in March and April.

If you need some more exercise, continue on up to **Geumosan** (323m), a rewarding and pleasant hike above Hyang-il-am. A circular track starts next to a **temple** and returns to the temple road 20m further down the track.

For bus details, see p244.

JINNAMGWAN 진남관

Right in the centre of town stands this national treasure and Korea's largest single-storey wooden structure (75m long and 14m high). This beautiful pavilion, with 68 pillars supporting its massive roof, was originally constructed for receiving officials and holding ceremonies. Later it was used as military quarters.

Ordinarily, this important structure would top our sightseeing recommendations, but it's due to be under repair until 2006. Until then, authorities are talking about placing a museum at the site.

Sleeping

Most bargain-basement options are clustered around the train station and have, shall we say, flavour.

Daedong Yeoinsuk (☎ 664 0089; r from W20,000; ☒) Typical of train-station-area lodgings, low rates are its chief virtue. No private facilities.

Haedong-jang (☎ 662 5577; d with ondol/bed W20,000/25,000; ☒) Don't be put off by the exterior; rooms are decent for the price, and you can't beat the location right in the city centre.

Lavender Motel (☎ 654 5293; fax 652 6234; d from W25,000; ☒) A new and quite pleasant option if you need to be by the bus terminal. Triple-pane windows and a side street location are designed to keep things quiet. It's next to E-mart supermarket.

Ilteung Motel (☎ 651 6700; d from W25,000; ☒) Plain but well-kept, across from Lavender.

Golden Park Motel (☎ 665 1400; d from W30,000; ☒) Above a fishmonger's on the Yeosu side of the bridge to Odongdo. Rooms are nothing special, but many come with nice views.

Hwangtobang (☎ 644 4353; d from W30,000; ☒) This is a great inn/restaurant in the tourist village near Hyang-il-am, built log-cabin-style and boasting deliberately rustic rooms. You can't quite see the sea from here, but views are a minute's walk away. There's a cheerful deck for eating, drinking and relaxing. *Haemul doenjang tchigae* (seafood and beancurd stew, W6000) and *haemultang* (spicy seafood hot pot, W30,000) are the most popular dishes.

Hotel Sky (☎ 662 7780; d from W35,000; ☒) This new inn is in a central location. The tile-work brightens the interior.

Yeosu Beach Hotel (☎ 663 2011; fax 664 2114; d, tw & ondol from W110,000, 20% weekday discount; ☒) Not on the beach but still the city's best high-end option. It was renovated in 2002, and most rooms have a city or hillside view. There's free Internet access in the lobby.

Eating

The area around the harbourfront is loaded with restaurants serving the local specialty (fish and seafood), alongside shops selling implements to catch the same. None is particularly fancy, but you're here for the food. You'll probably be served *gakkimchi*, leafy *kimchi* that is a nationally admired Yeosu delicacy.

Gubaek Sikdang (dishes W6000-20,000) One of the city's best regarded restaurants for *saengseongui* (grilled fish, W10,000) and *agutchim* (spicy fish with bean sprouts, W10,000). Some of the menu has been translated into English.

Mono Sikdang (dishes W10,000-20,000) Around the corner from Gubaek Sikdang, this place is less fuss but no less popular. Plus, you get harbour views. Try *saengseongui*, *sodaejwe* (sushi) or *saengsong chorim* (steamed seasonal fish with spicy sauce). There is no English menu.

Jeonju Sikdang (dishes W4500-6000) Serves a variety of more conventional Korean meals (*bibimbap, kimchi jjigae* etc) in a simple environment.

Uri Mandu (dishes W2500-4000) Serves a variety of *mandu* (dumplings) at budget prices. Budget travellers will also find fast-food and convenience store options nearby.

Getting There & Away
AIR
Yeosu airport has flights to Seoul and Jeju.

BOAT
The main pier for long-distance ferries is at the western end of the old fishing dock. See p258 for details of Jeju-do service.

BUS
The express and inter-city bus terminals are next to each other on the western side of the city, on the road out to the airport.

Express buses go to Seoul (W17,600, five hours, every 30 to 40 minutes) and Busan (W11,000, four hours, every two hours). Intercity buses go to:

Destination	Price (W)	Duration
Gwangju	8200	2hr
Hwa-eomsa	5900	2hr
Mokpo	13,400	3½hr

TRAIN
Trains from Seoul include *saemaeul* (W28,600 to W33,600, 5½ hours, three daily) and *mugunghwa* (W19,500 to W22,900, six hours, 12 daily).

Getting Around
TO/FROM THE AIRPORT
The airport is 17km north of town. Airport buses (W2500, 40 minutes, frequent) serve the town centre.

BUS
The express and intercity bus terminals are in the far north of town. City bus Nos 3, 5, 6, 7, 8, 9, 10, 11, 13 and 17 go past the two bus terminals, but probably the most useful is bus No 11, which connects the bus terminals with the train station via the centre of town.

Bus Nos 101, 111, 111-1 and 113 (W950) leave Yeosu approximately every 30 minutes for Hyang-il-am. If you want to catch the sunrise, the first bus departs Yeosu at around 5am.

BOSEONG 보성
Imagine standing on a mountainside, it slopes covered with rows and rows of green tea bushes. That is Boseong.

This town, squarely between Gwangju Yeosu and Mokpo, is best known for **Boseong Nokcha Dawon** (☎ 853 2595; admission free; ❀ plantation 24hr, office 9am-7pm May-Oct, to 6pr Nov-Apr), the tea plantation of Daehan, on of Korea's leading tea growers. It's quit an attractive place and visitors are free te ramble the tea-lined paths up the hillside fo a unique, rustic feeling and nice views of th surrounding slopes (signs request you don' walk between individual rows). Events suc as concerts are often held on the property.

There are many tea-drinking and tea dining places here, such as **Chamokwon** (mea W5000-11,000) where the house speciality i pork raised on green tea – try it *bulbaek* (*bulgogi* style) or as *saengsamgyeop* (grillee pork belly). There's also a **tea house** (tea W1000 for the regulation three cups poured by a pro, and a **drink bar** (drinks W2500) where mill shakes and lattes are made with…green tea – you were expecting a frappuccino?

Local buses to the tea plantation continue to the Yulpo coast, where **Yulpo Haesu Nokcha tang** (☎ 853 4566; admission W5000; ❀ 6am-8pm, las entry 7pm) offers you the chance to bathe in sea water or tea water. The tea bath is said to be good for skin diseases, hair, dandruff, acne and joint pain. Typical of Korean spas, the setting is more functional than luxurious, bu it's a unique opportunity. The facility was i the midst of an expansion on our visit, with swimming pools overlooking the sea.

Getting There & Around
Frequent buses go to Boseong termina from Gwangju (W4800, 1¾ hours), Mokpc (W6500, two hours) and Yeosu (W6800, 1¾ hours). From Boseong terminal, take a loca bus (every 30 minutes) to Daehan Daeop the tea plantation (W750, 10 minutes), o Yulpo (W1200, 20 minutes). It's less than 1(minutes' walk from the plantation bus stop to the grounds. To Yulpo there's a direct bus from Gwangju (W5300, 1¾ hours, hourly).

GANGJIN 강진
One of two important ceramic centres in Jeollanam-do, Gangjin has been associated with celadon for over 1000 years. Even back then, the combination of excellent clay soil

asy access to firewood and a long, narrow
way for shipping helped put Gangjin on the
map. Some 80% of the celadon pieces in the
Seoul National Museum are said to have been
made here. Across the Daegu-myeon district
are the ruins of some 190 historic kilns.

Gangjin is specifically known for etched
celadon, in which shallow patterns are cut
out of the piece while it's still wet and filled
in with special glazes through an inlay
process – pieces generally come out with
both whitish and bluish accents. Another
distinctive feature of Gangjin celadon: no
ice-crackles. Most celadon ware has crackles
because the soil and glazes are a tiny bit
mismatched – this wasn't the case in Gangjin;
both the oldest and most contemporary
Gangjin celadons are prized for their smooth-
ness. It takes 24 stages and an estimated 70
days to complete one celadon piece.

The centrepiece of the Korean Ceramic
Village is the extensive **Gangjin Ceramic
Museum** (☎ 430 3524; admission W1000; ꠜ 9am-6pm
Mar-Oct, to 5pm Nov-Feb). There are indoor and
outdoor exhibition spaces, a research and
experimental centre (where workers demonstrate the process from throwing the pots
to etching and glazing them). There's also a
workshop where visitors may try their hand
at various projects. Works can be glazed,
fired and shipped.

The Gangjin Ceramic Festival is held
during midsummer each year. At other
times, there are around a dozen studios
across from the museum, where local artisans peddle their wares.

If you need to stay in town, there are
numerous motels and *yeogwan* near the
Gangjin bus terminal.

Getting There & Around

Frequent buses travel to Gangjin's bus
terminal from:

Destination	Price (W)	Duration
Busan	18,000	5hr
Gwangju	6400	1½hr
Mokpo	3600	1hr
Seoul	15,900	5¼hr
Yeosu	9800	2½hr

For the ceramic village, take a local bus
bound for Maryang and get off at Misan
(W1400, 30 minutes, every 20 minutes).

MOKPO 목포

pop 246,000

The fishing port of Mokpo is the end of the
line for train and expressway traffic, and a
starting point for voyages at sea including
Jejudo and the western islands of Dadohae
Haesang National Park. Korea's National
Maritime Museum is appropriately located
here, and handsome Yudal Park rises up
Yudalsan mountain in the city centre. Not
surprisingly there's good seafood to be
had, an easygoing attitude and some nice
sea views.

Information

A **tourist information booth** (☎ 273 0536) sits opposite the Maritime Museum and is usually
staffed by a friendly English-speaking guide.
Other information desks are at the train station and international ferry terminal.

Sights

In 1983, a Goryeo period (estimated 11th-
century) Korean boat was discovered off
the island of Wando with a cargo of some
30,000 pieces of ceramic ware. This pottery
and the skeletal remains of the **Wando
Ship**, Korea's oldest known traditional ship, have
been preserved at the **Maritime Museum** (☎ 278
4271; admission W600; ꠜ 9am-6pm Tue-Fri, to 7pm Sat
& Sun Mar-Oct, closes 5pm Nov-Feb), and a small scale
replica is also here.

The museum also exhibits a Chinese
Yuan dynasty boat known as the **Sinan Ship**,
discovered in 1976 along the nearby Sinan
coast. The nine-year excavation revealed
over 20,000 pieces of ceramic ware. Visitors
may view the 34m vessel in partial restoration, as well as recovered food, spices and
coins. While the same wreck is covered at
the Gwangju National Museum (p234), the
focus there is almost entirely on ceramics.
The museum is along the harbour, east of
the town centre.

Opposite the Maritime Museum, the
Regional Cultural Hall (☎ 270 8367; admission
W1000; ꠜ 9am-8pm Mar-Oct, closes 7pm Nov-Feb)
mixes the random (natural stones in unusual shapes; currency collection) with the
highbrow (revered local artists works held
by the Yeo family and a handsome sculpture garden). A new **Natural History Museum**,
next to the Regional Cultural Hall, should
have opened by the time you read this, and
some of the items may be moved there.

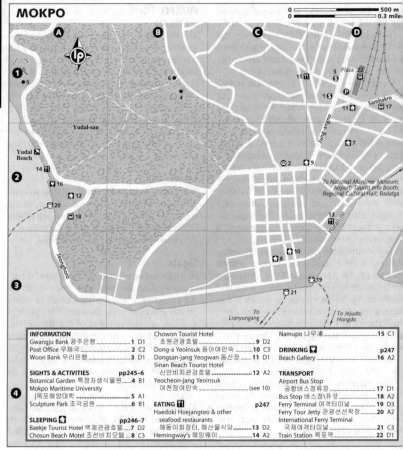

MOKPO

Catch local bus No 1 to the MBC Mokpo stop, then transfer to bus No 7 (about 30 minutes total). A taxi costs about W3000 from the train station.

YUDALSAN 유달산

In western Mokpo, overlooking the harbour, this mountain (229m) is a popular recreational area. A walk to the top affords good views, especially at sunset. The mountain's Yudal Park contains small temples, a **botanical garden** (☎ 270 8362; admission W700; ☼ 8am-7pm Mar-Oct, 8.30am-6pm Nov-Feb) and a **sculpture park** (☎ 270 8359; admission W1000; ☼ 8am-7pm Mar-Oct, 8.30am-6pm Nov-Feb). The beach is to the west. It's pretty basic, but the waterfront is nice for a stroll.

Sleeping

There's a cluster of inexpensive, undistinguished and handy lodgings near the ferry terminals.

Dong-a Yeoinsuk (☎ 244 1951; r W10,000) You want cheap, they've got cheap. The seven teensy rooms have TVs but no private bathroom.

Yeocheon-jang Yeoinsuk (☎ 244 7287; r W13,000) Rooms here have TV, fan and private facilities. Downside: cramped.

Chosun Beach Motel (☎ 242 0485; ondol/d W30,000/ 35,000; 🖭) It's a couple grades up, though hardly fancy; rooms are clean and comfy.

Elsewhere in town:

Dongsan-jang Yeogwan (☎ 244 4044; d W25,000) It doesn't look like much on approach, but rooms here have been recently renovated. By the station.

Baekje Tourist Hotel (☎ 242 4411; fax 242 9550; d from 40,000; ✕) Also near the station, this larger, more professional operation was being renovated as this book went to press. There's a restaurant on the premises for breakfast.

Shinan Beach Tourist Hotel (☎ 243 3399; www .shinanbeachhotel.com; mountain-/ocean-view r from W99,500/119,500; ✕) Traditionally Mokpo's top hotel, it towers above Yudal Beach, with a few restaurants, a pool (opens mid-July each year) and a sky lounge. In good weather, light sleepers may be sensitive to outdoor music from the waterside clubs below.

Chowon Tourist Hotel (☎ 243 0055; d W120,000; ✕) For European or North American-style comforts, this is a nice option in the town centre, with clean lines, wood floors and a cake shop.

Eating & Drinking

Haedoki Hwejangteo (dishes at market price) Mokpo specialises in seafood dishes, especially sashimi, and this restaurant is one of many good choices in a strip along the harbour, each with tanks full of the day's catch. Prices are not cheap at any of these places, but here's a strategy: state up front how much you want to spend.

Namupo (meals W5000-19,000) Not in a seafood mood? Try the grills at this thrillingly clean local favourite in the city centre. The meat of the namesake Namupo *galbi* is beautifully seasoned. Nearby are loads of cheap eats and convenience stores.

Badatga (dishes W6000-30,000) Located in the Maritime Museum building, this is a relaxing place for a meal or drink overlooking the bay. Choices include *bibimbap*, *donkasu* and filet 'minyon'. Many dishes are for sharing.

Hemingway's (meals W6000-15,000) The setting, on a bluff above Yudal beach, is ideal for ship-spotting, sunset-ogling and beer-nursing. Korean and Western cuisines are available here – both complete meals and drinking snacks.

Other bars and clubs front the water by the Shinan Beach Hotel. Among them, **Beach Gallery** (☎ 245 5736) has live music nightly and, weather permitting, outdoors.

Getting There & Away
AIR
Asiana flies the Seoul–Mokpo route. Both Asiana and Korean Air fly between Mokpo and Jejudo. The new Muan airport, 28km north of Mokpo, will eventually replace Mokpo airport, but the timing of the move has yet to be announced.

BOAT
Mokpo's boat terminals handle ferries to Jejudo and the smaller islands west and southwest of Mokpo. See the corresponding destination sections for details. Booking in advance for these ferries isn't usually necessary, except during the summer holidays (July to mid-August).

One international ferry serves Lianyungang, in Jiangsu, China. Service is intermittent, so check with KNTO (www .knto.or.kr) for details.

BUS
Mokpo's bus terminal is a considerable distance from the centre of town; take bus No 1. Departures include:

Destination	Price (W)	Duration
Busan	19,900	6hr
Daedunsa*	4900	1½hr
Gwangju	5700	1½hr
Haenam*	3600	1hr
Jindo	4500	2hr
Seoul	15,100	5hr
Wando	7200	2hr
Yeong-am	2100	50min

*for Duryunsan Provincial Park

TRAIN
From Seoul to Mokpo, you can catch many *saemaul* (W26,700 to W31,400, 4½ hours, three daily) and *mugunghwa* (W18,200 to W21,400, 5½ hours, 10 daily) trains. It's possible to train it from Gwangju to Mokpo (W2000, 1½ hours, once daily), though bus service is more convenient.

Getting Around
Airport buses (W2300, 30 minutes) depart from near the train station and are timed to flights. They also stop by the bus terminal.

Nearly all buses pass by the train station and the bus terminal (W720). Bus Nos 1,

1-2, 2, 101 and 102 run to Yudal's beach and park, or it's about a 10-minute walk from the station to the east side of the park.

DADOHAE HAESANG NATIONAL PARK
다도해 해상 국립공원

Consisting of more than 1700 islands and islets, Dadohae Haesang (Marine Archipelago) National Park occupies much of the coast and coastal waters of Jeollanam-do. Some of the isles support small communities with income from fishing and tourism; others are little more than rocks which surface only occasionally.

Mokpo is the park's major port. The most popular islands with Korean tourists are Hongdo and Heuksando. Among other things they're great places to beat the summer heat – temperatures rarely top 30°C. In summer months, advance booking of ferries and accommodation is virtually required, particularly for Hongdo.

You can visit lesser-known islands too, and there's no better way to get off the main tourist routes. For that sort of trip you really need a copy of the national bus, boat, rail and flight timetables booklet (*sigakpyo*). Armed with this booklet it's possible to work out a route and an approximate schedule, though it's all in Korean.

Hongdo 홍도

The most popular and beautiful of the islands west of Mokpo is Hongdo (Red Island; visitor fee W2300). Some 6km long and 2.5km wide, it rises precipitously from the sea and is bounded by sheer cliffs, bizarre rock formations and wooded hillsides cut by steep ravines. The main island is ringed by islets, and sunsets are spectacular on clear days. The hitch: the only way you can see most of it is by boat, because with the exception of the villages, Hongdo is a protected nature reserve; entry is prohibited.

Ferries to Hongdo land at Ilgu, the larger and more southern of the island's two villages, where the *minbak* and *yeogwan* are situated. Like Igu, its smaller neighbour to the north, a tiny cove provides shelter to fishing boats. A boat connects the two villages.

Hongdo Subsea Tour (☎ 246 3322; adult/child W25,000/15,000; ☷ hourly, conditions permitting) operates boats with windows below the surface for gazing at fish and coral, departing from Hongdo. Less formal boat tours also ply the waters (W15,000, two hours, twice daily).

SLEEPING

There's a good choice of *minbak* and *yeogwan* in Ilgu at the usual prices (except during the summer holiday period, when prices can double).

Royal-jang (☎ 246 3837; r off-peak/peak W20,000/35,000) It's clean and three minutes from the beach, but beware the karaoke downstairs.

Yuseong-jang (☎ 246 3723; ondol off-peak/peak W30,000/40,000; ☒) Next to the KT office, with all *ondol* rooms; meals can be arranged.

Heuksando 흑산도

Heuksando is a national park based on a small group of islands east of Hongdo, the largest is called **Daeheuksando** (Big Heuksando). It is larger, more populated and more accessible than Hongdo, and views from its peaks show why Dadohae Haesang means 'marine archipelago'. There are some villages on Daeheuksando and farming on the coast. The villages are linked by trails and walking around the island takes about nine hours. Local buses circle the island – a nice return trip is to the peak **Bonghwadae**, on the north coast mountain, Sangrasan.

The largest village, **Yeri**, has an excellent harbour, was formerly a whaling centre and is still an active fishing port (Heuksando exists for more than just tourists). It's also where ferries dock and where most of the island's accommodation is located. With sufficient demand, tourist boats will take you around the island (W13,000, two hours). The island's other major village is **Jinni**.

SLEEPING & EATING

The following options are in Yeri, by the post office.

Gecheonjang (☎ 275 9154; Yeri; d W25,000; ☒) This stone-fronted *yeogwan* has bright yet rustic rooms with views of the small-boat harbour.

Daedo Minbak (☎ 275 9340; Yeri; d W25,000; ☒) With just a few rooms, it's pleasant, unpretentious, tiny and recently renovated.

There are also a couple of *minbak* in Jinni and campsites elsewhere.

As you might expect, seafood is plentiful here, but prices can be steep. The big specialty is *hung-eo* (ray). Be sure to ask the price of a meal before you order.

GETTING THERE & AWAY
Hongdo is 115km west of Mokpo. Four daily ferries make the run (W30,200, 2¼ hours) between March and July, with additional departures in late summer and fewer in winter. All ferries between Mokpo and Hongdo call at Heuksando (Mokpo–Heuksando W24,800, 1½ hours; Heuksando–Hongdo W7250, 30 minutes). All ferries stop in Yeri and go on to Hongdo.

For details, ring **Mokpo ferry terminal** (☎ 243 0116) or KNTO (www.knto.or.kr).

YEONG-AM 영암
Believe it or not, in the 7th to 9th centuries this town east of Mokpo was on the waterfront, and its soil made for excellent claymaking. Add them together, and you've got the basis for trade with China and Japan, and an important historical centre of Korean ceramics.

One of the key kilns was in Gurim village. It was rediscovered in 1986, and in 1999 the **Yeong-am Pottery Culture Centre** (☎ 470 2566; admission free; ✆ 9am-6pm Mon-Fri, to 5pm Sat Apr-Oct, to 5pm Nov-Mar) opened on the historic site to showcase this unique work. Imaginative exhibits change a few times a year, but replicas of the ancient kiln and other implements are on display daily. Traditional glazes are brown-green or brown-black, and some pieces show white flecks, which are traces of the original red clay.

There's also a working studio where, with advance reservation, you can throw your own pot (W10,000), which can be fired and sent to you.

About 1km from the Pottery Culture Centre is the **birthplace of Wang-In** (☎ 470 2560; admission W800; ✆ 9am-6pm Mar-Oct, to 5pm Nov-Feb), a 6th-century scholar credited with introducing Chinese writing and teaching methods to Japan. The site is of particular interest to those with a background in Japanese culture; others may find it a bit impenetrable. Arguably the best time to visit is during the Wang-In festival (www.wangin.org), held during cherry blossom season.

Getting There & Around
There are buses from both Mokpo (W2100, 50 minutes, every 15 minutes) and Gwangju (W4400, 70 minutes, every 15 minutes) to Yeong-am bus terminal. Some buses stop at Gurim for the pottery centre and the

birthplace of Wang-In; otherwise it's a quick local bus from Yeong-am (W750).

WOLCHULSAN NATIONAL PARK
월출산 국립공원
South and east of Yeong-am, 42-sq-km **Wolchulsan** (☎ 473 5210; wolchul@npa.or.kr; admission W2500), Korea's smallest national park, invites a day of hiking. There are crags and spires, steel stairways on the trail and at one point, a steel bridge (52m) crossing a huge gap between rocks. Beautiful and rugged rock formations include the park's highest peak, **Cheonwangbong** (809m). The park is small enough to hike from the eastern entrance to **Dogapsa** (☎ 473 5122; ✆ 7am-7pm Mar-Oct, 8am-6pm Nov-Feb) in the west in under five hours. Dogapsa dates to AD 661 and is associated with a long line of Zen masters. Tracks are well signposted. The ascent is steep and strenuous, but you'll be rewarded with great views. There is a pleasant teahouse below Dogapsa, where you can sip a refreshing cup of green tea.

Sleeping
Camping (W3000) is available at Cheonhwangsa (the park's eastern side) and should be booked ahead for weekends and holidays on the park's website. *Minbak* accommodation is plentiful around the park entrances.

Getting There & Away
Access to the park is via Yeong-am. There are six buses a day from Yeong-am terminal or a taxi costs W3500 to W4000. There's also direct service to the park from Gwangju or Mokpo (one hour). See p249 for transit info. Contact KNTO (www.knto.or.kr) for the latest details and schedules.

DURYUNSAN PROVINCIAL PARK
두륜산 도립공원
One highlight of this park, southeast of Gangjin, is **Daedunsa** (Daeheungsa; ☎ 534 5502; admission W2000; ✆ sunrise-sunset), a major Zen temple complex. The temple is thought to date back to the mid-10th century, but it remained relatively unknown until it became associated with Seosan, a warrior monk who led a group against Japanese invaders in 1592–98. Since then it's been very popular with Koreans, yet it maintains an atmosphere of rusticity. The complex also

contains a **museum** (🕑 8.30am-6pm Mar-Oct, to 5pm Nov-Feb, closed 2nd & 4th Sat each month) housing a Goryeo-period bell, some Buddhist treasures and a tea ceremony display (Sosan was also a tea master) but, unfortunately, no English descriptions. The temple is a 40-minute walk from the bus stop.

The park's highest peak, **Duryunbong** (700m), provides a dramatic backdrop. To climb it, turn left after the temple museum. It takes 1½ hours to reach the top. You are rewarded with a very picturesque view of Korea's southern coastline and, on clear days, out to Jejudo. Head back via the other trail and turn right at the first junction (20 minutes). It's another hour back down to Daedunsa, via Jinbulam.

Less hearty hikers may wish to cross the car park to the **cable car** (☎ 534-8992; one way/return W4000/6800; 🕑 7am-7pm) for similar views from the neighbouring peak, **Gogyebong** (638m). As this book went to press, cable car operators were experimenting with additional hours in summer.

Sleeping & Eating

There is a tourist village around the bus stop with the usual options, plus the following standouts:

Haenam Youth Hostel (☎ 533-0170; dm/r W6000/25,000) Uphill from the cable car entrance, it's your best budget option. Rooms are *ondol* or bed style, and some have bathrooms. However, it's often booked out with noisy school groups, so inquire ahead.

Yuseongwan (☎ 534 2959; d from W30,000) An idyllic traditional inn around a courtyard, handsomely renovated and filled with art. Reservations are virtually mandatory. It's about two-thirds of the way between the car park and Daedunsa. It also offers *hanjeongsik* (*table d'hote* for four people W64,000).

Jeonju Sikdang (meals from W6000) This place has received national coverage for its

mushroom dishes, particularly *pyogosanjeok* (translated as 'shiitake shish-kebab' but they're really more like glorious, thick mushroomy pancakes) and *pyogojeongol* (mushroom casserole). It's on the Daedunsa side of the tourist village.

Getting There & Around

Access to the park is from the nearby town of Haenam (W750, 15 minutes, every 30 minutes). A minibus runs from the parking lot to Daedunsa (W500).

Bus connections from Haenam include:

Destination	Price (W)	Duration
Busan	19,500	6hr
Gwangju	7300	1¾hr
Jindo	4000	1hr
Mokpo	3900	1hr
Wando	4000	1hr

WANDO 완도
pop 70,000

This relaxing group of over 150 islands (most uninhabited) occupies the southwestern tip of the Korean peninsula and is spread over 12 districts. There are both sandy and rocky beaches, plus some sites of cultural interest, and the region is famous throughout Korea for the quality of its seaweed (*gim*). Go at the right time and you'll see seaweed drying on racks around the island – at other times it's squid or fish.

The main island, Wando, has a quiet, rural atmosphere while its main town, Wando-eup (aka Kunnaeri) has a look of benign neglect. On the other hand, the town is so small that it's hard to get lost. Wando-eup is also where you catch the ferry to Jeju-do.

Sights

On Wando's south coast, the village **Jeongdo-ri** is home to the island's main

---

EXCERPT FROM 'THE FISHERMAN'S CALENDAR' by Yun Son-do

A new day warms itself, the bigger fish swim near the surface.
Pull the anchor, pull the anchor!
In twos and threes the seagulls rise, then glide low and rise again.
Chigukch'ong, chigukch'ong, oshwa!
The fishing rods are ready, where did we put the wine bottle?

JEOLLANAM-DO

WANDO-EUP

0 ———— 200 m
0 ———— 0.1 miles

To Mainland Ⓐ | Ⓑ
To Jejudo
Judo

To Jeongdo-ri;
Sanho Motel

Minor roads not depicted

| INFORMATION | |
| Gwangju Bank 광주은행 | 1 B2 |

SLEEPING 🏠	p251
Jea il Hotel 제일호텔	2 B1
Naju Yeoinsuk 나주여인숙	3 B1
Sydney Mote l 시드니모텔	4 A1

EATING 🍴	p251
BBQ 비비큐	5 B1
Ijosukbulgalbi 이촛숯불갈비	6 B1
Jinmi Hoetjip 진미횟집	7 B1

| SHOPPING 🛍 | |
| Laon Mart 라온마트 | 8 B1 |

TRANSPORT	
1st Pier 제1부두	9 B1
Bus Terminal 버스터미널	10 A1
Ferry Terminal 여객터미널	11 B1
Local Bus Stop 버스정빨장	12 B1

rocky beach **Gugyedeung** (Nine Steps; ☎ 554 1769; admission W1300; ticket office ⏰9am-6pm Mar-Oct, to 5pm Nov-Feb), also a nature preserve. Its name comes from the formation of ocean-swept stones said to have existed here. It's a good place for a picnic or a leisurely stroll, but the waters are considered too dangerous for swimming. As this book went to press, an observatory was in the works here.

Buses run every 40 minutes from the bus terminal (W750) or the town centre. Get off at Sajeong-ri. From there it's a 1km walk to the beach. Cafés and *minbak* are available both inside and outside the park.

Myeongsasimri (Myeongsajang) is a sandy beach on the nearby island of Sinjido. Getting there involves a trip by local ferry; however, they'll only sail if there's sufficient demand.

Ferries (W400, 10 minutes, every 30 minutes) leave from the local ferry terminal (locally known as the 1st Pier) about 600m north of the main ferry terminal in Wando-eup. In summer, buses wait for the ferries on Sinjido and take you from there to the beach.

Sleeping & Eating

Most of the island's options are in Kunnaeri. The rates at most inns rise substantially during summer.

Naju Yeoinsuk (☎ 554 3884; d/tr W15,000/17,000) Nicer than your average bare-bones inn. Although common areas are typically *yeoinsuk*-dingy, rooms (all *ondol*) have new flooring; and some have private facilities. It's just off the main street.

Jea Il Hotel (☎ 554 3251; fax 554 3250; d from W30,000; 🐾) In the town centre, some rooms in this hotel have enclosed balconies overlooking the harbour and the tiny island, Judo.

Sydney Motel (☎ 554 1075; d/ondol W35,000/40,000; 🐾) Opened in 2003 and one of the spiffiest options in town. There's nice wood panelling and many rooms have sea views. All have shower stalls (hooray!); *ondol* rooms are larger.

Sanho Motel (☎ 552 4004; d from W30,000; 🐾) On a hill on the south coast and popular with Korean artists and entertainers, Sanho mostly offers *ondol* rooms, some of which are quite large. However, beds are available too. There's a coffee shop serving Korean and Western breakfasts, plus a karaoke room. Bonus: the owner can tour you through the marine hatchery across the street (closed to the public). Sanho is 900m from the entrance to Gugyedeung. Book well in advance.

Jeongdo-ri has many other options for *minbak*, near the entrance to Gugyedeung. There are also *minbak* on Bogildo, plus *yeogwan* on the island of Nohwado, a five-minute ferry ride away (W500, every 30 minutes).

Jinmi Hwetjip (meals W8000-15000) Wando's local specialty is raw seafood, and you can't get any fresher than a fish of your choosing scooped from the tank by the owner and prepared on the spot (market price). It's in the busy market alley.

Ijosutbulgalbi (dishes W5000-14000) Wonderful aromas emanate from here, including *dwaeji galbi* (pork BBQ), *dolsot bibimbap* (W5000) and *gangjang* (beef broth). For barbecue dishes, it follows the local custom of a minimum of three portions.

And if you just need a burger or chicken after a diet of Korean food, **BBQ** (dishes W1000-9000; ⏰Mon-Sat) is an informal option. Chicken comes fried, barbecued or smoked, and it also serves shrimp burgers. An English menu is available.

Getting There & Away

BOAT

Wando is connected to Jejudo by ferry (p258).

BUS

Buses depart from Wando for the following destinations:

Destination	Price (W)	Duration	Distance
Busan	23,500	6hr	454km
Gwangju	10,600	2¾hr	147km
Haenam*	4000	2hr	54km
Mokpo	7800	2hr	110km
Yeong-am**	6100	1½hr	94km

*for Duryunsan Provincial Park
**for Wolchulsan National Park

Getting Around

From the bus terminal, two routes circulate around the island, one heading east and south, the other north and west. Both terminate at the bridge from the mainland before heading back. To reach the Bogildo ferry, cross Wando to the port at Hwaheung Pohang (free shuttle bus, hourly); see following for details.

BOGILDO 보길도

This island south of Wando is a popular destination thanks to three fine beaches and thick pine groves. Everyone heads for sandy **Jung-ri** and **Tong-ri** beaches. **Yesong-ri Beach**, at the southern end of the island, is pebbly but also dramatic for its evergreen forest.

Bogildo was the home of Yun Son-do (1587–1671), a famed Joseon dynasty poet. It is said that Yun Son-do took temporary shelter from a typhoon here while on his way to Jejudo. He was so impressed by the beauty of the island that he stayed for the next 10 years. During that time, he is said to have built 25 buildings on the island and penned some of his best poems, including the 40-poem cycle 'Fisherman's Calendar'. **Boyongdong**, his garden retreat, is open to the public and makes a great side trip.

If you wish to stay on Bogildo, there are *minbak*. Other *yeogwan* are available on Nohwado, another island just north of Bogildo that's quickly reached by small boat across the channel.

Getting There & Away

Ferries between Bogildo and Wando (W7300, 1½ hours, nine daily) depart from 7am to 5pm. Between 15 July and 20 August, the schedule is increased. To reach this ferry, cross Wando to the port at Hwaheung Pohang (free shuttle bus, hourly). Note that a bridge is planned that will eventually connect the two islands.

JINDO 진도

pop 43,000

This long, wide island south of Mokpo boasts some of the largest tides in the world, but during low tide for a few days in early March each year, a 2.8km-long, 40m-wide land bridge appears, which connects to an island far off the southeastern coast. Some 300,000 people make the crossing each year – in long rubber boots (available for rent, naturally).

The experience is known as the *Ganjuyuk Gyedo* (Mysterious Sea Road), and it has long been celebrated among Koreans in legend and the Yeongdeung festival (coinciding with the crossing). With the spread of Christianity in Korea, the similarity to the Israelites' crossing of the Red Sea has only brought more enthusiasts.

THE LEGEND OF GRANDMOTHER BBONG

The Bbong family, en route to exile on Jejudo, was caught in a terrible storm and shipwrecked on a remote corner of Jindo. They soon discovered that the area was full of tigers and fled once again for the island of Modo, visible from shore. Only later did they realise that they had accidentally left their *halmeoni* (grandmother) behind on Jindo.

Pained with concern for her family, Bbong Halmeoni prayed and prayed, and she received word that if she went to the water her family would appear. Sure enough, she arrived at the shore to find a land bridge, with her family on the other side. She walked across to join them, but by the time they met in the middle, the exertion proved too much and she collapsed. Although she died in their arms, she was happy that the family had been reunited one last time.

Jindo is also famous for a unique breed of dog, the *Jindogae*. It's one of only two breeds designated as a precious national monument (and the only national monument we've encountered that can be described as faithful, brave and adorable). The **Jindo Dog Research Centre** (☎ 540 3396) is dedicated to their study and training. *Jindogae* shows (10 minutes) take place on an irregular basis (weather permitting) between 10am and 11.30am. It's best to phone before your arrival to confirm show times. Otherwise, the dogs can be viewed in their pens. The centre is about 20 minutes' walk from Jindo's bus terminal.

Getting There & Around

Buses connect Jindo-eup (Jindo's main town) with:

Destination	Price (W)	Duration
Busan	23,500	6¾hr
Gwangju	11,300	2¾hr
Mokpo	4400	1¼hr
Seoul	18,300	6hr

A free shuttle takes visitors to the Mysterious Sea Road during the festival. Otherwise, catch an hourly bus to Bbonghalme Dongsan (W700).

Jeju-do
제주도

Paradise, Hawaii, Disneyland…Jeju-do has been compared to all three, and all three comparisons have their place.

Jeju-do (the province) comprises Jejudo (the island), a large, subtropical volcanic mass off the southern tip of the Korean peninsula. While it was an agricultural outpost as late as the mid-20th century, these days it's tourism that's blooming. Jejudo has long been a favourite among Korean honeymooners – you can spot them by their matching outfits – and during peak times package tourists can fill the island as squid fill the local waters. (The two often meet for dinner at the island's ubiquitous seafood restaurants.)

Even if Jeju-do no longer feels remote and can be busy at peak times, there is still much to love here. For starters, topography: the almost 2000m-high extinct volcano of Hallasan is South Korea's highest mountain, and parts of the park around it are spectacular. The island is dotted with beaches, several impressive waterfalls and the dramatic volcanic Mt Seongsan, which rises up sheer from the ocean. Another unusual geographic feature is the rare lava-tube caves, formed when surface lava cooled and hardened while molten lava continued to flow like a river beneath the surface. The coasts are dotted with rock formations, which, depending on their shapes, locals categorise as dragons, tigers and even pickled ginseng.

As long as the weather cooperates, you'll find plenty of outdoor activities: hiking, cycling, golf, snorkelling, scuba diving, windsurfing, sailing, fishing, paragliding and horseback riding.

In sum, Jejudo is a beautiful and exciting place, and if you go during off-peak times (weekdays, any season but summer) you may well conclude that it is indeed a paradise.

HIGHLIGHTS

■ View unique **lava caves** (p265) at Manjanggul, the **volcanic crater** (p265) at Sangumburi, the sunrise over **Seongsan Ilchulbong** (p266) or the whole island from **Hallasan**, Korea's tallest mountain (p275)

■ Take in Jejudo's unique cultural heritage at **Jeju Folk Village** (p268) or **Seong-eup Folk Village** (p268)

■ Be awed by the power of nature on the **Yongmeori coastline** (p273), and the power of spirituality at the nearby mountainside temple, **Sanbanggulsa** (p273)

■ Unwind at the luxury resorts of **Jungmun** (p272) on the island's sun-drenched southern coast

■ Learn the ins and outs of bonsai (bunjae) at the **Bunjae Artpia** (p274) or tea at **O'Sulloc tea plantation and museum** (p274)

| ■ TELEPHONE CODE: 064 | ■ POPULATION: 540,000 | ■ AREA: 1847 SQ KM |

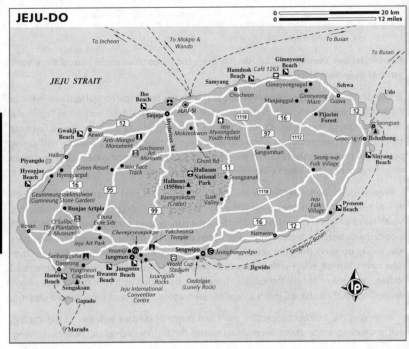

JEJU-DO

History

Despite being just 85km from the Korean mainland, Jejudo was little visited for centuries. As a result, it acquired its own history, traditions, dress, architecture and dialect.

Archaeologists place human habitation here as early as the middle Palaeolithic period, some 40,000 years ago, when the present island was believed to be part of a land mass that included China, Korea, Taiwan and Japan. Early Neolithic stones and arrowheads found on the island resemble those from the Jōmon period of Japan (roughly 10,000 BC to 300 BC), and the local belief system is known to have included shamanistic practices, which may have led to the *harubang*, 'grandfather stone' sculptures, that are now the island's best-known image (see the boxed text 'Harubang' following).

From the Silla period, the island came to be known as Tamra (aka Tamna), but in the early 12th century the Goryeo dynasty took over and, in the early 13th century, renamed the island Jeju, 'insignificant, faraway province.' Mongol herders arrived here in 1276, contributing both a tradition of horsemanship and quirks to the local dialect.

Over the years, Jeju developed a unique architectural style, in which different generations of families lived on the same property (as on the mainland), but each generation had separate cooking/heating facilities. Traditional clothing was made of hemp (or silk for royalty), and dyed with persimmon. You can still see orange-coloured clothing for sale today.

In 1653 a Dutch ship trading with Japan was shipwrecked here, and it is said that despite initial fears, the locals befriended the survivors. Nonetheless, the survivors were soon taken to Seoul by order of the Joseon king, where they remained imprisoned for 13 years for entering Korea illegally. (Then, as now, Korean authorities showed zero tolerance toward foreigners who violated immigration regulations.) The prisoners managed to escape and an account of those years, written by survivor Hendrick Hamel, became a bestseller and Europe's first accurate description of the 'Hermit Kingdom'.

Later in the Joseon period, Jeju-do became an exile territory for about 200 intellectuals and political undesirables, some of whom spent their time teaching the local people and are now among the island's – and Korea's – cultural giants.

Through it all locals existed on farming, and agriculture remains important here. The island is famous for tangerines (in season, it seems that roughly half of Korean mainlanders return home with a case), as well as barley, vegetables and tea, all grown on the coastal lowlands. Cactus is also cultivated as an ornamental plant and for making cactus tea, and the island produces most of Korea's mushrooms. Further inland, enormous pastures support horses and cattle.

Over the last few decades Jejudo has changed radically. Gone are the days when the locals had to earn a living by fishing or farming. The catalyst, of course, was tourism. Drawn by the warm climate and restrictions on travel abroad, well-to-do Koreans began taking their holidays here. By the 1970s the island became the favourite honeymoon destination for Korean couples and it remains so, even if nowadays many Koreans prefer to take their romantic interlude in Guam.

Climate

The island's climate is significantly different from that of the Korean peninsula – you can even find palm trees here. That's in part because Jejudo is the rainiest place in Korea –
however, while most of the nation gets up to 60% of its rainfall during the summer rainy season, Jejudo's is more spread out. Downpours are least likely during autumn.

Hallasan is the dividing line between the subtropical oceanic south side and the temperate north. Conditions on the peak can change rapidly, as it acts as a sort of cloud trap.

Despite the heavy rainfall, surface water is a rarity on Jejudo due to the island's porous volcanic rock. Ground water, by contrast, is abundant – Jejudo is basically one big sponge.

Swimmers: being 33° north of the equator, you'll want a wetsuit unless you confine your swimming to July and August – or to a nice swimming pool.

Orientation & Information

Jejudo is a long oval-shaped island, about 200km around the perimeter, but it may be easiest to think of it in four quadrants: north (Jeju-si and environs), south (Seogwipo, Jungmun and environs), west and east, with Hallasan National Park in the centre. While there's an assortment of historical and recreational attractions all around the island, generally speaking the southern side has a more easygoing, resort feel.

Jeju-si is the island's capital and largest town, while Seogwipo (the second-largest town) is the hub of traffic on the south coast; the luxury resorts of Jungmun are an easy drive from Seogwipo. A number of tourist

---

HARUBANG

Just as Easter Island and Okinawa are known for ancient stone statues of obscure origin, *harubang* (aka *dolharubang* or 'stone grandfather' statues) are the undisputed symbol of Jejudo. You'll find original *harubang* in strategic places island-wide, and *harubang* images grace every tourist pamphlet ever produced about the island, and even the sides of some local buses.

Whereas other ancient statuary can be mystical and stark, *harubang* actually look rather cheerful. Carved from lava-rock, *harubang* are substantial characters, up to 3m tall, and are typically seen with rounded, brimmed hats, large eyes and nose, and hands across the belly, one slightly higher than the other.

If the origin of *harubang* is unclear, so is their original purpose. One theory is that they served as village guardians; others speculate that there was a religious significance, that they were fertility symbols or simply location markers. Nowadays, some believe that if you hold the nose of a *harubang* and make a wish, the wish will come true.

There are 45 original *harubang* on Jejudo (including at the Seong-eup Folk Village, Meokseokwon and Samseonghyeol Shrine), plus two in the Gyeongbok Palace in Seoul. And if you want a *harubang* of your very own, there are, of course, innumerable re-creations, including some that will fit in your pocket.

FOOD

The island is famous for certain foods difficult to find elsewhere in Korea – horsemeat, for example. Various styles of grilled fish are created into popular dishes; other famous dishes are *haemuljeongol* (해물전골, seafood stew) and *haemuldolsotbap* (해물돌솥밥, seafood with rice in a hot stone pot). At the island's numerous raw-fish *(hoe)* restaurants, you might find live octopus (eat the tentacles first!), *jeonbokhoe* (전복회, abalone) and *seonggeguk* (성게국, sea urchin stew), plus tamer, pick-your-own-fish-from-a-tank experiences (don't worry – it will be prepared for you).

Even if you're just out sightseeing, you're likely to find *ajumma* (married or older women) selling raw seafood by the coast – served with hot sauce, *kimchi* (pickled and fermented vegetables) and perhaps a bottle of *soju* (distilled spirit, usually made from sweet potatoes) to wash it down.

roads radiate from Jeju-si towards destinations around the island, and a coastal road encircles the perimeter.

Although the coastline is generally rocky, it can be picturesque and there are a number of sandy coves and beaches (see Map p256). The midlands tend to be agricultural, rising to the mountain of Hallasan (1950m).

Jeju Tourism Information Service has offices at **Jeju Airport** (☎ 742 8866), the **Jeju Ferry Terminal** (☎ 758 7181), and in the resort town of **Jungmun** (☎ 738 0326). There are maller booths at popular tourist locations throughout the island.

Tours

The most readily available tours can be booked right in Jeju airport at the information counter. They depart daily from the airport between 9am and 10am and finish at around 6pm. One tour covers the west side of the island (W32,200), while the other does the east side (W29,700). Prices include admissions to the various sights. If you're with a large group, an English-speaking tour guide can be arranged. Otherwise, you can expect the tour to be in Korean only.

Many visitors (more Korean than foreign) opt for all-inclusive tours, including airfare, hotels and sightseeing.

Getting There & Away

AIR

Both **Korean Air** (☎ 752 2000) and **Asiana Airlines** (☎ 743 4000) operate domestic flights between Jeju airport (in Jeju-si) and numerous cities in Korea. There are also flights to several Japanese cities.

The main Korean Air office (Map p261) is opposite the KAL Hotel on Jung-angno. The Asiana Airlines main office (Map p263) is in Sinjeju. However, it's very easy to book tickets from the numerous travel agencies around town or at the airport.

BOAT

Ferries sail between Jeju-si and many destinations on the peninsula. Seas in the straits between Jejudo and the mainland are often quite rough – if you're not a good sailor it might be worth your while taking a fast ferry or even flying. Student discounts are often available if you ask for them.

Schedules vary seasonally, so it's important to check ahead of time.

FERRIES FROM JEJU-SI

Destination	Ship's name	Telephone	Price (W)	Duration	Frequency
Wando	Onbada lines	721 2171	14,850–26,000	5hr	2 daily
	Hanil Car Ferry No 1	751 5050	16,900	3½hr	daily Tue–Sun
	HanilCar Ferry No 2	751 5050	16,900–21,500	3hr	daily Mon–Sat
Mokpo	Orient Star I	758 4234	18,550–50,100	5½hr	daily Tue–Sun
	Car Ferry Rainbow	758 4234	18,550–50,100	4hr	daily Tue–Sun
	Continental lines	726 9542	21,300–39,500	3hr 10min	3 daily
Yeosu	Namhae Ferry	723 9700	18,500–58,800	7hr	daily Mon–Sat
Busan	Cozy Island	751 0300	from 26,800	11hr	Mon, Wed, Fri
	Orient Star II	751 1901	from 26,800	11hr	Tue, Thu, Sat
Incheon	Ohamana Ferry	721 2173	from 46,000	13hr	Tue, Thu, Sat
	Chonghaejin Ferry	721 2173	from 46,000	15hr	Mon, Wed, Fri

BUSES BETWEEN AIRPORT & JEJU-SI

Bus No	Major destinations	Fare (W)	Frequency
100	Sinjeju rotary, Jung-angno, ferry pier	700	every eight to 12 min
200	Sinjeju rotary, central Sinjeju, intercity bus terminal, Gwandeokjeong	700	every eight to 12 min
300	Yongdam rotary, Gwandeokjeong, intercity bus terminal, Sinjeju rotary, central Sinjeju	700	every eight to 12 min
500	Mokseokwon, City Hall, Jung-angno, Yongdam rotary	700	every eight to 12 min

BUSES BETWEEN AIRPORT & OTHER PARTS OF THE ISLAND

Bus No	Major destinations	Fare (W)	Frequency
600	Sinjeju, Yeomiji garden, Jungmun (major hotels)	3500 (Jungmun)	every 15min
	Seogwipo (downtown and major hotels)	4700 (Seogwipo)	
702	(westbound) Geumneung, Hallim Park	2400 (Geumneung)	every 45min
	(eastbound) Manjanggul, Gimnyeong, Seongsan	2100 (Hallim)	
		1700 (Gimnyeong)	
		3300 (Seongsan)	

Getting Around

TO/FROM THE AIRPORT

Jeju airport is adjacent to Jeju city (W2000 by taxi) and well connected by bus to points in town and around the island. Buses loop between the airport and Jeju-si every eight to 12 minutes (6.25am to 10.25pm) – see table above.

Two bus routes connect the airport with other parts of the island. Bus No 600 basically heads to the south coast, while bus No 702 runs across the north shore between west and east, stopping at the airport in the middle – see table above.

BICYCLE

If you're reasonably fit, you can propel yourself around the island (about 200km) in three or four days and visit all the hot tourist spots. Make sure you have some tools, a pump and patch kit in case you need to repair a flat tyre. A bike cable lock and rain gear are also necessities.

The Promotion Association of Bicycling for a new Life Environment (Pable; ☎ 02-2203 4225 in Seoul) publishes the awesome *Jeju Island Cycling Map*. Two rental shops in Jeju-si are **Sunkyoung Smart Bicycle** (Map p261; ☎ 751 2000), and Samcheonri (multiple locations). There are bike-rental shops in all the island's major cities.

BUS

Buses from Jeju's intercity bus terminal serve the whole island. Make sure you carry an ample supply of W100 and W500 coins, and W1000 notes. It gets a little confusing, as some buses to the same destinations may travel along different routes, this can mean different fares and travel times. You can pick up the latest bus information from tourist offices – see following page for table of what you generally can expect.

CAR

Given the rural nature of the island (though decidedly less so, year by year), renting a car almost makes sense. The cost is not excessive, especially if you can share the vehicle with a few others. The main drawback is the legal liability of renting a car and the numerous speed traps (don't exceed 80km/h anywhere on Jejudo). Walk-up rates range from about W42,000 for six hours to W76,500 per day.

Most up-market hotels have a car-rental desk in the lobby, or you can deal directly with the car rental agencies:

Dong-a	☎ 743 1515
Green	☎ 743 2000
Halla	☎ 755 5000
Hanseong	☎ 747 2100
Jeju	☎ 742 3301
Seongsan	☎ 746 3260
VIP (Avis)	☎ 747 4422
Woori	☎ 752 9600

TAXI

Hiring a taxi for a full day is a little more expensive than renting a car, but saves you much hassle. If you've got one or two companions to share the cost, so much the

BUSES FROM JEJU-SI INTERCITY BUS TERMINAL

Route	Destination	Fare (W)	Duration	Frequency
Via west tourist road (Rte 95)	Sincheonji Art Park	800	20min	every 20min
	Jeju Race Track	1200	30min	
Via east tourist road (Rte 97)	Sangumburi Crater	1800	25min	every 20min
	Seong-eup Folk Village	2200	35min	
	Jeju Folk Village	3300	1hr	
Via Jungmun Express Road (Rtes 95 & 1118)	Jungmun resort	2900	50min	every 20min
	Seogwipo	3600	70min	
Via 1100 road (Rte 99)	Eorimok (for Hallasan)	1900	30min	every 80min
	Yeongsil (for Hallasan)	3100	50min	
	Jungmun	4600	80min	
Via Ilju Road (Rte 12) west	Hallim	2100	50min	every 20min
	Jungmun	5500	2½hr	
	Seogwipo	6500	2¾hr	
Via Ilju Road (Rte 12) east	Gimnyeong (for Manjanggul)	1900	50min	every 20min
	Goseong (for Seongsan)	3400	1½hr	

better. In most cases, drivers are happy to act as your tour guide, though very few can speak English.

Figure on about W80,000 (negotiable) plus lunch (also negotiable), including petrol. Some drivers expect you to hire them for 1½ days, or perhaps two full days – the rate they quote you may be based on this assumption. If you spend the night somewhere, then you are responsible for the driver's lodging. Make sure that the details of the journey have all been talked through thoroughly so as to avoid misunderstandings later.

JEJU-SI 제주시
pop 294,000
Orientation
Jeju-si (Jeju City), the island's population and transit centre, sits at the middle of the north shore. There are two main districts: the town centre – aka Gujeju (old Jeju) – is a mere 2km east of Jeju airport. While Gujeju is hardly glam, it has a number of historic structures, plus shopping and restaurants, particularly in the town centre between the main street, Gwandeongno, and the waterfront. Chilseongno is the main pedestrianised street in this district. There's also a reasonably pleasant promenade, Sanjicheon, along the river.

Just south of the airport, or about 10 minutes' drive southwest of Gujeju, is Sinjeju, which dates all the way back to the…1970s. It's a high-rise district with some upscale hotels and the sort of nightlife and shopping found in other modern Korean cities.

Sights & Activities
GWANDEOKJEONG & MOK OFFICE
관덕정, 목관아
This complex combines two of Jeju's most interesting buildings. The open-sided, brightly painted, 15th-century pavilion **Gwandeokjeong** (Map p261; 24hr) is the oldest building of its type on the island and a national treasure. It was used for receiving official visitors and to host official banquets. Important murals here were due for restoration as we went to press, and there's an original *harubang* out front.

The spread-out **Mok Office** (Map p261; ☎ 702 3081; admission W1500; 9am-6pm, 9am-5pm Nov-Feb) was the island's administrative centre under the Joseon dynasty – responsibilities included investigating mistreatment of citizens and protection against Japanese pirates. It's been beautifully painted and restored. Rooms (closed in inclement weather) are decorated with scenes that represent what life during that period must have been like.

FOLKLORE & NATURAL HISTORY MUSEUM
민속 자연사 박물관
This worthy **museum** (Map p261; ☎ 722 2465; admission W1470; 8.30am-6pm, 8.30am-5pm Nov-Feb, closed Daeboreum & Juseok festivals) is set in Sinsan Park (spectacular during the brief cherry-blossom season in April). Inside, there is a re-creation of a traditional thatched house in the local style, local crafts, and folklore, flora, insect and marine displays. There's excellent English signage.

JEJU-DO

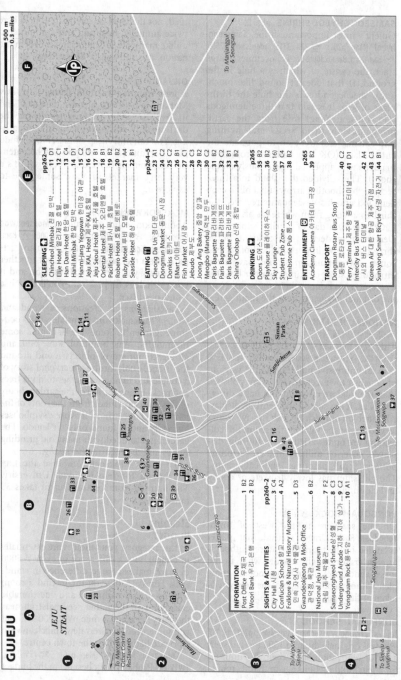

GUJEJU

JEJU STRAIT

To Marcello & Other Coastal Restaurants

To Airport & Sinjeju

To Sinjeju & Jungmun

To Manjanggul & Seongsan

To Mokseokwon & Seogwipo

JEJU-DO

SAMSEONGHYEOL SHRINE 삼성혈

Gujeju's most important shrine, **Samseonghyeol** (Map p261; ☎ 722 3315; admission W2500; 🕙 8am-7pm, 8am-6.30pm Dec-Jan) occupies a large tract, the centre of which is a hole in the ground. If that doesn't sound like much, know that legend calls this hole the birthplace of Jeju. It is said that three demigods (Go, Bu and Yang) rose from the earth, bringing with them seeds and hunting implements, and went on to populate the entire island (OK, they had help from three maidens who appeared mysteriously on the shore). They divided the island into three sections by shooting arrows up a hill – each demigod and his descendants received the third emanating from where his arrow fell.

On the 10th day of April, October and December, modern-day descendants of the three clans (and important local officials – some new population strains have been introduced since old times) gather here for a ceremony to honour their ancestors. Note the original *harubang* near the main gate.

NATIONAL JEJU MUSEUM
국립 제주 박물관

This new **museum** (Map p261; ☎ 720 8000; admission W400; 🕙 9am-6pm, 9am-5pm Nov-Feb, closed Mon) is in an impressive building, a little way out of Gujeju's town centre. It's more polished than the folklore museum and has a different focus. It has some 1300 items on display. Although on our visit English signage wasn't as good as at the folklore museum, the collections are quite varied and beautifully displayed, covering military history, furniture, pottery, scroll paintings and calligraphy. The gift shop has lovely trinkets of ebony and cloisonne.

YONGDUAM ROCK 용두암

On the seashore to the west of town, **Yongduam Rock** (Dragon's Head, Map p261) is lauded in the tourist literature. Although foreign visitors might wonder what all the fuss is about, no Korean honeymoon is complete without a photograph of the newlyweds taken at this spot.

CONFUCIAN SCHOOL 향교

Jeju-si's **hyanggyo** (Confucian school; Map p261; ☎ 757 0976) was originally built in 1392 but has seen a bit of renovation since then. It's unusual for a Jeju building of its age in that its roof is tiled, not thatched. A ceremony is held here twice annually, in spring and autumn, and unlike many other Confucian schools in the nation, it is still a place of learning.

OILJANG 오일장

A long-standing tradition, **Oiljang** (Five-Day Market) is held on calendar days that end in 'two' or 'seven'. It operates during the daytime only, and opens early in the morning. You can find cheap clothes, food, Jejudo plants, traditional *kimchi* pots, kitchen utensils and animals (alive or...otherwise). It's a very large market, so allow some time to explore it.

MOKSEOKWON 목석원

About 6km south of Gujeju, **Mokseokwon** (Map p256; ☎ 702 0203; admission W2000; 🕙 8am-6.30pm, 8am-5pm Dec-Jan) is both garden and artpark. It's a real labour of love, put together over many years by a local resident, and if your switch is flipped 'on', you'll find it a wondrous place.

Installations are creations of wood and stone ('Mokseokwon' translates as 'wood-stone garden'). Some are fanciful, some meaningful, some beautiful, some odd, and all are comprised of objects found around the island. Look for the apocryphal story of a couple and their life together told via trees and rocks in one section of the garden. Many of the works are made from the roots of the *jorok* (yew) tree, which, in Korea, symbolises longevity and is found only on Jejudo. The garden is also filled with many old grinding stones and the requisite *harubang*.

To reach Mokseokwon, take the city bus bound for Jeju National University. The journey from central Gujeju takes 30 minutes.

Sleeping
BUDGET

In this category, your choices are essentially in Gujeju, and a difference of even W5000 in price makes a large difference in standards. For W15,000 you might find a room with no private bathroom and questionable cleanliness in the rather seedy district near the ferry terminal, while W30,000 will get you someplace relatively new and clean with a private bathroom in the town centre.

Chincheol Minbak (Map p261; ☎ 755 5132; d W15,000) Probably your best bet in the budget category, near the ferry terminal and off the main street. It has received nice reviews from travellers who note that *chincheol* means 'friendly'.

Hanil Minbak (Map p261; ☎ 757 1598; d W15,000) Facing the street in front of Chincheol Minbak, Hanil's rooms have fans. Showers are communal and guests can use the kitchen.

Hanmi-jang Yeogwan (Map p261; ☎ 756 6555, 756 7272; r W25,000; ✂) This place has a commendably smiley *ajumma* (female proprietor) who doesn't speak English, but manages to be very sweet.

Han Dam Hotel (Map p261; ☎ 758 3385; r from W30,000; ✂) Despite its unconventional location (on the 5th floor of the Sun Office Building), it's clean and comfy, some staff speak English, and the surrounding neighbourhood has lots of local colour.

Ruby Motel (Map p261; ☎ 755 5565; r W30,000; ✂) Near the intercity bus terminal, Ruby Motel is friendly and has nicely sized rooms and some artwork in the halls. Look for the blue-tiled front.

Jeju Myeongdam Youth Hostel (Map p261; ☎ 721 8233; dm W8800) Big, hard to reach (you need

a taxi or your own transport) and generally booked out by thunderous school groups, this hostel is about 6km southeast of central Jeju.

MID-RANGE

As you get into the W100,000 range, many hotels offer discounts if you travel off-season or book through a travel agent.

Gujeju   **Map p261**
Elije Hotel (☎ 702 3595; fax 724 3598; d from W45,000) The purple exterior gives way to a somewhat gloomy lobby, but many rooms have recently been attractively renovated. Any unrenovated rooms that are left rent for W35,000.

Seaside Hotel (☎ 752 0091; r from W50,000; ✂) Hardly new but near the harbour and small amusement park, the Seaside has a couple of small cafés on the premises.

Jeju Seoul Hotel (☎ 752 2211; fax 751 1701; www.jejuseoul.co.kr; r with mountain/sea view W75,000/ 100,000; ✂) Down the block from the Seaside Hotel, it's a little older but well maintained.

Robero Hotel (☎ 757 7111; www.roberohotel .com; d from W100,000; ✂ 🖳) A modestly sized

JEJU-DO

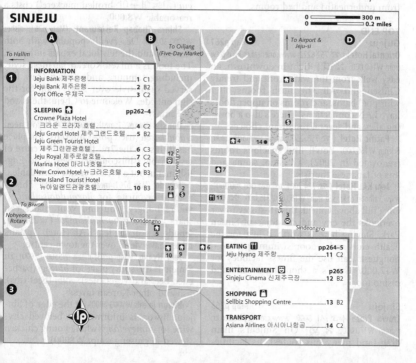

SINJEJU

0   300 m
0   0.2 miles

To Hallim

To Oiljang
(Five-Day Market)

To Airport &
Jeju-si

To Biwon

Nohyeong
Rotary

Yeondongno

Singwangno

Sindaero

Sindongno

Sindeongno

INFORMATION	
Jeju Bank 제주은행	1 C1
Jeju Bank 제주은행	2 B2
Post Office 우체국	3 C2

SLEEPING 🛏	pp262–4
Crowne Plaza Hotel	
크라운 프라자 호텔	4 C2
Jeju Grand Hotel 제주그랜드호텔	5 B2
Jeju Green Tourist Hotel	
제주그린관광호텔	6 C3
Jeju Royal 제주로얄호텔	7 C2
Marina Hotel 마리나호텔	8 C1
New Crown Hotel 뉴크라운호텔	9 B3
New Island Tourist Hotel	
뉴아일랜드관광호텔	10 B3

EATING 🍴	pp264–5
Jeju Hyang 제주향	11 C2

ENTERTAINMENT 🎭	p265
Sinjeju Cinema 신제주극장	12 B2

SHOPPING 🛍	
Sellbiz Shopping Centre	13 B2

TRANSPORT	
Asiana Airlines 아시아나항공	14 C2

high-rise of mid-'90s construction, opposite the Gwandeokjeong pavilion. Rooms are decent, there are Korean and Western restaurants, and guests can make use of a free Internet terminal in the lobby.

Sinjeju   **Map p263**
Marina Hotel (☎ 746 6161; www.marinahotel.co.kr; d W80,000;) Conveniently located at the entrance to Sinjeju, it's a wee bit austere and boxy, but rooms are a decent size for the area.

New Island Tourist Hotel (☎ 743 0300; www .newisland.co.kr; d & ondol W121,000;) A little older than some neighbouring hotels, but rooms compare favourably.

New Crown Hotel (☎ 742 1001; fax 742 7466; d from W150,000;) A high-rise on a quiet block above the centre of town; amenities include sauna and karaoke. Some rooms have sea views.

Jeju Green Tourist Hotel (☎ 742 0071; fax 742 0082; d W145,000;) Probably the sleekest on the island, it's just had a bold make-over with shiny black marble in the lobby. The hotel has both *ondol* (floor that is heated from underneath) and bed rooms.

TOP END
Gujeju   **Map p261**
Oriental Hotel (☎ 752 8222; www.oriental.co.kr; d & tw from W160,000;) Right in downtown, an easy walk from the waterfront and trendy Chilseongno. All 313 plush rooms offer whirlpool baths, and rooms on upper floors have LAN connections. There's also a bowling alley and several restaurant choices.

Pacific Hotel (☎ 758 2500; www.jejupacific.co.kr; d from W160,000) You'll find spacious rooms (renovated in 2002), a casino, sauna and lots of Japanese tourists.

Jeju KAL Hotel (☎ 724 2001; toll free 080 200 2001; www.kalhotel.co.kr; s/d from W160,000/215,000;) On a hill above Gujeju, this 18-storey tower overlooks the city and the adjacent Sinsan Park. Staying here is worth it just for the health club and indoor swimming pool – nonguests can use the fitness facilities for W17,000. There's a shopping arcade and casino too.

Sinjeju   **Map p263**
Crown Plaza (☎ 741 8000; www.crowneplaza.co.kr; r from W170,000;) On Sinjeju's main drag (and many bus routes), its facilities

include a fitness club, indoor pool, sun deck and casino. Each room is equipped with a computer, and most have ocean or mountain views.

Jeju Royal (☎ 743 2222; fax 748 0074; d & tw W184,500;) This tower is right in the centre of Sinjeju yet on a quiet block. Rooms are bright and cheerful. There are Japanese, Korean and Western restaurants, a nightclub and men's and women's saunas.

Jeju Grand Hotel (☎ 747 4900; www.oraresort.com; d & tw from W195,000;) This sprawling hotel occupies a whole city block and would be at home in any modern city in the world. There's a health club, a lovely pine garden, business centre and a golf club reached via free shuttle. There's also a free shuttle service to the airport.

Eating
Cheong Da Un (Map p261; meals W5,000-15,000) Lovers of grilled seafood will enjoy this casual spot overlooking the straits. It's well regarded for its summer dish of *mulhoe* (물회, marinated raw fish), and is often busy with tourists in summer. *Godeungeo gui* (고등어구이, broiled mackerel) costs a reasonable W8,000.

Shinra Chobap Restaurant (Map p261; dishes W5000-30,000) Deservedly popular with both Koreans and the few local expats in Jeju-si. The food is a mixed Korean-Japanese style, including tempura and *chobap* (raw fish served sushi-style over rice). Look for the sign outside: 'Welcome to Cheju, the island of Fantasy'.

Donkiss (Map p261; meals W5000-8500) If you need a *donkkaseu* (fried pork cutlet) fix, this place has it. It's on the 2nd floor in the centre of fashionable Chilseongno. There is no English menu, but a picture menu is available.

Jebudo (Map p261; meals W4000-10,000) This is a local favourite for *haemuldolsotbap*. If you're hungry, you and your mates can share a hulking *haemuljeongol* (W25,000). Jebudo is near the Jeju KAL Hotel. Upstairs tables have views over the town centre.

Jeju Hyang (Map p263; meals W5500-15,000) In Sinjeju is this spiffy place for *bulgogi* (barbecued beef and vegetables), *galbi* (beef ribs), fish and other Korean faves.

Biwon (meals W5000-8000) At the edge of Sinjeju, Biwon is informal but beloved citywide for *samgyetang* (whole young chicken stewed in ginseng soup, W8000).

Marcello (meals W7000-30,000) The coastal route west of Yongduam and north of the airport is rapidly developing as a restaurant row with both Korean and Western food. Typical is this two-storey spot that serves Western-style chicken and meat dishes, seafood and pasta. 'Entree' plates come with soup, salad and dessert. If you're looking for raw-fish restaurants, you should head to this district too.

For wholesome meals, visit Dongmun Market (Map p261), behind Dongmun Rotary bus stop in Gujeju. There are dozens of stalls here dishing out everything from *gimbap* (Korean version of sushi) to fried chicken. Aside from food, everything else you need in life is for sale here too.

Just outside the market entrance on the rotary, **Meogbo Mandu** (Map p261; dishes W2000-3500) is a tiny shop serving classic cheap eats: *mandu* (dumplings), *gimbap* and *naengmyeon* (buckwheat noodles in an icy beef broth, garnished with vegetables and half an egg).

Less adventurous eaters will find abundant bakeries and convenience stores in either Gujeju or Sinjeju. Joong Ang Bakery (Map p261) is the largest in Gujeju and has tables where you can enjoy your pastries with coffee or tea. Every district seems to have its local branch of Paris Baguette (Map p261). The big supermarket, down by the waterfront in Gujeju, is Emart (Map p261).

In central Sinjeju, Chinese and fried-chicken restaurants abound, and department stores have food halls.

Drinking

The **Playhouse** (Map p261; ☎ 726 9611) is a good place to start. It cultivates an internationalist atmosphere and is popular with expat English-language teachers. Drinks are reasonably priced and there is often live music.

Another good place to listen to music is the smaller basement pub the **Doors** (Map p261; ☎ 758 6316). There's a mixed Korean and foreign crowd and a fabulous CD collection.

Tombstone Pub (Map p261; ☎ 756 2622) is a country-and-Western bar, situated over several floors in the vibrant town centre; it's known for good drinks. Check out this area for its numerous *hofs* (beer pubs), shopping and local youth culture.

For higher-end drinks, literally and figuratively, the Sky Lounge (Map p261) at the Jeju KAL Hotel is Jejudo's only revolving restaurant (food prices match the sky-high location). It's famous for its cocktails, such as Singapore Sling or Blue Hawaii. Take the glass lift for the best view.

At the other end of the spectrum, there is a whole group of small pubs in the alleys just opposite City Hall. This is where Jeju's student population hangs out, and it's a great place to meet Korean students eager to practice English.

Entertainment

The Academy Cinema (Akademi Geukjang; Map p261) screens both Korean and foreign films.

EASTERN JEJUDO
Sangumburi 산굼부리 분화구

About halfway between Jeju-si and Seong-eup, this **volcanic crater** (Map p256; ☎ 783 9900; admission W2000; ☯ 9am-6pm) is some 350m in diameter and around 100m deep.

This is just one of the 360 so-called 'parasitic cones' (secondary volcanoes) found on Jejudo – the other 359 cones can be visited for free, but this one has the easiest access. It's a somewhat steep uphill climb on paved paths, but once you reach the crater, trails allow you to hike along the rim. Although you're not allowed inside the crater itself, inside it's lush and forested, with over 420 varieties of plants and several kinds of animals. In the distance, across the plains, there are good views of Jeju's other mountains.

Buses from Jeju-si to Seong-eup and Pyoseon pass right by the crater gate and will stop if you want to get off. You can't miss this place, as it's fronted by a huge parking lot and a tourist village near the entrance.

Manjanggul 만장굴

East of Jeju-si, and about 2.5km off the coast road from Gimnyeong Beach, is the world's longest system of **lava tube caves** (Map p256; ☎ 783 4818; admission W2200; ☯ 9am-7pm, 9am-5pm Nov-Feb). The cave system is 13.4km long, with a height and width varying from 3m to 20m. If you've never seen one of these before, don't miss this chance.

Take a sweater or windbreaker with you and a reasonable pair of shoes (your feet will get wet in sandals). It's damp down there (87% to 100% humidity) and the temperature rarely rises above a chilly 9°C. The cave is well-lit as far as a huge lava pillar (about 1km

SNAKES & VIRGINS

Jejudo's lava tubes are associated with an ancient legend of a huge snake that dwelled in them, threatening the nearby farms and villages.

The legend continues that local people annually sacrificed a 15- or 16-year-old virgin girl by throwing her into a lava tube cave, until the practice was stopped by a magistrate newly appointed to the area. He persuaded the reluctant villagers to perform the ritual without the sacrifice, whereupon the angry snake emerged, was killed by the villagers and burnt to ashes. For his pains, the magistrate inexplicably fell ill and died soon afterwards – but there was no reappearance of the snake.

from the entrance), which is as far as you're allowed to go without special permission.

Much closer to the turn-off from the main highway, but alongside the road that leads to Manjanggul, is another series of lava tube caves, known as the **Gimnyeongsagul** (김녕 사굴). They are especially unusual because there are actually two tubes, one on top of the other. These caves, however, are currently not open to the public.

GETTING THERE & AWAY
To get to Manjanggul, take a bus from Jeju-si going to Seongsan and get off at the Gimnyeong turn-off (signposted for the caves). From here there are local buses to Manjanggul, which run once or twice an hour. Alternatively, you can hitch a ride or walk.

Gimnyeong Maze 김녕 미로 공원
A short hop from the Manjanggul caves is this **hedge maze** (Map p256; ☎ 782 9266; admission W2000; ⏰ 8.30am-6.30pm) of the type normally seen in Europe. It has received a lot of press coverage in Korea on account of its design, history and owner, making it a popular, offbeat destination.

Much thought went into the design of this 1.6-hectare site and its 3km of paths. The maze's outline mirrors that of the island, and if you view it from above (maps provided) you can note icons pertinent to local culture: horse, ship, *taeguk* (the Korean national symbol) etc. Skilful maze-walkers should be able to get through it within 20 minutes.

The founder of the maze is Fred Dustin, an American who first came to Korea in 1952 as a soldier during the Korean War. After the war, he went back to the USA to study, but returned in 1955 and has been an expat ever since. He accepted a teaching position in Jejudo, and started growing the maze in 1987 using *leylandii* shrubs, a hybrid of cypress. Mr Dustin is still often on hand and has interesting tales to tell.

Most profits from the maze go to Jeju University.

If you're under your own power and need a relaxing coffee or tea, Café 1263 is a sophisticated yet quirky place near Gimnyeong Beach, about 6km from Manjanggul. This is no Starbucks; it's set up like a living room in a private home, and Mr Sung Chang-mo (who speaks excellent English) says he's happy to sell just half a dozen cups a day. A cup might set you back W4000 to 5000 – you're really paying for his time and some solitude.

Seongsan Ilchulbong 성산 일출봉
Seongsan-ri (Fortress Mountain Village) is at the extreme eastern tip of Jejudo, nestled at the foot of the spectacular extinct volcano known as **Ilchulbong** (Sunrise Peak; ☎ 784 0959; admission W2200; ⏰ before sunrise-sunset). The summit (182m) is shaped like a punch bowl, though there's no crater lake here because the volcanic rock is so porous. It is definitely one of Jejudo's most impressive sights.

Climbing the summit in time to catch the sunrise is a life-affirming journey for many Koreans – expect plenty of company on the trail. To do the sunrise expedition, you'll have to spend the night at a *yeogwan* (small family-run hotel) in Seongsan-ri. Most *yeogwan* owners will wake you up early so you can watch the sunrise. The path is quite clear, but if you're concerned you can carry a torch (flashlight). Not an early riser? It's also a popular day hike.

The sides of the mountain plunge vertically into the surf. Along the rugged shoreline, you can often see *haenyeo*, Jejudo's famous diving women, searching for seaweed, shellfish and sea urchin (see the boxed text p267). There are often boats (W5000) available to sail you around. They only sail when demand is sufficient and the sea is calm enough so that your *gimbap* stays where it belongs.

SLEEPING
There are a number of *yeogwan* and *minbak* (cheap rooms for rent) in Seongsan-ri, but most of them are undistinguished. A few exceptions:

Jeongli Minbak (☎ 782 2169; d W20,000) If you need to be near the entrance to Ilchulbong, you can't get much closer than this. *Ondol* rooms have simple bathing facilities and no air-con, but there are good breezes.

Jeonmang Joeun Hoetjip (☎ 784 1568; d W25,000, with ocean view W30,000) Small *minbak* with decent rooms above a fish restaurant facing the water. Other waterfront restaurant-*minbak* have comparable rooms for twice the price.

Yongkung Minbak (☎ 782 2379; d W30,000; ✷) Probably the newest and nicest in town. It's up a small hill, from a side street off the town centre. Many rooms offer in-your-face views of the mountain. Rooms are a decent size.

GETTING THERE & AWAY
There are frequent buses to Seongsan-ri departing from Jeju-si. The trip takes about 1½ hours.

Make sure that the bus you get on is going right into Seongsan-ri and not just to Goseong-ri, which is the town on the main coast road where you turn off for Seongsan-ri. From Goseong-ri, it's a 2.5km walk into Seongsan-ri.

Sinyang Beach 신양해수욕장
On the eastern shore, this half-moon shaped beach, about 1.5km in length, is the island's most sheltered. Many consider it Korea's best beach for windsurfing; you can rent sailboats and windsurfers and take lessons on how to use them. It's also a good staging post for climbing nearby Ilchulbong.

There are *yeogwan* and *minbak* in Sinyang-ri, the village adjacent to the beach, and even more in Seongsan-ri, which is about 3km to the north (see Sleeping earlier). Rates are typically W25,000.

Buses from Jeju-si do not go directly to Sinyang Beach. First take a bus to Goseong-ri, and there are hourly bus connections for the last 2km (six minutes). Otherwise you could walk it or take a taxi.

During the summer months the beach is patrolled by lifeguards and there are small kiosks dishing out drinks, snacks, postcards and other tourist paraphernalia.

Udo 우도
Northeast of Seongsan, just off the coast, is Udo (Cow Island) which is still very rural and relaxing despite its 1750 inhabitants, an increase in vehicular traffic and throngs of tourists. The superb views over to Ilchulbong are rewarding, and there are three **beaches** (one has white sand, one has black sand and the other is coral). An interesting twist is the small community of *haenyeo*, Jeju-do's famous **diving women**, who work in the cove below the lighthouse (see the boxed text following).

One popular way to see the island is by bicycle. Its 17km perimeter makes for a nice circuit. Hop-on-hop-off tourist buses (W4000) also leave from the ferry pier, though they can be quite crowded.

For a quieter experience, you can spend the night at one of numerous *minbak* or *yeogwan* (W20,000 and up).

HAENYEO
Female divers, or *haenyeo*, are found on a number of Korea's outlying islands. However, they are most well known (and numerous) on Jejudo.

Great physical stamina is a prerequisite. The divers use no scuba gear but are able to hold their breath underwater for two minutes and reach a depth of 20m. Their equipment is decidedly low-tech: fins, wetsuit, face mask, gloves, basket and net.

At their peak (in the 1950s), there were almost 30,000 *haenyeo* on Jejudo. By the 1980s their numbers were reduced to around 10,000, and by the year 2000 there were perhaps only 3000 left. The average age of the divers has been increasing – some of the women have continued to dive until reaching the age of 75.

That few young women are choosing to go into the diving profession is hardly surprising – it's never been an easy way to earn a living (headaches are a common symptom). More than anything, tourism may be the siren song that lures the *haenyeo* out of the ocean.

Udo Hoetjim (meals W6000) is a nationally famous restaurant, diagonally across the square from the ferry pier. Most people seem to order *hoedeupbap* (raw fish in a bowl with rice, vegetables and spicy sauce), *maeuntang* (spicy fish soup) or *seonggeguk* (성게국, sea urchin stew). All cost W6000, although more expensive options are also available.

GETTING THERE & AWAY

Frequent ferries (W2000, tax payable on outbound journey only W1000, bicycles W500) reach Udo from the port at Seongsan. Although a schedule technically exists, in peak season the real schedule seems to be 'according to demand'; peak season turnarounds can happen with lightning speed. The **ticket office** (☎ 782 5671) and pier are about 15 minutes' walk from the centre of Seongsan. Before boarding, you have to fill out a form including your name and passport number (passport itself not required). The fare per car is W8,800, but there's often quite a queue.

Seong-eup Folk Village
성읍 민속 마을

A short bus ride north of Pyoseon lies Jejudo's former provincial capital Seong-eup, which was founded in Goryeo times. It became the provincial headquarters in 1423 during the reign of King Sejong and remained such until 1914, when the administrative unit was abolished. Unlike some other folk villages, this one is an actual community where traditional architecture has been preserved with government assistance (W1,000,000 per year for each household). Modern intru-

sions include souvenir shops, car parks and a number of tourist restaurants, but otherwise it looks prodigiously old.

The village has a number of sections – take some time to explore them. Your bus, car or taxi may well be greeted by a local, inviting you on a free guided tour (in Korean). The catch is that they hope you'll buy some things from the souvenir shops. A major local product is five-flavours tea (W30,000 per jar).

Otherwise, you can just take off down the narrow lanes and discover the place for yourself. Remember that many of the houses are still occupied, so don't barge in and ask the 'staff' if you can cash a travellers cheque.

Jeju Folk Village 제주 민속촌

Just outside of Pyoseon and close to the town's fine beach, **Jeju Folk Village** (☎ 787 4501; admission W6000; ⏱ 8.30am-6pm, 8.30am-5pm Oct-Mar) is more re-creation than preservation, but in its way it's more educational than Seong-eup. Various sections cover Jejudo's historic culture, as seen in mountain, hill-country and fishing villages, from shamanism to officialdom. Some of the cottages were brought intact from other parts of the island and are 200 to 300 years old; even modern construction is done in authentically traditional style.

The folk village has diverse flora and fauna, and you may also be able to catch traditional song and dance performances.

There's relatively little signage in English, but the English-language audio guide (W3000) is well worth the investment.

The grounds also contain several popular restaurants.

Pyoseon Beach 표선 해수욕장

This beach, southernmost on the eastern shore, is wider than a football field and has good camping and some other lodging nearby. It is known for a distinctive pool of water which forms at high tide.

SOUTHERN JEJUDO
Seogwipo 서귀포
pop 84,300

Amid the tangerine groves on the lower slopes of Hallasan sits Seogwipo, Jejudo's second-largest city after Jeju-si. Compared to its northern neighbour, it's warmer, more tropical and more laid-back and its setting is quite spectacular. The city centre (up a steep

---

BUT SHOULD I BRING A GIFT?

At Jeju's folk villages, instead of gates in front of homes you'll probably encounter two stone pillars with a column of three holes carved through each. This is actually part of an ancient communication system through which fellow islanders could tell whether they were welcome. The key was whether, and how many, wooden poles connected the two sets of holes. Three poles straight across meant 'We're not home. Please stay away'. If one end of the top pole was in its hole and the other end was to the ground, it meant 'We'll be back soon'. All three poles down meant 'Come on in'.

SEOGWIPO

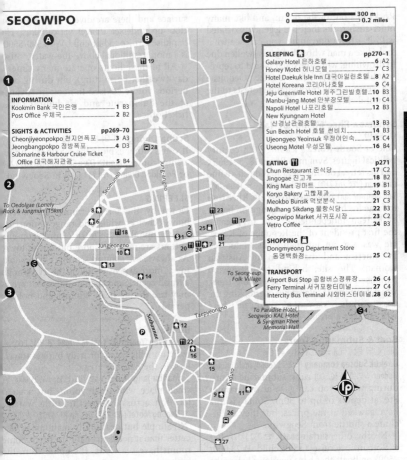

0 — 300 m
0 — 0.2 miles

INFORMATION
Kookmin Bank 국민은행 **1** B3
Post Office 우체국 **2** B2

SIGHTS & ACTIVITIES pp269–70
Cheonjiyeonpokpo 천지연폭포 **3** A3
Jeongbangpokpo 정방폭포 **4** D3
Submarine & Harbour Cruise Ticket
Office 대국해저관광 **5** B4

SLEEPING pp270–1
Galaxy Hotel 은하호텔 **6** A2
Honey Motel 허니모텔 **7** C3
Hotel Daekuk Isle Inn 대국아일란호텔 **8** A2
Hotel Koreana 코리아나호텔 **9** A2
Jeju Greenville Hotel 제주그린빌호텔 ... **10** B3
Manbu-jang Motel 만부장모텔 **11** C4
Napoli Hotel 나포리호텔 **12** B3
New Kyungnam Hotel
신경남관광호텔 **13** B3
Sun Beach Hotel 호텔 썬비치 **14** B3
Ujeongyeo Yeoinsuk 우정여인숙 **15** C4
Useong Motel 우성모텔 **16** B4

EATING p271
Chun Restaurant 춘식당 **17** C2
Jingogae 진고개 **18** B2
King Mart 킹마트 **19** B1
Koryo Bakery 고평제과 **20** B3
Meokbo Bunsik 먹보분식 **21** C3
Mulhang Sikdang 물항식당 **22** B3
Seogwipo Market 서귀포시장 **23** C2
Vetro Coffee **24** B3

SHOPPING
Dongmyeong Department Store
동명백화점 **25** C2

TRANSPORT
Airport Bus Stop 공항버스정류장 **26** C4
Ferry Terminal 서귀포항터미널 **27** C4
Intercity Bus Terminal 시외버스터미널 ... **28** B2

To Oedolgae (Lonely
Rock & Jungmun (15km)

Seomuni-ro

Jung-ang-ro

Jungjeongno

To Seong-eup
Folk Village

Taepyeongno

Sohbannae

Paduro

To Paradise Hotel,
Seogwipo KAL Hotel
& Syngman Rhee
Memorial Hall

---

hill from the harbour area) is a short distance from some famous *pokpo* (waterfalls – this is one of the few places on the island where water is not immediately absorbed into the porous rock). It was just east of town that Korea's first president, Syngman Rhee, had his retreat.

SIGHTS & ACTIVITIES
Jeongbangpokpo 정방 폭포
These **waterfalls** (☎ 733 1530; admission W2000; ◷ 7.30am-6.30pm, until 5.30pm in colder months) are 23m high and it's claimed in the tourist literature that it is the only waterfall in Asia that falls directly into the sea (although others might dispute that). Still, if it's been raining recently these falls are an impressive sight,

and you might find yourself in spray even if you're standing several metres away. The falls are a 10- to 15-minute walk from the centre of town, down a steep flight of steps.

Cheonjiyeonpokpo 천지연 폭포
This **waterfall** (☎ 733 1528; admission W2200; ◷ 7am-11pm) is across town, en route to the cruise boat harbour. From the ticket booth, it's a 20-minute walk via a path through a beautifully forested, steep gorge. After a heavy rain, the waterfall can be impressive, but at other times it's only a trickle.

Oedolgae (Lonely Rock) 외 돌 개
About 2km west of Seogwipo, the 20m-tall volcanic basalt pillar of **Oedolgae** (Lonely

Rock) juts out of the ocean, and like many other such rocks there's a legend associated with it – from one angle, you can see what looks like a man whose belly has swollen due to drowning, while the pillar is said to represent his wife praying for his safety. Oedolgae is a pleasant walk through pine forests to the beautiful cliffside lookout.

Syngman Rhee Memorial Hall
이승만 기념관

One of South Korea's leading 20th-century political figures, Syngman Rhee (1875–1965), had his retreat on this site, and today it's a fine **museum** (☎ 763 2100; admission W2000; 🕑 10am-7pm, 9am-6pm Nov-Apr), dedicated to his life. Rhee rose to fame for his ceaseless campaign on behalf of Korean independence, and he became the first president of the Republic of Korea. He was also an internationalist, educated in America and married to an Austrian woman. The site, behind the Seogwipo Paradise Hotel, is lined with walking trails, which have spectacular views overlooking the coast, and there's a very pleasant café where you can take a break.

Boat & Submarine Tours
해상유람, 대국 해저 유람

Daekuk Subsea Company (☎ 732 6060; adult/primary student W51,000/30,200) runs submarine tours, during which you can gaze at underwater life, at depths of up to 30m. Some visitors have gawked at the prices, but they do include a shuttle from Seogwipo.

Nearby, other **surface boats** (☎ 732 1717) offer a Romantic Cruise (adult/child W23,000/ 9500) on boats that have windows below the surface and there are divers who show you close-up undersea images via cameras. The Paradise Cruise (adult/child W16,500/8500) is a more traditional above-the-water cruise.

All of these boats operate many times a day (weather permitting), but during peak periods you're advised to book in advance at the Submarine and Harbour Cruise ticket office.

Scuba Diving 다이빙 클럽

If you'd rather explore the sea floor without a ship, contact **Manta Dive School** (☎ 763 2264) or **Poseidon Diving** (☎ 733 1294) in Seogwipo.

SLEEPING

Down by the ferry terminal are several budget choices, while mid-range options are mostly uphill in the town centre. Top-end options are near the shore but out of town. As always, ask about discounts when booking at more expensive hotels (or try through a travel agent), and keep in mind that prices may rise during peak summer and holiday periods.

Budget

Ujeongyeo Yeoinsuk (☎ 762 7484; d W15,000) A truly no-frills place for truly budget travellers, in the harbour area.

Manbu-jang Motel (☎ 733 1315; r W25,000) A small place with small rooms but a good location, across the street from the water.

Useong Motel (☎ 732 5700; fax 732 5702; r W30,000 🏙) Simple but beautifully maintained, it's better than it needs to be for the price. Some rooms have sea views. It's uphill from the harbour.

WORLD CUP: HALF EMPTY OR HALF FULL?

Seogwipo was fortunate to be a 2002 World Cup host city – or was it? Among other things, the soccer tournament was supposed to bring many visitors to the city, and the modernist, open-topped 42,000-plus-seat Jeju World Cup Stadium was built east of central Seogwipo – its shape was said to resemble either a volcanic crater or a traditional Jeju fishing boat, depending on your perspective. However, only three matches ended up being played here, involving Brazil, China, Germany and Paraguay. To hear the locals tell it, three of those four nations were just too far away for there to be many visitors.

To make matters worse, in August 2002, within months of the World Cup, a monstrous typhoon tore off part of the stadium's roof, making it a leaky fishing boat indeed. Thankfully no-one was injured.

The good news is that football in Korea continues to grow in popularity. There are hopes that a professional team will base itself here, but there were no commitments as we went to press. Given Jeju's winning nature, we wouldn't count it out.

Galaxy Hotel (Eunha Hotel; ☎ 733 6678; d W30,000; ✗) This new place, adjacent to the fancy Hotel Daekuk Isle Inn in the town centre, is well kept and friendly. Upper rooms are bright and airy.

Honey Motel (☎ 763 6677; fax 733 5655; d W30,000; ✗) This multistorey place is surrounded by nightlife and restaurants. It's not fancy but in very good shape.

Mid-Range

Hotel Koreana (☎ 733 7007; fax 733 1114; d from W40,000) It's rambling, ageing and a little odd, but inside this timber-beamed shell you may luck out with a larger-than-average room, with lots of hardwood. It's the only decent place in this price range down by the harbour.

Napoli Hotel (☎ 733 4701; fax 733 4802; d peak/off-peak W60,000/40,000) A decent deal for the price. It's quite clean and at a major crossroads, and some rooms offer good views of Seogwipo harbour.

Jeju Greenville Hotel (☎ 732 8311; d W70,000; ✗ 🖳) Great value with newly renovated, handsome rooms near the town centre. Many have small balconies, and upper-floor rooms come with Internet terminals.

Sun Beach Hotel (☎ 763 3600; fax 732 0096; d/tw from W100,000/120,000) Rooms are bright and pleasant though not huge, and many have ocean views. Rooms in the annexe are newer and larger. There is karaoke and a nightclub on the premises.

Hotel Daekuk Isle Inn (☎ 763 0002; fax 763 0055; isleinn@isleinnhotel.co.kr; d from W120,000) Quiet, bright, cosy eight-storey hotel with a European feel and many Japanese guests.

New Kyungnam Hotel (☎ 733 2121; fax 733 2129; d & tw from W121,000) High-rise hotel, with restaurants, sauna and karaoke. *Ondol* rooms are available; both ocean- and mountain-view rooms cost the same.

Top End

Seogwipo KAL Hotel (☎ 733 2001; www.kalhotel.co.kr; d with mountain/ocean view W236,500/280,500; 🗨) A 225-room tower, on sprawling ocean-view grounds east of town. Facilities include several restaurants, indoor and outdoor swimming pools, tennis courts, sauna and a rainbow trout farm.

Paradise Hotel (☎ 763 2100; www.paradsehotel jeju.co.kr; d from W275,000; 🗨) Next to Sygnman Rhee's retreat (hotel guests admitted free),

this seems more intimate than the KAL, in a Spanish-colonial-ish style. Rooms have various motifs – Korean, American, European, Mediterranean, Scandinavian and African. The hotel has an inviting outdoor pool, restaurants, men's and women's health club/saunas and a shopping arcade.

EATING & DRINKING

Mulhang Sikdang (meals W4000-15,000) Above the harbour, this unpretentious place has both seafood and land food at fair prices. There are nice views to enjoy too.

Jingogae (meals W3000-25,000) Near the town centre, this restaurant is well regarded for Korean standards such as *bulgogi* (W10,000), *naengmyeon* (W5000) and *dolsotbibimbap* (rice, egg, meat and vegetables in hot sauce, in a stone hot pot; W5000).

Chun Restaurant (meals W6000-15,000) Descending to the basement, you'll find something quite unexpected: it looks like a brass-rail bar and grill, and serves both Korean and Western meals (eg steaks and grilled salmon).

For a simple breakfast, Koryo Bakery in central Seogwipo will do nicely, and when you need an iced café latte try comfy Vetro Coffee nearby.

Self-caterers will want to try Seogwipo Market, which has numerous stalls on an alley in the centre of town. If that's not your style, try the huge King Mart supermarket, on the northern fringe of the city. If you're after quick and cheap, tiny **Meokbo Bunsik** (dumplings from W2000), just south of the Seogwipo Market, specialises in dumplings.

You'll find a large selection of bars, karaoke establishments and *hofs* in the town centre.

Yakcheonsa 약천사

Although this **Buddhist temple** (☎ 738 5000; admission free; ⏰ 24hr, but ask permission if arriving late in the day) was only constructed between 1987 and 1997 (entirely from wood), it is one of Jejudo's most impressive buildings. Its main hall (four storeys) claims to be Asia's largest, and it is filled with vibrant murals of scenes from Buddhist teachings. Climb the stairs to the 3rd floor, and you'll also see cases containing some 18,000 tiny Buddhist figurines. Flash photography is not permitted (time exposures are OK).

Downhill from the temple, tangerine groves sprawl towards the sea.

Jusangjolli Rocks 주상절리

Less than 1km to the south of Yakcheonsa, this spectacular 2km stretch of coastline is known for hexagonal rock columns that look almost as if they were stamped out with a cookie cutter. These bizarre formations are the result of rapid cooling and contraction of lava (just what you'd expect to happen when molten lava pours into the sea); the black-rock and green-grass colour combination might remind you of parts of Maui.

You can admire Jusangjolli from the cliffs above the sea.

Jeju International Convention Centre
제주국제컨벤션센터

Although there's little reason for travellers to go here, business visitors may well find themselves here as Jeju builds up its convention business. The building itself (completed 2003) is an ocean-view glass cylinder. It's just west of Jusangjolli and near Jungmun resort; its Western restaurant is said to be the most reasonable in the Jungmun area.

Yeomiji & Vicinity 여미지

A massive complex said to be Asia's largest botanical gardens, **Yeomiji** (☎ 738 3828; admission W6000) boasts one of the world's largest greenhouses. Theme gardens on the site include Italian and Japanese (we'll leave you to assess their authenticity) and sections of the greenhouse mimic rainforest and desert, among other landscapes. There are some 800 species of plants on the grounds, and 1200 in the greenhouses. You can take advantage of the nice lawns if you bring a picnic.

Another major drawcard is **Cheonjeyeon-pokpo** (☎ 738 1529; admission W2700; ◐ sunrise-sunset), a cascade tucked deep inside the mountains. It's almost impossible to view except from an ornate footbridge that soars over an impressive gorge. There's also a large park on the premises. Note: not to be confused with Cheonjiyeonpokpo in Seogwipo.

Descending to the oceanside, you'll arrive at **Pacific Land**, which visitors with kids may enjoy for the **dolphin shows** (☎ 738 2888; adult/child W10,000/5000), although the complex looks as if it's seen better days. The shows are on four or five times per day.

Jungmun 중문

The main attraction of this town, west of Seogwipo, is its luxury resorts, and attractive resorts they are! If you're the sort of traveller who enjoys spending your days poolside, taking a car trip to visit local culture, or paying the island's top prices, this is the place for you. You'll have plenty of well-heeled company. **Jungmun tourist information office** (☎ 738 0326) can help with arrangements.

SLEEPING
Mid-Range

Jungmun does have some lodgings targeted at average travellers.

Hanguk Condominium (☎ 738 4000; rhdfyd79@ hanmail.net; r W120,000, W220,000 Jul-Aug; ✖ ▢) Popular with long-term holidaymakers, rooms (both *ondol* and beds) sleep up to five and have kitchens, making it a good deal. There's also a bakery and coffee shop onsite.

Jeju Hotel Hana (☎ 595 7070; fax 537 0116; d/t from W100,000/120,000; ✖) Unlike the condos, the Hana feels like an average hotel. The lobby is open and airy, and rooms are smaller and simpler than at Jungmun's ritzier lodgings, although many have nice views of...the other hotels. Steep discounts are often available.

Top End

Prices here may seem sky-high, but you can often get discounts when booking through travel agents.

Hyatt Regency Cheju (☎ 733 1234; www.cheju .regency.hyatt.com; d from W290,000; ✖ ▢ ▣) This beehive-shaped edifice around a soaring atrium was Jungmun's first luxury resort and it was recently renovated in mid-20th century modern style. There's a beautiful spa/fitness facility, and it's the closest to the beach among Jungmun's resorts. The setting of a famous Korean soap opera here has brought it renewed popularity.

Shilla Cheju (☎ 738 4466; toll free 1588 1142; fax 735 5415; r from W295,000; ▢ ▣) Cool and sleek, the Shilla would be at home on the Californian coast, with muted colours and generous spaces under a Spanish-style red-tile roof. Spacious rooms have blue, white and tan décor and nice bathrooms, while facilities include a casino, fitness club, spa/sauna, billiards, racquetball and tennis.

Lotte Hotel Jeju (☎ 738 7301; www.lottehotel.com; d from W320,000; ▢ ▣) If the Shilla is California, the Lotte is Las Vegas; a sprawling complex with huge rooms, waterways for boating and swimming, famous gardens and, incongruously, a Dutch-style windmill with

FERRIES TO/FROM GAPADO & MARADO

Destination	Departing from	Telephone	Return fare (W)	Duration (one-way)	Frequency
Gapado	Daejeong	794 3500	6400	30min	twice daily
Marado	Daejeong	794 3500	9600	50min	twice daily
Marado	Songaksan	794 6661	15,000	45min	7 daily

restaurant inside. Amenities include an aerobics room, sauna, and indoor and outdoor swimming pools. Even if you don't stay here, you can take in its Vegas-style volcano show, including buffet (W48,000, 8.30pm nightly except during heavy rains), which is a tourist attraction in its own right – advance booking is advised.

Sanbanggulsa & Yongmeori
산방굴사, 용머리 해안

Halfway up the southern slope of Sanbangsan (395m), overlooking the ocean, is a natural cave that was turned into a temple, **Sanbanggulsa** (☎ 794 2940; admission W2200; ☼ cave 24hr, office 8.30am-7pm) by a Buddhist monk during Goryeo times. It's a steep walk up, but the views are worth it, and the water flowing from the ceiling is said to be medicinal. Lower down, near the entrance, are two colourful temples of recent origin. In case you're wondering, Sangbanggulsa is only halfway up because the mountain is considered so holy, it should not be climbed to the summit.

Across the road, footpaths lead downhill towards the **Yongmeori** coastline, an oceanside promenade of soaring, weatherblown cliffs. Some are quite dramatic and beautiful, and you're likely to find local women selling raw seafood and *soju* if you're hungry. Note that Yongmeori closes during very high seas. Your Sangbanggulsa ticket admits you here as well.

Near the path, down toward Yongmeori, is the **Hamel Monument**, a simple plaque dedicated by the Korean and Dutch governments to commemorate the shipwreck of a Dutch merchant vessel in 1653 (see History, p256). Also near the path, construction of an **aquarium** has been stop-and-go for years. It was 'go' as we went to press, but it may be 'stop' again by the time you read this.

Jeju Art Park 제주 조각 공원
On an open meadow near Sanbangsan, **Jeju Art Park** (☎ 794 9680; admission W3000; ☼ 9am-7pm, 9am-5pm Nov-Mar) features more than 180 pieces of sculptured modern art in a naturalistic setting of ponds and trails. It claims to be the largest art park in Asia (430,000 sq metres).

Gapado & Marado 가파도, 마라도
Off Jejudo's southwest tip lie the islands Gapado and Marado – the latter is the most southern point of Korea. Gapado, the nearer and larger of the two, is flat and almost treeless, and crops have to be cultivated behind stone walls to protect them from high winds. Many of the inhabitants earn their living by fishing.

Unlike Gapado, Marado rises steeply from the sea, and though it is only half the size of Gapado, its grassy top supports cattle grazing. Some 20 families live there. It takes about 30 minutes to walk a circuit of the island, and it is popular for noodle and raw-fish restaurants.

GETTING THERE & AWAY
Transport to the islands is by ferry. The port of Daejeong serves both islands, while there's a ferry port at Songaksan with more frequent services to Marado. There's also a nice lookout atop a hill near the port at Songaksan.

Chusa Exile Site 추사 적거지
Those with an interest in Korean art and scholarship should check out this exile site of Kim Jeong-hi (pen name Chusa; 1786–1856), one of Korea's greatest calligraphers and a leading artist and Confucian scholar of his time. Like many other Joseon-era

---

MARADO'S FIRST INHABITANTS?

It is said that Marado's first inhabitants arrived in 1883, to escape gambling debts. This was considered a gutsy move as until then the island was thought to be haunted. However, the skilful flute-playing of one Mr Kim is said to have driven the bad spirits away, and now the island's residents live without fear.

intellectuals, he was exiled here (for nine years) and used the time to teach classics and tea etiquette to the locals. Given the reverence with which Korea treats its teachers, it is no surprise the respect he's accorded even today. His art is famous for combining painting and calligraphy. The **Chusa Exile Site** (☎ 794 3089; admission W500; ☺ 8.30am-6pm, 8.30am-5pm Dec-Jan) has some traditional stone and mud-thatched houses, and there are copies of his most famous works in the exhibition hall.

O'Sulloc Tea Museum
오'설록차 박물관
On the rolling, 52-hectare plantation of Sulloc, one of Korea's largest growers of *nok-cha* (green tea – also a cosmetics company), this teacup-shaped **museum** (☎ 794 5312; admission free; ☺ 10am-5pm) has swell views of tea fields and a rather on-the-nose video about tea. However, there is a great collection of ancient tea implements; some ceramic pieces date back to the 3rd century.

Visitors are welcome to stroll the fields, and in the shop you may enjoy green tea (W2000), a slice of green tea cake (W3000) or cone of green tea ice cream (W2000). The third Saturday of each month, tea-etiquette lessons take place three times daily – inquire whether English-language lessons are available.

WESTERN JEJUDO
Bunjae Artpia 분재 예술원
Bonsai (*bunjae* in Korean) may seem esoteric, but this **bonsai park** (☎ 772 3701; admission W7000; ☺ 8am-6.30pm, until 10pm late Jul–mid-Aug) helps humanise them and provides some stunning examples. It's the life's work of Mr Sung Bum-Young, originally from Gyeonggi-do, who opened the park in 1992 and has never looked back. The park has since hosted dignitaries from all over the world.

Mr Sung has filled it with hundreds of trees – the oldest is some 500 years old! Signs translated into English espouse his philosophy (eg 'to make nature more beautiful through exercising the aesthetic sense and personality of the grower'). You'll also get tips for appreciating the diminutive trees (eg bend at the waist and view from bottom to top). There's piped-in music (which you can try to ignore) and ponds busy with hungry koi (fish food per bag W500). Hungry

humans can fill up at a well-stocked Korea lunch buffet (W6000).

A quick walk-through can take 20 min utes, but some visitors make the most the experience (and the steep admissic fee), spending up to 1½ hours here, an walk away feeling blissed-out.

Equestrian Show
Jejudo pays tribute to the Mongolian herd ers who brought horses to the island, wit shows at the **Green Resort** (제주그린리조트 ☎ 792 6102; admission W12,000; ☺ 4 times daily, hou vary), a short hop from tourist road No 9: In an indoor arena, these hour-long show combine Chinese circus acrobatics (e tumbling, bicycle tricks, plate spinning and Mongolian acrobatics on horsebac (eg handstands on a horse at full gallop).

The cast is huge, so if the entry fe seems high, think of it as under W500 pe performer, not including the horses. Som of the tricks are quite amazing; others ma make you say 'that's gotta hurt' (and just tr to put a price on that!). Don't try to com pliment the performers in Korean (hint: tr Chinese).

Note: if you're sensitive to loud musi and announcers, bring ear plugs.

If you prefer a different kind of horse ac tion, **Jeju Racetrack** (제주경마장; ☺ weekend only) is on your way back to Jeju-si. Th horses raced here are *jorangmal*: unique small ponies native to Jejudo.

Hangmong Historical Site
항몽유적지
Jejudo was the last redoubt of a faction of th Goryeo army during the time of the Mon gol invasion of the 13th century (see His tory, p256). The soldiers were determine to resist the Mongol troops even after Kin Wonjong had made peace with the invader and returned to his capital at Gaesong. I 1273 an elite military force built a 6km-lon dual-walled fortress near what is today th town of Aewol on the northwest coast o the island, but the Mongols slaughtere the defenders to a man. Despite the defea islanders honoured their ancestors' braver by erecting an **Anti-Mongol Monument** (☎ 71 1968) on the battle site.

Another relic is a five-storey stone pagoda all that remains of the temple Wondangsa which had been built by the Mongols.

Shincheonji Art Museum
신천지 미술관

This **outdoor art park** (☎ 748 2137; admission W3000; ☺ 9am-6pm, 9am-6.30pm Jun-Aug, 9am-5.30pm Dec-Feb) features hundreds of sculptures by young and up-and-coming Korean artists. It's quite a large facility (99,000 sq metres), set into a hillside with paved and unpaved paths and piped-in classical music that's meant to complement the works. One section contains animal sculptures, another *harubang*. The grounds are lovely when wildflowers are in bloom.

Hallim Park 한림 공원

We strongly advise you to explore the whole island yourself, but if you are unable to, **Hallim Park** (☎ 796 0001; admission W5000; ☺ 8.30am-5.30pm) puts many of Jeju's greatest hits in one place.

The park is filled with beautiful plantings, most notably in a botanical garden full of local plants. There's also a mini folk-village, a bonsai garden and a lava tube cave.

The cave, Hyeopchaegul, was only discovered in 1981. It's one of the few lava tubes in the world with stalagmites and stalactites, usually only found in limestone caves. They're here thanks to the large quantities of pulverised seashells in the soil above the cave, which were blown in from the shore over thousands of years. Note that the rock is so porous it can 'rain' inside the cave (ie prepare to get wet). Two other lava-tube caves are in the vicinity, but they cannot be entered.

Minor downsides: piped-in music, a little precious. Major downside: lots of tourists. If any of that turns you off, please reread the beginning of this entry.

The entrance to Hallim Park is across the street from a nice **beach** overlooking Piyangdo, said to be Jeju's most recently formed islet (about 1000 years old). There are some 60-odd others off the Jeju coast. Another popular beach is Hyeopjae, a short bus ride towards Gosan.

Geumneungseokmulwon 금능석물원

A short drive from Hallim Park is the less touristed yet somehow more real **Geumneungseokmulwon** (Geumneung Stone Garden; ☎ 796 1361; admission free; ☺ 9am-6pm). Modern-day artists have played on the *harubang* theme with sculptures large and small.

Special features include small stone sculptures depicting traditional Jeju life, and, if you don't behave, a stone road to hell.

Mysterious & Ghost Roads
신비의 도로, 도깨비 도로

For a 'Twilight Zone' moment, drive on to one of these stretches of road, turn off the engine, shift to neutral, and your car will appear to roll uphill. If you pour water or roll a ball on the pavement, there's a similar effect. It's really a clever optical illusion due to the angle of the road relative to sight lines, but it certainly looks convincing. If you decide to test it, watch out for other vehicles trying the same thing!

The first stretch to be discovered (allegedly by a taxi driver taking a break) is **Sinbiui Dolo** (Mysterious Road), in the hills about 7km south of the airport. **Dokkaebi Dolo** (Ghost Road) is to the east. There are said to be many others, but their location, naturally, remains mysterious.

Hallasan National Park
한라산국립공원

Walking (or crawling) to the top of **Hallasan National Park** (☎ 742 3084; admission W1300; ☺) is one of the finest things you can do on Jejudo. At the time of writing the summit was closed for preservation, but it may have reopened by the time you read this. Even if it's still closed, the trip is well worth it. Parking up here costs W1800.

Make sure you get an early start. No matter how clear the skies may look in the morning, the summit is often obscured by clouds in the early afternoon, which is when you should be on the way down. Any reasonably fit person can do this trek and no special equipment is required. Just make sure you have a decent pair of jogging shoes or hiking boots and something warm (it gets remarkably windy and cold up here). Rain gear is also advised as the weather is very fickle. In winter Hallasan and its foothills can be covered with snow, even when it's warm in the towns below.

On the western side of the mountain are the two shortest trails leading to the summit, Yeongsil (3.7km) and Orimok (4.7km). It takes the average person about 2½ hours to climb to the top along either of these and about two hours to get back down again. The Gwaneumsa trail (8.7km)

HALLASAN NATIONAL PARK

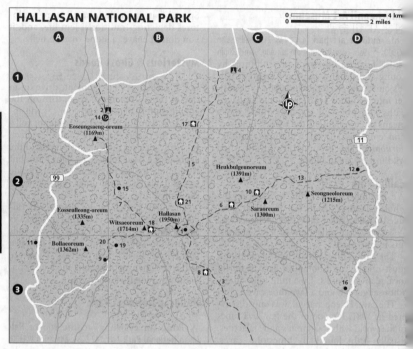

from the north and the Seongpan-ak trail (9.6km) from the east require a four- to five-hour slog to the summit. Close to all the trailheads or ticket offices, shops sell drinks, snacks and souvenirs.

There's a Buddhist temple – **Gwaneumsa** – close to the trail of the same name.

If you do reach the summit, you'll no doubt be delighted to find a crater lake, which is just about the only lake on Jejudo.

Jeollabuk-do
전라북도

CONTENTS

JEOLLABUK-DO

The western province of Jeollabuk-do (www.provin.jeonbuk.kr) is a rice-growing area, but national, provincial and county parks cover the more mountainous parts and offer some of Korea's finest hikes and scenery. It is hard to pick the best ones, but Maisan, Seonunsan and Naejangsan should not be missed. Jeonju city is well-known for its local food and alcohol specialities as well as its traditional culture – *hanok* houses, craft shops and museums. *Pansori* is a unique kind of opera featuring a singer and a drummer that is particularly associated with Jeollabuk-do. *Hanji* (paper made from mashed mulberry bark) and fans are popular buys. The province is dogged by two major environmental controversies – the Saemangeum reclamation project on the west coast and the storage of long-term nuclear waste on the island of Wido off Gyeokpo. For more information, see p49.

HIGHLIGHTS

- Spend a day in Jeonju's historic and fascinating **hanok district** (p279)
- Climb 'horse ear' mountain and wonder at the rock-art garden in **Maisan Provincial Park** (p284)
- Board a ferry in Gunsan to **Seonyudo** (p290), a beach island, or **Eocheongdo** (p290), a bird island
- Enjoy the fortress, ski resort and valley walk in **Deogyusan National Park** (p284)
- Take the cable car up to the skyline in **Naejangsan National Park** (p286)
- Amble along to an ancient rock-carved Buddha in Korea's prettiest provincial park, **Seonunsan** (p287)

★ Eocheongdo

Seonyudo ★

Jeonju ★

Deogyusan National Park ★

Maisan ★ Provincial Park

Seonunsan ★ Provincial Park

Naejangsan ★ National Park

| ▪ TELEPHONE CODE: 063 | ▪ POPULATION: 2 MILLION | ▪ AREA: 8050 SQ KM |

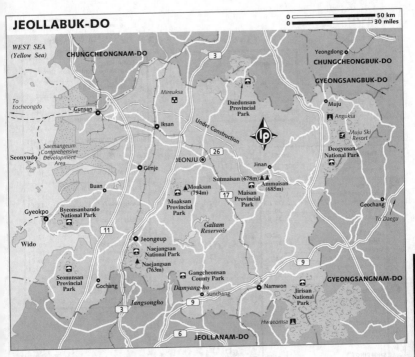

JEOLLABUK-DO

WEST SEA
(Yellow Sea)

CHUNGCHEONGNAM-DO

CHUNGCHEONGBUK-DO

GYEONGSANGBUK-DO

To Eocheongdo

Gunsan

Mireuksa

Daedunsan Provincial Park

Muju

Anguksa

Muju Ski Resort

Iksan

Under Construction

Deogyusan National Park

Saemangeum Comprehensive Development Area

JEONJU

Jinan

Seonyudo

Gimje

Sumaisan (678m)

Ammaisan (685m)

Geochang

Buan

Moaksan (794m)

Maisan Provincial Park

To Daegu

Moaksan Provincial Park

Gyeokpo

Byeonsanbando National Park

Galtam Reservoir

Jeongeup

Wido

Naejangsan National Park

Naejangsan (763m)

Gangcheonsan County Park

Namwon

GYEONGSANGNAM-DO

Seonunsan Provincial Park

Gochang

Damyang-ho

Sunchang

Jirisan National Park

Jangsongho

Hwaeomsa

JEOLLANAM-DO

JEOLLABUK-DO

JEONJU 전주

pop 622,000

Jeonju is the provincial capital of Jeollabuk-do and is famous for being the birthplace of two things – the Joseon dynasty and *bibimbap* (a dish of rice, meat and vegetables with some hot sauce). Centrally located, the city is a good base from which to explore Jeollabuk-do as bus services radiate from Jeonju to all parts of the province. The historical area of the city has many *hanok* buildings. All over Korea old-fashioned wood and tile buildings have been demolished and replaced with concrete apartment blocks and shopping malls. Jeonju is one of the few cities to have preserved its *hanok* houses and to open them up to tourists. Jeonju *bibimbap* and *kongnamulgukbap* (rice and beansprout soup) are two local specialities everyone should try.

Information

The main **Jeonju tourist information centre** (☎ 281 2939; www.jeonju.go.kr; ⏰ 9am-6pm) is located outside the express bus terminal while the main **Jeollabuk-do tourist information centre** (☎ 063 1330; ⏰ 9am-6pm) has free Internet and is near City Hall. There is another **tourist information centre** (☎ 281 2024; ⏰ 9am-6pm) at the train station and yet another **tourist information centre** (☎ 232 6293; ⏰ 9am-6pm) outside Gyeonggijeon.

Sights

JEONJU HANOK VILLAGE 전주 한옥 마을

This urban village is a historical area that can take all day to walk round. Ask at a tourist information centre for the excellent brochure on the area entitled 'Invitation to our Tradition', which includes a detailed map.

The **Traditional Wine Museum** (☎ 287 6305; admission free; ⏰ 10am-6pm Tue-Sun) has *gosori* (traditional stills for making fermented rice wine) exhibits and has alcohol for sale, but the main attraction is the beautiful old building. Some of the home-brews have interesting ingredients – Jeonju *guahaju* (a particular type of fermented rice wine) contains ginseng, bamboo leaves, glutinous rice, pine needles, chestnut, green peas and soy bean malt.

JEONJU

To Train Station
To Deokju Park, Jeonju Zoo,
Pan Asia Paper Museum,
Iksan & Gunsan

See Enlargement

Girinno
Paldalro
Jung-angno
To Jeonju National
Museum (4.5km) &
Geumsansa
Gyeonggiro
Jeonju
Hanok
Village
Jeonju-cheon

Gyeonggijeon (☎ 281 2790; admission free; ⏱ 9am-6pm) was originally constructed in 1410 and contains a portrait of Yi Seong-gye, the founder of the Joseon dynasty whose family came from Jeonju. Portraits of five other Joseon monarchs and some palanquins are also on display. Yi Seong-gye's ancestors were posthumously awarded royal titles to legitimise his overthrow of the Goryeo dynasty in 1392. A shrine (Jogyeongmyo) to these forebears is behind Gyeonggijeon but is not open to the public. In the garden is a 16th-century stupa that contains King Yejong's placenta.

Jeondong Catholic Church (☎ 284 322; admission free) was built on the spot where Korean Catholic martyrs were executed in 1781

and 1801. Built between 1908 and 1914, the architecture is a splendid fusion of Asian, Byzantine and Romanesque styles. The interior is equally interesting with stained glass windows portraying early martyrs. Entry is via a side door.

Gangnam Calligraphy Museum (☎ 285 7442; admission free; ⏱ 10am-5pm) houses the artwork and art collection of a well-known 20th-century calligrapher Song Sung-yong, whose pen name is Gangnam.

Jeonju Hanggyo (☎ 288 4548; admission free) is a Confucian school that dates back to 1603. Eighteen Korean and seven Chinese Confucian scholars are enshrined here. This is where the *yangban* (aristocratic) sons stayed in dormitories and were taught

Chinese characters and had to memorise the Confucian classics. Unfortunately, the buildings are invariably locked. See Hanggyo and Seowon boxed text.

The **Traditional Culture Centre** (☎ 280 7000; www.jtculture.or.kr; ☺ 10am-6pm) houses a theatre, classroom, **restaurant** (galbi W15,000, bibimbap or samgyetang W9000), wedding hall, **teashop** (teas W3000-6000) and outdoor area for traditional games.

Just past the centre, walk under the bridge to **Hanbyeokdang Pavilion**, originally built in 1404 and perched on rocks overlooking the river. Poets wrote and travellers rested here, but the peace and quiet is now disturbed by the traffic on the bridge. Herons, egrets and swallows can be seen by the river in summer.

Craft Treasures Centre (☎ 285 4403; admission free; ☺ 10am-6pm) has pottery-making demonstrations, embroidery exhibitions, and a display on making *hanji* paper. The *hanji* shop sells paper lanterns, papier-mâché dolls, and boxes and trays made out of paper. Jeonju is famous for its paper products and fans. Big sheets of Chinese characters cost just W500. The courtyard is a very pleasant place to rest, and on the nearby hill is **Omokdae**, a pavilion where Yi Seong-gye celebrated a victory over Japanese pirates in 1380. Cross over the bridge to **Imokdae**, a small monument.

Pungnammun, an impressive gate, is all that remains of Jeonju city's wall and four gates. First built in 1398, but renovated many times since then, it is a landmark on the edge of the *hanok* zone and marks the beginning of **Nambu Market**.

OTHER SIGHTS

Deokjin Park (☎ 281 2436; admission free; ☺ 4am-1am, 5am-11pm Nov-Feb) is a charming place with pavilions, paddle boats and lotus lilies in the lake, while the nearby **Jeonju Zoo** (☎ 281 2713; admission W500; ☺ 9am-7pm, 9am-6pm Nov-Feb) has 100 different types of animals and an amusement park.

The **Jeonju National Museum** (☎ 223 5051; adult/child W400/200; ☺ 9am-5pm Tue-Sun) is in the south of the city. At the **Pan Asia Paper Museum** (☎ 210 8103; admission free; ☺ 9am-5pm Tue-Sun) you can make your own sheet of *hanji* paper. A taxi there from the Core Hotel costs W4500 or you can take bus No 70-1, 77-1, 78-4 or 82 (W700). **Jeonbuk Art Hall** (admission free) has three art galleries and a theatre on the top floor.

> ### HANGGYO & SEOWON
>
> *Hanggyo* were neighbourhood schools established by *yangban* (aristocrats) to prepare their sons for the *seowon* (Confucian academies), which in turn prepared their pupils for the important government service exams. When *seowon* were first established in the 1500s they quickly became popular centres of learning. Their graduates were the Confucian scholars who became government bureaucrats and vied with the Joseon kings for political supremacy. During the 17th century there were over 600 *seowon* across the country, more than in China. But in the 1860s Regent Heungseon Daewongun forced most of them to close as he tried to reassert the king's authority. These schools and academies no longer function but some of the buildings still stand, symbols of Koreans' unwavering passion for education.

Sleeping

Many *yeoinsuk* (budget accommodation with shared facilities) and motels crowd around the bus terminals and new ones are being built.

Dongseong Yeoinsuk (☎ 274 2829; ondol W10,000) Tiny rooms (some without windows) with a fan and a TV.

Hosu Yeoinsuk (☎ 277 3827; ondol W10,000) Rooms here are tiny, have a TV but no fan, and there are bucket-and-bowl shared bathrooms.

Munhwatang Motel (☎ 251 5435; s & d W20,000; ✍) Old-fashioned but this *yeogwan* provides good cheap accommodation with satellite TV, although not on the same level as the modern motels. Next door is a **sauna** (W3300).

Sydney Motel (☎ 255 3311; s & d W30,000; ✍) One of many good motels, and the owner speaks a little English.

Tomato Motel (☎ 278 8703; s & d W30,000, Fri & Sat W35,000; ✍) A touch of luxury, as the modern and comfortable rooms have every facility you could imagine – including free soft drinks, toothpaste and toothbrushes.

Hanok Experience (☎ 287 6300; www.saehwagwan .com; s & d W50,000, s & d with en suite W80,000-100,000; ✍ ☲) Stay in the *hanok* area in a modern but traditional-style *yangban* house built around a courtyard, where you sleep in *ondol* rooms on a *yo* mattress on the floor.

Breakfast and bicycle hire are included. W50,000 rooms have a fridge and furniture but shared facilities, while the more expensive rooms are en suite. Music and tea ceremony lessons are available, but when we called by the staff had extremely limited English.

Jeonju Core Riviera Hotel (☎ 232 7000; fax 232 7100; s, d & tw incl tax & service W169,000; ☒) This comfortable hotel, next to the *hanok* area, has three restaurants, a bar, and the men's and women's **sauna** (W6600) and **exercise room** (W5000) are open to nonguests.

Core Hotel (☎ 285 1100; fax 285 5707; s, d & tw incl tax & service W150,000; ☒ ▣) A top local hotel in a downtown location, with three restaurants, a café, bar, nightclub and men's **sauna** (W6000 for nonguests; ✆ 6.30am-9.30pm).

Eating & Drinking

Banyadolsotbap (meals W6000-10,000) The meal here is a special *dolsotbap* for W6000 that consists of rice, vegetables, egg, lettuce, and *deodeok* root that you mix up with chives and spicy sauce in a delicious hotpot. It's served with beansprout soup and *mulkimchi* (cold kimchi soup). Scrape the burnt rice off the bowl and mix it with hot water to make an unusual drink. Serve yourself free coffee at the end. A tasty and highly recommended local speciality. A small bowl of sweet medicinal *moju* homebrew costs W1500.

Sambaekjip (meals W3500) This 50-year-old restaurant specialises in *kongnamulgukbap*, a local Jeonju dish of rice, egg, beansprouts and seasoning cooked in a stone pot. It comes with side dishes for W3500, and W1500 buys a bowl of *moju*, a sweet, gingery drink that's served warm. In Korea the alcoholic drinks look like teas. The *seonjigukbap* has dried blood as an extra ingredient.

Ijodolsotujoktang (meals W6000-12,000) Has a huge cauldron of *galbitang* (beef rib soup) and a bowl of it costs W6000. Other soups and *dolsotbibimbap* are the same price.

Andongjjimdak (meals W4500) Located next to Primus 9 multiplex cinema, this place offers cheap *jjimdak* – W9000 for two people. The chicken pieces, glass noodles and potatoes in *jjajangmyeon*-style sauce (a dark sauce) are spiced up with a generous helping of red chilli, but you can soothe your lips with cold *mulkimchi* soup. The food is freshly cooked, so you have to wait for it.

Gimbapmaeul (meals W2500) This small, clean place offers a wide range of freshly made *gimbap* (Korean sushi) at W2500 for 12 slices. Try octopus or *kimchi* along with the usual strips of egg, carrot and cucumber.

Dalsaeneundalmausaenggakhanda (Moon Bird Sings Only for the Moon; teas W4500) is a tiny teashop for goblin-sized people. *Yujacha* (citron tea) is good and comes with a sweet pancake snack.

Shopping

Core Department Store is next to the Core Hotel, while Nambu Market spreads from Pungnammun to the river. However the buzzing shopping area, especially for young people, is the traffic-quiet area behind Gaeksa that includes fashion malls, hundreds of small shops and a street of cinemas.

Getting There & Away

BUS

Destinations from the express bus terminal include:

Destination	Price (W)	Duration	Frequency
Daegu	9900	3½hr	hourly
Daejeon	4100	1½hr	every 30min
Gwangju	4800	1¼hr	every 30min
Incheon	10,300	3hr	hourly
Seoul (Gangnam)	9400	3¼hr	every 10min
Seoul (Nambu)	10,200	3¼hr	every 10min

Departures from the intercity bus terminal include:

Destination	Price (W)	Duration	Frequency
Buan	3300	1hr	every 15min
Daedunsan	4100	1¼hr	8 daily
Gangcheonsan	5000	1hr	4 daily
Gochang	4600	1½hr	hourly
Gunsan	3600	1hr	every 15min
Gurye (Jirisan)	6700	2hr	every 45min
Gyeokpo	5700	2hr	12 daily
Jeongeup	2800	1 hr	every 15min
Jinan	2900	50min	every 15min
Muju	6200	1½hr	hourly
Sunchang	4300	1hr	every 30min

TRAIN

There are four *saemaeul* (W20,900) and 1 *mugunghwa* (W14,200) trains to Seoul Station; the journey takes around 3½ hour

It's a comfortable ride and a better option than the buses, although you will probably need a short W1500 taxi ride to get to or from Jeonju train station. Trains also run south to Jeollanam-do.

Getting Around

Buses run every minute from the bus terminal area to downtown Jeonju. From the motels around the bus terminals you can walk to the Chonbuk University restaurant and entertainment area, but hop on any bus on the main road to get downtown. Taxis are plentiful and cheap (W1500 flag fall).

MOAKSAN PROVINCIAL PARK
모악산 도립공원

This **park** (☎ 548 1734; adult/youth/child W2600/1700/1000; ☘ 8am-7pm), which contains Moaksan (794m), is only 40 minutes from Jeonju and is a popular destination for hikers at weekends. The main attraction is **Geumsansa**, a temple that dates back to AD 599. The Maitreya Hall is unique and impressive – the only three-storey wooden temple building in Korea. Built in 1635 it retains an air of antiquity. The usual climbing route goes past the temple, up Janggundae and along the ridge to Moaksan peak. The hike is relatively easy and you can be up and down in three hours.

Sleeping & Eating

There is a free campsite 300m beyond the ticket office, and plenty of *minbak* (private homes with rooms for rent) and *yeogwan* (motels with small, well-equipped en suite rooms) near the bus stop.

Moaksan Youth Hostel (☎ 548 4401; fax 548 4403; dm/d/f W15,000/25,000/45,000; ☒) Housed in a traditional-style building at the park entrance, family rooms have their own TV, air-con and en suite facilities.

Hwarimhoegwan (meals W4000-10,000) This restaurant overlooking the car park offers Jinan black pig *samgyeopsal* for W15,000 (600g – enough for two or three people). *Geumsansongju* (금산송주) is the local pine needle brew (W5000 a bottle), which tastes better when mixed with water.

Jangsaganeungil (teas W3000-6000) Try the *dawonbulpaecha* (다원불패차, W6000), a home-made sweet, dark tea with lots of different nuts.

Getting There & Away

Moaksan is easily reached by bus from Jeonju. Local bus Nos 79-1, 79-2 and 887 (W1200, 40 minutes, every 10 minutes) provide a frequent service, and can be picked up at bus stops along the main street that runs to the Core Hotel and Chonbuk Art Hall. Don't get on buses such as bus No 77-2, which goes to the other end of Moaksan park. Ask for Geumsansa.

DAEDUNSAN PROVINCIAL PARK
대둔산 도립공원

Yet another of Korea's beautiful parks, **Daedunsan** (☎ 263 9949; adult/youth/child W1300/600/300; ☘ sunrise-sunset) offers craggy peaks with spectacular views over the surrounding countryside. Although relatively small, it's one of Korea's most scenic mountain areas.

Aside from the views, the climb to the summit of Daedunsan (878m) along steep, stony tracks is an adventure in itself. The main attraction for many hikers is the 50m-long cable bridge stretched precariously between two rock pinnacles, followed by a steep and long steel cable stairway. Vertigo sufferers should stick to the boulder-strewn trail instead!

It's a very popular place on weekends with locals huffing and puffing their way to the summit for the inevitable picnic. For the less active, a five-minute **cable car ride** (one way/return W2500/4500) can save you an hour's uphill hiking.

Sleeping & Eating

Daedunsan Tourist Hotel (☎ 263 1260; fax 263 8069; s & d W65,000, tw 75,000; ☒ ☐) This is the only luxurious place to stay and has a **hot spring bath** (guest/nonguest W3000/5000), the ideal way to soothe aching muscles and sore feet.

Nadeulmoksanjang (☎ 262 7170; s & d W25,000, Fri & Sat W30,000) This is one of a cluster of *yeogwan* at the park entrance.

Most restaurants serve *sanchae bibimbap* (mountain vegetables mixed with rice and hot pepper sauce) and the usual country-style food. Snacks like *beondegi* (boiled silkworm larvae) and *mettugi* (fried grasshoppers) are available, or for the less adventurous there's always ice cream.

Getting There & Away

Daedunsan can be reached by bus from Jeonju (W4100, 70 minutes, eight daily, leaving at 6.20am, 7.36am, 8.52am, 10.46am, 12.45pm, 2.34pm, 3.50pm and 6.12pm).

MAISAN PROVINCIAL PARK
마이산 도립공원

This is a must-see **park** (☎ 433 3313; adult/youth/child W2000/1500/900; ☉ sunrise-sunset). Maisan means Horse Ears Mountain, which is a good description of the two extraordinary rocky peaks as they appear from the access town of Jinan. The east peak, Sutmaisan, is considered male and reaches a height of 678m. The west peak, Ammaisan, is regarded as female and is slightly taller at 685m. Both ears are made of conglomerate rock, which is unusual in Korea. Only the female peak can be scaled. It is a steep half-hour climb, but a warning sign 'Climbing is forbidden to the old and the weak, the women, the children and the drunken' should not be taken seriously.

Tapsa (Pagoda Temple), at the base of the female ear, has a remarkable sculptural garden of 80 stone towers or pinnacles that were piled up by a Buddhist mystic, Yi Kap-myong (1860–1957). Up to 15m in height, they represent religious ideas about the universe and miraculously never seem to crumble, although no cement has been used. The diverse stone towers are an intriguing sight, evoking the atmosphere of a lost world.

Nearby is **Unsusa**, another temple that has a Dangun shrine, a centuries-old pear tree, attractive gardens and lots of *kimchi* jars – and you are allowed to bang the big drum.

An easy 1½-hour, 1.7km hike with a splendid view at the top and ever-changing views of Ammaisan starts by Tapsa and takes you back to the car park at the entrance. In spring the cherry trees around the nearby lake are a big attraction.

Eating & Drinking
Baekjejoegwan (meals W5000-10,000) Sells *pyogo-deopbap* (a hotpot containing mushrooms, cucumber, egg, rice and seasoning) with lots of side dishes.

Among the market stalls near Tapsa you can find a health drink, *haeryonggak*, which is made from seaweed and tastes better than you would expect.

Getting There & Away
There are frequent buses from Jeonju (W2900, 50 minutes, every 15 minutes) to the small town of Jinan. The route has attractive mountain scenery all the way. From Jinan, buses (W700, five minutes, hourly) run to the park entrance.

DEOGYUSAN NATIONAL PARK
덕유산 국립공원

The main highlights of this **park** (☎ 322 3174; adult/youth/child W2600/1200/600; ☉ sunrise-sunset) are an ancient mountain fortress, Muju ski and golf resort, and the Gucheon-dong Valley hike.

In the northwest of the park is **Jeoksang-sanseong**, a fortress which was rebuilt and enlarged in the 14th and 17th centuries. Encircled by the 8km wall are the ruins of a Joseon-dynasty archive, a reservoir and Anguksa, a temple that was built in the 1860s. A road runs from the access town of Muju to the fortress and circles the reservoir, but buses only run along the main road to Gucheon-dong, so get off at one of the access roads and walk (two to 4km depending on where you are dropped off). You can also leave the fortress by the west gate (Seomun) and climb down a steep footpath to a village from where buses go to Muju town.

Opened in 1990, **Muju Ski Resort** (☎ 322 9000; www.mujuresort.com) has become a popular ski resort attracting both Korean and foreign skiers and snowboarders. Despite being the most southerly (and warmest) ski resort on the peninsula, the facilities are excellent and it hosted the 1997 Universiade Winter Games. Snow-making machines are used if necessary. There are 26 ski slopes, ranging in difficulty from beginner to advanced, and 13 ski lifts. Sledding and night, free-style and cross-country skiing are possible. An all-day skiing package including lift pass and hire of skis, poles and boots starts from W50,000. The ski school conducts lessons in English, and facilities include skating rinks and a fitness centre, while evening entertainment includes various shows or disco dancing.

The best hike starts from the main tourist village of **Gucheon-dong**, along a paved track (1¾ hours, 6km) that follows the river valley to a small temple, Baengnyeonsa. On the way are 20 beauty spots – cascades, big boulders, pools and small waterfalls. Fairies

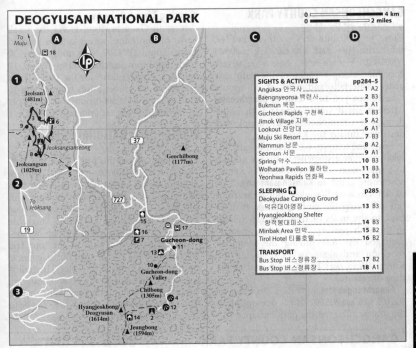

DEOGYUSAN NATIONAL PARK

SIGHTS & ACTIVITIES	pp284–5
Anguksa 안국사	1 A2
Baengnyeonsa 백련사	2 B3
Bukmun 북문	3 A1
Gucheon Rapids 구천폭	4 B3
Jimok Village 지목	5 A2
Lookout 전망대	6 A1
Muju Ski Resort	7 B3
Nammun 남문	8 A2
Seomun 서문	9 A1
Spring 약수	10 B3
Wolhatan Pavilion 월하탄	11 B3
Yeonhwa Rapids 연화폭	12 B3

SLEEPING	p285
Deokyudae Camping Ground 덕유대야영장	13 B3
Hyangjeokbong Shelter 향적봉대피소	14 B3
Minbak Area 민박	15 B2
Tirol Hotel 티롤호텔	16 B2

TRANSPORT	
Bus Stop 버스정류장	17 B2
Bus Stop 버스정류장	18 A1

are said to slide down rainbows to bathe in the pools. The valley is enchanting at any time of the year. The trail continues past Baengnyeonsa for a strenuous, steep, 1½-hour ascent of one of the highest peaks in South Korea, **Hyangjeokbong** (1614m). Yew trees, azaleas and alpine flowers adorn the summit. Although Hyangjeokbong is the name of the peak and Deogyusan is the whole mountain, you'll see both used on signposts.

Sleeping & Eating

Tirol Hotel (☎ 320 7617, fax 320 7609; s & d/tw Sun-Thu W150,000/180,000, Fri & Sat W200,000/230,000, s & d/tw in the ski season W220,000/250,000; ✗ ⬜ ⬜) This beautiful Austrian-style hotel with three restaurants and a sauna dominates the ski resort and starred in a $2 million Korean TV soap opera called *Summer Scent*.

Muju Resort (☎ 320 7830; s & d Sun-Thu W60,000, Fri & Sat W80,000, s & d in the ski season W190,000; ✗ ⬜) A cheaper alternative with an outdoor hot spring.

Two kilometres down the road from the resort is Muju Resort Village, with shops, restaurants, *yeogwan* and *minbak*. Expect to pay around W50,000 to W60,000 in the ski season, and about W20,000 to W30,000 at other times. If accommodation is full, take the free shuttle bus to Gucheon-dong, another 2km away, where prices are similar.

The large **camping ground** (W1000-2200) at Gucheon-dong is popular during the summer. Hyangjeokbong shelter costs W3000 a night.

Getting There & Away

Muju town is the gateway to Deogyusan National Park and is connected by bus to Seoul, Daegu, Daejeon and Yeongdong. Buses from Jeonju (W6200, 1½ hours, hourly) run to Muju, and two buses (at 9.25am and 2.55pm) go on to Muju Resort and Gucheon-dong. Otherwise catch the bus (W1700, 45 minutes, every 30 minutes) from Muju town to Gucheon-dong. Free yellow shuttle buses run from behind Muju bus terminal to Muju Resort and Gucheon-dong at 8am, 10.30pm, 2pm and 5pm, more often in August and during the ski season.

JEOLLABUK-DO

GANGCHEONSAN COUNTY PARK
강천산 군립공원

Close to Jeollabuk-do's southern border, this attractive **park** (☎ 650 1533; adult/child W1000/400; ☉ sunrise-sunset) has a relatively easy hike along a rocky ravine with cascades, waterfalls and lakes. A 20-minute hike brings you to a temple, **Gangcheonsa**, where a small stone pagoda with bullet damage is a reminder that the temple was destroyed during the Korean War.

From the temple, a 15-minute walk will take you over a suspension bridge and up to a small dam wall. From here it's a steep 45-minute climb to **Kumsongsanseong**. This 6km fortress wall snakes along the ridge line following the land contours. It dates back to the mists of time but was rebuilt in the 17th century. The fortress, heavily damaged in 1894 during the Donghak rebellion and again in 1950 during the Korean War, was being renovated at the time of research.

Gangcheongak Motel (☎ 652 9920; s & d Sep-Jun W25,000; Jul & Aug W35,000; ❄) is one option in the tourist village at the park entrance.

Getting There & Away

Access to Gangcheonsan is via the small town of Sunchang, which can be reached from Jeonju (W4300, one hour, every 30 minutes). From Sunchang buses (W750, 10 minutes, hourly) leave for the park. There are also a few direct buses from Jeonju to Gangcheonsan (W5000, one hour, four daily at 9.07am, 2.09pm, 3.30pm and 4.24pm).

NAEJANGSAN NATIONAL PARK
내장산 국립공원

The mountains in this **park** (☎ 538 7875; adult/youth/child W2600/1300/700; ☉ sunrise-sunset) are shaped like an amphitheatre. A spider web of trails leads up to the amphitheatre rim, but the fastest way up is by **cable car** (adult/child one way W2500/1500, return W3500/2000). The cable car takes you most of the way up Yeonjabong then you can walk to the top. The hike around the rim is great but strenuous, with splendid views all the way. The trail is a roller coaster ride, going up and down six main peaks and numerous small ones before you reach Seoraebong, from where you head down to the access road.

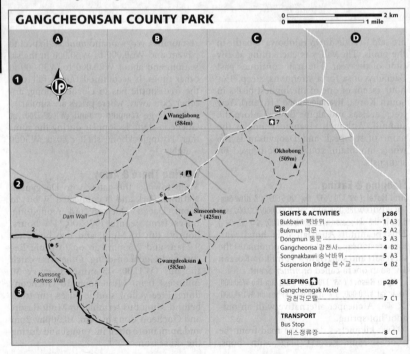

GANGCHEONSAN COUNTY PARK

| | 0 | 2 km |
| | 0 | 1 mile |

Ⓐ　Ⓑ　Ⓒ　Ⓓ

❶　❷　❸

▲Wangjabong (584m)

📷 8
🏠 7

Okhobong (509m) ▲

4 🏠

6

▲Sinseonbong (425m)

Dam Wall

2

● 5

Kumsong Fortress Wall

Gwangdeoksan ▲ (583m)

1

3

NAEJANGSAN NATIONAL PARK

There are metal ladders, bridges and railings to help you scramble over the rocky parts. Give yourself four hours to climb up and around the amphitheatre, with an hour for breaks and a picnic. If you find the hike too difficult you can turn right and follow one of the many trails down to Naejangsa.

An easy and picturesque 2km walk from Naejangsa goes through Geumsong valley, which becomes a steep ravine before leading to a cave, a natural rock arch and a waterfall.

At the entrance to the park is a large tourist village. A shuttle bus (W800) runs from the ticket office to Naejangsa and saves a 2½km, 30-minute walk.

Camping (W3000-6000) is available just outside the park.

Sarangbang Motel (☎ 538 8186; s & d W30,000, W40,000 Oct; 🖭) is one of the better motels.

Getting There & Away
Take a bus from Jeonju to Jeongeup (W2800, one hour, every 15 minutes). From there buses run to Naejangsan (W950, 20 minutes, hourly).

SEONUNSAN PROVINCIAL PARK
선운산 도립공원
According to one traveller, **Seonunsan** (☎ 563 3450; adult/youth/child W2600/1700/1200; 🖭 sunrise-sunset) is the most beautiful spot in Korea, if not the world! This is no doubt an exaggeration, even in autumn, but the area has inspired poets such as Sa Chong-ju:

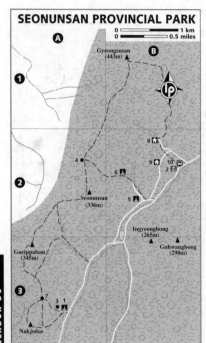

SEONUNSAN PROVINCIAL PARK

SIGHTS & ACTIVITIES	pp287–8
Dosolam 도솔암	1 A3
Folk Museum	
민속박물관	2 B2
Giant Buddha Rock Carving	
마애불상	3 A3
Maijae 마이재	4 A2
Seonunsa 선운사	5 B2
Soksangsa 속상사	6 B2
Yongmungul 용문굴	7 A3

SLEEPING	p288
Minbak Village 민박촌	8 B2
Seonunsan Youth Hostel	
선운산유스호스텔	9 B2

TRANSPORT	
Bus Stop 버스정류장	10 B2

Getting There & Away

Access to the park is via Gochang, which can be reached from Jeonju (W4600, 1½ hours, hourly). From Gochang there are buses (W1800, 35 minutes, every 30 minutes) to Seonunsa. While you are in Gochang, take a walk around the well-preserved 1.6km, 15th-century **fortress wall** (admission W500), with its gates and other buildings. It's only a 10-minute walk from Gochang bus terminal. Buses from Jeongeup also go to Seonunsan (W2300, 50 minutes, four daily).

BYEONSANBANDO NATIONAL PARK
변산 반도 국립공원

This coastal **park** (☎ 582 7808; adult/youth/child W2600/1300/700; ☼ sunrise-sunset) offers temples, a waterfall and easy hiking that is popular with school groups. **Naesosa** has not been over-renovated and the buildings look old, with lots of unpainted wood. Take a close look at the main hall, especially the lattice doors, the painting behind the Buddha statues and the intricately carved and painted ceiling with musical instruments, flowers and dragons among the motifs. A handful of monks still live there.

Every spring I go to Seonunsa
To see the camellia flowers
But this year they haven't bloomed yet
So I'm thinking about last year's visit
And the husky-voiced singing of a bar hostess.

A 20-minute walk along a rocky, tree-lined river brings you to **Seonunsa** and behind the temple is an ancient camellia forest that flowers around the end of April. Another 30 minutes further on is Dosolam and a giant folk-art Buddha that has been carved into a cliff, probably during the Baekje dynasty. The image is 13m high but its size and age are more impressive than its artistic merit. From there you can climb Nakjodae and carry on to Gaeippalsan and Seonunsan with views of the West Sea, before heading back down to Seonunsa.

A small **folk museum** (admission free) is near the entrance.

The usual tourist village is at the entrance to the park with restaurants, *yeogwan*, *minbak*, and the large **Seonunsan Youth Hostel** (☎ 561 3333; fax 561 3448; dm/f W12,000/44,000).

Hike up the unpaved road to Cheongneonam (20 minutes) for sea views, and another 15 minutes brings you to the ridge where you turn left for Gwaneumbong. From the peak follow the path which twists and turns, and goes up and down and over rocks for an hour, and you reach **Jiksopokpo**, a 30m high waterfall with a large pool that fills up with swimmers in the summer. Another pretty spot is **Sonyotang** (Angel Pool). From there walk along the unpaved access road past the ruins of Silsangsa, which was destroyed during the Korean War. You may need to hitch a lift as

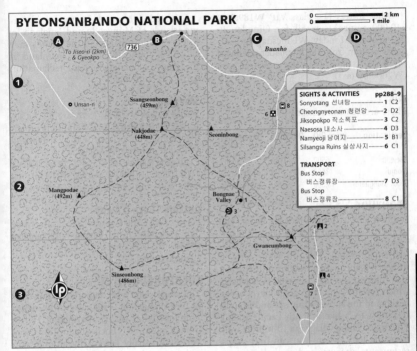

BYEONSANBANDO NATIONAL PARK

SIGHTS & ACTIVITIES	pp288–9
Sonyotang 선녀탕	1 C2
Cheongnyeonam 청련암	2 D2
Jiksopokpo 작소폭포	3 C2
Naesosa 내소사	4 D3
Namyeoji 남여지	5 B1
Silsangsa Ruins 실상사지	6 C1

TRANSPORT	
Bus Stop	
버스정류장	7 D3
Bus Stop	
버스정류장	8 C1

buses are infrequent. For a more challenging hike head up **Nakjodae**, which is famous for its sunset views.

Beaches along the coast attract crowds in summer. **Gyeokpo Beach** has dramatic stratified cliffs and caves as well as seafood restaurants. The beach is safe for swimming but the sea disappears from sight at low tide. Gyeokpo is also the starting point of ferries to **Wido**, a small island with a large sandy beach that is full of life in summer. Every house in the fishing village of Jinli is a restaurant-cum-*minbak*, and there is a supermarket, a hospital and a pool hall. There are plans to store nuclear waste on the island, but it may never happen.

Yeogwan and *minbak* can be found at Naesosa and at the beaches. Camping is another option at the beaches in July and August.

Getting There & Away

Take a bus from Jeonju to Buan (W3300, one hour, every 15 minutes). Then take a local bus to Naesosa (W1800, one hour, every 20 minutes). Buses (W1500, 40 minutes, eight daily) also run from Naesosa to Gyeokpo. Buses from Shilsangsaji are infrequent, so be prepared to hitch a lift. Direct buses (W5700, two hours hourly) run from Jeonju to Gyeokpo for the beach and ferry to Wido.

Ferries (W6500 one way, 40 minutes, three daily, six daily in July and August) run from **Gyeokpo terminal** (☎ 581 0023).

GUNSAN 군산

pop 280,000

Gunsan is a major port and industrial city that has an airport and a US airbase nearby. The main reason for coming here is to catch a ferry to Seonyudo, Eocheongdo or further afield to Jejudo or China. If you need to stay overnight **Jeiljang** (☎ 446 3227; s & d W25,000) behind the bus terminal has reasonable rooms. Nearby is a row of tent restaurant-bars *(bojangmacha)* serving up seafood and *soju* (Korean vodka)

Getting There & Away

BOAT

Ferry boats (adult W60,000 one way) sail down to Jejudo twice a day.

Other ferries (1st class/VIP W189,000/ 540,000 return) set sail for Qingdao in China every Monday, Wednesday and Saturday at 5pm from the **International Terminal** (☎ 467 2227), which is in the industrial area (W7000 by taxi).

BUS
There are bus connections to:

Destination	Price (W)	Duration	Frequency
Daejeon	6500	1½hr	hourly
Jeonju	3600	1hr	every 15min
Seoul (Gangnam)	10,600	3hr	every 20min

SEONYUDO 선유도
A 43km ferry trip from Gunsan brings you to the relaxing and pretty island of Seonyudo, surrounded by 24 mostly uninhabited small islands. The fine white sand of its beach is the main attraction, but you can also hike up the highest peak, **Mangjubong**, which rewards you with great views of the beach and the surrounding sea and islands. It almost feels like a South Pacific island. The main fishing village is a 10-minute walk from the jetty, where you can find shops, restaurants, *yeogwan* and *minbak*. You can walk round the island or hire a fishing boat for the day, which is an affordable option if you join a group (per person W10,000).

Seonyudo is connected to the neighbouring islands of Munyeodo and Jangjado by bridges. Unfortunately all the islands may soon be connected to the mainland if the giant Saemangeum land reclamation project is completed.

Sleeping
Seohae Minbak (서해민박; ☎ 465 8787; s & d Sun-Thu W20,000, Fri & Sat W25,000; ❄) It offers motel-like facilities but prices rise to W35,000 and W40,000 in July and August.

Jungang Minbak (중앙민박; ☎ 465 3450; s & d W30,000 Sep-Jun, W40,000 Jul & Aug; ❄) This one costs more but can be bargained down.

Getting There & Away
Ferries (W11,700 one way, two hours, twice daily) depart from **Gunsan Ferry Terminal** (☎ 446 7171) to Seonyudo at 11am and then again at 2pm.

EOCHEONGDO 어청도
This small island is becoming well-known for its bird population – view www.wbkenglish .com for all the twitcher information. Ferries from Gunsan to Eocheongdo (one way W21,800) usually leave daily around 8am and 3.30pm, but the times vary day-by-day depending on the tide – ask the tourist information centre in Jeonju for a monthly timetable.

Chungcheongnam-do
충청남도

Chungcheongnam-do (www.chungnam.net) was the site of two capitals of the ancient Baekje kingdom and houses a rich collection of cultural assets from the period in museums, tombs and fortresses. Scattered across the province are scenic mountain areas and temples. In summer the relatively unspoilt beaches along the province's west coast attract crowds of visitors, particularly Daecheon Beach and its famous mud festival. There are plans to decentralise government offices out of Seoul to the metropolitan area of Daejeon so the province may experience more rapid development in the future.

HIGHLIGHTS

- Be amazed by the Baekje treasures from King Muryeong's tomb in **Gongju** (p298)

- Tour the relics of Baekje's last capital, **Buyeo** (p301)

- Relax on **Daecheon beach** (p305) and the nearby islands of the **Taean Haean National Marine Park** (p307)

- Relive the struggle against Japanese colonial rule at the **Independence Hall of Korea** (p308)

- Cycle around **Magoksa** (p301), the remote and beautiful temple

- Get away from it all in **Gyeryongsan National Park** (p297)

| ■ TELEPHONE CODE: 041 | ■ POPULATION: 1.9 MILLION | ■ AREA: 8586 SQ KM |

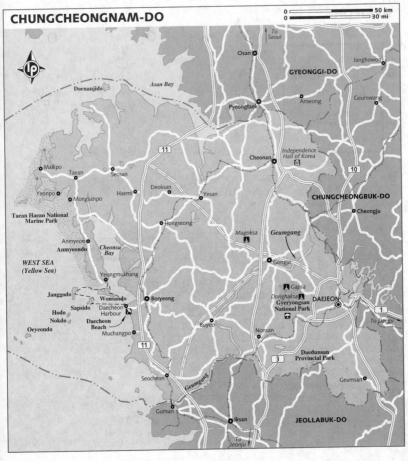

CHUNGCHEONGNAM-DO

| 0 | 50 km |
| 0 | 30 mi |

DAEJEON 대전

☎ 042 / pop 1.5 million / 539 sq km

Promoted as the science and technology capital of Korea, Daejeon hosted Expo '93, and although long past, the remnants of the once-proud pavilions still stand (rather neglected) in Expo Park. There is talk of moving central government offices out of Seoul to Daejeon, which is already an important transport hub, sitting at the junction where Korea's main north–south train line and expressway split for the southwest and southeast of the peninsula. With the opening of the new bullet train line from Seoul (planned for 2004 and eventually reaching as far as Busan) and the opening (maybe in 2006) of its own subway line, big changes will be coming to the city. Daejeon is a municipality independent of Chungcheongnam-do and has its own telephone code.

Orientation

The shops and markets are clustered around Daejeon train station, while new restaurants and bars have sprung up in Dunsandong. The best motels are in the Express/Dongbu bus terminal area and Yuseong to the west has hot spring hotels and restaurants. There are pleasant walks in the surrounding hills, such as Bomunsan.

Information

View www.daejeonweb.com for a lively expat website about the city.

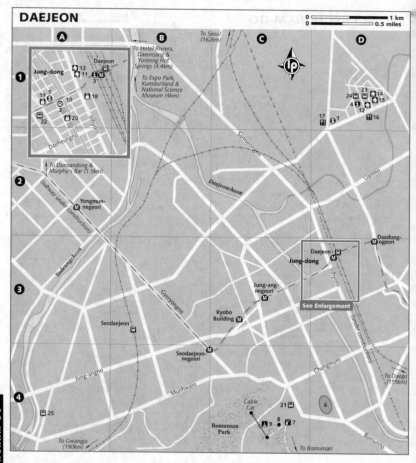

DAEJEON

See Enlargement

CHUNGCHEONGNAM-DO

Tourist information centre (☎ 632 1388; www.metro .daejeon.kr; express bus terminal; ⏱ 9am-6pm).
Tourist information centre (☎ 221 1905; train station; ⏱ 9am-6pm).

Sights

EXPO PARK AREA 엑스포 과학공원
Expo '93 ended long ago, but the pavilions of **Expo Park** (adult/youth/child W3000/2000/1000, per attraction W2500/2000/1500; ⏱ 9.30am-6pm) are still standing. Although IMAX and 3-D films are being shown, only a couple of pavilions are open.

Kumdoriland (adult/youth/child W3500/3000/2500, Big 3 W10,000/8000/6000, day pass W18,000/14,000/ 11,000; ⏱ 10am-8pm) is next door and is far more exciting with thrill rides providing

plenty of screams. The Big Three are the three main rides. A day pass gets you on every ride.

Connected with a pedestrian bridge to Expo Park is the **National Science Museum** (☎ 601 7979; www.science.go.kr; adult/child W1000/ 500; ⏱ 9.30am-5.30pm Tue-Sun Mar-Oct, 9.30am-4.30pm Tue-Sun Nov-Feb), which covers everything from dinosaurs to the Internet. **IMAX** (adult/child W1000/500) and **3-D films** (adult/child W1000/500) are shown and there are plenty of spacious displays. Although designed with children in mind, adults should find some exhibits of interest.

Bus No 103 (W1300, 30 minutes, every 15 minutes) leaves from outside the Express bus terminal. Get off at the museum.

YUSEONG HOT SPRINGS 유성 온천

In the west of Daejeon, near the World Cup Stadium, is Yuseong with 20 hot springs that are fed from 350m underground. The hot water has been gushing out since the Baekje era. A range of hotels allow you to rejuvenate tired limbs in therapeutic indoor hot pools. If you're not a guest, you can still enjoy a hot (and cold) pool for under W5000.

Bus No 103 (W1300, 45 minutes, every 15 minutes) runs to the Yuseong district from the Express bus terminal. Get off at the Riviera Hotel.

BOMUNSAN 보문산

Daejeon is encircled by a ring of hills that provide a scenic backdrop to the city. The most accessible hill is Bomunsan (457m) on the south side of the city. There are plenty of mature trees and on uncrowded weekdays you could do a spot of bird-watching on your way up to **Bomunsanseong**, a small 280m fortress that encircles the top of the hill and dates back to the Baekje era. In summer the outdoor swimming pool and small amusement parks are open. The **cable car** (adult/child one way W1500/1000) is not always working. Potable **spring water** and an **observation deck** with panoramic views of the city are other attractions.

To get there, catch bus No 724 (W700, 20 minutes, every 20 minutes) from the main road outside the express bus terminal or from outside the central train station. The bus drops you off near the tree-lined access road.

Tours

City tours (☎ 253 5960; tours W6000-10,000; ☯ 10am-4pm) depart from the small ticket office outside Dongbang Mart. The tours follow one of four different routes (with varying prices) but they all include the main sights.

Sleeping

Numerous comfortable and reasonably-priced new motels are clustered around the express and Dongbu intercity bus terminals.

Mannyeon Motel (☎ 633 7887; s & d Sun-Fri W25,000, Sat W30,000; ☒) Rooms are modern and quite luxurious and some have round beds. Room 505 is for homesick Aussies as a whole wall lights up with a photo of Sydney Harbour Bridge.

Also recommended are **Hwangtobang Park** (☎ 622 7500; s & d Sun-Fri W25,000, Sat W30,000; ☒) and **Daejeon Park** (☎ 631 2728; s & d Sun-Fri W25,000, Sat W30,000; ☒ 🖳) where rooms with a computer cost an extra W5000.

Accommodation around the train station is cheap but not very good. On a quiet street on the right of the station as you exit are:

Daejeon Yeoinsuk (☎ 252 7058; s & d W10,000) As cheap as you can find but guests share a squat toilet and shower, and rooms are tiny with just a TV and a *yo* mattress (a futon-style mattress) on the floor.

Chowonjang (☎ 255 6423; s & d W25,000; ☒) A bit tatty but OK at this price.

Other accommodation, mostly mid-range and top end, is concentrated in the Yuseong Hot Springs suburb.

Daeonjang (대온장; ☎ 822 0011; s & d W33,000; ☒) A good budget option in Yuseong. The hot spring here costs W2000/4000 for guests/non-guests but you should consider using the better spa at the Riviera or Yuseong hotels.

Hotel Riviera (호텔 리베라; ☎ 823 2111; fax 822 0071; s, d, tw & ondol incl tax & service W193,600; ☒ 🖳) This luxury hotel and spa offers a 30% discount on weekdays and has a nightclub. The hot spring pools are open to non-guests for W4500 but the sauna costs W9000.

Eating & Drinking

Dunsandong is a new restaurant and bar area, where many restaurants surround the express and Dongbu bus terminals.

Everything from chicken's feet to herbal medicine can be found at Jung-ang Sijang (Central Market) where you can eat well and cheaply at restaurants and street stalls. Dongbang Mart has a supermarket on the first floor and a food court on the second floor. There's also an Agricultural Cooperative Supermarket.

Pungjeon (meals W5000-7000) A busy restaurant with inside and outside seating that serves *samgyetang* with rice in the soup rather than in the chicken. The salad and cucumber side dishes are good too. Daejeon is famous for *dotorimuk* (acorn jelly, W5000).

Murphy's Bar (Dunsandong; ☺ 6.30pm-3am) It serves Guinness (W13,000) and has live music playing at 9pm and 11pm Monday to Saturday. The best way to get there is bus No 513 or by taxi.

Shopping

In front of the central train station is a large market plus the Galleria and Lotte department stores.

Getting There & Away
AIR

The nearest airport is Cheongju, a city 60km north of Daejeon in Chungcheongbuk-do, which is linked to Daejeon by bus (W3100, 45 minutes, five daily).

BUS

There are three bus terminals in Daejeon: the Seobu (west) intercity bus terminal, the Dongbu (east) intercity bus terminal and the *gosok teomineol* (express bus terminal). The latter two are located side by side on the eastern outskirts of town and are the terminals most used by travellers.

Buses depart the express bus terminal for:

Destination	Price (W)	Duration	Frequency
Busan	12,500	3¾hr	hourly
Cheonan	3300	1hr	every 20min
Daegu	6800	2hr	every 30min
Dong-Seoul	7600	2hr	every 30min
Gwangju	8,200	3hr	every 30min
Seoul Gangnam	7000	2hr	every 10min

From Dongbu intercity bus terminal, destinations include:

Destination	Price (W)	Duration	Frequency
Cheonan	3300	1hr	every 30min
Geumsan	2700	50min	every 10min
Gongju	2800	1hr	every 45min
Gunsan	6500	1½hr	hourly
Jeonju	4100	1½hr	every 30min
Taean	12,200	3½hr	every 20min

Departures from the Seobu intercity bus terminal include:

Destination	Price (W)	Duration	Frequency
Boryeong	7700	3hr	every 15min
Buyeo	4500	1¼hr	every 10min
Gongju	2800	1hr	every 10min

TRAIN

There are two train stations in Daejeon. Daejeon train station, in the centre of the city, serves the main line between Seoul and Busan and all trains en route to either city stop here. Seodaejeon station, in the west of the city, serves the line to Mokpo, via Ilsan and Jeongeup, though if you're heading for Gwangju you must change at Yeongsanpo.

Saemaeul trains (W12,600, 1¾ hours, hourly) run from Seoul to Daejeon as do *mugunghwa* trains (W8600, two hours, every 15 minutes). Trains to Busan cost W14,300 and take 3¼ hours.

Getting Around
BUS

From the central train station, bus No 841 goes to Seobu bus terminal while bus Nos 851 and 860 go to the Dongbu and express bus terminals. Bus No 102 heads to Yuseong Hot Springs while bus No 513 goes to the Dunsandong restaurant and bar area.

Bus No 724 (W700, every 20 minutes) links Dongbu bus terminal to the main train station and Bomunsan. The useful Bus No 103 (W700, every 15 minutes) links Dongbu terminal to Expo Science Park, Yuseong Hot Springs and Gyeryongsan National Park.

TRAIN

A subway system (to be opened in 2006) is currently being built to connect the city centre and Yuseong.

AROUND DAEJEON
Geumsan 금산
pop 65,000

The market town Geumsan (www.geumsan .chungnam.kr) is where 80% of the nation's *insam* (ginseng) is collected and marketed. Every market day 128 tons of ginseng and 66 tons of medicinal herbs worth billions of won are bought and sold. Ginseng biscuits, ginseng sweets, ginseng chocolate and ginseng wine are all popular buys. You can even have a ginseng sauna. Visit both the Geumsan Insam Gukje Sijang (Geumsan Ginseng International Market) and Geumsan Hanyak Sijang (Geumsan Medicinal Herb Market). The main market functions on the 2nd, 7th, 12th, 17th, 22nd and 27th days of every month. The main markets open on the 2nd. Not surprisingly, ginseng-based foods are a local specialty in Geumsan's stalls and restaurants. A heart-warming bowl of *samgyetang* (ginseng chickpea soup) or a medicinal variety are the most popular.

GETTING THERE & AWAY

The easiest way to get to Geumsan is by bus from Daejeon's Dongbu intercity bus terminal (W2700, 50 minutes, every 10 minutes).

Gyeryongsan National Park
계룡산 국립공원

The eastern entrance to **Gyeryongsan National Park** (☎ 825 3003; adult/youth/child W2600/1200/600; ☾ 6am-7pm) is just 18km from Daejeon.

The park contains two famous temples and forested hills, which give way to rocky cliffs towards the mountain peaks. It's a small but pretty park (the name translates as Rooster Dragon Mountain, apparently because some locals thought the mountain resembled a dragon with a rooster's head). **Donghaksa** (a nunnery) is only 1km from the park entrance. From there you can hike up to another temple, Gyemyeongjeongsa,

CHUNGCHEONGNAM-DO

GYERYONGSAN NATIONAL PARK

and then to Sambulbong and Gwaneum-bong mountain peaks before returning to Donghaksa via Eunseonpokpo (Eunseon Waterfall).

Gapsa is a temple at the western end of the park which is best approached from Gongju. A circular hike is possible from here too, and takes in a number of peaks and hermitages. Another option is to hike from one end of the park to the other (about four hours at a comfortable pace). A hiking map in English is being prepared.

SLEEPING & EATING

The bus to the eastern park entrance stops by a large tourist village of souvenir shops, a post office, convenience stores, restaurants, *minbak* (private homes with basic rooms for rent), *yeogwan* (motels with small, well-equipped en suite rooms), and stalls selling roast chestnuts in season and the Gyeryongsan version of *dongdongju* (fermented rice wine). There are small camping grounds at both entrances and **Eunseon Sanjang** (beds W3000), a simple 20-bed shelter.

Agnes Park Motel (☎ 825 8211; s & d Sun-Fri W33,000, Sat W50,000; 🐾) One of the better *yeogwan*, near the eastern park entrance.

Gyerong Youth Hostel (☎ 856 4666; dm/f W10,900/33,000) It's the cheapest place for solo travellers near the western entrance but there are plenty of *yeogwan* and *minbak* as well.

Mushroom (meals W5000-12,000) This musical and mushroom-shaped restaurant serves *beoseo ssambap* (W12,000) and plenty of other options.

GETTING THERE & AWAY

Bus No 103 (W1300, one hour, every 15 minutes) from outside Daejeon express bus terminal goes to the eastern end of the park via the National Science Museum and Yuseong Hot Springs, while bus No 102 goes there from the train station.

From Gongju take local bus No 2 (W830, 40 minutes, every 30 minutes) to the western park entrance.

GONGJU 공주
pop 140,000

Gongju was originally known as Ungjin, which became the second capital of the Baekje kingdom in AD 475, after the first capital, Hanseong, was abandoned. It was the Baekje capital for only 63 years before King Seong retreated south in 538 and moved the capital to Sabiseong (Buyeo).

At Gongju large tombs in Songsan district are tangible relics of the Baekje kingdom. More than a dozen tombs are clustered together, and in 1971 archaeologists accidentally made an exciting discovery – the undisturbed tomb of King Muryeong and his wife. It held a treasure trove of 3000 priceless artefacts that revealed a huge amount about the highly advanced artistic and technical culture of the Baekje kingdom. King Muryeong (the 25th Baekje king) ruled from AD 501 until his death in 523, at age 62. His wife died three years later in 526 and their tomb, sealed in 529, lay undisturbed for 1442 years.

Nowadays Gongju is a small provincial city and educational centre, but its brief golden age is celebrated every two years (in odd-numbered years) with a Baekje festival that is held at the beginning of October. It includes a large colourful parade down the main street, fireworks, and traditional dancing, games and sports. The festival is held in nearby Buyeo in even-numbered years.

Orientation

The tourist area is south of the river with accommodation and restaurants on or near Ungjinno, the main street. The tombs are 2km to the west, while Gongsanseong and the museum are on the eastern side.

Information

Tourist information centre (☎ 850 4548; www.gongju.go.kr; 🕑 9am-6pm Mar-Oct, 9am-5pm Nov-Feb) At the entrance to King Muryeong's tomb; has English-speaking staff.

Tourist information centre (☎ 856 7700; 🕑 9am-6pm Mar-Oct, 9am-5pm Nov-Feb) At the entrance to Gongsanseong.

Sights

GONGJU NATIONAL MUSEUM
공주국립 박물관

This **museum** (☎ 852 7714; adult/student W300/150; 🕑 9am-6pm Tue-Sun Mar-Oct, 9am-5pm Tue-Sun Nov-Feb) houses the finest collection of Baekje artefacts in Korea, including two golden crowns, part of a wooden coffin, gold, jade and silver ornaments, bronze mirrors and utensils, and white porcelain bowls. The Baekje kings as well as queens wore large gold earrings, and a silver bracelet with a

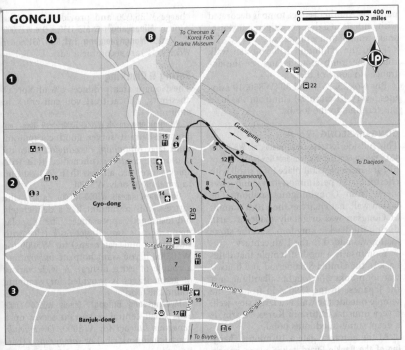

GONGJU

To Cheonan &
Korea Folk
Drama Museum

Geumgang

Gongsanseong

To Daejeon

Muryeong Wangreunggil

Jemincheon

Gyo-dong

Yongdanggil

Muryeongno

Unggogil

Gugogae

Banjuk-dong

To Buyeo

dragon design shows the great artistry of the craftsmen of 1500 years ago. Some designs reveal Mongolian as well as Buddhist and Chinese influences. Porcelain from China and coffins made of umbrella tree wood, that only grows in Japan, indicate that the Baekje dynasty traded with both of these nations. Most of the exhibits come from the tomb of King Muryeong and his wife. In 2004 the museum is likely to move to a new building behind the tombs in Songsan-ri.

TOMB OF KING MURYEONG 무령왕릉

The Baekje tombs are clustered together on a hill near Songsan-ri, a 25-minute,

2km walk from the centre of town. None of the burial chambers are open for viewing. These were sealed forever in 1997 to protect them from the moist warm air entering from the outside, that was causing deterioration of the patterned bricks and stonework inside.

Right at the entrance is the **Exhibition Hall** (☎ 850 4548; adult/youth/child W1000/700/500; ⏰ 9am-6pm Mar-Oct, 9am-5pm Nov-Feb), which contains replicas of some of the tombs as well as film footage of the King Muryeong tomb opening in 1971. One replica tomb is made of bricks decorated with lotus flower designs, which are symbols of Buddhist

paradise. Another replica tomb is decorated
with murals of a dragon, a tiger, a tortoise/
snake animal and a phoenix.

From the exhibition hall you can walk
round the tomb mounds and see the entrances to some of them.

Bus Nos 25, 25-1 and 30 (W850, 10 minutes, every 15 minutes) run from the local
bus terminal to the tombs.

GONGSANSEONG 공산성

This hillside **fortress** (adult/youth/child W800/600/
400; ☯ 9am-6pm Mar-Oct, 9am-5pm Nov-Feb) is full of
history and a pleasant place for a stroll with
chestnut and persimmon trees and river
views from Gongbungnu pavilion. The
2.4km wall that encircles the 110m summit
of Gongsan was originally made of earth
during the Baekje kingdom, and the stone
facing was added in the 17th century.

Yeonunsa is a modest temple that dates
back to the United Silla period and housed
warrior monks who fought valiantly against
the Japanese in the 1590's. In front of the
temple outside the wall is a large step-well,
a very unusual feature in Korea. Nearby is
a deep, stone-lined lotus pond.

At the entrance gate a 10-minute **Changing of the Baekje Guard** takes place hourly
between 2pm and 8pm on Saturday and
Sunday in April, May, June, September and
October. You can also dress up as a Baekje
warrior and try your hand at archery.

KOREA FOLK DRAMA MUSEUM
판소리 박물관

This **museum** (☎ 855 4933; adult W1500; www.folk
drama.net; ☯ 10am-6pm Tue-Sun Nov-Feb, 10am-5pm
Tue-Sun Nov-Feb) houses an impressive collection of puppets, dolls, masks, shamanist
implements and musical instruments from
Korea and other Asian countries.

Buses stop near the museum but it's
easier to take a taxi – a W3000, 10-minute
ride from the town centre.

Tours

A free day-long **bus tour** (☎ 856 7700) runs
every Sunday from April to October. It
departs from the fortress car park at 10am
and covers the main tourist sites.

Sleeping

The best place to stay is in one of the large
motels opposite the fortress entrance. They

charge W25,000 and provide good clean
rooms. **Minarijang** (☎ 853 1130; s & d W25,000;
☒) and **Mongnyeonjang** (☎ 856 7631; s & d
W25,000; ☒) are recommended.

Eating & Drinking

The Gongju area produces 8% of Korea's
chestnuts, a local treat you can enjoy in
autumn.

Pungmidang (meals W2000-5000; ☯ 9.30am-3am)
This restaurant serves good cheap food
until late. *Bibimbap, manduguk, kalguksu*
and spicy *sundubu* (uncurdled tofu with
spicy sauce) are all less than W4000 and
samgyetang is only W5000.

Gomanaru (meals W5000-10,000) Facing the
fortress, this restaurant has a deliberately
old-fashioned appearance. The popular
menu item is *ssambapjeongsik* (rice with
side dishes and leaf wraps) for W5000 (or
W10,000 if you want hotplate *bulgogi* and
a couple of extra dishes). A wide variety
of green leaves is provided for wrapping
round the food.

Myeongseong Bulgogi (meals W6000-12,000)
This small central restaurant serves up a
generous *bulgogi* for W8000. *Dwaejigalbi*
(barbecued pork ribs) or *samgyeopsal* (barbecued bacon-type pork) is W6000.

Nonttureongbattureong (meals W5000) This
has mud-hut decor and a small menu but
the local speciality *bamnaengmyeon* (chestnut *naengmyeon*) is a cooling W4000 lunch
on a hot day. The chestnut is in the noodles
but it's hard to detect.

World Beer House serves beers from
around the world. Guinness is W10,000
but others cost W6000 while local beer is
W3000.

Getting There & Away

The express and intercity bus terminals are
north of the river, but most buses will drop
you off in the town centre. A taxi between
the town centre and the bus terminals costs
W2000. Buses going to and from Daejeon
and Seoul stop at the bus stop marked on
the map.

Buses depart from the express bus
terminal for Seoul's Nambu bus terminal
(W5900, 2½ hours, every 20 minutes) and
Seoul Gangnam (W5900, two hours, every
20 minutes).

Departures from the intercity bus terminal include:

Destination	Price (W)	Duration	Frequency
Boryeong	4800	1¾hr	every 30min
Buyeo	2800	45min	every 30min
Cheonan	3500	1hr	every 20min
Daejeon	2800	1hr	every 10min
Taean	10,000	3hr	4 daily

Getting Around

Leaving from the local bus terminal, buses go to the western entrance of Gyeryongsan National Park (W830, 40 minutes, every 30 minutes) and to its eastern entrance (W830, 20 minutes, five daily). Local bus No 7 goes to Magoksa (W830, 45 minutes, every 35 minutes).

AROUND GONGJU

Magoksa (마곡사; adult/youth/child W2000/1500/1000; ☯ 6am-6.30pm) is another remote and historical temple, which lies northwest of Gongju off the main road. It was originally built by the Seon (Zen) Master Jajangyulsa during the reign of the first Silla queen, Seondeok (r AD 632–647), a major patron of Buddhism who introduced Chinese Tang culture into Korea.

Cross the 'mind-washing bridge' to the main hall **Daegwangbojeon**, which was last rebuilt in 1813 and has an intricately carved and decorated ceiling supported by huge beams and pillars. Behind it is an unusual and older two-storey prayer hall, **Daeungbojeon**, which was constructed in 1651. Another delight is **Yeongsanjeon** containing a thousand pint-sized white-painted devotees, each of them slightly different.

Next to the car park is a rack of **bicycles** (☯ 9am-6pm Mar-Oct, 9am-5pm Nov-Feb), which you can borrow for free and cycle along the hilly paths around the temple. Look for an office with a sign that reads '마곡사 관광지 관리 사무소' on the left. You need to leave your passport or some other form of identification.

Three circular **hiking trails** branch off from behind Magoksa. The longest trail (5km, 2½ hours) includes two peaks, Nabalbong (417m) and Hwalinbong (423m). The other trails are 2.5km and 4km long and should take 1½ hours and two hours respectively. The trails connect up with small hermitages scattered around the forested hillsides.

The small tourist village includes some interesting restaurants. **Chueokuisamhak** (meals W10,000-20,000) has *metdwaejigogi* (wild pig, W10,000), *ureongtang* (snail soup, W20,000) and *hanbang oribaeksuk* (duck in medicinal soup, W35,000), a dry version of *samgyetang* but with duck instead of chicken and served with a bland but medicinal rice soup which feeds three people. For connoisseurs of *dongdongju*, the local brew here is Gongju Albaminsamsul which contains pine needles, chestnut and ginseng. At W4000 for a 1.2L bottle, it's a good buy. Hunt around and you can spot a couple of *minbak* – look for a sign reading '민박'.

Bus No 7 (W830, 40 minutes, every 45 minutes) runs from Gongju's local bus terminal to Magoksa.

BUYEO 부여

pop 95,000

Buyeo is the site of the last capital of the Baekje kingdom, Sabi. The capital was moved there from Gongju in AD 538, and six kings ruled as the dynasty flourished until it was destroyed by the combined forces of Silla and the Tang (of China) in AD 660. General Gyebaek and his brave soldiers died trying to defend their country.

GENERAL GYEBAEK'S LAST STAND

General Gyebaek won many battles, but in AD 660 when he learnt of the size of the advancing Silla and Chinese armies, he feared defeat. Not wanting his family to face the suffering and disgrace of becoming slaves of the invaders, he personally killed his wife and children. After this extreme act he marched out with his small army of 5000 men to confront an enemy whose troops outnumbered his by ten to one. The general and his brave soldiers repulsed four enemy attacks on the Plains of Hwansanbeol, but the fifth attack resulted in the death of General Gyebaek and all his loyal soldiers. Their defeat meant the end of the Baekje kingdom. A statue of the general on horseback can be seen in central Buyeo, and by Gungnamji pond is a memorial to his final battle. The general and his men represent the unflinching martial spirit of the ancient kingdom of Baekje.

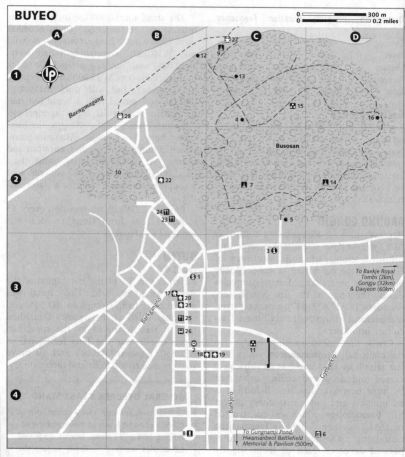

BUYEO

King Uija, the crown prince and 700 others were sent to China and held there as hostages.

Today Buyeo is a quiet and laid-back provincial town surrounded by wooded hills and rice fields, with friendly and traditional-minded inhabitants. Of the Baekje ruins not much remains – some burial mounds just out of town, a five-storey stone pagoda, and a cliff from which thousands of Baekje ladies jumped to their deaths. The best place to see relics of the Baekje kingdom is Buyeo National Museum southeast of the Jeongnimsa site.

Information

There are small tourist information kiosks at the Baekje tombs and outside Jeongnimsa. The useful main office of the **tourist information centre** (☎ 830 2523; ⊙ 9am-6pm) is outside the entrance to Busosan.

Sights

BUYEO NATIONAL MUSEUM

부여 국립 박물관

This **museum** (adult/youth & child W200/free; ⊙ 9am-6pm Mar-Oct, 9am-5pm Nov-Feb), which opened in 1993, has one of the best collections of Baekje artefacts in Korea. It also charts the development of the iron and bronze ages when people on the peninsula lived in pit houses in small villages and farmed. They made increasingly refined pottery and iron armour, and were buried in dolmens, jars and wooden coffins. The famous Baekje incense burner with its incredibly intricate and well-preserved metalwork and superb design is the outstanding item on display. Baekje designs on ordinary household items – kitchen pots with human faces and an animal-shaped chamber pot – are in stark contrast to the status symbols – gold crowns for the kings and queens, and gilt-bronze or silver ones for top government officials. A number of interesting stone relics – steles, baths, lanterns, and Buddha images – are in the museum's garden.

BUSOSAN 부소산

This **park** (adult/youth/child W2000/1100/1000; ⊙ 7am-7pm Mar-Oct, 8am-5pm Nov-Feb) covers the forested hill of Buosan (106m), where the last fortress bastion of the Baekje kings once stood. You can still see remains of the ancient earth wall. It also served as the palace garden and these days makes for a pleasant area to walk. Chipmunks, squirrels and birds have turned it into a nature reserve.

Temples, pavilions and shrines reflect Baekje history, and traces of carbonised food have been found in what was once a food storage area. A soldier's thatched pit-house has been reconstructed, and there is a shrine to General Gyebaek and two Baekje ministers whose warnings to the last Baekje monarch, King Uija (r 641–660) were ignored. See the boxed text (p301).

A wide river, Baengmagang, protected the northern side of the fortress, and the cliff above it was the setting for one of the most dramatic events in the Three Kingdoms period. The legend is that 3000 court ladies threw themselves off a large rock at the top of the cliff into the river. They preferred to die rather than face a life of slavery after the Baekje army was defeated by the invading Silla and Chinese forces in 660. The rock was later named Nakhwaam, 'falling flowers rock', in honour of those who chose death rather than dishonour.

At the bottom of the cliff is a small temple, Goransa. Behind it is a spring that provided the favourite drinking water of Baekje kings, and nearby is a plant that only grows near this spring. Slaves had to pick a leaf and put it in the water to show that the water came from this spring.

From Goransa, **ferries** (adult/child one way W2300/1100) connect to Gudurae sculpture park. The boats run daily from sunrise to sunset and the trip only takes 10 minutes. From Gudurae park it's a 15-minute walk to the town centre past some of Buyeo's best restaurants.

JEONGNIMSA 정림사

This small **temple site** (adult/youth/child W1000/600/400; ⊙ 7am-7pm, 8am-5pm Nov-Feb) located in the town centre contains a five-storey Baekje stone pagoda – one of the few that have made it to the 21st century. Buddhism was introduced to Baekje in the 4th century AD and their temples were usually simple affairs facing north–south with a wooden gate, a tiled main hall and a stone pagoda in the grounds. Dragons, monsters and lotus flowers were common motifs on roof and floor tiles. The biggest of the pagodas to remain standing is at Mireuksa near Iksan in Jeollabuk-do.

GUNGNAMJI POND & PAVILION 궁남지

A 15-minute walk past Jeongnimsa is a pavilion that was originally constructed by a Baekje king as a pleasure garden for the court ladies. The pavilion is in a lily pond, surrounded by flowers, willow trees and paddy fields. Nearby is a large memorial to the epic last battle of General Gyebaek and his 5000 Baekje troops who marched out of the fortress to confront the vastly superior combined forces of the Silla kingdom and their Chinese allies.

BAEKJE ROYAL TOMBS 백제 왕릉

These seven **royal tombs** (adult/youth/child W1000/600/400; ⏰ 7am-7pm Mar-Oct, 8am-5pm Nov-Feb), dating from 538 to 660, are on a hillside 4km from Buyeo along the road to Nonsan. It's not possible to enter them, but an **exhibition hall** has small-scale models of some of the tombs that have been excavated. One tomb has murals painted on the walls but they are not very distinct.

Adjacent to the tombs is the site of Neungsan-ri temple where in 1993 the superbly crafted metal incense burner now on display in the museum was unearthed. The tombs are just outside the high earthen ramparts that were part of the city's outer defence, and remnants can still be seen. The ramparts originally stretched for 8km and were wide enough to ride a horse along. Pheasants now wander where once Baekje soldiers marched.

To get there from the bus station or along the road that leads to Nonsan, hop on one of the frequent local buses to Nonsan (논산), which cost W850, or take a taxi (W4000).

Sleeping

There are three comfortable and inexpensive motels just north of the bus terminal.

Myeongseongjang (☎ 833 8855; s & d W25,000; ✗) The best and cheapest of the three motels north of the bus terminal, this has large, clean rooms adorned with attractive photographs, and an orchid-and-water feature in the hall.

Damyeongjang (☎ 835 3377; s & d W30,000; ✗) Features a fancy Lotte Hotel-style hallway.

New World Park (☎ 832 1755; s & d from W25,000; ✗) Also good.

Just south of the bus terminal is another good motel and a cheap *yeoinsuk* (family-run hotels with small rooms and shared bathroom).

Motel Sky (☎ 835 3331; s, d & ondol W25,000; ✗) This motel has a pebble-stoned facade and fancy furnishings.

Geumhwa Yeoinsuk (☎ 835 2936; s & d W10,000) Tiny rooms with a TV are grouped around a courtyard. There's shared squat toilets

and a bathroom where you splash yourself with water from a big plastic tub, but the price is as cheap as it gets.

Samjeong Buyeo Youth Hostel (☎ 835 3791; dm/f members W11,000/30,000, nonmembers W16,000/43,000; ✗ 🖥) This hostel has a kitchen, a children's pool (open July and August), a restaurant and a shop. It's nearer the town centre than most youth hostels.

Eating

The road down to the ferry is lined with interesting restaurants.

Gudurae Dolssambap (meals W5000-10,000) This popular restaurant has *dolssambap* and *bibimbap*.

Daega (meals W10,000) A restaurant that offers a wonderful roasted duck dish. Order the *hunjejeongsik* (W30,000, more if you want the duck soup included) which is enough for three people. Medicinal and garlic sauces, good side dishes, rice gruel, pickles and lettuce wrap make for a delicious meal.

Sinsedaebunsikjangteo (meals W1000-4000) This budget restaurant in the main street provides cheap meals in a clean environment – *gimbap*, *kalguksu*, *mandu*, *donkkaseu* and *seolleongtang*.

Getting There & Away

Intercity buses depart Buyeo bus terminal for:

Destination	Price (W)	Duration	Frequency
Boryeong	3300	1hr	every 45min
Daejeon	4500	1¼hr	every 10min
Gongju	2800	45min	every 30min
Seoul (Nambu)	10,000	2¾hr	every 20min

BORYEONG 보령

pop 122,000

Boryeong is the gateway to popular Daecheon beach and Daecheon harbour, from where ferries sail to nine of the nearby islands. The bus terminal, which houses express, intercity and several local buses, is just a five-minute walk from the train station. Turn left at the train station and exit. The **tourist information centre** (☎ 932 2023; www.boryeong.chungnam.kr; ⏰ 9am-6pm Mar-Oct, 9am-5pm Nov-Feb) is located inside the train station. The staff are helpful and some speak English.

Getting There & Away

BUS

Departures from Boryeong include:

Destination	Price (W)	Duration	Frequency
Buyeo	3300	1hr	every 45min
Cheonan	7400	2hr	every 30min
Daejeon	7700	2½hr	every 15min
Dong-Seoul	12,400	2½hr	9 daily
Gongju	4800	1½hr	every 30min
Gunsan	4600	1½hr	hourly
Hongseong	2700	¾hr	every 30min
Jeonju	8200	2½hr	8 daily
Seoul (Nambu)	13,000	2½hr	every 30min

TRAIN

There are three *saemaeul* (W14,500), 13 *mu-gunghwa* (W9900) and three *tongil* (W5500) trains to and from Seoul daily. The faster trains take 2½ hours. Confusingly the station in Boryeong is called Daecheon station.

DAECHEON BEACH 대천 해수욕장

Just 10km west of Boryeong is the best beach on the west coast. Although Daecheon Beach, boasting white sand and cleaner than most, is 3.5km long and 100m wide, it can still get crowded on summer weekends. The sea is shallow and calm and in the evening everyone gathers on the beach to watch the sunset and let off fireworks.

Daecheon beach has been heavily commercialised with amusement parks and row upon row of large brand-new but reasonably-priced motels, some of which have luridly-coloured plastic neon palm trees outside that light up at night. There are also *minbak*, *noraebang*, bars, nightclubs, cafés, shops and countless fish and seafood restaurants, but no banks. The restaurants are as big an attraction as the beach. Water sports are popular as is the annual mud festival.

Daecheon harbour, only 2km away, is packed with fishing boats and is the ferry terminal for visiting the unspoilt offshore islands, where the only residents are fisher folk.

Information

The **tourist information centre** (☎ 932 2023; ⏰ 9am-5pm) is located on the seafront by the main access road. The staff don't speak English.

Activities

Water-skiing, canoeing, windsurfing, horse-and-carriage rides along the beach and speedboat, banana-boat and jet-ski rides all take place in July and August.

Mud House (보령 머드하우스; ☎ 931 2930; www.mudhouse.co.kr; ⏰ 10am-3am) Provides a 40-minute face mudpack and face massage for W20,000. For an extra W5000 you can have an all-body mudpack. The local mud is full of health-giving minerals, and you can even buy mud cosmetics, such as mud soap (W2000) and mud shampoo (W6000).

Festivals & Events

The mid-summer madness culminates in the famous Boryeong Mud Festival. A mud bathtub, a mud slide, mud *ssireum* (wrestling), mud softball and a Mr Mud and Ms Mud contest are among the events held over six-days in late July.

Sleeping

Daecheon beach has hundreds of large, modern motels with lifts and quite luxurious rooms for W30,000 (W50,000 in July and August). If you want something cheaper go into an older *yeogwan* and bargain. Camping is possible behind the Mud House throughout the year and is free except in July and August when it costs W2000 to W4000. Showers cost W1000.

Daecheon Hyatt Motel (대천 하얏트 모텔; ☎ 934 9007; s & d W30,000; 🕸) It has good rooms and is on the main access road down to the beach. But prices increase to W50,000 on Friday and Saturday and W60,000 in July and August.

Daedong Motel (대동 모텔; ☎ 931 5950; s & d W30,000; 🕸) This typically smart motel is on the left-hand side of the main access road down to the beach. It has sea glimpses from some rooms and the heated floor in the bathroom is a nice touch.

Eating

Seafood restaurants stretch along the beachfront, and many have aquariums outside that are full of live sea creatures – fish, eels, blue crabs, shellfish and sea cucumbers. If you don't like raw fish or spicy *haemultang* (seafood soup), try steamed or grilled prawns and crabs, which are excellent. *Soju* (Korean vodka) is a popular accompaniment to the meals.

Yeonggwangsikdang (영광 식당; meals W5000-20,000) Just off the main access road, this restaurant serves up delicious *saeugui* (새우구이, 30 large prawns) cooked on salt on a hotplate at your table. Great taste and colour! The meal includes side dishes, *hwangtae* (dried fish soup) and self-serve coffee.

Nyumasanhoetjip (뉴마산 횟집; meals W7000-25,000) A typical seafront restaurant. Try *kkotgejjim* (꽃게찜, steamed blue crabs), which are not huge but are full of succulent meat. It costs W50,000 for two people and comes with side dishes – scallops, fish, corn, mushrooms and seaweed soup. You can also order rice (W1000).

Getting There & Away

Standard (W850) and deluxe (W1200) buses between Boryeong and Daecheon beach (10km) and harbour (12km) take 25 minutes and leave half-hourly. Look for '대천 해수욕장' (Daecheonhaesuyokjang) and '대천항' (Daecheonhang) on the buses which leave from outside the train station. Get off at the first stop in Daecheon beach for the main access road to the beach.

MUCHANGPO 무창포

This beach, 10km south of Boryeong, has become a popular tourist attraction on the four or five days every month when a low-tide phenomenon reveals a 1.5km natural causeway that connects the beach to a tiny off-shore island, Sokdaedo. It resembles the Biblical story of Moses parting the seas, but it's probably the prospect of picking up a lot of shellfish that really draws the crowds. The beach has some sand but low tide reveals lots of mud. Still there is beachfront accommodation and plenty of restaurants. Raw fish options range from W50,000 to W70,000 – 1kg of *ureok* (우럭) costs W60,000. *Kijogae* (키조개, razor clams) and *garibi* (가리비, scallops) are sometimes available.

If all this excites you, take a local bus from Boryeong local bus terminal (W850, one hour, nine daily) to Muchangpo – walk out of the train station and turn right for the bus stop. The buses go via Ungcheon – look for '무창포' on the bus.

SAPSIDO 삽시도

This island, 13km from Daecheon harbour, is peaceful (except for the barking dogs) with picturesque sea views and sandy beaches. The sea, encircled by countless islands both inhabited and uninhabited, is often as smooth as silk *hanbok*.

The island has a population of less than 300 sun-tanned residents and it takes 40 minutes to walk from one end to the other. There is no bus but there are some private vehicles. *Minbak*, huts, bungalows and shops are sprinkled around the island although the shops are not easy to spot as they are usually someone's lounge. **Geomeolneomeo Beach** in the north of the island has pine trees and some overpriced bungalows – even the better ones are just empty rooms with an en suite toilet and shower, and cost W40,000 in the off-season. More huts and *minbak* are clustered around **Bamseom Beach** in the south, such as **Uenhae Minbak Bungalows** (☎ 935 1082; bungalows Sep-Jun

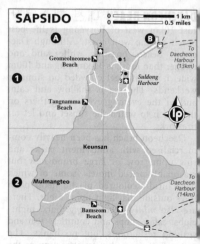

SAPSIDO

0 ─────── 1 km
0 ─────── 0.5 miles

SIGHTS & ACTIVITIES	pp306-7
Sapsido Primary School 삽시초등교 1 B1	

SLEEPING ⌂	pp306-7
Geomeolneomeo Beach Bungalows	
거멀너머해수욕장방갈로 2 A1	
Suwon Minbak 수원민박 3 B1	
Uenhae Minbak Bungalows	
은해민박방갈로 4 B2	

TRANSPORT	
Ferry Jetty 밤성선착장 5 B2	
Ferry Jetty 술동선착장 6 B1	

OTHER	
Store 수퍼 7 B1	

W40,000, Jul & Aug W50,000) which are nothing fancy and share facilities. In the evening you might see red-billed oystercatchers patrolling the sea's edge while ducks fly overhead.

Suwon Minbak (☎ 933 1617; s & d W35,000), near Suldong harbour in the north, is open all year and offers the usual bare rooms, but facilities include a washing machine, a kitchen and a TV lounge that adjoin the bedrooms which have *yo* mattresses on the floor. The toilet and shower is modern but shared. The owner speaks some English and offers Korean home cooking – W5000 for *baekban* featuring locally caught fish. Otherwise you could buy some local fish and cook it up in the kitchen.

Getting There & Away

Old car ferries run from **Daecheon harbour** (☎ 934 8772) to Sapsido and other nearby islands with extra services in July and August. Passengers have to sit on the floor. Ferries leave Daecheon harbour at 7.30am, 12.40pm and 4pm. The first two ferries take 40 minutes and cost W7800. The 4pm ferry goes to Sapsido (W10,450, one hour 40 minutes) via Anmyeondo (W6900, 35 minutes), Godaedo (W8650, 55 minutes) and Janggodo (W9900, 70 minutes). Children travel at half fare.

Other boats go to Wonsando (W3800, 15 minutes), which has a sandy beach and may become a resort island one day; Hwojado (W4100, 25 minutes); Hodo (W9050, one hour), Nokdo (W11,100, one hour 20 minutes) and Oeyeondo (W15,600, 1½ hours). Ferry times vary somewhat but they usually leave twice a day around 7.30am and 4pm.

Buses (W1200/850 one way, 25 minutes) depart every 20 minutes from 7am to 10.30pm for Daecheon beach and Daecheon harbour from outside Daecheon train station in Boryeong. Ask for Daecheonhang or look for '대천항' on the bus.

TAEAN HAEAN NATIONAL MARINE PARK 태안 해안 국립공원

This **marine park** (☎ 672 9737; adult/youth/child W2000/1500/700; ☼ sunrise-sunset) was established in 1978 and covers 329 sq km of land and sea. It includes 33 sandy beaches such as Mallipo, Yeonpo and Mongsanpo (which allow camping for W3000 to W6000 in July and August), and about 130 islands and islets. This is the nearest national park to Seoul to offer beachside scenery, so expect crowds (especially on summer weekends).

Anmyeondo 안면도

pop 13,000

This is the largest island in the park (87 sq km) and numerous beaches dot its western coast. Ferries run from Daecheon beach and Sapsido to **Yeongmukhang** on the southern tip of the island. Rugged buses (W1400, one hour, hourly) rattle over narrow unpaved roads that wind in and out of small villages surrounded by garlic fields and salt farms to the main town of **Anmyeon**. From Anmyeon bus terminal, buses (W1900, 30 minutes, hourly) run over a bridge to the mainland town of Taean. Buses also go from Anmyeon to Seoul's Nambu bus terminal (W11,500, 3½ hours, hourly).

Taean 태안

pop 25,500

Taean is the main gateway to the maritime park. Buses leaving from there include:

Destination	Price (W)	Duration	Frequency
Anmyeon	1900	30min	hourly
Cheonan	8200	3hr	every 15min
Daejeon	12,200	3½hr	every 20min
Haemi	2200	50min	every 30min
Mallipo	1300	35min	hourly
Seoul (Nambu)	9100	2½hr	every 20min

Mallipo Beach 만리포

Gorgeous Mallipo Beach has a rocky headland on one side and a small fishing harbour on the other. Eighteen kilometres from Taean, it's far less developed than Daecheon, but there are many seafood restaurants and some accommodation options.

Just 2.5km up the road is the privately-owned **Cheollipo Arboretum** (천리포 수목원; ☎ 672 9310; membership fee W60,000), a large botanical garden with plants and trees from around the world. It is only open to members. Travellers can join for W60,000.

Midong Park (미동 파크; ☎ 672 9050; s & d W30,000) – turn left when you reach the beach and you'll see it – is on the beach-front and has balconies with chairs. But the best place to stay is the smart and stylish **Pension Waltzheim** (펜션 월츠하임; ☎ 672 1371; www.waltzheim.co.kr; s & d W50,000; ⊠) is behind Midong Park but with sea and sunset views from the top floors.

Mujinjanghoetjip (무진장 횟집; meals W10,000-20,000) is a popular restaurant on the left-hand side of the access road. Try *ureok* (raw fish, W50,000), shellfish (W30,000) or octopus (W25,000). Brave souls can order *haemul-tang* (fish soup with lots of red pepper, W40,000). For something blander, order *hoedeopbap* (W10,000) – seafood rice. Most meals are meant for sharing.

Local shuttle and express buses (W1300, 35 minutes, hourly) provide a service from Taean to Mallipo (which is sometimes written 'Manripo'). There are also buses to Mallipo from Seoul's Nambu bus terminal (W10,400, 2¾ hours, nine daily) and seven from Daejeon.

HAEMI 해미
pop 9600

This small town is worth a stop to see the **town fortress** (admission free), a five-minute walk from the small bus terminal. The 1.4km fortress wall was originally constructed in 1418 to protect the local people against Japanese pirates who frequently attacked and looted coastal areas. Later a prison was built inside the walls but none of it remains except for some foundations. Korean Catholics were imprisoned and tortured there and in 1866 a thousand of them were executed in the prison. The fortress contains a small hill and some Joseon-style buildings.

Frequent buses pass through Haemi from Hongseong, Cheonan and Taean.

CHEONAN 천안
pop 403,000

Cheonan is the transit point for visiting Korea's largest museum, the Independence Hall of Korea (otherwise known as Dongnipginyeomgwan), which is 14km east of the city.

The Independence Hall of Korea
독립 기념관

The nation's largest **museum** (www.independence.or.kr; adult/youth/child W2000/1100/700; ◷ 9.30am-6pm Tue-Sun Mar-Oct, 9.30am-5pm Tue-Sun Nov-Feb) is definitely worth a visit. It highlights Korea's struggle for independence against Japanese colonialism from the 1870s to 1945, and gives a very different story to that presented in Japanese school history books. Built on a grand scale, it has seven exhibition halls and some English-language exhibit descriptions. The active collaboration with the Japanese colonialists at all levels of society, from ordinary policemen to the *yangban* elite, is not covered in the exhibition. One display says that 'the entire Korean population participated in the March 1st Movement'. This opposition movement was very widespread, but not all took part.

The Circle Vision Theatre has nine film projectors and 24 loudspeakers. It presents films on Korea's scenic beauty, traditions, customs and economic development, using the latest audiovisual techniques.

A pleasant wooded area surrounds the museum so you can take a picnic. Otherwise, you can eat in the museum's restaurant where meals cost around W5000, or buy a snack from a food stall.

City buses (W800, 20 minutes, every 10 minutes) head out to the museum from Cheonan. They depart from the front of the express bus terminal and the train station.

Getting There & Away

Cheonan intercity bus terminal is located in the basement of the Galleria department store, which is 150m north of the express bus terminal, in the north of Cheonan. Destinations from the intercity bus terminal include Gongju (W3500, one hour, every 20 minutes) and Taean (W8200, three hours, every 15 minutes). Buses depart the express bus station for Seoul's Nambu bus terminal (W3800, one hour, every 20 minutes) and Daejeon (W2800, one hour, every 15 minutes).

Chungcheongbuk-do
충청북도

CONTENTS

A region of small towns, lakes, mountains, hot springs and forests, Chungcheongbuk-do is South Korea's most rural province and the only one with no coastline. Three national parks (Songnisan, Woraksan and Sobaeksan) line its southwest border with Gyeongsangbuk-do, and no visitor should miss Suanbo Hot Springs and the pleasant lake-side resort town of Danyang with its nearby caves, mountains and temples. A two-hour ferry ride along Chungju lake is another highlight. Weekend trippers escaping from Seoul and other big cities flood into the province, but otherwise it's peaceful and relaxing.

HIGHLIGHTS

- Board a ferry on **Chungju Lake** (p316) for Korea's most scenic trip

- Stay in **Danyang** (p319) and visit limestone caves, Guinsa and mountain summits

- Relax in **Suanbo Hot Springs** (p317), savour pheasant, and hike or ski

- Enjoy the sights and student ambience of **Cheongju** (p311)

- Go on an antelope safari in **Woraksan National Park** (p318)

- Visit **Songnisan National Park** (p322), Beopjusa and its huge Buddha

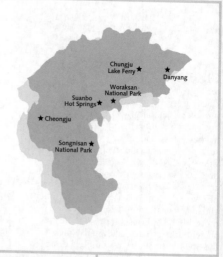

- TELEPHONE CODE: 043
- POPULATION: 1.5 MILLION
- AREA: 7432 SQ KM

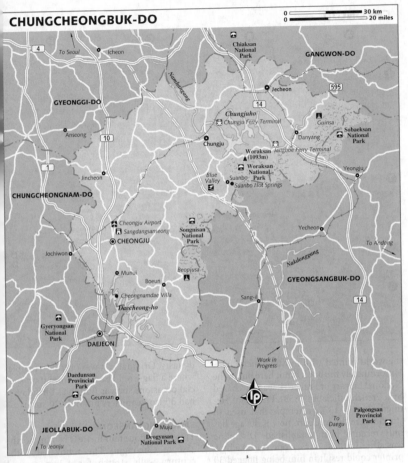

CHUNGCHEONGBUK-DO

0 ────── 30 km
0 ────── 20 miles

To Seoul · Icheon · 4

Chiaksan National Park

GANGWON-DO

Namhangang

Jecheon · 595

GYEONGGI-DO

14

Chungjuho
Chungju Ferry Terminal

Anseong · 10

Chungju · *Guinsa*

Danyang · Sobaeksan National Park

1 · Jincheon

Woraksan ▲ (1093m)
Woraksan National Park

Janghoe Ferry Terminal

Yeongju

CHUNGCHEONGNAM-DO

Blue Valley · Suanbo
Suanbo Hot Springs

Cheongju Airport
Sangdangsanseong

◎ CHEONGJU

Songnisan National Park

Yecheon

To Andong

Jochiwon

Nakdonggang

· Munui
Boeun · *Beopjusa*

GYEONGSANGBUK-DO

· *Cheongnamdae Villa*

Daecheong-ho

Sang-il

14

Gyeryongsan National Park

DAEJEON

1 · *Work in Progress*

Daedunsan Provincial Park

Geumsan

Palgongsan Provincial Park

JEOLLABUK-DO

To Daegu

Muju

To Jeonju · *Deogyusan National Park*

CHEONGJU 청주

pop 579,000

Cheongju is an education centre and the provincial capital of Chungcheongbuk-do, but can be confused with Chungju, 70km to the east, or Jeonju in Jeollabuk-do. It is served by an international airport and besides being the gateway to Songnisan National Park (1¾ hours away by bus), there are a few tourist attractions and a bargain-priced, student-oriented entertainment and restaurant zone. More expensive but more interesting restaurants are inside an ancient fortress, Sangdangsanseong. Near the bus terminals are new motels designed to look like castles which offer excellent accommodation at reasonable rates.

Orientation & Information

Frequent local buses run along Sajikro, the main road, to the student entertainment area (Jungmun), the market and the main shopping area which is over the bridge.

The well-stocked **tourist information centre** (☎ 233 8431; ⏰ 8.30am-7pm) is outside the intercity bus terminal where new motels are clustered.

Sights

EARLY PRINTING MUSEUM 고인쇄박물관

This small but modern **museum** (☎ 269 0556; adult/youth/child W800/600/400; ⏰ 9am-6pm Tue-Sun, 9am-5pm Nov-Feb) tells you everything you could want to know about *Jikji*, a book of Buddhist sayings that is the oldest book in

CHEONGJU

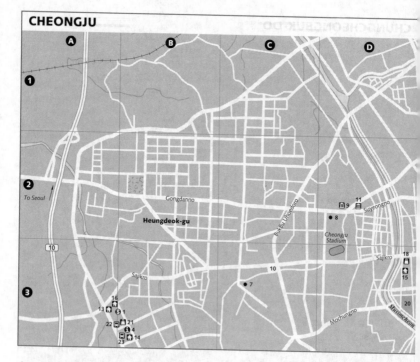

the world printed with movable metal type. Unfortunately the book is not here but in the National Library of France (it was purchased by a French official in 1853). Printed at Heungdeoksa in 1377, a temple that used to stand where the museum now is, its age has only recently been established. Discipline was strict in those days – one mistake by a printer could result in him being flogged 30 times, five errors and he lost his job.

To get there, catch any city bus that runs along the main street, get off at the stadium and walk for 10 minutes.

KOREAN CRAFT MUSEUM 한국 공예관
This **museum** (☎ 268 0255; admission free; 9am-7pm Tue-Sun) has displays of pottery and other craft and is next to the Early Printing Museum.

YONGDUSAJI IRON FLAGPOLE
용두사지 철당간
Standing rather incongruously outside a modern shopping mall is one of the oldest and tallest (13m) iron flag poles in Korea. According to the inscription on the base it was made in AD 962 during the Goryeo

dynasty. Originally, it was outside a temple, where a flag would be flown from it on special occasions such as Buddha's birthday; it had 30 iron canisters but only 20 survive.

SANGDANGSANSEONG 상당 산성
This large mountain fortress is 4km northeast of Cheongju. The renovated 18th-century walls stretch for 4.2km around wooded hillsides, with gates and pavilions that have also been rebuilt. Stroll around it (1½ hours) and build up an appetite to eat at one of the excellent traditional-style restaurants on the edge of a large pond. The restaurants serve duck stuffed with rice and medicinal herbs, rabbit, pheasant and locally reared black chicken. See Eating & Drinking later.

Bus Nos 231, 232, 233 and 590 (W800, 45 minutes, every 30 minutes) depart from outside Cheongju bus terminal. The last bus back leaves around 9pm.

Sleeping
Sting Motel (☎ 235 6668; s & d W30,000; ❄) This typical smart castle motel has large,

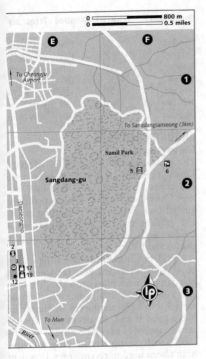

modern, fully-equipped rooms with large screen TVs as well as free coffee, drinking water, soft drinks, toothbrushes, toothpaste and condoms. It also has a lift.

Hilton Motel (☎ 236 3400; s & d W30,000; ✗ 🖳) The Hilton offers reasonable rooms if you don't fancy staying in a Disneyland castle.

Baekje Tourist Hotel (☎ 236 7979; fax 236 0979; d/tw/ste incl tax & service W85,000/105,000/140,000; ✗ 🖳) Most rooms have a computer and facilities include a Korean restaurant, a bar and a coffee shop.

Hotel Royal (☎ 221 1300; fax 221 1319; s/d W72,000/75,000, tw & ondol W86,000, ste W120,000; ✗) A mid-range downtown option near the pedestrianised shopping area, in a street of hardware stores. Prices include tax and service, and a US-style breakfast costs W7000.

Eating & Drinking
JUNGMUN
In the Jungmun entertainment area outside Chungbuk University, restaurants and stalls compete to offer the lowest prices. Some restaurants list over 40 meals between W2000 and W4000, and one sells *bibimbap* (rice, egg, meat and veggies in hot sauce) for just W2000. At tent stalls *gimbap* (Korean sushi) and *tteokbokki* (rice cakes in spicy sauce) are W1000. A convenience store offers sofas outside where you can relax and drink beer at shop prices.

Gongpoui (공포의; meals W3000-5000) Offers a good *samgyeopsal* (barbecued bacon-type pork) for an unbelievable W3000, or try the novel *gochujang bulgogi* – pork, some *ramyeon* (noodles) and sauce are cooked in a foil tray, and you can mop up the sauce with a mixture of rice, lettuce and dried seaweed.

Lakota (라코타) has a special offer with *donkkaseu* (pork with rice and veggies) and dessert for W3000.

The Jungmun area also has bars, live music, *noraebang* (karaoke rooms), PC and DVD rooms, board game cafés and who knows what else.

Woodstock (우드스탁) has beer for W2500, scribbles on the wall and a barman who speaks English, loves Jimi Hendrix and plays your requests from his collection of 1800 LPs.

0 Bar (오바; ⏱ 6pm-2am Sun-Thu, 6pm-6am Fri & Sat) Has rock music, a pool table, outside balconies, beers at W3000 and live music twice a month. It's popular at the weekend with expat English-language teachers.

Pearl Jam (펄잼) plays rock music, but all kinds of live bands play on Fridays at 11pm. Beers are W3500.

To get to Jungmun, take a city bus along the main street to Sachang intersection.

SANGDANGSANSEONG

Sangdangjip (상당집; meals W10,000) The menu is in English. The excellent black chicken (*ogolgye*) has black meat and bones, comes from a nearby farm and is cooked in a broth of bark, roots and cloves, and served with *bindaetteok* (mung bean pancake), rice and good side dishes. It tastes like *samgyetang* (ginseng chicken soup) but better. A local brew made from red dates, *daechusul* (W5000), adds another flavour to the meal. *Tokkitang* (rabbit soup, W33,000) is enough for three or four people, as is *hanbang oribaeksuk* (W28,000), duck stewed with rice and herbs. A side dish of *ureongmuchim* (river snails) is W10,000.

Shopping

The covered market is one of many markets close to the Hotel Royal. **Carrefour** (⏱ 10am-midnight) is a megastore with a large supermarket. This area of pedestrianised streets also contains Cheongju department store, APM fashion mall and Lotte Mart and is usually packed with young shoppers.

Getting There & Away

AIR

Cheongju Airport has services to Jejudo and China.

BUS

Departures from Cheongju express bus terminal include:

Destination	Price (W)	Duration	Frequency
Busan	14,100	4¼hr	hourly
Daegu	9200	2¾hr	hourly
Dong-Seoul	6100	1½hr	hourly
Gwangju	9500	2¾hr	hourly
Seoul (Gangnam)	5600	1¾hr	every 30min

Departures from the intercity bus terminal include:

Destination	Price (W)	Duration	Frequency
Chuncheon	12,300	3½hr	hourly
Chungju	5700	1¼hr	every 20min
Daejeon	2800	½hr	every 15min
Danyang	11,300	3½hr	every 30min
Gyeongju	14,000	3hr	6 daily
Seoul (Nambu)	5600	1½hr	every 20min
Songnisan	5500	1¾hr	every 20min

AROUND CHEONGJU

Cheongnamdae 청남대

The **holiday villa** (☎ 220 4999; tour free) of South Korea's presidents overlooks Daecheongho (Daecheong Lake) and was built by President Chun Doo-hwan in 1983. A two-hour guided tour (in Korean) covers the extensive gardens and the house, which has a modest and old-fashioned décor of pale shades and natural wood.

President Chun liked ice skating on the pond, while President Roh Tae-woo was a golf fanatic who played on the five-hole golf course and would order beef to be served to all his employees whenever he had a good round. President Kim Young-sam disapproved of golf because of its association with corruption and the golf course hasn't been used in recent years. President Kim Dae-jung planted the honeysuckle (the Korean word for it means 'overcoming hardship', which was his nickname) and built the thatched pavilion containing mementos from his hometown in Jeollanam-do. President Roh Moo-hyun opened the residence to the public in 2003.

You must reserve a place on the guided tour in advance as the villa is not always open to tourists – find a Korean speaker to telephone, or contact Cheongju tourist information centre (see p311). Bring your passport on the tour for ID purposes.

The **Munui Cultural Centre** (문의 문화재단지; admission free; ⏱ 9am-6pm Tue-Sun, 9am-5pm Nov-Feb) is a small folk village with traditional houses, a roof museum (no English), a blacksmith making tools, a fortress gate and a good view of the lake. It's a 10-minute walk from the Cheongnamdae shuttle bus parking lot.

GETTING THERE & AWAY

Take local bus No 300, 301 or 302 (W1140, 50 minutes, hourly) from outside Cheongju intercity bus terminal to Munui, 15km south of Cheongju. Walk out of the bus depot, turn left and in a couple of minutes you'll reach the parking lot and ticket office for the guided tours of Cheongnamdae. The shuttle buses leave every 20 minutes between 9.40am and 4pm, but numbers are limited and you must make a prior reservation. The tours are new and these arrangements may alter.

SONGNISAN NATIONAL PARK
속리산 국립공원

This **park** (☎ 542 5267; adult/youth/child W3200/1500/1000; ⏱ 5am-8pm) covers one of the finest scenic areas in central Korea with forested mountains and rocky granite outcrops. Its name means 'Remote from the Ordinary World Mountain', which refers to its famous temple Beopjusa. A **tourist information centre** (☎ 542 5267; ⏱ 9am-6pm) is in the park's bus terminal building and a map of Songnisan was being produced in English at the time of research.

Beopjusa is one of the largest temple complexes in the country, and dates back to AD 553. The temple was burnt to the ground in 1592 during the Japanese invasion, rebuilt in 1624 and has been renovated often since then. **Daeungbojeon** with its large golden Buddha statues and **Palsangjeon**, a unique five-storeyed wooden pagoda, are outstanding features. The huge 33m **bronze standing Buddha** weighs 160 tonnes and was completed in 1990 at a cost of US$4 million.

Ancient relics include stone lanterns, an elegant Unified Silla seated Buddha hewn out of rock, a massive bell and a vast iron cauldron that was cast in AD 720 and was used to cook rice for the thousands of monks who once lived at Beopjusa.

Beyond the temple, **hiking trails** extend up to a series of 1000m-high peaks. A favourite hike is the relatively easy climb up Manjangdae (1033m), which King Sejo was carried up in a palanquin in 1464. It's three hours up and takes two hours to get down. If you still have the energy at the top, you can continue on to Munsubong and Sinseondae, and as far as Ipseokdae and Birobong. The highest peak Cheonhwangbong (1058m) is a bit too far away.

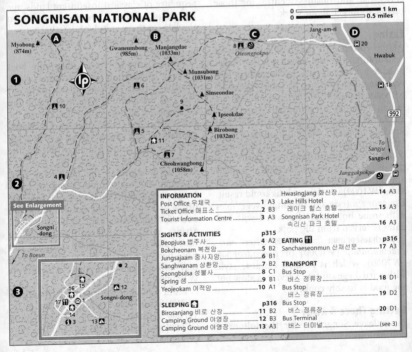

SONGNISAN NATIONAL PARK

CHUNGCHEONGBUK-DO

Sleeping

The park has a large tourist village at its entrance, with *yeogwan* (motels with small, well-equipped en suite rooms), food and souvenir shops, stalls and a post office. The two camping grounds (free) are open in July and August.

Birosanjang (☎ 543 4782; s & d Sun-Thu W30,000, Fri & Sat W40,000) This privately run accommodation in the mountains has *yeogwan*-style rooms. You can hike up to it (one hour) or else the owners will pick you up from the park entrance.

Hwasingjang (☎ 543 6241; s & d W20,000) The rooms are *ondol*-style and small, but clean and tidy with en suite facilities.

Songnisan Park Hotel (☎ 542 3900; s & d W39,000; ✖) You can usually bargain down the price of the clean and comfortable Western and *ondol* rooms here.

Lake Hills Hotel (☎ 542 5281; www.lakehills.co.kr; s, d, tw & ondol incl tax & service from W129,000; ✖ 💻) Rooms are discounted 20% on weekdays in the off-season but increase at peak times. Stylish rooms afford superb views of the forest, and facilities include a restaurant, coffee bar and business centre, for those unable to forget about work.

Eating

At the entrance to the park, hundreds of restaurants offer the usual tourist-village-outside-a-national-park meals such as *bulgogijeongsik* (barbecued beef and vegetables with side dishes, W15,000), *sanchaejeongsik* (small banquet of mountain vegetables, W12,000), *beoseot jeongsik* (W15,000) and *sanchaebibimbap* (rice and mountain vegetables with some hot sauce), which often contain *pyogo* (mushroom). Snacks include the usual rice crackers (W1000 a packet) and Frisbee-sized toffee, sesame and nut slabs (W1000) but dentist bills could result. *Dongdongju* (rice and mountain vegetables with some hot sauce) flavoured with red dates is served from big pots.

Sanchaeseonmun (meals W7000) Offers *sanchaebibimbap* (W6000) or *pyogodeopbap* (W7000), which is cooked Chinese style with a fried egg on top. Service is slow but the food is freshly cooked.

Getting There & Away

Buses leave Songnisan for the following destinations:

Destination	Price (W)	Duration	Frequency
Cheongju	5500	1¾hr	every 20min
Daejeon	5100	1½hr	every 20min
Dong-Seoul	11,600	3½hr	12 daily
Seoul (Nambu)	11,100	3½hr	7 daily

CHUNGJU 충주

pop 220,000

Chungju (www.chungju.chungbuk.kr) is the gateway to the Chungjuho (Chungju Lake) ferries, Woraksan National Park and Suanbo Hot Springs, but the latter, just 21km away, is a better place to stay. Every autumn the week-long World Martial Arts Festival brings groups of Korean and international martial art experts to the city where they demonstrate their skills and compete against one another.

Chungju Lake 충주호

The two-hour, 52km **boat ride** (☎ 851 6771; adult/child under-12 W16,000/8000) along this large artificial lake from Danyang to Chungju is a highlight with constantly changing scenery that on misty days looks like a sequence of classical Joseon-era landscape paintings. A lot of boats zip up and down the lake so there are plenty of alternatives, some of which depend on the water level in the lake.

From Danyang it is a 30-minute boat journey to Janghoe ferry terminal where the rocky cliffs are particularly scenic. If you exit the terminal here, turn right and continue for 200m, you will come to the ticket office for the western part of **Woraksan National Park** (adult/youth/child W1300/600/300) and you can enjoy a 1.8km hike to the Eoreungol Valley.

From Janghoe to the next ferry pier, Cheongpung, takes another half an hour. Nearby is a folk village and across the bridge is a resort with a bungee jump and other facilities. After another hour the boat arrives at Chungju ferry terminal. Only nine buses a day (W850, 30 minutes) run from here to Chungju bus terminal so you may have to wait some time. A taxi costs W12,000.

From Chungju ferry terminal boats go to Woraksan ferry terminal (Map p318, W7000 return, one hour), Cheongpung (W8000), Janghoe (W11,000) and Danyang (W16,000).

Getting There & Away

Chungju's brand new bus terminal, conveniently located in the town centre, incorporates a Lotte Mart and a hospital clinic. Local buses leave from across the street; bus No 240 goes to Suanbo Hot Springs (W900, 35 minutes, 20 daily). Local buses also depart for two areas in Woraksan National Park – Songgye (two daily) and Naesongye (eight daily). Buses (W850, 30 minutes, nine daily) also leave from here to Chungjuho ferry pier – see p316 for this highly recommended trip.

From the bus terminal itself, destinations include:

Destination	Price (W)	Duration	Frequency
BCheongju	5700	1¾hr	every 10min
Daejeon	7400	2¼hr	13 daily
Danyang	5600	1½hr	hourly
Dong-Seoul	6100	2hr	every 20min
Seoul (Gangnam)	8100	2¼hr	every 30min

SUANBO HOT SPRINGS 수안보

Suanbo is a hot spring resort town 21km southeast of Chungju, which is small enough to walk round on foot. Nearby is Woraksan National Park and a ski resort with a golf course. The town has a relaxing atmosphere with restaurants that specialise in rabbit, duck and pheasant meals. Near the tourist information centre is a stone pagoda and figure (possibly from the Goryeo era), which were nearly taken home by a Japanese police officer but the Japanese surrender came just in time. At the far end of town is a botanical garden with a zoo and an aquarium (admission free).

Information

The **tourist information centre** (☎ 845 7829; 9am-6pm) is on the main street near the bus terminal and has helpful, English-speaking staff.

Sleeping

Sinheung Hotel (☎ 846 3711; fax 846 1760; small/medium/large s & d W30,000/50,000/70,000; ☒) An old-fashioned hotel one-minute's walk from the tourist information centre. The cheapest rooms are a bit run-down, but the *oncheon* (hot spring bath) in the basement is free to guests and open from 6am to 8pm. The spring water contains a long list of minerals (hopefully all health-promoting).

Suanbo Sangrok Hotel (☎ 845 3500; fax 845 7878; s, d, tw & ondol incl tax & service W98,000; ☒ ▯) This centrally located smart hotel has a good sauna and *oncheon* (W3000 for guests). Massages are W40,000.

Eating

Numerous restaurants offer pheasant (*kkwongdoritang*, 꿩도리탕), duck (*oritang*, 오리탕) and rabbit (*tokkidoritang*, 토끼도리탕) stew for W30,000 to W40,000, which can be shared by two or three people. See 'Something Special' p317 for details of a gourmet pheasant meal. For vegetarians another local speciality is *sundubu* (uncurdled tofu with spicy sauce, W4000). Snacks include local dried persimmons.

Getting There & Away

Intercity buses depart from Suanbo bus terminal to destinations such as Cheongju (W6700, two hours, hourly) and Dong-Seoul (W9200, 2½ hours, hourly).

AROUND SUANBO HOT SPRINGS
Blue Valley Ski Resort
블루 밸리 스키 리조트

Only 2km from Suanbo Hot Springs, this **ski resort** (☎ 846 0750; fax 846 1789) is modest in size, which is a handicap in a country that believes that bigger is better. There are seven slopes and three lifts, and ski equipment can be hired. Night skiing is also possible. There is a youth hostel near the slopes but the best plan is to stay in Suanbo and use the free shuttle buses between the ski resort and Suanbo that run during the ski season.

WORAKSAN NATIONAL PARK
월악산 국립공원

Woraksan means 'Moon Crags Mountains' and this **park** (☎ 653 3250; adult/youth/child W1300/600/300; ☼ sunrise-sunset) receives relatively few visitors by Korean standards. While lacking dramatic granite cliffs and pinnacles, the park still offers fine hiking through picturesque forests and the chance to see an endangered goral antelope (see 'Save the Goral!' p319).

A road runs all the way through the park so access is no problem. Mireuk-ri, the tourist village at the southern entrance to the park, is only 11km southeast of Suanbo Hot Springs. Scattered near the tourist village is **Mireuksaji**, the remains of Mireuksa, a temple that was originally built in the late-Silla or early-Goryeo period. A couple of stone pagodas and an interesting stone Buddha are the main relics, though a new temple was being built at the time of writing. The most popular **hiking course** does not leave from there but further into the park at another small tourist village, **Deokju**, which has a camping ground. Follow the trail up to Dongmun, the east gate of an ancient mountain **fortress**, whose walls stretched for 10km, that dates back to the Goryeo dynasty. Parts of it were being renovated when we came through. Further on is a temple, Deokjusa, after which you bear left to 960m-bong, a peak with an uninspiring name – there are so many mountain peaks in Korea that they've run out of names. Carry on to Woraksan (1093m) and then descend the steep slope back down to the access road and Songgye-ri. This is another tourist village at the northern entrance to the park. The total distance is around 10km and takes about six hours.

Chungjuho ferries dock at Worak ferry terminal, which provides an alternative

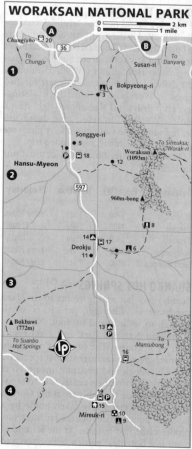

WORAKSAN NATIONAL PARK

Goral antelopes have been a protected species in South Korea since 1967, but their numbers have declined in recent years. Most of the 700 or so that live in the wild can be found in Seoraksan National Park or the DMZ, while less than 20 can be found in zoos. However Woraksan National Park has been identified as an ideal habitat for these brownish-grey animals that have short horns and look like goats. Ten goral antelopes live in the park – six were released into the park and four have been born there. Some antelope wear radio transmitters and unlike the bears introduced into Jirisan National Park, they never cause any problems. Keep a look out for them when you are hiking in the park, but they are shy creatures and not many hikers spot one.

way of visiting the park. It's a 4km walk to Songgye-ri from the pier but you should be able to hitch a ride.

Sleeping & Eating

There are shops, restaurants and *minbak* (private homes with rooms for rent) in Songgye-ri, Deokju and Mireuk-ri, and two camping grounds (W3000 to W6000 per night). You ought to find a *minbak* room for W20,000, while a camp site is W4500.

Getting There & Away

Local buses (W900, 10 minutes, seven daily) run from a bus stop in Suanbo's main street to Mireuk-ri and through the park to Songgye-ri.

JECHEON 제천
pop 148,000

Jecheon is another useful transit point in the northern part of Chungcheongbuk-do.

From Jecheon's Dongbu express bus terminal there are buses to Seoul Gangnam (W7200, 2¼ hours, every 40 minutes). From the intercity bus terminal there are buses to Cheongju (W9000, three hours, every 20 minutes), Chungju (W3300, one hour, every 15 minutes), Danyang (W2300, 45 minutes, six daily), Dong-Seoul (W8700, two hours, every 30 minutes), Jeongseon (W5900, three hours, seven daily).

Twelve daily *mugunghwa* trains connect Jecheon and Seoul's Cheongnyangni station (W10,000, three hours).

DANYANG 단양
pop 41,000

Danyang is an attractive resort town nestled in the mountains on the edge of an artificial lake (Chungjuho) and within 50km of three national parks. The lake stretches almost all the way to the city of Chungju and is Korea's most scenic inland waterway. Ferry boats whiz along it and taking a ride on one is highly recommended. There are plenty of good-quality, reasonably priced motels in Danyang along the lake and you can spend a couple of pleasant days exploring the sights. Visit at least one of the limestone caves and don't miss the awesome temple complex, Guinsa. The town itself is modern as the old town of the same name was partially submerged in 1986 under the artificial lake. The train station is still in old Danyang, 3km from the new town, but buses and taxis connect them.

The guy with bushy eyebrows, who you'll see all over Danyang, is Ondal. Born in the Three Kingdoms period he was the local fool, but he married a princess who turned him into an educated and skilled soldier. He became a general but was killed by soldiers from Silla. Education and a good wife turned him from a mocked fool into a respected hero.

Located on the far side of the bridge, the **tourist information centre** (☎ 422 1146; 9am–6pm) has helpful, English-speaking staff.

Sleeping

Hoseong Yeoinsuk (☎ 422 1674; s, d & ondol W10,000) The cheapest place in town where you sleep on a *yo* in a room with just a TV. Facilities (squat toilets and showers) are shared. You have to request the owner for hot water – *tteugeounmul* (뜨거운 물).

Cinderella Motel (☎ 423 3018; s & d W30,000;) Just one of the excellent new motels along the lakefront.

Seongsujang (☎ 421 2345; s & d W30,000;) Small rooms but smart, new and clean. Room 208 has a balcony overlooking the lake.

Rivertel (☎ 422 2619; www.erivertel.com; s, d & ondol W30,000;   ) Good rooms with a bath and cable TV, and the owner speaks a bit of English.

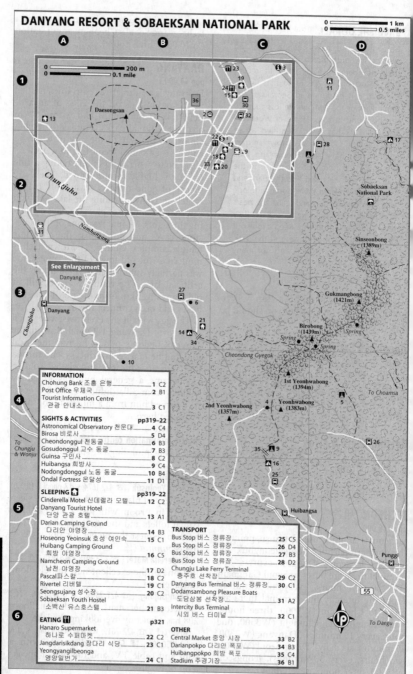

DANYANG RESORT & SOBAEKSAN NATIONAL PARK

INFORMATION
Chohung Bank 조흥 은행...................................**1** C2
Post Office 우체국..**2** B1
Tourist Information Centre
관광 안내소...**3** C1

SIGHTS & ACTIVITIES pp319–22
Astronomical Observatory 천문대..............**4** C4
Birosa 비로사..**5** D4
Cheondonggul 천동굴.....................................**6** B3
Gosudonggul 고수 동굴..................................**7** B3
Guinsa 구인사..**8** C2
Huibangsa 희방사..**9** C4
Nodongdonggul 노동 동굴...........................**10** B4
Ondal Fortress 온달성...................................**11** D1

SLEEPING pp319–22
Cinderella Motel 신데렐라 모텔...................**12** C2
Danyang Tourist Hotel
단양 관광 호텔..**13** A1
Darian Camping Ground
다리안 야영장...**14** B3
Hoseong Yeoinsuk 호성 여인숙...................**15** C1
Huibang Camping Ground
희방 야영장...**16** C5
Namcheon Camping Ground
남천 야영장...**17** D2
Pascal파스칼...**18** C2
Rivertel 리버텔..**19** C1
Seongsujang 성수장.......................................**20** C2
Sobaeksan Youth Hostel
소백산 유스호스텔.......................................**21** B3

EATING p321
Hanaro Supermarket
하나로 수퍼마켓..**22** C2
Jangdarisikdang 장다리 식당.......................**23** C1
Yeongyangilbeonga
영양일번가...**24** C1

TRANSPORT
Bus Stop 버스 정류장....................................**25** C5
Bus Stop 버스 정류장....................................**26** D4
Bus Stop 버스 정류장....................................**27** B3
Bus Stop 버스 정류장....................................**28** D2
Chungju Lake Ferry Terminal
충주호 선착장...**29** C2
Danyang Bus Terminal 버스 정류장...........**30** C1
Dodamsambong Pleasure Boats
도담삼봉 선착장...**31** A2
Intercity Bus Terminal
시외 버스 터미널...**32** C1

OTHER
Central Market 중앙 시장..............................**33** B2
Darianpokpo 다리안 폭포.............................**34** B3
Huibangpokpo 희방 폭포..............................**35** C4
Stadium 주경기장..**36** B1

Pascal (☎ 646 9933; s & d Sun-Thu W45,000, Fri & Sat W55,000; 🖳) Smart, new and by the lakeside.

Danyang Tourist Hotel (☎ 423 9911; s & d incl tax & service W99,000; 🖳 🖳) A 20% discount is possible from Sunday to Thursday. This upmarket hotel is out of town and facilities include a sauna, sports massage, restaurant and nightclub.

Eating

Jangdarisikdang (meals W10,000) The electronic hotpot cooker can heat up 24 hotpots at a time. The speciality is *ondal* (garlic rice), which comes with 18 side dishes and plenty of garlic, including a strong *kimchi* garlic. *Bulgogi* is another option.

Yeongyangilbeonga (meals W6000-10,000) Try *chueotang* (minced fish soup), which is a healthy Korean soup including mushroom, potato and rice cakes. It's cooked at your table in a large pot (minimum of two people) and costs W6000. It's best to avoid the goat stew, and don't forget that *yeongyangtang* (영양탕) or 'health soup' is actually a euphemism for *bosintang*, dog soup.

Getting There & Away

BOAT

The ferry terminal for boats to Chungju is on the lakefront in the centre of town. The ferry takes two hours and costs W16,000 (children under-12 W8000).

BUS

Buses connect Danyang to:

Destination	Price (W)	Duration	Frequency
Chungju	5600	1½hr	hourly
Daejeon	13,000	3hr	5 daily
Dong-Seoul	11,000	3½hr	hourly
Guinsa	2300	30min	hourly
Jecheon	2300	45min	6 daily

TRAIN

Trains go from here to Seoul station (W14,000) and to Seoul's Cheongnyangni station (W9200).

AROUND DANYANG

Daesongsan 대송산

Just behind Danyang is this wooded hill that is covered with a network of easy walking trails.

Gosudonggul 고수 동굴

This spectacular limestone **cave** (☎ 422 3072; adult/youth/child W4000/2500/1500; ⏰ 9.20am-5.20pm) is one of the most famous and popular in Korea. Endless metal catwalks and spiral staircases allow you to see the varied formations up close, and the subdued lighting is effective. Discovered in the 1970s the cave system is 1.7km long so allow at least an hour to look round. As many as 24 small creatures live in the cave so keep a look out for them. The stalagmites usually grow about 1cm every five to 10 years, so you can estimate their age.

By the entrance is the usual tourist village. You can buy local honey (W10,000 for a small pot) or try *ma* juice (W1000 a glass), which is good for your stomach and tastes like coconut cream. Korea has more health drinks than the rest of the world put together.

The cave is just a 10-minute walk from Danyang – walk across the bridge and turn right.

Nodongdonggul 노동 동굴

Not as grand or as crowded as Gosudonggul, this **cave** (adult/youth/child W4000/2500/1500; ⏰ 9.20am-5.20pm) also has plenty of limestone formations that have built up slowly over the centuries, and the steel staircases and catwalks give you a good view of them.

Unfortunately this cave has a very poor bus service – local buses (W750) leave from outside Danyang bus terminal at 9.25am and 2pm but return at 2.30pm and 5.50pm.

Cheondonggul 천동굴

Yet another **cave** (☎ 422 2972; adult/youth/child W4000/2500/1500; ⏰ 9.20am-5.20pm), this one is more of an adventure as you have to squeeze through narrow clefts and crawl through low tunnels. It's only 470m long and was discovered in 1977. In the shops and stalls that surround the entrance, seekers of the unusual can find *jinesul*, an alcoholic health beverage with a millipede in it, no doubt recommended for back or leg ache.

The cave is a 10-minute walk from the nearby bus stop and a 15-minute walk from the entrance to Sobaeksan National Park. Buses (W750, 10 minutes, 14 daily) leave from outside Danyang bus terminal for Cheondong-ri.

SOBAEKSAN NATIONAL PARK
소백산 국립공원

Sobaeksan means 'Little White Mountain' and this **park** (☎ 423 0708; adult/youth/child W1300/600/300; ☽ 8am-6pm) is one of Korea's largest. It's on a par with the better-known Seoraksan National Park, but lacks the latter's dramatic cliffs and unusual rock formations. Nevertheless, the park is rich in flora and offers good hiking trails through dense forests. The climbs are not particularly steep or dangerous, but can be hard work. Take some Sobaeksan *dongdongju* (fermented rice wine) to help you along.

Birobong (1439m) is the highest peak in the park and is most easily reached from Cheondong-ri (three hours up and two hours down if you're fit) in the northwest of the park. This route follows a picturesque 6.5km trail along the beautiful Cheondong Valley. The peak is famous for azaleas, which bloom around late May.

Guinsa 구인사

Deep in the mountains stands the isolated and impressive headquarters of the Cheontae sect of Korean Buddhism. The order was re-established by Sangwol Wongak in 1945, based on an interpretation of the Lotus Sutra made by an ancient Chinese monk called Jija Daesa. The **temple complex** (admission free) consists of more than 30 multistorey concrete buildings that line a narrow road and are connected by elevated walkways. The buildings are squeezed into a steep, narrow, thick-wooded valley. The opulence is obvious and building work is continuing

at a hectic pace. Carry on past the buildings and you reach the founder's tomb.

The temple has the atmosphere of a utopian community – everything is spotless, the gardens are beautiful, and the monks, nuns and lay members are dressed in loose-fitting grey trousers and shirts. The followers of this sect appear to be uniformly quiet, polite and well-behaved. The communal kitchen serves simple but free vegetarian meals three times a day and visitors are welcome. Hundreds sit down together to share meals of rice, soup, lettuce and vegetables.

Sleeping

Camping is available at Cheondong-ri, Namcheon-ri and Huibang. There are plenty of *minbak* that charge from W20,000 at the park entrances, but no mountain shelters inside the park.

Sobaeksan Youth Hostel (☎ 421 5555; f W50,000; ☙) Near the park entrance at Cheondong-ri, this hotel has no dormitory beds but has an outside pool (open in July and August).

Getting There & Away

Buses (W750, 10 minutes, 14 daily) leave from outside Danyang bus terminal for Cheondong-ri. Express buses (W2300, 30 minutes, hourly) leave Danyang bus terminal hourly for Guinsa. There are also direct buses to Guinsa from Dong-Seoul (W12,200, three hours 40 minutes, hourly). Local buses depart from outside Danyang bus terminal for other entry points into the park.

North Korea

TONY WHEELER

North Korea

Continuing to defy the odds stacked heavily against it, North Korea is a land where ancient myths bend to modern political reality, where the mysterious dictator Kim Jong Il is believed to control the weather, and his father, dead for a decade, remains head of state.

The Cold War may just be a distant memory to most of us, but here time is frozen somewhere in the early 1980s. There is no other country on earth where visitors must be escorted at all times outside their hotel by two guides, and where mobile phones and the Internet are against the law. These zealous measures to keep the country isolated make North Korea a magnet for those seeking to experience something truly different; and while travel here is neither easy nor cheap, the rewards for making the trip are abundant.

The communist state – turned feudal kingdom by the Kim dynasty – allows a small influx of tourists each year to witness a few of its fascinating show-piece cities and inspiring alpine resorts. Tourism in North Korea is strictly on the government's own terms, the dual purposes being to promote the Kim dynasty among impressionable foreigners and to bring foreign currency to an economically crippled nation.

Reactions to the Democratic People's Republic of Korea – the official name of North Korea – differ widely. Much has been said, both true and false about North Korea, but visiting yourself gives you the opportunity to make up your own mind.

HIGHLIGHTS

- Be amazed at **Pyongyang's** (p344) vast architectural wealth
- Feel the full force of Cold War tensions in a visit to the Demilitarized Zone at **Panmunjeom** (p351)
- Enjoy pristine mountain walks in the stunning resort of **Kumgangsan** (p353)
- Revisit the past at the ancient Korean capital of **Kaesong** (p350)
- Explore the remote far north and Korea's highest peak and holy mountain **Paekdusan** (p354)

FAST FACTS:

- Area: 120,540 sq km
- Population: 23 million
- Currency: North Korean won (170KPW = €1) on the black market
- Percentage of GDP spent on the military: 31.3%
- Number of movies Kim Jong Il owns: 20,000
- Minimum military service for men: 6 years
- Percentage of the country that is uninhabitable mountain: 80%
- Number of Internet cafes: 1

GETTING STARTED

North Korea is one of the world's most unusual destinations – while visiting it will instantly make you the most interesting person you know, it's one that can hit you where it hurts financially. Aside from the money, the other hindrance is whether or not you will be granted a visa (see p360).

Once there, however, the trips usually run like clockwork. Two guides will accompany you everywhere you go outside the hotel and control what you see and the spiel you hear while seeing it. Forward planning is a must – almost everything you want to see needs to be approved before your arrival – ad hoc arrangements make the guides very nervous and thus less fun to be around. Being accompanied is non-negotiable, and if you are not prepared to be controlled throughout the duration of your stay, North Korea is not a destination you should consider. By far the best option is to enjoy a positive and friendly relationship with your guides, as once they trust you and like you, they will help you make the most of your trip.

When to Go

Like South Korea, the North has four distinct seasons. Winters are dry but colder than in the South, while the summers are humid and often rainy. As North Korean tours can be fairly arduous, those who suffer from the heat may want to avoid the sticky height of summer in July and August. Tourists are not usually admitted in December and early January; while the energy crisis remains critical, visitors would be best avoiding all the freezing winter months, although it's highly unlikely that hotels used by foreigners would be affected by power cuts.

The best time to plan a trip is during one of Pyongyang's Mass Games or during a national holiday. Special performances, which have been rehearsed for months, can be included in the itinerary. During these periods train and plane tickets are harder to obtain, so ensure that you have booked well in advance. In general, the most pleasant months for a visit are April, May, June, September and October.

Costs & Money

As a tourist, North Korea is no budget destination. Opportunities to cut costs by staying in youth hostels do not exist. As well as paying for your bed and board in advance, you will also have to pay for two guides and a driver – which makes group tourism one of the few measures that can save you money.

As a rough guide, solo travellers should bank on paying about €170 per day for guides, hotel and full board. This is reduced

---

DON'T LEAVE HOME WITHOUT...

Anything medical or electrical that you will need during your stay; this includes simple everyday products such as pain killers, tampons, condoms and soap. Everything from film to batteries for your camera are best brought in too – such basic items are available but their price and quality can be quite different from elsewhere. As most trips are no longer than a week, bringing fruit from China is a great idea for snacking between sights – even a bag of apples is a luxury item in Pyongyang. Just as important is what not to bring, as these rules are quite strict. Mobile phones and laptop computers are all best left at home. Small token gifts for your guides are a good idea – pens, postcards of your hometown or chocolates will always go down well. Most of all bring a very good sense of humour and an open mind – you'll need both to make North Korea enjoyable and rewarding.

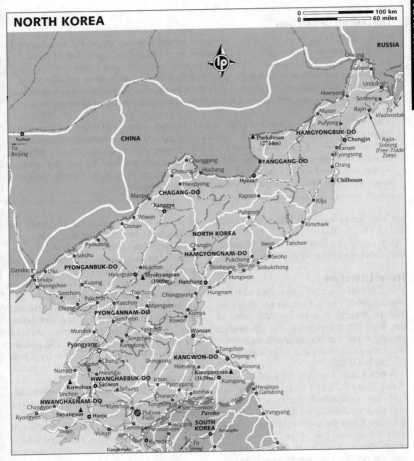

NORTH KOREA

to between €125 and €85 per day if you go as part of a group, and can be further reduced the larger the tour group. Note that the Euro is the accepted currency for visitors to use (see p358).

Once in North Korea, the only major expenses will be the souvenirs and other gifts that are on sale at every tourist attraction. Apart from evening drinks and telephone/fax costs, there is little opportunity to spend your money elsewhere.

Tours

Every visitor to North Korea must book all their accommodation, guides and transport with the government monolith Ryohaengsa – North Korea's version of Intourist for anyone

lucky enough to have visited pre-perestroika Russia. Booking your tour through a travel agent will simply mean that they have the job of dealing with Ryohaengsa on your behalf. The advantage of this is that travel agents are IATA (International Air Transport Association) bonded and will return your money if your trip is cancelled – always a very real possibility with North Korea – whereas Ryohaengsa will not. The number of North Korean specialists is very limited – but those who run tours are listed on p361. The main office of **Ryohaengsa** (☎ +86-10-6437 6666/3133; fax 6436 9089; Korean International Travel Company, 2nd fl, Yanxiang, No A2 Jiangtai Rd, Chaoyang District, Qionghuating) in Beijing is the office most used to dealing with individual travellers. Ryohaengsa also

---

THE LEGEND OF TAN'GUN

In the year 2333 BC, a son of the Lord of Heaven named Hwanung descended from heaven with 3000 retainers to the mountain of Taebaeksan and established a 'City of God' on its summit. Modern scholarship has been unable to locate this 'Taebaeksan', and Korean traditionalists have varying opinions: some favour the great mountain with the same name in Gangwon-do, South Korea; more favour Myohyangsan, just north of Pyongyang; but most hold that Paekdusan must have been the spot, being closest to heaven and having such outstanding natural features (see p354).

According to the story, a bear and a tiger desired to become human, and beseeched 'Heavenly King Hwanung'. He gave them bundles of garlic and mugwort (a green medicinal herb, common in Korea) and directed them to eat those foods (the first *kimchi*!) while avoiding the sun for 100 days. The tiger failed the test, but the bear succeeded and emerged from the cave as a young woman. She mated with Hwanung and produced a son named Tan'gun. He became the first Korean king, establishing his capital at the walled city of Pyongyang.

---

has branches in Dandong, Liaoning Province and in Yanji in Jilin.

See Solo Travellers (p359) for information about travelling on your own.

Travel Literature

The choice of evocative literature and travel writing about North Korea is severely limited. In general, it is far better to turn to the Web for travelogues and up-to-date writing about the country, although there are some good books that offer a glance at life inside DPRK.

North Korea Through the Looking Glass (Kong Dan Oh, Ralph C. Hassig, Kongdan Oh) has established itself as a classic overview of DPRK politics and society, although it has the usual limitations of any work concerning one of the most secretive governments on earth – much is conjecture and cannot be adequately supported by documented evidence. For that, it's still a fascinating introduction to the country.

Bruce Cummings has written over a dozen books about Korea, the division of the peninsula and its future. Highly recommended is *War and Television* that recounts his experiences recording interviews in North Korea for a documentary on the Korean War. His other authoritative histories of the peninsula include *Korea's Place in the Sun*, one chapter of which gives an impressive analysis of the DPRK's political culture.

For a very readable, yet still substantial account of North-South relations since 1948, Don Oberdorfer's *The Two Koreas* is excellent. Oberdorfer puts the politics of both countries squarely in the context of constant efforts by both governments to reunify the peninsula, by peaceful means or otherwise.

Perhaps the closest North Korea has come to its own Gulag Archipelago is the horrific *The Aquariums of Pyongyang: Ten Years in the North Korean Gulag* by Kang Chol-hwan. This book describes the hell on earth that is life as a political prisoner here. Not for the faint-hearted, but definitely recommended for anyone seeking the whole picture. *Pyongyang: The Hidden History of the Hidden Capital* by Chris Springer is a newly published city guide. This glossy and informative work tells the stories behind the mysterious buildings, monuments and ministries of the capital, and is by far the most detailed guide to Pyongyang available. There's also a plethora of guides produced within North Korea.

Internet Resources

The scarcity of information from North Korea has created a large Web community of DPRK-watchers, and although every subject from annual grain production to Kim Jong Il jokes are covered, the bias of each website should always be borne in mind – few people are indifferent towards North Korea. The following sites offer the best coverage of events and developments from the hermit state.

www.pyongyangsquare.com One of the very best sites for North Korean news and views. Despite being a little dry, it gives a simple and intelligent overview of all economic, political and diplomatic developments from the DPRK.

www.nautilus.org The website of a very highbrow US research fund called the Nautilus Institute for Security and

Kim Jong Il admires Mt Chilbo (p329) scenery

Pyongyang metro (p346)

Reunification Highway (p351)

TONY

Pyongyang (p340) city skyline

Mansudae Grand Monument (p341),
Pyongyang

TONY WHEELER

TONY

Kim Il Sung, Kim Jong Il and grateful farmers
survey the bountiful harvest, North Korea (p323)

Sustainability. Its stated mission is to 'solve interrelated critical global problems' – and this puts North Korea at the top of the agenda.

www.korea-np.co.jp The North Korean government's mouthpiece in Japan. Along with eulogies of the Great Leader and anti-American diatribes, there are some useful news archives and information, giving the official version of international events. A good introduction to the world the way Pyongyang sees it.

www.chosunjournal.com Maintained largely by Koreans living and studying in the United States. Its focus is on human rights abuse and the injustices of life in DPRK – essential reading, although unsurprisingly focused on the negatives.

www.stat.ualberta.ca/people/schmu/nk.html Lists the best selection of DPRK travelogues from the

Web. These include two particularly good recent ones by Arne Eilers and Scott Fisher, a witty South Korean resident whose linguistic abilities made him quite a handful for his guides.

SNAPSHOT

After decades of icy deadlock, the North and South appeared to make a huge step towards reunification in June 2000, when then South Korean President Kim Dae-jung flew to Pyongyang for a three-day summit with Kim Jong Il. The stated aim of both governments since division in the 1940s, reunification is still the burning issue for North Koreans. However, political change in both Seoul and Washington since the

---

TONY DOES THE DPRK by Tony Wheeler

I have a fascination with cities and countries that seem to exist at a 90-degree angle to reality. In the world today North Korea is undoubtedly the best example of the phenomenon, and when George W Bush – himself a denizen of a strange parallel universe – decided to skewer North Korea on his axis of evil I simply had to go.

Unfortunately a solo visit to the hermit kingdom is really impossible – you can go by yourself but it's still on an organised tour – but one glance at the group which assembled under Nicholas Bonner's watchful eye at the Beijing railway station was enough to confirm this would be no ordinary group tour.

Day 1 – Our overnight train from Beijing arrived at the Chinese border town of Dondang in the early morning. Remarkably there's a giant Mao statue still standing in the square outside the railway station. That evening (the train is very slow) we arrived in Pyongyang and immediately went to pay homage to the Great Leader's Mansudae statue.

Day 2 – Apart from our little group, Pyongyang International Airport was deserted. We flew up to the northwest corner of the country then took a bus along the beautiful coastline and in to the forested mountains of Outer Chilbo.

Day 3 – Another flight took us to the Paekdu region where Lake Chon's icy surface crosses the border into China. It was here where Kim Jong-Il was *said* to be born.

Day 4 – Back in Pyongyang we go to the Arirang Mass Games in the 150,000-seat May Day Stadium, the world's biggest stadium. In the stands opposite 20,000 kids flip open card-books with synchronised precision to make a steady stream of pictures, while tens of thousands more children, women, men and soldiers dance across the stadium floor. If wars are ever decided by whose army dances best the North Koreans have it wrapped up.

Day 5 – A day's solid sightseeing covers everything from the Fatherland Liberation War Museum (see how North Korea almost singlehandedly defeated the Japanese in WWII) to the Great People's Study Hall and the spyship USS *Pueblo* before we end the evening in the Egypt Palace Karaoke Bar in the hotel basement. For me the day's highlight was a chance to wander unescorted for 45 minutes in the shopping delights of Department Store No 1.

Day 6 – A bus takes us across the peninsula to the port town of Wonsan. At our hotel, the restaurant staff have moved some dividers between our table and a tour group of well-lubricated Chinese who are singing loudly. Nick leaps from his seat and pulls the dividers aside, yelling in Chinese 'We will have no divisions here!'. A roar goes up and at their invitation we render our own drinking songs.

Day 7 – After a visit to a collective farm and a park temple we cross back over the peninsula to Pyongyang. We were all so knocked out by our visit to the Mass Games that we organise a second showing.

Day 8 – We barrel down the six-lane (but extremely empty) highway to the perhaps somewhat inaccurately named DMZ, there's nothing very demilitarized about it. On the way back to Pyongyang we make an all too brief stop in the provincial town of Kaesong and at the beautiful hillside Kongmin mausoleums just outside the town.

Day 9 – The airport is rather busier today when we fly out to Shenyang in China. Remarkably an Air Korea flight from Seoul taxis in right behind us; the bags from North and South are jumbled together on the luggage carousel.

summit has meant that the momentum of 2000 has been severely reduced and deadlock has again set in.

Still, the economic reforms of 2002 point to the possible future liberalisation of the country's economy, if not its political system. While workers enjoyed vast wage increases, they were also required to pay market prices for their apartments and electricity for the first time since the country's formation. The reforms include a scaling back of the public distribution system for food – therefore increasing the role of the already important private markets in the country. The policy suggests a North Korean attempt to emulate China under Deng Xiaoping, when market reforms were introduced while social control remained absolute. Inflation is the obvious worry in such a climate, and within the first six months of the reforms, the price of rice had indeed rocketed by 4000%. Yet commentators are unanimous that things can hardly get any worse: diplomats in Pyongyang have indicated that North Korean industry is running at about 10–15% capacity, and this could be Kim Jong Il's last chance to save the beleaguered regime.

Propaganda is on every corner in North Korea, and a unique interpretation of affairs will be revealed by speaking to anyone you meet or reading any official mouthpieces or other publications. You will be told that the United States started the Korean War, that South Korea is a scandal-ridden puppet regime, and that it is in the West where everyone is being lied to. Evidence cited for South Korea's corruption runs from the availability of pornography to the fact that women smoke in public.

North Korea is one of the most highly militarised societies on earth. Men and women in uniform are everywhere, particularly visible in Pyongyang. Both sexes are obliged to devote years of military service to the state, and the army is the subject of most films, songs, books and art here. Moreover, the military is key to Kim Jong Il's tenure on the DPRK leadership – his ascendancy seems to have seen a strengthening of the military's role in government and his position as supreme commander is popularly considered to be his real power base, rather than the weakened Korean Worker's Party.

After 50 years of total repression, there are no surviving networks of dissent. Apart from the social divisions inside the country, daily life is marked at all levels by the obligatory attendance of political education meetings most nights of the week. City streets are deserted after nightfall, as there is often no electricity to power the streetlights, and, even more significantly, nothing to do. A standard North Korean evening will involve listening to TV or radio reports of joyful masses surpassing their grain quotas or the latest proclamation of the Great Leader.

Yet part of the excitement and fascination of the country is trying to divine the real from the fake and attempting to see past the ideology. While you may be horrified, amazed or awe-struck by what you see in North Korea, you won't be able to help yourself seeing the world from a different perspective once you've been here.

HISTORY

The geopolitical divide of the Korean peninsula since 1945 could be seen as an interesting reflection of the historic differences between the North and South. While ethnically homogenous, Koreans in the north had been the poorer cousins of those in the south long before the tragic 20th-century split. In this sense, while still a source of great bitterness to both the North and South, the division of Korea is perhaps not as completely without foundation as that of Germany or Vietnam.

In AD 668, the far-southeastern Silla kingdom, in alliance with Tang China, conquered the more sophisticated northern Goguryeo kingdom (comprising the northern half of the peninsula and most of Manchuria), losing most of Goguryeo lands to China in the process. From the northern point of view, this was only the first of a long string of betrayals of the Korean nation to foreign powers by southerners acting for their own benefit. Silla proceeded to oppressively rule what remained of Goguryeo for 250 years, sowing seeds of resentment that still bloom today.

The Goryeo dynasty (918–1392), which succeeded the Silla, was founded by a general of north-central origins, and some northern families gained importance in its government but, overall, southern

THE GENERAL SHERMAN & USS PUEBLO

During the 'hermit kingdom' phase of the Joseon dynasty, one of Korea's first encounters with Westerners was the ill-fated attempt of the American ship the *General Sherman* to sail up the Taedong River to Pyongyang in 1866. It arrogantly ignored warnings to turn around and leave, and insisted on trade. When it ran aground on a sand bar just below Pyongyang, locals burnt it and killed all those on board, including a Welsh missionary and the Chinese and Malay crew. An American military expedition later pressed the Seoul government for reparations for the loss, then the incident was otherwise virtually forgotten in the South. However northerners have always regarded it with great pride, as being their first of many battles with, and victories over, the hated Yankee imperialist enemy.

Also of great pride to the North Koreans is the 'fact' that none other than the Great Leader's great-grandfather had not only participated in burning the ship, but had been instrumental in the defeat of the Yankees in Pyongyang. Today, all that is left of the *General Sherman* is a plaque. The site is over-shadowed by the nearby ship the *Pueblo*. This US surveillance vessel was seized by the North Koreans off the east coast of Korea in January 1968 during a heightening of tensions between the North and South. For a fee you can step aboard and hear another lecture on the violations of the cease-fire agreement by the US.

clans maintained their socio-economic dominance.

Northerners felt especially mistreated by southerners throughout the Joseon dynasty (1392–1910), while ruled by a Jeolla-do clan and their mostly southern cronies in an openly subservient relationship to China. Northerners had fewer chances to advance to the ruling class and bore the brunt of frequent raids and invasions from Manchuria; they saw very few benefits in exchange for their onerous tax payments. With Korea's economy based on rice, the south, being less mountainous, warmer and better watered, was naturally wealthier. Little was ever done to redress the imbalance, or pull the northern populace back from the brink of starvation during their frequent famines. The government only seemed to acknowledge the worth of the taller, stronger, tougher northern mountain-dwellers when they needed soldiers to fight off another 'barbarian' incursion.

At the end of the Joseon dynasty, after Korea had opened up to foreigners, almost the only successful Western economic venture was a large gold mine north of Pyongyang. By providing difficult and dangerous jobs for northern workers at very low wages, with all profits sent to Seoul and abroad, it came to be seen as southsanctioned foreign theft of the North's resources. At the same time, American Christian missionaries found the northern regions to be fertile (spiritual) soil, rapidly gaining converts by exploiting the resentment of poor northerners towards the corrupt and exclusive Confucian culture of Seoul.

Japanese Occupation

The Japanese occupation of the Korean peninsula between 1910 and 1945 was one of the darkest periods in Korean history; the occupation forces press-ganged Koreans into slave labour teams, to construct factories, mines and heavy-industry – particularly in the north. Moreover, the use of Korean girls as 'comfort women' for Japanese soldiers – a euphemism for enforced prostitution – remains a huge cause of resentment.

The Japanese conquest of Korea was, in northern eyes, the result of yet another sell-out of the national sovereignty by corrupt southern officials. Most of the guerrilla warfare conducted against the Japanese police and army took place in the northern provinces and neighbouring Manchuria; northerners are still proud of having carried a disproportionate burden in the anti-Japan struggle. In fact, modern history books from Pyongyang imply that Kim Il Sung defeated the Japanese nearly single-handedly (with a bit of help from loyal comrades and his infant son).

While his feats have certainly been exaggerated, Kim Il Sung was a strong resistance leader, although not a strong enough force to rid Korea of the Japanese. This was left to the Red Army, who, in the closing days of WWII, entered Manchuria and Northern Korea, as the Japanese forces retreated. The United States suddenly realised that the strategic importance of the peninsula was too great for it to be left in Soviet hands. Despite an agreement at Yalta to give joint custodianship of Korea to the USSR, USA and China, no concrete plans had been made to this end, and the State Department assigned the division of the country to two young officers, who, working from a *National Geographic* map, divided Korea across the 38th parallel.

American forces gradually moved in from Japan, while Soviet forces kept to the dividing line. The intention to have democratic elections across the whole peninsula soon became hostage to Cold War tensions, and after the North refused to allow UN inspectors to cross the 38th parallel, the Republic of Korea was proclaimed in the South on 15 August 1948, while the North proclaimed the Democratic People's Republic just three weeks later on 9 September 1948.

The People's Republic

Stalin, it is rumoured, personally chose the 33-year-old Kim Il Sung to lead the new republic. The ambitious and fiercely nationalistic Kim was an unknown quantity, although Stalin is said to have favoured him due to his youth. He would have had no idea that Kim would outlive not only him and Mao Zedong, but communism itself, to become the world's longest serving head of state. As soon as Kim had assumed the leadership of North Korea, he applied to Stalin to sanction an invasion of the South. The

man of steel refused Kim twice in 1949, but, perhaps bolstered by Mao's victory over the nationalists in China and the USSR's own A-bomb project bearing dangerous fruit, he gave Kim the green light a year later.

The brutal and pointless Korean War of 1950–1953 saw a stunning North Korean advance into the South, where it almost drove US forces into the sea, followed by an equally impressive counter-attack by the United States and United Nations, which managed to occupy most of North Korea. As the situation began to look bleak, Kim advocated retreating to the hills and waging guerrilla warfare against the South, unaware that China's Mao Zedong had decided to covertly help the North by sending in the People's Liberation Army in the guise of 'volunteers'. Once the PLA moved in and the balance of powers stabilised again, the North pushed the front down to the original 38th parallel, and, with two million dead, the original stalemate was more or less retained. The armistice agreement obliged both sides to withdraw 2000m from the ceasefire line, thus creating a huge nature reserve in the form of the Demilitarized Zone, still in existence today.

Despite the Chinese having alienated Kim by taking control of the war – Chinese commander Peng Dehuai apparently treated Kim as a subordinate, much to the future Great Leader's anger – the Chinese remained in North Korea and helped with the massive task of rebuilding a nation all but razed to the ground by bombing.

Simultaneously, following his ill-fated attempt to reunite the nation, Kim Il Sung began a process of political consolidation

---

TIME LINE

1392 The start of the Joseon dynasty, unsympathetic to northerners
1866 The *General Sherman* goes aground on the Taedong River, all on board are killed
1910 Japanese occupation begins
1948 Declaration of the Democratic People's Republic of Korea
1950 North Korean invasion of South Korea
1953 Korean War ends in stalemate
1980 Kim Jong Il anointed 'Dear Leader' and successor to his father
1983 North Korean bomb kills many South Korean cabinet members in Rangoon
1994 Kim Il Sung dies
1995 Floods devastate North Korea
2000 Kim Dae-jung and Kim Jong Il meet in an unprecedented summit in Pyongyang
2002 President George W Bush labels North Korea part of his 'Axis of Evil'

and brutal repression. He executed his foreign minister and those he believed threatened him in an attempt to take overall control of the Korean Workers' Party. Following Khrushchev's 1956 denunciation of Stalin's personality cult, Central Committee member Yun Kong-hum stood up at one of its meetings and denounced Kim for similar crimes. Yun was never heard from again, and it was the death knell for North Korean democracy.

Unlike many communist leaders, Kim's outlandish personality cult was generated almost immediately – the sobriquet *suryong* or 'Great Leader' was employed in everyday conversation in the North by the 1960s – and the initial lip-service paid to democracy and multiparty elections was soon forgotten.

The first decade under Kim Il Sung saw vast material improvements in the lives of workers and peasants. Literacy and full health care were soon followed by access to higher education and the full militarisation of the state. However, by the 1970s, North Korea slipped into recession, one from which it has never recovered. During this time, in which Kim Il Sung had been raised to a divine figure in North Korean society, an *éminence grise* referred to only as the 'party centre' in official-speak began to emerge from the grey anonymity of Kim's henchmen. At the 1980 party congress this enigmatic figure, to which all kinds of wondrous deeds had been attributed, was revealed to be none other than the Great Leader's son, Kim Jong Il. He was awarded several important public posts, including a seat in the politburo, and even given the honorific title 'Dear Leader'. Mini-Me was designated hereditary successor to the Great Leader, and in 1991 made supreme commander of the Korean Army although he had never served a day in it. From 1989 until 1994, Kim father and son were almost always pictured together, praised in tandem and generally shown to be working in close proximity, preparing the North Korean people for a hereditary dynasty far more in keeping with Confucianism than communism.

Beyond Perestroika

It was during the late 1980s, as communism shattered throughout Eastern Europe, that North Korea's development began to differ strongly from that of other socialist nations. Its greatest sponsor, the Soviet Union, disintegrated in 1991, leaving the North at a loss for the subsidies it ironically needed to maintain its façade of autarky.

North Korea, having always played China and the USSR off against one another, turned to the Chinese, who have reluctantly played godfather to the DPRK ever since. Quite why the People's Republic has done so has never been explicit. Chinese 'communism' has produced the fastest expanding economy in the world and any ideological ties with Maoism remain purely surface, while China's increasingly close relationship to both the South and Japan also makes its reluctant support for the Kim regime all the more incongruous. Yet China remains the North's one trusted ally, although several times since the early nineties, Beijing has laid down the law to Pyongyang, even withholding oil deliveries to underscore its unhappiness at the North's continuous brinkmanship.

The regime's brinkmanship did pay off in 1994 however, when North Korea negotiated an agreement with the Clinton administration in which it agreed to cancel its controversial nuclear programme in return for US energy supplies in the short term. This was to be followed by an international consortium constructing two light water reactors for North Korean energy needs in the long-term. All in all, a diplomatic victory for the North who had negotiated on equal terms with the United States.

Midway through negotiations, Kim Il Sung, founding father of North Korea, gave way to a massive heart attack and died. In another tragic irony, he had spent the day personally inspecting the accommodation being prepared for the planned visit of South Korean president Kim Young-sam. This summit between the two leaders would have been the first ever meeting between the heads of state of the two nations, and Kim Il Sung's stance towards the South had noticeably changed in the last year of his life.

The Great Leader's death rendered the North weaker and even less predictable than before. Optimistic Korea-watchers, including many within South Korea's government, expected the collapse of the regime to be imminent without its charismatic leader. In a move that was to further derail the reunification process, Kim Young-sam's government in Seoul did not therefore send condolences for Kim's death to the North – something even President Clinton felt obliged to do. This slight to a man considered (officially, at least) to be a living god, was a miscalculation that set back any progress another five years.

While the expected collapse did not occur, neither did any visible sign of succession by the Dear Leader. North Korea was more mysterious than ever, and in the three years following Kim Il Sung's death, speculation was rampant that a military faction had taken control in Pyongyang, and that continuing power struggles between them and Kim Jong Il meant that there was no overall leader.

Kim Jong Il finally assumed the mantle of power in October 1997, after a three-year mourning period. Surprisingly, the presidency rested with the late Kim Il Sung, making him the world's only dead head of state, not to mention the longest serving, currently standing at 56 years, out-serving even Fidel Castro and Queen Elizabeth II. Kim Jong Il's power-base is believed to be centred on his control of the military rather than his role in government. As supreme military commander and chairman of the National Defence Commission, he holds sway over the nation's all-powerful third estate.

However, the backdrop to Kim Jong Il's succession was horrific. While the North Korean economy had been contracting since the collapse of vital Soviet supplies and subsidies to the DPRK's ailing industrial infrastructure in the early 1990s, the terrible floods of 1995 led quickly to disaster. Breaking with a strict tradition of self-reliance (of course, one that had never reflected reality – aid had long been received secretly from both communist allies and even the South two months previously), the North appealed to the United Nations and the world community for urgent food aid.

So desperate was the Kim regime that it even acceded to unprecedented UN demands for access to the whole country for their own field workers, something that would have previously been unthinkable in North Korea's staunchly secretive military

climate. Aid workers were horrified by what they saw – malnutrition everywhere, and the beginnings of starvation, which led, over the next few years, to the death of between one and two million people.

Towards Engagement?

Kim Jong Il's pragmatism and relative openness to change came to the fore in the years following the devastation, and a series of initiatives to promote reconciliation with both the South and the United States were implemented. These reached their height with a swiftly convened Pyongyang summit between the South's Kim Dae-jung and the Dear Leader in June 2000; the first ever meeting on such a level between the two countries. The two leaders, their countries ready at any second to launch holocaust against one another, held hands in the limousine from the airport to the guesthouse in an unprecedented gesture of solidarity. The summit paved the way for US Secretary of State Madeleine Albright's visit to Pyongyang later the same year. Kim Jong Il's aim was to have his country legitimised through a visit from the American president himself. However, as Clinton's second term ended and George W Bush assumed power in Washington, the climate swiftly changed.

In his 2002 State of the Union address, President Bush labelled the North as part of an 'Axis of Evil' – a phrase that has since passed into everyday language and haunted the DPRK leadership. The year that followed was to signal yet another low in the beleaguered nation's diplomatic endgame.

New lows were reached in 2002, when North Korea resumed its nuclear programme, claiming it had no choice due to American oil supplies being stopped and the two promised light water reactors remaining incomplete. Since then a climate of containment has once again predominated.

Against all odds, North Korea has survived the decade since the end of the Cold War, and the Kim regime seems to be in full control of the country – once more going against the predictions of many Korea-watchers. How long the status quo can go on remains a mystery, but the fact that Kim Jong Il saw the country through its most devastating famine on record, complete

KIM JONG IL AND THE SUCCESSION

Kim Jong Il has provoked much conjecture, myth and rumour. Several members of his inner circle who defected in the 1980s and 1990s have spoken out about the recluse, giving fascinating glimpses of his luxurious lifestyle, as well as insight into his personality.

His early years were spent shielded from reality in his father's palaces. His mother died in childbirth, and his younger brother drowned at a young age. By the 1970s, the adult Kim was living a playboy lifestyle, apparently riding a Harley Davidson, womanising and drinking. Yet, by the end of the 1970s, he was involved in the everyday running of North Korea. When anointed successor to his father in 1980, Kim Jong Il was put in charge of the North's espionage and thus terrorist networks, and it is believed that he gave instructions for the assassination of South Korean cabinet ministers in Rangoon in 1983, and ordered the bombing of a South Korean airliner in 1987.

His university tutor Hwang Jang Yop defected to the South in 1997, and gave the following portrait of the diminutive demagogue: 'He has only been worshipped by the people without being controlled by anyone...As a result he has become impatient and has a violent character... He considers the party and military his own and does not care about the national economy.'

Kim's appearance, at 5'2" in heels, with a pompadour more befitting a Regency dandy, has been the subject of much ridicule, not least from the Dear Leader himself. 'What do you think of my physique?' he asked kidnapped South Korean actress Choi Eun-Hee, 'Small as midget's turd, aren't I?' he answered for her. Yet not fitting the average dictator's profile has proved an advantage. His famous reticence – the only phrase uttered in public was, 'Glory to the people's heroic military' at a parade in 1992 – has meant he has been feared as a volatile unknown quantity the world over.

His diplomatic blitz in 2000 and 2001 therefore amazed the world, whose leaders admitted that they were dealing with a sharp, good humoured and flexible leader, albeit one in absolute control of his country. Indeed, his adopted daughter, Lee Nam-ok, who also defected in 1997 described the Dear Leader as a calm and caring man, whom she had never seen angry or inebriated.

The next big question is who will follow Kim Jong Il? In his sixties, it is likely that the succession will be decided shortly, and the two main contenders are his sons, half-brothers Kim Jong-Nam and Kim Jong-Chol.

Kim Jong-Nam, had a similar childhood to his father – cloistered away, apparently as Kim Il Sung did not approve of Jong-Nam's actress mother, and never acknowledged his grandson.

Until recently Jong-Nam was believed to be the first choice as successor. However, this changed in 2001, when a man claiming to be Kim Jong-Nam, and looking surprisingly like the Dear Leader, was arrested in Japan for travelling on a forged Dominican passport. He told police that he wanted to see Tokyo and Disneyland. Jong-Nam has never returned to Pyongyang and is believed to be living in Russia.

Since then, a new movement in Pyongyang has elevated Kim Jong Il's current wife, Ko Yong-Hee, to that of a political entity. Ko is mother to Kim's second son Kim Jong-Chol, and it seems almost certain that he is being promoted as the next *suryong* or Great Leader. In his early twenties, Jong-Chol is still an unknown quantity, but this seems to be a requisite for North Korean demagogues-to-be.

international isolation and recurring energy crises suggests that the quick dissolution of the hermit state is far from certain.

THE CULTURE
The National Psyche

The North Koreans are a fiercely nationalistic and proud people. Most refugees confirm that the popular affection for Kim Il Sung was largely genuine, while Li'l Kim has not endeared himself to the populace in the same way. While North Koreans will always be polite to foreigners, there remains a large amount of antipathy towards both the United States and Japan. Both due to propaganda and the very real international isolation they feel, North Koreans have a sense of being hemmed in on all sides – threatened particularly by the South and the United States, but also by Japan. The changes over the past decade in both China and Russia have also been cause for concern. These two big brothers who guaranteed survival and independence have both sought rapprochement with the South.

On a personal level, Koreans are very good humoured and hospitable, yet remain conservative socially, the combination of centuries of Confucianism and decades of communism. By all means smile and say hello to people you see on the streets, as North Koreans have been instructed to give foreigners a warm welcome, but do not think about taking photos of people without the explicit permission of both your guide and subject. Similarly, giving gifts to ordinary people could result in very unpleasant consequences for them, so ask your guide at any point what is appropriate.

Kids are remarkably forthcoming and will wave back and smile ecstatically when they see a foreign tour group. Personal relationships with North Koreans who are not your tour guides or business colleagues will be impossible. Men should bear in mind that any physical contact with a Korean woman will be seen as unusual, so while shaking hands may be acceptable, do not greet a Korean female with a kiss in the European manner.

Korea is still a very patriarchal society, and despite the equality of women on an ideological level, this is not the case in day-to-day life.

Lifestyle

Trying to give a sense of day-to-day North Korean life is a challenge indeed. It's difficult to overstate the ramifications of half a century of Stalinism – and it is no overstatement to say that North Korea is the most closed and secretive nation on earth. Facts meld with rumour about the real situation in the country, however, power cuts and food shortages are still everyday events in DPRK – although North Koreans are told to attribute both to American imperialism, leading to the comic tradition of Koreans shouting 'blame America!' whenever the lights go out. Chilling campaign titles such as 1992's 'Let us eat two meals a day' give a good sense of what the Korean Workers Party is doing to the population food-wise.

The system of political apartheid that exists in North Korea has effectively created a three-strata society. All people are divided up by *taedo*, a curious post-feudalist caste system, into loyal, neutral or hostile categories in relation to the regime. The hostile are deprived of everything, and often end up in forced labour camps in entire family groups, maybe for nothing more than having South Korean relatives or for one family member being caught crossing into China. The neutral have little or nothing, but are not persecuted, while the loyal enjoy everything from Pyongyang residency and desk jobs (at the lower levels) to Party membership and the privileges of the nomenclature. At the top of the tree, the Kim dynasty and its vast array of courtiers, security guards, staff and other flunkies enjoy great wealth and luxury.

It's hard to overstate the importance of the military in North Korean culture – as witnessed by the Military First campaign, which sees priorities in all fields going to the army. North Korea has the world's fifth-largest standing army and the social status of anyone in uniform is very high – rations increase in proportion to the individual's importance to the regime's survival.

North Korea is predictably austere – the six-day week and obligatory political education classes in the evenings make for an exhausted populace – but this makes Sundays a real event, and Koreans visibly beam as they relax, go on picnics, sing songs and drink in small groups all over the country. A glance at the showcase shops and department stores in Pyongyang confirms that there is a tiny number of imported goods available to the general population. The few lucky enough to have access to special party shops can enjoy foreign luxuries. Testimonies taken from North Korean refugees in China give a picture of daily life in the rural north of the country – many refugees' hair has fallen out due to malnourishment and they tell stories of surviving on eating grass and rats.

While in the 20 years following the Korean War it could genuinely be claimed that Kim Il Sung's government increased the standard of living in the North immensely, bringing literacy and health care to every part of the country, the regression since the collapse of communism throughout the world has been just as spectacular, and people are now just as materially poor as their grandparents were in the early 1950s. Outside Pyongyang the standard of living is far worse and this is visible on the street, although the carefully planned tour routes will never fully expose the poverty of the nation to the casual tourist.

Population

The current population of North Korea is anyone's guess. Officially it stands at 23 million, but the devastation wrought by the famine in the late 1990s has had untold effects on the country and its people. In a watershed announcement in 1999, the North Korean government shocked the world by admitting that as many as 3 million people had died of starvation since 1995. How closely this corresponds to the real figure is still completely unknown. Terrifyingly enough, some North Korean defectors in China have suggested that the population could have dropped to as little as 15 million over the past decade.

All of the 2.2 million inhabitants of Pyongyang are from backgrounds deemed

to be loyal to the Kim regime – and with a complete lack of free movement in the country (all citizens need special permission to leave their town of residence) no visitor is likely to see those termed 'hostile' – anyway, most people in this unfortunate category are in hard labour camps miles from anywhere. All North Korean citizens have been obliged to wear a 'loyalty' badge since 1970 featuring Kim Il Sung's portrait. Since the 1980s, Kim Jong Il badges have also been worn. You can be certain that anyone without one is a foreigner.

Sport

North Korea looked on jealously when Seoul hosted the 1988 Olympics, and in the ultimate unsporting act, blew up a South Korean airliner to frighten people from attending. However, the bad feeling generated by the South's popularity with the rest of the world was put to one side when both North and South marched under a pan-peninsula flag at the Sydney Olympics. Soccer remains the most popular spectator sport, and seeing a match in Pyongyang is often a possibility, as well as offering the chance to get as close

---

NORTH-KOREA SPEAK

It's a good idea to familiarise yourself with some of the linguistic and idiomatic quirks peculiar to the North – although your ever-zealous tour guide will be delighted to fill in any ideological gaps that become apparent.

Chollima Speed Nothing it seems, in North Korea, is capable of moving with anything other than Chollima speed. Not simply a grand way of saying 'fast', Chollima Speed dazzles and amazes. Whether you feel like it or not, you too will be dazzled and amazed when various buildings, factories or monuments are described to you in terms of their amazingly brief construction periods. Chollima is an ancient Korean myth, a Pegasus who was capable of travelling 1000 *ri*, or 400 km, in one day, and could not be tamed by any rider. The Chollima movement, launched in the shadow of China's equally disastrous Great Leap Forward, engaged the population in trying to over-fulfil already ridiculously ambitious production targets. While its results were impressive on paper, the reality was of course, somewhat different. However, the myths, both ancient and modern, remain, and if you really want to please your guide, say *jongmal Chollima soktoimnida* ('that really is Chollima speed').

Juche Pronounced 'joo-chay', this is the cornerstone of North Korean philosophy, as witnessed by the Tower of the Juche Idea, the vast Pyongyang phallus designed by the Dear Leader himself. Juche encompasses many things – none of which are in any way related to DPRK's grim reality. Juche essentially stresses self-reliance and the individual's role in forging his/her own destiny, although no doubt it gets a cool reception at the concentration camps. Likewise, your guide will be delighted at your ideological progress if you say *Igosun Juchejog-imnida* ('It is Juche oriented').

The Great Leader This universally employed phrase describes Kim Il Sung (1912–94) who founded the DPRK and over five decades in power, sought to apotheosise himself and his son.

The Dear Leader This reverential title refers to Kim Jong Il, the first person to lead a communist country by primogeniture. To confuse matters, since his father's death he has also been referred to as the 'Great Leader'. To make your guide's day, try to throw the phrase *widaehan ryongdoja Kim Jong Il tongji-ui mansumugang-ul samga chugwon hamnida* into the conversation ('I wish the Great Leader Comrade Kim Jong Il a long life in good health').

to ordinary North Koreans as is generally possible for foreign visitors. North and South Korean national teams played each other for the first time in over a decade in 2002 in Seoul. With true diplomatic flair, the 'reunification game' ended in a 0-0 draw. The South's stellar display in the 2002 World Cup was sketchily reported in the North, a rare display of nationalism overcoming political differences.

The North's greatest sporting moment came at the 1966 World Cup in England, however, when they thrashed favourites Italy and stunned the world. They subsequently went out to Portugal in the quarter-finals. The story of the team is told in a strangely touching documentary – one of the few ever to be made by Western crews in DPRK – *The Game of Their Lives* (refer to www.thegameoftheirlives.com).

Weightlifting and martial arts are the only other sporting fields in which North Korea has created any international impact. However, one home-grown sporting phenomenon (for want of a more accurate term) that should not be passed over if the opportunity to see it arises is the Arirang Mass Games, held annually at the world's largest stadium, the May Day Stadium, in Pyongyang. These mass gymnastic displays involve over 100,000 soldiers, children and students holding up coloured placards to form enormous murals in praise of North Korea's achievements, truly an amazing sight.

Religion

In North Korea, all traditional religion is regarded, in accordance with Marxist theory, as an expression of a 'feudal mentality', an obsolete superstitious force opposing political revolution, social liberation, economic development and national independence. Therefore, it has been effectively proscribed since the 1950s. However, as the Kim regime became more and more deified in the 1990s, official propaganda against organised religion accordingly stopped.

THE MILLION MEMBER MOVEMENT

By the end of the Joseon dynasty, the Pyongyang area and some other parts of northern Korea were the most successful centres on the peninsula for American Protestant missionary work. Pyongyang

was the epicentre of the 'Great Revival' of 1907 and the origin of the subsequent nationwide 'Million Member Movement'. These evangelical outbreaks were partly an emotional response to the surrender of Korea's sovereignty to Japan, which began in 1905; but regardless of the cause they resulted in a heavy concentration of Christians in northern areas.

Until Kim Il Sung came to power, that is. The near total suppression of religion and traditional customs that he imposed from 1946 onwards led to a mass exodus of Christians – especially priests, ministers and lay leaders – to the South before and during the Korean War. Many of those who would not or could not flee were executed outright or died in labour camps.

TRADITIONAL RELIGIONS

The northern version of Korean shamanism was individualistic and ecstatic, while the southern style was hereditary and based on regularly scheduled community rituals. As far as is known, no shamanist activity is now practised in North Korea. Many northern shamans were transplanted to the South, chased out along with their enemies the Christians, and the popularity of the services they offer (fortune-telling, for instance) has endured there. Together with the near-destruction of southern shamanism by South Korea's relentless modernisation, we have the curious situation where the actual practice of northern Korean shamanism can only be witnessed in South Korea.

Northern Korea held many important centres of Korean Buddhism from the 3rd century through the Japanese occupation period. The Kumgangsan and Myohyangsan mountain areas in particular hosted large Zen-oriented (Jogye) temple-complexes left over from the Goryeo dynasty. Under the communists, Buddhism in the North (along with Confucianism and shamanism) suffered a fate identical to that of Christianity.

Some historically important Buddhist temples and shrines still exist, mostly in rural or mountainous areas. The most prominent among them are Pyohon Temple at Kumgangsan, Pohyon Temple at Myohyangsan, and the Confucian Shrine in the Songgyungwan Neo-Confucian College just outside of Kaesong (p350).

Arts

Largely due to Kim Jong Il's lifelong interest in celluloid, the North Korean film industry has had money pumped into it since the founding of the nation. Kim Jong Il's input has been all encompassing and hands-on – he is listed as the executive producer of many films produced in the country, and is believed to have many actors, actresses and directors among his palace courtiers.

The only North Korean film that can be seen with ease in the West is Shin Sang-Ok's *Pulgasari* – a curious socialist version of Godzilla made by the kidnapped South Korean director, who escaped back to the South in 1986 (see 'Kidnap Victims', p351). The on-going *Nation* and *Destiny* series of films is supposed to be a series of 100, so far 56 have been released. Far more interesting is the 1999 epic *Forever in Our Memory* that, surprisingly, tackles the mass starvation of the mid-1990s. The climax of the film sees a big flood threatening the harvest and soldiers and farmers standing on top of a dam to create a human dyke with their bodies, all the while screaming 'Long Live Kim-Il Sung' and waving the North Korean flag. You can request a visit to the Pyongyang Film Studios when booking your tour – and you may even be lucky enough to see an agitprop classic in production.

North Korean literature has not profited from the Kim dynasty, which has done little to encourage original writing. Despite an initial artistic debate in the 1950s, all nonparty controlled forms of expression were quickly repressed.

Kim Il Sung was a fierce nationalist, relentlessly emphasising the superiority of Korean culture. Tourists with an interest in traditional arts can benefit – visits to performances of traditional Korean music, singing and dance can easily be arranged. Some even argue that in terms of traditional culture, the North is the 'real Korea', untainted by the Americanisation of the South. Exhibitions of traditional or modern pottery, sculpture, painting and architecture can be viewed on request, and it is highly recommended to include a visit to a cinematic, theatre or opera performance in your itinerary. If one hasn't been pre-arranged for you, your guide should be able to organise a visit to a performance for a token extra charge, as long as you give some warning.

While the performances are unlikely to be cutting edge, or even comprehensible to the non-Korean speaker, Pyongyang does have a small opera and theatre scene. Again, it's a question of asking your guides and preferably your travel agent before you go, but it may be possible to spend the evening at one of Pyongyang's cultural institutes.

ENVIRONMENT

A trip to North Korea makes an interesting comparison to the South. While South Korea suffers from some serious environmental problems, there is little visible pollution in the North. The one thing that strikes most visitors to North Korea is its squeaky-clean appearance. This is a function not just of the lack of consumer goods and their packaging but of determined policies that keep it that way. The streets are washed down twice a week, and before dawn each day street cleaners are out sweeping up any litter or leaves. You'd be hard pressed to find a single piece of paper on the streets, despite the absence of litter-bins. Even in the countryside, locals are assigned a particular stretch of the main road to sweep – each and every day.

North Korea boasts a diverse range of plants and animals. The varying climatic regions have created environments that are home to subarctic, alpine and even subtropical plant and tree species. Most of the country's fauna is contained within the limited nature reserves around the mountainous regions, as most of the lower plains have been converted to arable agricultural land. An energetic reforestation programme was carried out after the Korean War to replace many of the forests that were destroyed by the incessant bombing campaigns. A notable exception being the area to the north of the DMZ, where defoliants are used to remove vegetation for security purposes. The comparatively low population has resulted in the preservation of most mountainous regions.

Only recently has the international community looked at assisting the North in assessing and monitoring the country's biodiversity. Three areas of particular focus are the DMZ, the wetlands of the Tumen River and the Paekdusan mountains. For those people interested in participating in a tour of North Korea with a greater emphasis on flora and fauna, then it is possible to organise an appropriate itinerary with your Korean tour company. Bird-watching endeavours to some of the wetland habitats of migratory birds are the most popular. These tours, however, often involve greater expenses, especially if a chartered flight is necessary.

Two particular flora species have attracted enormous attention from the North Koreans and neither of the flowers are native. In 1965, President Sukarno named a newly developed orchid after Kim Il Sung – *kimilsungia* – popular acclaim overcoming Kim's modest reluctance to accept such an honour. Kim Jong Il was presented with his namesake, *kimjongilia*, a begonia developed by a Japanese horticulturist, on his 46th birthday. The blooming of either flower is announced annually as a tribute to the two Great Leaders and visitors will notice their omnipresence throughout official tourist sites.

Environmental Issues

The main challenges to the environment are from problems that are harder to see. The devastating floods and economic slowdown during the 1990s wreaked havoc not only on property and agricultural land, but also on the environment. Fields were stripped of their topsoil, which, combined with fertiliser shortages, forced authorities to expand the arable land under cultivation. Unsustainable and unstable hillside areas, river banks and road edges were brought under cultivation, further exacerbating erosion, deforestation, fertiliser contamination of the land and rivers and the vulnerability of crops.

One advantage of its isolation is the pristine natural environment to be found in the mountains, untouched by commercialism or mass tourism. However, there has been substantial deforestation due to the famine. Fried leaves is a dish served very regularly in rural areas of DPRK – and some refugees have reported that their biggest surprise on finally reaching the South was to find that the hillsides were so lush and full of greenery. Due to food and fuel shortages, many areas of DPRK have simply been left desolate by plunder.

FOOD & DRINK
Staples & Specialities

While tour groups eat sumptuously by North Korean standards, the standard fare is decidedly mediocre and varies depending on the food situation at the time. Recent visitors have reported being served scrappy off-cuts that would not ordinarily be offered, although others have been very satisfied with the fare. There is no danger of tourists going hungry, but many will automatically be served Western food unless they specifically request Korean – a better idea, as the North Korean take on Western food is distinctly bland.

Drinks

In a surprise move for a country with millions of malnourished children, in 2000 North Korea purchased the Ushers brewery in Trowbridge, England, dismantled it, shipped it to Nampo and rebuilt it on the outskirts of Pyongyang. The $2 million deal is probably good news for North Korean beer lovers. Pyongyang and Taedonggang beers are the most popular brands.

Other drinks on offer include a pleasant range of North Korean fruit juices and sodas, although Coke and Fanta are also available now in some Pyongyang hotels, as are imported Japanese beers.

Soju is the classic Korean rice wine drunk at dinners, although it's rather strong stuff. Visitors might prefer Korean blueberry wine; the best is apparently made from Mount Paekdu blueberries. Blueberry wine comes in two forms – the gently alcoholic, which tastes like a soft drink, and the reinforced version, which could stun an elephant.

Kim Jong Il famously favours a Hennessey whiskey at €500 per bottle, according to many anti-Kim websites.

PYONGYANG

☎ 02 / pop 2,741,260 / 200 sq km

Pyongyang is an extraordinary city, the mother of all political statements wrapped in marble, bronze and concrete; part defiant display of strength, part socialist realist melodrama. While it is possible to sense the power in the air as palpably as in Moscow or Washington, the chaos and charisma of a national capital is conspicuously absent in Pyongyang's eerily quiet streets.

All tours begin and end in the national capital, and here at least foreigners are just a novelty rather than the aliens they are elsewhere in North Korea. The guides will be falling over themselves to show you a succession of monuments, towers, statues, and buildings that apotheosise the Juche idea and propagate the achievements of the Kim regime. These include the Tower of the Juche Idea, the Chollima Statue and the Mansudae Grand Monument, a vast rendering of the Great Leader in bronze to which every visitor is expected to pay floral homage.

While these are all impressive, if surreal, the real delights of Pyongyang are to be had in the quieter moments when you can get glimpses of everyday life. If possible, suggest walking between sights rather than driving which the guides prefer; a gentle stroll on Pyongyang's relatively relaxed Moran Hill, for example, will reveal that the locals have picnics, play music and idle away sunny afternoons. Despite the best attempts of the Korean Workers' Party, there is a semblance of normality surviving in the capital.

PYONGYANG HIGHLIGHTS

- Ride the express lift to the top of the **Tower of the Juche Idea** (p345) for a spectacular view of the sprawling cityscape on a clear day
- Ride one station on the spectacularly designed but empty **Pyongyang metro** (p346) and decide if it's all just for show or not
- See where Kim Il Sung lies in state at the **Kumsusan Memorial Palace** (p344) – by invitation only, but it makes Lenin's mausoleum look like a shoebox
- Visit the staggering **Grand People's Study House** (p345) and enjoy one of 30 million books being delivered mechanically to your desk
- Escape the relentless grandeur of the city centre and have a walk on **Moran Hill** (p345)

HISTORY

It seems incredible to think it, given its architectural similarities to Minsk and Brasilia, but Pyongyang is ancient, stretching back to when the Goguryeo dynasty built its capital here in AD 427. By the 7th century the kingdom of Goguryeo had started to collapse under the strain of successive, massive attacks from Sui and Tang China. Cutting a deal with the Tang Chinese, the Silla kingdom in the South was able to conquer Goguryeo in 668, creating the first unified Korea.

Later, during the Goryeo dynasty, Pyongyang became the kingdom's secondary capital. The city was to be completely destroyed by the Japanese in 1592 and then again by the Manchus at the beginning of the 17th century. Pyongyang thenceforth remained a relative backwater until the arrival of foreign missionaries, who constructed over 100 churches in the city. Pyongyang was once again destroyed during the Sino-Japanese War (1894–95) and was to remain neglected until the occupying Japanese developed industry in the region.

The US practically wiped Pyongyang out between 1950 and 1953, and yet as the capital of the DPRK under Kim Il Sung, modern Pyongyang rose from the ashes with inimitable 'Chollima speed'. Few historic buildings remain but there are some in evidence, including a couple of temples and pavilions, the Taedong Gate and a few sections of the Goguryeo kingdom's inner and northern walls.

ORIENTATION

Pyongyang today is an imposing city. The regime has created a showpiece capital employing its own grandiose style of architecture, which borrows much from the Soviet model, and it's one that rarely fails to impress.

The larger part of the city is on the northern bank of the Taedong River that curves gracefully off to the suburb of Mangyongdae to the west. The city is centred on Kim Il Sung Square, which faces the Tower of the Juche Idea across the river. All the hotels where foreigners are put up are centrally located and not more than a few minutes' drive from the major sights of the city. Arriving by train, tourists will alight

PYONGYANG

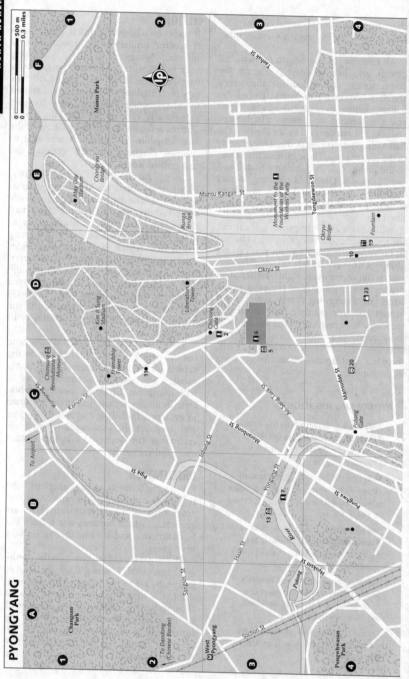

Changsan Park

To Airport

To Dandong
(Chinese Border)

West
Pyongyang

Sangsin St

Hasin St

Sochon St

Pongwhwasan
Park

Putong
River

Hyoksin St

Pipa St

Idung St

Morangbong St

Yongsin St

Pongwha St

13

7

8

Sangsin St

Kwangbok St

Kim Il Sung
Stadium

Chonsung
Revolutionary
Museum

Friendship
Tower

Kaeson St

An Sang Taek St

1

6
2

Chitsong
Gate

Liberation
Tower

May Day
Stadium

Chongyu
Bridge

Munsa Park

Runga
Bridge

Munsu-Kangan St

Okryu St

Okryu
Bridge

Taehak St

Monument to the
Foundation of the
Workers' Party

Tongdaewon St

Fountain

19

10

23

5

Mansudae St

Potong
Gate

20

0   500 m
0   0.3 miles

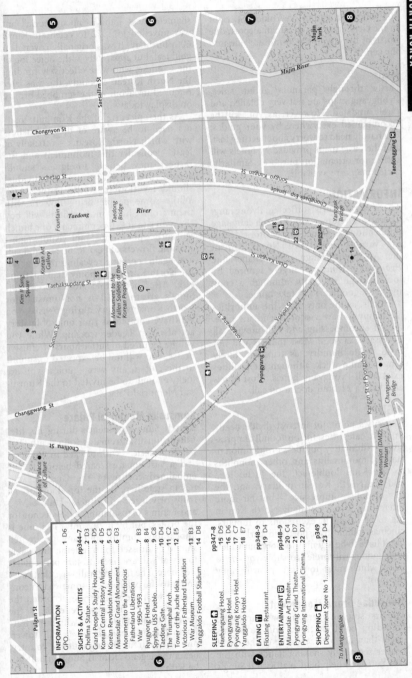

People's Palace of Culture

Pulgun St

Cheollima St

Changgwang St

To Mangyongdae

To Panmunjom (DMZ)/
Wonsan

Chongnyon St

Juchetap St

Taedong

Fountain

Korean Art
Gallery

Kim Il Sung
Square

Taehaksupdang St

Samun St

Taedong
Bridge

River

Monument to the
Fallen Soldiers of the
Korean People's Army

Songyo Kangan St

Chongbaek Esplanade

Olan Kangan St

Yanggwang St

Yokjon St

Pyongyang

Yanggak
Bridge

Yanggak

Chungsong
Bridge

Kangan St of Pyongchon

Saesallim St

Mujin River

Mujin
Park

Taedonggang

INFORMATION	
GPO............................	1 D6
SIGHTS & ACTIVITIES	**pp344–7**
Chollima Statue.............	2 D3
Grand People's Study House.	3 D5
Korean Central History Museum.	4 D5
Korean Revolution Museum..	5 C3
Mansudae Grand Monument..	6 D3
Monument to the Victorious	
Fatherland Liberation	
War 1950–1953............	7 B3
Ryugyong Hotel..............	8 B4
Spyship USS Pueblo.........	9 C8
Taedong Gate................	10 D4
The Triumphal Arch.........	11 C2
Tower of the Juche Idea....	12 E5
Victorious Fatherland Liberation	
War Museum...............	13 B3
Yanggakdo Football Stadium.	14 D8
SLEEPING	**pp347–8**
Haebangsang Hotel..........	15 D5
Pyongyang Hotel............	16 D6
Pyongyang Koryo Hotel.....	17 C7
Yanggakdo Hotel............	18 E7
EATING	**pp348–9**
Floating Restaurant.........	19 D4
ENTERTAINMENT	**pp348–9**
Mansudae Art Theatre.......	20 C4
Pyongyang Grand Theatre....	21 D7
Pyongyang International Cinema..	22 D7
SHOPPING	**p349**
Department Store No 1......	23 D4

at Pyongyang station on Yokjon St, right in the city centre. From Sunan airport, due north of the city, it's a 20-minute ride into the centre.

Maps

Partly through paranoia about spies, Pyongyang maps are not very detailed and rarely updated. However, as you will be accompanied everywhere by your guides, you hardly need to worry about getting lost, and the basic maps provided by hotels will suffice for orientation purposes. Similarly, metro maps are available.

INFORMATION

There is no tourist office in Pyongyang. There are numerous English-language publications designed for visitors detailing various aspects of North Korean life. An English-language newspaper, the *Pyongyang Times*, is largely ignored by local foreign residents, although a copy may be a good curio to take home.

Hotels, as the only place the authorities are happy to have visitors spend any time, are all encompassing and will provide all necessary services. Most tourists will not need to do laundry, as trips are rarely longer than a week, although the facilities exist in all Pyongyang hotels. Most hotels also have a 24-hour doctor on call.

SIGHTS

The city's points of interest divide neatly into two categories: the profoundly impressive yet ultimately pointless proliferation of statues, monuments and other monoliths to the Kim double-act, the Juche Idea and the North Korean military; and the less obviously impressive – but far more interesting – slices of daily North Korean life to be found in excursions to funfairs, cinemas, public transport and parks. You don't have to be a genius to work out which your guides will prefer to show you, or to guess which most tour groups will enjoy the most.

Mansudae Grand Monument

The first stop on every visitor's trip (often preceding hotel check-in) will be to this larger-than-life bronze statue of the Great Leader seemingly shaking hands with the sky. You can't help blanch at Kim Il Sung's

shamelessness – this is no memorial, but was unveiled in 1972 to celebrate Kim's 60th birthday. It was originally covered in gold leaf, but apparently at the objection of the Chinese, who were effectively funding the North Korean economy, this was later removed in favour of the scrubbed bronze on display today.

As the epicentre of the Kim cult, visitors need to be aware of the seriousness with which North Koreans – officially at least – consider this monument and the respect they believe foreigners should accord it. Each tour group or individual should lay flowers at the statue's feet. While some people bring flowers with them from China, most visitors will buy them on site at €10 per bunch – one bunch will suffice per group. Some visitors report that the flowers appear to be resold again and again, perhaps revealing more about the North Korean economy than anything else. After being told stories of Kim Il Sung's greatness (it is not unusual for North Koreans to cry during a visit), you will have completed your only obligatory act of Great Leader worship. While you will be required to suffer hours of effusive praise, you will not be expected to submit to the cult in any way – unless you are lucky enough to be invited to the Kumsusan Memorial Palace.

Kumsusan Memorial Palace

Kim Il Sung's residence during his lifetime, Kumsusan remains so in death. The palace is eerie – with bricked in windows and a vast square cleared before it. The embalmed corpse of the Great Leader lies in state here on the top floor for the truly privileged to witness. Unlike Mao and Lenin's mausoleums, access is not for the proles, but by invite only. The tone is unbearably sombre and anyone invited should be dressed for a funeral; those able to cry at will are likely to fare particularly well here. The moving walkways that carry you into the palace seem somewhat incongruous with the seriousness accorded the visit, however. Even more eerie is the **Tower of Immortality**, under which the traffic to the palace must pass. This tower, one of hundreds throughout the country, bears the legend 'Kim Il Sung will always be with us'.

Tower of the Juche Idea

On the other side of the Taedong River from Kim Il Sung Square, this honours Kim Il Sung's philosophy Juche (see 'North-Korea Speak', p337), which expounds the theory of economic self-sufficiency as vital to national sovereignty. The tower stands at 170m and a trip to the top by lift (€10) is well worth it, providing a great view over the capital on a clear day. The pavilions surrounding the tower feature a trio of workers holding aloft the emblem of the DPRK and in the river immediately in front are two water jets that reach 150m on the rare occasions when they are working.

Chollima Statue

Less obviously impressive, but an interesting example of how the Kim regime has sought to incorporate traditional Korean myths into its socialist cult, is the bronze statue of the Korean Pegasus, the steed Chollima. According to legend Chollima could cover hundreds of kilometres a day and was untameable (see 'North-Korea Speak', p337). Kim Il Sung appropriated the myth in the period of reconstruction following the Korean War – the zeal of the North Korean workers to rebuild their shattered nation and construct vast and pointless monuments to the leadership became known as 'Chollima speed'. When North Korea broke through to the quarterfinals of the World Cup in 1966, it was apparently because Kim senior had urged them to play 'Chollima football'.

The Triumphal Arch

Your guides will tell you with barely concealed glee that the Triumphal Arch is 3m higher than its cousin in Paris, making it the largest in the world. Similarly, Kim Il Sung Square was enlarged to make it bigger than Red Square in Moscow.

The arch marks the site where Kim Il Sung first addressed the liberated Koreans after the end of Japanese occupation in 1945. The gloss you hear will omit the fact that the Soviets liberated Pyongyang, not Kim Il Sung's partisans, who themselves gave all credit to the Soviets at the time.

Kim Il Sung Square

This vast plaza would be the packed hub of any other world capital, but Pyongyang's central square and marching ground is strange in its emptiness, the open spaces seemingly cowed by the massive buildings surrounding it. Most impressive of these is the **Grand People's Study House** – the country's largest library and national centre of Juche studies. This is one of Pyongyang's most striking buildings, a socialist realist structure melded with traditional Korean architecture.

With over 30 million books, finding what you want is inevitably quite a challenge – and you will be proudly shown the incredible system of conveyer belts that can deliver books right to your desk. All foreign publications are viewable with special permission only, while even North Korean literature over 15 years old is proscribed to conceal the historical rewrites.

Historic Pyongyang

To see something of Pyongyang's prewar history is a challenge. The **Taedong Gate** was the eastern gate to the original walled city of Pyongyang, and built in the 6th century. The current gate was rebuilt in 1635, but is one of the oldest remaining structures in the city – a reminder that Pyongyang was once a traditional Asian city rather than the post-Soviet monolith it is today. Nearby are the other major historical sites – the **Pyongyang Bell**, a bronze early warning system for fire and invasion dating from 1726 and the beautiful **Ryongwang Pavilion**, originally built in 1111 and rebuilt in 1670.

Mangyongdae Children's Palace

This centre for extra-curricular activity – from martial arts to the playing of traditional instruments – can make a great visit. Note the model of a 'North Korean' space shuttle at the entrance, a replica of the Soviet *Buran*. The palace visit will include displays of incredibly talented martial artists, gymnasts and musicians, all beaming at you as they perform. The tour usually culminates in the huge main auditorium with a stellar display of fantastically regimented youth. The grand finale is usually a loyalty song to Kim Jong Il.

Moran Hill

This is Pyongyang's top recreation ground for the masses. Couples wander, families picnic and there are people who even play musical instruments in an incongruously relaxed area of the capital. It's particularly busy on a Sunday and a lovely place to stroll and absorb something of daily life.

Pyongyang Metro

Finally, one other visit that is often included on a city tour is a trip on the impressive **Pyongyang Metro**. It's a good idea to request this in advance of travel, as it's definitely a highlight. The network, which is made up of two lines, has a simultaneous function as a nuclear bunker in the event of the long-awaited American invasion. Stations are deep below ground, and you can even see blast doors that will close if Pyongyang comes under nuclear bombardment (see 'The Pyongyang Metro', p347).

Museums

Pyongyang's museums unsurprisingly offer the regime's version of history. While one or two can be very interesting for a totally new perspective on events, the novelty can soon wear thin. A visit to the **Korean Revolution Museum** is likely to be included on your itinerary. This shows the anti-Japanese struggle, including numerous action exhibits depicting the fiercest of the battles.

The **Party Founding Museum** is located on the southern slope of Haebang Hill and originally housed the Central Committee of the Korean Workers' Party, as well as Kim Il Sung's office from where he 'led the building of a new democratic Korea'. Next door is the Great Leader's conspicuously modest residence, used after coming to power and presumably before the masses demanded he build himself numerous palaces.

Korean Central History Museum is all rather tedious and predictable – a large number of exhibits about the North's struggle against imperialism and oppression. On the other hand, the **Victorious Fatherland Liberation War Museum** is a fascinating place. The key battles of the Korean War are depicted vividly in dioramas, and there's some fascinating military hardware from war-damaged tanks and aircraft to torpedo boats used by both sides. These were all placed in the basement and the museum was then built around them. Opposite the little Potong tributary of the Taedong, there is the impressive **Monument to the Victorious Fatherland Liberation War 1950–1953**, which was unveiled in 1993

to mark the 40th anniversary of the war's end. The sculptures reflect the different battles of the war – the Victory Sculpture is the centrepiece.

The Tomb of Tan'gun

History continues to evolve in North Korea, with new 'revolutionary discoveries' being made every year. While the government announced in 1993 that its archaeologists had discovered the tomb of Tan'gun, the founder of the first Korean kingdom, it wasn't until recently that North Korean historians made the incredible discovery that Tan'gun was in fact a member of the Kim clan.

During North Korea's more rational communist period, the government had agreed with most scholars of Korean history that Tan'gun was a mythical figure and that his kingdom of KoChoson (ancient Korea) with its capitals Pyongyang and Asadal was in fact located in Northeast China, if it indeed existed. However, it's been recently 'discovered' that KoChoson was northern Korea, its capital was right where theirs now stands, Tan'gun was a real man, and a Kim at that; they have also discovered his skeletal remains.

Those decayed bones (and those said to be of his wife) are on display at a grandly constructed tomb just outside of Pyongyang. A small museum stands nearby, displaying 'artefacts' from Tan'gun's times, said to have been found in and around the tomb.

Mangyongdae

The closest North Korea has to a Kim Il Sung Disney World is the suburb of Mangyongdae, one of the many cottage industries created by and simultaneously bolstering the ever-growing personality cult of Great Leaders one and two. Just 12km from the centre of Pyongyang, Mangyongdae has long been a destination for day-trippers from the capital, due to its idyllic setting amid the gentle hills where the Sunhwa River flows into the Taedong. The suburb now houses the place of Kim Il Sung's birth – an interesting place to visit, as much to see the pretty setting, the funfair and the relaxing Pyongyangites, as for the flourishing Kim cult.

Kim Il Sung's Birthplace is a collection of mud huts – a typical Korean peasant house

THE PYONGYANG METRO

There can be no better example of the Kim regime's prioritisation of the military-industrial complex than the fascinating Pyongyang metro. While two lines exist for civilian use, there are believed to be several government-only lines linking key ministries and military installations, capable of withstanding a full-scale American bombardment. Since the system opened in 1973, each station has doubled as a nuclear bunker, and there are frequent air-raid drills in Pyongyang, in which citizens make their way into the stations and the triple blast doors shut behind them.

As tourists, visiting the Pyongyang metro will involve a one-stop trip between Puhung (Reha-bilitation) and Yongwang (Glory) stations. All state visitors, from US Secretary of State Madeleine Albright to former South Korean President Kim Dae-jung, were given the same show trip, giving rise to a rumour that power cuts and lack of repair have meant that the rest of the system no longer functions on a day-to-day basis. Other travellers have reported that the ordinary Koreans on the metro looked like actors – beautifully attired and seemingly travelling without purpose. While this fits the profile of many North Korean sights, it seems unlikely in a city with a dearth of transport options – at rush hours the trains are apparently absolutely packed.

The entire system's construction was overseen by the Great Leader, who offered his 'on the spot guidance'. A guidebook to the Metro describes his wise words on opening the new network in 1973:

'The Great Leader President said to officials in a thoughtful tone "I think it is difficult to build the metro, but it is not to cut the tape." Hearing his words, which considered the trouble of builders first, the participants in the opening ceremony felt a lump in their throats and gave enthusiastic cheers, waving bundles of flowers.'

Ultimately it's just another of the many North Korean enigmas – but the trip should not be missed. One of the deepest metros in the world, it is also one of the most elaborately decorated – marble platforms, vast chandeliers and impressive murals extolling the virtues of Juche and detailing yet more of the heroic activities of guess who...

with a thatched roof and a block of living rooms, as well as a small barn. The emphasis is very much on the president's humble origins, and indeed, it's an open question as to whether Kim Il Sung was really born here at all. The **Mangyongdae Revolutionary Museum**, located nearby, continues the theme of the Great Leader's childhood and makes the point that all his family members were Korean patriot revolutionaries of the humblest possible order.

You may also be lucky enough to visit the **Mangyongdae Revolutionary School**, where Pyongyang's elite sons are trained for the next generation of leadership. This can be a fun tour through the various classrooms and gymnasiums, where children look at you wide-eyed with wonder. To relax after the relentless propaganda, the **Mangyongdae Funfair** is a pleasant nonpoliticised oasis built around the base of Song Hill, where you can relax with some day-trippers from the capital. While the guides insist that the fair gets 100,000 visitors a day at the weekends, it consistently seems to be pleasantly empty!

SLEEPING

Pyongyang has the largest range of hotels of any North Korean city. They are, like much of the city's architecture, built to impress, and while their façades are often striking, their interiors are all fairly uninspiring. The city's skyline is dominated by the fabulously impressive pyramidal Ryugyong Hotel – designed to be the world's largest luxury hotel in the 1980s. As you approach it, it becomes clear that it is a skeleton, with no windows or interiors. The project ran out of money and the vast structure now sits as a derelict monument to overly ambitious central planning. Of the functioning Pyongyang Hotels, the deluxe options are listed following.

Yanggakdo Hotel (☎ 381 2134; fax 381 2930/1; s/d €175/290; 🛏 🍴) A new 45-floor hotel on Yanggak islet, the Yanggakdo is now the default hotel for tour groups. The anti-American photo displays in the lobby might not be the most welcoming, but the rooms are large and comfortable, often with superb views over the city. As well as a pool and sauna, there is also a bowling alley, three pool tables and a foreigners-only disco. The staff is largely Chinese – spare a thought for them, as they are not allowed to leave the island.

Pyongyang Koryo Hotel (☎ 381 4397; fax 318 4422; s/d €175/290; ✖ ✔) This 1985 orange-bronze structure is the preferred place to lodge UN functionaries and business people and is possibly the most luxurious option in the city. Each of its twin towers has a revolving restaurant on top and its location is better than the Yanggakdo's, on the relative bustle of Changgwang St, a short walk from Pyongyang train station.

Potonggang Hotel (☎ 381 2229; fax 381 4428) First-class options include the Potonggang, the only hotel in North Korea to get CNN. It is owned by Unification Church leader Reverend Moon, who negotiated directly with Kim Il Sung in 1991 for its purchase, and is situated by the small Pothong River, about 4km from the city centre.

The Sosan Hotel is also 1st class and opened in 1989, while the 2nd-class Pyongyang Hotel, opposite the Pyongyang Grand Theatre, seems to be the preferred place to billet budget travellers. Other hotels, all of remarkably similar quality, are the pyramidal Ryanggang and the high-rise Chongnyon (Youth).

The 3rd-class Haebangsan Hotel on Sungni St is the cheapest option of all. However, depending on the prevailing mood at Ryohaengsa the day you book, there may be reluctance to let foreigners stay here.

EATING & DRINKING

Pyongyang is by far the best place to eat in the country, offering both variety and decent fare if you know where to go. Unless you request otherwise, you will have dinner in your hotel, but it is possible to eat out as a group for the sake of variety. Any restaurant outside your hotel that you are taken to will be the exclusive preserve of foreigners and the party elite – there doesn't seem to be a visible restaurant scene for the ordinary people.

One of the most popular restaurants is the vast Okryu Restaurant overlooking the Taedong. The speciality here is cold noodles, a traditional Pyongyang dish. Similarly, the Chongryu Restaurant, weirdly fashioned from concrete to resemble a giant boat, is famous for its barbecues.

Those seeking the authentic Korean experience may be interested in sampling dog meat. This is most famously served at **Dangogo Gukjib** (Tongil St), where a dog 'from brain to tail' will set you back €30. You are expected to eat the dog's penis as well, and the unfortunate mutt's brain usually comes as dessert.

The last night of each trip usually involves a farewell dinner of delicious barbecued duck, a definite highlight. Other restaurants to be recommended include the Chinese restaurant in the basement of the Yanggakdo Hotel – there's no view here, but the vegetables are brought in fresh from China. The fancy Japanese-owned Mokran Restaurant at the Pottonggang Hotel gets great reviews. There is also a popular café and patisserie in the foyer of the Pottonggang where tasty crepes are served. The Pyongyang Boat Restaurant is moored on the bank of Kim Il Sung Square and will cruise the Taedong at meal times, for around €25 per person, making a very pleasant excursion if the weather is good.

Nightlife in Pyongyang is almost non-existent, although the large diplomatic and NGO presence in town means that there are some private clubs where foreigners can relax away from the strictures of everyday Pyongyang life. Both the Diplomatic Club ('the diplo' to any self-respecting foreign resident) and the Random Access Club (RAC) are located in the diplomatic district of Munsudong. While you would not be stopped entering as a foreigner, your guide is unlikely to agree to take you. The RAC is in the World Food Program building and is a members club for NGO workers. Tourists and diplomats can only go by invitation.

An easier place to meet some foreign residents is the 2nd-floor billiards room at the Koryo Hotel, where a mixture of businesspeople, diplomats and journalists meet to hang out. There is also the smart but expensive disco in the basement of the Yanggakdo Hotel, complete with a casino.

ENTERTAINMENT

The nature of visiting North Korea is that the most mundane everyday things become instantly fascinating. Given that contact with locals is kept to a necessary minimum, while in Pyongyang you should take advantage of the relatively wide choice of evening entertainment to see how locals like to relax. Of course, what you will and won't be able to do depends on your guides, and so let them know any requests as early on as possible, and, of course, try and stay in their good books. There will often be a nominal charge of €10 for extra activities in the evening.

The Pyongyang Circus gets glowing reviews from visitors – it is mainly a human circus, and you may hear vicious rumours that during the famine many of the animals ended up on plates. The Pyongyang Zoo is a depressing and uninspiring place, best avoided.

Perhaps one suitably military pastime is a trip to the Pyongyang shooting range off Chongchun St, where all Pyongyang's sporting facilities are concentrated. It costs €1 for three bullets using a 2.2mm rifle or pistol. It makes a fun evening out for nationals of nonmilitarised countries.

Cinema, theatre and opera trips are also possible, and while neither films, operas or plays are likely to be of a particularly gripping order, again it's the experience that is interesting. The main theatres are the Pyongyang Grand Theatre, the East Pyongyang Grand Theatre and the Mansudae Art Theatre, although spectacles vary little from one to the other. Musical 'classics' such as The Flower Girl and A Daughter of the Party are in constant rotation. Seeing a North Korean film is even more surreal – their emotive subjects (the vast majority are war films depicting the Japanese occupation or American imperialism) mean that Koreans in the audience frequently jeer and stamp their feet. The Pyongyang International Cinema is a six-screen complex on Yanggak Islet, near the Yanggakdo Hotel. The biennial Pyongyang Film Festival is held here every September in even-numbered years. Other cinemas include the **Taedongmun** (Sungri St) and the Kaeson Cinema near the Triumphal Arch.

Football, a very popular local spectator sport, is a good way to spend an evening with ordinary Koreans. Ask if there are any matches on at Yanggakdo Football Stadium during your stay. For anyone interested in the surreal, a round at Pyongyang Golf Course will make a great anecdote for years to come – how many people can say they've played 18 holes in North Korea? Other sports are possible by prior arrangement – the Olympic Pool, among the impressive sporting centres of Chongchun St, is open to foreigners on Saturday.

Karaoke and a visit to the sauna remain your guide's preferred evening activity for you, and most hotels offer both. However, the Chinese sauna at the Yanggakdo is a 'special service' sauna for tired businessmen, so it's best to stick to the normal sauna, unless you are looking for more risqué activities.

SHOPPING

There are plenty of souvenir shops at the main tourist venues. Out where the masses shop, there are scarcely any consumer goods at all on the shelves. Nevertheless, North Korea does offer plenty of unique souvenirs that make fantastic conversation pieces. Books and videos on the immortal achievements of Juche and the Great/Dear Leaders may be your best picks.

Just to the south of the Pyongyang Koryo Hotel is a place selling postage stamps (the sign is in English), and it's definitely worth your time to stop in here as North Korean stamps are spectacular propaganda pieces.

Many tourists have expressed an interest in purchasing the metal badge which every North Korean wears, with the Great Leader's picture printed on it; however, these are not for sale.

Insam, or ginseng, is for sale in hotels but prices seem ridiculously high. It claims to be from Paekdusan; insam from there has a high value for all Koreans. You may be able to pick up some more cheaply in Kaesong, ask your guide for advice. However, you can buy all grades of insam much more cheaply in the South.

GETTING AROUND

The usual restrictions exist with Pyongyang's network of buses, trams and metro trains: in theory you are free to use them all, providing your guides are with you. As a rule, they seem very reluctant to show you anything other than the two approved metro stations. Indeed, given that you will have a car or coach, they may think you mad to want to brave Pyongyang's overcrowded mass-transit network. However, if they agree, the flat fare throughout the city is KPW2.

Both buses and trams have a substantial network throughout the city, but are hugely overcrowded and slow. The metro is fast and convenient, but the network is limited. While the government has made it clear that it plans to extend the lines further out to the suburbs, there is no evidence of this happening in the near future.

Taxis are available outside all hotels for you to travel in with your guide, should the need arise. Reception can also book taxis for you if there are none outside the hotel. Unlike in China, bicycles are not widely used in North Korea.

AROUND NORTH KOREA

North Korean cities are, often for no clear reason, 'open' or 'closed' to tourists. Some, for example, the strategically important port cities of Nampo and Wonsan, change status frequently, while others, such as Panmunjeom, Myohyangsan and Kumgangsan are nearly always open to visitors. Either way, only cities or towns with tourist hotels are possible to visit (unless you arrange a day trip), as staying elsewhere is not an option.

KAESONG
pop 330,000

Named Koryo when it was the fine capital of the Goryeo dynasty, this is an interesting place to spend some time. It's a two-hour drive down the expressway from Pyongyang, and is usually combined with a trip to **Panmunjeom** where the DMZ seethes with military readiness. Recently, itineraries have tended to keep any visit to Kaesong very brief, although the reason for this is far from clear. It's a pity, as there is plenty of interest in the city as an ancient capital. Kaesong is famous for being a centre of Buddhism (until Kim Il Sung's ascendancy) and also has a reputation as having the most beautiful women in Korea.

You won't see many relics of antiquity here due to the unfortunate effects of neglect and three major wars which each left little but rubble. At least there is the **Songgyungwan Neo-Confucian College**, which was originally built in AD 992 and rebuilt after

being destroyed in the 1592 Japanese invasion. Today it is host to the **Koryo Museum** of celadon pottery and other Buddhist relics; re-enactments of Confucian ceremonies are very occasionally held here. The buildings surround a wide courtyard dotted with ancient trees, and the surrounding grounds are very pleasant to walk around. It's a short drive northeast of town.

Kaesong may be your only chance while in the DPRK to see an authentic Korean royal tomb. The best one by far is the **Tomb of King Kongmin** (the 31st Goryeo king, who reigned between 1352 and 1374) and his queen. It is richly decorated with traditional granite facing and statuary. It's a very secluded site about 13km west of the city centre; there are splendid views over the surrounding tree-covered hills from a number of vantage points.

The third great tourist site is the 37m-high **Pakyon Falls**, one of the three most famous in North Korea. It's found in a beautiful natural setting some 24km north of town. Theoretically at least, some great hiking can be done around here: from the falls to the **Taehungsan Fortress**, to the mid-Goryeo **Kwanum Temple** (with cave) and the **Taehung Temple**.

Kaesong itself is a modern city with wide streets – of scant interest, though it does have an interesting older section consisting of traditional tile-roofed houses, sandwiched between the river and the main street. Within the town are a number of lesser tourist sights: the **Sonjuk Bridge**, a tiny clapper bridge built in 1216 and opposite, the **Songin Monument**, which honours Neo-Confucian hero Chong Mong-ju; the **Nammun** (South Gate) which dates from the 14th century and houses an old Buddhist bell; the **Sungyang Seowon** (Confucian academy); and **Chanamsan**, on the summit of which stands a massive bronze statue of – guess who?

If you stay over in Kaesong, you'll be based at either the Chanamsan Hotel near the Sonjuk Bridge or the Kaesong Minsok (Folk) Hotel. If you have a choice, definitely choose the latter, which is built in the traditional Korean *yeogwan* (motels with small, well-equipped en suite rooms) style and has a charming stream running through it. Both hotels are rated 3rd class.

KIDNAP VICTIMS

Nobody could accuse the North Korean government of being lacking in pragmatism. Need to teach spies Japanese? The simple solution is to kidnap Japanese civilians and employ them to do the job. By their own sheepish admission in 2002, the DPRK government kidnapped 13 Japanese nationals between 1977 and 1983, including couples enjoying romantic walks on desolate beaches and even tourists visiting Europe.

The Japanese government is unlikely to normalise relations with North Korea and pay billions of dollars in compensation for its colonial rule of the peninsula until the DPRK gives a fuller and more truthful account of the fate of its kidnap victims. As well as Japanese citizens, more than 400 South Koreans, mainly fishermen, have been abducted by the North and their fates remain unknown.

The most sensational kidnap of all was orchestrated by Kim Jong Il. The keen cineaste, appalled by the state of film production in the North, ordered that South Korean director Shin Sang-ok and his movie star wife Choi Eun-hee be kidnapped and brought north to make films. After surviving four years in the gulag for attempting to escape, Shin and Choi were brought before Kim Jong Il who greeted them like old friends, explaining how much he needed them. Given unlimited funds and the elite lifestyle exclusive to the inner circle of Kim Jong Il, Shin made seven films before managing to escape with Choi during a visit to Vienna. His autobiography *Kingdom of Kim* makes for some chilling reading about life in North Korea's heart of darkness.

PANMUNJEOM

For many, a visit to the 38th parallel is the highlight of their trip – military historians and anyone interested in the Cold War will be fascinated by this hangover from the 20th century. You don't have to be an expert, however, to appreciate the weirdness of the site where the bloody Korean War ended in an unhappy truce. Seeing the situation from the North, facing off against US troops to the south is a unique chance to witness things from a new perspective.

The eerily quiet drive down the six-lane Reunification Highway gives you a sense of what to expect – the road is deserted save for military checkpoints. Just before you exit to the DMZ, the sign saying 'Seoul 70km' makes your spine tingle. Incidents of the Korean Army demanding payment of up to €25 per person from day-trippers have been on the increase. Talk to your guides, but it's worth stumping up the cash.

On arrival, after reminders of the usual dos and don'ts about photography and sticking together as a group, military staff will escort you to the border area. Being at the very centre of the biggest military face-off on earth is rather like being at the eye of a storm – tension is in the air, but it is so peaceful as to make the very idea of imminent combat seem ridiculous. South Korean and American soldiers eyeball their northern counterparts as they have done everyday

since 1953. Do not be fooled by the prevailing air of calm, though; any attempt to even approach the border proper will result in you being shot on the spot, possibly from both sides. In the 1980s however, a Soviet tourist found a unique way to flee the communist block, and defected amid gunfire from both sides. Unless you are really short of time, this is not an advisable way to get to Seoul.

Having soaked up the Cold War fumes, you will be taken into the small blue huts used for negotiations unless they are busy with meetings, and then on to the main building to visit a display outlining the North Korean version of events over the last 50 years. A plaque in red script standing next to the DMZ best sums up the North Korean version of the ceasefire. It reads:

> It was here on July 27, 1953 that the American imperialists got down on their knees before the heroic Chosun people to sign the ceasefire for the war they had provoked June 25, 1950.

Bile against the US imperialist forces is particularly strong at Panmunjeom, although it's moderated with the disclaimer that the Korean people hate the US military, not its citizens.

Throughout the 1970s and 1980s, the North Koreans tunnelled under the DMZ into South Korean territory. The largest was discovered in 1975, and US military experts estimated that 10,000 men per hour could pass through the tunnel into the South. The last tunnel was discovered in 1990 – although the persistent phenomenon gave the Pentagon such headaches that they had even hired psychics to help them find tunnels.

The other interesting sight at the DMZ is the **Korean Wall**, a US-constructed antitank barrier that runs the length of the entire 248km border. It has been hijacked as an emotive propaganda weapon by the North who since 1989 have been comparing it with the Berlin Wall. Indeed, the issue has proven an emotive one in the South as well, where students demand it be dismantled.

MYOHYANGSAN

A trip to this pretty resort area, just 150km north of Pyongyang is often the first chance visitors will have to experience the pristine North Korean countryside, completely untouched by mass tourism. Mount Myohyang and the surrounding area of hills, mountain trails and waterfalls make for a charming trip, and if you begin to miss the relentless pomp and propaganda of Pyongyang, the **International Friendship Exhibition** (IFE) will remind you that you are still very much in North Korea.

Myohyangsan means 'mountain of mysterious fragrance' and it's certainly no misnomer. The scenery is quite wonderful, and in summer awash with flowers. The focus of all trips are, however, the two vast shrines that make up the IFE. The first one contains all the gifts presented to the eternal president Kim Il Sung. Before entering the vast traditional building, you will be asked to put on shoe covers in keeping with the reverential attitude shown by one and all. A member of your group may be honoured with the task of opening the vast doors that lead into the exhibit – after putting on ceremonial gloves to protect the polished door knob.

Kim Il Sung's gifts are very impressive – particularly noteworthy is the beautiful armoured train carriage presented to him by Mao Zedong and a limousine sent to Kim by that great man of the people, Josef Stalin. The exhibits are arranged geographically, although you will thankfully only be shown the highlights of over 100,000 gifts spread over 120 rooms. Gifts from heads of state are displayed on red cloth, those from other officials on blue and gifts from individuals on brown. The undeniable highlight is a stuffed crocodile holding a tray of wooden glasses, presented to the Great Leader by the Sandinistas.

The tone of the visit is very strict and sombre, so avoid the very real temptation to ice-skate across the ridiculously over-polished floor in your foot covers. The most reverential and surreal part of the exhibit (quite an achievement) is the final room in which there is a grinning life-size waxwork of the Great Leader to which you will be expected to bow your head before leaving respectfully. The waxwork itself was apparently a gift from the Chinese and Kim Il Sung is depicted standing against a 3D landscape of bucolic idyll, replete with birdsong, gentle breeze and elevator music. The tone is so remarkably odd that you'll have to concentrate not to get the giggles, especially when your guide insists how serious it all is.

Next is Kim Jong Il's similarly spectacular warehouse. Since taking over as leader on his father's death, an incredible array of gifts have been showered upon the Dear Leader and are housed in a vault built into the cave wall, recalling the secret lair of one of the Bond villains. There is a noticeable shift away from the grand fraternal gifts of fellow communist dictators that characterise Kim Il Sung's exhibit. Instead, Kim Jong Il's smacks of corporate and political gesture – characterising much of his reign since 1994. For example, where Kim Snr received gifts from Ceausescu and Honecker, Kim Jnr has gifts from Hyundai and CNN, as well as a good luck note from Jimmy Carter and a basketball from Madeleine Albright. Indeed, some parts of the exhibit look like any up-market electronics showroom – row after row of wide screen televisions and stereo equipment donated by industrialists.

The highlight of Kim Jong Il's Friendship Exhibition is one of the only statues of the Dear Leader in the country. It depicts the Marshall seated benevolently, back-lit with pink soft-tone lighting.

Having completed a tour of both exhibits, the perfect way to unwind from the seriousness is with some walking on the beautiful mountain trails. Sangwon Valley is the most common place for a hike and is directly northeast of the IFE. You climb via a clearly defined pathway, stone steps and a suspension footbridge past the **Kumgang**, **Taeha**, **Ryongyon** and **Cheonsin waterfalls** (with the **Sanju Falls** an option off to the right). Past the humble **Sangwon Hermitage**, you'll arrive at the pretty **Cheonsin Pavilion**. From there you can descend back the same way or head east to the **Oseon Pavilion**, and then back to civilisation via **Pulyong Hermitage**, **Ryongju Peak**, and **Poyun Hermitage**. If you're not yet tired and there's enough daylight you can proceed 3km upwards from the Cheonsin Pavilion past **Nungin Hermitage** to the **Peobwang Peak**, which offers an astounding view of the entire region.

But at any rate don't miss **Pohyon Temple**, the most historically important Buddhist temple in western North Korea. The temple complex dates back to 1044, with numerous renovations over the centuries. It's just a short walk from the IFE, at the entrance to Sangwon Valley, and features several small pagodas and a large hall housing images of the Buddha, as well as a museum that sports a collection of woodblocks from the Buddhist scriptures the Tripitaka Koreana.

It is common for tours to visit the **Ryongmun Big Cave** either prior or after a visit to Myohyangsan. This 6km-long limestone cave boasts some enormous caverns and a large number of stalactites. Enjoy sights like the Pool of Anti-Imperialist People's Struggle, the Juche Cavern and the Mountain Peak of the Great Leader.

Sleeping

Tourists are usually put up at the deluxe Hyangsan Hotel, a 15-storey pyramidal building that is now in a rather poor state of repair. It's well located though, just below the IFE and a short walk onto mountain trails. In keeping with North Korean hotel tradition, there is a revolving restaurant on the top floor, complete with net curtains, from which absolutely nothing is visible in the evenings due to the hotel's isolated mountain location. The other possibility is the Chongchon Hotel, a small traditional-style 2nd-class hotel. However, we've never heard of foreign tour groups staying there.

KUMGANGSAN

South of the port city of Wonsan on the east of the Korean peninsula, the most dramatic scenery in the entire country begins to rise. The Diamond Mountains (Kumgangsan) have exerted a strange hold over people for centuries, including the notoriously insular Chinese, who conceded to include Kumgangsan among the five most beautiful in the known world (the other four ranges were in China). Located just north of the 38th parallel, the area has also been annexed for very heavily controlled South Korean tourism by the Hyundai Corporation (see p374).

Kumgangsan is divided into Inner, Outer and Sea Kumgang regions. The main tourist activities (at least theoretically) are hiking, mountaineering, boating and sightseeing. The area is peppered with former Buddhist temples and hermitages, waterfalls, mineral springs, a pretty lagoon, and a small museum. Maps of the area are provided by park officials to help you decide where you want to go among the dozens of excellent sites.

If your time here is limited, the best places to visit in the Outer Kumgang Region are the **Samil Lagoon** (try hiring a boat, then rest at Tanpung Restaurant); the **Manmulsang Area** (fantastically shaped crags) and the **Kuryong** and **Pibong Falls** (a 4.5km hike from the Mongnan Restaurant). In the Inner Kumgang Region, it's worth visiting the impressively reconstructed **Pyohon Temple** (founded in AD 670 and one of old Korea's most important Zen monasteries). Hiking in the valleys around Pyohon Temple or, really, anywhere in the park would be rewarding and memorable. You won't need to carry drinking water, but bring plenty of film. **Pirobong** (1639m) is the highest peak out of at least a hundred.

Getting There & Away

The usual route to Kumgangsan is by car from Pyongyang to Onjong-ri via Wonsan along the new highway (around 315km, a four-hour drive). Along the way to Wonsan, your car or bus will stop off at a teahouse by Sinpyeong Lake. From Wonsan, the road more or less follows the coastline south, and you'll get glimpses of the double-wired electric fence that runs the entire length of the east coast. There may also be a stop for tea at Shijung Lake.

Your final destination is the village of Onjong-ri and the 1st-class Kumgangsan Hotel. The hotel is quite a rambling affair consisting of a main building and several outer buildings that include chalets, a shop, a dance hall and bathhouse (fed by a hot spring). The food served here is good, especially the wild mountain vegetable dishes.

PAEKDUSAN

Mount Paekdu, one of the most stunning sights on the Korean peninsula, straddles the Chinese-Korean border in the very far northeastern tip of DPRK. Apart from it being the highest mountain in the country at 2744m, and an amazing geological phenomenon – an extinct volcano now containing a vast crater lake at its centre – it is also of huge mythical importance to the Korean people.

Paekdusan is not included on most tours, as it involves chartering an internal flight to the city of Chongjin and then travelling into the mountains from there. However, if you have the time and money to include a visit on your trip, you will not be disappointed.

The natural beauty of the extinct volcano now containing one of the world's deepest lakes is made all the more magical by the mythology that surrounds the lake, both ancient and modern. The legend runs that Hwanung, the Lord of Heaven, descended onto the mountain in 2333 BC, and from here formed the nation of Choson – 'The Land of Morning Calm', or ancient Korea. It therefore only seems right and proper that four millennia later Kim Jong Il was born here 'and flying white horses were seen in the sky' according to official sources. In fact, Kim Jong Il was probably born in Khabarovsk, Russia, where his father was in exile at the time, but the necessity of maintaining the Kim myth supersedes such niggling facts.

Much like Myohyangsan, an area of spectacular natural beauty is further enhanced by revolutionary 'sights' such as **Jong-Il peak** and the **Secret Camp** from where Kim Il Sung supposedly directed some of the key battles during the anti-Japanese campaigns of WWII, despite the fact that no historians outside DPRK have ever claimed that the area was a battle scene. North Korea's current history books also claim that he established his guerrilla headquarters at Paekdusan in the 1920s, from where he defeated the Japanese. To prove this, you'll be shown declarations that the Great Leader and his comrades carved on the trees. More and more of these 'slogan-bearing trees' are being discovered every year, some so well preserved you'd think they were carved yesterday. The North Korean book *Kim Jong Il in His Young Days* describes the Dear Leader's difficult childhood during those days of ceaseless warfare at Paekdusan:

> His childhood was replete with ordeals. The secret camp of the Korean People's Revolutionary Army in the primeval forest was his home, and ammunition belts and magazines were his playthings. The raging blizzards and ceaseless gunshots were the first sounds to which he became accustomed. Day in and day out fierce battles went on and, during the breaks, there were military and political trainings. On the battlefield, there was no quilt to warmly wrap the new-born child. So women guerrillas gallantly tore cotton out of their own uniforms and each contributed pieces of cloth to make a patchwork quilt for the infant.

Visitors here will be shown the secret camp beneath Jong-Il Peak, said to be the Dear Leader's birthplace, which features a log cabin, and plenty of monuments commemorating patriotic fighters and glorious battles. But the real reason to come here is the glories of nature – vast tracts of virgin forest, abundant wildlife, lonely granite crags, fresh springs, gushing streams and dramatic waterfalls – and, for those able to make the steep and treacherous climb, the astounding **Jong-Il peak**, where heaven indeed seems close and the mundane world is so very far away. Few foreign travellers make it here at all, due to the formidable costs involved, and that is unlikely to change until a highway or train line is built.

Sleeping

Hotels in this area include the 2nd-class Pegaebong Hotel located in the middle of the forest in Samjiyon County, a nice place built for mountain climbers in lodge style.

NORTH KOREAN REFUGEES IN CHINA

Since the early 1990s, there has been an increasing number of North Korean refugees making it across the heavily guarded border with China. The reasons are mainly economic – working for a few months in China can earn enough money to support a North Korean family through the winters by buying food from the private markets, and often refugees return to North Korea once they've saved some money in China.

In 2000, under pressure from the DPRK government, the Chinese authorities launched their harsh 'Strike Hard' campaign. The aim is to forcibly repatriate any North Koreans found in Northern China and send already malnourished individuals back to a country where at the very least they will be imprisoned, but perhaps executed. Even those lucky enough not to get caught often fall victim to people traffickers who force women into prostitution or marriage.

Those lucky enough to survive and make the journey to South Korea are forming refugee support networks, such as Life Funds for North Korean Refugees (www.northkoreanrefugees.com). These vital networks provide financial and emotional support for those who have managed to escape the 'worker's paradise'. For a first-hand account, read Soon Ok-Lee's incredible life story at www.soonoklee.com.

Further away, you can also stay in the town of Hyesan, at the 2nd-class Hyesan Hotel.

Getting There & Away

Paekdusan is only accessible from around late June to mid-September; at all other times it is forbiddingly cold and stormy. Access to the mountain is by air only, followed by car. There are charter flights available which can hold up to 30 people, for €4600 per round-trip flight. At €150 per person that isn't unreasonable, but it's a bit much for a solo trip. Unfortunately, this flight is currently the only transport offered to Paekdusan.

You can also visit the mountain and crater lake from the Chinese side – a trip that's now popular with South Korean tourists. A five-day tour (€425) departs from the South's port of Sokcho in Gangwon-do to the Russian port of Zarubino. The tour then travels by land to Hunchun, Yanji and finally Paekdusan, remaining in Chinese territory. Paekdusan is called Changbaishan in Chinese and the crater lake is called Tianchi (Lake of Heaven). For more details, contact **Dongchun Ferry Company** (☎ 02-720 0101; fax 734 7474) in Seoul.

WONSAN
pop 300,000

The port city of Wonsan on the East Sea is not a huge tourist draw itself, but is an interesting stop en route to the Kumgangsan mountains. As it's not usually a destination it reflects real North Korean life to a good extent. The city is an important port, a centre of learning with 10 universities and a popular holiday resort for Koreans, with beaches at nearby **Lake Sijung** and **Lake Tongjong**. An overnight stop can be pleasantly rewarding.

The city, 200km east of Pyongyang, is surrounded by verdant mountains. It is modern with high-rise buildings, but also pleasantly attractive, especially during the summer months. The two main tourist hotels are the Songdowon Tourist Hotel and the Tomgmyong Hotel, both 2nd class.

The nicest part of Wonsan is the suburb of Songdowon on the northwestern shore. There is a clean sandy beach here set among pines where the Jokchon Stream runs into the East Sea, and a small **zoo** and **botanical garden** – which are both pleasant enough to walk in.

NAMPO
pop 730,000

On the Taedong delta, 55km southwest of Pyongyang is Nampo, North Korea's most important port and centre of industry. Nampo has made its name for being the 'birthplace of the Chollima movement' after the workers at the local steel plant supposedly 'took the lead in bringing about an upswing in socialist construction' according to local tourist pamphlets.

In fact the most impressive sight in town is the **West Sea Barrage**, built across an 8km estuary of the Taedong, and solving the irrigation and drinking water problems in the area. There is little to see in the city itself, but there are nice beaches about 20km from the city on the other side of the barrage. Here if you are lucky enough to go, you will see the locals enjoying volleyball and swimming. It would be unusual to overnight here unless you were on business or taking a ferry to China, but the tourist accommodation is at the 2nd-class Hanggu Hotel situated near Wau islet.

NORTH KOREA DIRECTORY

ACCOMMODATION

Accommodation in North Korea is graded into four classes – deluxe, 1st, 2nd and 3rd. Deluxe accommodation is roughly equivalent to Western four-star hotels, 1st class to three-star and so on. Tourists are always encouraged to stay in the higher bands, but sometimes you can stay in cheaper 2nd- and 3rd-class hotels, particularly off the beaten tourist track where the deluxe variety are not an option. In general, hotels are clean and comfortable, although often in need of redecoration. If your bath is filled with water when you arrive, it is generally because the water supply can be cut regularly, and it's a good way to store water. Similarly, you may be left a bucket for flushing the toilet.

Hotel rooms should always be assumed to be bugged and phone lines tapped, so do not give vent to a day's pent-up anti-Kim frustration once back in your room, as the consequences could be serious.

CHILDREN

While North Koreans love children and often spoil them rotten, a DPRK tour is not suitable for kids. The long days and endless sightseeing may tire out even diehard Kimophiles, and they are likely to bore a child to tears. Equally, the lack of creature comforts and facilities for foreign children would make residents think twice before bringing their families.

CUSTOMS

North Korean customs procedures vary in severity from general polite inquiries to thorough goings over. The last edition of this book was sometimes, but not routinely

confiscated on entry. There are, however, some very strict rules about bringing other items into the country. Most importantly are modems and mobile phones. If you are entering and exiting at the same point, you can hand them over for storage and collect them on exit – this seems to be perfectly safe. Video cameras have on occasion been confiscated, although they are not officially proscribed. The following, however, are:

- telescopes and magnifiers with over x6 magnification
- wireless apparatus and parts, including mobile phones, camcorders or video cameras and transistor radios
- tobacco seeds, leaf tobacco and other seeds
- publications, video tapes, recording tapes, films, photos and other materials which are hostile to the North Korean socialist system or harmful to the North Korean political, economic and cultural development and disturb the maintenance of social order

Note that they are very serious about the last of these prohibitions, which may include any foreign-printed information you have about either North or South Korea.

DANGERS & ANNOYANCES

There have been consistent reports that petty crime is on the increase due to the dire economic situation in the country. That said North Korea must be one of the safest places on earth due to the Stalinist terror that instils social order almost without exception. As a foreigner you will be both conspicuous and unfathomably wealthy compared to the average local. Be as vigilant as you would be anywhere else, but realistically, your chances of being a victim of crime are very low. Pyongyang's Sunan airport seems to be one place where petty theft could be a problem.

The major potential for disaster is thoughtless visitors openly criticising the regime while in the country. In 2002, according to rumours an American aid worker was incarcerated for two months after asking why Kim Jong Il was so plump while ordinary North Koreans were so skinny. It is to be hoped that most readers would have more sense than to make such a remark. If in doubt, bite your tongue – likewise on the phone, by fax and in your hotel room, all of which can be monitored.

Similarly, spare a thought for both your guides and the few locals you will come in contact with. Despite being the official representatives of a brutal Stalinist regime, your guides are vulnerable to persecution themselves. Running away from them, disobeying them or otherwise going against the grain will be far more dangerous for them than for you. When meeting North Koreans in the street, take your lead from the guides. Ask before you take photographs, do not give them any gifts that could incriminate them in imperialist flunkeyism and generally proceed with caution.

DISABLED TRAVELLERS

North Korean culture places great emphasis on caring for the disabled, especially as the Korean War left such a brutal legacy among young recruits. Popular songs such as *I Love an Unmarried Disabled Soldier* encourage marrying the war-wounded, and so disabled visitors need not fear a lack of local understanding. Facilities are basic, but manageable and even in situations where disabled access is a problem, the guides are likely to find some locals to help out.

EMBASSIES & CONSULATES

Despite decades of diplomatic isolation when North Korea only had links with its communist allies and some African countries, a furious few years of diplomatic progress has seen several significant new embassies open in Pyongyang. North Korea now enjoys full diplomatic relations with all EU countries save France and Ireland, although most have not opened embassies in Pyongyang yet. North Korean embassies abroad are largely useless for the average tourist, although in theory they can all process visa applications. Moreover, they tend to favour anonymity – perhaps to avoid human rights activists – and even finding their details can be near impossible. The Beijing Embassy remains the most useful, as well as the only embassy used to dealing with tourists.

North Korean Embassies & Consulates

Canada (☎ 613 232 1715; 151 Slater St, 6th fl, Ottawa K1P5H3)

China (☎ 10-6532 1186/1189, visa section ☎ 6532 4148/6639; fax 6532 6056; Ritan Beilu, Jianguomenwai, Chaoyang District, Beijing) This is the most useful embassy in the list. Ryohaengsa travel usually has a worker (☎ 6532 4862) within the consular and visa section of the embassy. The entrance to the consular section is on the east side of the building at the northern end of the fruit and vegetable stalls.

France (☎ 0417475385; fax 0417476141; 47 rue du Chaveau, 92200 Neuilly-sur-Seine)

Germany (☎ 229 3189/3181; fax 229 3191; Glinka str 5-7, D-10117 Berlin) An Interest Section for the DPRK is its unofficial embassy in Berlin. It is also possible to contact the DPRK's consular section through this office.

Hong Kong (☎ 2803 4447; Consulate General of DPRK, 20/F Chinachem Century Tower, 178 Gloucester Rd, Wanchai) It may be possible to arrange North Korean visas and tours from here.

Indonesia (☎ 21-521 1081; fax 526 0066; Embassy of the DPRK, Chancery, J1 HR Rasuna Said, Kav X-5, Kuningan, Jakarta 12950)

Russia Moscow (☎ 95-143 6249/9063; ulitsa Mosfilmovskaya 72, RF-117192); Nakhodka Consulate (☎ 423-665 5210; ulitsa Vladivostokskaya 1)

Sweden (☎ /fax 76703836; Norra Kungsvägen 39, 181 31 Lindingö)

Switzerland (☎ 31 951 6621; Pourtalèsstrasse 43, 3074 Muri bei Bern)

UK (☎ 20-8992 4965; fax 8992 2053; 73 Gunnersbury Ave, London W5 4LP)

USA (Permanent Representative of the DPRK to the UN; ☎ 212-972 3105; fax 972 3154 820; 2nd Ave, New York, NY 10017) At the time of writing, the USA and the DPRK had no diplomatic representatives, but North Korea does maintain an office in New York for the UN that may be useful for information regarding contacts and other information.

Embassies & Consulates in North Korea

The few embassies that might be of help to travellers are listed following. The UK Embassy represents the interests of Australians, New Zealanders, Canadians, US citizens and EU citizens whose own country does not have a legation in Pyongyang. Most embassies are located in the Munsudong diplomatic quarter.

China (☎ 390 274)
Germany (☎ 381 7385; fax 381 7397)
India (☎ 317277; fax 3817619)
Russia (☎ 381 3101)
Sweden (☎ 381 7908, 382 7908; fax 381 7258)
United Kingdom (☎ 382 7980, out of hours ☎ 381 7993)

In recent times, Italy, Australia and Canada have established diplomatic relations with

Pyongyang, but at the time of writing were operating through their Beijing embassies. Their contact details in Beijing:

Australia (☎ 10-6532 2331; www.austemb.org.cn; 21 Dongzhimenwai Dajie, Sanlitun, Beijing 100600)

Canada (☎ 10-6532 3536; www.canada.org.hk; 19 Dongzhimenwai Dajie, Chaoyang District, Beijing 100600)

Italy (☎ 10-6532 2131~5; www.italianembassy.org.cn; San Li Tun 2, Dong Er Jie, Beijing 100600)

USA (☎ 10-6532 3431/3831; www.usembassy-china.org .cn; 2 Xiu Shui Dong Jie, Beijing, 100600) This is the best place for details regarding US visitors to North Korea.

FESTIVALS & EVENTS

Public holidays include:

New Year's Day 1 January
Kim Jong Il's birthday 16 February
Kim Il Sung's birthday 15 April
Armed Forces Day 25 April
May Day 1 May
The Death of Kim Il Sung 8 July
Victory in the Fatherland Liberation War 27 July
National Liberation (from Japan) Day 15 August
National Foundation Day 9 September
Korean Workers' Party Foundation Day 10 October
Constitution Day 27 December

Note that North Korea does not celebrate Christmas or the Lunar New Year, or many of South Korea's major traditional holidays.

Foreign tourists are usually not welcome, unless by special invitation, around the birthdays of the Kims (16 February and 15 April). By all means try to be in Pyongyang during May Day or Liberation Day. Both holidays are celebrated with huge extravaganzas called Mass Games, featuring military-style parades and mass-gymnastics performances. These rank among North Korea's most memorable sights.

INTERNET ACCESS

It is illegal to bring modems, and thus most laptops, into the DPRK. The foreign community in Pyongyang has a degree of access to the Web via satellite, although it's expensive, and not really a possibility for foreigners. Internet access from the World Food Program office costs €45 per hour, although that was recently reduced by special offer to €8 per hour. In an emergency you may be able to use this service, but otherwise it's very unlikely your guide will agree to take you to the diplomatic quarter.

LEGAL MATTERS

It is highly unlikely that a tourist will come into serious contact with the North Korean authorities, save the guides who accompany you everywhere. For the police to become involved in a matter, a serious transgression of DPRK law will have been committed, such as slander against the Great Leader. If for whatever reason this does occur, stay calm and ask to speak to your country's diplomatic representative in North Korea. Usually, tourists who break the law in North Korea are deported immediately. However, due to the regime's unpredictability, you cannot always count on this.

MAPS

Plans of all cities and towns are available at hotels, although you will have little chance for independent exploration. There are few good quality maps of North Korea available outside the country; the best on offer from travel specialists is the general map of Korea published by Nelles Maps.

MONEY

The unit of currency is the North Korean won (KPW) which, following the economic reforms of 2002, is valued at approximately KPW125 to the euro. There are one, five, 10, 50, 100, 500, 1000 and 5000 bank notes. However, visitors do not usually deal with the won – although they may use the Foreign Exchange Certificates issued during periods of (relatively) heavy tourism, such as the Mass Games. The euro is now the currency all visitors will use. Therefore, to avoid disadvantageous exchange rates, bring only euros with you to spend. You may be given change in Chinese Renminbi, Japanese Yen or even chewing gum by North Korean shop staff. While you are unlikely to use the won, it may be possible to get some from your guides as a souvenir (although it's officially illegal to take it out of the country).

Credit cards not issued by American banks can be used to pay for hotels and for cash advances in Pyongyang. However, it makes best sense to carry all the cash you will need with you in euros, as the situation can change at any time. Travellers cheques are more trouble than they are worth.

PHOTOGRAPHY & VIDEO
Film & Equipment
You can buy colour-print film at reasonable prices from the hard-currency gift shops, but everything else is expensive, so bring what you need. There are modern photo-processing facilities on the 2nd floor at the Koryo Hotel, but you'd probably be better off waiting until you return to China or back home.

Restrictions
Always ask first before taking photos and obey the reply. North Koreans are especially sensitive about foreigners taking photos of them without their permission. Not only are Koreans camera shy, they are acutely aware of the political power of an image in the Western press. Your guides are familiar with the issue of tourists taking photos that end up in a newspaper article that contains anti-DPRK content. The repercussions of such an event could be quite serious for your guides and the tour company that is sponsoring you.

Avoid taking photos of soldiers or any military facilities.

Video
If you are able to get a video camera into North Korea, the restrictions are similar to those with a camera. But, as a number of journalists have made video documentaries about the country in the guise of simply filming tourist sights, the guides and customs officers have become far stricter about their use. Although there is no blanket ban as such, if you are unlucky, they may confiscate your video camera at customs.

POST
Like all other means of communication, the post is monitored. It is however, generally reliable and the colourful North Korean stamps, featuring everything from tributes to the Great Leader to Princess Diana commemoratives, make great souvenirs. Sending postcards anywhere in the world costs 80 euro cents. Some people have suggested that postcards arrive more quickly as they do not need to be opened by censors. In either medium, keep any negative thoughts about the country to yourself to ensure your letter gets through. Poste restante service is not available, and

given the near impossibility of Internet use, telephone and fax remain the best means of communication.

SOLO TRAVELLERS
The concept of 'solo traveller' in North Korea is somewhat redundant – as even when 'alone' you are with two official guides, which can be intense. Combined with the fairly constant vilification of all things Western and capitalist, along with the deification of the Great and Dear Leaders, solo travellers can find long trips in North Korea trying and vastly expensive. However, if you want your own itinerary or need to travel when there are no tours, travelling solo is your only option. Most travel agencies offering group tours to DPRK, such as those listed on p374, will also be happy to negotiate tailor-made itineraries for individuals via Ryohaengsa.

TELEPHONE & FAX
Some refugees have reported that it is illegal for North Koreans to have telephones in their homes. Certainly, it's unlikely you will need to call anywhere within the country – if the need arises, your guide is most likely to call on your behalf. North Korean telephone numbers are divided into 381 numbers (international) and 382 (local). It is not possible to call a 381 number from a 382 number or vice versa. International calls start at €1.50 per minute to China and €4 to Europe. To dial North Korea, the country code is 850.

International calls made from your hotel are extremely expensive, although calls to China are more reasonable. Mobile phones are illegal although a network has been established in Pyongyang for the party elite. Make sure you leave yours in China or at the border.

Faxing is still popular in a land without email. From Pyongyang hotels it's not exactly cheap though – one page to China will cost you €4.50, while a page to Europe will set you back €13! Following pages are slightly less expensive.

TIME
The time in Korea is Greenwich Mean Time plus nine hours. When it is noon in Korea it is 1pm in Sydney or Melbourne, 3am in London, 10pm the previous day in

New York and 7pm the previous day in Los Angeles or San Francisco.

You will also see years such as Juche 8 (1919) or Juche 93 (2004). Three years after the death of Kim Il Sung, the government adopted a new system of recording years, starting from Juche 1 (1912) when Kim No 1 was born.

TOILETS

In Pyongyang and around frequently visited tourist sites, toilet facilities are basic but sanitary. There are regular cuts in the water supply outside Pyongyang, and often a bucket of water will be left in your hotel room for this eventuality. As human waste is used as fertilizer in much of the country, toilets off the beaten tourist path are exceptionally grim – wooden shacks with a raised area about a foot off the ground from where the waste can be gathered for agricultural use. Toilet paper is supplied in hotels, but it's always a good idea to carry tissues for emergencies, especially as diarrhoea is a common problem for visitors.

VISAS

Visas for North Korea will not be issued to US or South Korean citizens (unless they travel on the Hyundai programme, see p374) and journalists need special visas. They cannot travel on tourist ones, although there have been cases of journalists posing as tourists successfully in the past. Each visa must be approved by Pyongyang, so applications need to be made well in advance of travel (preferably allow two months). The embassy usually asks for a one-page résumé listing all education and employment, and may well contact your current employers to verify your status.

Tour groups usually have their visas issued in Beijing the day before travel and it's not unusual to meet in Beijing only to be told that the trip has been cancelled (often due to internal political strife or other diplomatic machinations) – it is therefore important to have good insurance coverage and a contingency plan in China.

The embassy charges between €30 and €80 processing charge, which seems to vary for no good reason. So as not to prejudice your entry to either the South or the United States, North Korean visas are not put into passports, but are separate

documents, taken from you when you exit the country. If you want a souvenir, make a photocopy.

WOMEN TRAVELLERS

While communist ideology dictates equality of the sexes, this is still far from everyday reality in a traditionally patriarchal society. However, women travellers will have no problem at all in the country, as no North Korean would be foolhardy enough to get themselves in trouble for harassing a foreigner. There are an increasing number of female guides being employed by Ryohaengsa and it is possible to request them for individual travel.

TRANSPORT

GETTING THERE & AWAY

Beijing is now the only real transport hub for people entering North Korea, offering both regular trains and flights to Pyongyang. Traffic entering through Russia from Vladivostok – which is still a theoretical possibility – has fallen off to a trickle. This situation is exacerbated by the fact that tourists are often obliged to pick up their visas in Beijing, thus making the use of other routes impossible.

Entering the Country

Immigration is rather severe, but straightforward, as the major hurdle is getting the visa in the first place. Your guides will take your passports for the duration of your stay in North Korea. This is totally routine, so do not worry about them being lost.

AIR

The national airline Koryo Air, running a fleet of old Soviet Tupolevs and Ilyushins, flies to Beijing, Shenyang, Moscow, Berlin, Vladivostok, Macao and Bangkok. The most popular route is from Beijing, from where flying time to Pyongyang is just over an hour. There are two flights per week on a Tuesday and Saturday in each direction and a return flight costs €330. Their international flight codes are JS151 and JS152. The weekly flight from Vladivostok is the second most popular, going in both directions every Thursday. Pyongyang's airport code is FNJ.

4경 인민 의

The dancing army, Arirang Mass Games (p337), Pyongyang

Chickens and eggs, Arirang Mass Games (p337), Pyongyang

The women in blue, Arirang Mass Games (p337), Pyongyang

Waterfalls near Paekdusan (p354)

The Triumphal Arch (p345), Pyongyang

'Long live the Great Victory of the Military Force Policy', Pyongyang (p340)

Koryo Air Office (☎ 10-6501 1557/1559; fax 6501 2591) in Beijing is located inside the Swissotel building, Hong Kong–Macau Center, Dongsi Shitau Lijiao, Beijing 100027. This building adjoins the Swissotel, but the entrance is around the back. You must have a visa before you can pick up your ticket, or Korea International Travel Company (KITC) can pick it up for you (it charges 10% commission).

Koryo Air also has inbound and outbound flights from Shenyang, Liaoning Province, on Thursday and Saturday. Tickets cost €80 one-way.

At the time of writing, China Northern Airlines had suspended their Beijing–Dalian–Pyongyang route.

Aeroflot and Air China no longer fly to Pyongyang, although both may offer chartered flights from time to time.

TRAIN

There are four trains per week in either direction between Beijing and Pyongyang via Tianjin, Tangshan, Jinxi, Dandong and Sinuiju. They run Monday, Wednesday, Thursday and Saturday. On each day, train No 27 leaves Beijing at 5.48pm and arrives at Pyongyang the next day at 6.05pm (about 23 hours). Going the other way, train No 26 departs from Pyongyang at 10.10am arriving in Beijing at 9am. The fare each way is €75 for a soft sleeper. In contrast to the plane, it's possible to pick up your train tickets to Pyongyang without a DPRK visa.

The North Korean train is actually just two carriages attached to the main Beijing–Dandong train, which are detached at Dandong (Chinese side) and then taken across the Yalu River Bridge to Sinuiju (Korean side), where more carriages are added for local people. Non-Koreans remain in their original carriages.

The trains usually spend about four hours at the border for customs and immigration – two hours at Dandong and two hours at Sinuiju. You may wander around the stations and take photos, but ask permission first and obey the directives of signs and officials about going outside.

Sinuiju station will be your first introduction to North Korea and the contrasts with China will be quite marked. Everything is squeaky-clean and there are no vendors plying their goods. A portrait of the Great Leader looks down from the top of the station, and at all other train stations in North Korea.

Soon after departing Sinuiju, you will be presented with a menu (complete with colour photographs) of what's for dinner. The food is excellent and the service is fine. Make sure you have some small denomination euro notes to pay for the meal (about €5), as this is not usually included in tours. There are no facilities for changing money at Sinuiju or on the train. The dining car is for the use of non-Koreans only.

Your guide will meet you on arrival at Pyongyang train station and accompany you to your hotel. Likewise, when you leave North Korea, your guide will bid you farewell at Pyongyang train station or the airport and you then travel to China unaccompanied.

When leaving North Korea, you can link up with the *Trans-Siberian* at Dandong, China. To make this connection you need to reserve your tickets with CITS (China International Travel Company) or KITC in Beijing beforehand. There's also a chance of crossing directly from North Korea into Russia in the northeast via Hasan and then taking the *Trans-Siberian* to Moscow. KITC will let you know if this is possible.

Leaving the Country

If you are travelling without a tour, you should make your reservations for departure from North Korea before you arrive. The government tourist agency, Ryohaengsa (p361) can easily do this for you as long as you inform them in advance. Ensure you reconfirm your departure reservations through your guide.

If departing by air, your guide will accompany you to the airline office so you can buy your ticket, or to reconfirm your outbound flight if you've already bought one. You must pay an airport departure tax of €15 at the airport, while there is no departure tax for the train.

GETTING AROUND

All accommodation, guides and transport must be booked through the government-run Ryohaengsa. You can also book through a travel agent and they will then deal Ryohaengsa on your behalf. The main office of **Ryohaengsa** (☎ +86-10-6437 6666/3133; fax 6436 9089; Korean International Travel Company, 2nd fl, Yanxiang, No A2 Jiangtai Rd, Chaoyang District, Qionghuating) is in Beijing and there are also branches in Dandong, Liaoning Province and in Yanji in Jilin.

Some tour operators:

Chollima Group (☎ 020-7243 3829; www.chollima -group.com; 86 Ralph Ct, Queensway, London W2 5HU) This UK-based company was founded in 2002 and boasts very close links to the DPRK (Democratic People's Republic of Korea) authorities on its impressive website. The company also has a sideline in mail order DPRK products, from Kim Il Sung's works to videos and CDs. It offers a good choice of hotels for all budgets in DPRK – and its standard week-long group tour is €1500 all-inclusive from Beijing.

Hyundai Asan (☎ 02-3669 3000) offers three-day tours to Mount Kumgangsan, crossing into the North from South Korea by ferry. A typical tours costs between 300,000 and 350,000 South Korean won. Highly regimented, with no contact with the real North whatsoever, these trips are laid on for South Koreans interested in visiting the North. However in the past, foreigners including Americans have been able to join these tours as well. See http:// english.tour2korea.com/sightseeing/theme/ggs/list06.asp for more details.

Koryo Group (☎ 10-6416 7544; www.koryogroup .com; Room 43, Red House Hotel, 10 Tai Ping Zhuang, Chun Xiao Lu, Chun Xiu Lu, Dong Zhi Men Wai, Chao Yang District, 100027 Beijing) Nick Bonner's Beijing-based company has been offering DPRK tours for over a decade. It is the undoubted specialist and enjoys a very good working relationship with Ryohaengsa. Its tours

can be tailored to meet the most specialist of interests and it can also arrange individual travel. Its website is an excellent place to start for any tourist, as it is packed with information and infectious enthusiasm for all things DPRK. A standard five-night tour of North Korea is €1275 all-inclusive from Beijing.

Regent Holidays (☎ 20-2921 1711; www.regent -holidays.co.uk; 15 John St, Bristol BS1 2HR) Regent Holidays specialises in obscure destinations and has been taking groups into North Korea since the late eighties. A fully inclusive eight-night tour costs £1110 (starting from Beijing). It also offers an interesting 18-day tour of both North and South Korea – taking a ferry from Dandong in China to Inchon. Starting from London this tour is a substantial £2450.

VNC Travel (☎ 030-231 15 00l; www.vnc.nl; Cathari-jnesingel 70, Postbus 79, 3500 AB Utrecht) This Dutch company specialises in travel to Asia, and includes both group and individual tours to North Korea. It seems to be slightly cheaper than Koryo, but without the flair for the country. A 14-day trip, starting and ending in Amsterdam and including four nights in Beijing is available for €2595.

Some other operators that offer North Korean tours include **Infohub** (www.infohub.com; 38764 Buckboard Common, Fremont, CA 94536), **Marco Polo Reisen** (☎ 089-1500190; www.marco-polo-reisen .com; Riesstrasse 25, D-80992 Munich) and **Tin Bo Travel Services** (☎ 613 238 7093; www.tinboholidays.com; 2nd fl, 725 Somerset St W, Ottawa, Ontario K1R 6P7). None of these is a specialist, but all have good contacts with Ryohaengsa.

Directory

ACCOMMODATION

Backpacker guesthouses are nearly all located in Seoul, but 50 youth hostels are scattered throughout the country near national parks and other tourist areas, and offer dormitory beds from W7000 to W15,000. *Yeoinsuk* (family-run hotels with small rooms and shared bathroom; W10,000 to W25,000) are another cheap option in towns but facilities are poor. In the countryside and at the seaside, *minbak* (private homes with rooms for rent) offer bare budget rooms (W20,000 to W25,000) with shared facilities. These cheaper options often have only a quilt for

bedding so you might want to bring a pair of sheets. Every city and town has budget *yeogwan* – motels with small but well-equipped en suite rooms. They are usually clustered around bus terminals or train stations and at W25,000 to W35,000 for a room they provide a good deal, although the owners rarely speak English and some double up as 'love hotels'. Mid-range hotels can be hard to find, but recently built motels provide a good standard at the cheaper end of mid-range. Luxury hotels can be found in the big cities with a very wide choice available in Seoul.

Accommodation is invariably charged per room with no discount for single travellers. Rooms have beds or the traditional

---

PRACTICALITIES

- The *Korea Herald* has political and business press agency stories, and Saturday's 'Weekender' section is worth a look.

- Radio Gugak broadcasts traditional music to Seoul on 99.1FM or log onto www.gugakfm.co.kr.

- KBS1, KBS2, MBC, SBC and EBS are the five Korean-language TV networks.

- Arirang (www.arirang.co.kr) is a cable channel that broadcasts mainly educational programmes in English.

- AFN (http://afnkorea.com), run by the American military, broadcasts American TV shows and action films on cable, and provides radio broadcasts on 1530AM and 102.7FM – mainly country music and sports events.

- The video system is NTSC – rental charges are cheap and videos are not usually dubbed into Korean.

- Electricity supply is 220V at 60Hz and uses two round pins with no earth although a few ancient *yeogwan* may still be wired for 110V and have two flat pins.

- The metric system rules, but real estate is measured in *pyeong* (3.3 sq metres) and markets still use wooden measuring boxes.

system of a *yo* (a special mattress similar to a futon) on an *ondol* floor that is heated from underneath in cold weather. A third person can usually be squeezed into the room for an additional modest fee. Prices can rise on Friday and Saturday nights, and in July and August near the coast, and near national parks in summer and autumn.

Budget accommodation is defined as rooms that cost W39,000 or less, mid-range is rooms from W40,000 to W150,000, and top end is anything over W150,000.

Backpacker Guesthouses

Seoul has a dozen small guesthouses that cater specifically for budget-conscious foreigners. The staff are friendly and speak English. They offer dormitory accommodation (W15,000 per night) and double rooms (W35,000), and provide a TV and video lounge, a kitchen, access to a free washing machine, a free breakfast and free Internet access. Toilets and showers are usually shared. They are good places to meet other travellers.

Camping & Mountain Huts

Camping grounds with basic facilities (water, toilets and sometimes cold showers) are generally only open in July and August, and can be found at the entrance to national and county parks. Popular beaches have official and unofficial camping grounds. Prices are very cheap (W3000 for a three-person tent in the national parks) but facilities are very limited. For keen hikers, mountain huts are available in most national parks, which also have basic accommodation in a variety of huts (W3000 per night in older style huts, W5000 in newer ones). Huts and camping grounds can get booked-up at weekends and peak times – log on to www.npa.or.kr to make a reservation.

Homestays

Some Korean families offer rooms in their apartments or houses to foreigners. The cost for bed and breakfast is around US$30 a night for a single person and US$50 for a couple. It's a particularly good deal for singles although not all families are keen on hosting single males. Rates are greatly reduced if you stay for a month. Homestay offers visitors the chance to experience Korean food, customs and family life at close quarters; guests are often treated like royalty and you might become life-long friends with your host family. Booking online at least two weeks before your arrival date is the best method of making a reservation. The registration fee is usually US$30. Find out more at www.labostay.or.kr, www.komestay.com, www.seoulhomestay.co.kr or www.korea homestay.com.

Hanok

Staying in a traditional wooden and tiled house or *hanok* is a unique experience. Small rooms are built around a courtyard and you sleep on a *yo* mattress on an *ondol*-heated floor. Some rooms also have traditional furniture or paintings to let you really experience the *yangban* (aristocratic) lifestyle.

Hotels

Luxury hotels are scarce outside the major cities, and mid-range hotels may not exist in smaller towns. You can usually bargain down the price in these hotels, and lots of websites offer heavily discounted prices – try www.koreahotels.net, www.khrc.com or www.hotelwide.net.

Luxury hotels usually have half a dozen restaurants, a bar, nightclub, sauna and fitness centre, indoor pool, coffee shop, karaoke lounge and Internet access. Rooms and furnishings are international standard. The upper mid-range tourist hotels usually have a restaurant, coffee shop, bar and maybe a sauna. Mid-range hotels are suffering because new motels offer small but quite luxurious rooms at a much cheaper price. Top-end and mid-range hotels invariably add 21% (10% service plus 10% VAT) to all bills, although there is a recent tendency to quote prices that include service and tax.

Minbak & Yeoinsuk

Minbak provide basic accommodation (and usually meals) on islands, near ski resorts, in rural areas and near beaches and national parks. Expect to pay up to W25,000 a room but double that in peak season. You sleep on a *yo* mattress on an *ondol* floor with only a TV and a heater or fan in the room. Facilities are shared and lots of people can share one room – an extra person usually costs W5000. The view usually makes up for any discomfort.

Yeoinsuk have disappeared in Seoul but can be found in other cities and towns. They can cost as little as W10,000 a room, but they are tiny with just *yo* mattresses and a TV. Facilities are shared and the décor and cleanliness are usually of a poor standard. Better ones cost up to W25,000 but their low price is usually their only good point.

Rental Accommodation

Most foreign workers live in accommodation supplied by their employers, but a few live in a guesthouse, homestay or *yeogwan* on a monthly basis and negotiate a reduced daily cost. Apartment sharing is another option in Seoul although spare rooms are difficult to find – try the notice boards on the Seoul government or newspaper websites, such as www.koreaherald.co.kr or http://english.metro.seoul.kr.

Renting an apartment is difficult because of the traditional payment system. *Chunsee* is when you loan W100 million to W300 million (70% of the value of the property) to the landlord and get it all back at the end of the rental period. *Wolse* is when you pay a smaller returnable deposit of W3 million to W10 million (a year's rent) plus a monthly rental fee. However some accommodation is available to foreigners on the Western system, with a small returnable deposit and a monthly rent.

If you are looking to rent, take note that real estate is measured in *pyeong* (1 *pyeong* is 3.3 sq metres). A medium-sized apartment is about 30 *pyeong*, though smaller budget ones of 15 *pyeong* to 20 *pyeong* are common.

Temple Stays

Overnight stays in temples throughout Korea were started during the soccer World Cup finals in 2002 but the programme is being continued. They usually run from 4pm to 10am the next day and cost around W50,000. Participants wear Buddhist robes and stay in single-sex dormitory-style accommodation, sleeping on padded quilts on the floor. Don't go to bed late because you have to get up at 3am the next day to join the monks at prayer.

Sweeping paths, making stone rubbings and hiking in the mountains could also be

---

> **BUDDHIST PRAYER BEFORE EATING A MEAL**
>
> Now we take our meal that caused no harm to any sentient beings.
> Let us consider whether our behaviour deserves this meal.
> Let us cultivate our minds away from greed, anger and foolishness.
> We eat this meal to become enlightened.

---

on the schedule, as well as meditation, temple meals and a tea ceremony. Temple stays are an enlightening experience providing genuine insights into the lifestyle and beliefs of Korean monks. Contact **KNTO** (Korean National Tourism Organisation; Map pp72-4; ☎ 02-757 0086; www.knto.or.kr; ☸ 9am-8pm) in Seoul for details.

Yeogwan & Motels

The rooms may be small but they have en suites and are full of facilities: TV, video, fridge, telephone, drinking water, air-conditioning, heating, even toothbrushes, shampoo and hairdryers. They offer double beds or *ondol*-style rooms with *yo* mattresses on the floor. If you want twin beds you will have to ask for the latter. Note that single rooms are usually double rooms with no discount. The owners rarely speak English and there are no restaurants, bars, kitchens or laundry facilities. You just get a room and maybe some videos that you can borrow for free, although the selection rarely strays from action and X-rated films. *Yeogwan*, *jang* (inns) and motels are all similar and don't add any tax or service charge to the bill. They are identified by the symbol:

Unfortunately the same symbol is also used by public baths and saunas, which can cause confusion.

If you want an inexpensive room, look for a *yeogwan* in an older-style building. However, *yeogwan* in more modern buildings offer smarter and better rooms for only W5000 or W10,000 extra. If you see a fairyland castle, it's a love motel which caters for short-term stays by couples but also accepts conventional guests. They often offer

DIRECTORY

the best deal if you don't mind a round bed, satin sheets and a boudoir décor with stars painted on the ceiling.

Youth Hostels

Fifty large youth hostels are spread around the country but are not always conveniently located in terms of public transport. They are not used to dealing with foreigners but are worth considering by solo budget travellers as dormitory beds generally cost W7000 to W15,000 (W22,000 in Seoul). Family rooms are W35,000 to W55,000 (W70,000 in Seoul), but motels are better. Membership costs W20,000 – see www.kyha .or.kr for more details.

ACTIVITIES
Hiking

Tramping around densely forested national parks, coming across monks living in remote hermitages, and scaling mountain peaks for that top-of-the-world feeling are frequently the highlights of a journey through Korea. So many parks are outstanding, with well-marked paths, unspoilt vistas, waterfalls, autumn colours and cascading rivers. Reliable and frequent buses make it all easily accessible.

Hot Spring Baths & Saunas

Don't leave Korea without experiencing the therapeutic effects of a hot spring bath. If you are in Seoul take a bus to Icheon (p127), 50km to the southeast, to soak in an *oncheon* – a hot bath fed from mineral-laden hot spring water, or take the subway west to Incheon and a ferry to Yeongjongdo (p132) for a seawater hot bath. Yuseong (p295), Suanbo (p317), Osaek (p153) and Busan (p211) all make expansive therapeutic claims for their hot spring water. Prices vary with the luxuriousness of the facilities but are normally reasonable.

There are plenty of ordinary hot water public baths, known as *tang*, in every town in the country. *Tang* have the same symbol as *yeogwan* which causes confusion. The rather spartan *tang* bathhouses only cost around W4000, which is less than half the price of the more palatial facilities offered by some hotels and smart new *jjimjilbang* (modern-style saunas with luxurious facilities).

Undress in the locker room and then take a shower, as you must clean yourself

thoroughly before getting into the bath. Soap and shampoo is supplied, as well as toothbrushes and toothpaste. A thorough clean is part of the bath experience. The ladies section has hairdryers, foot massagers and all sorts of lotions and perfumes. You can often have your hair cut as well.

The water in the big public baths varies from hot to extremely hot, but there may also be a cold bath (including a 'waterfall' shower). Relaxing and wrinkling-up in a hot bath is good therapy, especially on a cold winter's day. The heat soaks into weary bodies, soothing tired muscles and minds.

Most *tang* also have saunas – some made of wood, some of stone – but all are as hot as a pizza oven. If you want to suffer more, you can be pummelled by a masseur. But check the price first as massages are usually expensive. Many bathers also take a nap lying down on a wooden floor with a block of wood for a pillow. Some places allow you to stay all night.

Try to find an *oncheon* with an outdoor section, which is a real Garden of Eden experience, although the Adams and Eves are separated. It's the perfect way to relax after a hike in the mountains.

Pool & Four Ball

There are pool halls all over the country that cost around W6000 an hour. (Look for the obvious signs outside.) They often have pool (called 'pocketball' in Korea) and tables for games of 'four ball', which is similar to billiards, but there are no pockets and players must hit cannons. Two red balls and two white ones are used. The players (any number) hit the white balls in turn. The object of the game is to hit both of the red balls in one shot without hitting the other white ball. It sounds easy but it isn't.

You score minus one if you are successful, and you also get to take another turn. You score nothing if you hit just one red, and you score plus one if you hit the other white ball or miss everything. Beginners start with a score of three points and when you improve you start with five points, then eight and so on. When your score reaches zero, to finish you must do a more difficult shot – hit one red and two side-cushions or two reds and one side-cushion without hitting the other white ball.

Scuba Diving

Diving is not a major activity in Korea, but view www.scubainkorea.com for general information and www.bigblue33.co.kr for details of a dive company in Seogwipo on the south coast of Jeju-do, which is probably the best diving spot – see p270. A two-tank dive costs W60,000.

Skiing

The cold winters and mountainous terrain make Korea an ideal country for winter sports, and the main ski season runs from December to February. Prices are reasonable and increasing numbers of ski resorts offer plenty of facilities; accommodation ranges from youth hostels and *minbak* to condominiums and luxury hotels. Korea only just missed out to Vancouver (53 votes to 56) on hosting the 2010 Winter Olympics. Most resorts are in Gyeonggi-do or Gangwon-do and the most southerly one is near Muju in Jeollabuk-do. It's easy to hire ski clothes and equipment, and ski instructors speak English. Expect to pay around W40,000 for a day lift pass and W25,000 for ski equipment hire or W35,000 for snowboarding gear. Package deals from Seoul start at W75,000. Snowboarding and night skiing are usually available. Ski resorts are reviewed in the regional chapters. View www.visitseoul.net for information on ski resorts. Otherwise contact **KNTO** (☎ 757 0086; www.knto.or.kr) or a travel agent.

Taekwondo, Sunmudo & Gicheon

Korean martial arts are attracting world-wide interest. For information about taekwondo see p92, and for information about *sunmudo* see Golgulsa on p183. *Gicheon* is another indigenous Korean martial art. You can learn more about *gicheon* at www24.brinkster.com/thefringe; Lee Ki-tae, a *gicheon* instructor, can be contacted on ☎ 016-420 0509 or gicheonmaster@yahoo.com.

BUSINESS HOURS

For most government and private offices, business hours are from 9am to 6pm Monday to Friday, and from 9am to 1pm on Saturday. From November to February government offices usually close an hour earlier. However, a five-day week is gradually being introduced, so fewer offices will be open on Saturday mornings. Tourist information centres are usually open from 9am to 5pm daily while national parks are open daily from sunrise to sunset.

Banking hours are from 9.30am to 4pm Monday to Friday. Post offices are open from 9am to 6pm Monday to Friday from March to October, and 9am to 5pm November to February. On alternate Saturdays they open from 9am to noon but this could soon end.

Department stores traditionally open from 10.30am to 7.30pm six days a week (the day they are closed varies from store to store). Nowadays some open every day, and a few open until late evening. New youth-oriented shopping malls tend to stay open until 10pm. Small general stores often stay open until midnight even in suburban areas, and many convenience stores are open 24 hours. Shops are generally open from 10am to around 9pm every day. Travel agents may take Sunday off.

Restaurants usually open from 10am to 10pm every day. Cinemas traditionally open at 11am, with the last show ending at 11pm, but a few run later.

Pubs and bars open daily from 6pm to midnight but they close later on Friday and Saturday. Some open at noon for the thirsty early birds.

There is plenty for night owls to do in Korean cities – some saunas, Internet and DVD rooms, convenience stores, bars and nightclubs open all night. In Seoul some markets, malls, cinemas and restaurants stay open all night too.

CHILDREN

Lonely Planet's *Travel with Children* is recommended. Foreigners travelling with young children are a novelty but, once they have got over their surprise, expect the locals to be helpful and intrigued. View www.travelwithyourkids.com for general advice and a first-hand report on Seoul for kids, which gives the city a thumbs-up.

Practicalities

Only luxury hotels are likely to be able to organise a cot, but infants could sleep on a *yo* mattress on the floor. Bring your own car safety seat and bicycle helmets as they are not common. Few restaurants have high-chairs. Nappy-changing facilities are common in Seoul toilets but less so in the provinces. Bring your own baby food unless

DIRECTORY

you can decipher *hangeul* labels. Baby-sitting services are almost non-existent, except in Lotte World Hotel in Seoul, which charges US$9 an hour. Breastfeeding in public is not a local custom, although you may see it occasionally in a park.

Sights & Activities

Zoos, funfairs and parks can be found in most cities along with cinemas, DVD rooms, Internet rooms, video game arcades, ten-pin bowling alleys, *noraebang* (karaoke rooms) and board-game cafés. Children will rarely be more than 100m away from an ice-cream or a fast-food outlet. In winter go skiing, snowboarding and sledding, and in summer head for the beaches. The Seoul area has plenty of fun activities for kids – see p94. Busan has an aquarium (p213) on Haeundae Beach, and for Bugok Hawaii near Busan, see p223.

CLIMATE CHARTS

Korea has four distinct seasons – spring is mid-March to the end of May, summer is from June to August, autumn is September to November and winter goes from December to mid-March. Temperature varies extremely between midsummer and midwinter, moreso in the northern half of the country. Winters in Seoul are colder than in the more southerly Busan or Jeju-do. Rainfall in the northern part generally arrives in the summer monsoon season (late June to August) while rainfall in Jeju-do is more evenly spread throughout the year. See p9 for advice about the best times to visit.

COURSES

See p94 for cooking and Korean language courses in Seoul. Korean language courses are available all over the country – visit your nearest university or log on to www.knto.or.kr for more information.

CUSTOMS

You must declare all plants, fresh fruit and vegetables that you bring in. Bringing in meat is not allowed. If you have more than US$10,000 in cash and travellers cheques, this should be declared and you have to fill in a form. Gifts worth more than US$400 should also be declared.

When leaving the country, the duty-free allowance is 1L of alcohol, 200 cigarettes and 59ml (2oz) of perfume. Antiques of

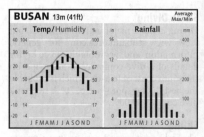

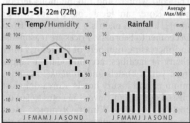

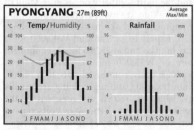

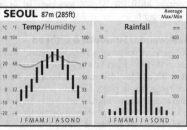

national importance are not allowed to be exported, so if you are thinking of buying a very expensive genuine antique, check with the **Cultural Properties Appraisal Office** (☎ 662 0106). View www.customs.go.kr for further information.

DISABLED TRAVELLERS

In the past, Korea did not cater for disabled travellers as Koreans with disabilities tended to stay at home, and there were few disabled foreign tourists. But in Seoul and some other cities this is changing. Most subway stations in Seoul now have lifts, elevators and toilets with wheelchair access and handrails. Tourist attractions, especially government-run ones, offer generous discounts or even free entry for disabled people and a helper. A useful brochure in Seoul is the *Accessible Seoul* map, available from the KNTO office in Seoul. More information is available on www.easyaccess.or.kr.

DISCOUNT CARDS

Bring your student or pensioner card if you have one. A youth hostel membership card provides a few discounts. Some government-run tourist attractions offer discounts or free entry to people over 65 years. Other organisations may restrict discounts to local residents but it is always worth trying.

EMBASSIES & CONSULATES
South Korean Embassies & Consulates

Australia (☎ 06-270 4100; 113 Empire Circuit, Yarralumla, ACT 2600)

Canada (☎ 613-244 5010; www.emb-korea.ottawa.on.ca; 150 Boteler St, Ottawa, ON K1N 5A6)

China (☎ 10-6532 0290; 4th Ave East, Sanlitun, Chaoyang District, Beijing 100600)

France (☎ 01 47 53 01 01; 125 rue de Grenelle, Paris 75007)

Germany (☎ 30-260 65432; www.koreaemb.de; Kurfurstenstrasse 72-74, Berlin 10787)

Hong Kong (☎ 2529 4141; 5th fl, Far East Finance Centre, 16 Harcourt Rd, Central)

Ireland (☎ 01-660 8800; 15 Clyde Rd, Ballsbridge, Dublin 4)

Japan (☎ 03-3452 7611; 1-2-5 Minami-Azabu, 1-chome, Minato-ku, Tokyo 106-0047)

Netherlands (☎ 070-358 6076; Verlengde Tolweg 8, the Hague 2517 JV)

New Zealand (☎ 04-473 9073; 11th fl, ASB Bank Tower Bldg, 2 Hunter St, Wellington)

Philippines (☎ 02-811 6139; 10th fl, the Pacific Star, Makati Ave, Makati, Metro Manila)

Russian Federation (☎ 095-956 1474; ulitsa Spiridonobka Dom 14, Moscow)

Singapore (☎ 65-6256 1188; 47 Scotts Rd, 08-00 Goldbell Towers, Singapore 228233)

Taiwan (visa office ☎ 02-2758 8320; Room 1506, 333 Keelung Rd, Section 1, Taipei)

Thailand (☎ 0-2247 7537; 23 Thirmruammit Rd, Ratchadapisek, Huay Kwang, Bangkok 10320)

UK (☎ 020-7227 5500; 60 Buckingham Gate, London SW1E 6AJ)

USA (☎ 202-939 5600; www.koreaembassyusa.org; 2450 Massachusetts Ave NW, Washington DC 20008)

YOUR OWN EMBASSY

It's important to realise what your own embassy – the embassy of the country of which you are a citizen – can and can't do to help you if you strike trouble. Generally speaking, it won't be much help in emergencies if the trouble you're in is remotely your own fault. Remember that you are bound by the laws of the country you are in. Your embassy will not be sympathetic if you end up in jail after committing a crime locally, even if such actions are legal in your own country.

In genuine emergencies you might get some assistance, but only if other channels have been exhausted. If you need to get home urgently, a free ticket home is very unlikely – the embassy would expect you to have insurance. If you have all your money and documents stolen, it might assist with getting a new passport, but a loan for onward travel is out of the question.

Some embassies used to keep letters for travellers or have a small reading room with home newspapers, but these days a mail-holding service is rare and newspapers generally tend to be out of date.

Embassies & Consulates in South Korea

Log on to a site such as www.embassy world.com for contact details on embassies worldwide. There are a number of embassies in Seoul:

Australia (Map pp72-4; ☎ 2003 0100; www.australia .or.kr; 11th fl, Kyobo Bldg, Jongno 1-ga, Jongno-gu)

Canada (Map pp76-7; ☎ 3455 6000; www.korea .gc.ca; 9th fl, Kolon Bldg, 45 Mugyo-dong, Jung-gu)

China (Map pp72-4; ☎ 738 1193; www.chinaemb .or.kr; 9th fl, Kyobo Bldg, Jongno 1-ga, Jongno-gu)

France (Map pp70-1; ☎ 3149 4300; ambassade.france.or.kr; 30 Hap-dong, Seodaemun-gu)

Germany (Map pp72-4; ☎ 748 4114; www.gembassy .or.kr; 308-5 Dongbinggo-dong, Yongsan-gu)

Ireland (Map pp76-7; ☎ 774 6455; www.irelandhouse-korea.com; 15th fl, Daehan Fire & Marine Insurance Bldg, 51-1 Namchang-dong, Jung-gu)

Japan (Map pp72-4; ☎ 2170 5200; www.kr.emb -japan.go.jp; 18-11 Junghak-dong, Jongno-gu)

New Zealand (Map pp72-4; ☎ 730 7794; www.nz embassy.com; 18th fl, Kyobo Bldg, Jongno 1-ga, Jongno-gu)

Russian Federation (Map pp82-3; ☎ 552 7096; 1001-13 Daechi-dong, Gangnam-gu)

Singapore (Map pp76-7; ☎ 744 2464; 19th fl, Samsung Taepyeongno Bldg, 310 Taepyeongno 2-ga, Jung-gu)

Taiwan (Map pp72-4; ☎ 399 2767; 6th fl, Gwanghwa-mun Bldg, Jongno-gu)
UK (Map pp76-7; ☎ 3210 5500; www.britishembassy
.or.kr; 4 Jeong-dong, Jung-gu)
USA (Map pp72-4; ☎ 397 4114; http://usembassy
.state.gov/seoul; 6322 Sejongno, Jongno-gu)

FESTIVALS & EVENTS

Festival dates and months are constantly altered, so check before you go.

Snow Festival (January) Held in Taebaeksan (p162) and other mountain areas. There are giant ice sculptures, sledding opportunities and igloo restaurants.

Cherry Blossoms (April) The date that the cherry trees blossom depends on the weather and where you are in Korea, but every region has streets and parks where people go to enjoy the sight.

Buddha's Birthday Parade (May) Held in Seoul (p96), it's the country's biggest street parade.

Modern Dance Festival (May) Held in Daehangno, Seoul.

International Mime Festival (May) Held in the lakeside city of Chuncheon (p142).

Dano Festival (22 June 2004, 11 June 2005, 31 May 2006, 19 June 2007, 8 June 2008) Held according to the lunar calendar, this traditional festival features shamanist rituals, mask dances and a market; Gangneung (p154) is the best place to experience it.

Mud Festival (July) Held on Daecheon Beach with lots of muddy fun and games (p305).

Gwangju Biennale (usually autumn) A two-month festival of avant garde art (http://gwangju-biennale.org) held in even-numbered years (see p237).

UNUSUAL FESTIVALS

Some of Korea's more unusual festivals you may want to check out:

- Gangneung's **Cuttlefish Festival** – includes a catch-a-cuttlefish-by-hand competition
- Chodang's **Uncurdled Tofu Festival** – a good one for vegetarians
- Jeong-eup's **Bullfighting Festival** (May) – more pushing than fighting
- Muju's **Firefly Festival** (August) – the smallest festival star
- Gimje's **Horizon Festival** (October) – because all the other festival topics have been taken.

Contact the KNTO (www.knto.or.kr) for information on when these festivals are held.

World Ceramics Biennale (autumn) Held in odd-numbered years in Icheon.

World Martial Arts Festival (September to October) Held in Chungju (p316), the birthplace of *taekgyeon* (the original form of taekwondo).

Mask Dance Festival (September to October) A 10-day festival that involves over 20 traditional dance troupes and is held in Andong (p193).

Baekje Festival (October) Running since 1955 and held in Buyeo in even-numbered years and in Gongju (p298) in odd-numbered years.

Pusan Film Festival (October) Korea's leading film festival (www.piff.org) is held in Busan (p215). Don't let Pusan/Busan fool you – the film festival has retained the old spelling.

FOOD

Exploring Korea's unique and very diverse cuisine is one of the pleasures of any visit – see p50. Western, Japanese and Chinese food is also widely available. Price definitions for Eating listings in this book:

Budget Most meals under W7000.
Mid-range Most meals in the W7000 to W18,000 range.
Top end Most meals cost more than W18,000.

GAY & LESBIAN TRAVELLERS

Korea has never passed any laws that overtly discriminate against homosexuals. But this should not be taken as a sign of tolerance or acceptance. Korean law does not mention homosexuality because it is considered so bizarre and unnatural that it is unmentionable in public. Many older Koreans insist that there are no gays in Korea. Recent attempts by gays and lesbians to come out of the closet have met with hostility but their situation is improving because younger people are less prejudiced than their parents.

Virtually all Korean gays and lesbians keep their sexual orientation a secret from their family, work colleagues and friends. Major cities have several gay clubs, bars and particularly saunas, but they maintain a low profile. Despite some discussion on the issue, it is generally a taboo topic, especially for the older generation. Gay and lesbian travellers who publicise their preferences can expect some shocked and hostile reactions.

View www.utopia-asia.com for the most current news on gay and lesbian issues, and listings of bars and events in Korea's bigger cities. See p108 for information on the gay scene in Itaewon, Seoul.

HOLIDAYS
Public Holidays
Nine Korean public holidays are set according to the solar calendar and three according to the lunar calendar, meaning that they fall on different days each year. The government may reduce the number of public holidays (moving Children's Day and Arbour Day to Saturday) because of the introduction of a five-day working week. The five-day week will cause tourist sites to become even more crowded at weekends. School holidays don't cause any particular problems for tourists.

New Year's Day (1 January) Bells ring out at midnight.

Lunar New Year (9 February 2005, 30 January 2006, 18 February 2007, 7 February 2008) Korea grinds to a halt during this three-day holiday when everybody returns to their hometown, visits relatives, bows to their elders, and eats rice cakes and other goodies. Trains and planes are booked up months ahead and expressways are one long traffic jam.

Independence Movement Day (1 March) The anniversary of the day in 1919 when nation-wide protests against Japanese rule began.

Arbour Day (5 April) Plant a tree to beautify the country.

Children's Day (5 May) Take the kids out for a day and load them up with gifts.

Buddha's Birthday (26 May 2004, 15 May 2005, 5 May 2006, 24 May 2007, 12 May 2008) Colourful lanterns decorate all the Buddhist temples.

Memorial Day (6 June) Honours those who died for their country.

Constitution Day (17 July) Commemorates the founding of the Republic of South Korea in 1948.

Liberation Day (15 August) Celebrates the day the Japanese surrendered to Allied forces in 1945, marking the end of their 35-year rule of Korea.

Chuseok (Thanksgiving; 28 September 2004, 18 September 2005, 6 October 2006, 25 September 2007, 14 September 2008) The Harvest Moon Festival, a three-day holiday when families get together, eat crescent-shaped rice cakes and visit their ancestors' graves. Avoid travelling at this time.

National Foundation Day (3 October) Dangun, the legendary founder of the Korean nation, was born on this day in 2333 BC.

Christmas Day (25 December) Grandfather Santa hands out presents.

INSURANCE
A policy covering theft, loss, medical expenses and compensation for cancellation or delays in your travel arrangements is highly recommended. If items are lost or stolen, make sure you get a police report straightaway – otherwise your insurer might not pay up. There is a wide variety of policies available, so check the small print. See p385 for health insurance and p382 for car insurance.

INTERNET ACCESS
There are Internet rooms with high-speed access on almost every street in the country. They charge around W1000 per hour – look out for the 'PC 방' signs. Some tourist information centres, cafés, and other establishments provide free Internet access, as do the more expensive hotels. Internet Service Providers (ISPs) can offer you an English-language home page and continuous access for around W35,000 a month. Lonely Planet's eKno email account service can help you keep in touch. See p10 for some useful websites.

LEGAL MATTERS
The Korean police tend to be easy-going with foreigners, and most legal problems involve visa violations or illegal drugs. In the case of visa transgressions, the penalty is normally a fine and possible expulsion from the country. As for using or selling narcotics, think twice: you could spend a few years researching the unpleasant living conditions in a South Korean prison.

MAPS
The Korean National Tourism Organisation (KNTO) and tourist information centres in every province give out free tourist maps which are good enough for most purposes. Ask at the ticket booths at national and provincial parks for hiking maps, which usually contain some English and cost only W1000. High-quality maps are not available in English.

LEGAL AGES

Women can get married at 16 but men have to wait until they are 18, while the age of consent for sex (outside marriage) is 18. To drive a car or vote you must be 20 years old, although it is being debated whether to reduce the voting age to 18 or 19. Anyone under 20 is not allowed to buy or drink alcohol nor to buy or smoke cigarettes.

MONEY

The South Korean unit of currency is the won (W), which comes in W10, W50, W100 and W500 coins. Notes come in denominations of W1000, W5000 and W10,000. The highest-value note is worth less than US$10 at the current exchange rate, so be prepared to carry around a thick wad of notes. See p10 for the cost of everyday items, and the inside front cover for exchange rates at the time of printing. View www.keb.co.kr for up-to-date exchange rates.

Banks in every high street offer foreign exchange services, although it often takes some time. Tourist shops and hotels exchange money, but compare their rates and commissions with the banks before using their services. US dollars are the easiest to exchange but any major currency is accepted. The Korea Exchange Bank accepts 49 currencies in the form of cash and 28 currencies in the form of travellers cheques. Travellers cheques have a slightly better exchange rate than cash. There is a black market in Busan but the risks outweigh the benefits. Don't forget to reconvert your surplus won into another currency before you leave the country, as exchanging won outside Korea is often impossible. If you reconvert more than US$2000 worth of won at Incheon airport, you will have to show bank receipts to prove you exchanged the money.

ATMS

Korean ATMs are a little strange. If you have a foreign credit card, you need to find an ATM with a 'Global' sign and the logo of your credit card company. Some of the Global ATMs have all their instructions in Korean, so you may need help. ATMs can be found outside banks and post offices and inside deluxe hotels, subway stations, convenience stores and department stores. Restrictions on the amount of money you can withdraw vary from machine to machine. It can be as low as W100,000 or W300,000 per day, but many ATMs have a W700,000 limit. Another problem is that ATMs have time restrictions and most only operate between 9am and 10pm. If you use an ATM after 10pm or even outside banking hours you may be charged a higher commission. Itaewon subway station (Map p75; Line 6) has a Global ATM that has instructions in English, is open 24 hours and has a withdrawal limit of W300,000.

Credit Cards

More and more hotels, shops and restaurants in cities and tourist areas accept foreign credit cards, but there are still plenty of *yeogwan*, restaurants and small businesses that don't accept them. Be prepared to carry around plenty of cash, especially if you're touring around outside the cities.

PHOTOGRAPHY & VIDEO

The major film brands are readily available for around W4000 (36 exposures, 100 ISO). Processing facilities are high quality, fast and cost around W1000 plus W200 a print. Slide film isn't as easy to find due to lack of demand. All the major camera and video brands are available including the local ones, such as Samsung, which are challenging the Japanese manufacturers. Yongsan Electronics Market and Techno Mart in Seoul are the best places to buy the latest camera and video equipment – see p111.

Most people do not mind being photographed, but market traders, riot police and monks are among those who may not want to be photographed, so always ask first. Never take photographs of shamanist ceremonies without asking permission. In the DMZ you can take photos, but always follow the advice of your guide or you might spark off World War III. For professional hints on how to improve your pictures purchase Lonely Planet's *Travel Photography*.

POST

Korean postal services (www.koreapost.go .kr) are reliable and reasonably cheap. Domestic postal rates are W160 for a postcard, W190 for a letter, W1170 for a registered letter and W1500 for a package weighing less than 2kg. Local mail is usually delivered in two days or so, but letters with the address in English can take a day or two longer. Postcards are W350 and aerograms W400 to any country, but international letter and parcel rates vary according to the destination. Airmail letters (10g) cost W580 (for zone three: North America, Europe, Australia and New Zealand). For zone three a 2kg airmail packet costs W18,000, and a 10kg parcel costs W86,200 by airmail and W28,000 by surface mail. Don't seal your package if you want to take advantage of the lower rate that applies to sending printed papers only. Larger post offices have a packing service that costs from W2000 to W5500, and may have free Internet access. Except in Seoul and large cities it is probably better not to rely on the poste restante system.

SOLO TRAVELLERS

Solo travellers are at a disadvantage in Korea because no motels and few hotels have single rooms, and solo travellers pay the same or almost the same as a couple. When travelling solo around the country, budget travellers should consider staying at youth hostel dormitories, although they are not always conveniently located.

Another problem faced by singles is that many traditional Korean meals are for sharing and are not available in single portions, so find a companion if you want to enjoy *hanjeongsik* (Korean-style banquet), *bulgogi* (marinated barbecued beef), *galbi* (barbecued beef ribs), *samgyeopsal* (barbecued pork belly wrapped in lettuce) or *jjimdak* (steamed chicken in a spicy sauce).

TELEPHONE & FAX
Fax
If you want to send a fax, first ask at your guesthouse, *yeogwan* or hotel, but if they can't help you, try the nearest stationery store or photocopy shop.

Mobile Phones
Mobile phones can be rented at Incheon International Airport. Charges are around W20,000 for the initial rental and then W2000 to W4000 a day. Incoming calls are free and outgoing domestic calls currently cost around W350 a minute.

Phone Codes
Korea's nine provinces and seven largest cities have their own area codes. South Korea's country code is ☎ 82. Do not dial the first zero of the area codes if you are calling from outside Korea.

Province/City	Code
Busan	☎ 051
Chungcheongbuk-do	☎ 043
Chungcheongnam-do	☎ 041
Daegu	☎ 053
Daejeon	☎ 042
Gangwon-do	☎ 033
Gwangju	☎ 062

Province/City	Code
Gyeonggi-do	☎ 031
Gyeongsangbuk-do	☎ 054
Gyeongsangnam-do	☎ 055
Incheon	☎ 032
Jeju-do	☎ 064
Jeollabuk-do	☎ 063
Jeollanam-do	☎ 061
Seoul	☎ 02
Ulsan	☎ 052

Phonecards
Telephone cards usually give you a 10% bonus and can be bought at convenience stores and many small shops. There are two types of cards so if your card does not fit in one type of phone, try a different-looking phone. A few phones accept credit cards. Dial KT (☎ 001), Dacom (☎ 002) and Onse (☎ 008) to call abroad, and you can make international calls from many telephone booths. Much cheaper international rates are offered by other providers whose call-back telephone cards are available in Itaewon and elsewhere.

TIME
South Korea has one time zone, which is Greenwich Mean Time (GMT) plus nine hours. When it is noon in Seoul it is 1pm in Sydney, 3am in London, 10pm the previous day in New York and 7pm the previous day in San Francisco. See the time-zone world map at the back of this book. Korea does not have a daylight-saving period.

TOILETS
Korea's public toilets are improving and there are more and more clean, modern and well-signposted ones. Virtually all toilets are free of charge and some are decorated with flowers and pictures. The cleaning staff generally do an excellent job. All tourist attractions, parks, subway stations, train stations and bus stations have public toilets. Even when you go hiking in the mountains there are lots of toilets although some are very basic. Asian-style squat toilets are losing their battle with European-style ones with seats, but there are still a few around. Face the hooded end when you squat. Always carry tissues around with you as not all of the restrooms supply toilet paper.

TOURIST INFORMATION

In Seoul KNTO operates an excellent **tourist information centre** (Map pp72-4; ☎ 757 0086; www.knto.or.kr; 9am-6pm, 9am-5pm Nov-Feb), which has stacks of brochures on every region, as well as helpful and well-informed staff. They can book hotels for you and advise you about anything.

A useful **tourist phone number** (☎ 1330) connects you with Seoul's KNTO office. Dial ☎ 02-1330 if you're on a mobile phone or are outside Seoul. If you want to contact a tourist information centre elsewhere, dial the provincial/metro code first – so for information on Gangwon-do, dial 033-1330. Many tourist areas throughout the country have their own tourist information centres, so it's not a problem to find one.

For tourist information in the provinces and metropolitan areas log on to the following websites:

Busan www.pusanweb.com
Chungcheongbuk-do www.cb21.net
Chungcheongnam-do www.chungnam.net
Daegu www.thedaeguguide.com
Daejeon www.metro.daejeon.kr
Gangwon-do www.gangwon.to
Gwangju www.gwangju.go.kr
Gyeongsangbuk-do www.gyeongbuk.go.kr
Gyeonggi-do www.gyeonggi.go.kr
Gyeongsangnam-do www.gsnd.net
Incheon www.incheon.go.kr
Jeju-do www.cheju.go.kr
Jeollabuk-do www.provin.jeonbuk.kr
Jeollanam-do www.jeonnam.go.kr
Seoul www.seoul.go.kr
Ulsan www.ulsan.go.kr and www.theulsanweb.com

Goodwill Guides (www.goodwillguide.com) is an organisation that provides volunteer guides for foreign tourists. You pay only for your guide's expenses such as transportation, admission tickets and food. Apply at least two weeks in advance. There are 3000 registered guides and it's a good way to meet an English-speaking local.

TOURS

Hyundai Asan (☎ 02 3669 3000; see p362) operates tours to Geumgangsan in North Korea by boat from Sokcho in Gangwon-do. It costs around W450,000 to W600,000 for a three-day/two-night tour, but a government subsidy may reduce the cost. Geumgangsan (spelled 'Kumgangsan' in North Korea) is a famous scenic area of towering mountain peaks, granite pinnacles and waterfalls (see p353). Bookings must be made 10 days ahead and you stay on the boat or on a floating hotel. Hiking, a hot spa bath (US$12), a circus ($25) and shopping are available on the tour.

The same company started to run cheaper overland coach tours across the DMZ to Geumgangsan in February 2003. Although North Korea suspended them almost immediately, they recommenced later in the year. No visas are required. If you share a dormitory (six people) a three-day/two-night tour costs W230,000, while the same tour costs W350,000 per person if you share a double room at Haegeumgang Hotel. The tour is like the boat tour above.

Phone for more information, log on to www.knto.or.kr (click on 'sightseeing', 'theme tours' and 'North Korea Tour') or find a travel agent who handles these tours. Other tours of the North may be available soon but no doubt they will be highly supervised and restricted, and all your money will go to the government.

See p95 for details on tours around the South.

VISAS

With a confirmed onward ticket, visitors from nearly all West European countries, New Zealand, Australia and around 30 other countries receive 90-day permits on arrival. Visitors from the USA and a handful of countries receive 30-day permits, citizens of Italy and Portugal receive 60-day permits, and Canadians receive a six-month permit.

About 30 countries – including the Russian Federation, China, India, the Philippines and Nigeria – do not qualify for visa exemptions. Citizens from these countries must apply for a tourist visa, which allows a stay of 90 days. You cannot extend your stay beyond 90 days except in rare cases such as a medical emergency; if you overstay the fine starts at W100,000. Log on to www.moj.go.kr or www.mofat.go.kr to find out more.

Applications for a work visa can be made inside Korea and are processed in as little as a week, but you must leave the country to pick up the visa. Most applicants fly or take the Busan ferry to Fukuoka in Japan, where it usually takes two days to process the visa. You can also apply for a one-year work visa before entering Korea but it can take a few weeks to process. Take note that the visa authorities will want to see originals (not photocopies) of your educational qualifications. This is to make it easier to detect fake degree certificates.

You don't need to leave Korea to renew a work visa as long as you carry on working for the same employer. But if you change employers you must normally apply for a new visa and pick it up outside Korea.

If you don't want to forfeit your work or study visa, you must apply at your local immigration office for a re-entry permit before making any trips outside South Korea. The fee is W30,000 for a single re-entry or W50,000 for multiple re-entry, but permits are free for some nationalities.

If you are working or studying in Korea on a long-term visa it is necessary to apply for an alien registration card within 90 days of arrival, which costs W10,000. This is done at your local immigration office and requires your fingerprints.

WOMEN TRAVELLERS

Korea is a safe country for everyone, including women, but the usual precautions should be taken. Korea is a very male-dominated society, so female visitors can expect some interesting discussions about sex equality. Another legacy from the past is that higher standards are expected of women than of men, so it is generally regarded as bad manners for women to smoke, shout, display affection or reveal too much of themselves publicly. At times Korea resembles America in the 1950s (conservative and innocent).

WORK

South Korea is a popular place for English-language teachers to find work. The job pays around W30,000 per hour and income tax is low. English teachers on a one-year contract can expect to earn W1.9 million a month, with a furnished apartment, medical insurance, return flights, paid holiday and completion bonus all included in the package. Koreans have an insatiable appetite for studying English so finding an English teaching job should not be too difficult.

Most English teachers work in a *hagwon* (private language school) but some are employed by universities or government schools. Private tutoring, company classes and even teaching via the telephone are also possible. Teaching hours in a *hagwon* are usually around 30 hours a week and involve some evening and Saturday classes. Overtime is usually possible if you want it.

A degree in any subject is sufficient as long as English is your native language. However it is a good idea to obtain some kind of English teaching certificate before you arrive, as this increases your options and you should be able to get (and do) a better job.

Some *hagwon* owners are less than ideal employers, so check out the warnings on the websites following before committing yourself. One point to keep in mind is that if you change employers, you will usually need to obtain a new work visa, which requires you to leave the country and fly or take a ferry to Japan to pick up your new visa.

The English-language newspapers have very few job advertisements, but hundreds of English teaching vacancies are advertised on the Internet. Some websites:

www.englishspectrum.com Has job offers, information on living and working in Korea, and a bulletin board with accommodation options.

www.eslcafe.com Lots of job vacancies in Korea and masses of other teacher stuff.

www.eslhub.com Contains teaching jobs and other classifieds.

www.eslunderground.com Has job vacancies, classifieds and useful links.

www.pusanweb.com Offers jobs in Busan and elsewhere – click on 'community classifieds'.

Volunteer Work

Willing Workers on Organic Farms (WWOOF; ☎ 723 4458; www.wwoofkorea.com; KPO Box 1516, Seoul 110-601) has about 40 farms and market gardens on its books. Volunteers work four to five hours per day in return for their board and food, but some of the people who advertise in the booklet don't speak any English. The minimum period of stay is a few days and the maximum is by mutual agreement between volunteers and their host. Joining costs W15,000 and you receive a list of farms and orchards that you can apply to.

Volunteer teachers are also needed to teach English to some of the 26,000 children in Korean orphanages. Log on to www.yheesun.com for information about becoming a volunteer teacher for a couple of hours per week. Just meeting a foreigner brings cheer to their lives.

Transport

CONTENTS

THINGS CHANGE

The information in this chapter is particularly vulnerable to change: Prices for international travel are volatile, routes are introduced and cancelled, schedules change, special deals come and go, and rules and visa requirements are amended. You should check directly with the airline or a travel agent to make sure you understand how a fare (and ticket you may buy) works and be aware of the security requirements for international travel.

The upshot of this is that you should get opinions, quotes and advice from as many airlines and travel agents as possible before you part with your hard-earned cash. The details given in this chapter should be regarded as pointers and are not a substitute for your own careful, up-to-date research.

GETTING THERE & AWAY

ENTERING THE COUNTRY

Disembarkation in Korea is a straightforward affair, but you have an extra form to fill in if you are carrying more than US$10,000 in cash and travellers cheques (see also p368).

Passport

There are no restrictions when it comes to citizens of foreign countries entering Korea. Most visitors don't need a visa, but if your country is not on the visa-free list, you will need one (see p374).

AIR

Airports & Airlines

Most international flights leave from Incheon International Airport but there are six regional airports that provide some international flights, mainly to China and Japan. View www.airport.co.kr for information on all the airports.

Korea's own carrier is Korean Air (www.koreanair.com). Many airlines serve Korea:

Aeroflot (☎ 02-551 0321, airport 032-744 8672; www.aeroflot.com; airline code SU; hub Moscow)

Air Canada (☎ 02-3788 0100, airport 032-744 0898; www.aircanada.ca; airline code AC; hub Pearson International Airport, Toronto)

Air China (☎ 02-774 6886, airport 032-744 3256; www.air-china.com; airline code CA; hub Beijing)

Air France (☎ 02-318 3788, airport 032-744 4900; www.airfrance.com; airline code AF; hub Charles de Gaulle International Airport, Paris)

All Nippon Airways (☎ 02-752 5500; airport 032-744 3200; www.fly-ana.com; airline code NH; hub Narita Airport, Tokyo)

Asiana Airlines (☎ 02-1588 8000, airport 032-744 2134; www.flyasiana.com; airline code OZ; hub Incheon International Airport, Seoul)

Cathay Pacific Airways (☎ 02-311 2800, airport 032-744 6777; www.cathaypacific.com; airline code CX; hub Hong Kong International Airport)

China Eastern Airlines (☎ 02-518 0330, airport 032-744 3780; www.ce-air.com; airline code MU; hub Shanghai)

China Southern Airlines (☎ 02-3455 1600, airport 032-744 3270; www.cs-air.com; airline code CZ; hub Guangzhou)

Garuda Indonesia Airways (☎ 02-773 2092, airport 032-744 1990; www.garuda-indonesia.com; airline code GA; hub Soekarno-Hatta International Airport, Jakarta)

Japan Airlines (☎ 02-757 1711, airport 032-744 3601; www.japanair.com; airline code JL; hub Narita Airport, Tokyo)

KLM Royal Dutch Airlines (☎ 02-2011 5500, airport 032-744 6700; www.klm.nl; airline code KL; hub Schiphol Airport, Amsterdam)

Korean Air (☎ 02-1588 2001, airport 032-744 5132; www.koreanair.com; airline code KE; hub Incheon International Airport, Seoul)

Lufthansa Airlines (☎ 02-3420 0400, airport 032-744 3400; www.lufthansa.com; airline code LH; hub Frankfurt Airport)

Malaysia Airlines (☎ 02-777 7761, airport 032-744 3501; www.malaysiaairlines.com; airline code MH; hub Kuala Lumpur International Airport)

Northwest Airlines (☎ 02-7321 2700, airport 032-744 6300; www.nwa.com; airline code NW; hub Detroit Metro Airport)

Philippine Airlines (☎ 02-744 3581, airport 032-744 3720; www.philippineair.com; airline code PR; hub Manila Airport)

Qantas Airways (☎ 02-777 6872, airport 032-744 3283; www.qantas.com.au; airline code QF; hub Kingsford-Smith Airport, Sydney)

Singapore Airlines (☎ 02-755 1226, airport 032-744 6500; www.singaporeairlines.com; airline code SQ; hub Changi International Airport)

Thai Airways International (☎ 02-3707 0011, airport 032-744 3571; www.thaiair.com; airline code TG; hub Bangkok International Airport)

United Airlines (☎ 02-757 1691, airport 032-744 6666; www.ual.com; airline code UA; hub Los Angeles International Airport)

Tickets

Be sure you research the options carefully to make sure you get the best deal. The Internet is an increasingly useful resource for checking airline prices.

Automated online ticket sales work well if you're doing a simple one-way or return trip on specified dates, but are no substitute for a travel agent with the low-down on special deals, strategies for avoiding layovers and other useful advice.

Paying by credit card offers some protection if you unwittingly end up dealing with a rogue fly-by-night agency in your search for the cheapest fare, as most card issuers provide refunds if you can prove you didn't get what you paid for. Alternatively, buy a ticket from a bonded agent, such as one covered by the Air Travel Organisers' Licensing (ATOL; www.atol.org.uk) scheme in the UK. If you have doubts about the service provider, at the very least call the airline and confirm that your booking has been made.

There are a number of websites to search for the cheapest fares to Korea when booking online:

www.airbrokers.com Round-the-world ticket specialists.
www.cheapestflights.co.uk Cheap worldwide flights from the UK.
www.cheapflight.com Excellent site with links to many countries and fast access to fares to Korea.
www.eltexpress.com Flight quotes from the US and Germany.
www.expedia.msn.com Microsoft's travel site with access to world-wide fares.
www.statravel.com American site that has links to worldwide STA sites.
www.travelocity.com Search fares quickly and easily from virtually anywhere to anywhere.

There is some confusion about whether Korean departure taxes are included in the ticket price, so check with your travel agent. Departure tax from Incheon International Airport is W17,000 for foreigners (W27,000 for Korean nationals) but it should be included in the ticket price. Other Korean international airports charge less – W12,000 at Gimhae (Busan).

Ticket prices listed are off-peak. Prices from Korea can increase 30% to 40% in July and August, and special deals are less common at peak times.

INTERCONTINENTAL TICKETS & AIR PASSES

These round-the-world tickets can provide good deals if you have plenty of money and time and don't mind making a few stopovers – eg a Los Angeles–London–Paris–Bombay/Delhi–Bangkok–Seoul–Los Angeles ticket costs US$1400.

The All Asia Pass is worth considering if you only have a short time. The basic deal is that you can visit up to 18 cities in Asia, including Seoul, in three weeks. The price used to be around US$1200 from the USA or C$1900 from Canada, but a price war has been going on, so check for up-to-date prices – fares as low as US$699 from the USA may be possible.

From Australia

The cheapest return flights from Sydney to Seoul (Incheon International Airport) are usually around A$1200 – try Singapore Airlines.

Two well-known travel agents in Australia are **Flight Centre** (☎ 133 133; www.flightcentre.com.au) and **STA Travel** (☎ 1300 733 035; www.statravel.com.au), which have offices all round the country.

Return flights from Seoul to Sydney, Brisbane or Cairns generally start from around W750,000.

TRANSPORT

From Canada

Return flights from Toronto to Seoul usually cost just over C$2000 but special offers can go down to C$1600 or less – try United Airlines or Air Canada. From Vancouver flights are cheaper at around C$1500, with some special deals going under C$1200.

Travel Cuts (☎ 1-866-246 9762; www.travelcuts.com) is one of the largest discount travel agents in Canada, with offices in more than 10 cities. The website lists addresses and phone numbers of its offices.

Return flights from Seoul to Toronto start at W850,000, and to Vancouver they start at W720,000.

From China

Return flights from Beijing to Seoul start at around RMB5700, while flights from Shanghai are similar and cost around RMB5500. There are also flights from Shenyang, Dalian, Guangzhou, Qingdao, Yantai and Tianjin. All seven international airports in Korea have links to Chinese cities.

Return flights from Seoul to Beijing and Shanghai start at W390,000.

From Continental Europe

The cheapest return flights from Continental Europe to Seoul are usually around €700 to €750 although ultraspecials can be less than this – try Aeroflot, KLM or Lufthansa. In Germany check **STA Travel** (☎ 03 0311 0950; www.statravel.de) for up-to-date fare details.

In France contact **Usit Connect Voyages** (☎ 01 4329 6950; www.usitconnections.fr), **OTU Voyages** (☎ 08 9268 8363; www.vdm.com) and **Nouvelles Frontieres** (☎ 08 2500 0825; www.nouvelles-frontieres.fr) for reliable travel agencies with branches nationwide.

In Holland the place to call is **NBBS Reizen** (☎ 020 620 5071; www.nbbs.nl) or **Holland International** (☎ 070 307 6307; www.hollandinternational.nl) for flight information.

Return flights from Seoul to Continental Europe usually cost around W850,000 but look out for W750,000 special offers.

From Hong Kong

Return flights from Hong Kong to Seoul are about HK$3500, but special offers can drop to HK$2600 – try Thai Airways.

To book flights try **Phoenix Travel Services** (☎ 2722 7378; fax 2369 8884) in the Tsimshatsui district of Hong Kong, which receives good reviews from travellers. Check the classifieds in the English-language newspapers for a guide to current prices.

Return flights from Seoul to Hong Kong start at around W300,000.

From Japan

Japanese tourists make up the majority of foreign visitors to Korea and increasing numbers of Koreans are flying to Japanese cities, sometimes just for the weekend. There are direct nonstop flights from 19 Japanese cities to Seoul, but flights from Tokyo are usually the cheapest, starting at around ¥32,000 on Northwest or United Airlines. Fares tend to go up and down with the seasons, and fares in Golden Week and August cost up to twice the price of low-season fares. Flights are also available from Japan to airports in Busan, Daegu and Jeju-do.

Across Traveller's Bureau (☎ 03-3374 8721), **STA Travel** (☎ 03-5391 2922; www.statravel.co.jp) and **Just Travel** (☎ 03-3207 8311) have English-speaking staff who can help you find discounted fares. Also check classified advertisements in the *Japan Times* newspaper or on its website (www.japantimes.co.jp), as well as in the *Tokyo Journal* monthly magazine.

Return flights from Seoul to Tokyo and Osaka start at W250,000 but special deals are sometimes available at W200,000.

From New Zealand

Return flights from Auckland to Seoul cost about NZ$1400 to NZ$1700 and airlines take it in turn to offer the lowest fare.

Flight Centre (☎ 0800 243 544; www.flightcentre.co.nz) and **STA Travel** (☎ 0508 782 872; www.statravel.co.nz) are travel agents with offices in the main cities.

Return flights from Seoul to New Zealand start at around W800,000.

From Singapore

The cheapest return flights to Seoul are often around S$900 but look out for cutprice bargains – try Malaysian Airlines.

STA Travel (☎ 6737 7188; www.statravel.com.sg) has offices in Singapore, and other travel agents advertise special offers in the classified columns of the *Straits Times*.

Return flights from Seoul to Singapore are generally around W360,000 but look our for special offers.

From the UK

In the UK, discount travel agents are sometimes known as 'bucket shops'. The cheapest return flights to Seoul from London are usually between £400 and £450 – try Lufthansa.

London has hundreds of discount travel agents including **Trailfinders** (☎ 020-7938 3939 www.trailfinders.co.uk), who has offices in nine cities, and **STA Travel** (☎ 0870 160 0599; www.sta travel.co.uk). **WorldPlus** (www.worldplus.co.uk) specialises in flights to the Far East so check their prices.

Return flights from Seoul to London start at around W750,000.

From the USA

From New York the cheapest return flight to Seoul is usually around US$900 but look out for US$650 specials – try United, North West or Malaysian Airlines.

From Los Angeles return flights usually start at around US$800 but again look out for discounted fares from US$500.

Check out **STA Travel** (☎ 800-781 4040; www .statravel.com) for cheap fares.

Return flights from Seoul to New York generally cost around W750,000, while return flights from both Seoul and Busan (Gimhae International Airport) to Los Angeles start at around W650,000.

LAND

Having North Korea as a neighbour has turned South Korea into a virtual island. However if North Korea does ever relax its isolationist policies, the South could be linked by rail and road through the North to China, Russia and beyond. It's an exciting prospect but unlikely to happen soon. One day buses will run from Seoul to Beijing, but when is anyone's guess.

SEA

International ferries are worth considering if you're travelling around North Asia – you can catch a ferry to Incheon in South Korea from a number of Chinese ports, travel around South Korea, and then leave on a fast ferry from Busan to Japan. Another ferry option is travelling to or from Russia via Sokcho in Gangwon-do. See following for details on China–South Korea–Japan combined rail-and-ferry tickets.

To/From China

Many ferries sail from various China ports to Incheon. Some are crowded with petty traders but they provide an option to flying. Some of the cheapest fares offer a thin floor mattress rather than a bunk bed, while the more expensive fares give you a small cabin with a TV. Child fares are usually half the adult fare, and some ferry companies have 20% discounts for students. There is a W1000 harbour tax and a W1000 departure tax when exiting Incheon, but they can be included in the ticket price. Prices listed are for one-way tickets and sailing times are subject to variation. Most ferries leave Incheon from Yeon-an Pier, but the larger

KOREA–CHINA FERRIES

Ferries leaving from Incheon's Yeon-an Pier:

Destination	Phone	Price (W)	Departures	Duration
Dalian	032 891 7100	115,000–230,000	4.30pm Tue & Thu, 6pm Sat	17hr
Dandong	032 891 3222	115,000–210,000	5pm Mon, Wed & Fri	16hr
Shidao	032 891 8877	84,000–200,000	6pm Mon, Wed & Fri	12hr
Yantai	032 891 8880	110,000–336,000	6pm Tue, Thu & Sat	14hr
Yingkou	032 891 5555	115,000–220,000	7pm Tue, noon Sat, 11am Sun, 6pm Wed	23hr

Ferries leaving from Incheon's International Terminal 2 are:

Destination	Phone	Price (W)	Departures	Duration
Qingdao	032 777 0490	120,000–160,000	1pm Mon, Wed & Thu	20hr
Tianjin	032 863 9181	115,000–250,000	1pm Tue, 7pm Fri	24hr
Weihai	032 777 0490	110,000–160,000	7pm Tue, Thu & Sat	14hr

TRANSPORT

boats depart from International Terminal 2. See www.knto.or.kr for more information on ferries between China and South Korea.

A ferry-and-train package is available from cities in Korea to Beijing, Shanghai, Hangzhou or Shenyang in China via the Incheon–Tianjin ferry – see www.korail.go .kr for details. Ferries from China also run to Gunsan in Jeollabuk-do and Mokpo in Jeollanam-do but they are not as frequent or convenient.

To/From Japan

A number of ferry lines link Japan with Busan's international ferry terminal near Jungang subway station. Combined rail-and-ferry tickets cost W292,900 for the Seoul–Busan–Shimonoseki–Tokyo route – see www.korail.go.kr. There is a W1100 departure tax from Busan that is not included in the ticket price.

On the Busan to Hakata (Fukuoka) route, the *Beetle Jetfoil* operates twice daily to Chuo Futoh Wharf in Hakata. It's fast and takes only three hours at a cost of W85,000 from Busan and ¥13,000 from Hakata. A slow overnight ferry runs daily but takes 14½ hours and costs from W75,000.

One-way tickets on other ferries leaving from Busan:

Destination	Price (W)	Duration
Hiroshima	95,000	17hr
Hitakatsu	55,000	2½hr
Izuhara	55,000	2½hr
Kokura	80,000	4hr
Osaka	110,000	18hr
Shimonoseki	75,000	14hr

To/From Russia

Dongchun (☎ 033-639 2632) operates a ferry twice a week from Zarubino in Russia to Sokcho in Gangwon-do that takes 18 hours. With the cheaper fares (W156,000 to W204,000 one way, W265,000 to W346,000 return) you sleep on the floor and share facilities. The more expensive fares (W216,000 to W300,000 one way, W367,000 to W510,000 return) entitle you to a cabin for two or four people with your own bed, TV and bathroom. You can connect to the Trans-Siberian railway although most passengers are on a package tour to Paekdusan on the Chinese/North Korean border. These package tours cost from W299,000 for six nights (1 March to 31 May) or from W489,000 for five nights (1 June to 30 September).

GETTING AROUND

South Korea is a public-transport dream come true and everything is reasonably priced. Planes, trains and express buses link major cities, and local buses, subways and taxis make getting around cities easy. Long-distance and local buses reach every national park and village, and ferries ply numerous routes to offshore islands.

Comparing the three forms of transport, Seoul to Busan (444km) costs W18,400 by ordinary bus and W27,500 by deluxe bus and takes 5½ hours, while the *mugunghwa* (limited express) class train costs W22,900 and takes five hours. Flying costs W65,500 and only takes an hour, but travelling to and from the airports takes another 1½ hours.

AIR
Airlines in Korea

South Korea has only two domestic carriers – **Korean Air** (☎ 1588 2001; www.koreanair.com) and **Asiana Airlines** (☎ 1588 8000; www.flyasiana.com). Fares charged by both companies are virtually identical and very reasonable. Flights to the southern holiday island of Jeju-do leave from a dozen airports around the country and cost from W46,000 to W78,900, and the longest flight time is just over an hour. Korean Air has the more extensive network – the only route covered exclusively by Asiana is Jeju-do to Pohang. Fares are cheaper from Monday to Thursday when seats are easier to get. Flights on public holidays have a surcharge and are often booked out, so avoid travel on those days if possible. There are discounts for students and children. Foreigners should carry their passports on all domestic flights for ID purposes. Domestic airports have a W4000 departure tax (W5000 from Incheon) which is usually included in the ticket prices. See the Domestic Air Fares map for details of routes.

BICYCLE

Cycling around mountainous Korea is not recommended due to the local driving habits, but hiring a bike for short trips in areas

DOMESTIC AIR FARES – SOUTH KOREA

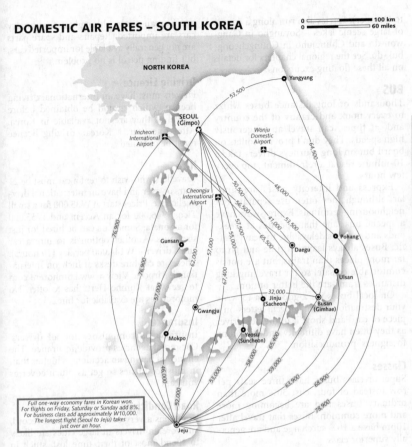

NORTH KOREA

Incheon International Airport

SEOUL (Gimpo)

Yangyang

Wonju Domestic Airport

Cheongju International Airport

Gunsan

Pohang

Daegu

Ulsan

Gwangju

Jinju (Sacheon)

Busan (Gimhae)

Mokpo

Yeosu (Suncheon)

Jeju

Full one-way economy fares in Korean won.
For flights on Friday, Saturday or Sunday add 8%.
For business class add approximately W10,000.
The longest flight (Seoul to Jeju) takes just over an hour.

TRANSPORT

with bike paths or little traffic is a good idea – see p91 for cycling in Seoul and individual destination chapters for some cycling opportunities in the provinces. Bicycle hire is W2000 an hour but try for a discount for a day's hire. You will have to leave your passport or negotiate some other ID or deposit. Safety helmets are not available and it's a good idea to bring your own padlock. Cycling around Jeju-do is the only long-distance ride that could be an enjoyable experience – see p259.

BOAT

Korea has an extensive network of ferries that connects hundreds of offshore islands to the mainland. The large

southern island of Jeju-do can be reached from Mokpo (from W18,550, 3¼ to 5½ hours), Yeosu (from W18,500, seven hours), Wando (from W14,850, three to five hours), Busan (from W26,800, 11 hours) and Incheon (from W46,000, 13 to 15 hours). On the west coast, ferries from Incheon's Yeon-an Pier service a dozen nearby and more-distant islands, while other islands further south can be reached from Daecheon Beach, Gunsan and Gyeopko. Mokpo, Wando, Yeosu and Busan provide access to the many islands strung along the south coast. Remote Ulleungdo off the east coast can be reached by ferry from Pohang (from W51,100, three hours) or Mukho-Donghae (from W42,000, daily from March to October). Ferries also run along a couple of large scenic lakes – Soyangho in Gangwon-do and Chungjuho in Chungcheongbuk-do. See the regional chapters for details on all these floating excursions.

BUS

Thousands of long-distance buses whizz to every nook and cranny of the country and, at times, can travel at dangerously high speeds. They don't provide toilets on board but on long journeys drivers take a 10-minute rest at a refreshment stop every few hours.

Express and intercity buses are similar, although they often use separate but neighbouring terminals. Expressways have a special bus lane that operates at weekends and reduces delays due to heavy traffic. Buses always leave on time and go to far more places than trains, but are not as comfortable or safe, so for travelling long distances trains are the better option.

On local buses it's a good idea to write your destination in big *hangeul* letters on a piece of card and show it to the bus driver as they often have difficulty understanding foreigners' pronunciation.

Classes

Superior-class buses have three seats per row instead of four, cost 50% more than ordinary buses and are becoming more and more common. Buses that travel after 10pm have a 10% surcharge and are generally superior class.

Costs

See p114 for sample bus fares.

Reservations

Buses are so frequent that it's not necessary to buy a ticket in advance, except perhaps on holidays and weekends. Reservations can be made at the bus terminal that the bus departs from.

CAR & MOTORCYCLE
Bring Your Own Vehicle

Contact customs (www.customs.go.kr) for information on regulations concerning importing your own car, but don't be surprised if you have problems finding out the details as it's not a question that is often asked. Nearly all the cars running in the country are Korean-made although a few luxury cars are imported. Repairs and spare parts are not generally available for imported cars, but finding petrol is no problem.

Driving Licence

Drivers must have an international driving licence, which should be obtained before arrival as they are not available in Korea. After one year, a Korean driving licence must be obtained.

Hire

Travellers who wish to rent a car must be 21 years or over and have an international driving licence. Prices start at W35,000 for a small Tico, W46,000 for an Accent and W55,000 for a Sonata. Some cars can be hired for just six hours. Another option is to hire a car and a driver – W144,000 per day (10 hours). There are car-hire desks at Incheon International Airport. View www.kumhorent.com to see what Kumho-Hertz has to offer. No motorcycles are available for hire.

Insurance

Insurance is compulsory for all drivers. Car rental agencies provide insurance. The chance of having an accident is higher than in most countries so get as much cover as you can.

Road Conditions

Korea has a very bad road accident record, and foreign drivers in large cities are likely to spend most of their time lost, stuck in traffic jams or looking for a parking space. Impatient and careless drivers are a major hazard everywhere. Driving in rural areas or on Jeju-do is more feasible but public transport is so good that few visitors get behind a steering wheel.

Road Rules

Vehicles drive on the right side of the road. The driver and front-seat passengers must wear seatbelts, drunk drivers receive heavy fines and speed cameras are as common as *kimchi*. Victims of road accidents are often paid a largish sum by drivers who don't want to face a court case.

HITCHING

Hitching is not a local custom and there is no particular signal for it, but the country is relatively crime-free so if you get stuck in a rural area, stick out your thumb and the chances are that someone will soon give you a lift and go out of their way to help you. Normally bus services are frequent enough and cheap enough even in the countryside that hitching isn't necessary. Accepting a lift anywhere always has an element of risk.

LOCAL TRANSPORT
Bus
Local city buses provide a frequent and inexpensive service, and although rural buses provide a less-frequent service, many run on an hourly or half-hourly basis, so you don't usually have to wait for long. The main problem is getting on the right bus because bus timetables, destination signs on buses and bus stop names are rarely in English and bus drivers don't speak any English. Writing your destination in big *hangeul* letters on a piece of card can be helpful (as well as amusing). Local tourist information centres usually have English-speaking staff and are the best places to find out about which local bus number goes where.

Regular buses with only a few seats and lots of standing space cost around W800, while the limited-stop buses with coach-style seating cost around W1400. All buses have one fare irrespective of the distance travelled. Put the money in the glass box next to the driver – you will need plenty of W1000 notes because the machines only give coins in change. If you only have a W10,000 note, you may have to hunt around the bus passengers for someone who can change it into smaller notes.

Subway
Seoul, Busan, Daegu and Incheon have a subway train system and Gwangju and Daejeon are building systems. The subway is a cheap and very convenient way of getting around large cities, and signs are in Korean and English, which makes the subway system easy to use.

Taxi
Taxis are numerous almost everywhere and are so cheap that they are often cheaper than buses for short journeys by two or more people. Even if you never use taxis in other countries, you should consider using them in Korea. Fares vary slightly in different areas. Every urban taxi has a meter, tipping is not a local custom and some drivers even insist on giving you change. Taxi drivers are more honest than politicians.

Regular taxis *(ilban)* cost around W1600 for the first 2km, while deluxe taxis *(mobeom)*, which are black with a yellow stripe, cost around W4000 for the first 3km. Note that the meters work on a time basis when the vehicle is stuck in a traffic jam. The regular taxis have an after-midnight surcharge of 20% but the deluxe taxis don't. Since few taxi drivers speak English it is useful to write down your destination in *hangeul* letters. Any expressway tolls are added to the fare. In the countryside check the fare first as there are local quirks, such as surcharges or a fixed rate to out-of-the-way places with little prospect of a return fare. A few taxis, known as bullet taxis *(chongal)* because the drivers go fast, can be found at remote tourist sites or at bus terminals after the buses have stopped running. Negotiate the price with the driver before you start.

TRAIN
South Korea has an excellent train network operated by **Korea National Railroad** (☎ 1544 7788; www.korail.go.kr) that connects all major cities and the towns along the way. Trains are clean, safe, punctual and inexpensive, and just about every station has a sign in Korean and English. Compartments are nonsmoking, but smoking is allowed in the area between compartments. Trains are the best option for long-distance travel and *mugunghwa* trains cost less than deluxe buses. A new high-speed train service from Seoul to Daejeon is due to begin in 2004 and should be extended to Busan in 2008, halving the journey time. Developed in Korea, the new bullet trains can travel at over 300km/h. Talks about reopening rail links between North and South Korea are continuing, but this depends on the agreement of the North Korean government. If the rail link ever started running, it would open the way to the development of a Seoul–London and even a Seoul–Singapore rail link, but this is probably a distant dream.

TRANSPORT

Classes

There are three classes of trains. The fastest and most luxurious are *saemaeul* trains, but they only stop in major towns. *Mugunghwa* trains stop more often and are almost as comfortable and fast. *Tongil* trains are cheapest and stop at every station, but only run infrequently on certain routes and are unfortunately dying out. *Saemaeul* trains have a dining car while *mugunghwa* trains have *gimbap* (Korean sushi), lunch boxes and a snack trolley.

Costs

Saemaeul class is nearly 50% more expensive than *mugunghwa* class, which is 80% more expensive than *tongil* class. First-class seats (not available on *tongil* trains) are 30% extra. Tickets are discounted 15% from Tuesday to Thursday and standing tickets (*ipseokpyo*) are discounted 15% to 30% depending on the length of the journey. With a standing ticket you are allowed to sit on any unoccupied seats. Children travel for half price. See p115 for some sample train fares.

Reservations

The railway ticketing system is computerised and you can get tickets up to one month in advance at many travel agents as well as railway stations. There are less trains than buses so seat reservations are sensible and necessary at weekends, holidays and busy times.

Train Passes

Foreigners can buy a KR Pass at overseas travel agents – try STA Travel who sells them in 15 countries – or from the Korea National Railroad website, www.korail.go.kr. The KR Pass offers unlimited rail travel for three/five/seven/10 consecutive days at a cost of US$47/70/89/102, or you can select travel days within a one-month period. Couples or larger groups are entitled to a 10% discount and students aged under 25 receive a 20% discount. You can travel the length of the country for around US$20 so it's not really worth buying a pass unless you plan to spend most of your holiday on a train. Using a mixture of buses and trains or planes is the best way to get around.

Health

CONTENTS

Health issues and the quality of medical care vary significantly depending on whether you stay in Seoul or venture into rural areas.

Travellers tend to worry about contracting infectious diseases whilst abroad, but infections are a rare cause of serious illness or death whilst overseas. Pre-existing medical conditions such as heart disease, and accidental injury (especially traffic accidents), account for most life-threatening problems. Becoming ill in some way, however, is relatively common. Fortunately most common illnesses can either be prevented with some common-sense behaviour or be treated easily with a well-stocked traveller's medical kit.

The following advice is a general guide only and does not replace the advice of a doctor trained in travel medicine.

BEFORE YOU GO

Pack medications in their original, clearly labelled, containers. A signed and dated letter from your physician describing your medical conditions and regular medications (use generic names), is also a good idea. If carrying syringes or needles, be sure to have a physician's letter documenting their medical necessity. If you have a heart condition bring a copy of your ECG taken just prior to travelling.

If you take any regular medication bring double your needs in case of loss or theft. In Korea you need a local doctor's prescription to buy medication, and it may be difficult to find some of the newer drugs, particularly the latest anti-depressant drugs, blood pressure medications and contraceptive pills.

INSURANCE

Even if you are fit and healthy, don't travel without health insurance – accidents do happen. Declare any existing medical conditions you have – the insurance company WILL check if your problem is pre-existing and will not cover you if it is undeclared. You may require extra cover for adventure activities. If your health insurance doesn't cover you for medical expenses abroad, consider getting extra insurance – check Lonely Planet's subwwway (www.lonelyplanet.com) for more information. If you're uninsured, emergency evacuation is expensive, bills of over US$100,000 are not uncommon.

Find out in advance if your insurance plan will make payments directly to providers or reimburse you later for overseas health expenditures. (In many countries doctors expect payment in cash.) Some policies offer lower and higher medical-expense options; the higher ones are chiefly for countries that have extremely high medical costs, such as the USA. You may prefer a policy that pays doctors or hospitals directly rather than you having to pay on the spot and claim later. If you have to claim later, make sure you keep all documentation. Some policies ask you to call back (reverse charges) to a centre in your home country where an immediate assessment of your problem is made.

RECOMMENDED VACCINATIONS

Specialised travel-medicine clinics are your best source of information; they stock all available vaccines and will be able to give specific recommendations for you and your trip. The doctors will take into account factors such as past vaccination history, the length of your trip, activities you may be undertaking and underlying medical conditions, such as pregnancy.

Most vaccines don't produce immunity until at least two weeks after they're given, so visit a doctor four to eight weeks before departure. Ask your doctor for an International Certificate of Vaccination (otherwise known as the yellow booklet), which will list all of the vaccinations you have received.

MEDICAL CHECKLIST

The following are recommended items for personal medical kits. (* Indicates items most commonly used by travellers.)

- Antifungal cream (eg Clotrimazole)
- Antibacterial cream (eg Muciprocin)
- If you are planning on visiting rural areas then antibiotics – one for skin infections (eg Amoxicillin/Clavulanate or Cephalexin) and another for diarrhoea (eg Norfloxacin or Ciprofloxacin)
- Antihistamine – there are many options (eg Cetrizine for daytime and Promethazine for night)
- Antiseptic* (eg Betadine)
- Anti-spasmodic for stomach cramps (eg Buscopan)
- Contraceptive method
- Decongestant* (eg Pseudoephedrine)
- DEET-based insect repellent
- Diarrhoea* – consider an oral rehydration solution (eg Gastrolyte), diarrhoea 'stopper' (eg Loperamide) and anti-nausea medication (eg Prochlorperazine)
- First-aid items such as scissors, elastoplasts, bandages, gauze, thermometer (but not mercury), sterile needles and syringes, safety pins and tweezers*
- Anti-inflammatory (eg Ibuprofen)
- Indigestion tablets (eg Quick Eze or Mylanta)
- Iodine tablets (unless you are pregnant or have a thyroid problem) to purify water
- Laxative (eg Coloxyl)
- Migraine medicine – sufferers should take their personal medicine
- Paracetamol*
- Permethrin to impregnate clothing and mosquito nets
- Steroid cream for allergic/itchy rashes (eg 1% to 2% hydrocortisone)

RECOMMENDED VACCINATIONS

There are no required vaccinations for North or South Korea. The World Health Organization recommends the following vaccinations for travellers to Korea:

Adult diphtheria and tetanus Single booster recommended every 10 years. Side effects include sore arm and fever.

Hepatitis A Provides almost 100% protection for up to a year, a booster after 12 months provides at least another 20 years protection. Mild side effects such as headache and sore arm occur in 5% to 10% of people.

Hepatitis B Now considered routine for most travellers. Given as three shots over six months. A rapid schedule is also available, as is a combined vaccination with Hepatitis A. Side effects are mild and uncommon, usually headache and sore arm. In 95% of people three shots results in lifetime protection.

Measles, mumps and rubella Two doses of MMR required unless you have had the diseases. Occasionally a rash and flu-like illness can occur a week after receiving the vaccine. Many young adults require a booster.

Typhoid Recommended unless your trip is less than a week and only in Seoul. The vaccine offers around 70% protection, lasts for two to three years and comes as a single shot. Tablets are also available, however the injection is usually recommended as it has fewer side effects. Sore arm and fever may occur.

Varicella If you haven't had chickenpox discuss this vaccination with your doctor.

The following immunisations are recommended for long-term travellers (more than one month) or those at special risk:

Japanese B Encephalitis Three injections in all. Booster recommended after two years. Sore arm and headache are the most common side effects. Rarely an allergic reaction comprising hives and swelling can occur up to 10 days after any of the three doses.

Rabies Three injections in all. A booster after one year will then provide 10 years protection. Side effects are rare – occasionally headache and sore arm. This is recommended for animal handlers.

Tuberculosis TB is only relevant for North Korea. A complex issue. Adult long-term travellers are usually recommended to have a TB skin test before and after travel, rather than vaccination. Only one vaccine given in a lifetime.

- Sunscreen and hat
- Throat lozenges*
- Thrush (vaginal yeast infection) treatment (eg Clotrimazole pessaries or Diflucan tablet)
- Ural or equivalent if you're prone to urine infections

ONLINE RESOURCES

There is a wealth of travel health advice on the Internet. For further information, Lonely Planet (www.lonelyplanet.com) is a good place to start. The **World Health Organization** (WHO; www.who.int/ith) publishes a superb book called *International Travel & Health*, which is revised annually and is available online at no cost. Another website of general interest is **MD Travel Health** (www.mdtravelhealth.com), which provides complete travel health recommendations for every country and is updated daily. The **Centers for Disease Control and Prevention** (CDC; www.cdc.gov) website also has good general information.

FURTHER READING

Pick up a copy of Lonely Planet's *Healthy Travel Asia & India*. Other recommended references include *Traveller's Health* by Dr Richard Dawood and *Travelling Well* by Dr Deborah Mills – check out the website (www.travellingwell.com.au).

IN TRANSIT

DEEP VEIN THROMBOSIS (DVT)

Deep vein thrombosis occurs when blood clots form in the legs during plane flights, chiefly because of prolonged immobility. The longer the flight, the greater the risk. Though most blood clots are reabsorbed uneventfully, some may break off and travel through the blood vessels to the lungs, where they may cause life-threatening complications.

The chief symptom of DVT is swelling or pain of the foot, ankle, or calf, usually but not always on just one side. When a blood clot travels to the lungs, it may cause chest pain and difficulty in breathing. Travellers who find that they have any of these symptoms should immediately seek medical attention.

To prevent the development of DVT on long flights you should walk about the cabin, perform isometric compressions of the leg muscles (ie contract the leg muscles while sitting), drink plenty of fluids, and avoid alcohol and tobacco.

JET LAG & MOTION SICKNESS

Jet lag is common when crossing more than five time zones; it results in insomnia, fatigue, malaise or nausea. To avoid jet lag try drinking plenty of fluids (non-alcoholic) and eating light meals. Upon arrival, seek exposure to natural sunlight and readjust your schedule (for meals, sleep etc) as soon as possible.

Antihistamines such as dimenhydrinate (Dramamine), prochlorperazine (Phenergan) and meclizine (Antivert, Bonine) are generally the first choice for the treatment of motion sickness. Their major side effect is drowsiness. A herbal alternative is ginger, which works like a charm for some people.

IN KOREA

AVAILABILITY & COST OF HEALTHCARE

South Korea is a relatively well-developed country and the quality of medical care reflects this. In Seoul the quality is high, however in rural areas you cannot expect to find Western standards of care.

North Korea is poverty-stricken and medical care is inadequate throughout the country, including in Pyongyang. Shortages of routine medications and supplies are a common problem.

A recommended hospital in Seoul is the government-run **Samsung Medical Center and International Health Service** (☎ 822-3410 0200; 50 Ilwon-Dong, Kangnam-Ku).

HEALTH

INFECTIOUS DISEASES

Filariasis
A mosquito-borne disease that is very rare in travellers; mosquito-avoidance measures are the best way to prevent this disease. It's widespread in rice growing areas in southeast Korea.

Hantavirus
This is transmitted by breathing in droplets from infected rat or mouse urine or faeces. It causes fever, headache, abdominal and back pain and dizziness but is very rare in travellers. It is diagnosed by specific blood tests. Prevention is by avoiding areas with rodent droppings.

Hepatitis A
A problem throughout the country, this food- and water-borne virus infects the liver, causing jaundice (yellow skin and eyes), nausea and lethargy. There is no specific treatment for hepatitis A, you just need to allow time for the liver to heal. All travellers to Korea should be vaccinated against hepatitis A.

Hepatitis B
The only sexually transmitted disease that can be prevented by vaccination, hepatitis B is spread by body fluids, including sexual contact. Up to 10% of the population are carriers of hepatitis B, and usually are unaware of this. The long-term consequences can include liver cancer and cirrhosis.

HIV
HIV is also spread by body fluids. Avoid unsafe sex, sharing needles, invasive cosmetic procedures such as tattooing and needles that have not been sterilised in a medical setting.

Influenza
Influenza (flu) symptoms include high fever, muscle aches, runny nose, cough and sore throat. It can be very severe in people over the age of 65 or in those with underlying medical conditions such as heart disease or diabetes – vaccination is recommended for these individuals. There is no specific treatment, just rest and paracetamol.

Japanese B Encephalitis
This viral disease is transmitted by mosquitoes, but is rare in travellers. Most cases occur in rural areas and vaccination is recommended for travellers spending more than one month outside of cities. There is no treatment, and a third of infected people will die while another third will suffer permanent brain damage. The highest risk is in the southwest rice growing areas.

Leptospirosis
Leptospirosis is contracted after exposure to contaminated fresh water (eg rivers). Early symptoms are very similar to the 'flu' and include headache and fever. It can vary from a very mild to a fatal disease. Diagnosis is through blood tests and it is easily treated with Doxycycline.

Lyme Disease
This tick-borne disease occurs in the summer months. Symptoms include an early rash and general viral symptoms, followed weeks to months later by joint, heart or neurological problems. Prevention is by using general insect avoidance measures and checking your self for ticks after walking in forest areas. Treatment is with Doxycycline.

Malaria
For such a serious and potentially deadly disease, there is an enormous amount of misinformation concerning malaria. You must get expert advice as to whether your trip puts you at risk. Limited risk occurs in some areas close to the border between North and South Korea, and only during the spring and summer months. The medicine Chloroquine protects against malaria in this area.

Malaria is caused by a parasite transmitted by the bite of an infected mosquito. The most important symptom of malaria is fever, but general symptoms such as headache, diarrhoea, cough, or chills may also occur. Diagnosis can only be made by taking a blood sample.

Two strategies should be combined to prevent malaria – mosquito avoidance, and anti-malaria medications. Most people who catch malaria are taking inadequate or no anti-malarial medication. Travellers are advised to prevent mosquito bites by taking these steps:

■ Use a DEET-containing insect repellent on exposed skin. Wash this off at night, as long as you are sleeping under a mosquito net. Natural repellents such as Citronella can be effective, but must be applied more frequently than products containing DEET.

- Sleep under a mosquito net impregnated with permethrin.
- Choose accommodation with screens and fans (if not air-conditioned).
- Impregnate clothing with permethrin in high-risk areas.
- Wear long sleeves and trousers in light colours.
- Use mosquito coils.
- Spray your room with insect repellent before going out for your evening meal.

Rabies

This uniformly fatal disease is spread by the bite or lick of an infected animal – most commonly a dog or monkey. You should seek medical advice immediately after any animal bite and commence post-exposure treatment. Having pre-travel vaccination means the post-bite treatment is greatly simplified. If an animal bites you, gently wash the wound with soap and water, and apply iodine based antiseptic. If you are not pre-vaccinated you will need to receive rabies immunoglobulin as soon as possible.

STDs

Sexually transmitted diseases are common throughout the world and the most common include herpes, warts, syphilis, gonorrhoea and chlamydia. People carrying these diseases often have no signs of infection. Condoms will prevent gonorrhoea and chlamydia but not warts or herpes. If after a sexual encounter you develop any rash, lumps, discharge or pain when passing urine seek immediate medical attention. If you have been sexually active during your travels have an STD check on your return home.

Tuberculosis

Only North Korea has significant risk. While rare in travellers, medical and aid workers, and long-term travellers who have significant contact with the local population should take precautions. Vaccination is usually only given to children under the age of five, but adults at risk are recommended pre- and post-travel TB testing. The main symptoms are fever, cough, weight loss, night sweats and tiredness.

Typhoid

This serious bacterial infection is spread via food and water. It gives a high and slowly worsening fever and headache, and may be accompanied by a dry cough and stomach pain. It is diagnosed by blood tests and treated with antibiotics. Vaccination is recommended for all travellers spending more than a week in Korea and travelling outside of Seoul. Be aware that vaccination is not 100% effective so you must still be careful with what you eat and drink.

Typhus

Scrub typhus is present in the scrub areas of Korea. This is spread by a mite and is very rare in travellers. Symptoms include fever, muscle pains and a rash. Following general insect avoidance measures when walking in the scrub will help you avoid this disease. Doxycycline works as a prevention and treatment for typhus.

TRAVELLER'S DIARRHOEA

Traveller's diarrhoea is the most common problem which affects travellers – between 10% and 20% of people visiting South Korea will suffer from it. The risk in North Korea is greater at 40% to 60%. In the majority of cases, traveller's diarrhoea is triggered by a bacteria (there are numerous potential culprits), and therefore responds promptly to treatment with antibiotics. Treatment with antibiotics will depend on your circumstances – how sick you are, how quickly you need to get better, where you are etc.

Traveller's diarrhoea is defined as the passage of more than three watery bowel-actions within 24 hours, plus at least one other symptom such as fever, cramps, nausea, vomiting or feeling generally unwell. Treatment consists of staying well-hydrated; rehydration solutions like Gastrolyte are the best for this. Antibiotics such as Norfloxacin, Ciprofloxacin or Azithromycin will kill the bacteria quickly.

Loperamide is just a 'stopper' and doesn't get to the cause of the problem. It can be helpful, for example if you have to go on a long bus ride. Don't take Loperamide if you have a fever, or blood in your stools. Seek medical attention quickly if you do not respond to an appropriate antibiotic.

HEALTH

Giardiasis

Giardia is a parasite that is relatively common in travellers. Symptoms include nausea, bloating, excess gas, fatigue and intermittent diarrhoea. 'Eggy' burps are often attributed solely to Giardia, but work in Nepal has shown that they are not specific to Giardia. The parasite will eventually go away if left untreated but this can take months. The treatment of choice is Tinidazole, with Metronidazole being a second line option. Giardia is not common in South Korea.

ENVIRONMENTAL HAZARDS
Air Pollution

Air pollution, particularly vehicle pollution, is an increasing problem in Seoul. If you have severe respiratory problems speak with your doctor before travelling to any heavily polluted urban centres. This pollution also causes minor respiratory problems such as sinusitis, dry throat and irritated eyes. If troubled by the pollution, leave the city for a few days and get some fresh air.

Food

Eating in restaurants is the biggest risk factor for contracting travellers' diarrhoea. Ways to avoid it include eating only freshly cooked food and avoiding shellfish and food that has been sitting around in buffets. Peel all fruit, cook vegetables, and soak salads in iodine water for at least 20 minutes. Eat in busy restaurants with a high turnover of customers.

Insect Bites & Stings

Insects are not a major issue in Korea, however there are some insect-borne diseases present.

Ticks are contracted after walking in rural areas. Ticks are commonly found behind the ears, on the belly and in armpits. If you have had a tick bite and experience symptoms such as a rash at the site of the bite or elsewhere, fever or muscle aches, you should see a doctor. Doxycycline prevents and treats tick-borne diseases.

Bee and wasp stings mainly cause problems for people who are allergic to them. Anyone with a serious bee or wasp allergy should carry an injection of adrenaline (eg an Epipen) for emergency treatment. For others pain is the main problem – apply ice to the sting and take painkillers.

DRINKING WATER

- Never drink tap water
- Bottled water is generally safe – check the seal is intact at purchase
- Avoid ice
- Avoid fresh juices – they may have been watered down
- Boiling water is the most efficient method of purifying it
- The best chemical purifier is iodine. It should not be used by pregnant women or those with thyroid problems.
- Water filters should also filter out viruses. Ensure your filter has a chemical barrier such as iodine and a small pore size (eg less than four microns).

Parasites

The most common parasite in Korea is Clonorchis. Infection occurs after eating infected fresh-water fish – these may be raw, pickled, smoked or dried. Light infections usually cause no symptoms, however heavy infections can cause liver problems. In some areas up to 20% of the local population are infected.

Skin Problems

Cuts and scratches can become easily infected when travelling. Take meticulous care of any cuts and scratches to prevent complications such as abscesses. Immediately wash all wounds in clean water and apply antiseptic. If you develop signs of infection (increasing pain and redness) see a doctor.

Rashes can be often very difficult to diagnose, even for doctors. If you develop a rash you should seek medical advice as soon as possible.

WOMEN'S HEALTH

In most well developed areas of Korea, supplies of sanitary products are readily available. Birth control options may be limited so bring adequate supplies of your own form of contraception. Heat, humidity and antibiotics can all contribute to thrush. Treatment is with antifungal creams and pessaries such as Clotrimazole. A practical alternative is a single tablet of Fluconazole (Diflucan). Urinary tract infections can be precipitated by dehydration or long bus journeys without toilet stops; bring suitable antibiotics.

Pregnant women should receive specialised advice before travelling. The ideal time to travel is in the second trimester (between 16 and 28 weeks), when the risk of pregnancy-related problems are at their lowest and pregnant women generally feel at their best. During the first trimester there is a risk of miscarriage and in the third trimester complications such as premature labour and high blood pressure are possible. It's wise to travel with a companion. Always carry a list of quality medical facilities available at your destination and ensure you continue your standard antenatal care at these facilities. Avoid rural travel in areas with poor transportation and medical facilities. Most of all, ensure travel insurance covers all pregnancy-related possibilities, including premature labour.

Traveller's diarrhoea can quickly lead to dehydration and result in inadequate blood flow to the placenta. Many of the drugs used to treat various diarrhoea bugs are not recommended in pregnancy. Azithromycin is considered safe.

TRADITIONAL & FOLK MEDICINE

Traditional medicine in Korea is known as Oriental medicine and is based on Traditional Chinese Medicine (TCM). Although Korean Traditional medicine is heavily influenced by TCM, it has developed its own unique methods of diagnosis and treatment. Acupuncture techniques and herbal medicines are widely used.

Unique to Korean Traditional Medicine is Sasang Constitutional Medicine, which classifies people into four types (Taeyangin, Taeumin, Soyangin and Soeumin) based on their body type, and treats each differently according to their constitution. In Korea 'fusion medicine', which combines both traditional and western medical systems, is increasingly popular. The World Health Organization has more than one research facility looking into traditional medicine in Seoul.

Be aware that 'natural' doesn't always mean 'safe', and there can be drug interactions between herbal medicines and Western medicines. If you are utilising both systems ensure you inform both practitioners what the other has prescribed.

HEALTH

Sverdrup
(Norway)

Zemlya Frantsa-Iosifa
(Russia)

Severnaya Zemlya
(Russia)

Novaya Zemlya
(Russia)

KARA
SEA

LAPTEV
SEA

Novosibirskie
Ostrova (Russia)

EAST SIBERIAN
SEA

BARENTS
SEA

Sweden
1pm

Norway

2pm

Finland

Denmark

3pm

Latvia

Poland

Belarus

Germany

Ukraine

Austria

Romania

Italy

4pm

Kazakhstan

Russia

5pm

6pm

7pm

9pm

10pm

11pm

12am

SEA
OF
OKHOTSK

BERING
SEA

3am

2am

Greece

Turkey

Uzbekistan

Kyrgyzstan

Mongolia

Tunisia   MEDITERRANEAN
SEA

Syria

Iraq

Turkmenistan

4pm

China

8pm

North Korea

South
Korea

Japan

NORTH
PACIFIC
OCEAN

Algeria

Libya

Egypt

Iran
3.30pm

Afghanistan
4.30pm

Tibet (China)

5pm

Pakistan

Nepal
5.45
pm

EAST
CHINA
SEA

Taiwan

Niger

Chad

Saudi
Arabia

India

6.30
pm

Myanmar

Northern
Mariana
Is (US)

9pm

Marshall
Is (US)

12am

Nigeria

Sudan

Eritrea Yemen

Oman

5.30
pm

Thailand

Vietnam

Philippines

Kiribati

Central African
Republic

Ethiopia

3pm

ARABIAN
SEA

BAY OF
BENGAL

6pm

5.30pm

Malaysia

Palau

Federated States
of Micronesia
11pm

Congo

Somalia

Kenya

Sri Lanka

Maldives

Nauru   EQUATOR

Gabon 1pm

Congo
(Zaire)

Tanzania

Indonesia

East
Timor

Papua New
Guinea

Solomon Is

SOUTH
PACIFIC
OCEAN

Angola

Malawi

Seychelles
4pm

6.30
pm

Cocos (Keeling)
Is (Aust)

Vanuatu

New Caledonia (Fr)

Fiji

Zambia

Namibia

Zimbabwe

Madagascar

Mauritius

INDIAN OCEAN

11.30
pm

Botswana

Mozambique

Reunion
(Fr)

9.30
pm

Norfolk Is
(Aust)

South
Africa

Australia

10.30
pm

Lord Howe
Is (Aust)

Prince Edward Is
(S. Africa)

French Southern &
Antarctic Territories (Fr)

New Zealand

TASMAN
SEA

SOUTHERN OCEAN

Heard &
McDonald Is
(Aust)

International Date Line

Mon
Sun

| 1pm | 2pm | 3pm | 4pm | 5pm | 6pm | 7pm | 8pm | 9pm | 10pm | 11pm | 12am |

Language

CONTENTS

Korean is a knotty problem for linguists. Various theories have been proposed to explain its origins, but the most widely accepted is that it is a member of the Ural-Altaic family of languages. Other members of the same linguistic branch are Turkish and Mongolian. In reality Korean grammar shares much more with Japanese than it does with either Turkish or Mongolian. Furthermore, the Koreans have borrowed nearly 70% of their vocabulary from neighbouring China, and now many English words have penetrated the Korean lexicon.

Chinese characters (hanja) are usually restricted to use in maps, government documents, the written names of businesses and in newspapers. For the most part Korean is written in hangeul, the alphabet developed under King Sejong's reign in the 15th century. Many linguists argue that the Korean script is one of the most intelligently designed and phonetically consistent alphabets used today.

Hangeul consists of only 24 characters and isn't that difficult to learn. However, the formation of words using hangeul is very different from the way that Western alphabets are used to form words. The emphasis is on the formation of a syllable, and the end result bears some resemblance to a Chinese character. For example, the first syllable of the word hangeul (한) is formed by an 'h' (ㅎ) in the top left corner, an 'a' (ㅏ) in the top right corner and an 'n' (ㄴ) at the bottom, the whole syllabic grouping forming a syllabic 'box'. These syllabic 'boxes' are strung together to form words.

ROMANISATION

In July 2000, the Korean government adopted a new method of Romanising the Korean language. Most of the old Romanisation system was retained, but a few changes were introduced to ensure a more consistent spelling throughout Korea and overseas. The main changes to the system are:

- the diacritical breve (ŏ or ŭ) has been dropped and the letter **e** placed in front of the **o** or **u**; eg Inch'ŏn and Chŏngŭp become Incheon and Jeongeup
- the letter ㅈ is transliterated as **j**; the consonants ㄱ/ㄷ/ㅂ are transliterated as **g**, **d**, and **b** respectively when they occur before a vowel (eg Pusan and Kwangju become Busan and Gwangju), and **k**, **t**, and **p** respectively when they are word-final or followed by a consonant
- the voiceless consonants ㅋ/ㅌ/ㅍ/ㅊ are still be transliterated by the letters **k/t/p/ch** but lose their apostrophe. Previously, voiceless or aspirated consonants (those accompanied by a puff of air) were indicated by an apostrophe, as in P'ohang or Ch'ungju; under the new system these will be written Pohang and Chungju respectively.
- the form 시 is no longer be written 'shi', but simply 'si'; eg Shinch'on becomes Sinchon
- official names of persons and companies remain unchanged, but for all new names the new Romanisation system will be used
- hyphens are rarely used, except where confusion may arise between two syllables, eg Chungangno becomes Jung-angno. Hyphens have been retained for administrative units; eg Gyeonggi-do and Suncheon-si.

The new system has been energetically promoted throughout the government and tourist bureaus, but it will take a long time for the whole country to fall into line. Local governments have until 2005 to change all the road signs around the country, and the central government is also actively encouraging the adoption of the new system overseas.

Travellers will have to be careful with Romanisation during the next few years of transition. Lonely Planet has adopted the new Romanisation style throughout this book, but you will come across many spelling variations. To avoid confusion it's always best to go back to the original Korean script. In fact, it's well worth the few hours required to learn the Korean alphabet. To help make travel easier, we have provided Korean script throughout this book for map references and points of interest.

Once you're familiar with *hangeul*, the next step towards Korean competency is listening to the way Koreans pronounce place names and trying to repeat their pronunciations.

PRONUNCIATION

In the words and phrases included in this chapter, the use of the variants **ga/i, reul/eul** and **ro/euro** depends on whether the preceding letter is a vowel or a consonant respectively.

Vowels

ㅏ	a	as in 'are'
ㅑ	ya	as in 'yard'
ㅓ	eo	as the 'o' in 'of'
ㅕ	yeo	as the 'you' in 'young'
ㅗ	o	as in 'go'
ㅛ	yo	as in 'yoke'
ㅜ	u	as in 'flute'
ㅠ	yu	as the word 'you'
ㅡ	eu	as the 'oo' in 'look'
ㅣ	i	as the 'ee' in 'beet'

Vowel Combinations

ㅐ	ae	as the 'a' in 'hat'
ㅒ	yae	as the 'ya' in 'yam'
ㅔ	e	as in 'ten'
ㅖ	ye	as in 'yes'
ㅘ	wa	as in 'waffle'
ㅙ	wae	as the 'wa' in 'wax'
ㅚ	oe	as the 'wa' in 'way'
ㅝ	wo	as in 'won'
ㅞ	we	as in 'wet'

ㅟ	wi	as the word 'we'
ㅢ	ui	as 'u' plus 'i'

Consonants

Unaspirated consonants are generally difficult for English speakers to render. To those unfamiliar with Korean, an unaspirated **k** will sound like 'g', an unaspirated **t** like 'd', and an unaspirated **p** like 'b'.

Whether consonants in Korean are voiced or unvoiced depends on where they fall within a word. The rules governing this are too complex to cover here – the following tables show the various alternative pronunciations you may hear.

Single Consonants

The letter ㅅ is pronounced 'sh' if followed by the vowel ㅣ, even though it is transliterated as **si**.

In the middle of a word, ㄹ is pronounced 'n' if it follows ㅁ (**m**) or ㅇ (**ng**), but when it follows ㄴ (**n**) it becomes a double 'l' sound (**ll**); when a single ㄹ is followed by a vowel it is transliterated as **r**.

ㄱ	g/k
ㄴ	n
ㄷ	d/t
ㄹ	r/l/n
ㅁ	m
ㅂ	b/p
ㅅ	s/t
ㅇ	–/ng
ㅈ	j/t
ㅊ	ch/t
ㅋ	k
ㅌ	t
ㅍ	p
ㅎ	h/ng

Double Consonants

Double consonants are pronounced with more stress than their single consonants counterparts.

ㄲ	kk
ㄸ	tt
ㅃ	pp
ㅆ	ss/t
ㅉ	jj

Complex Consonants

These occur only in the middle or at the end of a word.

ㄱㅅ –/ksk/–
ㄴㅈ –/nj/n
ㄴㅎ –/nh/n
ㄹㄱ –/lg/k
ㄹㅁ –/lm/m
ㄹㅂ –/lb/p
ㄹㅅ –/ls/l
ㄹㅌ –/lt/l
ㄹㅍ –/lp/p
ㄹㅎ –/lh/l
ㅂㅅ –/ps/p

POLITE KOREAN

Korea's pervasive social hierarchy means that varying degrees of politeness are codified into the grammar. Young Koreans tend to use the very polite forms a lot less than the older generation, but it's always best to use the polite form if you're unsure. The sentences in this section employ polite forms.

ACCOMMODATION

I'm looking for a ...
... reul/eul chatgo isseoyo   ...를/을 찾고 있어요
  guesthouse
  yeogwan/minbak jip   여관/민박집
  hotel
  hotel   호텔
  youth hostel
  yuseu hoseutel   유스호스텔

Where is a cheap hotel?
ssan hoteri eodi isseoyo?
싼 호텔이 어디 있어요?
What is the address?
jusoga eotteoke dwaeyo?
주소가 어떻게 돼요?
Could you write the address, please?
juso jom jeogeo juseyo?
주소 좀 적어 주세요?
Do you have any rooms available?
bang isseoyo?
방 있어요?

I'd like (a) ...
... ro/euro juseyo   ...로/으로 주세요
  bed
  chimdae   침대
  single bed
  singgeul chimdae   싱글 침대
  double bed
  deobeul chimdae   더블 침대
  twin beds
  chimdae dugae   침대 두개

room with a bathroom
yoksil inneun bang juseyo   욕실있는 방 주세요
to share a room
gachi sseuneun bang   같이 쓰는 방
Western-style room
chimdae bang juseyo   침대 방 주세요
a room with sleeping mats
ondol bang juseyo   온돌 방 주세요

How much is it ...?
e ... eolma eyo?   에...얼마에요?
  per night
  harutbam   하룻밤
  per person
  han saram   한사람

May I see it?
bang jom bolsu
isseoyo?   방 좀 볼수 있어요?
Where is the bathroom?
yoksiri eodi-e
isseoyo?   욕실이 어디에 있어요?
I'm/We're leaving now.
jigeum tteonayo   지금 떠나요

Making a reservation
(for written or phone requests)

To ...   e-ge ...   에게...
From ...   buteo ...   부터...
Date   naljja   날짜

I'd like to book ...
(see the list on this page for bed and room options)
  ... yeyak haryeogo haneundeyo ...
  예약 하려고 하는데요...
in the name of ...
  ireum euro ...   이름으로...
for the night/s of ...
  naljjalro ...   날짜로...
credit card ...
  sinyong kadeu ...   신용 카드...
  number
  beonho   번호
  expiry date
  manryo il   만료일

Please confirm availability and price.
sayonghal su inneunji wa gagyeok hwaginhae juseyo
사용할 수 있는지 와 가격 확인해 주세요

CONVERSATION & ESSENTIALS

Hello. (polite)
annyeong hasimnikka
안녕 하십니까

Hello. (informal)
annyeong haseyo
안녕 하세요

Goodbye. (to person leaving)
annyeong-hi gaseyo
안녕히 가세요

Goodbye. (to person staying)
annyeong-hi gyeseyo
안녕히 계세요

Yes.
ye/ne 예/네

No.
aniyo 아니요

Please.
juseyo 주세요

Thank you.
gamsa hamnida 감사 합니다

That's fine/You're welcome.
gwaenchan seumnida 괜찮습니다

Excuse me.
sillye hamnida 실례 합니다

Sorry (forgive me).
mian hamnida 미안 합니다

See you soon.
tto mannayo/najung-e bwayo 또 만나요/나중에 봐요

How are you?
annyeong haseyo? 안녕 하세요?

I'm fine, thanks.
ne, jo-ayo 네 좋아요

May I ask your name?
ireumeul yeojjwobwado doelkkayo 이름을 여쭤봐도 될까요?

My name is ...
je ireumeun ... imnida 제 이름은...입니다

Where are you from?
eodiseo oseosseoyo? 어디서 오셨어요?

I'm from ...
jeoneun ... e-seo wasseumnida 저는...에서 왔습니다

I (don't) like ...
jeoneun ... jo-a hey/ ... jo-a haji anhayo 저는...좋아해요/ ...좋아하지 않아요

Just a minute.
jamkkan manyo 잠깐만요

DIRECTIONS

Where is ...?
... i/ga eodi isseoyo? ...이/가 어디 있어요?

Go straight ahead.
ttokbaro gaseyo 똑바로 가세요

Turn left.
oenjjogeuro gaseyo 왼쪽으로 가세요

Turn right.
oreunjjogeuro gaseyo 오른쪽으로 가세요

at the next corner
da eum motungi e-seo 다음 모퉁이에서

at the traffic lights
sinhodeung e-seo 신호등에서

SIGNS	
입구 *ipgu*	Entrance
출구 *chulgu*	Exit
안내 *annae*	Information
영업중 *yeong eop jung*	Open
휴업중 *hyu eop jung*	Closed
금지 *gumji*	Prohibited
방있음 *bang isseum*	Rooms Available
방없음 *bang eopseum*	Full/No Vacancies
경찰서 *gyeongchalseo*	Police Station
화장실 *hwajangsil*	Toilets
신사용 *sinsayong*	Men
숙녀용 *sungnyeoyong*	Women

behind ...	*... dwi-e*	...뒤에
in front of ...	*... ap-e*	...앞에
far	*meolli*	멀리
near	*gakka-i*	가까이
opposite	*bandae pyeon-e*	반대편에
beach	*haesu yokjang* *haebyeon*	해수욕장 해변
bridge	*dari*	다리
castle	*seong*	성
cathedral	*seongdang*	성당
island	*do*	도
	(when used with a proper name)	
	seom	섬
	(when used as a noun)	
market	*sijang*	시장
palace	*gung*	궁
ruins	*yetteo*	옛터
sea	*bada*	바다
tower	*ta-wo/tap*	타워/탑

HEALTH

I'm ill.
jeon apayo 저 아파요

LANGUAGE

It hurts here.
yeogiga apayo 여기가 아파요

I'm ... *... isseoyo* ...있어요
asthmatic *cheonsik* 천식
diabetic *dangnyo byeong-i* 당뇨병이
epileptic *ganjil byeong-i* 간질병이

I'm allergic to ...
... allereugiga isseoyo
...알레르기가있어요
antibiotics *hangsaengje* 항생제
aspirin *aseupirin* 아스피린
penicillin *penisillin* 페니실린
bees *beol* 벌
nuts *ttang kkong* 땅꽁

antiseptic *sodong yak* 소독약
condoms *kondom* 콘돔
contraceptive *pi imyak* 피임약
diarrhoea *seolsa* 설사
hospital *byeongwon* 병원
medicine *yak* 약
sunblock cream *seon keurim* 선크림
tampons *tampon* 탐폰

EMERGENCIES

Help!
saram sallyeo! 사람살려!
There's been an accident.
sago nasseoyo 사고 났어요
I'm lost.
gireul ireosseoyo 길을 잃었어요
Go away!
jeori ga! 저리가!

Call ...!
... bulleo juseyo! ...불러 주세요!
a doctor *ui-sareul* 의사를
the police *gyeongchareul* 경찰을
an ambulance *gugeupcha jom* 구급차좀

LANGUAGE DIFFICULTIES

Do you speak English?
yeong-eo haseyo?
영어 하세요?
Does anyone here speak English?
yeong-eo hasineunbun gyeseyo?
영어 하시는 분계세요?
How do you say ... in Korean?
... eul/reul hangug-euro eotteoke malhaeyo?
...을 한국어로 어떻게 말해요?

What does ... mean?
... ga/i museun tteusieyo? ...가/이무슨 뜻 이에요?
I understand.
algeseoyo 알겠어요
I don't understand.
jalmoreugenneun deyo 잘 모르겠는데요
Please write it down.
jeogeo jusillaeyo 적어 주실래요
Can you show me (on the map)?
boyeo jusillaeyo 보여 주실래요?

NUMBERS

Korean has two counting systems. One is of Chinese origin, with Korean pronunciation, and the other is a native Korean system – the latter only goes up to 99 and is used for counting objects, expressing your age and for the hours when telling the time. They're always written in *hangeul* or digits, but never in Chinese characters. Sino-Korean numbers are used to express minutes when telling the time, as well as dates, months, kilometres, money, floors of buildings; numbers above 99 and can also be written in Chinese characters. Either Chinese or Korean numbers can be used to count days.

	Sino-Korean		Korean	
1	*il*	일	*hana*	하나
2	*i*	이	*dul*	둘
3	*sam*	삼	*set*	셋
4	*sa*	사	*net*	넷
5	*o*	오	*daseot*	다섯
6	*yuk*	육	*yeoseot*	여섯
7	*chil*	칠	*ilgop*	일곱
8	*pal*	팔	*yeodeol*	여덟
9	*gu*	구	*ahop*	아홉
10	*sip*	십	*yeol*	열

	Combination	
11	*sibil*	십일
12	*sibi*	십이
13	*sipsam*	십삼
14	*sipsa*	십사
15	*sibo*	십오
16	*simnyuk*	십육
17	*sipchil*	십칠
18	*sippal*	십팔
19	*sipgu*	십구
20	*isip*	이십
21	*isibil*	이십일

22	isibi	이십이
30	samsip	삼십
40	sasip	사십
50	osip	오십
60	yuksip	육십
70	chilsip	칠십
80	palsip	팔십
90	gusip	구십
100	baek	백
1000	cheon	천

PAPERWORK

name	ireum/ seongmyeong	이름/ 성명
nationality	guk jeok	국적
date of birth	saengnyeon woril/ saeng-il	생년월일/ 생일
place of birth	chulsaengji	출생지
sex (gender)	seongbyeol	성별
passport	yeogwon	여권
visa	bija	비자

QUESTION WORDS

Who? (as subject)	nugu	누구
What? (as subject)	mu-eot	무엇
When?	eonje	언제
Where?	eodi	어디
How?	eotteoke	어떻게

SHOPPING & SERVICES

I'd like to buy ...
... reul/eul sago sipeoyo ...를/을 사고 싶어요

How much is it?
eolma yeyo? 얼마예요?

I don't like it.
byeollo mam-e andeuneyo 별로 맘에 안드네요

May I look at it?
boyeo jusillaeyo? 보여 주실래요?

I'm just looking.
geunyang gugyeong haneungeo-eyo 그냥 구경 하는 거에요

It's cheap.
ssa-neyo 싸네요

It's too expensive.
neomu bissayo 너무 비싸요

I'll take it.
igeoro haraeyo 이걸로 할래요

Do you accept ...?
... jibul haedo dwaeyo? ...지불해도 돼요?
  credit cards
  keurediteu kadeu-ro 크레디트 카드로
  travellers cheques
  yeohaengja supyo 여행자 수표

more	deo	더
less	deol	덜
smaller	deo jageun	더작은
bigger	deo keun	더큰

I'm looking for ...
... reul/eul chatgo isseoyo ...를/을 찾고 있어요
  a bank
  eunhaeng 은행
  a church
  gyohoe 교회
  the city centre
  sinae jung simga 시내 중심가
  the ... embassy
  dae sigwan 대사관
  the market
  sijang 시장
  the museum
  bangmulgwan 박물관
  the post office
  uche-guk 우체국
  a public toilet
  hwajangsil 화장실
  the telephone centre
  jeonhwa guk 전화국
  the tourist office
  gwan gwang annaeso 관광 안내소

I want to change ...
... reul/eul bakku ryeogo haneun deyo
...를/을 바꾸려고 하는데요
  money
  don 돈
  travellers cheques
  yeohaengja supyo 여행자 수표

TIME & DATES

What time is it?
jigeum myeot si-eyo? 지금 몇시 에요?

It's (10 o'clock).
(yeol) siyo (열)시요

in the morning	achim-e	아침에
in the afteroon	ohu-e	오후에
in the evening	jeonyeok-e	저녁에
When?	eonje	언제
today	o-neul	오늘
tomorrow	nae-il	내일
yesterday	eo-je	어제

Monday	woryoil	월요일
Tuesday	hwayoil	화요일
Wednesday	suyoil	수요일
Thursday	mogyoil	목요일
Friday	geumyoil	금요일

Saturday	toyoil	토요일
Sunday	iryoil	일요일
January	irwol	일월
February	iwol	이월
March	samwol	삼월
April	sawol	사월
May	owol	오월
June	yu-gwol	육월
July	chirwol	칠월
August	parwol	팔월
September	guwol	구월
October	siwol	시월
November	sibirwol	십일월
December	sibiwol	십이월

TRANSPORT
Public Transport
What time does the ... leave/arrive?
... i/ga (eonje tteonayo/eonje dochak-haeyo)?
...이/가 언제 떠나요/언제 도착해요?

airport bus	gonghang beoseu	공항버스
boat (ferry)	yeogaekseon	여객선
bus	beoseu	버스
city bus	sinae beoseu	시내버스
intercity bus	si-oe beoseu	시외버스
plane	bihaeng-gi	비행기
train	gicha	기차

Two other types of intercity bus are:

gosok beoseu 고속 버스
(high frequency express bus)
u-deung beoseu 우등 버스
(less frequent, more comfortable and a little more expensive)

I'd like a ... ticket.
... hanjang juseyo ...한장 주세요

one-way	pyeondo pyo	편도표
return	wangbok pyo	왕복표
1st class	il-deung seok	일등석
2nd class	i-deung seok	이등석

I want to go to ...
... e gago sipseumnida
...에 가고 싶습니다
The train has been (delayed).
gichaga (yeonchak) doe-eosseumnida
기차가 (연착) 되었습니다.
The train has been (cancelled).
gichaga (chwiso) doe-eosseumnida
기차가 (취소) 되었습니다

the first
cheot 첫

the last
maji mak 마지막
bus station
beoseu jeongnyu jang 버스정류장
platform number
peuraetpom beonho 플랫폼번호
subway station
jihacheol yeok 지하철역
ticket office
pyo paneun got 표 파는곳
ticket vending machine
pyo japangi 표 자판기
timetable
sigan pyo 시간표
train station
gicha yeok 기차역

Private Transport
I'd like to hire a/an ...
... reul/eul billi-go sipeoyo
...를/을 빌리고 싶어요
car
jadongcha 자동차
(or simply *cha*, 차)
4WD
jipeu cha 지프차
motorbike
otoba-i/moteo sai-keul 오토바이/모터사이클
bicycle
jajeongeo 자전거

Is this the road to ...?
i-gil daragamyeon ... e galsu isseoyo?
이길 따라가면...에갈수 있어요?
Where's a service station?
annae soga eodi isseoyo?
안내소가 어디있어요?
Please fill it up.
gadeuk chaewo juseyo
가득 채워 주세요
I'd like (30) litres.
(samsip) liteo neo-eo juseyo
(삼십)리터 넣어 주세요

diesel	dijel	디젤
leaded petrol	gayeon	가연
unleaded petrol	muyeon hwi baryu	무연휘발유

(How long) Can I park here?
eolmana jucha halsu isseoyo?
얼마나 주차 할수 있어요?
Where do I pay?
eodiseo jibul hamnikka?
어디서 지불합니까?

I need a mechanic.
jeongbi gong-i biryo haeyo
정비공이 필요해요
The car/motorbike has broken down (at ...)
... eseo chaga/otoba-i ga gojang nasseoyo
…에서 차가/오토바이가 고장 났어요
The car/motorbike won't start.
chaga/otoba-i ga sidong-i geolli-ji annayo
차가/오토바이가 시동이 걸리지
않아요
I have a flat tyre.
taieo-e peongkeu nasseoyo
타이어에펑크났어요
I've run out of petrol.
gireumi tteoreo jeosseoyo
기름이 떨어졌어요
I've had an accident.
sago nasseoyo
사고 났어요

ROAD SIGNS

우회로	Detour
uhwoe-ro	
길없음	No Entry
gil-eupseum	
추월금지	No Overtaking
chuwol geumji	
주차금지	No Parking
jucha geumji	
입구	Entrance
ipgu	
접근금지	Keep Clear
jeopgeun geumji	
통행료	Toll
tonghaeng-ryo	
톨게이트	Toll Gate
tol geiteu	
위험	Danger
wi heom	
서행	Slow Down
seo haeng	
일방통행	One Way
il-bang tonghaeng	
나가는길	Freeway Exit
naganeun gil	

TRAVEL WITH CHILDREN
Is there (a/an) ...
... isseoyo?   ...있어요?
I need (a/an) ...
piryo haeyo   ...필요해요
　baby change room
　gijeogwi galgosi   기저귀 갈 곳이

baby car seat
yu-a jadongcha   유아자동차안전의자
anjeon uija
child-minding service
agi bwajuneun seobiseu 아기봐주는 서비스
children's menu
eorini menyu   어린이 메뉴
(disposable) nappies/diapers
ilhoeyong gijeogwi   일회용 기저귀
formula (milk)
bunyu   분유
(English-speaking) babysitter
agi bwajuneun saram   아기 봐주는 사람
highchair
agi uija   아기의자
potty
agi byeon-gi   아기변기
stroller/pusher
yu-mocha   유모차

Do you mind if I breastfeed here?
yeogi-seo agi jeotmeok yeodo doenayo?
여기서 아기 젖먹여도 되나요?
Are children allowed?
eorinido doennikka?
어린이도됩니까?

Also available from Lonely Planet:
Korean phrasebook

Glossary

A

ajumma – a married or older woman; a term of respect for a woman who runs a hotel, restaurant or other business
am – hermitage
anju – snacks eaten when drinking alcohol; can be expensive in a nightclub

B

bang – room; a PC *bang* is an Internet room and a DVD *bang* is a room where you can watch DVDs
bawi – large rock
bong – peak
buk – north
buncheong – Joseon-era pottery with simple folk designs

C

cha – tea
cheon – small stream

D

da bang – tearoom
dae – great, large
Dangun – mythical founder of Korea
DMZ – the Demilitarized Zone that runs along the 38th parallel of the Korean peninsula, separating North and South
-do – province
do – island
-dong – ward
dong – east
donggul – cave

E

-eup – town

G

-ga – section of a long street
gang – river
geobukseon – 'turtle ships'; iron-clad warships of the late 16th century
gil – small street
-gu – urban district
gugak – traditional Korean music
gun – county
gung – palace
gyotongkadeu – subway and bus travel card

H

hae – sea
haenyo – female divers of Jejudo
hagwon – private schools where students study after school or work
hanbok – traditional Korean clothing
hangeul – Korean phonetic alphabet
hanji – traditional Korean hand-made paper
hanok – traditional Korean one-storey wooden house with a tiled roof
harubang – 'grandfather stones'; Easter Island–like statues found on Jejudo
ho – lake

I

insam – ginseng

J

jaebol – huge family-run corporate conglomerate
jeon – hall of a temple
jeong – pavilion
Juche – North Korean ideology of economic self-reliance

K

KNTO – Korean National Tourism Organisation

M

minbak – private homes with rooms for rent
mobeom – deluxe taxi
mugunghwa – limited express train
mun – gate
-myeon – township
myo – shrine

N

nam – south
neung – tomb
no – large street, boulevard
noraebang – a room for singing songs to a backing track
nyeong – mountain pass

O

oncheon – hot-spring bath
ondol – underfloor heating

P

pansori – traditional Korean solo opera
pokpo – waterfall
pyeong – a unit of measurement equal to 3.3 sq metres

R

reung – tomb
-ri – village
ro – large street, boulevard
ROK – Republic of Korea (South Korea)
ru – pavilion
ryeong – mountain pass

S

sa – temple
saemaeul – luxury express train
san – mountain
sanjang – mountain hut
sanseong – mountain fortress

seo – west
Seon – Korean version of Zen Buddhism
seong – fortress
seowon – Confucian academy
si – city
ssireum – Korean-style wrestling

T

taekwondo – Korean martial art
tang – a public bathhouse that usually includes a sauna
tap – pagoda
tongil – slow local train

Y

yangban – aristocrat
yeogwan – motels with small, well-equipped en suite rooms
yeoinsuk – small family-run budget hotel with shared toilets and bathrooms
yo – padded quilt used as mattress for sleeping on the floor

Behind the Scenes

THIS BOOK

Korea was first published in 1988. The last edition of this guide was written by Robert Storey and Eunkyong Park. This 6th edition was updated by Martin Robinson, Andrew Bender and Rob Whyte. The Health chapter was written by Dr Trish Batchelor.

THANKS from the Authors

Martin Robinson Thanks to KNTO, Ji Il-hyun, Yi Sang-woo, Park Young-hee, Jang Young-bok, Hank Kim, Han Joon-yeob, Park Seok-jin, Jang Kyung-hee, Han Sang-hoon, Park So-young, Lee Jin-hyeong, Park Soon-kap, Hong Seok-chun, Kim Young-ja, Timothy Lee, Antony Stokes, Hong Jae-sun, Hwang Geum-joo, Mr Jang, my co-authors, commissioning editor Michael Day and everyone else who helped me. Special thanks to Mr BJ Song and my dad and special special thanks to my wife, Marie.

Andrew Bender Thanks, first of all, to the entire crew at the KNTO in Los Angeles (Messrs Kim, Jo and Hong, Monica Poling and Aliza Rosenberg), without whose assistance none of this would have been possible. And boundless gratitude goes to my helpers and new friends on the ground in Korea, especially Kim Hee-A in Jeju-do, Joseph Kim and Mr Kim Jin-don in Daegu, Sophie Park in Gyeongsanbuk-do, Ms Kim Bog-hee in Gwangju and Sharon Park in Jeollanam-do, as welt the ever-professional and incomparably smiley Mr Lee. Thanks to Diana Rosen for her knowledge of tea and to all the monks, docents, ticket-takers, desk clerks, chefs, waiters and waitresses who ever put up with my niggling questions. Finally, thanks to Michael Day, Martin Robinson, and Emma Koch, who made working on this book a pleasure.

Rob Whyte Many thanks to my wife, Kyoung-mi, for her patience and ability to proofread my poor Korean writing with alacrity. To my daughter Genieve who, at the tender age of seven, has blossomed into a capable Korean–English translator for her dad. On the road, thanks to Ian Pringle (Baekseju connoisseur), Kim Yong-young, So Eun-young, Park Mi-ja, Kim Ohk-bin, Lee Ha-jin, Moon Jeong-ee, Kim Eun-mi (for her raw-fish eatery insights) and Lee Koum-sook, one of Geoje Island's finest tour guides. Final thanks to Dr. Bruce Hocking, healer, humanist and inspiration on the road less travelled.

CREDITS

Korea 6 was commissioned and developed in Lonely Planet's Melbourne office by Michael Day. Cartography for this guide was developed by Corie Waddell, and the project was managed by Chris Love and Charles Rawlings-Way.

Coordinating this book were Emma Koch (editorial), Hunor Csutoros (cartography), and Yvonne Bischofberger and Steven Cann (layout). Emma was assisted by Yvonne Byron, Helen Christinis, Jocelyn Harewood, Susannah Farfor, Simone Egger, Lara Morcombe, Melissa Faulkner, Katrina Webb and Carolyn Boicos. Quentin Frayne prepared the Language chapter. Managing editor Jane Thompson provided guidance and support

THE LONELY PLANET STORY

The story begins with a classic travel adventure: Tony and Maureen Wheeler's 1972 journey across Europe and Asia to Australia. There was no useful information about the overland trail then, so Tony and Maureen published the first Lonely Planet guidebook to meet a growing need.

From a kitchen table, Lonely Planet has grown to become the largest independent travel publisher in the world, with offices in Melbourne (Australia), Oakland (USA), London (UK) and Paris (France).

Today Lonely Planet guidebooks cover the globe. There is an ever-growing list of books and information in a variety of media. Some things haven't changed. The main aim is still to make it possible for adventurous travellers to get out there – to explore and better understand the world.

At Lonely Planet we believe travellers can make a positive contribution to the countries they visit – if they respect their host communities and spend their money wisely.

throughout production. Ben Handicott provided editorial production assistance.

Hunor was assisted by Marion Byass, Celia Wood, Daniel Fennessy, Valentina Kremenchutskaya, Bonnie Wintle, Nick Stebbing, Kim McDonald and Herman So. Managing cartographer Corie Waddell lent her support as needed. Maria Vallianos designed the cover.

Cris Gibcus, Nick Stebbing and Sally Darmody assisted Yvonne Bischofberger and Steven Cann. Adriana Mammarella and Kate McDonald oversaw layout.

Series Publishing Manager Virginia Maxwell oversaw the redevelopment of the country guides series with help from Maria Donohoe. Regional Publishing Manager Virginia Maxwell steered the development of this title. The series was designed by James Hardy, with mapping development by Paul Piaia. The series development team included Shahara Ahmed, Susie Ashworth, Gerilyn Attebery, Jenny Blake, Anna Bolger, Verity Campbell, Erin Corrigan, Nadine Fogale, Dave McClymont, Leonie Mugavin, Rachel Peart, Lynne Preston and Howard Ralley.

THANKS from Lonely Planet
Many thanks to the travellers who used the last edition and wrote to us with helpful hints, useful advice and interesting anecdotes:

A Daniel af Ekenstam, Magued Abdel-Maaboud, Jadwiga Adamczuk, Joony An, Crispin Anderlini, Richard Anderson, Mark Andrews, Maja Rom Anjer, Angus Arnell, Charlotte Arrington, Tim Athan, Carl Atteniese **B** Sylvia Baars, Jesse Baehm, Chris Bagley, Sarom Bahk, David Balcanquel, Ben Ball, Jennifer Barclay, Geoff Barton, Mike Bartos, John & Clare Bartram, Amy Berman, Aart Biewenga, Grace Blake, M J Blanchard, Mark Bodak, Adam Bohnet, Emily Bone, Michel Bourbon, Glyne Bourne, Geoff Brooks, Jacinta Brown, Lyndal & Murray Brown, Theo Bruening, Aafke & Dennis Bruin, Fabienne Brütt, Rowland Burley **C** Adam Carlson, Centre for Korean Studies, Peter Chang, Ramon Chang, Quek Hong Cheang, Kyungsil Choi, Jong-Won Choo, Ha Chung Bong, David Corlett, Ainsley Corp, David Covill, Alison Crump, John Cushing **D** Elizabeth Davison, Nikki Dawson, Francesco Diodato, Marion Donaldson, Hugues Donato, Emily Donville, Christina Dunigan, D Duprez **E** Frazer Egerton, Richard & Sung Hui Elberfield, Hong Eun-mee, Tim Eyre **F** Macdara Ferris, Joseph Fette, Yamuna Flaherty, Del Ford, Nigel Foster, Timothy Fowell, Mike Fowler **G** Anthony & Michele Gain, Steven Galbraith, Mike Galvin, Patrick Gaudio, Gustav Gautshci, Previe Gauvin, Jennifer Georges, Aya Gomez **H** Adrian Haas, Shirley Hackam, Angela Hansen, Leigh Hardy, Tim L Hedges, Barry Heinrich, Marlene Helfert, Trevor Hemsley, Jan Henckens, Geoffrey Hibbert, Roger Hodgerson, Tara Hoffman, John Holmes, Clifton Hood, H Matthew Howarth, Lim Hsing **I** Lee Jeong Im, Otto Insam, John Iseppi, Musashi Iwamoto **J** Jurgen Jacoby, Mirte Jansen, Kim Jayune, H K Jeong, V Jezusek, Lee Myung Jin, Tina Joh, Ulf-Arne Johannessen, Mary Jones, Terry & Rob Jordens, Sim Jui Luang **K** Anna Keaschuk, Yorgos Kechagioglou, Ute Keck, Jason Keith, David Kendall, Dennis Kim, Hyunsuk Kim, Insun Kim, Ms Kim, Shidon Kim, Dave Kimber, Jay Klawier, Nick Knight, Geertje Koeman, Alex Koolhof, Bartosz Kozik, Nikolaus Kratzat **L** Lawrence Kriese, Christopher Laine, Cedric LaMar Joyner, Anna-Maree Laney, Mark Lang, Lorna Larson, Alex Lee, Hwa Pyung Lee, Jae-ho Lee, James Lee, Ji-Hyun Lee, Dominic Leonard, JoAnn Lichtenberger, Jeremy Lifton, Jonathan Lim, Ethan Lincoln **M** Kari Makelainen, Danielle Marchand, Mike Martin, Rob Martin, Peter Martyn, David R Mathieu, Walsh McGuire, Heather McKee Hutwitz, Nathan McMurray, Jann McPherson, Jarrod McPherson, Elizabeth McZeo, Stan Meihaus, Esther Merrick, Jared Millar, Brandon Miller, Gavin Mills, Hong Minsuk, Sofia Mitoraj **N** Sean Moriarty, Shin Nara, Andrea Nesbitt, Patricia Neyman, Jean Nicca, Jens Niedzielski, Henrik Skov Nielsen **O** Gee O'Conner, Sven-Olof & Yue Ohlsson, Dax Oliver, Bryan Olson, Jason Orchyk, Tony Osborne **P** Ramon Pacheco Pardo, Aristea Parissi, Ryan Parker, Sruti Patel, Cory Pettit, Shaun Petty, Dick Pluim, Laura Pohl, Abel Polese, Ian C Potter, Volker Preusser, Sarah Prunier **R** Christine Rae, Debra Richardson, Jim Richardson, Michael Richter, Jennifer Roberts, Nuno Miguel Romao, Jean

---

SEND US YOUR FEEDBACK

We love to hear from travellers – your comments keep us on our toes and help make our books better. Our well-travelled team reads every word on what you loved or loathed about this book. Although we cannot reply individually to postal submissions, we always guarantee that your feedback goes straight to the appropriate authors, in time for the next edition. Each person who sends us information is thanked in the next edition – and the most useful submissions are rewarded with a free book.

To send us your updates – and find out about LP events, newsletters and travel news – visit our award-winning website: **www.lonelyplanet.com**.

Note: We may edit, reproduce and incorporate your comments in Lonely Planet products such as guidebooks, websites and digital products, so let us know if you don't want your comments reproduced or your name acknowledged. For a copy of our privacy policy visit www.lonelyplanet.com/privacy.

Pierre Rosay, Joshua Ross, Steve Rowan, Ji-Hong Ryu **S** Nadia Sbaihi, Patti Schaffer, Lisa Scheinin MD, Harald Schubert, Peter Scott, Marcus Sheehan, Melinda Sherwood, Minjung Shin, Susan Shin, Pauline Shiu, Brandon Si, Christian Sickermann, Reda Sijiny, Paul Silvester, Aileen Simarro, Clayton Simpson, Anze Slosar, Paul Smeaton, Leif Soderlund, Alistair Spratt, Brian Stanley, Joshua Stanton, Mathieu Stewart, Jasmine St-Laurent, Chris Stuart-Vanderburg, Joanne Sugiono, Sonia Sumner, Park Sung Deug, Kim Sun-Ju, Eric Sustad **T** Joshua Taaffe, Huihong Tang, Nicky Taylor, Mathilde Teuben, Barbara Theiler, Aairam Thomas, Peter Thomson, Ken Tidwell, Wim Timmermans, Linda Tisue, Tasha Tower, Lee Towndrow, Eugene Trabich, Melissa Tremblay, Mimi Tresman, Steven P Tseng **U** Laura Upton **V** Nick van der Leek, Floris van der Tak, Frank Villante, Vicky Vitallo **W** Cooper Walden, Dr. Mari Watanabe, Andy Westall, Anthony P White, Sam Whittington, Robert J Wilhoyt, Josephine Williams, Michael A Witt, Choo Jong Won, Clayton Wood, Beth Woollam, Alister Wright, Nancy Wright **Y** Derek Yokota, **Z** Ruth Zanker, Alfons Zeegers, Oliver Zoellner, Seth Zuckerman, David Zuman

ACKNOWLEDGMENTS

Many thanks to the following for the use of their content:

Images used with kind permission of APL Corbis (p8) & Masterfile (adjacent to p64).

Index

INDEX

000 Map pages
000 Location of colour photographs

MAP LEGEND

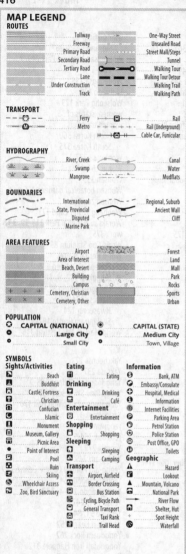

ROUTES

Tollway	One-Way Street
Freeway	Unsealed Road
Primary Road	Street Mall/Steps
Secondary Road	Tunnel
Tertiary Road	Walking Tour
Lane	Walking Tour Detour
Under Construction	Walking Trail
Track	Walking Path

TRANSPORT

Ferry	Rail
Metro	Rail (Underground)
	Cable Car, Funicular

HYDROGRAPHY

River, Creek	Canal
Swamp	Water
Mangrove	Mudflats

BOUNDARIES

International	Regional, Suburb
State, Provincial	Ancient Wall
Disputed	Cliff
Marine Park	

AREA FEATURES

Airport	Forest
Area of Interest	Land
Beach, Desert	Mall
Building	Park
Campus	Rocks
Cemetery, Christian	Sports
Cemetery, Other	Urban

POPULATION

⊙ CAPITAL (NATIONAL)	⊛ CAPITAL (STATE)
● Large City	● Medium City
° Small City	° Town, Village

SYMBOLS

Sights/Activities
- Beach
- Buddhist
- Castle, Fortress
- Christian
- Confucian
- Islamic
- Monument
- Museum, Gallery
- Picnic Area
- Point of Interest
- Pool
- Ruin
- Skiing
- Wheelchair Access
- Zoo, Bird Sanctuary

Eating
- Eating

Drinking
- Drinking
- Café

Entertainment
- Entertainment

Shopping
- Shopping

Sleeping
- Sleeping
- Camping

Transport
- Airport, Airfield
- Border Crossing
- Bus Station
- Cycling, Bicycle Path
- General Transport
- Taxi Rank
- Trail Head

Information
- Bank, ATM
- Embassy/Consulate
- Hospital, Medical
- Information
- Internet Facilities
- Parking Area
- Petrol Station
- Police Station
- Post Office, GPO
- Toilets

Geographic
- Hazard
- Lookout
- Mountain, Volcano
- National Park
- River Flow
- Shelter, Hut
- Spot Height
- Waterfall

LONELY PLANET OFFICES

Australia
Head Office
Locked Bag 1, Footscray, Victoria 3011
☎ 03 8379 8000, fax 03 8379 8111
talk2us@lonelyplanet.com.au

USA
150 Linden St, Oakland, CA 94607
☎ 510 893 8555, toll free 800 275 8555
fax 510 893 8572, info@lonelyplanet.com

UK
72–82 Rosebery Ave,
Clerkenwell, London EC1R 4RW
☎ 020 7841 9000, fax 020 7841 9001
go@lonelyplanet.co.uk

France
1 rue du Dahomey, 75011 Paris
☎ 01 55 25 33 00, fax 01 55 25 33 01
bip@lonelyplanet.fr, www.lonelyplanet.fr

Published by Lonely Planet Publications Pty Ltd
ABN 36 005 607 983

© Lonely Planet 2004

© photographers as indicated 2004

Cover photographs by Lonely Planet Images: a tall stone Buddha, Beopjusa, Songnisan National Park, John Banagan (front); a neon forest of advertising, Gwangju, Bill Wassman (back). Many of the images in this guide are available for licensing from Lonely Planet Images: www.lonelyplanetimages.com.

Printed through Colorcraft Ltd, Hong Kong.
Printed in China